Freedom of Speech
Volume I

The International Library of Essays in Law and Legal Theory
Second Series
Series Editor: Tom D. Campbell

Titles in the Series:

Freedom of Speech
Volume I: Foundations

Edited by

Larry Alexander

University of San Diego

Ashgate

DARTMOUTH

Aldershot • Burlington USA • Singapore • Sydney

Published by
Dartmouth Publishing Company Limited
Ashgate Publishing Limited
Gower House
Croft Road
Aldershot
Hants GU11 3HR
England

Ashgate Publishing Company
131 Main Street
Burlington
Vermont 05401
USA

Ashgate website: http://www.ashgate.com

British Library Cataloguing in Publication Data
Freedom of speech : volumes 1 and 2. – (The international
   library of essays in law and legal theory)
   1. Freedom of speech 2. Freedom of speech – Philosophy
   I. Alexander, Larry
   342'.0853

Library of Congress Cataloging-in-Publication Data
Freedom of speech / edited by Larry Alexander.
            p.   cm.
      Includes index.
      Contents: v. 1. Foundations — v. 2. Doctrine.
      ISBN 1-84014-771-7 (hardback)
      1. Freedom of speech—United States. 2. Freedom of speech.
   I. Alexander, Lawrence A.
   KF4772.F475 1999
   342.73'0853—dc21

99-16906
CIP

ISBN 1 84014 771 7

Printed and bound by Athenaeum Press, Ltd.,
Gateshead, Tyne & Wear.

Contents

Acknowledgements

The editor and publishers wish to thank the following for permission to use copyright material.

Academic Press, Inc. for the essay: Larry Alexander (1998), 'Freedom of Speech', *Encyclopedia of Applied Ethics*, **2**, pp. 299–305. Copyright © 1998 Academic Press, Inc. All rights reserved.

Columbia University for the essays: David A. Strauss (1991), 'Persuasion, Autonomy, and Freedom of Expression', *Columbia Law Review*, **91**, pp. 334–71. Copyright © 1991 Columbia University; Kent Greenawalt (1989), 'Free Speech Justifications', *Columbia Law Review*, **89**, pp. 119–55. Copyright © 1989 Columbia Law Review.

Constitutional Commentary, Inc. for the essay: Larry Alexander (1995), 'Free Speech and Speaker's Intent', *Constitutional Commentary*, **12**, pp. 21–28.

Harvard Law Review Association for the essay: John Hart Ely (1975), 'Flag Desecration: A Case Study in the Roles of Categorization and Balancing in First Amendment Analysis', *Harvard Law Review*, **88**, pp. 1482–508. Copyright © 1975 Harvard Law Review Association.

Indiana Law Journal and William S. Hein & Co Inc. for the essay: Robert H. Bork (1971), 'Neutral Principles and Some First Amendment Problems', *Indiana Law Journal*, **47**, pp. 1–35.

The Journal of Philosophy for the essay: Alvin I. Goldman (1991), 'Epistemic Paternalism: Communication Control in Law and Society', *Journal of Philosophy*, **88**, pp. 113–31. Copyright © 1991 The Journal of Philosophy, Inc.

Northwestern University School of Law for the essays: Lawrence Alexander and Paul Horton (1984), 'The Impossibility of a Free Speech Principle', *Northwestern University Law Review*, **78**, pp. 1319–57. Copyright © 1984 Northwestern University School of Law. Reprinted by special permission of Northwestern University School of Law, *Law Review*, **78** (5), 1984; Frederick Schauer (1984), 'Must Speech be Special?', *Northwestern University Law Review*, **78**, pp. 1284–318. Copyright © 1984 Northwestern University School of Law. Reprinted by special permission of Northwestern University School of Law, *Law Review*, **78** (5), 1989; Larry Alexander (1989), 'Legal Theory: Low Value Speech', *Northwestern University Law Review*, **83**, pp. 547–54. Copyright © 1989 Northwestern University School of Law. Reprinted by special permission of Northwestern University School of Law, *Law Review*, **83** (3), 1989.

O'Brien Center for Scholarly Publications for the essay: Larry A. Alexander (1993), 'Trouble on Track Two: Incidental Regulations of Speech and Free Speech Theory', *Hastings Law Journal*, **44**, pp. 921–62. Copyright © 1993 University of California, Hastings College of the Law.

Preface to the Second Series

The first series of the International Library of Essays in Law and Legal Theory has established itself as a major research resource with fifty-eight volumes of the most significant theoretical essays in contemporary legal studies. Each volume contains essays of central theoretical importance in its subject area and the series as a whole makes available an extensive range of valuable material of considerable interest to those involved in research, teaching and the study of law.

The rapid growth of theoretically interesting scholarly work in law has created a demand for a second series which includes more recent publications of note and earlier essays to which renewed attention is being given. It also affords the opportunity to extend the areas of law covered in the first series.

The new series follows the successful pattern of reproducing entire essays with the original page numbers as an aid to comprehensive research and accurate referencing. Editors have selected not only the most influential essays but also those which they consider to be of greatest continuing importance. The objective of the second series is to enlarge the scope of the library, include significant recent work and reflect a variety of editorial perspectives.

Each volume is edited by an expert in the specific area who makes the selection on the basis of the quality, influence and significance of the essays, taking care to include essays which are not readily available. Each volume contains a substantial introduction explaining the context and significance of the essays selected.

I am most grateful for the care which volume editors have taken in carrying out the complex task of selecting and presenting essays which meet the exacting criteria set for the series.

TOM CAMPBELL
Series Editor
The Faculty of Law
The Australian National University

Introduction

This is the first of a two-volume collection of theoretical essays on the topic of freedom of speech. My task was to collect what are, in my opinion, the most important of such essays written during the past 30 years or so. Such a task is especially daunting for two reasons. First, there is an enormous literature on freedom of speech – a literature that includes far too many fine essays for ten volumes, much less two. This means that I have had to exclude theoretical essays on all but a couple of specific doctrinal areas, and to confine the collection mainly to essays that transcend specific doctrines. Moreover, even so confined, the collection omits many essays worthy of inclusion, some because they were too long[1] and others because choices had to be made. No one will find all of his or her favourite theoretical pieces in the collection.

Second, within a literature so rich, any assessment of which are the most important theoretical essays on freedom of speech will inevitably be idiosyncratic – a reflection of the anthologer's specific view of the topic. I have tried to be open-minded and catholic, and to attend to an essay's reputation in the scholarly community as well as to my own judgement of its worth, but I am sure that the collection reveals as much about my view of freedom of speech as it does about the literature. Moreover, the collection contains several works of mine that I am reasonably certain would not all be included by a different anthologer. I include them for the same reason I wrote them – namely, because I believed they make theoretical points not discussed in the extant literature.

Volume I, 'Foundations', begins with my 1998 encyclopedia entry, 'Freedom of Speech', which functions as an overview of the topic. I begin with the question of the scope of freedom of speech and conclude that freedom of speech should be thought of as freedom of communication. I turn then to the question of who has the right to freedom of speech, arguing that the primary right belongs to the recipients of the communication. Next, I survey the principal justifications for freedom of speech: consequentialist (the attainment of 'truth', the maximization of autonomy and so on); deontological; and democratic. Finally, I classify the governmental acts that implicate freedom of speech: various type of regulations of content; incidental restrictions on speech; governmental speech and subsidies of private speech; and laws permitting private suppression of speech.

Part II deals with justificatory theories of freedom of speech. It begins with Thomas Scanlon's highly influential 1972 essay, 'A Theory of Freedom of Expression' (Chapter 2), Scanlon argues that, at its core, freedom of expression protects the right not to have government interdict communications on the grounds that the audience might be moved to act harmfully by the reasons given in the communication, or that the audience might come to have false beliefs as a result of it. He defends the core right, which he calls the Millian Principle, by arguing that it is a right which an autonomous person would insist on as part of the social contract. He also argues that the Millian Principle cannot account for all of freedom of speech and must be supplemented with consequentialist considerations.

In his 1991 essay, 'Persuasion, Autonomy, and Freedom of Expression' (Chapter 3), David

Strauss puts forward a principle very similar to Scanlon's, which Strauss calls the *persuasion principle*. This principle prohibits government from banning expression on the ground that it might persuade others to commit proscribable acts. Strauss finds support for the principle in US Supreme Court case law. He also argues that deontological principles that are protective of autonomy rather than consequentialist ones are the most plausible justification for the persuasion principle.

C. Edwin Baker, in his 1978 essay, 'Scope of the First Amendment: Freedom of Speech' (Chapter 4), argues on behalf of what he calls the *liberty model* of freedom of speech, which he distinguishes from the *classic model* and the *market failure model*. The latter models are both versions of the case for freedom of speech that rests on its promotion of truth through the 'marketplace of ideas'. Baker argues that the classic model of the marketplace of ideas 'depends on implausible assumptions' and that the market failure model is 'unworkable, dangerous, and inconsistent with a reasonable interpretation of the first amendment'. On the other hand, the liberty model, which protects 'a realm of liberty roughly corresponding to noncoercive, nonviolent action', provides a maximally coherent theory of freedom of speech. Baker, in contrast to Scanlon and Strauss, emphasizes the autonomy of the speaker rather than that of the audience. Audience interests enter into the analysis primarily as limits to the speaker's freedom of speech, as is the case where the speech is coercive.

In 'The Value of Free Speech', published in 1982, Martin Redish (Chapter 5) advances a theory of freedom of speech that focuses on the value of individual self-realization and makes that value the core of the freedom. All other contending values – protecting the 'political process', 'checking' official conduct and maintaining the 'marketplace of ideas' – are in reality subvalues that depend on the primary value of individual self-realization. And that primary value is established not by *a priori* moral reasoning, but by reasoning from the assumptions underlying our democratic system of government. Redish distinguishes his theory from Baker's by emphasizing its greater breadth, including its protection of audience self-realization.

Robert Bork's oft-cited 'Neutral Principles and Some First Amendment Problems' (Chapter 6), published in 1971, links freedom of speech not to autonomy, liberty, or self-realization, but to a particular political system – namely, democracy. However, unlike Redish, who finds a higher value from which democracy itself is derived to be the basis of freedom of speech, Bork begins and ends his analysis with the political process and its demands. Although his argument rests largely on constitutional interpretation rather than normative theory, one can infer a good deal of scepticism about normative theory from his words. Bork concludes that freedom of speech – or at least that freedom of speech that is constitutionalized – is a relatively narrow liberty that primarily encompasses political speech and speech that bears other than tangentially on matters of democratic decision-making. It does not protect speech such as advocacy of violence that aims at subverting democratic processes or laws democratically enacted.

As his 1989 essay title, 'Free Speech Justifications', implies, Kent Greenawalt is a pluralist when it comes to providing a justification for freedom of speech. Greenawalt 'maintains that efforts to arrive at any single unifying justification risk either simplifying or obscuring the complex values undergirding freedom of expression'. He finds both consequentialist and non-consequentialist justifications at work in this area, the former referring to reasons dependent on empirical grounds, the latter referring to non-empirical normative reasons. He usefully canvasses the various consequentialist and non-consequentialist values that freedom of speech might serve and points out the areas where the justifications overlap and reinforce one another.

Alvin Goldman, in his 1991 essay 'Epistemic Paternalism: Communication Control in Law and Society' (Chapter 8), focuses on restricting communication in order to improve the audience's epistemic prospects. Goldman's analysis is applicable to all governmental restrictions on speech based on fear that the audience will misevaluate it. He does not take a categorical position on epistemic paternalism, finding it relatively unproblematic in the context of the rules of evidence, but much more problematic in other contexts. Goldman identifies a variety of factors that should bear on the evaluation of epistemic paternalism.

In 'The Impossibility of a Free Speech Principle' (Chapter 9), which Paul Horton and I published in 1984, we express doubt that any principle can justify special protection for speech. We critique Frederick Schauer's 'negative', distrust-of-government free speech principle, as presented in his *Free Speech: A Philosophical Enquiry*, as well as various 'positive' free speech principles, both consequentialist and deontological. We agree with Schauer's focus on government's *motive* to *suppress a message* as key to freedom of speech, but we believe that Schauer does not apply his own framework consistently. We also argue that Schauer needs a positive theory like Scanlon's to buttress his government-motive centred theory. Finally, we conclude that Schauer's theory leaves completely unprotected all incidental regulations of speech – those not aimed at suppressing messages – no matter how great their impact on communication.

Frederick Schauer, in his 1984 essay 'Must Speech Be Special?' (Chapter 10), finds that theories of freedom of speech that emphasize individual self-realization or fulfilment fail as theories of the First Amendment because they are too broad to explain the 'specialness' of speech. Schauer believes that no single value can justify freedom of speech. Rather, the best chance for justifying special protection for freedom of speech lies in the convergence of a number of different values. Such a multivalued theory of freedom of speech would, in a sense, represent a cluster of different 'First Amendments', each a response to a different evil or problem.

Part III shifts from general theories of freedom of speech to a derivative question – namely, what kinds of acts raise freedom of speech concerns? In other words, is freedom of speech's focus on a specific kind of activity – 'speech' – that government might regulate, or is it instead on a specific kind of *reason* government might have for regulating *any* activity?

The *locus classicus* on this issue is John Ely's 1975 essay, 'Flag Desecration: A Case Study in the Roles of Categorization and Balancing in First Amendment Analysis' (Chapter 11). Ely argues that laws prohibiting flag desecration violate freedom of speech not because the underlying conduct which they target is immune from regulation – in many cases, the conduct is punishable under some valid statute, such as one prohibiting setting fires on public streets and pavements – but because government's *reason* for enacting flag desecration laws is to prevent receipt of an ideological message. The key to the application of freedom of speech is not the ontology of the conduct regulated but the teleology of the regulation.

In 'Trouble on Track Two: Incidental Regulations of Speech and Free Speech Theory' (Chapter 12), published in 1993, I explore the implications of focusing freedom of speech on government's reasons for regulating. I follow Ely in holding that government's desire to suppress a message is at the core of freedom of speech, but I also point out that the very concern that makes presumptively invalid government actions so motivated should also render government action not so motivated immune from judicial invalidation on free speech grounds. The latter category of governmental actions includes everything that government does and has vastly greater impact on communication – what gets said by whom to whom and with what effect – than does governmental action aimed at suppressing messages. The reason that these incidental regulations of speech must be immune from judicial invalidation on free speech grounds is that invalidation would require the courts to assign the communicative impact a weight, and that in turn would entail having the government – the courts – evaluate messages.

In 'Legal Theory: Low Value Speech', published in 1989, I explore another implication of focusing free speech inquiry on government's reasons for regulating rather than on the nature of the conduct being regulated. I argue that such a focus precludes the courts, deeming some speech to be 'low value' and other speech to be 'high value'. If, for example, government regulates pornography because it wishes to prevent the audience from drawing a political conclusion about the status of women, then the government's regulation should be viewed as a regulation of political speech. Likewise, a medical text's primary audience may be using it voyeuristically. Audiences may derive all sorts of ideas from all sorts of objects, many, and perhaps most, of which were never intended by an author; and government might be worried about such messages even when the messages are being derived from objects never intended to convey them. I conclude that, although the notion of a 'low value *idea*' makes sense (even if it is constitutionally suspect), the notion of 'low value *speech*' does not.

I continue this theme in my 1995 essay, 'Free Speech and Speaker's Intent' (Chapter 14), this time looking at the role of the speaker's intent in free speech analysis. Just as freedom of speech should not focus on the nature of the conduct or object regulated, neither, I argue, should it focus on what message the speaker intended to communicate through the conduct or object. If the government is regulating the conduct or object because of the message government believes or fears the audience is deriving from it, then it should make no difference whether the speaker intended that message or, indeed, any message whatsoever. In the case of pornography, for example, if government regulates because of fear of a political message, then core freedom of speech values are implicated even if the pornographer did not intend such a message.

Note

1   Only its length caused the omission of Kent Greenawalt's superb essay, 'Speech and Crime', *American Bar Federation Reserve Journal*, 1980, p. 645.

Part I
Overview

[1]

FREEDOM OF SPEECH

Larry Alexander
University of San Diego

GLOSSARY

autonomy The condition of being self-governing.
compossible Describing the ability of individuals' rights to coexist without conflicting in any possible situation.
consequentialist Referring to theories of ethical justification that base ethical assessment of acts exclusively on their consequences.
deontological Referring to theories of ethical justification that base ethical assessment on features of acts other than and in addition to their consequences.
incidental restrictions Restrictions on speech that are not aimed at its communicative aspect.

FREEDOM OF SPEECH is widely held to be a moral right and almost as widely recognized as a legal right. It was defended by John Milton in the 17th century and enshrined in the Constitution of the United States in 1791 as part of the First Amendment. Some form of recognition of freedom of speech is expressed in almost every modern constitution and international protocol regarding human rights. Yet, as revealed by the jurisprudence under the First Amendment of the United States Constitution—which is by far the most developed free speech jurisprudence—and the enormous body of philosophical and legal commentary on freedom of speech, the justification(s) for and the contours of freedom of speech are much mooted. Moreover, there are some, even in liberal democracies, who deny any special importance to freedom of speech, and there are others who deny its coherence as a concept.

I. THE SCOPE OF FREEDOM OF SPEECH: WHAT IS "SPEECH"?

Freedom of speech has always been thought to cover more than what is literally speech, that is, spoken language. For example, no one disputes that it covers written language as well as spoken language. Moreover, it is difficult to see how it could be withheld from sign language, pictographs, pictures, movies, plays, and so forth, and indeed the legal protection afforded freedom of speech has been extended to all of these media of communication and expression, as well as to abstract artistic and musical performances. Usually, then, freedom of speech refers to—and is frequently referred to as—freedom of expression or freedom of communication.

It is a commonplace to distinguish between "speech" and "symbolic speech." As the previous paragraph should make clear, however, that distinction is illusory. All speech employs symbols, whether they be sounds, shapes, gestures, pictures, or any other tangible medium. There is thus no such thing as nonsymbolic speech; there is only speech that employs symbols that are less or more conventional. The same point also applies to any purported distinction between speech and "conduct" or "action." All speech requires conduct of some sort, and any conduct can be communicative. The conclusion to be drawn is that freedom of speech should be thought of as freedom of communication.

II. WHO HAS THE RIGHT TO FREEDOM OF SPEECH?

It is most natural to think that if there is a right to freedom of speech, it must be the right of the speaker. Thus, when the government threatens S with punishment if he attempts to give certain information to A, we are tempted to regard this as a violation of S's right to freedom of speech.

On most accounts of why freedom of speech should be protected, however, it is A's freedom of speech that is violated whether or not S's freedom of speech is also violated. For assume that S is the author of a book and is now dead (or the citizen of a foreign country). He has no freedom of speech now in A's country. If A's government is violating anyone's rights by prohibiting the dissemination of S's book, it is A's (the audience's) rights. Moreover, if A's government prohibited A from watching sunsets because it feared A would be inspired to have subversive thoughts, freedom of speech would arguably be implicated, *even though there is no speaker*.

In suggesting that the right to freedom of speech is best thought of as belonging to the audience, I do not mean to imply that people have a claim right against the government or anyone else that they be spoken to or provided with information. If the right of freedom of speech ultimately belongs to the audience, it is in the form of a right not to be prevented from obtaining information or ideas that are otherwise available to it.

In saying that free speech is best thought of as a right of the audience, I also am not saying that speakers have no standing to object to having their speech suppressed. Frequently it will best serve the audience's right to hear if speakers are given a derivative right to speak. Indeed, in most cases where government interdicts a communication between a willing speaker and

her audience, the speaker will be in the best position to assert the right to freedom of speech, both because the audience may be unaware of the attempted communication and because the audience's right depends upon the speaker's being willing to speak. (The right is not a claim right against the speaker that she speak.)

III. WHAT ARE THE JUSTIFICATIONS FOR FREEDOM OF SPEECH?

There are numerous theories regarding the justification(s) for freedom of speech. Each theory produces a different conception of what freedom of speech encompasses and when it is violated. I shall lump the theories into four broad groupings.

A. Consequentialist Theories

1. The Search for Truth

One common justification advanced on behalf of freedom of speech is that such freedom is instrumental to the discovery of truth. Freedom to disseminate new information and to criticize prevailing views is necessary for eliminating misconceptions of fact and value.

Although this justification is frequently criticized as resting on a philosophically naive realist view about facts and values, that criticism is off the mark. The justification for free inquiry as a means for discovering truth is not tied to any particular metaphysical view about fact or value.

The real problem with this justification is not in what it assumes about the nature of truth but in what it assumes is the best procedure for obtaining truth. In domains in which obtaining truth is the principal value—for example, in legal proceedings—speech is regulated and circumscribed. Even in the area of scientific inquiry, professional journals refuse to publish claims that the editors believe are not properly substantiated, and faculties and laboratories refuse to employ those who hold what in the opinion of the faculties and laboratories are outlandish views.

Moreover, it is a mistake to assume that truth is something quantifiable, so that we can assess alternative regimes based on how much "truth" each produces. There is no *single thing* called Truth that we can obtain, either absolutely or in varying degrees. To ask whether a regulation promotes or impedes Truth is to ask a question that is essentially meaningless, like asking how many individual things there are in the universe. All regulations, and all failures to regulate, produce different environments, and each environment reveals some truths and obscures others.

Of course the truthseekers might want to see the question posed differently. Instead of posing the question in a way that invokes Truth, one might pose a specific truth-seeking question: whether a specific regulation promotes or impedes a scientific truth.

One should concede that there are specific truths—"right answers" to specific truth-seeking questions. One should concede that some of those specific truths can be viewed as particularly important to obtain. These concessions having been made, it would follow that if (1) a governmental regulation interferes with the search for the answer to a particular question—a particular truth—and if (2) obtaining the answer to that particular question is viewed as very important, then (3) the regulation is unjustified unless (4) the other values served, or "truths" revealed, by the regulation are equally as important as obtaining the answer to that particular question.

For example, one might believe that forbidding the publication of the *Pentagon Papers* substantially obstructs the search for the truth about U.S. involvement in Vietnam, and that the "truths" and other values served by keeping the *Pentagon Papers* secret are less important than the truth about that involvement. If one subscribes to this belief, then one will condemn any attempt to restrain the publication of the *Pentagon Papers,* even though, because of other values that would be implicated, one might not allow citizens to search the Pentagon looking for those papers, or one might punish those whose thievery was responsible for their publication.

The problem with the "quest for truth" as a theory of free speech in the "specific truths" sense is that one cannot extrapolate from the quest for specific truths to any recognizable general theory of free speech. The quest for specific truths demonstrates only that some speech does help answer some questions that are relatively important, and that regulation of speech sometimes will be unjustified. Other speech contributes little toward answering some questions; some activities other than speech contribute a great deal toward answering some questions; and answering some questions is less important than, and occasionally is downright destructive of, other values that even avid specific-truth seekers would want to protect or maximize.

2. Maximization of Other Values

There are other values besides Truth that freedom of speech might advance. These values are various; they include individual self-rule, individual self-develop-

ment, and political self-rule. To the extent that we can characterize these theories as based on the general value of autonomy, they seek to maximize autonomy rather than to treat it as some absolute or near-absolute side constraint.

The autonomy these theories seek to maximize, however, is not affected only by regulations aimed at communicative impact, that is, by regulations designed to prevent audiences from learning certain information or hearing certain arguments or opinions. Autonomy also is affected by any regulation that affects the information and opinions one receives—that is, by all governmental regulations. All of government's regulations—those affecting access to information; access to the indefinite diversity of the media of communication; access to private property in others' possession that may be useful for communicating generally, certain ideas, or in a particular form—affect the ideas that individuals receive. Hence, *all* government regulations influence individuals' self-rule and self-development. And, of course, the interests that government balances against speech—such as security of person, security of property, and protection of privacy—all affect autonomy values.

Thus, these consequentialist theories all require some sort of balancing mechanism. Balancing is required so that government can, for example, decide whether allowing Able to burn Baker's dollar bill without Baker's consent (in order, say, to protest inflation in front of a particular audience and with a particular communicative effect) advances autonomy more than not allowing Able to do so (with the resulting benefits of protecting security of property while permitting whatever speech would result if property allocations were undisturbed, and so forth).

Consequentialist theories require that speech be assigned a "proper value" in furthering autonomy. They likewise require that other values be assigned "proper weights" relative to autonomy. Surely "speech" has some value, and surely the value of "speech" varies with its truth, its importance, and so forth. Therefore, these theories require some government agency—ultimately courts or legislatures—to assess speech for its truth, importance, and so forth, as well as to balance the value of "speech" against other values.

None of these theories justifies the special treatment of "speech" as distinguished from other activities that contribute to autonomy. None of them justifies distinguishing courts from primary governmental decision makers, either by treating courts as more trustworthy balances or by recognizing a special need for a second opinion from the courts with respect to "speech" but

not with respect to other activities. None of these theories even presents a comprehensive scheme for balancing speech against other activities that contribute to
autonomy. None of them, indeed, presents a comprehensive scheme for balancing "autonomy" against
other values.

B. Democratic Theories

Freedom of speech is usually thought of as a right
to be asserted against the government, even when,
as, for example, in the United States, that government
is democratic in nature. Yet a very prominent group
of justificatory theories of freedom of speech find the
central justification of that freedom to be its affiliation
with democratic decision making. One idea is that
democratic decision making requires an informed
citizenry, and an informed citizenry requires freedom
of speech. A separate idea is that democratic (in
form) decision making is legitimate (and truly democratic) only if public opinion is not itself shaped by
the government.

Versions of democratic justifications of freedom of
speech vary in scope. Some versions are very narrow,
treating freedom of speech as concerned only with
communications about governmental policies and personnel. Others are much broader, arguing that informed self-rule requires protection of scientific, literary, artistic, and other types of speech along with
the overtly political. The broadest of these theories
are operationally indistinguishable from either those
which justify freedom of speech as maximizing autonomy, as already discussed, or those which justify
it as a deontological side constraint, as discussed
further on.

The problem with justifying freedom of speech by
its relation to democratic decision making is that both
being democratic and being informed are matters of
degree. A regime that protects freedom of speech from
democratically passed restrictions is in one sense—an
informed citizenry—more democratic, and in another
sense—democratic laws are struck down—less democratic, than a regime in which democratic decision making is unlimited. Moreover, no citizenry is ever perfectly
informed about anything; all information about some
things comes at a cost, including the cost of displacing
information about other things, and all laws, including
laws restricting freedom of speech, bring some new
information and opinions into the world at the same
time that they eliminate other information and
opinions.

C. Deontological Theories

The last group of justificatory theories view freedom
of speech as justified, not by its ability to maximize
some value such as truth or autonomy, and not by
its association with a particular form of government,
but by an argument from an asserted moral right not
to have government prevent people from having certain ideas because of its fear that they will not respond
to those ideas appropriately. The right is deontological
in character. Its recognition is not something to
be maximized. Rather, it is a side constraint on
government's action.

These deontological theories logically require that
we look not at government's laws per se, but at government's reasons for enacting those laws. If the reasons
are to prevent people from having certain ideas, then
freedom of speech is implicated, even if there is no act
of communication in the normal sense. Thus, a law
banning rallies in residential neighborhoods because of
concern with noise or traffic would not implicate freedom of speech under these theories. On the other hand,
a law banning toy soldiers based on a concern about
creating positive views of militarism would. The root
idea is that people have a right that government not
take action predicated on its concern that they may
otherwise possess ideas that they will act on in harmful ways.

D. Other Theories of Proscribed
Government Motives

A final group of theories would have us look at government's reasons for acting, not because people have a
deontological right that government not concern itself
with their thoughts, but because it is improper for other
reasons or dangerous for government to be permitted
to act on its views about the worthiness or harmfulness
of ideas. Some of these theories are deontological in
form, positing, for example, a duty on government to
treat ideas with equal respect. Others are consequentialist in orientation, arguing that government is more
likely to overestimate the benefits and underestimate
the costs of trying to affect what people think
through coercion.

Some of these motive theories would have courts
ferret out the forbidden motives behind laws directly.
Others would have the courts do so indirectly, through
various presumptions and burdens of proof. Some, indeed, find the first amendment jurisprudence in the
United States most explicable on this latter basis.

IV. THE MAJOR CLASSIFICATIONS OF GOVERNMENT ACTS IMPLICATING FREEDOM OF SPEECH

A. Laws Directed at the Content of Speech

At the core of freedom of speech is a concern over laws directed at the content—the communicative impact—of speech. If any type of law violates freedom of speech, it is a law that picks out certain ideas and prohibits or restricts their communication.

Nonetheless, even laws aimed at interdicting the communication of certain ideas are frequently deemed not to violate freedom of speech. To understand why, it is most useful to examine the linkage between the communication of the idea and the ultimate harm that is the government's concern.

1. Harms That Government May Not Legitimately Seek to Prevent

Freedom of speech itself is usually deemed to make certain "harms" matters with which government has no legitimate concern. For example, government has no legitimate concern with whether people think well of it. Nor does government have a legitimate concern with the religious and political ideas and values of its adult citizens, or their cultural tastes, at least not to the extent that would license governmental attempts to suppress communication.

2. Harms Caused in Two Steps

Frequently when government suppresses speech based on its content, it is seeking to prevent a harm that it may legitimately attempt to prevent. Thus, if S incites A to kill government officials, the government may legitimately prevent A from doing so, and punish A if he attempts to do so.

Here, the ultimate harm that the government may legitimately prevent—killing government officials—is connected to the inciting speech in two steps: The inciting speech communicates the idea to A, and A then decides to act on the idea. The question for freedom of speech is whether the government may seek to prevent the harm more effectively by targeting the first step in addition to the second step.

Laws against inciting or soliciting crimes, advocating the overthrow of the government by force, provoking another to fight, revealing information useful to domestic terrorists or other criminals, and the like are examples of laws suppressing speech based on its content in order to prevent a harm that requires a still further

step. The free speech jurisprudence of the United States was largely developed in response to laws of this type, at least into the 1960s.

3. Harms Caused in One Step

Frequently, once information has been communicated to A, there is nothing further the government can do to prevent harm, either because mere possession of this information by A is itself harmful, or because, although the harm will not eventuate without further action by A, government cannot legitimately prevent that further action.

Examples of such harms caused by the content of speech are numerous. They include revelation of secret, confidential, or private information; defamation; infringement of copyright or other property interests in speech; offense; interference with a fair trial; coercion; deception; assault; and adverse effects on the morale or efficiency of governmental operations. (The content of speech can bring about these last harms by causing friction among government employees, causing loss of confidence in government employees among the public clientele, or revealing disloyal or inappropriate attitudes of public employees.) In each of these cases, the question is whether the speech interests of S and A override the competing values.

B. Incidental Restrictions on Speech

Laws directed at the content of speech obviously raise freedom of speech issues. But such laws are not by any means the exclusive determinants of what gets said, by whom, to whom, and with what effect. Indeed, *all laws* have effects on what gets said, by whom, to whom, and with what impact. That is, all laws have information effects.

Thus, arguably the domain of free speech includes not only restrictions on obstructing traffic while speaking or demonstrating, using amplifying devices in residential neighborhoods, posting signs on utility poles, burning draft cards, or sleeping in parks, but also includes tort, contract, and property law, the tax code, and the multitude of criminal and regulatory laws and administrative regulations. For example, laws determining who owns what property under what restrictions or the price and availability of various resources will also determine what gets said, by whom, to whom, and with what effect—that is, the laws will have information effects. A change in the laws of any region of the corpus juris will have information effects. Laws equalizing income would surely have dramatic information effects. Any law, however, and any change in law, will have cognizable effects which will translate into information of some kind.

The courts of the United States have treated some incidental regulations of speech as raising free speech issues, though the jurisprudence has been murky, the number of cases finding free speech violations few, and the choice of which laws to review apparently unprincipled. There is a reason for these problems. If all laws have information effects, then all alternatives to those laws will also have information effects. For example, the setting of the marginal tax rate affects my income, which, if greater, I might devote to increased speaking. The courts could rule that if the government's interest in the present rate is not significant, and the rate adversely affects my speech, the government must abandon that rate in favor of another rate. But any other rate the government chooses will affect somebody's speech—it may result in lower transfer payments, adversely affecting the communication between poorer speakers and their audience—and, thus, it will have to serve a significant interest as well.

If all laws—and therefore all alternative sets of laws—have information effects, then courts assessing such laws in terms of freedom of speech need some Archimedean point from which to evaluate such laws and sets of laws. But if freedom of speech functions principally as a bar to government's imposing an evaluation on the content of speech—and since courts are part of the government—freedom of speech arguably and paradoxically requires the courts to forgo reviewing incidental restrictions on speech, even though incidental restrictions have far more important information effects than content restrictions.

Such a conclusion is consistent with the deontological justifications for freedom of speech. They make freedom of speech an issue when and only when government's acts are motivated by government's desire to keep audiences from having certain information or ideas. On the other hand, consequentialist and democratic justifications would arguably require evaluation of information effects across the board, regardless of the type of law (content-directed or incidental restriction) in question.

C. Government Speech and Subsidies of Private Speech

Another area where freedom of speech is arguably implicated is where the government itself "speaks." That area includes not only such acts as government's issuing pamphlets describing laws and programs and govern-

ment's advertising opportunities in government employment and the military, but also government's running the public schools and universities. Still more broadly it includes government's subsidizing those private speakers who deliver government's message, so long as we are dealing with a true subsidy rather than a penalty on those who refuse to deliver the message.

Some believe that the principle of freedom of speech renders all or some of these acts illegitimate. Others believe that such acts are entirely consistent with freedom of speech. The latter argue that freedom of speech is restricted to coercive government action. The former respond that government action is always coercive in that it involves resources involuntarily extracted from the citizenry that could be devoted to alternative communication and information.

D. Private Suppression of Speech

Although as a legal matter freedom of speech is usually concerned with laws and other governmental acts, it is common to refer to freedom of speech in purely private contexts as well. Thus, if our (private) employer forbids us to discuss politics on the job, or asks us to donate to her political party if we wish to be promoted, we are quite likely to argue that such directives violate our freedom of speech—so, too, if a private residential organization refuses to let pamphleteers enter a gated community, or if a private shopping center bans petition gathering from its premises.

Under the deontological justification theories, the question is whether the private employer or landowner is exercising *its* rights. If so, then, assuming deontological rights are compossible, it is not violating any free speech rights. Of course, it may be acting wrongly even if within its rights. And the autonomy value that lies behind the deontological right of freedom of speech may explain the wrongness even if it does elevate it to the level of rights violation.

The consequentialist theories would not in principle exempt private speech suppression from their purview. Indeed, if the private speech suppression is permitted by law, then *its* free speech status is really just another way of putting the status of those laws that permit it, a matter already touched on in the section on incidental restrictions on speech.

Also See the Following Articles

AUTONOMY • CENSORSHIP • CONSEQUENTIALISM AND DEONTOLOGY

Bibliography

Alexander, L. (1993). Trouble on track two: Incidental regulations of speech and free speech theory. *Hastings Law J.* 44, 921–962.

Garvey, J., and Schauer, F. (1996). "The First Amendment," 2nd ed. West, St. Paul, MN.

Kagan, E. (1996). Private speech, public purpose: The role of govern-mental motive in first amendment doctrine. *Univ. Chicago Law Rev.* 63, 413–517.

Post, R. (1995). Recuperating first amendment doctrine. *Stanford Law Rev.* 47, 1249–1281.

Schauer, F. (1992). Uncoupling free speech. *Columbia Law Rev.* 92, 1321–1357.

Sunstein, C. R. (1993). "Democracy and the Problem of Free Speech." The Free Press, New York.

Part II
Freedom of Speech

[2]

Thomas Scanlon

A Theory of Freedom of Expression[1]

> Persecution for the expression of
> opinions seems to me perfectly logical.
> If you have no doubt of your premises
> or your power and want a certain result
> with all your heart you naturally express
> your wishes in law and sweep away all
> opposition. To allow opposition by speech
> seems to indicate that you think the
> speech impotent, as when a man says
> that he has squared the circle, or that
> you do not care wholeheartedly for the
> result, or that you doubt either your
> power or your premises. But. . . .
> —Oliver Wendell Holmes[2]

I

The doctrine of freedom of expression is generally thought to single
out a class of "protected acts" which it holds to be immune from
restrictions to which other acts are subject. In particular, on any very
strong version of the doctrine there will be cases where protected
acts are held to be immune from restriction despite the fact that they
have as consequences harms which would normally be sufficient to
justify the imposition of legal sanctions. It is the existence of such
cases which makes freedom of expression a significant doctrine and
which makes it appear, from a certain point of view, an irrational
one. This feeling of irrationality is vividly portrayed by Justice Holmes
in the passage quoted.

To answer this charge of irrationality is the main task of a philosophical defense of freedom of expression. Such an answer requires,
first, a clear account of what the class of protected acts is, and then
an explanation of the nature and grounds of its privilege. The most
common defense of the doctrine of freedom of expression is a con-

1. This paper is derived from one presented to the Society for Ethical and
Legal Philosophy, and I am grateful to the members of that group, as well as
to a number of other audiences willing and unwilling, for many helpful comments and criticisms.
2. Dissenting in Abrams v. United States, 250 U.S. 616 (1919).

sequentialist one. This may take the form of arguing with respect to a certain class of acts, e.g., acts of speech, that the good consequences of allowing such acts to go unrestricted outweigh the bad. Alternatively, the boundaries of the class of protected acts may themselves be *defined* by balancing good consequences against bad, the question of whether a certain species of acts belongs to the privileged genus being decided in many if not all cases just by asking whether its inclusion would, on the whole, lead to more good consequences than bad. This seems to be the form of argument in a number of notable court cases, and at least some element of balancing seems to be involved in almost every landmark first amendment decision.[3] Thus one thing which an adequate philosophical account of freedom of expression should do is to make clear in what way the definition of the class of protected acts and the justification for their privilege depend upon a balancing of competing goals or interests and to what extent they rest instead on rights or other absolute, i.e., nonconsequentialist, principles. In particular, one would like to know to what extent a defender of freedom of expression must rest his case on the claim that the long-term benefits of free discussion will outweigh certain obvious and possibly severe short-run costs, and to what extent this calculation of long-term advantage depends upon placing a high value on knowledge and intellectual pursuits as opposed to other values.

A further question that an adequate account of freedom of expression should answer is this: To what extent does the doctrine rest on natural moral principles and to what extent is it an artificial creation of particular political institutions? An account of freedom of expression might show the doctrine to be artificial in the sense I have in mind if, for example, it identified the class of protected acts simply as those acts recognized as legitimate forms of political activity under a certain constitution *and* gave as the defense of their privilege merely a defense of that constitution as reasonable, just, and binding on those to whom it applied. A slightly different "artificial"

---

3. The balancing involved in such decisions is not always strictly a matter of maximizing good consequences, since what is "balanced" often includes personal rights as well as individual and social goods. The problems involved in "balancing" rights in this way are forcefully presented by Ronald Dworkin in "Taking Rights Seriously," *New York Review of Books*, 17 December 1970, pp. 23-31.

account of freedom of expression is given by Meiklejohn,[4] who finds
the basis for the privileged status of acts of expression in the fact
that the right to perform such acts is necessary if the citizens of a
democratic state are to perform their duties as self-governing citizens.
On his view it appears that citizens not expected to "govern themselves"
would lack (at least one kind of) right to freedom of expression. In
contrast to either of these views, Mill's famous argument offers a defense of "the liberty of thought and discussion" which relies only on
general moral grounds and is independent of the features of any particular laws or institutions. It seems clear to me that our (or at least
my) intuitions about freedom of expression involve both natural and
artificial elements. An adequate account of the subject should make
clear whether these two kinds of intuitions represent rival views of
freedom of expression or whether they are compatible or comple-
mentary.

Although I will not consider each of these questions about freedom of expression in turn, I hope by the end of this discussion to
have presented a theory which gives answers to all of them. I begin
with an oblique attack on the first.

II

The only class of acts I have mentioned so far is the class "acts
of expression," which I mean to include any act that is intended by
its agent to communicate to one or more persons some proposition
or attitude. This is an extremely broad class. In addition to many
acts of speech and publication it includes displays of symbols, failures to display them, demonstrations, many musical performances,
and some bombings, assassinations, and self-immolations. In order
for any act to be classified as an act of expression it is sufficient that
it be linked with some proposition or attitude which it is intended
to convey.

Typically, the acts of expression with which a theory of "free
speech" is concerned are addressed to a large (if not the widest
possible) audience, and express propositions or attitudes thought to
have a certain generality of interest. This accounts, I think, for our

4. Alexander Meiklejohn, *Political Freedom*, 2nd edn. (New York, 1965).
See esp. p. 79.

reluctance to regard as an act of expression in the relevant sense the communication between the average bank robber and the teller he confronts. This reluctance is diminished somewhat if the note the robber hands the teller contains, in addition to the usual threat, some political justification for his act and an exhortation to others to follow his example. What this addition does is to broaden the projected audience and increase the generality of the message's interest. The relevance of these features is certainly something which an adequate theory of freedom of expression should explain, but it will be simpler at present not to make them part of the definition of the class of acts of expression.

Almost everyone would agree, I think, that the acts which are protected by a doctrine of freedom of expression will all be acts of expression in the sense I have defined. However, since acts of expression can be both violent and arbitrarily destructive, it seems unlikely that anyone would maintain that as a class they were immune from legal restrictions. Thus the class of protected acts must be some proper subset of this class. It is sometimes held that the relevant subclass consists of those acts of expression which are instances of "speech" as opposed to "action." But those who put forward such a view have generally wanted to include within the class of protected acts some which are not speech in any normal sense of the word (for instance, mime and certain forms of printed communication) and to exclude from it some which clearly are speech in the normal sense (talking in libraries, falsely shouting "fire" in crowded theaters, etc.). Thus if acts of speech are the relevant subclass of acts of expression, then "speech" is here functioning as a term of art which needs to be defined. To construct a theory following these traditional lines we might proceed to work out a technical correlate to the distinction between speech and action which seemed to fit our clearest intuitions about which acts do and which do not qualify for protection.[5]

To proceed in this way seems to me, however, to be a serious mistake. It seems clear that the intuitions we appeal to in deciding whether a given restriction infringes freedom of expression are not

5. This task is carried out by Thomas Emerson in *Toward a General Theory of the First Amendment* (New York, 1966). See esp. pp. 60-62.

intuitions about which things are properly called speech as opposed to action, even in some refined sense of "speech." The feeling that we must look for a definition of this kind has its roots, I think, in the view that since any adequate doctrine of freedom of expression must extend to some acts a privilege not enjoyed by all, such a doctrine must have its theoretical basis in some difference between the protected acts and others, i.e., in some definition of the protected class. But this is clearly wrong. It could be, and I think is, the case that the theoretical bases of the doctrine of freedom of expression are multiple and diverse, and while the net effect of these elements taken together is to extend to some acts a certain privileged status, there is no theoretically interesting (and certainly no simple and intuitive) definition of the class of acts which enjoys this privilege. Rather than trying at the outset to carve out the privileged subset of acts of expression, then, I propose to consider the class as a whole and to look for ways in which the charge of irrationality brought against the doctrine of freedom of expression might be answered without reference to a single class of privileged acts.

As I mentioned at the start, this charge arises from the fact that under any nontrivial form of the doctrine there will be cases in which acts of expression are held to be immune from legal restriction despite the fact that they give rise to undoubted harms which would in other cases be sufficient to justify such restriction. (The "legal restriction" involved here may take the form either of the imposition of criminal sanctions or of the general recognition by the courts of the right of persons affected by the acts to recover through civil suits for damages.) Now it is not in general sufficient justification for a legal restriction on a certain class of acts to show that certain harms will be prevented if this restriction is enforced. It might happen that the costs of enforcing the restriction outweigh the benefits to be gained, or that the enforcement of the restriction infringes some right either directly (e.g., a right to the unimpeded performance of exactly those acts to which the restriction applies) or indirectly (e.g., a right which under prevailing circumstances can be secured by many only through acts to which the restriction applies). Alternatively, it may be that while certain harms could be prevented by placing legal restrictions on a class of acts, those to whom the restriction would apply are not responsible for those harms and hence cannot be restricted in order to prevent them.

Most defenses of freedom of expression have rested upon arguments of the first two of these three forms. In arguments of both these forms factors which taken in isolation might have been sufficient to justify restrictions on a given class of acts are held in certain cases to be overridden by other considerations. As will become clear later, I think that appeals both to rights and to the balancing of competing goals are essential components of a complete theory of freedom of expression. But I want to begin by considering arguments which, like disclaimers of responsibility, have the effect of showing that what might at first seem to be reasons for restricting a class of acts cannot be taken as such reasons at all.

My main reason for beginning in this way is this: it is easier to say what the classic violations of freedom of expression have in common than it is to define the class of acts which is protected by that doctrine. What distinguishes these violations from innocent regulation of expression is not the character of the acts they interfere with but rather what they hope to achieve—for instance, the halting of the spread of heretical notions. This suggests that an important component of our intuitions about freedom of expression has to do not with the illegitimacy of certain restrictions but with the illegitimacy of certain justifications for restrictions. Very crudely, the intuition seems to be something like this: those justifications are illegitimate which appeal to the fact that it would be a bad thing if the view communicated by certain acts of expression were to become generally believed; justifications which are legitimate, though they may sometimes be overridden, are those that appeal to features of acts of expression (time, place, loudness) other than the views they communicate.

As a principle of freedom of expression this is obviously unsatisfactory as it stands. For one thing, it rests on a rather unclear notion of "the view communicated" by an act of expression; for another, it seems too restrictive, since, for example, it appears to rule out any justification for laws against defamation. In order to improve upon this crude formulation, I want to consider a number of different ways in which acts of expression can bring about harms, concen-

trating on cases where these harms clearly can be counted as reasons for restricting the acts that give rise to them. I will then try to
formulate the principle in a way which accommodates these cases. I
emphasize at the outset that I am not maintaining in any of these
cases that the harms in question are always sufficient justification
for restrictions on expression, but only that they can always be taken
into account.

   1. Like other acts, acts of expression can bring about injury or
damage as a direct physical consequence. This is obviously true of
the more bizarre forms of expression mentioned above, but no less
true of more pedestrian forms: the sound of my voice can break
glass, wake the sleeping, trigger an avalanche, or keep you from
paying attention to something else you would rather hear. It seems
clear that when harms brought about in this way are intended by the
person performing an act of expression, or when he is reckless or
negligent with respect to their occurrence, then no infringement
of freedom of expression is involved in considering them as possible
grounds for criminal penalty or civil action.

   2. It is typical of the harms just considered that their production
is in general quite independent of the view which the given act of
expression is intended to communicate. This is not generally true of a
second class of harms, an example of which is provided by the common law notion of assault. In at least one of the recognized senses
of the term, an assault (as distinct from a battery) is committed
when one person intentionally places another in apprehension of
imminent bodily harm. Since assault in this sense involves an element of successful communication, instances of assault may necessarily involve expression. But assaults and related acts can also be
part of larger acts of expression, as for example when a guerrilla
theater production takes the form of a mock bank robbery which
starts off looking like the real thing, or when a bomb scare is used
to gain attention for a political cause. Assault is sometimes treated
as inchoate battery, but it can also be viewed as a separate offense
which consists in actually bringing about a specific kind of harm.
Under this analysis, assault is only one of a large class of possible
crimes which consist in the production in others of harmful or unpleasant states of mind, such as fear, shock, and perhaps certain

kinds of offense. One may have doubts as to whether most of these harms are serious enough to be recognized by the law or whether standards of proof could be established for dealing with them in court. In principle, however, there seems to be no alternative to including them among the possible justifications for restrictions on expression.

3. Another way in which an act of expression can harm a person is by causing others to form an adverse opinion of him or by making him an object of public ridicule. Obvious examples of this are defamation and interference with the right to a fair trial.

4. As Justice Holmes said, "The most stringent protection of free speech would not protect a man in falsely shouting fire in a theater and causing a panic."[6]

5. One person may through an act of expression contribute to the production of a harmful act by someone else, and at least in some cases the harmful consequences of the latter act may justify making the former a crime as well. This seems to many people to be the case when the act of expression is the issuance of an order or the making of a threat or when it is a signal cr other communication between confederates.

6. Suppose some misanthropic inventor were to discover a simple method whereby anyone could make nerve gas in his kitchen out of gasoline, table salt, and urine. It seems just as clear to me that he could be prohibited by law from passing out his recipe on handbills or broadcasting it on television as that he could be prohibited from passing out free samples of his product in aerosol cans or putting it on sale at Abercrombie & Fitch. In either case his action would bring about a drastic decrease in the general level of personal safety by radically increasing the capacity of most citizens to inflict harm on each other. The fact that he does this in one case through an act of expression and in the other through some other form of action seems to me not to matter.

It might happen, however, that a comparable decrease in the general level of personal safety could be just as reliably predicted to result from the distribution of a particularly effective piece of political propaganda which would undermine the authority of the govern-

6. In Schenck v. United States, 249 U.S. 47 (1919).

ment, or from the publication of a theological tract which would lead to a schism and a bloody civil war. In these cases the matter seems to me to be entirely different, and the harmful consequence seems clearly not to be a justification for restricting the acts of expression.

What I conclude from this is that the distinction between expression and other forms of action is less important than the distinction between expression which moves others to act by pointing out what they take to be good reasons for action and expression which gives rise to action by others in other ways, e.g., by providing them with the means to do what they wanted to do anyway. This conclusion is supported, I think, by our normal views about legal responsibility.

If I were to say to you, an adult in full possession of your faculties, "What you ought to do is rob a bank," and you were subsequently to act on this advice, I could not be held legally responsible for your act, nor could my act legitimately be made a separate crime. This remains true if I supplement my advice with a battery of arguments about why banks should be robbed or even about why a certain bank in particular should be robbed and why you in particular are entitled to rob it. It might become false—what I did might legitimately be made a crime—if certain further conditions held: for example, if you were a child, or so weak-minded as to be legally incompetent, and I knew this or ought to have known it; or if you were my subordinate in some organization and what I said to you was not advice but an order, backed by the discipline of the group; or if I went on to make further contributions to your act, such as aiding you in preparations or providing you with tools or giving you crucial information about the bank.

The explanation for these differences seems to me to be this. A person who acts on reasons he has acquired from another's act of expression acts on what *he* has come to believe and has judged to be a sufficient basis for action. The contribution to the genesis of his action made by the act of expression is, so to speak, superseded by the agent's own judgment. This is not true of the contribution made by an accomplice, or by a person who knowingly provides the agent with tools (the key to the bank) or with technical information (the combination of the safe) which he uses to achieve his ends. Nor

would it be true of my contribution to your act if, instead of providing you with reasons for thinking bank robbery a good thing, I
issued orders or commands backed by threats, thus changing your
circumstances so as to *make* it a (comparatively) good thing for you
to do.

It is a difficult matter to say exactly when legal liability arises
in these cases, and I am not here offering any positive thesis about
what constitutes being an accessory, inciting, conspiring, etc. I am
interested only in maintaining the negative thesis that whatever
these crimes involve, it has to be something more than merely the
communication of persuasive reasons for action (or perhaps some
special circumstances, such as diminished capacity of the person
persuaded).

I will now state the principle of freedom of expression which
was promised at the beginning of this section. The principle, which
seems to me to be a natural extension of the thesis Mill defends
in Chapter II of *On Liberty*, and which I will therefore call the Millian
Principle, is the following:

> There are certain harms which, although they would not occur
> but for certain acts of expression, nonetheless cannot be taken
> as part of a justification for legal restrictions on these acts. These
> harms are: (a) harms to certain individuals which consist in
> their coming to have false beliefs as a result of those acts of ex-
> pression; (b) harmful consequences of acts performed as a result
> of those acts of expression, where the connection between the
> acts of expression and the subsequent harmful acts consists mere-
> ly in the fact that the act of expression led the agents to believe
> (or increased their tendency to believe) these acts to be worth
> performing.

I hope it is obvious that this principle is compatible with the
examples of acceptable reasons for restricting expression presented
in 1 through 6 above. (One case in which this may not be obvious,
that of the man who falsely shouts "fire," will be discussed more
fully below.) The preceding discussion, which appealed in part to
intuitions about legal responsibility, was intended to make plausible
the distinction on which the second part of the Millian Principle

rests and, in general, to suggest how the principle could be reconciled with cases of the sort included in 5 and 6. But the principle itself goes beyond questions of responsibility. In order for a class of harms to provide a justification for restricting a person's act it is not necessary that he fulfill conditions for being legally responsible for any of the individual acts which actually produce those harms. In the nerve-gas case, for example, to claim that distribution of the recipe may be prevented one need not claim that a person who distributed it could be held legally responsible (even as an accessory) for any of the particular murders the gas is used to commit. Consequently, to explain why this case differs from sedition it would not be sufficient to claim that providing means involves responsibility while providing reasons does not.

I would like to believe that the general observance of the Millian Principle by governments would, in the long run, have more good consequences than bad. But my defense of the principle does not rest on this optimistic outlook. I will argue in the next section that the Millian Principle, as a general principle about how governmental restrictions on the liberty of citizens may be justified, is a consequence of the view, coming down to us from Kant and others, that a legitimate government is one whose authority citizens can recognize while still regarding themselves as equal, autonomous, rational agents. Thus, while it is not a principle about legal responsibility, the Millian Principle has its origins in a certain view of human agency from which many of our ideas about responsibility also derive.

Taken by itself, the Millian Principle obviously does not constitute an adequate theory of freedom of expression. Much more needs to be said about when the kinds of harmful consequences which the principle allows us to consider can be taken to be sufficient justification for restrictions on expression. Nonetheless, it seems to me fair to call the Millian Principle the basic principle of freedom of expression. This is so, first, because a successful defense of the principle would provide us with an answer to the charge of irrationality by explaining why certain of the most obvious consequences of acts of expression cannot be appealed to as a justification for legal restrictions against them. Second, the Millian Principle is the only plausible principle of freedom of expression I can think of which applies to expression in general and makes no appeal to special rights (e.g., political rights) or to the value to be attached to expression in some particular domain (e.g., artistic expression or the discussion of scientific ideas). It thus specifies what is special about acts of expression as opposed to other acts and constitutes in this sense the usable residue of the distinction between speech and action.

I will have more to say in section IV about how the Millian Principle is to be supplemented to obtain a full account of freedom of expression. Before that, however, I want to consider in more detail how the principle can be justified.

III

As I have already mentioned, I will defend the Millian Principle by showing it to be a consequence of the view that the powers of a state are limited to those that citizens could recognize while still regarding themselves as equal, autonomous, rational agents. Since the sense of autonomy to which I will appeal is extremely weak, this seems to me to constitute a strong defense of the Millian Principle as an exceptionless restriction on governmental authority. I will consider briefly in section V, however, whether there are situations in which the principle should be suspended.

To regard himself as autonomous in the sense I have in mind a person must see himself as sovereign in deciding what to believe and in weighing competing reasons for action. He must apply to these tasks his own canons of rationality, and must recognize the need to defend his beliefs and decisions in accordance with these canons. This does not mean, of course, that he must be perfectly rational, even by his own standard of rationality, or that his standard of rationality must be exactly ours. Obviously the content of this notion of autonomy will vary according to the range of variation we are willing to allow in canons of rational decision. If just anything counts as such a canon then the requirements I have mentioned will become mere tautologies: an autonomous man believes what he believes and decides to do what he decides to do. I am sure I could not describe a set of limits on what can count as canons of rationality which would secure general agreement, and I will not try, since I am sure that the area of agreement on this question extends far beyond anything which will be relevant to the applications of the notion of autonomy that I intend to make. For present purposes what will be important is this. An autonomous person cannot accept without independent consideration the judgment of others as to what he should believe or what he should do. He may rely on the judgment of others, but when he does so he must be prepared to advance independent reasons for thinking their judgment likely to be correct, and to weigh the evidential value of their opinion against contrary evidence.

The requirements of autonomy as I have so far described them are extremely weak. They are much weaker than the requirements Kant draws from essentially the same notion,[7] in that being autonomous in my sense (like being free in Hobbes's) is quite consistent with being subject to coercion with respect to one's actions. A coercer merely changes the considerations which militate for or against a certain course of action; weighing these conflicting considerations is still up to you.

An autonomous man may, if he believes the appropriate arguments, believe that the state has a distinctive right to command him. That is, he may believe that (within certain limits, perhaps) the fact that the law requires a certain action provides him with a very strong reason for performing that action, a reason which is quite independent of the consequences, for him or others, of his performing it or refraining. How strong this reason is—what, if anything, could override it—will depend on his view of the arguments for obedience to law. What is essential to the person's remaining autonomous is that in any given case his mere recognition that a certain action is required by law does not settle the question of whether he will do it. That question is settled only by his own decision, which may take into account his current assessment of the general case for obedience and the exceptions it admits, consideration of his other

7. Kant's notion of autonomy goes beyond the one I employ in that for him there are special requirements regarding the reasons which an autonomous being can act on. (See the second and third sections of *Foundations of the Metaphysics of Morals*.) While his notion of autonomy is stronger than mine, Kant does not draw from it the same limitations on the authority of states (see *Metaphysical Elements of Justice*, sections 46-49).

duties and obligations, and his estimate of the consequences of obedience and disobedience in this particular case.[8]

Thus, while it is not obviously inconsistent with being autonomous to recognize a special obligation to obey the commands of the state, there are limits on the *kind* of obligation which autonomous citizens could recognize. In particular, they could not regard themselves as being under an "obligation" to believe the decrees of the state to be correct, nor could they concede to the state the right to have its decrees obeyed without deliberation. The Millian Principle can be seen as a refinement of these limitations.

The apparent irrationality of the doctrine of freedom of expression derives from its apparent conflict with the principle that it is the prerogative of a state—indeed, part of its duty to its citizens—to decide when the threat of certain harms is great enough to warrant legal action, and when it is, to make laws adequate to meet this threat. (Thus Holmes's famous reference to "substantive evils that Congress has a right to prevent.")[9] Obviously this principle is not acceptable in the crude form in which I have just stated it; no one thinks that Congress can do *anything* it judges to be required to save us from "substantive evils." The Millian Principle specifies two ways in which this prerogative must be limited if the state is to be acceptable to autonomous subjects. The argument for the first part of the principle is as follows.

The harm of coming to have false beliefs is not one that an autonomous man could allow the state to protect him against through restrictions on expression. For a law to provide such protection it would have to be in effect and deterring potential misleaders while the potentially misled remained susceptible to persuasion by them. In order to be protected by such a law a person would thus have to concede to the state the right to decide that certain views were false and, once it had so decided, to prevent him from hearing them

---

8. I am not certain whether I am here agreeing or disagreeing with Robert Paul Wolff (*In Defense of Anarchism* [New York, 1970]). At any rate I would not call what I am maintaining anarchism. The limitation on state power I have in mind is that described by John Rawls in the closing paragraphs of "The Justification of Civil Disobedience," in *Civil Disobedience: Theory and Practice*, ed. Hugo Bedau (New York, 1969).

9. In Schenck v. United States.

advocated even if he might wish to. The conflict between doing this and remaining autonomous would be direct if a person who authorized the state to protect him in this way necessarily also bound himself to accept the state's judgment about which views were false. The matter is not quite this simple, however, since it is conceivable that a person might authorize the state to act for him in this way while still reserving to himself the prerogative of deciding, on the basis of the arguments and evidence left available to him, where the truth was to be found. But such a person would be "deciding for himself" only in an empty sense, since in any case where the state exercised its prerogative he would be "deciding" on the basis of evidence preselected to include only that which supported one conclusion. While he would not be under an obligation to accept the state's judgment as correct, he would have conceded to the state the right to deprive him of grounds for making an independent judgment.

The argument for the second half of the Millian Principle is parallel to this one. What must be argued against is the view that the state, once it has declared certain conduct to be illegal, may when necessary move to prevent that conduct by outlawing its advocacy. The conflict between this thesis and the autonomy of citizens is, just as in the previous case, slightly oblique. Conceding to the state the right to use this means to secure compliance with its laws does not immediately involve conceding to it the right to require citizens to believe that what the law says ought not to be done ought not to be done. Nonetheless, it is a concession that autonomous citizens could not make, since it gives the state the right to deprive citizens of the grounds for arriving at an independent judgment as to whether the law should be obeyed.

These arguments both depend on the thesis that to defend a certain belief as reasonable a person must be prepared to defend the grounds of his belief as not obviously skewed or otherwise suspect. There is a clear parallel between this thesis and Mill's famous argument that if we are interested in having truth prevail we should allow all available arguments to be heard.[10] But the present argument does not depend, as Mill's may appear to, on an empirical

10. In chap. II of *On Liberty*.

claim that the truth is in fact more likely to win out if free discussion is allowed. Nor does it depend on the perhaps more plausible claim that, given the nature of people and governments, to concede to governments the power in question would be an outstandingly poor strategy for bringing about a situation in which true opinions prevail.

It is quite conceivable that a person who recognized in himself a fatal weakness for certain kinds of bad arguments might conclude that everyone would be better off if he were to rely entirely on the judgment of his friends in certain crucial matters. Acting on this conclusion, he might enter into an agreement, subject to periodic review by him, empowering them to shield him from any sources of information likely to divert him from their counsel on the matters in question. Such an agreement is not obviously irrational, nor, if it is entered into voluntarily, for a limited time, and on the basis of the person's own knowledge of himself and those he proposes to trust, does it appear to be inconsistent with his autonomy. The same would be true if the proposed trustees were in fact the authorities of the state. But the question we have been considering is quite different: Could an autonomous individual regard the state as having, not as part of a special voluntary agreement with him but as part of its normal powers qua state, the power to put such an arrangement into effect without his consent whenever *it* (i.e., the legislative authority) judged that to be advisable? The answer to this question seems to me to be quite clearly no.

Someone might object to this answer on the following grounds. I have allowed for the possibility that an autonomous man might accept a general argument to the effect that the fact that the state commands a certain thing is in and of itself a reason why that thing should be done. Why couldn't he also accept a similar argument to the effect that the state qua state is in the best position to decide when certain counsel is best ignored?

I have already argued that the parallel suggested here between the state's right to command action and a right to restrict expression does not hold. But there is a further problem with this objection. What saves temporary, voluntary arrangements of the kind considered above from being obvious violations of autonomy is the fact that they can be based on a firsthand estimation of the relative reliability of the trustee's judgment and that of the "patient." Thus the person whose information is restricted by such an arrangement has what he judges to be good grounds for thinking the evidence he does receive to be a sound basis for judgment. A principle which provided a corresponding basis for relying on the state qua state would have to be extremely general, applying to all states of a certain kind, regardless of who occupied positions of authority in them, and to all citizens of such states. Such a principle would have to be one which admitted variation in individual cases and rested its claim on what worked out best "in the long run." Even if some generalization of this kind were true, it seems to me altogether implausible to suppose that it could be rational to rely on such a general principle when detailed knowledge of the individuals involved in a particular case suggested a contrary conclusion.

A more limited case for allowing states the power in question might rest not on particular virtues of governments but on the recognized fact that under certain circumstances individuals are quite incapable of acting rationally. Something like this may seem to apply in the case of the man who falsely shouts "fire" in a crowded theater. Here a restriction on expression is justified by the fact that such acts would lead others (give them reason) to perform harmful actions. Part of what makes the restriction acceptable is the idea that the persons in the theater who react to the shout are under conditions that diminish their capacity for rational deliberation. This case strikes us as a trivial one. What makes it trivial is, first, the fact that only in a very farfetched sense is a person who is prevented from hearing the false shout under such circumstances prevented from making up his own mind about some question. Second, the diminished capacity attributed to those in the theater is extremely brief, and applies equally to anyone under the relevant conditions. Third, the harm to be prevented by the restriction is not subject to any doubt or controversy, even by those who are temporarily "deluded." In view of all of these facts, the restriction is undoubtedly one which would receive unanimous consent if that were asked.[11]

11. This test is developed as a criterion for justifiable paternalism by Gerald Dworkin in his essay "Paternalism," in *Morality and the Law*, ed. Richard Wasserstrom (Belmont, Cal., 1971).

This is not true, however, of most of the other exceptions to the Millian Principle that might be justified by appeal to "diminished rationality." It is doubtful, for example, whether any of the three conditions I have mentioned would apply to a case in which political debate was to be suspended during a period of turmoil and impending revolution. I cannot see how nontrivial cases of this kind could be made compatible with autonomy.

The arguments I have given may sound like familiar arguments against paternalism, but the issue involved is not simply that. First, a restriction on expression justified on grounds contrary to the Millian Principle is not necessarily paternalistic, since those who are to be protected by such a restriction may be other than those (the speaker and his audience) whose liberty is restricted. When such a restriction is paternalistic, however, it represents a particularly strong form of paternalism, and the arguments I have given are arguments against paternalism only in this strong form. It is quite consistent with a person's autonomy, in the limited sense I have employed, for the law to restrict his freedom of action "for his own good," for instance by requiring him to wear a helmet while riding his motorcycle. The conflict arises only if compliance with this law is then promoted by forbidding, for example, expression of the view that wearing a helmet isn't worth it, or is only for sissies.

It is important to see that the argument for the Millian Principle rests on a limitation of the authority of states to command their subjects rather than on a right of individuals. For one thing, this explains why this particular principle of freedom of expression applies to governments rather than to individuals, who do not have such authority to begin with. There are surely cases in which individuals have the right not to have their acts of expression interfered with by other individuals, but these rights presumably flow from a general right to be free from arbitrary interference, together with considerations which make certain kinds of expression particularly important forms of activity.

If the argument for the Millian Principle were thought to rest on a right, "the right of citizens to make up their own minds," then that argument might be thought to proceed as follows. Persons who see themselves as autonomous see themselves as having a right to make up their own minds, hence also a right to whatever is necessary for them to do this; what is wrong with violations of the Millian Principle is that they infringe this right.

A right of this kind would certainly support a healthy doctrine of freedom of expression, but it is not required for one. The argument given above was much more limited. Its aim was to establish that the authority of governments to restrict the liberty of citizens in order to prevent certain harms does not include authority to prevent these harms by controlling people's sources of information to insure that they will maintain certain beliefs. It is a long step from this conclusion to a right which is violated whenever someone is deprived of information necessary for him to make an informed decision on some matter that concerns him.

There are clearly cases in which individuals have a right to the information necessary to make informed choices and can claim this right against the government. This is true in the case of political decisions, for example, when the right flows from a certain conception of the relation between a democratic government and its citizens. Even where there is no such right, the provision of information and other conditions for the exercise of autonomy is an important task for states to pursue. But these matters take us beyond the Millian Principle.

IV

The Millian Principle is obviously incapable of accounting for all of the cases that strike us as infringements of freedom of expression. On the basis of this principle alone we could raise no objection against a government that banned all parades or demonstrations (they interfere with traffic), outlawed posters and handbills (too messy), banned public meetings of more than ten people (likely to be unruly), and restricted newspaper publication to one page per week (to save trees). Yet such policies surely strike us as intolerable. That they so strike us is a reflection of our belief that free expression is a good which ranks above the maintenance of absolute peace and quiet, clean streets, smoothly flowing traffic, and rock-bottom taxes.

Thus there is a part of our intuitive view of freedom of expression which rests upon a balancing of competing goods. By contrast with the Millian Principle, which provides a single defense for all kinds of expression, here it does not seem to be a matter of the value to be placed on expression (in general) as opposed to other goods. The case seems to be different for, say, artistic expression than for the discussion of scientific matters, and different still for expression of political views.

Within certain limits, it seems clear that the value to be placed on having various kinds of expression flourish is something which should be subject to popular will in the society in question. The limits I have in mind here are, first, those imposed by considerations of distributive justice. Access to means of expression for whatever purposes one may have in mind is a good which can be fairly or unfairly distributed among the members of a society, and many cases which strike us as violations of freedom of expression are in fact instances of distributive injustice. This would be true of a case where, in an economically inegalitarian society, access to the principal means of expression was controlled by the government and auctioned off by it to the highest bidders, as is essentially the case with broadcasting licenses in the United States today. The same might be said of a parade ordinance which allowed the town council to forbid parades by unpopular groups because they were too expensive to police.

But to call either of these cases instances of unjust distribution tells only part of the story. Access to means of expression is in many cases a necessary condition for participation in the political process of the country, and therefore something to which citizens have an independent right. At the very least the recognition of such rights will require governments to insure that means of expression are readily available through which individuals and small groups can make their views on political issues known, and to insure that the principal means of expression in the society do not fall under the control of any particular segment of the community. But exactly what rights of access to means of expression follow in this way from political rights will depend to some extent on the political institutions in question. Political participation may take different forms under different institutions, even under equally just institutions.

The theory of freedom of expression which I am offering, then, consists of at least four distinguishable elements. It is based upon the Millian Principle, which is absolute but serves only to rule out certain justifications for legal restrictions on acts of expression. Within the limits set by this principle the whole range of governmental policies affecting opportunities for expression, whether by restriction, positive intervention, or failure to intervene, are subject to justification and criticism on a number of diverse grounds. First, on grounds of whether they reflect an appropriate balancing of the value of certain kinds of expression relative to other social goods; second, whether they insure equitable distribution of access to means of expression throughout the society; and third, whether they are compatible with the recognition of certain special rights, particularly political rights.

This mixed theory is somewhat cumbersome, but the various parts seem to me both mutually irreducible and essential if we are to account for the full range of cases which seem intuitively to constitute violations of "free speech."

v

The failure of the Millian Principle to allow certain kinds of exceptions may seem to many the most implausible feature of the theory I have offered. In addition to the possibility mentioned earlier, that exceptions should be allowed in cases of diminished rationality, there may seem to be an obvious case for allowing deviations from the principle in time of war or other grave emergency.

It should be noticed that because the Millian Principle is much narrower than, say, a blanket protection of "speech," the theory I have offered can already accommodate some of the restrictions on expression which wartime conditions may be thought to justify. The Millian Principle allows one, even in normal times, to consider whether the publication of certain information might present serious hazards to public safety by giving people the capacity to inflict certain harms. It seems likely that risks of this kind which are worth taking in time of peace in order to allow full discussion of, say, certain scientific questions, might be intolerable in wartime.

But the kind of emergency powers that governments feel entitled to invoke often go beyond this and include, for example, the power to cut off political debate when such debate threatens to divide the country or otherwise to undermine its capacity to meet a present threat. The obvious justification for such powers is clearly disallowed by the Millian Principle, and the theory I have offered provides for no exceptions of this kind.

It is hard for me at the present moment to conceive of a case in which I would think the invocation of such powers by a government right. I am willing to admit that there might be such cases, but even if there are I do not think that they should be seen as "exceptions" to be incorporated within the Millian Principle.

That principle, it will be recalled, does not rest on a right of citizens but rather expresses a limitation on the authority governments can be supposed to have. The authority in question here is that provided by a particular kind of political theory, one which has its starting point in the question: How could citizens recognize a right of governments to command them while still regarding themselves as equal, autonomous, rational agents? The theory is normally thought to yield the answer that this is possible if, but only if, that right is limited in certain ways, and if certain other conditions, supposed to insure citizen control over government, are fulfilled. I have argued that one of the necessary limitations is expressed by the Millian Principle. If I am right, then the claim of a government to rule by virtue of this particular kind of authority is undermined, I think completely, if it undertakes to control its citizens in the ways that the Millian Principle is intended to exclude.

This does not mean, however, that it could not in an extreme case be right for certain people, who normally exercised the kind of authority held to be legitimate by democratic political theory, to take measures which this authority does not justify. These actions would have to be justified on some other ground (e.g., utilitarian), and the claim of their agents to be obeyed would not be that of a legitimate government in the usual (democratic) sense. Nonetheless most citizens might, under the circumstances, have good reason to obey.

There are a number of different justifications for the exercise of coercive authority. In a situation of extreme peril to a group, those in the group who are in a position to avert disaster by exercising a certain kind of control over the others may be justified in using force to do so, and there may be good reason for their commands to be obeyed. But this kind of authority differs both in justification and extent from that which, if democratic political theory is correct, a legitimate democratic government enjoys. What I am suggesting is that if there are situations in which a general suspension of civil liberties is justified—and, I repeat, it is not clear to me that there are such—these situations constitute a shift from one kind of authority to another. The people involved will probably continue to wear the same hats, but this does not mean that they still rule with the same title.

It should not be thought that I am here giving governments license to kick over the traces of constitutional rule whenever this is required by the "national interest." It would take a situation of near catastrophe to justify a move of the kind I have described, and if governments know what they are doing it would take such a situation to make a move of this sort inviting. For a great deal is given up in such a move, including any notion that the commands of government have a claim to be obeyed which goes beyond the relative advantages of obedience and disobedience.

When the situation is grave and the price of disorder enormous, such utilitarian considerations may give the government's commands very real binding force. But continuing rule on this basis would be acceptable only for a society in permanent crisis or for a group of people who, because they could see each other only as obedient servants or as threatening foes, could not be ruled on any other.

[3]

PERSUASION, AUTONOMY, AND FREEDOM OF EXPRESSION

*David A. Strauss**

The government may not suppress speech on the ground that it is too persuasive. Except, perhaps, in extraordinary circumstances, the government may not restrict speech because it fears, however justifiably, that the speech will persuade those who hear it to do something of which the government disapproves. If speech brings about bad consequences through other means—by attracting crowds or causing litter, for example—those bad consequences can justify restrictions on the speech.[1] But bad consequences that come about because the speech persuades people to do certain things cannot justify suppression.

This principle has, I believe, been extremely important in the development of the law governing freedom of expression in the United States. Several of the most important and controversial first amendment issues of today turn on whether this principle is correct. My objective in this Article is to consider whether it is correct.

In Part I, I will define this principle, which I call the persuasion principle. The central idea is that the government may not justify a measure restricting speech by invoking harmful consequences that are caused by the persuasiveness of the speech. But "persuasion" denotes a rational process. That is, not every kind of inducement through speech should be considered persuasion. I will trace the pervasive influence of this principle in the American system of freedom of expression.

In Part II, I will address the argument, commonly used to defend the persuasion principle, that suppression is unnecessary because counter-persuasion—answering arguments—will cure any evils caused by persuasion. This defense of the persuasion principle is related to several prominent theories about freedom of expression, including the famous "marketplace of ideas" metaphor. I will argue that this attempted justification for the persuasion principle does not succeed.

In Part III, I will make what seems to me the best argument for the

* Professor of Law, the University of Chicago. I thank Larry Kramer, Louis Michael Seidman, Geoffrey Stone, Cass Sunstein, Mark Tushnet, Paul Kahn, David Friedman, Albert Alschuler, and Richard Posner for their comments on an earlier draft. I benefitted from presenting this paper at a Georgetown University Law Center faculty workshop, the University of Maryland Legal Theory Workshop, and the University of Chicago Legal Theory Workshop. I am also grateful to Jacqueline Bennett, Michael Faris, and Reid Prouty for their research assistance and advice, and to the Kirkland & Ellis Faculty Research Fund at the University of Chicago Law School for financial support.

1. See, e.g., Heffron v. International Soc'y for Krishna Consciousness, Inc., 452 U.S. 640, 650 (1981); Schneider v. State, 308 U.S. 147, 160–61 (1939).

persuasion principle. This argument rests on a conception of autonomy—a notoriously vague notion that I will try to define relatively
clearly. Specifically, I will suggest that a violation of the persuasion
principle is wrong for essentially the same reasons (although not to the
same degree) that it is wrong deliberately to lie to a person.

In Part IV, I will suggest two important respects in which the persuasion principle must be qualified. One is that it can be overridden if
the consequences of following it are too severe. The autonomy justification provides a way of determining when the consequences are too
severe without engaging in open-ended balancing. The other qualification is that the persuasion principle has what might be called a libertarian bias: it is sensitive only to wrongs done by the government and
systematically underemphasizes comparable wrongs done by private
parties.

In Part V, I will suggest how this bias might be corrected. In particular, I will describe how government actions affecting expression
should be evaluated to determine if they are consistent with the autonomy rationale that underlies the persuasion principle. In this connection, I will suggest that the persuasion principle is rooted in—and raises
the same questions as—the central features of certain forms of
liberalism.

I. The Persuasion Principle and Its Influence

The persuasion principle, as I define it, holds that the government
may not suppress speech on the ground that the speech is likely to persuade people to do something that the government considers harmful.
Put another way, harmful consequences resulting from the persuasive
effects of speech may not be any part of the justification for restricting
speech.

"Persuade," however, does not mean simply "induce." "Persuasion" denotes a process of appealing, in some sense, to reason. Speech
persuades when it induces action through a process that a rational person would value.

The clearest example of speech that might induce action by nonrational means is a false statement of fact. A rational person never wants
to act on the basis of false information.[2] When a false statement induces action, therefore, what is taking place is not the rational process
of persuasion as I define it. Another candidate for exclusion from the
persuasion principle is speech that seeks to precipitate an ill-considered
reaction. Obviously this category is unclear and troublesome in many
respects, for reasons I will discuss in Part IV. But provisionally, I will
define the persuasion principle to exclude these two categories of
speech that move people to action by means other than the rational

---

2. This statement should be qualified, but the qualifications do not affect my argument. See infra note 77 and accompanying text.

process of persuasion: false statements, and speech that seeks to elicit action before the hearer has thought about the speech and possible answering arguments.

In this Part, I will try to show that this principle, so defined, unifies much of first amendment law. In subsequent discussion I will consider whether the principle I have defined in this way can be justified.

A. *The Principle*

A famous passage in Justice Brandeis's concurring opinion in *Whitney v. California*[3] states the central idea of the persuasion principle:

> [T]he fitting remedy for evil counsels is good ones. . . . [N]o danger flowing from speech can be deemed clear and present, unless the incidence of the evil apprehended is so imminent that it may befall before there is opportunity for full discussion. If there be time to expose through discussion the falsehood and fallacies, to avert the evil by the processes of education, the remedy to be applied is more speech, not enforced silence.[4]

Justice Brandeis's opinion is notable in many respects[5]—there are several ideas implicit even in this brief passage—but this passage does contain a clear statement of the persuasion principle. Justice Brandeis is, first, concerned with the evils that result from persuasion. He speaks of "evil counsels"—speech that threatens to bring about evil by counselling evil. He is not addressing government action that restricts speech for other reasons, such as because it is too noisy or even because the audience reacts with hostility to the speaker. Those are not restrictions aimed at "evil counsels."

In addition, Justice Brandeis describes one of the exceptions to the persuasion principle when he specifically withholds protection from speech that does not "counsel" but rather precipitates ill-considered action by bringing about its evil objective "imminent[ly] . . . before there is opportunity for full discussion." While Justice Brandeis does

---

3. 274 U.S. 357 (1927).

4. Id. at 375–77 (Brandeis, J., concurring).

In the literature, the most prominent statement of a principle that resembles the persuasion principle is the "Millian principle" advanced by T.M. Scanlon in A Theory of Freedom of Expression, 1 Phil. & Pub. Aff. 204 (1972) [hereinafter Freedom of Expression], but then repudiated by Scanlon in Freedom of Expression and Categories of Expression, 40 U. Pitt. L. Rev. 519, 530–35 (1979) [hereinafter Categories of Expression]. In note 62, infra, I discuss the relationship between the persuasion principle, as I define it, and the "Millian principle." Other discussions of similar principles (focusing on the Brandeis opinion) are found in Stone, Content Regulation and the First Amendment, 25 Wm. & Mary L. Rev. 189, 213 (1983); Wellington, On Freedom of Expression, 88 Yale L.J. 1105, 1135–36 (1979).

5. See Blasi, The First Amendment and the Ideal of Civic Courage: The Brandeis Opinion in *Whitney v. California*, 29 Wm. & Mary L. Rev. 653 (1988), for an interesting discussion of the themes of this opinion.

not explicitly except false statements of fact from the principle,[6] such statements are, as I will explain, properly assimilated to (in fact, they are the clearest case of) statements that bring about ill-considered action.

Justice Brandeis's dictum states unequivocally that the government may not suppress evil counsels on the ground that they are too effective. That is the persuasion principle. But Justice Brandeis adds something to the persuasion principle by specifying the government's alternative remedy: it is to use "more speech" or "good counsels." This is an effort—unsuccessful, I will argue in Part II—to justify the persuasion principle on the ground that suppression is unnecessary because counter-persuasion is a better way to accomplish the same objectives.

B. *The Influence of the Persuasion Principle*

In several respects, the persuasion principle is central to the American system of freedom of expression. On a general level, the persuasion principle captures much of the essence of freedom of expression. More specifically, the persuasion principle unifies several important and apparently disparate areas of first amendment law. While it would be an oversimplification to suggest that the persuasion principle can explain every aspect of the American system of freedom of expression,[7] the explanatory power of the persuasion principle is very great.

1. *In General.* — On a general level, freedom of speech is valued precisely because speech has the capacity to persuade. When speech causes litter or traffic problems, or when it prompts a hostile audience to threaten the speaker with violence, those are undesirable by-products, even if they sometimes must be tolerated. They are not the reasons speech merits special protection. The reason we value speech—in large part, at least—is that it persuades people to do or believe things.

To put the point another way, tyrants suppress speech because they fear it will be persuasive. There would be little left of the first amendment, as we understand it, if the government could suppress speech whenever it plausibly believed that the speech might, at some point and in some way, persuade people to do things of which the government disapproved. As Holmes and Brandeis said in their famous opinions of the 1910s and 1920s, almost any dissident speech increases the likelihood that some people will be persuaded to break the law.[8]

---

6. Indeed, Brandeis says that the "remedy" for "falsehood" is "more speech, not enforced silence," 274 U.S. at 377, but it seems more plausible to read that as referring to "false" ideas, rather than false statements of fact. See infra notes 76–78 and accompanying text.

7. See infra note 64 and accompanying text.

8. See, e.g., *Whitney*, 274 U.S. at 376 (Brandeis, J., concurring); Gitlow v. New York, 268 U.S. 652, 673 (1925) (Holmes, J., dissenting); Abrams v. United States, 250 U.S. 616, 630 (1919) (Holmes, J., dissenting).

Consequently, if freedom of speech is to mean anything, it must mean that speech may not be restricted simply because it persuades people to engage in harmful actions.

Moreover, suppose, as a thought experiment, we could construct a device that would automatically enforce the persuasion principle—it would automatically preclude the government from ever considering consequences that are the result of persuasion. We might not need anything else to ensure freedom of expression as we understand it. The many other first amendment doctrines that have developed are, arguably, designed to guard against the danger that the government is only pretending to be concerned about noise, litter, offensiveness, or a hostile audience reaction but in fact is reacting to the feared persuasiveness of the speech that it seeks to suppress. If the danger of violating the persuasion principle were eliminated, the political process alone might be sufficient to ensure that other kinds of restrictions on expression do not become unacceptable.

2. *Specific Doctrines.* — A wide range of first amendment doctrines can be understood as a reflection of the persuasion principle. The Supreme Court has not always been explicit in relying on some statement of the persuasion principle, but its decisions consistently vindicate that principle.

a. *The Prohibition Against Political Censorship.* — The government may not suppress speech on the ground that the speech will persuade people to cast a vote for a candidate or position of which the government disapproves. This fundamental principle is so well accepted that it is essentially never questioned; the government does not attempt to justify restrictions of speech on this ground.[9] Although this rule is consistent with many understandings of the first amendment, it can be seen as a straightforward application of the persuasion principle.

b. *Speech Advocating Unlawful Conduct.* — What Brandeis urged in *Whitney* has become the law today: speech advocating unlawful conduct may not be suppressed unless it creates a clear and present—by which Brandeis meant probable and imminent—danger of law violation.[10]

---

9. Cf. H. Kalven, A Worthy Tradition 6–19 (1988) (discussing "The Consensus on Untouchable Content").

10. The current formulation is even more protective of speech than what Brandeis proposed:

[T]he constitutional guarantees of free speech and free press do not permit a State to forbid or proscribe advocacy of the use of force or of law violation except where such advocacy is directed to inciting or producing imminent lawless action and is likely to incite or produce such action.

Brandenburg v. Ohio, 395 U.S. 444, 447 (1969).

Although this standard literally applies to all speech advocating unlawful action, in fact, it probably applies only to speech that has a political component. In all of the relevant cases—*Brandenburg* itself, other cases in which the Supreme Court has either invalidated restrictions on speech advocating unlawful conduct or has acknowledged that such restrictions present substantial first amendment questions, and the cases in which the separate Holmes and Brandeis opinions established the foundations of first

The persuasion principle, as I have defined it, directly justifies the requirement of imminence: the risk of law violation can justify suppression of speech only if the speech brings about the violation by
bypassing the rational processes of deliberation. If people are truly *persuaded* to violate the law—in the sense in which I defined "persuasion"
above—the government may not punish the speech that persuaded
them.

    c. *Defamation*. — The core of defamation doctrine was summarized
in *Gertz v. Robert Welch, Inc.*:[11]

> Under the First Amendment there is no such thing as a false
> idea. However pernicious an opinion may seem, we depend
> for its correction not on the conscience of judges and juries
> but on the competition of other ideas. But there is no consti-
> tutional value in false statements of fact.[12]

The precept that pernicious opinions are to be corrected only by other
ideas is a paraphrase of Brandeis's dictum in *Whitney* and directly reflects the persuasion principle: suppression is not an acceptable way to
combat the persuasive effects of speech. The second part of the *Gertz*
formulation is also consistent with the persuasion principle; it reflects
the notion that because false statements of fact do not appeal to reason,
their use does not constitute persuasion and they are therefore not protected by the persuasion principle.

    When *Gertz* was decided, the Court's embrace of the persuasion
principle in this context seemed uncontroversial; the Court characterized it as "common ground."[13] The controversy concerned how far the
law would protect false statements of fact in order to avoid chilling true
statements. But today there is renewed concern over two issues that
directly implicate the application of the persuasion principle to what
Gertz called "pernicious opinions": regulation of speech that incites ra-

---

amendment doctrine—the speech in question not only advocated unlawful action but
expressed a political view. Indeed, it is striking that the entire development of the doctrine took place in cases involving overtly political speech: Abrams v. United States, 250
U.S. 616 (1919); Gitlow v. New York, 268 U.S. 652 (1925); Whitney v. California, 274
U.S. 357 (1927); DeJonge v. Oregon, 299 U.S. 353 (1937); Herndon v. Lowry, 301 U.S.
242 (1937); Dennis v. United States, 341 U.S. 494 (1951); Yates v. United States, 354
U.S. 298 (1957); Bond v. Floyd, 385 U.S. 116 (1966); Watts v. United States, 394 U.S.
705 (1969); Hess v. Indiana, 414 U.S. 105 (1973); NAACP v. Claiborne Hardware, 458
U.S. 886 (1982); cf. Kingsley Int'l Pictures Corp. v. Regents, 360 U.S. 684, 688–89
(1959) (artistic depiction of adultery).

    The Supreme Court has never considered a first amendment challenge to laws for-
bidding garden-variety criminal solicitation, but it seems clear that such speech could be
punished even if it did not meet the *Brandenburg* standard. See K. Greenawalt, Speech,
Crime, and the Uses of Language 110–26 (1989). This apparent exception to the persuasion principle is probably best understood as an instance in which the harmful consequences of following the principle are sufficient to overcome the values it serves. See
infra Part IV.A.

    11. 418 U.S. 323 (1974).
    12. Id. at 339–40 (citation omitted).
    13. Id. at 339.

cial hatred, and suppression of non-"obscene" pornography. To the extent the government seeks to justify measures of this kind on the ground that the speech causes people to hold harmful attitudes toward women or minority groups, the persuasion principle, as captured in the *Gertz* formula, decisively forbids such measures: they constitute efforts to restrict speech on the ground that the speech will persuade people to adopt attitudes that the government considers undesirable.[14]

d. *The Regulation of Campaign Finance.* — The expenditure of money in connection with political campaigns may be regulated to avoid corruption or the appearance of corruption. But it may not be regulated to reduce the effectiveness of the speech that is more effective because it is supported by larger expenditures. As the Supreme Court said in *Buckley v. Valeo*,[15] and has repeated many times since: "[T]he concept that government may restrict the speech of some elements of our society in order to enhance the relative voice of others is wholly foreign to the First Amendment . . . ."[16]

---

14. On pornography, compare American Booksellers Ass'n v. Hudnut, 771 F.2d 323, 332–34 (7th Cir. 1985), aff'd, 475 U.S. 1001 (1986) and Stone, Anti-Pornography Legislation as Viewpoint Discrimination, 9 Harv. J.L. & Pub. Pol'y 461 (1986) with C. Mackinnon, Feminism Unmodified, 127–213 (1987) and Sunstein, Pornography and the First Amendment, 1986 Duke L.J. 589. On racial hate literature, see, e.g., Matsuda, Public Response to Racist Speech: Considering the Victim's Story, 87 Mich. L. Rev. 2320 (1989). Compare Delgado, Words that Wound: A Tort Action for Racial Insults, Epithets, and Name-Calling, 17 Harv. C.R.-C.L. L. Rev. 133 (1982) with infra notes 22–23 and accompanying text.

Beauharnais v. Illinois, 343 U.S. 250 (1952), seems to permit restrictions on racial hate speech on the ground that it may cause bad attitudes. If that is the rationale of *Beauharnais* (as opposed to a concern with the psychic impact of the speech on the defamed group), *Beauharnais* is inconsistent with the persuasion principle. See infra notes 22–23 and accompanying text. But it is doubtful that this aspect of *Beauharnais* remains good law. See Collin v. Smith, 578 F.2d 1197, 1204–05 (7th Cir. 1978), cert. denied, 439 U.S. 916 (1978).

Such restrictions on speech might be justified not just as efforts to prevent the speech from persuading people to adopt bad attitudes but also as efforts to prevent the speech from inflicting a certain kind of psychic wound on minority groups or women. See infra note 22 and accompanying text. The second justification is not precluded by the persuasion principle, and I do not address the question whether it is otherwise acceptable. If the government offers more than one justification, or if there is a risk that the government may be relying on an impermissible justification, doctrinal rules must take into account the danger that government action purporting to have a proper justification in fact violates the persuasion principle. I discuss this point in greater detail infra notes 18–19 and accompanying text.

15. 424 U.S. 1 (1976).

16. Id. at 48–49. The Court reiterated this point in Meyer v. Grant, 486 U.S. 414, 426 & n.7 (1988); Citizens Against Rent Control v. Berkeley, 454 U.S. 290, 295 (1981); First Nat'l Bank v. Bellotti, 435 U.S. 765, 790–91 (1978).

In Austin v. Michigan Chamber of Commerce, 110 S. Ct. 1391 (1990), which upheld a state statute forbidding certain corporations from making expenditures in connection with political campaigns, the dissents attacked the Court for, in effect, violating the persuasion principle. See, e.g., id. at 1408 (Scalia, J., dissenting) ("the Court today endorses the principle that too much speech is an evil that the democratic majority can

The Court has not explained why this "concept" is so foreign to the first amendment. The persuasion principle provides an explanation: when the government restricts expenditures on campaigns because it fears that those with more money will have too much influence, its concern is with the persuasiveness of the speech. It is concerned that the people who spend more will circulate their ideas more widely and more effectively, and will thereby convince more voters. Under the persuasion principle, this justification for restricting expenditures is not legitimate.

e. *Offensive Speech.* — Although more than the persuasion principle is at work in this area,[17] established first amendment law governing offensive speech not only is fully consistent with the persuasion principle but also confirms its importance.

There are different ways in which speech might be offensive. Sometimes people are offended by speech because they believe it will persuade some of those who hear it to do bad things. The persuasion principle of course forbids the government from suppressing speech because it is offensive in this way.

But speech might also be "intrinsically" offensive, that is, offensive without regard to its persuasive effect on anyone. Such intrinsically offensive speech covers a spectrum from speech that is just distasteful (in the way that offensive sights, odors, or noises other than speech might be distasteful) to, at the other extreme, speech that is so offensive that it can be said to inflict a psychic wound on the listener. A common-law assault, although not ordinarily thought to present a first amendment issue, is an example of intrinsically offensive expression of this kind. Blasphemy, ethnic slurs, and profane language are other likely examples of intrinsically offensive speech: in general (although not always) people who object to such speech would find it offensive even if they

---

proscribe"). While the basis of the Court's decision in *Austin* is not entirely clear, it seems best understood as resting not on this ground but on a different premise: that the capacity to organize in corporate form is a kind of subsidy that the government may choose not to confer on organizations that engage in political speech, at least when there are readily available alternative means through which those connected with the corporation may speak. See id. at 1397–98.

17. In particular, there is a significant theme in the history of the first amendment suggesting that the offensiveness of speech is not an undesirable by-product of the system of free expression but something affirmatively desirable. For an original and important statement of this view, see L. Bollinger, The Tolerant Society (1986). For a suggestion that even highly offensive speech is valuable because it signals the range of views held by members of society, see Farber, Civilizing Public Discourse: An Essay on Professor Bickel, Justice Harlan, and the Enduring Significance of *Cohen v. California*, 1980 Duke L.J. 283, 301.

For an argument suggesting that regulating speech on the ground of offensiveness threatens the neutrality required by a system of "public discourse," see Post, The Constitutional Concept of Public Discourse: Outrageous Opinion, Democratic Deliberation, and *Hustler Magazine v. Falwell*, 103 Harv. L. Rev. 603 (1990).

were convinced that the speech would have no persuasive effect on anyone.

The persuasion principle does not, of its own force, prohibit the government from restricting "intrinsically" offensive speech of this kind. If the government is truly concerned with speech because it is intrinsically offensive in one of these ways, the consequences at which the government is aiming are not caused by the persuasive effect of the speech.[18]

For two reasons, however, the persuasion principle requires that the government's power to act against intrinsically offensive speech be limited. First, of course, a government with unlimited latitude to suppress speech on grounds of intrinsic offensiveness could violate the persuasion principle by acting pretextually. The government might claim, for example, that it is restricting profane political criticism because the profanity is intrinsically offensive, while it is actually concerned that unsuppressed criticism of that form will rally those who agree with the substance of the criticism. Second, and more subtly, even if there were no danger of pretextual action by the government, these two kinds of concern—with intrinsic offensiveness and with persuasive effects—are not always easy to disentangle even as a psychological matter. Blasphemy and flag burning are examples; even the people who object to these forms of expression will often find it difficult to determine whether their objection is rooted in the intrinsic offensiveness of the speech or in the concern that the speech will undermine religious faith or patriotism.

Consequently, the persuasion principle calls for a general, but not unrelenting, hostility to measures that restrict speech on the ground of offensiveness.[19] The persuasion principle suggests that such measures are acceptable only when there is a low risk that the government's real concern is the persuasive effect of the speech.

That is roughly what the law is. In general, the government may not restrict speech simply because it is offensive.[20] The hostility to such restrictions is greatest when there is the greatest danger that the real objection is to the message and its possible persuasive effects—as in the case of political speech or proselytizing religious speech.[21]

---

18. Here and elsewhere, when I refer to "the government's" concerns, objectives, or reasons for acting, I of course do not mean just the concerns and objectives of government officials. The government's actions will often reflect the desires and concerns of people in society. The persuasion principle is violated if *whoever* is controlling governmental power—officials, powerful private groups, or dominant opinion in society—seeks to restrict speech because of concern with its persuasive effects.

19. For a discussion of how existing doctrine, particularly the focus on "communicative impact," attempts to prevent pretextual actions, including pretextual violations of the persuasion principle, see Stone, supra note 4, at 207–17.

20. See, e.g., Texas v. Johnson, 109 S. Ct. 2533, 2544 (1989) (citing numerous cases).

21. On political speech, see id.; Hustler Magazine v. Falwell, 485 U.S. 46 (1988);

There are, however, a few instances in which it is clear that speech can be restricted because of the psychic wound it inflicts—so clear that such speech is often not even seen as raising a first amendment issue. Assaults, racial and sexual harassment, and fighting words are examples.[22]

The persuasion principle accounts for the disparate treatment of these kinds of expression. When wounding words are spoken directly to the victim, with little or no other audience, there is little chance that any persuasion is occurring. The government's well-established power to punish harassment, fighting words, and assaults—forms of expression that are directed at a victim who is face-to-face with the speaker—is therefore consistent with the persuasion principle. When speech is addressed to a larger audience, however, there is a greater danger that the government is actually concerned not with the wounds that the speech inflicts, but with the possibility that the speech will have a persuasive effect on the audience. This explains why the government's power to restrict group defamation or speech that induces a hostile audience reaction is so limited.

The law governing offensive speech is, therefore, roughly what a consistent commitment to the persuasion principle would require. There are a few, more controversial instances in which the Supreme Court has permitted speech to be restricted on grounds of offensiveness; but on each such occasion the Court has emphasized that the government's real concern was not with the persuasive effect of the speech.[23] The Court's assessment of the government's concern in these cases might have been wrong, but the fact that the Court considered it necessary to reach such a conclusion in each case reflects the importance of the persuasion principle.

f. *Commercial Speech*. — Some of the Supreme Court's strongest affirmations of the persuasion principle have occurred in cases concerning commercial speech. In *Virginia State Board of Pharmacy v. Virginia Citizens Consumer Council*,[24] and *Linmark Associates, Inc. v. Township of Willingboro*,[25] for example, the Court invalidated bans on certain forms of advertising, declaring unacceptable the government's argument that the advertising in question would cause people to take actions that the government considered harmful to society.[26]

Linmark, in particular, is a high-water mark for the persuasion prin-

---

Cohen v. California, 403 U.S. 15 (1971). On religious proselytizing, see Cantwell v. Connecticut, 310 U.S. 296 (1940).

22. See Meritor Sav. Bank v. Vinson, 477 U.S. 57, 65 (1986) (sexual harassment); Chaplinsky v. New Hampshire, 315 U.S. 568, 574 (1942) (fighting words). On assaults, see K. Greenawalt, supra note 10, at 90–91.

23. See, e.g., City of Renton v. Playtime Theatres, Inc., 475 U.S. 41, 47–49 (1986); FCC v. Pacifica Found., 438 U.S. 726, 745–46 (1978) (plurality opinion); Young v. American Mini Theatres, Inc., 427 U.S. 50, 63–64, 70 (1976) (plurality opinion).

24. 425 U.S. 748 (1976).

25. 431 U.S. 85 (1977).

26. Id. at 96–97; 425 U.S. at 771–73.

ciple. In that case a township that was trying to remain racially integrated sought to ban "sold" and "for sale" signs on front lawns, on the ground that such signs encouraged panic selling by whites who feared that their neighborhoods were about to become predominantly black. The Court unanimously disapproved this argument, saying that it revealed a basic "constitutional defect" in the township's actions and quoting Justice Brandeis's language.[27]

Overall, however, the persuasion principle has had mixed fortunes in the area of commercial speech. In cases subsequent to *Linmark*, the Court questioned the persuasion principle explicitly,[28] and in *Posadas de Puerto Rico Associates v. Tourism Co. of Puerto Rico,*[29] the Court dealt the persuasion principle an unequivocal setback.[30] *Posadas* upheld a Puerto Rico statute that forbade gambling casinos from advertising in Puerto Rico on the ground that Puerto Rico has a legitimate interest in not encouraging its citizens to gamble. *Posadas* has been severely criticized precisely on the ground that it slights the persuasion principle.[31]

Here again, the persuasion principle is crucial to the resolution of

---

27. 431 U.S. at 96–97 (quoting Brandeis's concurring opinion in *Whitney*).

28. See Central Hudson Gas & Elec. Corp. v. Public Serv. Comm'n, 447 U.S. 557, 563 (1980).

29. 478 U.S. 328 (1986).

30. Even during the period when *Virginia State Board* and *Linmark* established strong protection for commercial speech on the basis of the persuasion principle, the Supreme Court endorsed, without seriously questioning, the rule that commercial speech proposing an illegal transaction can be suppressed. See, e.g., Brown v. Hartlage, 456 U.S. 45, 55 (1982); Village of Hoffman Estates v. Flipside, 455 U.S. 489, 496 (1982) (upholding ordinance concerning, inter alia, proximity of drug paraphernalia and drug-related literature); Virginia State Bd. of Pharmacy v. Virginia Citizens Consumer Council, 425 U.S. 748, 772–73 (discussion of illegal transactions in general); Pittsburgh Press Co. v. Pittsburgh Comm'n on Human Relations, 413 U.S. 376, 388 (1973) (designating employment advertisement by sex).

At first glance it is difficult to square this rule with the persuasion principle: it seems that the reason for suppressing the advertisements is that they might encourage people to engage in the illegal activity. (These cases did not discuss the persuasion principle or address the tension with *Linmark* or the central holding of *Virginia State Board*.) But, arguably, speech proposing an illegal transaction is not protected under the persuasion principle because it is an inseparable part of the illegal activity, in the way that an agreement to fix prices is an illegal act consisting entirely of speech. See K. Greenawalt, supra note 10, at 271. That is why there is a difference between (suppressible) speech *proposing* an illegal transaction and (protected) speech *advocating* an illegal transaction, such as advocacy of drug use. See supra note 10.

Alternatively, as in the case of nonpolitical criminal solicitation, the potential harmful consequences of speech proposing an illegal transaction may warrant abrogating the persuasion principle. See infra Part IV.A.

31. See Kurland, *Posadas de Puerto Rico v. Tourism Company:* " 'Twas Strange, 'Twas Passing Strange; 'Twas Pitiful, 'Twas Wondrous Pitiful," 1986 Sup. Ct. Rev. 1, 2–3. For a discussion of *Posadas* from a different angle, suggesting the possibility that the government's motives may not have been to reduce gambling by local citizens but something less admirable, such as inhibiting competition among casinos, possibly for racial reasons, see Strauss, Constitutional Protection for Commercial Speech: Some Lessons from the American Experience, 17 Can. Bus. L.J. 45, 46–48 (1990).

a current controversy: periodically, there are efforts to prohibit the advertising of tobacco or alcohol on the ground that the advertising will persuade people to do things that are harmful to their health.[32] If, notwithstanding *Posadas*, the persuasion principle continues to operate in the area of commercial speech, the resolution of this issue is straightforward: the government may not prohibit advertisements for this reason.

*   *   *

Several features of the persuasion principle heighten its attractiveness as a governing principle in the first amendment area. Unlike many constitutional doctrines, it does not just call for amorphous balancing. It really decides actual hard cases—as the examples of pornography, racial hate literature, campaign finance, and tobacco advertising show. In addition, the persuasion principle, especially in the Brandeis formulation, expresses a vigorous, optimistic view that avoids defensiveness:[33] the government must allow even the most persuasive speech, confident in its ability to counter-persuade.

Some cases clearly inconsistent with the persuasion principle have been discredited.[34] In other areas, substantial argument would be needed to defend the proposition that current law is consistent with the persuasion principle.[35] But outside the area of commercial advertising,

---

32. See infra Part IV.A and accompanying text on the issues raised by restrictions on tobacco advertising.

33. This is a principal theme of Blasi, supra note 5, especially at 693–94.

34. See supra note 14 (discussing *Beauharnais v. Illinois*). Dennis v. United States, 341 U.S. 494 (1951), has not been expressly overruled and indeed was cited in *Brandenburg* as support for the test that the Court adopted in that case. But the approach taken by the plurality opinion in *Dennis* (which followed Judge Learned Hand's opinion for the Second Circuit) cannot be reconciled with *Brandenburg*, which requires the government to show both imminence of harm and the use of words of incitement before it may suppress advocacy of law violation. By contrast, *Dennis* required courts to balance the benefits of speech against the potential harm, discounted by the improbability of that harm. See id. at 510 (plurality opinion). Imminence and incitement might affect the discounted magnitude of harm, but under *Dennis* they are not necessary conditions without which speech may not be suppressed. In fact, it is not clear that this aspect of *Dennis* survived Yates v. United States, 354 U.S. 298, 320–24 (1957).

It may, of course, be just a fortuity that cases in which the Supreme Court would not apply the persuasion principle have not yet come before it. It is reasonably certain, for example, that the persuasion principle does not apply to garden-variety criminal solicitation, and it is a happenstance that such cases have not come before the Court. See supra note 10. In Part IV, I will discuss some of these arguable exceptions and suggest that they may in fact be consistent with the persuasion principle, once the foundations of the principle are worked out.

35. The first amendment exception for obscenity presents a particularly difficult case. To some extent, obscenity may be regulated because of its intrinsic offensiveness. See Paris Adult Theatre I v. Slaton, 413 U.S. 49, 59 (1973). That rationale does not implicate the persuasion principle. But there is also an element of the justification for regulating obscenity that is based on the danger that obscenity will encourage the commission of crimes, see id. at 58, 60–63, and also a more general concern with the moral tone of society and the way in which society views sex. See, e.g., id. at 59, 63. This is

which is widely viewed as being at most of peripheral concern to freedom of expression,[36] it can fairly be argued that not a single Supreme Court decision now accepted as good law has violated the persuasion principle, as I have interpreted it.

The persuasion principle is an appealing, optimistic notion, cloaked with the authority of Brandeis's extraordinary opinion; it arguably expresses the central concern of the first amendment; it produces specific answers to hard problems; it defends an important liberty; it is the governing principle in several of the most important areas of first amendment law; and an advocate can assert that not a single Supreme Court decision worth bothering about is inconsistent with it. This combination of circumstances gives the persuasion principle extraordinary influence in the law and rhetoric of freedom of expression.

II. Consequentialist Justifications and Their Weaknesses

Is this exceptionally influential principle correct? In this Part, I will consider the argument, suggested by Brandeis's opinion in *Whitney* and much other literature on freedom of expression, that the persuasion principle can be justified on consequentialist grounds. These justifica-

---

close to a concern that obscene speech will persuade people to act, or to alter their views, in an undesirable way.

Perhaps the best way to understand the prohibition against obscenity, however, is that it rests on the premise that sexually oriented speech is peculiarly likely to make a manipulative, nonrational appeal that cannot be resisted by answering speech. See id. at 67 ("Preventing unlimited display or distribution of obscene material . . . is distinct from a control of reason and the intellect."). See also Schauer, Speech and "Speech" — Obscenity and "Obscenity": An Exercise in the Interpretation of Constitutional Language, 67 Geo. L.J. 899, 910–19 (1979). It is not easy to explain exactly what idea this manipulative appeal seeks to advance; presumably it involves a suggestion that a certain attitude toward sex is appropriate, and it may also concern an attitude toward women (although that is more directly the basis for feminist proposals to regulate pornography) and perhaps toward deferred gratification and similar matters. See generally Grey, Eros, Civilization, and the Burger Court, 43 Law & Contemp. Probs. 83 (1980). Indeed, perhaps the very difficulty of articulating the message involved in obscenity supports the notion that the message is being conveyed in such a way that reason cannot address it.

If the basis for the regulation of obscenity is that sexually oriented speech is peculiarly likely to produce a nonrational response then the regulation of obscenity would fit within the exception to the persuasion principle for speech that precipitates an ill-considered reaction. See infra notes 77–78 and accompanying text.

36. See, e.g., Central Hudson Gas & Elec. Corp. v. Public Serv. Comm'n, 447 U.S. 557, 562–63 (1980) ("The Constitution . . . [provides] a lesser protection to commercial speech than to other constitutionally guaranteed expression.").

I should note that the persuasion principle, at least as I have defined it so far, does not explain why commercial expression should be only of peripheral concern to freedom of expression. Parts IV and V, which discuss the possibility that private speech can create some of the same dangers that the persuasion principle is designed to avoid, may suggest a basis for concluding that commercial speech is peripheral to freedom of expression. But I do not argue in this Article that the persuasion principle necessarily dictates the peripheral status of commercial expression.

tions have in common the claim that following the persuasion principle will produce good consequences in the long run, even though the persuasion principle protects speech that produces bad consequences in the short run.

I will argue in this Part that this justification fails. In Part III, I will describe a justification, based on a Kantian notion of autonomy, that is more successful.

A. *The "Remedy" of "More Speech"*

I have stated the persuasion principle as a prohibition: the government may not invoke certain grounds for suppressing speech. The famous passage from Brandeis's opinion in *Whitney* is, conspicuously, much more affirmative. Brandeis's point is not just that the government's power is limited to providing answering speech; he also suggests that answering speech will be effective. "Good [counsels]" are a "remedy" for "evil counsels." The point of discussion is "to expose . . . the falsehoods and fallacies, to avert the evil." The suggestion is that "more speech" can accomplish practically everything that suppression could accomplish. There is no need to suppress persuasive speech because the government can simply counteract the effects of such speech with its own answering speech.[37]

If this were true, the persuasion principle would be easy to justify. If suppression and "more speech" are equally effective ways of averting evil consequences, then of course "more speech" is preferable.

But there will be many occasions on which this optimistic view is an illusion. The problem with the "more speech" approach is that it is not unusual for people to be persuaded to do bad things, and it will not always be possible to talk them out of it. At the very least, appeals to self-interest or base motives can persuade people to take antisocial actions. People can, for example, be persuaded to commit crimes. "Counterspeech" appealing to altruistic or socially conscious motives (or reminding people that they may be punished for bad acts) will not always talk them out of it.[38]

There are many possible examples: *Linmark Associates, Inc. v. Township of Willingboro*[39]—the case in which the Supreme Court, without dissent, invalidated a ban on "for sale" signs—is one. If the homeowners who see such signs are prompted to sell their own homes, it is wholly unrealistic to think that the township will be able to change their minds with "wise counsels" aimed at convincing the homeowners that they should sacrifice what they perceive—perhaps correctly—to be their

---

37. Although this seems to be a fair reading of Brandeis's *Whitney* opinion, it is not the only reading. See, e.g., Blasi, supra note 5, at 674–77 (urging that Brandeis himself did not hold this view).

38. See Posner, Free Speech in an Economic Perspective, 20 Suffolk U.L. Rev. 1, 33 (1986).

39. 431 U.S. 85 (1977).

economic interest.[40] If *Linmark* is correct, it must be because allowing the signs to stay serves some other value important enough to outweigh the harmful consequences that the Township feared the signs would cause. It is simply a mistake to believe that "more speech" will be sufficient to avert those consequences.

B. *The Consequentialist Justifications*

Perhaps it is unfair to attribute to Brandeis a position that seems so obviously incorrect.[41] But Brandeis's optimistic view—that "good [counsels]" and "more speech" are the "remedy" for "evil counsels" because they can "avert the evil"—has exerted a powerful hold on first amendment rhetoric.[42] It has exerted such a hold because there is a family of theories about freedom of expression, all of which suggest in some way that "more speech" will "remedy" the evils caused by persuasive speech. These theories are less determinate and less self-assured than the view I have attributed to Brandeis. They emphasize, for example, that while "more speech" might not fully remedy the evils of evil counsels, "more speech" is on balance, or in the long run, a better remedy than suppression. Some of these theories are important and instructive, but none provides a satisfactory basis for the persuasion principle.

1. *The Marketplace of Ideas.* — Justice Holmes's famous aphorism—"[T]he best test of truth is the power of the thought to get itself accepted in the competition of the market"[43]—would, if correct, justify the persuasion principle. So long as all ideas are available and in competition with each other, the good counsels will prevail. It follows that there is no warrant for restricting speech that might persuade people to

---

40. There are several reasons why seeing "for sale" signs might persuade other owners to sell their own homes. Some owners might not want to live in an integrated neighborhood under any circumstances. In their case, the "wise counsels" would take the form of urging the virtues of integration. Some owners might be willing to live in an integrated neighborhood but believe that others are not willing to do so; those owners would fear that the amount their property could command on the market would fall as integration progressed. Still others might not have either of these concerns but might fear that their neighbors have such concerns and are "panic selling" at low prices. In these latter two cases it is possible that the owners have correctly perceived the facts. "Wise counsels" would therefore have to persuade them to make a financial sacrifice. Finally, it is possible that the situation is solely a collective action problem: a sufficient number of the owners would be willing to stay if each was convinced that the others were willing to stay. The "wise counsels," which would attempt to overcome this failure of coordination, would have to urge each owner to risk a financial loss in the hope that sufficient others could be persuaded not to sell. In none of these cases are the "wise counsels" likely to be very effective.

41. See supra note 37.

42. The principal opinions in which the Brandeis dictum is cited are collected in Blasi, supra note 5, at 683 n.107.

43. Abrams v. United States, 250 U.S. 616, 630 (1919) (Holmes, J., dissenting).

do harmful things; it is only necessary to provide competing, good ideas.

The market metaphor is powerful and attractive because it is untroubled by self-interested action. In well-functioning economic markets, self-interested action produces an outcome that is in some sense good for society as a whole. The notion of a "marketplace of ideas" suggests that self-interested behavior in the realm of ideas—such as efforts to persuade people to do apparently harmful things by appealing to their self-interest—can similarly be turned into social benefit. Superficially the market metaphor is alluring; just as force and fraud are impermissible in economic markets, making a false statement of fact or coercing a person to adopt a view are impermissible in a well-functioning system of freedom of expression.

This metaphor has received its share of criticism, much of which emphasizes the "market failures" in the first amendment area.[44] But the real problem with the market metaphor is more fundamental. There is a theory about how economic markets lead to outcomes that are in some sense desirable: if certain conditions hold, then we know that the market will produce an efficient outcome. There is no such theory for the so-called marketplace of ideas.

We do not know what constitutes perfect competition or the equivalent of market power in the realm of ideas. No matter how we define the ground rules, there is no theory that explains why competition in the realm of ideas will systematically produce good or truthful or otherwise desirable outcomes. Is a well-functioning market one in which each idea is equally represented? What does it mean to say that ideas are "equally" represented? How does one even individuate ideas? And why is equal representation (whatever that is) desirable? Among the ideas that are underrepresented because no one seriously advocates them, some have been rightfully rejected and deserve to be underrepresented; others are wrongly ignored and should receive a stronger defense.

It is even misleading to speak of "market failures" in the marketplace of ideas. Since we do not have a theory of what a well-functioning first amendment "market" would look like, it gives false comfort to suggest that the problem is ascertainable "failures" that need only be eliminated in order to generate good outcomes. On the level of theory we do not know when the system of free expression will produce good outcomes.

2. *The Peculiar Dangers of Government Intervention.* — Another defense of Brandeis's "more speech" idea, common to many arguments for

---

44. See, e.g., Barron, Access to the Press—A New First Amendment Right, 80 Harv. L. Rev. 1641, 1641 (1967); Ingber, The Marketplace of Ideas: A Legitimizing Myth, 1984 Duke L.J. 1, 4–5. For an argument that the "market failure" criticism does not go far enough, see C.E. Baker, Human Liberty and Freedom of Speech 12–24 (1989).

constitutional protection of expression, is that while "more speech" may not literally remedy the ills caused by speech that induces harm, any other supposed remedy that the government attempts will be worse. The government's assessment of the dangers caused by speech is likely to be so systematically biased that it is better, on the whole, to place suppression off limits; however ineffective "more speech" is, it should be the only "remedy" open to the government.[45]

Whether the premise is true—that the dangers of government regulation of speech are in fact systematically greater than the dangers posed by unregulated private speech—is a difficult question, and I return to it below.[46] But even assuming that this premise is correct, it does not satisfactorily justify the persuasion principle because it does not explain why the consequences that are caused by *persuasion* should be treated differently from other consequences. Undoubtedly, government officials' assessments of the harmful consequences caused by speech will often be biased. Moreover, it seems likely that there will be systematic biases toward, for example, overestimating the harm caused by speech advocating unlawful conduct or politically unpopular points of view. But these biases will exist whether the harmful consequences result from persuasion or from some other property of the speech. Government officials are likely to overstate the dangers of hostile audience reactions, the propensity of proponents of certain speech to engage in violence, the likelihood that speech will interfere with the government's ability to carry out its various functions (ranging from foreign affairs to traffic control), and so on. Certain kinds of regulation—such as regulation directed at the content of speech—may be especially likely to present these dangers of government overreaction. But there is no reason to think that harmful consequences caused by persuasion are especially likely to be overestimated, compared with harmful consequences that have other causes.

3. *The Imperatives of Democratic Self-Government.* — This view, associated with Alexander Meiklejohn, holds that democracy requires that the people, and not the government, be allowed to decide which views about political issues will prevail.[47] If the government is allowed to suppress certain ideas, then the people are not free to choose how to govern themselves. Freedom of speech is therefore "a deduction from the basic American agreement that public issues shall be decided by universal suffrage."[48]

This theory certainly reflects a plausible understanding of the cen-

---

45. See, e.g., L. Bollinger, supra note 17, at 76–103; F. Schauer, Free Speech: A Philosophical Enquiry 81–82 (1982); Blasi, The Checking Value in First Amendment Theory, 1977 Am. B. Found. Res. J. 521, 538–44.

46. See infra Part IV.B.2.

47. See, e.g., A. Meiklejohn, Free Speech and Its Relation to Self-Government (1948).

48. Id. at 39.

tral meaning of democratic self-government. But even assuming that it is correct, it justifies the persuasion principle only in certain very limited respects; it does not explain why the persuasion principle should extend throughout first amendment law.

First, the Meiklejohn view would justify the persuasion principle only in the area of political speech. Of course, as Meiklejohn himself argued, political speech may be a much broader category than it appears to be at first.[49] But the persuasion principle applies to all speech. For the Meiklejohn view to justify the persuasion principle, therefore, one would have to make the argument that all speech is "political" in the relevant sense. As Meiklejohn's critics have pointed out, his thesis becomes much less plausible when it is broadened in this way.[50]

Second, and more important, even within the realm of political speech the Meiklejohn view does not justify all applications of the persuasion principle. In fact, it only justifies an entirely uncontroversial application of the persuasion principle—what I referred to earlier as the prohibition against political censorship.[51] The Meiklejohn theory does not absolutely prohibit all restrictions on political speech. It permits some time, place, and manner restrictions, for example. All Meikeljohn's theory absolutely forbids is restrictions that are premised on the government's conclusion that a certain outcome of an election, or other political controversy, would be the "wrong" outcome.

Thus the Meiklejohn view does not justify the application of the persuasion principle to invalidate, for example, restrictions on campaign financing. Those restrictions purport to be based not on the concern that the outcome of the election will be "wrong" (that is, an outcome that the government opposes) but on the concern that the process will not be fair, or truly democratic. Because the Meiklejohn view prohibits only government actions that attempt to preclude certain possible outcomes, it cannot prohibit—in fact, to some extent it must welcome—efforts to maintain the integrity of the democratic process.

The Meiklejohn view would limit the government's power to regulate campaign financing if one believed that, in the guise of eliminating an unfair imbalance in campaign expenditures, the government would be too likely to attempt covertly to control the results of elections. But this argument against campaign finance laws no longer reflects the persuasion principle. It no longer explains why there is something special about the process of persuasion. In the area of campaign finance, this approach will lead to the same conclusion as the persuasion principle, but it will not explain why the persuasion principle is correct.

---

49. Political speech might include art that is not overtly political, for example. See Meiklejohn, The First Amendment Is an Absolute, 1961 Sup. Ct. Rev. 245, 256, 263.

50. See, e.g., Bork, Neutral Principles and Some First Amendment Problems, 47 Ind. L.J. 1, 27 (1971); Chaffee, Book Review, 62 Harv. L. Rev. 891, 899–900 (1949); see also Kalven, The Metaphysics of the Law of Obscenity, 1960 Sup. Ct. Rev. 1, 15–16.

51. See supra note 9 and accompanying text.

There is a final way in which the Meiklejohn view provides only limited support for the persuasion principle. The Meiklejohn theory explicitly relies on the "basic American agreement" on popular sovereignty. Most of us would say, however, that freedom of expression is morally required even if, for some reason, democracy is not appropriate for a society. Or at least we would want to defend freedom of expression even to people who do not believe in democratic self-government. And we would want to say that punishing people for their speech is an additional wrong, distinct from (and probably worse than) the undemocratic nature of the government. In Part III, I will suggest a defense of the persuasion principle that, unlike the Meiklejohn view, does not presuppose acceptance of democracy.

4. *Theories of Deliberative Rationality.* — Other justifications for the persuasion principle rest on theories that hold that truth—political, moral, or scientific—can best be discovered through the free exchange of ideas. Although these theories take a variety of specific forms, the theme that free inquiry advances the search for truth (somehow defined) is common in liberal thought.[52]

These theories fall into two categories. One approach adopts an independent criterion of what constitutes truth (or some other desirable outcome) and asserts that the process of free inquiry leads to this desirable result. If truth is defined as correspondence to nature, for example, the theory would assert that free inquiry (perhaps called "scientific method") promotes truth in this sense.[53] The second approach does not independently define a desirable outcome. Instead, it defines a process of free inquiry and asserts that the outcomes of that process are ipso facto desirable. By this view, truth can be defined only as what emerges from a certain process of free inquiry.[54]

The first category of theories is vulnerable to the same criticism I made of the "marketplace of ideas" metaphor. It is certainly plausible to say that, in general, truth is promoted by free inquiry; unquestionably there are instances in which the suppression of ideas has impeded the search for truth, however that term is defined. The problem arises

---

52. The classic statements are found in J. Milton, Areopagitica (J. Hales ed. 1944), and J.S. Mill, On Liberty (C. Shields ed. 1982). In the pragmatist tradition, see, e.g., J. Dewey, Freedom and Culture 128–29 (1939); R. Rorty, Philosophy and the Mirror of Nature 373–79 (1979); C.S. Peirce, The Scientific Attitude and Fallibilism, *in* Philosophical Writings 42–59 (Buchler ed. 1955). The (now out of fashion) scientist liberalism of Popper is another example. See, e.g., 2 K. Popper, The Open Society and Its Enemies 200–11 (1945). Perhaps the best-known contemporary exponent of the view is Habermas. See, e.g., 1 J. Habermas, The Theory of Communicative Action (T. McCarthy trans. 1984). For a more recent statement, see P. Chevigny, More Speech (1988).

53. See, e.g., K. Popper, The Poverty of Historicism (1948); K. Popper, supra note 52.

54. See, e.g., J. Habermas, Communication and the Evolution of Society (1979); J. Habermas, Legitimation Crisis 107–08 (1973).

when one tries to move from these general statements to specifying precisely the conditions of "free inquiry" that will promote truth (or some other desirable outcome). We can specify precisely the conditions that will promote economic efficiency. But we simply do not know what specific institutional arrangements, what "market conditions," or what form of government "regulation," will best promote truth, or morality, or some other independently specified desirable outcome.

The second category of theories is not vulnerable to this criticism, because these theories *define* a desirable outcome as that which emerges from a certain process of free inquiry—for example, a process in which "no force except that of the better argument is exercised; and . . . all motives except that of the cooperative search for truth are excluded."[55] This second category of theories is, therefore, no longer consequentialist. Theories of this kind do not justify free expression by saying that a system of free expression will produce better consequences than a system in which restrictions are permitted. Instead, these theories try to justify a process on some other ground; the consequences produced by that justified process are then ipso facto good consequences. These theories assert that the process of free inquiry makes the outcomes desirable, not that the outcomes make the process of free inquiry desirable.

The problem with theories in this second category is to define, and to justify, the conditions that constitute the process of free inquiry that is said to be intrinsically desirable. Why should we accept the outcomes of *this* process—instead of some other process? The autonomy-based argument I make in Part III can be seen as a defense of one such process. In that sense, my approach is not at odds with—indeed, it reinforces—certain nonconsequentialist theories of deliberative rationality.

III. The Autonomy Justification of the Persuasion Principle

A. *Autonomy, Lying, and Manipulation*

Since speech will sometimes persuade people to do harmful things, isn't the persuasion principle simply irrational? Since it is chimerical to believe that "more speech" will always solve the problems created by "evil counsels," why shouldn't the government be allowed to suppress the evil counsels?

Brandeis's opinion in *Whitney*, in addition to suggesting a consequentialist argument, uses terms that we would today say reflect a conception of human autonomy: "the final end of the State" is to make people "free to develop their faculties," and liberty is valuable "both as an end and as a means."[56] Autonomy has been the basis of attempted

---

55. J. Habermas, Legitimation Crisis, supra note 54, at 108.
56. Whitney v. California, 274 U.S. 357, 375 (1927) (Brandeis, J., concurring).

justifications of principles comparable to the persuasion principle.[57] But autonomy is a notoriously vague notion; there is a danger that any attempt to justify a principle in terms of autonomy will slip into question-begging assertions about the nature of truly free and rational human beings.

In this Part, I will argue that the persuasion principle can be defended on autonomy grounds in the following way: Violations of the persuasion principle are similar in kind (although not in degree) to lies that are told for the purpose of influencing behavior. Violating the persuasion principle is wrong for some of the reasons that lies of this kind are wrong: both involve a denial of autonomy in the sense that they interfere with a person's control over her own reasoning processes. This justification of the persuasion principle can be characterized as Kantian.

Consider the case in which *A* lies to *B* in order to get *B* to do what *A* wants her to do. Suppose, for example, that *A* induces *B* to do her a favor by saying that she is ill, when in fact she is just lazy.[58] This deception is morally wrong (unless there are unusual circumstances) in part because it is disrespectful to treat *B* in this way. *B* is entitled to feel that *A* treated her as something less than a person—as a mere instrument of *A*'s will. *A* has manipulated *B*; she has used *B* as a tool, instead of treating her as a person.[59]

A manipulative lie of this kind has something in common with coercion. Both are ways of exerting control over the victim. Both are deliberate efforts to make a person do not what that person wants but what another person—the liar or coercer—wants. This is the sense in which the victim's autonomy is at stake.

In fact, in one respect lying is worse than outright coercion, because it is more insidious: the victim does not even know that he or she has been taken over and is being manipulated. At least in cases of outright coercion, the victim's mind is free. The victim of a lie is denied that freedom. In making decisions, the victim is pursuing the liar's ends, not the victim's own. Lying creates a kind of mental slavery that is an offense against the victim's humanity for many of the reasons that physical slavery is. While it is hard to argue that lying is worse than physical slavery, lying has a peculiarly offensive quality because it denies the victim even the knowledge that he or she is being used by

---

57. See Scanlon, Freedom of Expression, supra note 4; see also infra note 62 (discussing Scanlon's "Millian principle").

58. I do not use Kant's example (obtaining money by promising to repay it, knowing that one will not be able to, see I. Kant, Foundations of the Metaphysics of Morals 40, 48 (L. Beck trans. 1959)) because it involves an element of breach of promise as well as falsehood.

59. In this discussion I am indebted to C. Korsgaard, The Right to Lie: Kant on Dealing with Evil, 15 Phil. & Pub. Aff. 325, 330–37 (1986).

Freedom of Speech I

PERSUASION AND AUTONOMY

another.[60]

This Kantian account gives relatively clear content to the notion that lying is wrong because it violates human autonomy. Lying forces the victim to pursue the speaker's objectives instead of the victim's own objectives. If the capacity to decide upon a plan of life and to determine one's own objectives is integral to human nature, lies that are designed to manipulate people are a uniquely severe offense against human autonomy.

This account suggests that there is a difference between lies that are manipulative and false statements made for different reasons. False statements that are not manipulative lack the element of control and domination. An inadvertently false statement, for example, or a false statement made solely for the purpose of protecting a confidence, is less objectionable because it does not involve the same degree of manipulation as a false statement made for the purpose of influencing behavior or thought. This distinction parallels the difference between, on the one hand, coercing someone, and, on the other hand, acting in a way that is not designed to be coercive but happens to prevent a person from doing what she wants.

B. *Government Manipulation*

1. *Restrictions on Speech*. — The same autonomy-based argument justifies the persuasion principle. The persuasion principle singles out restrictions on speech that are manipulative; it does not speak to nonmanipulative restrictions on speech. It prohibits the government from deliberately denying information to people for the purpose of influencing their behavior.[61] Deliberately denying information for this

---

60. The crucial passage in Kant is as follows:

[H]e who intends a deceitful promise to others sees immediately that he intends to use another man merely as a means, without the latter containing the end in himself at the same time. For he whom I want to use for my own purposes by means of such a promise cannot possibly assent to my mode of acting against him and cannot contain the end of this action in himself. This conflict against the principle of other men is even clearer if we cite examples of attacks on their freedom and property. For then it is clear that he who transgresses the rights of men intends to make use of the persons of others merely as a means, without considering that, as rational beings, they must always be esteemed at the same time as ends, i.e., only as beings who must be able to contain in themselves the end of the very same action.

I. Kant, supra note 58, at 48 (citation omitted) (quoted in part in Korsgaard, supra note 59, at 331).

The view that the "mental slavery" brought about by lying is in some ways worse than physical slavery is related to the defense of the privilege against self-incrimination offered in Seidman, Rubishov's Question: Self-Incrimination and the Problem of Coerced Preferences, 2 Yale J.L. & Hum. 149 (1990). See especially id. at 167–68, suggesting that it is more dangerous to give the government the power to coerce (manifestations of) states of mind than to give it the power to coerce behavior.

61. As I noted earlier, when I refer to manipulation by "the government" to pro-

reason is not the same thing as lying, but it is a form of attempting to control the audience's mental processes.

Ordinarily, withholding information is not as effective as lying because a lie affirmatively throws the hearer off the track. When information is simply withheld, there is usually a greater chance that the victim will discover the information for herself. But the difference is only one of degree; both a manipulative denial of information and a manipulative lie invade the victim's autonomy.

Thus there is a clear sense in which violations of the persuasion principle infringe human autonomy: they manipulate people by, in part, taking over their thinking processes in somewhat the same way as (although to a lesser degree than) lying. When the government violates the persuasion principle, it has determined that people will, to a degree, pursue its—the government's—objectives, instead of their own.[62]

This Kantian justification provides a further defense of my provi-

---

mote "the government's" objectives, I of course do not mean simply the objectives of government officials. See supra note 18.

62. The "Millian principle" advanced in Scanlon, Freedom of Expression, supra note 4, at 215–24, and subsequently repudiated in Scanlon, Categories of Expression, supra note 4, at 530–35, has some similarities to the persuasion principle. Both principles forbid the government from invoking certain categories of consequences caused by speech as a justification for restricting speech, and both rest on a notion of autonomy.

But Scanlon's approach differs from mine in both its prescriptions and its foundations, and the differences make my approach better able to survive the objections that caused Scanlon to alter his. First, the Millian principle, unlike the persuasion principle, is not limited to speech that achieves its result through a rational process of persuasion. The Millian principle prohibits the government from considering certain categories of bad consequences—false beliefs and harmful acts—whenever they are "a result of" expression. Scanlon, Freedom of Expression, supra note 4, at 213. Consequently, Scanlon's view has problems with prohibitions against false statements of fact, as Scanlon acknowledged in his repudiation. See Scanlon, Categories of Expression, supra note 4, at 532 (discussing deceptive advertising). Scanlon's theory also should have problems with defamation, cf. Scanlon, Freedom of Expression, supra note 4, at 211, hostile audience reactions, and perhaps even "harmful acts" like crowding the streets and littering.

Second, Scanlon's notion of autonomy is very different from mine. It is not linked to the wrongness of lying. Instead, it rests on a conception of the proper relationship between the government and the citizen; as Scanlon said, his view was a generalization of Meiklejohn's theory that a democratic government may not dictate to its citizens what they shall believe about politics. See id. at 221; Scanlon, Categories of Expression, supra note 4, at 530–31, 535. Under the Kantian conception of autonomy, by contrast, the evil to be avoided is the manipulation of the individual by any actor, private or governmental. This conception focuses on what is happening to the listener rather than on what the government is doing.

Scanlon abandoned his principle in substantial part because he concluded that private actions as well as government actions can endanger autonomy. See id. at 527, 533. Because his conception of autonomy focused on the limitations of the government's power over citizens, it had no way to accommodate private threats to autonomy. By contrast, the Kantian conception of autonomy—because it prohibits manipulation by any source—has no difficulty recognizing that private manipulation is threatening. In Part IV.B, I discuss how the persuasion principle should be qualified to take into account private threats to autonomy.

sional definition of the persuasion principle, under which I excluded false statements and statements that precipitate ill-considered action. The persuasion principle does not apply to government restrictions of false statements of fact because those restrictions do not manipulate or deny autonomy. No one wants to make decisions on the basis of false information. When the government prevents people from making decisions on the basis of false information, it does not manipulate their mental processes to serve the government's ends. Rather, it enables those processes to function as they should, to promote the ends of the listener.

Similarly, restricting speech in a way that effectively prevents a person from making ill-considered decisions does not deny her autonomy in the way that lying to her does.[63] It does not manipulate the person and cause her to pursue the government's ends instead of her own. She remains free to decide what she wants to do on the basis of reasoned discussion. Such a restriction on speech may deny listeners something they value—people may enjoy being moved to impulsive action—but it does not control the listeners by causing them to pursue the government's ends instead of their own.[64]

2. *Withholding Information.* — It might be objected that the persuasion principle cannot be justified in the way I have suggested—as a means of protecting individuals against government actions designed to manipulate them by denying them information—because the first amendment is not generally thought to forbid the government from manipulatively denying access to information in the government's own possession.[65] In fact, one might say that the government constantly denies people information by failing to take steps to make it available to

---

63. Of course, the assumption that a class of ill-considered decisions can be identified is both essential and controversial. See infra notes 77–78 and accompanying text.

64. At this point, other first amendment principles besides the persuasion principle may become important. In particular, limiting speech that precipitates ill-considered action, or even factually false speech, might infringe upon important interests of the speaker that deserve first amendment protection—including interests that are called autonomy interests, although they differ from the Kantian notion that I have described. See, e.g., C.E. Baker, supra note 44, at 58–59; D. Richards, Toleration and the Constitution 188–95 (1986). The essential idea behind this conception of autonomy is that there are "capacities central to human rationality" that an autonomous person must be free to exercise. Richards, Free Speech and Obscenity Law: Toward a Moral Theory of the First Amendment, 123 U. Pa. L. Rev. 45, 62 (1974).

I do not intend to suggest that such interests are not to be protected. As I said earlier, while the persuasion principle is centrally important to the American system of freedom of expression, it would oversimplify that system to suppose that no other principles bear upon it. My concern here is not to describe exhaustively what the first amendment protects, but to examine the extent to which the persuasion principle should be accepted as a reason to forbid restrictions on speech.

65. See, e.g., Houchins v. KQED, Inc., 438 U.S. 1, 8–16 (1978) (media does not have first amendment right of access to state-run penal facilities); Pell v. Procunier, 417 U.S. 817, 829–35 (1974) (statutory limitation on contact between media and prison inmates does not violate first amendment).

them. Indeed, governments sometimes tell outright lies, and that is not thought to violate the first amendment—even though lying is the clearest example of the kind of manipulation that the autonomy rationale of the persuasion principle forbids.

Not all government lying, and certainly not all government refusals to release information, are manipulative. For example, the government may make false statements, or fail to disclose information, in order to protect an individual's privacy. The failure to disclose information will often reflect simply a desire to save resources. In addition, even if the government's action (or inaction) is manipulative, the object of the manipulation might be someone who cannot claim constitutional rights against the government, such as a foreign power. But when the government makes false statements or fails to disclose information for the purpose of manipulating its own citizens, its conduct is wrong (other things equal) for the same reasons that violations of the persuasion principle are wrong. If the persuasion principle were carried out to the limits of its logic, it would condemn this conduct.

The fact that the first amendment is not enforced in this way does not, however, substantially undermine my claim that the persuasion principle is central to our system of freedom of expression. Many theories of the first amendment are unable fully to explain why the government's false statements and failures to disclose information pose less of a threat to first amendment values than the government's suppression of private speech. For example, false statements by the government, or the government's refusal to disclose information in its possession, can seriously hamper the discussion necessary for democratic self-government that, according to the Meiklejohn theory, the first amendment was designed to protect.[66]

That an apparent weakness of the persuasion principle is shared by other justifications of freedom of expression suggests that some institutional factor—something about the way in which the theoretical concerns underlying the first amendment are translated into practice — may be at work. Specifically, prohibitions against government lying and manipulative government nondisclosure may be examples of a principle of free expression that is underenforced by the courts.[67] Although the principles underlying the first amendment (under either the persua-

---

66. See generally DuVal, The Occasions of Secrecy, 47 U. Pitt. L. Rev. 579, 587 (1986) (discussing "reasons for restricting the acquisition and dissemination of knowledge"). But see BeVier, An Informed Public, an Informing Press: The Search for a Constitutional Principle, 68 Calif. L. Rev. 482 (1980).

67. See, e.g., Sager, Fair Measure: The Legal Status of Underenforced Constitutional Norms, 91 Harv. L. Rev. 1212 (1978).

It might be thought that the reason the courts do not enforce a prohibition against government lying is that the language of the first amendment does not authorize such a prohibition. But as a matter of language it is not implausible to say that the government "abridg[es] the freedom of speech" when it deliberately lies about a matter of great public concern for the purpose of preventing a full public debate.

sion principle or the Meiklejohn theory) should prohibit government action of this kind, that is not a limitation that the courts can implement.

For the courts to enforce a prohibition against government lying or nondisclosure, they would have to make a delicate and complex inquiry into precisely what information was in the government's possession. They would then have to determine the government's reasons for the nondisclosure or false statements. The great detail of the Freedom of Information Act[68]—which has numerous exceptions designed by Congress, many of which have given rise to complex judicial interpretations, and which do not even apply to the most difficult cases (such as false statements made to the public by high officials)—suggests that courts would find such a prohibition too difficult to enforce. Institutional concerns, therefore, rather than any theoretical weakness, explain why the autonomy justification for the persuasion principle has not given rise to a judicially enforced first amendment prohibition against false statements by the government or manipulative government failures to disclose information.

C. *Why the Greater Does Not Include the Lesser*

The autonomy justification answers one of the most superficially appealing arguments against the persuasion principle: if the Constitution does not forbid the government from prohibiting an action, it should not be interpreted to forbid the government from taking the "lesser" step of merely banning speech that might persuade people to engage in the action. If the action in question is constitutionally protected, of course, this argument does not apply. But this argument would permit restrictions on speech in the wide range of cases in which the government could prohibit the action that the speech encourages.

This "greater includes the lesser" rationale persuaded the Supreme Court in *Posadas de Puerto Rico Assocs. v. Tourism Co. of Puerto Rico*,[69] the one case other than those that have been discredited in which the Court explicitly rejected the persuasion principle. *Posadas* upheld a ban on advertisements for casinos. The Constitution does not generally prohibit the government from paternalistic action; that is well settled.[70] Thus the government would be free to ban gambling even on strictly paternalistic grounds. How can it possibly be a greater invasion of human freedom for the government to ban only speech advocating gambling, when it leaves people free to gamble?

The autonomy justification provides an answer because it explains that a lie—and, by extension, a manipulative restriction on access to information—is a different kind of affront from outright coercion. One

---

68. 5 U.S.C. § 552 (1982).
69. 478 U.S. 328 (1986).
70. See, e.g., Paris Adult Theatre I v. Slaton, 413 U.S. 49, 68 & n.15 (1973).

might dramatize the distinction by saying that outright coercion affects what people do, but restrictions on information affect what people are. For the government to frustrate the desire to gamble, for example, is different from the government manipulating the flow of information so that some people who would otherwise have developed that desire never do so.

Which imposition is worse may depend on the facts of the specific case. But the restriction on information imposes a different *kind* of control on people. That is enough to answer the "greater includes the lesser" argument. There is a value in being able to hold a belief or desire even if one cannot act on it. That is why "thought control" is such an odious notion. It is different from, and often worse than, behavior control. When the government violates the persuasion principle, it is engaged in a form of thought control. Even if the government can forbid people from acting in certain ways, it does not follow that it may try to prevent them from believing that such actions are proper, or from wanting to engage in those actions.[71]

Suppose that the government could manipulate people's minds directly, by irradiating them in a way that changed their desires. No one would say that the power to ban an activity automatically included the "lesser" power to irradiate people so that they no longer had the desire to engage in that activity. Violations of the persuasion principle, unless justified in some other way, are objectionable for the same reason (although, because they are less effective, not to the same degree) as such imaginary thought-expunging radiation.

IV. THE LIMITS OF THE PERSUASION PRINCIPLE

This discussion shows that the persuasion principle can be securely justified and should play an important role in the system of freedom of expression. But I do not want to suggest that the current state of the law, in which the persuasion principle plays such a significant role, is fully satisfactory. On the contrary, the persuasion principle must be qualified in at least two ways.

A. *Averting Very Bad Consequences*

Even if violating the persuasion principle is as bad as manipulative lying, manipulative lying is not always wrong. If the consequences of not lying are very bad, it is acceptable, and sometimes morally obligatory, to lie. It follows that the persuasion principle can be overridden if the consequences of permitting the speech are sufficiently harmful.

This result is not surprising; few principles hold absolutely, regardless of consequences. But basing the persuasion principle on auton-

---

71. See Stanley v. Georgia, 394 U.S. 557, 565 (1969) ("Our whole constitutional heritage rebels at the thought of giving government the power to control man's minds.").

omy gives some sense of how severe the consequences must be before
they allow the principle to be overridden. Roughly, the question is
whether the consequences are so severe that it would be acceptable to
engage in manipulative lying or deception to prevent them.

Consider, for example, the debates over whether the Constitution
would permit prohibitions against tobacco advertising, or against
speech that might encourage discrimination against minorities. These
debates tend to focus on one of the polar positions. Some say that such
restrictions are utterly inconsistent with the first amendment because
they constitute attempts by the government to manipulate behavior by
controlling ideas. Others urge that such prohibitions are unproblematic because the greater power to ban the activity includes the
lesser power to ban speech that encourages the activity.

But if the persuasion principle rests on an autonomy rationale—
that violations of the persuasion principle are wrong for approximately
the same reason that lying is wrong—then neither of these polar positions is correct. Instead, according to the autonomy rationale, the
question is roughly whether it would be acceptable to engage in manipulative lying in order to prevent the conduct in question (discrimination
or smoking). This does not decisively resolve the question, but it nar-
rows and focuses the inquiry. One should not manipulatively deceive
someone casually, but manipulative lying is certainly justified to prevent serious harms. It follows that a serious social problem could justify manipulation of the kind that the persuasion principle forbids.

B. *The Libertarian Bias of the Persuasion Principle*

The other limit on the persuasion principle is more complex and
problematic. It derives from what might be called the libertarian bias
of the persuasion principle. The persuasion principle focuses on the
dangers that government action creates, without considering whether
private action might present comparable dangers or whether the government might help overcome the dangers created by private action.[72]
This bias does not undermine the persuasion principle, but it does require that the principle be qualified.

These qualifications are not easy to specify. As I will discuss in
Part V, the question of how the government should be allowed to respond to private speech that threatens listeners' autonomy is exceptionally complex. It raises both empirical questions—When is there a
problem of private autonomy-threatening speech? How likely is government action to correct the problem instead of making it worse?—

---

72. The argument that current first amendment doctrine does not give the government sufficient power to combat private threats to the values underlying free expression
is increasingly common in the literature. See, e.g., Fiss, Free Speech and Social Structure, 71 Iowa L. Rev. 1405, 1415 (1986); Schneider, Free Speech and Corporate Freedom: A Comment on *First National Bank of Boston v. Bellotti*, 59 S. Cal. L. Rev. 1227, 1287
(1986).

and theoretical questions about exactly what it means to say that private speech threatens listeners' autonomy. But before addressing these questions, I will defend the assertion that the persuasion principle reflects a libertarian bias; consider various arguments that suggest (with partial but not complete success) that the libertarian bias is justified; and describe some ways in which the persuasion principle, as I have stated it, already attempts to correct for the libertarian bias.

1. *Private Manipulation and the Libertarian Bias*. — Private speakers commonly try to manipulate their listeners. If they do so by making false statements of fact, the persuasion principle permits their speech to be restricted. But the manipulation might take the form of withholding opposing arguments, or distorting the truth in ways that do not amount to outright falsehoods, or appealing to the listener in a subliminal way.

Private manipulation of this kind is endemic. It occurs not only in obvious places like advertising but in virtually all forms of private discourse. Every speaker who tries to gain an advantage by using his or her superior resources (including intellectual and rhetorical abilities as well as material resources), instead of just offering the arguments for what they are worth on the merits, is engaged in a form of manipulation of the kind I described in justifying the persuasion principle.[73] Such a speaker is trying to take over the mind of the listener, to make her pursue the speaker's ends instead of her own. In every such case, the private speaker is doing something that is akin to coercion.

But the persuasion principle forbids the government from restricting private speech on the ground that the speech is manipulative; such a government restriction would be directed at consequences resulting from the persuasiveness of the speech. Manipulation is one of the many harmful consequences that, under the persuasion principle, the government may not take into account.[74] For example, the persuasion principle would forbid the government from restricting racial hate propaganda even if it could be demonstrated that the propaganda, by skillfully presenting evocative images and one-sided data, manipulated people into thinking that certain groups were intrinsically inferior.

Thus the persuasion principle seems to leave the government helpless against endemic private autonomy-invading manipulation. The paradoxical effect of the persuasion principle is that the autonomy of the listener—precisely what the persuasion principle is supposed to protect—will be invaded, but by private speakers. The persuasion prin-

---

73. See 1 J. Habermas, supra note 52, at 85–95, 285–88 (contrasting "communicative action," which is "oriented to reaching understanding," with uses of speech oriented to achieving the speaker's objectives, including "strategic" and "dramaturgical" (or "[t]he manipulative production of false impressions")).

74. I leave aside for now the exceptions for false statements of fact and speech that attempts to precipitate an ill-considered reaction. As I will explain, see infra notes 76–77 and accompanying text, those exceptions are rudimentary efforts to address the problem of private manipulation.

ciple will, in this instance, detract from autonomy rather than enhance it. The source of the problem is that the persuasion principle is blind to private manipulation and bars only government manipulation.

2. *Can the Libertarian Bias Be Justified?* — Although private manipulative speech is ubiquitous, this problem is not as severe at it might seem at first. Several factors mitigate the problem and partially justify the libertarian bias of the persuasion principle. These factors do not, however, eliminate the problem of private manipulation or justify the libertarian bias completely.

First, manipulative private speech on one side of an issue may counteract manipulative speech on the other side. Private speakers will sometimes have an incentive, financial or otherwise, to supply the arguments, facts, or perspectives omitted by others. Competitors and consumer groups try to correct the distortions they see in advertising. Political factions answer one another. The net effect on the audience may be the same as if there had been no manipulation at all.

If manipulative private speech were always available to correct other manipulative private speech, the libertarian bias of the persuasion principle would be justified. It makes sense for the persuasion principle to forbid the government from engaging in manipulative suppression—since suppression prevents any private speech from counteracting the government's manipulation—while leaving private parties free to engage in manipulative speech, since counteracting private speech will be available.

But there is, of course, no reason to think that an unregulated system of private expression will be self-correcting in this way. The content and quantity of speech in circulation depends on the inclinations and resources of potential speakers. So far as the promotion of truth is concerned, these are arbitrary factors. There is no reason to think that they will generate a self-correcting system. Certain points of view may be underrepresented or wholly unrepresented. It follows that sometimes private speech can threaten—and government restrictions can therefore serve—the values that the persuasion principle is intended to protect.

Second, sometimes the listener will know that the speaker is attempting to manipulate her and will make the necessary adjustments. The listener will seek out opposing points of view or will correct for the distortion in her own thinking. This will also mitigate the problem of private manipulative speech and partially justify the libertarian bias of the persuasion principle. A listener will ordinarily be less able to overcome the effects of government restrictions because those restrictions prevent her from even encountering speech that might enable her to make the necessary adjustments. A listener will usually be more able to overcome private distortions.

But the listener's ability to adjust can be a complete solution only in a world of unlimited, or at least very great, resources. In such a world, before making any decisions people could uncover all possible counter-arguments, including those not already in circulation, and fully consider every argument and counter-argument. But in a world in which people have only limited resources (especially time) to devote to each of the many decisions they must make, people will be vulnerable to manipulation. They will be unable to consider every way in which the information and arguments presented to them might be distorted.

Third, the government really can "remedy" the manipulative character of private speech by providing "more speech." If private speakers attempt to manipulate people by omitting information or counter-arguments, the government can supply what is missing.[75] Even after the government supplies what is missing, the speech may still persuade people to do bad things, as I argued in Part III. But autonomy-invading manipulative distortions can be corrected by "more speech" supplied by the government. Again, this is a partial solution to the problem, and it suggests that the libertarian bias of the persuasion principle is defensible.

Again, however, this "more speech" remedy will not be a complete solution in a world of limited resources. Correcting manipulative private speech by supplying "more speech"—for example, by providing public funding for political campaigns—is costly. Correcting manipulative private speech by suppressing it, on the other hand, will be nearly cost-free to society in monetary terms, assuming—obviously a big assumption—that the government restrictions do no more than correct for private distortions.

It is tempting to say that if society is not willing to pay the costs of more speech, then the threat that the private speech poses to autonomy cannot be serious. But the fact that people consider other needs to be more pressing does not mean that the private speech that happens to be in circulation is free of serious, manipulative distortions. Unless some other argument can show why government suppression is undesirable, the assertion that "more speech" can remedy manipulative private speech, even if accurate, does not require that the government must choose that remedy instead of suppression.

Finally, the libertarian bias of the persuasion principle might be justified on the ground that even if private speakers are manipulating their audiences, government restrictions of the private speech will do more harm than good. The government itself has biases; in the guise of correcting private manipulation, the government may distort the debate in a way that manipulatively serves its own purposes.

This danger is most apparent when distinctively governmental in-

---

75. See Capital Broadcasting Co. v. Mitchell, 333 F. Supp. 582, 587 (D.D.C. 1971) (Wright, J., dissenting) (citing evidence that before cigarette advertising was banned from television and radio, FCC "fairness doctrine" that mandated antismoking advertising effectively decreased number of smokers), aff'd sub nom. Capital Broadcasting Co. v. Acting Attorney Gen., 405 U.S. 1000 (1972).

terests are affected, for example when the restricted speech criticizes
government officials or threatens to unseat incumbents from office.
But it can also happen in other cases, when no distinctively governmental interests are at stake, such as in cases of commercial speech or
speech that incites hatred toward a particular group in society. In such
cases, private parties might use the government not just to correct for
the distortions and manipulation of their opponents but manipulatively
to restrict speech in order to serve their own purposes.

This danger is certainly important, and again it mitigates the problem of the libertarian bias in the persuasion principle: it suggests that
the bias does not wholly undermine the soundness and usefulness of
the persuasion principle. But this argument, like the other limitations,
does not completely solve the problem of the libertarian bias.

Sometimes government intervention will do more harm than good.
But there is no reason to think that that will always be true, or that
government intervention is so harmful so often that the best course is
to bar it entirely. There may be occasions when the danger of continuing to allow private manipulation is greater than the danger of allowing
the government to restrict the manipulative private speech. Whether
this is true will depend on several complex empirical and theoretical
issues, some of which I will address below. But there is simply no basis
for saying that there is no definable category of cases in which government intervention will, on balance, improve protection for autonomy.
The persuasion principle, with its libertarian bias, implicitly makes this
statement.

3. *False Statements and Statements Prompting Ill-Considered Action*. — As
I have defined the persuasion principle, it does not protect false statements of fact or statements that seek to precipitate ill-considered action. When the government restricts such statements in order to
prevent the bad consequences that they induce, it does not violate the
persuasion principle.

There were many reasons for defining the persuasion principle in
this way. These built-in exceptions are not ad hoc but rather cohere
with the idea that the government may not interfere with a rational process of persuasion. Without these exceptions, the persuasion principle
would not fit first amendment doctrine. Indeed, Justice Brandeis's
Whitney concurrence is itself the source of the exception for speech that
induces ill-considered action; Justice Brandeis suggested that the government may restrict speech when there has been no "opportunity for
full discussion." And the autonomy justification for the persuasion
principle seems to validate these exceptions; there is a clear sense in
which the government does not infringe on autonomy when it restricts
these kinds of speech.

Most important, this aspect of the persuasion principle—the exceptions for false statements of fact and statements that seek to precipitate ill-considered reactions—addresses the problem of private

manipulation. That is, these exceptions partially overcome the libertarian bias. The exceptions permit the government to intervene in certain circumstances when private speakers are attempting to manipulate their audience.

This point is made most clearly in connection with false statements of fact. Lying is the clearest case of the coercion-like, autonomy-invading manipulation that the persuasion principle is intended to prevent. When a speaker tells a lie in order to influence the listener's behavior, the metaphor of commandeering the listener's mind, and making it serve the speaker's ends instead of the listener's, seems especially appropriate. The speaker really does inject her own false information into the thought processes of the listener for the purpose of making those processes produce the outcome that the speaker desires.

Consequently, false statements of fact seem to present an especially clear instance in which the libertarian bias is unjustified; it seems more likely here than anywhere else that allowing the government to restrict false statements of fact by private speakers, while it does present some risks of government abuse, will do more good than harm. If the category of false statements of fact is not defined very narrowly, it can, of course, become highly problematic.[76] But there is a core area in which the harm of private manipulation seems great enough to justify government restrictions on speech.

Speech that seeks to induce ill-considered action—assuming for the moment that such a category can be defined—presents similar dangers to autonomy. This speech manipulates listeners by causing them to act in ways that the speakers want them to act, before they have a chance to consider whether the action will advance their own ends. In that sense, speech that induces ill-considered action is a violation of autonomy, akin to coercion, in the way I discussed in Part III. As in the case of false statements, government suppression of private speech can protect the listeners' autonomy.

Speech that induces ill-considered action is different from false speech, however, in one significant respect. It is a fair generalization that no rational person ever wants to act on the basis of a false statement of fact.[77] But there are occasions when a rational person would

---

76. For example, many statements made in political debate—about candidates' records, the economy, the progress that can be made in solving problems over the next few years—are literally false statements of fact.

77. There are instances in which a rational person might want to be lied to. In such cases, a manipulative falsehood does not invade the listener's autonomy. I leave these instances aside because they seem too unusual and peripheral to implicate the basic institutional structure governing freedom of expression.

One reason that a rational person might choose to be lied to is that we cannot always control what we think, and hearing certain statements might involuntarily stimulate unpleasant thoughts. A person might prefer the risk of being lied to, to the risk of having a true statement force an unpleasant thought before her mind. Thus, for exam-

want to be moved to spontaneous or impulsive action.[78] If, in such cases, the government restricts speech because the speech will bring about an ill-considered reaction, the government deprives the listeners of something they value—the capacity to be moved to spontaneous action.

But such a restriction is not a deprivation of the kind of autonomy that underlies the persuasion principle. Depriving a person of the capacity for spontaneous action does not constitute manipulation; the government is not causing the listener to pursue its aims instead of the listener's own aims. It is inflicting a different kind of harm on the listener.

The true problem with allowing the government to restrict speech that precipitates an ill-considered reaction is a deeper one. It is that *every* action is to some degree ill-considered. Because resources are scarce, people seldom, if ever, consider every possible counter-argument and ramification before they act. At some point they must make a decision even though their information is incomplete. There is virtually never an opportunity for truly "full discussion" (to use Brandeis's phrase). Thus whenever a speaker tries to manipulate her audience— by providing a tendentious or distorted view, or even by not fully presenting counter-arguments—the speech might be said to be attempting to induce ill-considered action.

That is why this category is so ill-defined—because potentially it includes all manipulative private speech, a very broad category indeed. Brandeis's qualification for "full discussion" attempts to correct for the libertarian bias by allowing the government to suppress manipulative private speech. But manipulative private speech is endemic. Brandeis's qualification identifies the problem, rather than solving it.

The problem is: how far should the government be allowed to go in restricting private speech because it is manipulative? False statements of fact, at least if the category is narrowly defined, present a relatively easy case for government intervention. And the mitigating factors previously discussed suggest that denying the government the authority to restrict manipulative private speech is not quite as serious a problem as it might initially seem. But because manipulative private

---

ple, it can be rational for a person to prefer to be told that she does not have an untreatable and deadly disease, even if that statement is false.

A person who makes such a choice pays a price in uncertainty. In the example given, the listener will not know whether the good news she is certain to receive—the statement that she does not have the disease—is true or false. But it is not necessarily irrational to prefer that uncertainty to the unpleasant thoughts that will be involuntarily induced by bad news.

78. Two disparate examples are a response to a *true* cry of fire in a theater, and a response to a charismatic religious (or other) figure. In the first instance the weighing of pros and cons, while it would be desirable if possible, is too costly. In the second instance, the weighing of pros and cons is intrinsically undesirable because it detracts from the quality of the experience.

COLUMBIA LAW REVIEW [Vol. 91:334

speech is so prevalent, a serious problem remains, and beyond the category of false statements of fact it is unclear what the answer to that problem might be. In the next Part, I offer some thoughts on this issue.

V. AUTONOMY AND LIBERALISM

A. *Eliminating the Libertarian Bias*

Any effort wholly to eliminate the libertarian bias of the persuasion principle will raise questions of extraordinary difficulty. Suppose the government were to restrict private speech of a certain kind—say, speech that made derogatory assertions about particular groups in society, or advertising for certain products, or large expenditures in connection with political campaigns—on the ground that the speech was too one-sided and manipulative. The argument would be that although this government restriction is superficially inconsistent with the persuasion principle, it actually furthers the objectives of the persuasion principle because it averts a threat to the autonomy of those who might be influenced by this private speech.

In order to evaluate this argument, it would not be enough to conclude that some private speakers were engaged in manipulative or distorting arguments. One would have to consider: whether other private speech corrected those distortions; whether the listeners themselves could correct for the distortions; and if not, whether the government action really corrected them or instead merely imported distortions favorable to the government.

These inquiries raise difficult, but perhaps manageable, empirical questions; the aspects of first amendment doctrine that do not fit the persuasion principle may even reflect a rough effort to come to grips with these empirical issues.[79] But there is a more fundamental prob-

---

79. See supra notes 28–36 and accompanying text (aspects of first amendment doctrine that seem not to fit the persuasion principle).

There are some circumstances—what might be called "laboratory conditions"—in which it is easier to assess precisely what speech is in circulation on different sides of an issue. In these cases, there is a greater chance that government action will not overreach but will simply correct for imbalances (and that any government overreaching can be set aside). Criminal solicitation, see supra note 10, at least in private, may be an example. The notion of "laboratory conditions" (used in a different but related way) is part of the justification that the Supreme Court gives for its approach in cases involving speech in connection with representation elections under the National Labor Relations Act, in which the usual first amendment principles are essentially suspended. See, e.g., NLRB v. Gissel Packing Co., 395 U.S. 575, 616 (1969).

Another example is the restrictions imposed on speech by advocates in a trial. Certain statements may not be made in arguing to a jury precisely because they are too likely to persuade the jury by means that are thought to be manipulative. See generally the discussion in L. Bollinger, supra note 17, at 56. This is perhaps the best example of a situation in which both the speech in circulation and the effects of the government's restrictions on speech can be so carefully monitored that government overreaching becomes less of a concern than private manipulation.

lem. How would we know when we had a system of expression free of manipulation? As I said earlier, there is no theory of what a well-functioning speech "market" consists of. There is no theory that tells us what mixture of speech and restrictions is optimal, at least in the short run. Without such a theory, it will be very difficult to specify how the persuasion principle should be qualified to eliminate the libertarian bias.

I cannot offer either a complete theory or concrete prescriptions for specific cases. But it may be helpful at least to identify the point of view from which the problem should be considered. In moral philosophy, if not in law, this is often all that can be accomplished. To show that an issue should be addressed from a particular point of view—for example, that of a utilitarian ideal observer who seeks to maximize the sum of utility in society,[80] or that of an individual who does not know her particular circumstances but must design rules to govern a society[81]—advances the discussion, even if one cannot say specifically what such a hypothetical individual would do in concrete situations.

My suggestion is that in trying to decide how far the government can go in restricting private speech on the ground that it is manipulative, we should adopt the point of view of a (hypothetical) individual who has no interests or desires other than to reach the best decision about the subject under discussion. Perhaps the best way to understand this construct is to draw an analogy to a judge or any other impartial arbiter. Ideally, a judge should have no desire other than to decide cases correctly.

The best way to understand the persuasion principle is by analogy to the ideal judge. The autonomy rationale underlying the persuasion principle requires government actions affecting speech to be assessed from the point of view of an individual who is self-interested, but whose only operative desire is to reach the correct decision about what she should do or believe. For example, suppose one were trying to determine whether unquestionably manipulative advertising for a certain product should be forbidden. In making this determination, one would try to adopt the point of view of an individual whose only interest is in reaching a correct decision, and ask: does the information currently available—taking into account both the manipulative advertising and all other relevant speech—deviate substantially from what that hypothetical individual would desire? If so, could that individual, operating under normal conditions of scarcity, compensate for the deficiency herself? If not, does the proposed government restriction make it more

---

80. The classic utilitarian impartial observer theories are D. Hume, Treatise of Human Nature Book II, Pt. I, Sec. XI; Book III, Pt. I, Secs. I and VI; 316–20, 575–60, 582–84, 618– 19 (Selby-Bigge ed. 1888); D. Hume, An Enquiry Concerning the Principles of Morals, 218–32, 268–78 (Selby-Bigge ed. 1975); A. Smith, The Theory of Moral Sentiments (D. Raphael & A. Macfie eds. 1976).

81. See J. Rawls, A Theory of Justice 17 (1971).

likely, from the point of view of that individual, that she will be able to reach the correct decision, or does it simply substitute the government's manipulation for that of the private parties? These questions are, of course, highly abstract, far removed from specific doctrines that might resolve specific cases. But they provide a framework for considering the issues.

B. *Liberalism and the Persuasion Principle*

Focusing the question in this way also reveals the liberal theoretical roots of the persuasion principle in the American system of freedom of expression. The ideal observer position that I described reflects certain classic liberal virtues. It is abstracted from any particular desires, attachments, or ways of life. In that sense it is an impartial or neutral point of view. It is also, like certain forms of liberalism, highly rationalistic; from the point of view I have described, speech is valuable only to the extent that it furthers *rational* decision making.

It is not part of my argument that these aspects of liberalism—its abstraction from particular desires and its rationalism—are correct. My suggestion is only that a central principle in the American system of freedom of expression is distinctively liberal at its core. Indeed, the liberal ideal observer construct I have described may not even be coherent. Real individuals have more than a bare desire to decide correctly what candidates they should vote for, or what views to hold about others in society, or what occupation they should pursue, or what products they should buy. They have concrete desires and views about products and candidates and occupations. It is possible that unless one knows what those concrete desires are, one cannot make sense of the question: what information would this person want in circulation? The bare desire to reach a correct decision may leave that question unanswerable in principle.

This objection echoes a common objection to liberalism: liberalism mistakenly attempts to deduce moral principles from too "thin" or "unsituated" a conception of human nature, a conception that views people simply as rational beings without particular attachments.[82] If this objection to liberalism is correct, it follows from the argument I

---

82. This is today perhaps the most common criticism of (certain forms of) liberalism. For representative examples, see M. Sandel, Liberalism and the Limits of Justice 59 (1982); Galston, Defending Liberalism, 76 Am. Pol. Sci. Rev. 621 (1982); Sen, Justice: Means versus Freedoms, 19 Phil. & Pub. Aff. 111 (1990).

This problem is parallel to the question whether liberalism can support a coherent theory of education. See Gutmann, What's the Use of Going to School?, in Utilitarianism and Beyond 261 (A. Sen & B. Williams eds. 1982). A "thin" theory of human nature like the one described in text suggests that people should be educated simply to use their rational faculties. (I understand the effort in A. Gutmann, Democratic Education (1987) to be along these lines.) That may be insufficient to generate any useful account of what an education should consist of. But any more complete conception threatens to mold people too much, in a way that endangers their autonomy.

have made here that the theory of freedom of expression reflected in the first amendment is fundamentally flawed. My argument has been that that theory incorporates a principle—the persuasion principle—that is derived from a Kantian notion of autonomy, according to which the autonomous individual is an unmanipulated individual. If one cannot make sense of the idea of an individual whose only desire is to decide correctly, then perhaps one cannot make sense of the idea of an unmanipulated individual. In that case, this component of the first amendment theory of freedom of expression collapses. But even if that happens, it is useful to understand the connection between a concrete legal principle and the deeper presuppositions of liberalism. As long as we must enforce the first amendment—within a liberal system—the approach I have outlined may be the best we can do.

CONCLUSION

I have suggested that a single theoretical premise—that freedom of expression is designed to protect the autonomy of potential listeners, with autonomy defined in Kantian terms—generates a doctrinal principle that unifies much of current first amendment law and that helps resolve specific current controversies. I have also argued that when considered in light of its justification, that doctrinal principle, which I have called the persuasion principle, must be qualified in two significant ways.

First, the persuasion principle does not hold when the consequences of following it are too severe. The connection between the persuasion principle and the prohibition against lying gives some sense of how severe the consequences must be in order to override the principle. Second, the persuasion principle is insensitive to the danger that private parties, and not just the government, infringe autonomy. I have tried to specify a point of view from which institutions should be evaluated to determine if they are consistent with the autonomy rationale that underlies the persuasion principle.

There is a serious question whether that point of view is too disembodied and rationalistic, too abstracted from specific desires and attachments. If it is, however, that reflects the connection between the persuasion principle, and, therefore, the American system of freedom of expression, and a common form of liberalism. The strengths and weaknesses of the persuasion principle are the strengths and weaknesses of the system of freedom of expression, and of the political culture that gives freedom of expression its prominent place.

[4]

SCOPE OF THE FIRST AMENDMENT
FREEDOM OF SPEECH

C. Edwin Baker*

   This paper develops three theories of the scope of speech protected by the first amendment: two different marketplace of ideas
theories, which I will call the *classic model* and the *market failure
model*, and a third, the *liberty model*. The classic model depends
on implausible assumptions for its coherence. The market failure
model is unworkable, dangerous, and inconsistent with a reasonable interpretation of the purpose of the first amendment. Although the Court consistently has used and proclaimed the classic
theory and though most modern reformist proposals recommend a
market failure model, the liberty model provides the most coherent theory of the first amendment. Adoption of this theory,
which delineates a realm of individual liberty roughly corresponding to noncoercive, nonviolent action, would have major, salutary
implications for judicial elaboration of the first amendment.

   The classic marketplace of ideas model argues that truth (or
the best perspectives or solutions) can be discovered through robust debate, free from governmental interference. Defending this
theory in *On Liberty*,[1] John Stuart Mill argued that three situations are possible: 1) if heretical opinion contains the truth, and if
we silence it, we lose the chance of exchanging truth for error; 2) if
received and contesting opinions each hold part of the truth, their
clash in open discussion provides the best means to discover the
truth in each; 3) even if the heretical view is wholly false and the

   * Assistant Professor of Law, University of Oregon. Thomas I. Emerson, Er-
nestine Magagna Baker, and Falcon O. Baker encouraged and aided me in writing
earlier versions of this paper. Margaret Jane Radin, Jennifer Friesen, Paula Wilk and
the editors of UCLA Law Review have made helpful comments on recent drafts The
help of those and other teachers is much appreciated. This article is scheduled to
appear as one of a series of essays in CONSTITUTIONAL GOVERNMENT IN AMERICA
(R. Collins ed. 1979).
   1. J. S. MILL, ON LIBERTY (1956) [hereinafter cited as ON LIBERTY]. Mill's argument was made in a long chapter, *Of the Liberty of Thought and Discussion, id.* at
19-67, which he intended to serve as an example of his defense of liberty in general. In
fact, his argument for liberty in general rests on different assumptions and is not
subject to the criticisms I will make of his defense of liberty of thought and discussion.

orthodoxy contains the whole truth, the received truth, unless debated and challenged, will be held in the manner of prejudice or
dead dogma, its meaning may be forgotten or enfeebled, and it
will be inefficacious for good.[2] Moreover, without free speech, totally false heretical opinions which could not survive open discussion will not disappear; instead, driven underground, these
opinions will smolder, their fallacies protected from exposure and
opposition.[3] In this model, the value of free speech lies not in the
liberty interests of individual speakers but in the societal benefits
derived from unimpeded discussion.[4] This social gain is so great,
and any loss from allowing speech is so small, that society should
tolerate no restraint on the verbal search for truth.

Just as real world conditions prevent the laissez-faire economic market—praised as a social means to facilitate optimal allocation and production of goods—from achieving the socially
desired results, critics of the classic marketplace of ideas theory
point to factors that prevent it from successfully facilitating the
discovery of truth or generating proper social perspectives and decisions.[5] Because of monopoly control of the media, lack of access
of disfavored or impoverished groups, techniques of behavior manipulation, irrational response to propaganda, and the nonexis-
tence of value-free, objective truth, the marketplace of ideas fails

---

2. *Id.* at 64. *See also* New York Times v. Sullivan, 376 U.S. 254, 279 n.19
(1964); ON LIBERTY, *supra* note 1, at 33-36, 41-43.
    3. ON LIBERTY, *supra* note 1, at 41; *see* Dennis v. United States, 341 U.S. 494,
584 (1951) (Douglas, J., dissenting).
    4. Were an opinion a personal possession of no value except to the owner,
    if to be obstructed in the enjoyment of it were simply a private injury, it
    would make some difference whether the injury was inflicted only on a few
    persons or on many. But the peculiar evil of silencing the expression of an
    opinion is that it is robbing the human race, posterity as well as the existing
    generation—those who dissent from the opinion still more than those who
    hold it.

ON LIBERTY, *supra* note 1, at 21. For the same view, see Z. CHAFEE, FREE SPEECH IN
THE UNITED STATES 33-35 (1964); A. MEIKLEJOHN, POLITICAL FREEDOM 26-27
(1965).
    5. The analogy between the perceived need to correct for failures in the eco-
nomic market and the idea market is, I think, more than accidental. Most advocates
of the market failure model of the first amendment would probably also advocate
considerable government regulation of the economy; typically, this group sees the
government as facilitating compromises among individuals and groups having competing desires and as administering programs technically designed to achieve pre-
ordained objectives. In contrast, "conservatives" advocating decreases in government
regulation recommend that the "liberals" should have the same faith in economic
markets as they do in the unregulated market place of ideas. *See* Coase, *Advertising
and Free Speech,* 6 J. LEGAL STUD. 1 (1977); Coase, *The Market for Goods and the
Market for Ideas,* 64 AM. ECON. REV.: PAPERS & PROC. 384 (1974); Director, *The
Parity of the Economic Market Place,* 7 J. L. & ECON. 1 (1964). Elsewhere, I have
argued that the analogy should be rejected. *See* Baker, *Ideology of the Economic
Analysis of Law,* 5 PHILOSOPHY & PUB. AFF. 3 (1975) [hereinafter cited as *Economic
Analysis*]; Baker, *Commercial Speech: A Problem in the Theory of Freedom,* 62 IOWA
L. REV. 1 (1976) [hereinafter cited as *Commercial Speech*].

to achieve the desired results. Therefore, the advocates of the market failure model conclude that objective social realities require state intervention in the speech arena, just as in the economic arena, in order to correct for these market failures;[6] only then will freedom of speech promote socially desirable perspectives and decisions.

The liberty model holds that the free speech clause protects not a marketplace but rather an arena of individual liberty from certain types of governmental restrictions. Speech is protected not as a means to a collective good but because of the value of speech conduct to the individual. The liberty theory justifies protection because of the way the protected conduct fosters individual self-realization and self-determination without improperly interfering with the legitimate claims of others. Of course, the liberty theory must specify what conduct is protected. After investigating the nature of speech—its uses and the manner in which it typically affects the world—and after reviewing generally accepted notions of the values of first amendment protected activities, I argue that the constitutional protection of free speech bars certain governmental restrictions on noncoercive, nonviolent, substantively valued conduct, including nonverbal conduct. In this liberty interpretation, first amendment protections of speech, assembly, and religion are merely different markers illustrating or bounding a single realm of liberty of self-expression and self-determination. Although any one of these three concepts illuminates this realm, the concept of protected speech most clearly delineates its scope.[7] Finally, the broadened scope of protection required by the liberty theory cures the major inadequacies of the marketplace of ideas as a model for finding or creating societal "truth," thereby providing protection for a progressive process of change.

I will proceed by developing and evaluating each of these theories in turn.

---

6. *See, e.g.*, Barron, *Access—The Only Choice for the Media?*, 48 TEX. L. REV. 766 (1970); Barron, *Access to the Press—A New First Amendment Right*, 80 HARV. L. REV. 1641 (1967). *See also* Columbia Broadcasting Sys. v. Democratic Nat'l Comm., 412 U.S. 94, 170-204 (1973) (Brennan & Marshall, JJ., dissenting).

7. Some readers may object to my extending the concept of speech to cover some nonverbal conduct. This objection is, I believe, adequately met by the arguments that nonverbal conduct *with the same uses* as constitutionally protected verbal conduct should be treated as speech. *See* notes 42-68 & accompanying text *infra*. Even if this conclusion is rejected, the recommended scope of protection would be justified on the basis of a proper interpretation of the free exercise and freedom of assembly clauses. The analysis in this article is an important step in developing a proper interpretation of these clauses because 1) it develops a criticism of the marketplace of ideas paradigm that currently improperly dominates the interpretation of the free exercise of religion and freedom of assembly clauses and 2) it suggests an alternative paradigm for and resolves certain difficulties in interpreting these clauses. *See* Part V *infra*.

I. THE CLASSIC MARKETPLACE OF IDEAS THEORY

A. *The Theory*

According to classic theory, truth is discovered through its competition with falsehood for acceptance. This result depends on certain crucial assumptions. First, truth must be "objective" or "discoverable." Truth is able to outshine falsity in debate or discussion only if truth is there to be seen. If, instead, truth were subjective, chosen or created, an adequate theory must explain why the competition among various viewpoints leads to the "best choice" or why protecting this competition provides a proper or legitimate process of choice or creation. Second, people must possess the capacity correctly to perceive truth or reality. One can distinguish two aspects of this rationality assumption. First, people's social location must not control the manner in which they perceive or understand the world. If perceptions are social creations and if people's social experiences are radically different, then mere discussion would be inadequate for discovering what truth or which perspectives are correct or best; one could not hope that employing reason in discussion would provide an unbiased insight into reality. Instead, perceptions of truth would vary, and dominance of one perception over another would depend on arbitrary circumstances and power relations among social groups. Second, people's rational faculties must enable them to sort through the form and frequency of message presentation in order to evaluate the core notions. Otherwise, the marketplace of ideas would only promote acceptance of those perspectives which were adequately packaged and promoted.

The premise that this marketplace of ideas uniformly promotes human interests implies that cultural pluralism will be progressively diminished and that no intractable conflict of values exists in society. Intractable value conflicts and permanent or progressive diversity would imply either a lack of uniform, stable content of truth or the insufficiency of truth as a basis for human action; the usefulness of the robust debate could not then be assumed but would depend on whether it operated to advance or obstruct the interests of the group whose values one adopts. Nevertheless, given the theory's assumptions about the objective nature of truth, the rational capabilities of humans, and the unity of the real aims of people, limiting the marketplace of ideas necessarily undermines the discovery and recognition of truth and impedes wise, well-founded decision making. Given the theory's assumptions, the presentation of conflicting arguments and insights aids people in discovering the truth in each position.[8]

---

8. These three assumptions are all explicit in ON LIBERTY, note 1 *supra*. First, truth is objective; this assumption is clearly suggested by the language Mill uses to

B.   *Judicial Adoption*

The Supreme Court steadfastly relies upon a marketplace of ideas theory in determining what speech is protected.[9] Marketplace imagery (competition of ideas, the value of robust debate) pervades Court opinions and provides justification for their first amendment "tests." Brief review of three prominent tests can illustrate this judicial reliance on the theory.

Holmes and Brandeis grounded the clear and present danger test[10] on the classic marketplace model: "[T]he ultimate good desired is better reached by free trade in ideas—that the best test of truth is the power of thought to get itself accepted in the competition of the market . . ."[11] and "freedom to think as you will and to speak as you think are means indispensable to the discovery and spread of political truth."[12] Holmes' and Brandeis' language suggests the model's three assumptions concerning the nature of truth, human rationality, and society; and the logic of their test parallels the implications of the classic marketplace of ideas model. The danger must be "clear," as Brandeis indicated, in order to prevent suppression on the basis of irrational fear, like the fear of witches exhibited by men when they burned women.[13] And it must be "present"—because if "there is opportunity for full dis-

---

describe truth: persons "rediscover" truth, *id.* at 36; "give truth a chance of reaching us," *id.* at 26. Second, human rationality is necessary. The "doctrine is meant to apply only to human beings in the *maturity of their facilities." Id.* at 13 (emphasis added). *See also id.* at 25. Finally, a decrease in pluralism and an absence of intractable value conflicts is expected and applauded by Mill. In agreement with the "best of men," he concludes that "no belief which is contrary to truth can be really useful," *id.* at 28; and that "the well-being of mankind may almost be measured by the number and gravity of truths which have reached the point of being uncontested." *Id.* at 53. *See also* J. S. MILL, UTILITARIANISM 40-48 (1957). A person "still needs to be conscious that his real aim and theirs do not conflict." *Id.* at 43.

9. The Court usually cites either its earlier opinions or people, such as Jefferson, who may have influenced the drafters of the first amendment. However, Mill is occasionally cited. *See* Columbia Broadcasting Sys. v. Democratic Nat'l Comm., 412 U.S. 94, 189 n.25 (1973) (Brennan & Marshall, JJ., dissenting); Furman v. Georgia, 408 U.S. 238, 467 (1972) (Rehnquist, J., dissenting); Red Lion Broadcasting Co. v. F.C.C., 398 U.S. 367, 392 n.18 (1969); New York Times v. Sullivan, 376 U.S. 254, 272 n.13, 279 n.19 (1964); Poe v. Ullman, 367 U.S. 497, 514-15 (1961) (Douglas, J., dissenting); Barenblatt v. United States, 360 U.S. 109, 151 n.22 (1959) (Black & Douglas, JJ., and Warren, C.J., dissenting). *See also* Paris Adult Theatre I v. Slaton, 413 U.S. 49, 68 n.14 (1973) (rejecting Mill's argument for liberty in general).

I refer to Mill to exemplify the marketplace theory because he provides its best formulation.

10. Speech is not constitutionally protected when there is (or, in the case of attempts, when the speaker intends that there be) "a clear and present danger that [the speech] will bring about the substantive evils that Congress has a right to prevent." Schenk v. United States, 249 U.S. 47, 52 (1919).

11. Abrams v. United States, 250 U.S. 616, 630 (1919) (Holmes & Brandeis, JJ., dissenting).

12. Whitney v. California, 274 U.S. 357, 375 (1927) (Brandeis & Holmes, JJ., concurring), *overruled*, Brandenberg v. Ohio, 395 U.S. 444 (1968).

13. *Id.* at 376.

cussion" or "if there be time to expose through discussion the falsehood and fallacies, . . . the remedy to be applied is more speech."[14] If the danger is not "present," the gravity of the evil and the probability of its occurrence[15] must be irrelevant because, given the faith in reason and discussion, the evil must be accepted as best if people choose it after hearing both sides: "If in the long run the beliefs expressed in proletarian dictatorship are destined to be accepted . . . the only meaning of free speech is that they should be given their chance and have their way."[16] In other words, protection must be given *as long as* the market place continues to operate. "Harms" resulting from speech cannot justify suppression as long as the harm results from people being convinced by the robust debate. (If the "right" side failed to participate, they, not those spreading evil counsel, are at fault; in this situation, governmental restriction must not be allowed.)

In fact, the development of the clear and present danger test by Holmes and Brandeis merely repeats the conclusion of the classic formulation of the marketplace of ideas theory. John Stuart Mill had already noted that:

> [E]ven opinions lose their immunity when the circumstances in which they are expressed are such as to constitute their expression a positive investigation to some mischievous act. An opinion that corn dealers are starvers of the poor . . . ought to be unmolested when simply circulated through the press, but may justly incur punishment when delivered orally to an excited mob assembled before the house of a corn dealer, or when handed about among the same mob in the form of a placard.[17]

---

14. *Id.* at 377.

15. Learned Hand's test, "whether the gravity of the 'evil', discounted by its improbability, justifies such invasion of free speech as is necessary to avoid the danger," was adopted in Dennis v. United States, 341 U.S. 494, 510 (1951). The test, implicitly for the majority and explicitly in Frankfurter's concurrence, involves a "balancing" approach to determine the protection to be given speech. This judicial adoption of a legislative type balancing approach has been properly criticized. *See, e.g.*, T. EMERSON, TOWARD A GENERAL THEORY OF THE FIRST AMENDMENT 53-56 (1966) [hereinafter cited as GENERAL THEORY]; Frantz, *The First Amendment in the Balance*, 71 YALE L.J. 1424 (1962). However, balancing itself involves no theory of what or why speech is protected. In fact, the Court made clear in *Dennis* that they continued to rely on the marketplace of ideas as the central concept of the first amendment. 341 U.S. at 503, 545-46, 549-50, 553.

16. Gitlow v. New York, 268 U.S. 652, 673 (1925) (Holmes & Brandeis, JJ., dissenting).

17. ON LIBERTY, *supra* note 1, at 67-68. *See also id.* at 117 (if there is no time to warn another of danger then one can temporarily stop the other from crossing the unsafe bridge).

In *Roth v. United States*,[18] Mr. Justice Brennan denied obscenity constitutional protection precisely because obscenity does not contribute to the marketplace of ideas. And although many liberals quarrel with this factual perception, it is crucial for the Court's conclusion that obscenity is "utterly without redeeming social importance." "All *ideas* having even the slightest redeeming social importance . . . have full protection . . . ."[19] In regulating speech, the government must be neutral towards different ideas. Content discrimination amounts to forbidden censorship that is avoided only if all communications containing messages or conveying ideas are protected.[20] The allegedly obscene communication meets the redeeming social importance criterion and is thereby protected if, but only if, the publication participates in the marketplace of ideas. "The protection given speech and press was fashioned to assure unfettered interchange of ideas for the bringing about of political and social changes desired by the people."[21] "[T]he First Amendment's basic guarantee is of freedom to advocate ideas, including unorthodox ideas, controversial ideas, even ideas hateful to the prevailing climate of opinion."[22]

In rejecting two obvious objections to its analysis, the Court further highlights its reliance on the marketplace theory. First, Mr. Justice Douglas asks:

---

18. 354 U.S. 476 (1957). *See also* Memoirs v. Massachusetts, 383 U.S. 413 (1966).

19. 354 U.S. at 484 (emphasis added).

20. *See, e.g.*, Chicago Police Dep't v. Mosley, 408 U.S. 92 (1972). Licensing and other time, place and manner restrictions traditionally have been upheld only if they do not permit the government to discriminate among communications. Shuttlesworth v. Birmingham, 394 U.S. 147 (1969); Cox v. Louisiana, 379 U.S. 536 (1965); Cox v. New Hampshire, 312 U.S. 569 (1941). The current Court may be abandoning its rejection of content discrimination. *See* Young v. American Mini Theatres, 427 U.S. 50 (1976); Lehman v. Shaker Heights, 418 U.S. 298 (1974). For an anaysis of this development, see Goldman, *A Doctrine of Worthier Speech:* Young v. American Mini Theatres, 21 St. Louis L.J. 281 (1977).

Within the liberty theory developed below, some content based time, place and manner restrictions may be acceptable. Since different uses of speech serve different values, a permissible restriction would be one that did not impede people's use of speech to further that value. Thus, content restrictions on "advocacy" speech would never be allowed; but where speech is used essentially for entertainment purposes and where the speaker only wants to reach those who desire receipt of the speech, content restrictions that do not significantly limit the availability of the speech may be an acceptable method of promoting community values. *Compare* Paris Adult Theatre I v. Slaton, 413 U.S. 49, 112-13 (Brennan, Stewart & Marshall, JJ., dissenting) (1973) (suggesting that unconsenting adults can be protected from obscenity) *with* Cohen v. California, 403 U.S. 15, 21 (1971) (in context of political or "advocacy" speech, state cannot protect unconsenting viewers). The different treatment does not relate to any lesser value of entertainment speech but to whether the government did, or had a purpose to, abridge the speech.

21. Roth v. United States, 354 U.S. at 484.

22. Kingsley Int'l Pictures Corp. v. Regents of New York, 360 U.S. 684, 688-89 (1959).

When the Court today speaks of "social value," does it mean a "value" to the majority? Why is not a minority "value" cognizable? The masochistic group is one; the deviant group is another . . . . [I]f the communication is of value to the masochistic community or to others of the deviant community, how can it be said to be "utterly without redeeming social importance"? "Redeeming" to whom? "Importance" to whom?[23]

Douglas finds "social value" not in the contribution advocacy of masochism makes to the pursuit of truth in the marketplace of ideas, but in the contribution the material makes to "the needs of this group."[24] Douglas could have further argued that people's willingness to pay money for the material proves that it has some value to them—any obscenity which sells has "social value." The Court must employ the marketplace theory to avoid Douglas' constitutional conclusion without rejecting his factual observation. The Court can conclude that the willingness to pay only indicates the value of obscenity for the entertainment "needs of the group," but that only the literature's *advocacy* of a way of life and not its use *within* a way of life, only its presentation of an argument, even if ineloquent, for a set of ideas and not merely its manifestation of certain ideas, is relevant to the literature's contribution to or its redeeming value in the marketplace of ideas. Because of this focus on the marketplace of ideas, "to equate the free and robust exchange of ideas and political debate with commercial exploitation of obscene material demeans the grand conception of the First Amendment . . . ."[25] And, despite liberal protests, most would agree with the Court's assessment that obscenity does not contribute to the marketplace of ideas.[26]

Second, the Court often says that speech is protected because of its role in "bringing about political and social change." Yet a major argument for banning obscenity is that it contributes to social change.[27] Some think that obscenity leads to criminal conduct, and most would agree that its use can, and does, affect the moral or cultural tone of the community. The Court's reliance on the marketplace model explains its refusal to protect obscenity despite its contribution to bringing about social change. In the mar-

---

23. Ginzburg v. United States, 383 U.S. 463, 489-90 (1966) (Douglas, J., dissenting).

24. *Id.* at 489.

25. Miller v. California, 413 U.S. 15, 34 (1973).

26. The Court emphasized this factor when it concluded that the method of advertising the publication, pandering, provided evidence that it was designed for the pleasure, not the opinion, market. Ginzburg v. United States, 383 U.S. at 474-75.

27. The state interest lies in protecting the "community environment, the tone of commerce . . . and, possibly, the public safety itself." Paris Adult Theatre I v. Slaton, 413 U.S. 49, 58 (1972). *See also id.* at 63-64.

ketplace theory, speech must bring about change by the (at least partly) rational process of convincing people of ideas or opinions, not by its use in disapproved entertainment practices.

In *Paris Adult Theatre I v. Slaton*, Mr. Justice Brennan correctly objects that the Burger Court's altered standard ("serious literary, artistic, political, or scientific value") "jeopardize[s] the analytic underpinnings of the entire scheme."[28] The jeopardy results because now the government through the courts must evaluate the worth of the speech, the importance, and the "seriousness" of the ideas; in the earlier approach, the government, in theory, was required to be agnostic. Nevertheless, the new majority, although it explicitly rejects Mill's argument for liberty in general,[29] repeatedly reaffirms its allegiance to "the free and robust change of ideas," "the unfettered interchange of ideas,"[30] the prohibition of state "control of reason and the intellect," and the protection of the "communication of ideas."[31] The Court still relies upon the marketplace theory although, by its implicit balancing, the Court avoids the analytic consequences of fully accepting the theory.

The Court's basic constitutional analysis of defamation invokes Mill's marketplace of ideas theory to justify its conclusion. At least in the case of defamation of public officials, the first amendment gives absolute protection to the speaker unless the false, defamatory statement is made "with knowledge that it was false or with reckless disregard of whether it was false or not."[32] The Court explained that the first amendment "was fashioned to assure unfettered interchange of ideas," and emphasized the Constitutional faith "in the power of reason as applied through public debate."[33] In *New York Times v. Sullivan*, the Court quotes Mill for the practical point that erroneous statements are inevitably made, even in good faith, during discussions;[34] and, therefore, the erroneous statements must be protected to provide the breathing space needed by the marketplace of ideas. The Court also cites Mill's argument that falsehoods can serve a useful function by bringing about "the clear perception and livelier impression of truth, produced by its collision with error."[35] Still, the marketplace logic does not require that all defamation be protected. The Court can justify the *New York Times* rule that limits protection

---

28. *Id.* at 96 (Brennan, Stewart & Marshall, JJ., dissenting).
29. *Id.* at 68 n.14. However, Mill's argument for liberty in general rests on entirely different premises than does his argument for freedom of speech.
30. Miller v. California, 413 U.S. at 34.
31. Paris Adult Theatre I v. Slaton, 413 U.S. at 67.
32. New York Times v. Sullivan, 376 U.S. 254, 280 (1964).
33. *Id.* at 269, 270 (quoting from Justice Brandeis's concurring opinions in *Roth* and *Whitney*).
34. *Id.* at 272 n.13.
35. *Id.* at 279 n.19.

to those who are concerned about the truth of their statements on the ground that only these people are engaged in any search for truth or "any exposition of ideas." The first amendment protects speech totally, but only if the speech stems from honest participation in the marketplace of information and ideas.[36]

In recent cases in which the Court often undertakes explicit legislative-like balancing, the Court has developed a not-yet-complete complex of rules to cover speech injuries to non-public figures.[37] Despite abandoning the strict requirements of marketplace logic, the Court continues to emphasize the marketplace theory in order to explain the role and value of speech. For example, in *Gertz v. Robert Welch, Inc.*,[38] Mr. Justice Powell opens his discussion of the First Amendment by noting that we depend for the correction of pernicious opinions "on the competition of other ideas."[39] A "false statement of fact," which Powell distinguishes from ideas, has "no constitutional value," because it does not "materially advanc[e] society's interest in 'uninhibited, robust, and wide-open' debate on public issues"; still, false statements of fact are sometimes protected because they are "inevitable in free debate."[40] Thus, although the Court does not extend the *New York Times* degree of protection, it retains *New York Times'* reliance on the classic marketplace of ideas theory of speech.

The logic of these "tests" illustrates the judicial adoption of the classic marketplace of ideas model. Other examples could be given. Marketplace notions are not the only strains to be heard in the chorus of Court pronouncements on the first amendment. Some Court opinions suggest the "liberty theory." And individual justices clearly adopt the liberty theory in some situations. Nevertheless, the marketplace theory dominates; and its rejection

---

36. Note that one could reject the Court's approach without rejecting the marketplace model. For example, Goldberg with Douglas concurring, argued that the Court's analysis "is not responsive to the real issue presented by this case, which is whether that freedom speech which all agree is constitutionally protected can be effectively safeguarded by a rule allowing the imposition of liability upon a jury's evaluation of the speaker's state of mind." 376 U.S. at 300. This danger of the majority's approach is illustrated by its compatibility with the argument that communists should not be protected because they are not interested in truth. *See* Dennis v. United States, 341 U.S. 494 (1951). Following Goldberg, Emerson emphasizes the need to consider the system context. GENERAL THEORY, *supra* note 15, at 16-46. Emerson notes: "Most of our efforts in the past have been seriously defective through failure to take into consideration the realistic context in which such limitations are administered." *Id.* at 16.

37. Gertz v. Robert Welch, Inc., 418 U.S. 323, 348-50 (1974). One reason the Court gave for differentiating between public and private parties is their differential access to the media. *Id.* at 344. This explanation partially relies on the market failure model. *See* Part II *infra*.

38. 418 U.S. 323 (1974).

39. *Id.* at 340.

40. *Id.* (citations omitted).

would have major implications for first amendment interpretation.

C. *Failure of Assumptions*

The assumptions on which the classic marketplace of ideas theory rests are almost universally rejected today. Because of this failure of assumptions, the hope that the marketplace leads to truth, or even to the best or most desirable decision, becomes implausible. First, truth is not objective. Even in the sciences, the presumed sanctuary of objectively verifiable truth, often only those values to which the scientists personally give allegiance provide criteria for judging between competing theories.[41] Criteria for choice of paradigms include the theory's ability to provide answers to currently pressing questions, its usefulness in suggesting further applications or new investigatable problems, and its simplicity or aesthetic appeal. The moderns appear unwilling to believe in Platonic forms or intelligible essences. Instead, knowledge depends on how people's interests, needs, and experiences lead them to slice and categorize an expanding mass of sense data. In fact, the greater diversity and conflict in people's social interests, needs, and experiences may explain why social life has a greater number of, and more constant conflict among, competing paradigms than is usually the case within a "science." And even if "rational" debate can play some role in advancing understanding within a given paradigm, discussion appears insufficient by itself to evaluate different paradigms. This failure of discussion results, in part, precisely because the value oriented criteria—interests, desires, or aesthetics—which guide the development of perceptions, appear ungrounded, incapable of objective demonstration.[42] However, one premise of my latter constructive argument will be that one must assume the value of the free development of people's humanity;[43] and that this value provides an initial basis from which something can be said about differing paradigms and even more can be said about the desirable features of a structure of paradigm conflict and about the process of developing or creating knowledge. One could also, but I will not here, argue that this value of free development of people's humanity has been progressively unfolding in human history.[44]

---

41. *See* T. KUHN, THE STRUCTURE OF SCIENTIFIC REVOLUTION (2d ed. 1970); M. POLYANI, PERSONAL KNOWLEDGE (1964).

42. For both a description of the modern view of knowledge and a discussion of the problems with it, see R. UNGER, KNOWLEDGE AND POLITICS (1975).

43. This assumption serves in my argument the same function served by Mill's assumption that nothing contrary to truth can really be useful. *See* ON LIBERTY, *supra* note 1, at 28.

44. *See* R. UNGER, *supra* note 42, at 146-47, 234, 243-45, 248. *But see id.* at 230-31.

The adequacy of the marketplace of ideas must be reconsidered if one rejects the assumption of objective truth and assumes that people's perspectives and understanding are chosen or created rather than "discovered." First, the contribution of the marketplace in discovering truth or reaching "better" choices would depend, in part, on the respective role of discussion and analysis as contrasted with experience in determining what perspectives we adopt. Unless reason operating in discussion can control or dominate the perspectives resulting from experience, progress in understanding would depend on the content of people's experiences and their everyday practices as much as on discussion. But if experience contributes, then restrictions on experience-generating conduct are as likely as restrictions on robust debate to stunt the progressive development of understanding; and no principle would explain why the marketplace of ideas is more deserving of constitutional protection than is expressive, experience-producing conduct. These same observations answer what at first seems a less ambitious defense of free speech: Protecting free speech insures that the individual will have more information and, thus, be able to make a more informed choice. The problem with this defense is that the individual is as likely to find needed information in experiences as in speech. Again, no objection is made to protecting verbal interchange; rather, the objection is that protection of verbal interchange is inadequate to promote the functions or values which justify protection of this realm of liberty.

Second, if truth or understanding are created or chosen, an evaluation of the marketplace must consider whether the values of different people or groups are furthered by the choice or creation of the same truth or understanding. If a unity of interest exists, the differential contribution of various people or groups to the creation of understanding and perspectives may be unimportant. However, if groups have divergent interests concerning the choice of perspectives, one can presume that the marketplace of ideas (and other activities which might be protected) leads to the "best" or "proper" or "progressive" understanding only if the marketplace favors those groups who should be favored or "properly" distributes influence among various people or groups such that optimal compromises are reached. For example, Herbert Marcuse concluded that in the present historical circumstances the marketplace of ideas would work properly only if the rich and powerful were completely excluded and access were limited to progressive, leftist elements;[45] others argue for more or less equal

---

45. R. WOLFF, B. MOORE, JR., H. MARCUSE, A CRITIQUE OF PURE TOLERANCE 109-111 (1968).

access for all groups to the market place.[46]

This observation about the consequences of rejecting the assumption of "objective truth" leads directly to an evaluation of the other assumptions of the model. The first aspect of rationality required by the marketplace model, that people can use reason to comprehend a set reality, is undermined once one rejects the assumption of objective truth, for no set reality exists for people to understand. The sociology of knowledge provides a more precise basis for a critique of this rationality assumption. People's perspectives and understanding are greatly influenced, if not determined, by their experiences and their interests, both of which reflect their location in a specific, historical socio-economic structure.[47] Two implications of the sociology of knowledge should be relatively uncontroversial. First, dialogue cannot completely eliminate conflicts and divergences between people's perspectives as long as the social structure is such that people have very different experiences and conflicting interests. More specifically, social change—changes in the family, social, economic, or political order—not the marketplace of ideas, will have the greater impact on these divergent notions of "truth." Second, and in consequence of the first comment, not only will robust discussion be insufficient for advancing understanding (since it is at best one determinant of understanding), but also, if one continues to hope for a process of progressive development of understanding (the classic model's search for truth), the process of development will depend on the existence of a realm in which new experiences and interests can become actualities; thus, progress requires protection of some realm of conduct and of everyday activity beyond mere discussion.

The classic model also requires that people be able to use their rational capacities to eliminate distortion caused by the form and frequency of message presentation and to find the core of relevant information or argument. This assumption cannot be accepted. Emotional or "irrational" appeals have great impact; "subconscious" repressions, phobias, or desires influence people's assimilation of messages; and, most obviously, stimulus-response mechanisms and selective attention and retention processes influence understanding or perspectives. In fact, these psychological processes partially explain at the level of the individual what the sociology of knowledge observes at the level of the group. One is

---

46. *See* Part II *infra.*

47. *See, e.g.,* P. BERGER & T. LUCKMAN, THE SOCIAL CONSTRUCTION OF REALITY (1967); K. MANNHEIM, IDEOLOGY AND UTOPIA (1954); C. MILLS, POWER, POLITICS, AND PEOPLE (1967). *See also* P. WINCH, THE IDEA OF SOCIAL SCIENCE AND ITS RELATION TO PHILOSOPHY (1958). This entire field, of course, owes a tremendous debt to the writings of Karl Marx.

rewarded for adopting perspectives that further one's interests. Since interests vary with social position, the perspectives that are reinforced will also vary. These differential rewards explain *why* the sociology of knowledge finds that people maintain perspectives which promote one's interest even when presented with contrary information or alternative perspectives. The psychological technique of selective attention and retention, as well as the insights of cognitive dissonance and balance theories, suggest *how* people preserve these perspectives.

These psychological insights, extensively relied upon in practice by advertisers and propagandists,[48] eviscerate the faith in the ability of the marketplace of ideas to lead to the "best" truths or understandings. Even if one assumes that some understandings are best, one has no reason to expect these to be discovered in the marketplace of ideas. Instead, the understandings resulting from the robust debate will depend on the form and quantity of inputs, on the mechanisms by which people process these inputs, and on people's interests and experiences. Without the dominance of a rationality that can evaluate the merit of positions, people's processing of inputs cannot, in itself, be expected to lead to the best perspectives.[49] Given this diminished confidence in people's ability to *process* inputs, faith in the marketplace requires acceptance of one of two assumptions about the inputs into the robust debate. One must assume either that the quality of the resulting

---

48. The propagandist aware of the findings of the behavioral sciences no longer has as much confidence as his counterparts from the late eighteenth to the early twentieth century had in the ability of rational arguments or even of catchy slogans to influence human behavior. The evolution of psychoanalysis, clinical psychology, and experimental research on communication has made it clear that reactors' responses are affected not only by the immediate input of symbols but also (and often more powerfully) by three other sets of forces: (1) the stored residues of, and associations to, previous inputs of related symbols, which often give the reactor a predisposition and capacity to ignore or to rationalize away the current flow of symbols; (2) economic inducements . . . and coercive inducements . . . and (3) the coercive structures and processes in the surrounding social systems . . . .
12 INT'L ENCYCLOPEDIA OF THE SOC. SCI. *Propaganda*, at 585 (1968) [hereinafter cited as *Propaganda*].

49. A defense of the market model might suggest that, although not all people reason rationally all the time, progress results because some people are sometimes sufficiently insightful to reach an improved understanding and their gains are carried forward. However, the last step, how people demonstrate their new insights to others, is not explained. Two explanations seem plausible. First, historical developments may make others desirous or in need of the new insights or perspectives. *See* T. KUHN, note 41 *supra*; Wallace, *Revitalization Movements*, 58 AM. ANTHROPOLOGIST 264 (1956). Second, if the new insights are put into practice, they may provide modes of interaction which people will find more appealing or useful than dominant practices and, therefore, people would convert. Note that both explanations crucially depend not merely on the intellectual persuasiveness of the new viewpoints but on the appeal of the implementation of the insights. This suggests that faith in the marketplace might be reasserted, but only if dissenting or minority groups are free to implement their perspectives. *See* Part IV-C *infra*.

perspectives will not depend upon the source of input or that whatever input opportunities that happen to exist are fair or, at least, acceptable. Neither alternative can be maintained: First, as the sociology of knowledge shows, people will favor divergent perspectives and, therefore, it *does make a difference who has opportunities* to exercise influence; second, no one has seriously suggested that the existing distribution of access opportunities, which surely are most available to the rich and powerful, is fair or is apportioned in accordance with the contribution each group can make to a "best" understanding of the world.

Furthermore, apart from the purported function of the marketplace of ideas as a means to provide for the best understanding, the theory cannot be defended on the grounds that it provides a "fair" or otherwise justifiable process for regulating the struggle between opposing groups.[50] The incredible inequalities of opportunity to use the marketplace cause a fairness defense to fail.[51] The marketplace of ideas appears improperly biased in favor of presently dominant groups, both because these groups have greater access to the marketplace and because these dominant groups may legally restrict the opportunities for dissident groups to develop patterns of conduct in which new ideas would appear plausible.[52]

Of course, unless processes or perspectives can be evaluated as better or worse, criticisms of the marketplace of ideas would seem pointless. Many people—maybe, in their everyday lives, most people—believe such evaluations can be made and defended. Many, including myself, would assert that these evaluations can be made on the basis of a fundamental long range unity of human interests. However, this belief neither necessarily nor even normally leads to acceptance of a marketplace of ideas as an adequate process for moving toward these better "understandings." For example, Roberto Unger, who maintains faith in some sort of long term basic unity of humanity and who also presents a vibrant defense of speculative thought, specifically argues that discussion itself is insufficient for reaching this better understanding; instead, improved understanding *depends* on political action and

---

50. On the notion of pure procedural justice, see J. RAWLS, A THEORY OF JUSTICE 84-87 (1971).

51. *See* Part II *infra. See also*, Baker, *Counting Preferences in Collective Choice Situations*, 25 UCLA L. Rev. 381 (1978).

52. The power of dominant groups to legally restrict opportunities to practice alternatives, thereby developing alternative perceptions or knowledge can occur in two ways: 1) through legal prohibitions of certain behavior, *see* Part IV *infra*; or 2) through legal control of economic resources enabling them to limit work experience, *see* Gintis, *Consumer Behavior and the Concept of Sovereignty: Explanations of Social Decay*, 62 AM. ECON. REV.: PAPERS & PROC. SUPP. 267, 271 (1972).

social change.[53] Thus, if, as the classic marketplace model asserts, the first amendment protects a process for achieving improved understandings, then first amendment protection must extend to aspects of human action other than mere discussion.

Given that the assumptions underlying the classic marketplace of ideas theory are so clearly incorrect, one wonders why the theory has had such popularity and so many advocates. One answer might be that its popularity is primarily limited to writers, academics and other intellectuals who have a professional interest in supporting faith in rationality, rational discussion or debate, and the intellectual pursuit of knowledge.[54] Although the classic statements of faith by people such as Brandeis caution against too quickly dismissing the theory as an ideological construct, one constantly wonders whose interests this marketplace promotes. Since so much modern communication takes place through mass communication media, an insight into the social role of the marketplace theory of speech may be gained by considering how the constitutionally protected mass communication media influence people's attitudes or behavior.

Two relatively clear results of modern social science research are: 1) that "the most common effect of mass communication is to reinforce its audience's pre-existing interests, attitudes, and behavior";[55] and 2) that "the media appear to be extremely effective in creating new opinions," possibly because "the audiences have no existing opinions to be guarded by the conscious or subconscious play of selective exposure, selective retention, or selective perception."[56] Only in changing people's existing conceptions—the normal goal of the critics of the status quo—does the media falter.[57] If the mass media primarily either reinforce already held views or create views where people had no prior opinion, then those who previously held the views that are reinforced, those who hold the new views created by the media, and those who wanted these views reinforced or created, are likely to conclude that the marketplace is working. This includes almost everyone except critics of the status quo. Since media are inherently least effective in changing existing perspectives, this bias in favor of the status quo would result even if every one had equal input. Nevertheless, equal input does not exist. The bias in favor of the status quo is

---

53. R. UNGER, *supra* note 42, at 103, 242-44, 253, 255.

54. *See* Coase, note 5 *supra*; Director, *supra* note 5, at 6.

55. 3 INT'L ENCYCLOPEDIA OF THE SOC. SCI. *Communications, Mass*, at 82 (1968).

56. *Id.* at 85.

57. Jaffe, *The Editorial Responsibility of the Broadcaster: Reflections on Fairness and Access*, 85 HARV. L. REV. 768, 769-70 (1972). Each of the conclusions in the text concerning the effects of the mass media are supported by Professor Jaffe's brief survey of communications theory.

magnified because the three main sources of media views are: the mass audience which must be willing to buy (or, at least, receive) the communication; the present power elites, who usually own or manage the media; and the dominant economic groups, whose advertisements largely finance the media. These overlapping groups seldom radically oppose status quo perspectives.[58] In fact, these groups usually want either to reinforce existing attitudes or, occasionally, to stimulate new views, such as desires for new products that business is marketing. Thus, for most elements in society, the market is doubly determined to appear successful: 1) "natural" participation counts—those groups who most frequently participate in the marketplace find that it "correctly" advances their interests or views; and 2) the process works—the marketplace validates those views that generally appear to be correct; that is, it reinforces currently dominant views. These observations support the conclusion that the marketplace of ideas theory is merely an ideological construct—the unregulated marketplace of ideas promotes the dominant group's interests and reflects its experiences of reality. The workings of the marketplace confirm the dominant group's self-serving belief that in the marketplace of ideas "the best ideas for the society will find the most takers."[59]

Dissenters must be expected to perceive the situation differently. Their views are least likely to be presented by the media and, when presented, are least likely to have an effect on society. Two reactions are plausible. If dissidents place faith in the individual and emphasize the value of individual expression or choice, they may be unwilling to reject the marketplace of ideas, which

---

58. Conflict could potentially arise between a class conscious mass audience and power elites or dominant economic groups. In case of conflict, the second groups appear in control. The most the mass audience can hope for may be the set of communications they most prefer that are also consistent with the interests of the power elite. At present the mass audience appears to demand little that is inconsistent with status quo relations. As noted, preferences reflect patterns of social interaction. As long as dominant groups control the character and content of social experience—for example, the demeaning, hierarchical nature of the work experience or the exchange nature of both economic and personal value—a congruence of mass desires and status quo promises can be expected. This congruence may be ruptured, however, if the system has important dysfunctional characteristics. *See, e.g.*, J. HABERMAS, LEGITIMATION CRISIS (1975); C. REICH, GREENING OF AMERICA (1970). In addition constitutional protection of opportunities for people to develop alternative patterns of interaction might provide a basis for change in the mass audience's perspectives.

59. In *Propaganda, supra* note 48, at 587, the author, who explained how people are not rational but are controlled by other factors, still hoped that the marketplace would work:

By definition, a healthily functioning democracy is a polity in which opposition to propaganda is habitually expressed primarily through peaceful counterpropaganda. It is assumed that a variety of propagandists will compete vigorously in "the marketplace of ideas," and it is hoped that the ideas best for society will find the most takers in the long run.

One wonders if this faith is sustained precisely because the marketplace aids in preserving the existing order.

claims to affirm this faith. Instead, these dissidents would conclude that market failures exist and that the functioning of the
market needs to be improved—possibly by government intervention.[60] Alternatively, if the dissenters view the government as an
instrument of the dominant groups and perceive existing values as
products of conscious or unconscious manipulations of these dominant groups, then they would postulate false consciousness and,
at least under current historical conditions, would place little confidence in the power of mere speech or the workings of any marketplace of ideas.[61]

II. THE MARKET FAILURE MODEL

Society has found that the invisible hand does not always
produce the results desired in the marketplace of goods; various
forms of market failures require state intervention to achieve efficient allocations or desired distributions. Critics of the classic
marketplace of ideas theory, relying either on the failure of the
assumptions described in Part I or specifically on failures of the
economic market (such as monopolization of communication
channels or difficulties of organizing interest groups), have advocated various forms of governmental intervention to improve market functioning. The specific solutions proposed relate to the
particular problem or market failure identified—identifications
which have varied considerably among the critics.

A. *The Reform Proposals*

To clarify the content of the market failure model(s) I will
outline the major reform positions, analyze the assumptions justifying each, and give a few examples of specific reform proposals.
Reformers generally take one of four positions: 1) that economic
market failures be corrected to the extent possible without restricting anyone's speech freedom; 2) that all viewpoints be guaranteed
adequate, but not necessarily equal, access to the market; 3) that
all viewpoints have equal access to the marketplace of ideas (e.g.,
equal time for each candidate); or 4) that all individuals have
equal access. (I should note that implementing many proposals
suggested by the first two positions would be compatible with, but
not necessarily required by, the liberty theory of the first amendment advanced in Part III.)

The first view—that economic market failures require government intervention—is based on the observation that inefficient
resource allocations to speech activities may be caused by monopolization or by the difficulty which racial, sexual, or ethnic groups,

---

60. *See* Part II *infra.*
61. *See* R. WOLFF, B. MOORE, JR., H. MARCUSE, note 45 *supra.*

consumers, the poor, or environmentalists, and other large, unorganized groups have, due to organization costs and freeloading, in achieving efficient levels of advocacy. Often, critics of this form of market failure propose invigorated enforcement of anti-trust laws or subsidies for advocacy by various difficult-to-organize groups.[62] However, these proposals, motivated by economic efficiency concerns, do not require or imply any particular theory of free speech; thus, they are outside the scope of the present paper. Moreover, these reform proposals raise no first amendment issues unless the economic corrective measures involve placing restrictions on activities protected within some first amendment theory.

The assumptions which require guaranteeing adequate, but not equal, presentation of all (serious?) viewpoints are very similar to those of the classic model. In fact, in *On Liberty*, Mill recommended that we search for devices to assure the forceful presentation of viewpoints that, without our positive efforts, would not be adequately presented.[63] Like the classic model, this approach must assume that reason dominates. Only if people use reason to analyze disputes will their conclusions not be controlled by the form and frequency of inputs. This approach assumes that people will use their intellect to find the core of insight, if any, in each message. It merely notes the absence of meaningful access opportunities for certain positions and advocates that these views be guaranteed adequate access to the marketplace.[64] Of course, the practical problem with this position as a constitutional standard rather than as a legislative policy is the difficulty of determining what amounts to an adequate or meaningful presentation opportunity.

This conclusion that an adequate presentation of each view is the constitutional goal points to an interesting fact about, and pos-

---

62. *See, e.g.*, B. OWEN, ECONOMICS AND FREEDOM OF EXPRESSION (1975) (arguing for structural reform including anti-trust enforcement); Cooper, *The Tax Treatment of Business Grassroots Lobbying: Defining and Attaining the Public Policy Objectives*, 68 COLUM. L. REV. 801, 841-59 (1968) (suggesting method of using tax laws as incentives for political speech of private groups, particularly relatively poor groups).

63. ON LIBERTY, *supra* note 1, at 46.

64. In Red Lion Broadcasting Co. v. FCC, 395 U.S. 367 (1969), the Court upheld the "fairness doctrine," which was considered to be a method of assuring that the most important views would be aired on the electronic media. In various cases the Court has suggested that it would assure that effective channels of communication exist for all positions. Linmark Assoc., Inc. v. Township of Willingboro, 413 U.S. 85, 93 (1977) (one of two grounds for decision); Columbia Broadcasting Sys. v. Democratic Nat'l Comm., 412 U.S. 94, 193-96 (1973) (Brennan, & Marshall, JJ., dissenting); United States v. O'Brien, 391 U.S. 367, 388-89 (1968) (Harlan, J., concurring); Kovacs v. Cooper, 336 U.S. 77, 102-03 (1949) (Black, J., dissenting). *See also* Columbia Broadcasting Sys. v. Democratic Nat'l Comm., 412 U.S. at 122 (opinion of Court) (where the Court, quoting Meiklejohn, suggests that assuring an effective forum for all viewpoints is constitutionally crucial: " '[W]hat is essential is not that everyone shall speak, but that everything worth saying shall be said.' ").

sibly an objection to, both this market failure theory and the classic market model. Given that some expression of a viewpoint suffices to assure its proper evaluation, a restraint on the speech of some individuals would not obstruct the search for truth as long as others forcefully express the views of those individuals. Unless persuaded by rule utilitarian objections—for example, that it would be costly to prevent or correct predictable misapplications of the power to restrict or censor individuals—government restraints on individuals, as long as the individual's message were adequately presented by others, would be unobjectionable. Despite marketplace rhetoric, a theorist's objection to such restraints often reveals an underlying concern with individual liberty that supersedes the theorist's concern for the workings of the market place.[65]

Equal access for all viewpoints is a quite unusual interpretation of a properly functioning marketplace of ideas. It makes sense, however, if truth (or a best or correct solution) exists but if people's rational faculties are too feeble to avoid or neutralize distortions caused by propagandists' use of quantity or packaging techniques. In other words, this model relies upon the classic model's truth assumption but rejects the second aspect of its rationality assumption, that people are able to sort through the form and frequency of message presentation to evaluate the core notions.[66] Equalizing the presentation opportunities for each potentially true or best viewpoint (in contrast to equalizing the opportunity for each speaker) enables each position to use quantity and packaging to neutralize the other's use. Provision for equal funding of all political candidates attempts, at least in the context of political campaigns, to accomplish that goal. (Or, if

---

65. The Court has struck down restraints that would prohibit some people from speaking as much as they desire even though the position of those people may already be adequately expressed in the market place. Buckley v. Valeo, 424 U.S. 1 (1976). It has also struck down laws and rejected proposals to assure some access to print or broadcast media as being contrary to, or at least not required by, the first amendment. Miami Herald Publishing Co. v. Tornillo, 418 U.S. 241 (1974); Columbia Broadcasting Sys. v. Democratic Nat'l Comm., 412 U.S. 94 (1973). *But cf.* Red Lion Broadcasting Co. v. FCC, 395 U.S. 367 (1969) (upholding "fairness doctrine," requiring each side of public issues to be given equal presentation by the media). These decisions are inconsistent with the market failure model, and although the Court continued to invoke marketplace language, *see, e.g.*, Miami Herald Publishing Co. v. Tornillo, 418 U.S. at 529 (White, J., concurring), the decisions are best explained by a liberty theory. *See Commercial Speech, supra* note 5, at 41-42 n.144.

66. This model develops difficulties if an information overload, too much "noise," decreases people's ability or willingness to assimilate messages. If even a minimal presentation of all viewpoints would produce dysfunctional levels of "noise," instead of guaranteeing presentation opportunities for all viewpoints, one might hope that the messages most often presented will be closer to truth than those not presented; or one could impose limits on how much a given message could be presented in the hope of reducing "noise" distortion. *But cf.* Buckley v. Valeo, 424 U.S. 1 (1976) (invalidating expenditure limits).

passing some threshold level of support provides evidence that a candidate is potentially the best choice, that is, the one who would win if presentation opportunities were equalized, then the state should assure equal resources to those candidates who meet this threshold requirement.[67])

Equal access for all individuals is the most logical version of the market failure theory. Each of the faulty assumptions of the classic model is replaced with a new one. First, truth is chosen or created not made. Second, reason exists but normally does not control or dominate people's response to debate. Instead, people normally can not divorce their understanding from their experiences in a particular social location; moreover, people respond to packaging, quantity, and context aspects of messages. Third, societal choices must fairly respond to people's different needs and groups' conflicting interests, whether or not the conflict is permanent. Given these assumptions, success in "rational" debate does not provide criteria for judging the merit of particular proposals or perspectives—at least, unless the debate is "fair." Cut adrift from the logic which explained how the marketplace of ideas advances truth, and instead assuming that truth is chosen, at least in part, on the basis of inputs into the marketplace, the democratic notion provides a solution: The marketplace works if and only if all people are equally able to participate in making or influencing the choice. Moreover, providing each person a roughly equal opportunity to generate equal quantities of carefully packaged messages increases the role of reason; the equalization neutralizes the advantage which packaging presently gives to well-financed perspectives. At first, the failure of the classic model's assumptions appeared to make faith in the market place of ideas incoherent. However, once one concludes that the purpose of the market is to provide legitimate scope for differing, often conflicting, interests rather than to promote the discovery of objective truth, and once one accepts a democratic notion that equal individual influence gives legitimate scope for differing interests, then the marketplace of ideas seems perfectly coherent as long as people have equal opportunities (*e.g.*, equal resources) for participating.

Reliance on this equality standard rather than the existing wealth (market) criterion for determining individual opportunities is not the norm in our basically capitalistic society. The area where we most commonly claim to adopt the equality standard is in the political sphere—"one person, one vote." Thus, the equality standard for individual input will seem most appropriate for

---

67. Federal Election Campaign Act of 1971, 2 U.S.C. §§ 431-456 (1976); 47 U.S.C. §§ 801-805 (Supp. II 1972), *as amended by* Pub. L. No. 93-443, 88 Stat. 1263 (1974).

speech which relates to what are perceived as political decisions, *i.e.*, collective decisions which will affect the rights as well as the values of the members of the collective.[68] For example, this could explain why the Court has concluded that wealth should not affect one's ability to vote (participate politically) even though generally wealth is, unless the political system concludes otherwise, assumed to be the proper criterion for allocating other goods.[69]

To achieve equality of opportunity for individual input requires either a combination of subsidies and expenditure restrictions or a method of making speech a free good, *i.e.,* making any amount of communication the speaker desires costless to the speaker. Some campaign reform proposals, for example, giving everyone an equal amount of government money to spend on election campaigns, can be interpreted as a *partial* move toward such an egalitarian system.[70]

B. *Evaluation*

Some criticisms apply only to specific versions of the market failure theory. For example, the second market failure theory, requiring adequate access for all viewpoints, or the third, requiring equal access for all viewpoints, rely respectively on the classic model's rationality or its truth assumptions. Thus, each of the reformulations is subject to the criticisms of the specific assumption of the classic model upon which it relies. Here, I intend first to develop criticisms which apply to all versions (possibly with differing force). Then, I will note serious practical difficulties with guaranteeing equal access for all individuals. This equal access argument merits special attention since, by reversing each of the classic model's assumptions, it apparently escapes all the theoretical criticisms directed against the classic model.

The most fundamental objection to the market failure theories applies when they require interference with the speech freedom of some people. This objection starkly poses the question whether equalizing "real opportunities" to speak justifies restricting speech or certain other forms of personal liberty. Since this objection is not so much a criticism of the logic of the equal access arguments as a claim that other values are more basic, the force of

---

68. *See Economic Analysis, supra* note 5, at 32-41.
69. Harper v. Virginia Bd. of Elections, 383 U.S. 663 (1966) (striking down poll tax). *See also* Lubin v. Panish, 415 U.S. 709 (1974); Bullock v. Carter, 405 U.S. 134 (1972); *see generally* Baker, *Utility and Rights: Two Justifications for State Action Increasing Equality,* 84 YALE L.J. 39 (1974); Michelman, *On Protecting the Poor Through the Fourteenth Amendment,* 83 HARV. L. REV. 7 (1969).
70. For example, this is accomplished by giving people full credit against their taxes for political expenditures (contributions) up to a certain level and, for people who do not pay taxes, by directly giving them rebates for political expenditures. Absent this second procedure, the law should succumb to an equal protection attack.

the objection will depend on the appeal of the liberty model—and, therefore, evaluation of this objection must be postponed until the liberty model is examined. However, several preliminary observations deserve attention.

If, as I have argued,[71] the same ethical principle requires collective concern both for individual liberty and for an egalitarian distribution of resources, these two values, equality and liberty, interpreted in light of this ethical principle, will not be incompatible. Government respect for, and treatment of, individuals as equals is necessary in order to morally justify legal obligation.[72] Respect for individuals as equals requires a concern for people's liberty (for restrictions on liberty disrespect a person's autonomy as a moral agent) and for people's opportunities (which implies a concern with the distribution of opportunities, with equality). However, both conceptually and in our constitutional system, the two values, liberty and equality, do different work.[73] The first amendment provides the best constitutional base for delineating a protected realm of liberty. Other constitutional texts, particularly the equal protection clause, provide the best basis for recognizing equality claims. For example, respecting people as equals, although consistent with considerable economic inequality, may require that certain "merit goods" be provided up to a certain level.[74] Thus, if "merit goods" properly include some opportunity to communicate one's views to a large audience, the fourteenth amendment's equal protection clause, not some market failure version of the first amendment, provides the proper constitutional base for the argument. And, fortunately, this basis avoids the serious practical difficulties, identified below, which make application of the market failure model objectionable.[75]

The correction of market failures requires criteria to guide the state in its intervention. If provision of *adequate* access is the goal, the lack of criteria for "adequacy" undermines the legitimacy of government regulation. For the government to determine what access is adequate involves the government implicitly judging what is the correct resolution of the marketplace de-

71. Baker, note 51 *supra*; Baker, note 69 *supra*.

72. R. Dworkin, Taking Rights Seriously, 150-205 (1977); Baker, *supra* note 69, at 48-55.

73. Baker, note 51 *supra*.

74. Michelman, note 69 *supra*. *See* San Antonio Independent School Dist. v. Rodriguez, 411 U.S. 1, 23-24, 25 n.60, 36-37 (1973).

75. *See* text accompanying notes 76-82 *infra*. These comments are not a defense of a fourteenth amendment right to a minimum opportunity to communicate. Instead, I suggest that if an argument is made to require governmental action assuring everyone such a minimum opportunity, the analysis ought to be based on the fourteenth amendment notion that individuals be respected as equals rather than on a first amendment marketplace of ideas theory (or on the first amendment notion that persons be respected as autonomous individuals).

bates—or, more bluntly, allows the government to define truth. If a purpose of the first amendment is to protect unpopular ideas that may eventually triumph over the majority's established dogma, then allowing the government to determine adequacy of access stands the first amendment on its head. (In other versions, where equality of input provides the criterion, the parallel problem will be defining equality.)

Harlan's concurrence in *United States v. O'Brien*,[76] the draft card burning case, illustrates the problem of determining adequacy of access. Harlan apparently agreed that a constitutional right to have one's view adequately presented to the public might justify violating an otherwise valid law, if the violation were necessary in order to present one's view.[77] Presumably, Harlan and O'Brien disagreed precisely over whether other "adequate" opportunities for presenting O'Brien's view were available. No criteria exist for making this determination. And the differing determinations by Harlan and O'Brien illustrate the danger of using makeshift criteria. Judges (as arms of the state), particularly given that judges are drawn almost exclusively from the dominant classes in society, will normally find that the dissidents have had adequate opportunity and that they have lost in the debate because their position is unpersuasive. In other words, state determination of adequacy will usually favor the status quo.[78]

O'Brien's defiance indicates an additional problem created by the market failure approach. Recognizing individual rights which focus on achieving results (particularly imprecisely defined results such as having society reach the best or "proper" decision) converts the right into a guaranteed adequate means to an end. This instrumentalist conception of fundamental rights inherently tends toward justifying violent or otherwise objectionable conduct. Dissenters, like O'Brien, who firmly believe reason con-

---

76. 391 U.S. 367 (1968).

77. This "passage does not foreclose consideration of First Amendment claims . . . [where a regulation] has the effect of entirely preventing a 'speaker' from reaching a significant audience with whom he could not otherwise lawfully communicate." 391 U.S. at 388-89 (Harlan, J., concurring).

78. Interestingly, the clearest example of the Court relying on this adequacy of access argument involved a situation where those excluded were not political dissidents but were presumably quite middle class. Linmark Assoc., Inc. v. Township of Willingboro, 431 U.S. 85, 93 (1977) (one—the weakest—ground for invalidating a ban on "For Sale" signs on homes was that the homeowners did not have "satisfactory" alternative means of communication). The civil rights protest cases might appear to contradict the generalization in the text. However, when these cases favored the dissidents, the Court usually relied either on discriminatory enforcement (content discrimination) or on statutory vagueness or overbreadth grounds to set aside the convictions—not adequacy of access arguments. Unless the Court fully adopts the perspective of the dissidents, these faults are more easily seen and are more easily corrected by judicial decrees than is the inadequacy of access opportunities. These two factors suggest why the Court did not employ inadequacy of access arguments.

firms their views, are told by marketplace theory that a *properly functioning marketplace* of ideas would lead people to accept correct beliefs, their beliefs, *e.g.*, to reject the war. Under the market failure analysis, since the war continues, and given that they firmly believe their views are correct, these dissenters must conclude that the state has violated their constitutional right to a properly functioning market. Then, either because violation of this important right, until corrected, ends the legitimacy of their obligation to obey the laws of the state or because, as Harlan suggested, they have a right to take the steps required to vindicate their right, the dissenters are justified in breaking rules to do what is necessary to achieve the acceptance in the marketplace of ideas to which they are constitutionally entitled. Law breaking or violence, however, cannot be expected to stop here. Important disputes usually produce at least two sides which are firmly convinced that they are right. Thus, any success on one side will appear to the other side to justify their making an even more forceful response, thereby providing the logic for an escalating use of increasingly extreme, possibly violent, means. These normally illegal activities appear necessary to correct for the denial of one's right to a properly functioning marketplace of ideas.[79]

The argument for equality of individual access provides an apparently clear criterion for proper market functioning. But the clarity of the criterion is deceptive. Here, I will only note some key problems. For example, one can not easily identify communication activities. Virtually all activities undertaken in a context where another will be aware of the activity communicate something; and requiring equality of resources for all publicly performed activities, an *extreme* egalitarian requirement, greatly aggravates all the problems noted below. But let us assume that communication activities can be identified. To equalize the amount that both rich and poor can speak, the state could employ a combination of subsidies and legal restrictions or could make speech a free good, costless for everyone. Either approach raises numerous problems. First, the restrictions in the subsidy-restriction approach impose an objectionable restraint on liberty. Second, this subsidy-restriction approach *unequally* burdens the speech of the rich if only the rich must pay for their speech.

---

79. The situation was much calmer in the classic theory that assumed that the marketplace would not fail (unless *because* of government censorship) and, therefore, the government had no need to guarantee a properly functioning market. Thus, in the classic model, "when men have realized that time has upset many fighting faiths, they may come to believe even more than they believe the very foundations of their own conduct that the ultimate good desired is better reached by free trade in ideas—that the best test of truth is the power of the thought to get itself accepted in the competition of the market . . . ." Abrams v. United States, 250 U.S. 616, 630 (1919) (Holmes & Brandeis, JJ., dissenting).

Third, the intensity of people's desire to speak or communicate (at different levels of communication) varies; it is not apparent that allowing two people to do the same thing, when their desire to do it differs, actually treats them equally. Moreover, whether one utilizes the subsidies or a universally "free good" approach, the resulting equality involves an inefficient use of resources, *e.g.*, those subsidized who are relatively uninterested in speech activities would have rather used these resources for other purposes.[80] Even theorists as egalitarian as John Rawls would object if the inefficiency were so great that the worst-off group would prefer less equality.[81] Fourth, if one justification for the first amendment lies in its contribution to the proper formulation of community values and improved collective decision making, guaranteeing equality of access will be objectionable. Both the subsidy restriction and the free good approach promote expression of weakly held viewpoints as compared to strongly held viewpoints, thereby preventing the marketplace of ideas from accurately reflecting the collective values or perspectives of the community.

Finally, it is unclear why the sought after equality should refer to opportunities for input as opposed to opportunities for influence.[82] If truth is chosen or created and if people diverge in their conclusions about what should be created, equality would apparently require that each be able to exercise equal influence. Since the same expenditure of money enables different people to exercise different degrees of influence, an equality of influence standard would require that the "naturally" influential be allowed even less resources for communication purposes than the non-influential. This is a curious constitutional standard. Most people would assume that it is desirable, not objectionable, to allow people with wisdom and experience to exercise greater noncoercive influence and to allow some specialization in being opinion leaders or information spreaders. In fact, if the marketplace of ideas is not to further merely random changes, those attuned to the needs for change must exercise greater influence.

In summary, all the market failure theories should be rejected as first amendment doctrine and, particularly, should be rejected as justifications for restricting liberty. Arguments for providing either "adequate" or equal access for all viewpoints rely on assump-

---

80. Each of the above faults are suggested by Winter, *Poverty, Economic Equality, and the Equal Protection Clause*, 1972 SUP. CT. REV. 41. Certain faults in Winter's analysis, *see, e.g.*, Baker, *supra* note 69, at 44 n.17, are less likely to apply if the subsidy is constitutionally required rather than legislatively chosen and if the subsidy attempts to achieve rather than absolute equality a minimal level of "merit good" availability rather than absolute equality.

81. J. RAWLS, *supra* note 50, at 302-03.

82. The Court noted that this "inequality" of equality of opportunity is a serious problem. Buckley v. Valeo, 421 U.S. 1, 56-57 (1976).

tions rejected in the earlier analysis of the classic marketplace model; moreover, they generate serious practical problems. Only equality of individual opportunities for communication relies on plausible assumptions. The most important objection to this equality standard is that it improperly subordinates liberty. Moreover, this equality standard is unworkable as it cannot be coherently defined; and, on any definition, it requires tremendous scope of state intervention. This equality standard is also objectionable as it leads to very inefficient use of resources and to serious distortions in the representation of community values or perspectives. Finally, according to the analysis in Part I, even if implemented, a "properly functioning" market of ideas will favor the status quo[83] because an equality standard that is tied to speech provides inadequate protection for dissenting perspectives to develop.

III. THE LIBERTY MODEL

My thesis is that the first amendment protects a broad realm of nonviolent, noncoercive activity. The method for determining the scope of protection proceeds, first, by determining the purposes or values served by protected speech. These values, however, are also served by violent and coercive activities. Thus, I conclude that constitutional protection of speech is justified not merely because of the values served by speech but because freedom of speech serves these values in a particular, humanly acceptable manner, *e.g.*, nonviolently and noncoercively. Describing these methods is the second step of the analysis. Finally, I argue in Part IV, that when nonverbal conduct advances the same values in a relevantly similar manner, the nonverbal conduct should be viewed as speech and should receive protection.[84]

A. *First Amendment Values or Purposes*

In the marketplace theories, a single value—discovery of truth or reaching the "best" societal or individual decision—justified and defined the scope of protection. This focus is too limited. Professor Emerson, probably the most thoughtful and influential first amendment scholar, finds first amendment freedom essential for four values: 1) individual self-fulfillment, 2) advancement of knowledge and discovery of truth, 3) participation in decision making by all members of the society (which "embraces the right to participate in the building of the whole culture"), and 4) achievement of a "more adaptable and hence

---

83. *See* text accompanying notes 54-61 *supra*.
84. *See* notes 124-41 & accompanying text *infra*.

stable community."[85]

Emerson's list is acceptable. However, it is informative to see that the first value, self-fulfillment, and the third, participation in change, are key values and to understand why conduct promoting these two values ought to receive constitutional protection.

The values of self-fulfillment and participation in change impose somewhat different requirements on a satisfactory theory. The emphasis on "self" in self-fulfillment requires the theory to delineate a realm of liberty for self-determined processes of self-realization. The participation in change value requires the theory to specify and protect activities essential to a democratic, participatory process of change. Emerson's other two values are derivative. Given that truth is chosen or created, not discovered, advancement of knowledge and discovery of truth are merely aspects of participation in change.[86] Also, one apparently achieves a "more flexible and thereby more stable community" by providing for individual self-fulfillment and participation in change. Thus, henceforth, I will refer to individual self-fulfillment and participation in change as the key first amendment values.

Why should these two values receive constitutional protection? I will briefly summarize an answer I have advanced elsewhere.[87] Obligation exists only in relationships of respect. To justify legal obligation, the community must respect individuals as equal, rational and autonomous moral beings. For the community legitimately to expect individuals to respect collective decisions, *i.e.*, legal rules, the community must respect the dignity and equal worth of its members. One can elaborate this core truth of social contract doctrines in order to explain both the propriety of and proper limits on utilitarian policies.[88] And determining the proper limits on utilitarian policies is crucial for identifying constitutional rights because having constitutional protection means that the right prevails over preference maximization policies. The justification for welfare maximization policies is that, in decision making, the state should weight each person's concerns *equally*, thereby respecting the equal worth of each. This required respect for people's equal worth also explains the major limit on adopting welfare maximization policies, *i.e.*, the state's policy must respect

85. T. EMERSON, THE SYSTEM OF FREEDOM OF EXPRESSION 6-7 (1971) [hereinafter cited as FREEDOM OF EXPRESSION]; GENERAL THEORY, *supra* note 15, at 3-15.

86. Since *democratic participation* in change focuses on the individual's freedom to participate, if the speech is not chosen by anyone, if it is not a manifestation of the speaker's values, even though the speech may cause change or advance knowledge, it does not serve this liberty value and is not protected. *See Commercial Speech*, note 5 *supra*.

87. Baker, *supra* note 5, at 413-15.

88. *See* R. DWORKIN, note 72 *supra*; J. RAWLS, note 50 *supra*; Baker, note 69 *supra*.

people's integrity as rational, equal, autonomous moral beings, it must respect people as ends and not just as means. This requires that people's choices, their definition and development of *themselves*, must be respected—otherwise they become mere objects for manipulation or means for realizing someone else's ideals or desires. This respect for defining, developing or expressing one's self is precisely Emerson's value of self-realization. Moreover, since group decisions significantly influence both one's identity and one's opportunities, respecting people's autonomy as well as people's equal worth requires that people be allowed an equal right to participate in the process of group decision making—which is precisely Emerson's other key value, participation in collective decision making. Without trying to further develop this justification for the centrality of these two values, below I will merely rely on the widely accepted conclusion that *individual self-fulfillment and participation in change are fundamental purposes of the first amendment*. If, however, one accepts the justification offered here, it would help explain why utilitarian balancing does not justify limiting first amendment rights.

B. *Uses of Speech*

An exploration of the uses of speech will clarify both *how* and *when* speech contributes to the key values of the first amendment. A complete elaboration of the uses of speech is impossible. But in surveying the uses of speech one must take care not to adopt a too narrow or misguided vision. A very insightful article by Professor Scanlon illustrates the problems resulting from too narrow a vision. Scanlon not only argued "that all protected acts will be 'acts of expression,'" which he defines as "any act that is intended by its agent to communicate to one or more persons some proposition or attitude," but also that "almost everyone would agree" with this conclusion.[89] He is, I think, very wrong in his limitation of the category of properly protected acts although he is, possibly, correct that most would agree to his error.

Scanlon's ready acceptance of a marketplace of ideas theory, as evidenced by his emphasis on the intended communication of propositions or attitudes, illustrates the dominance of this model in our thinking. But his categorization of protected acts of expression is inadequate in three respects. First, it excludes many uses of speech. People continually speak or write without intending any person to hear their speech or see their writing.

---

89. Scanlon, *A Theory of Freedom of Expression*, 1 PHILOSOPHY & PUB. AFF. 204, 206-07 (1972). Most thoughtful commentators agree with Scanlon's categorization. *See, e.g.*, L. TRIBE, AMERICAN CONSTITUTIONAL LAW 601, 605 (1978); Nimmer, *The Meaning of Symbolic Speech Under the First Amendment*, 21 UCLA L. REV. 29, 36 (1973).

Moreover, people's "solitary" uses of speech—to record by keeping a diary, to organize by outlining or cataloguing, to understand by problem solving, to amuse or relax by singing or making up a story, to perform a duty by praying, or to order one's behavior by writing oneself a note—contribute to self-fulfillment and often to individual or social change. And, although this fact should not be relevant for determining the scope of the first amendment, the government sometimes attempts to control or regulate these solitary uses of speech—for example, if, as in Orwell's *1984*,[90] the government believes the speech is an aspect of, or contributes to, resistance to the government, or if society considers the speech to be anti-social or immoral,[91] or if the government fears the speech might lead to new knowledge or capabilities, like nuclear weapon or genetic research, that the government wants to control or suppress.

Second, many uses of speech—for example, story telling where the purpose of the story telling is to entertain rather than to promote insight—are best described as the speaker intending to do something.[92] Attempting to force such uses of speech into the category of communicating propositions or attitudes is strained. "The paradox disappears only if we make a radical break with the idea that language always functions in one way, always serves the same purpose: to convey thoughts—which may be about houses, pains, good and evil, or anything else you please."[93]

Third, Scanlon duplicates the marketplace model's emphasis on *content*. The speech is protected if, and because, it contains *propositions* or *attitudes* relevant to public debate. Instead, the first amendment values of *self*-fulfillment and *popular participation* in change emphasize the *source* of the speech in the self, and make the choice of the speech by the self the crucial factor in justifying protection.

In describing an alternative to Scanlon's categorization, Wittgenstein's warning should be kept in mind. He writes:

> But how many kinds of sentence are there? Say assertion, question, and command?—There are *countless* kinds: *countless different kinds of use of what we call*

---

90. G. ORWELL, 1984 (1948).

91. *Cf.* Stanley v. Georgia, 394 U.S. 557 (1969) (statute banning private possession of obscene material held unconstitutional). According to some, the Court only protected the pornography to the extent that no communication between people, at least people outside the home, was involved. United States v. Thirty-Seven Photographs, 402 U.S. 363, 382 (1971) (Black & Douglas, JJ., dissenting). Compare praying in a state that wants to promote aetheism.

92. Compare Karl Marx's report that in ancient India the "poet . . . in some communities replaces the silversmith, in others the school master." K. MARX, CAPITAL 357-58 (1967).

93. L. WITTGENSTEIN, PHILOSOPHICAL INVESTIGATIONS § 304 (3d ed. 1958).

"symbols," "words," "sentences." And this multiplicity
is not something fixed, given once for all; but new types
of language, *new language-games,* as we may say, *come
into existence,* and others become obsolete and get forgotten . . . . Here the term "language-game" is meant to
bring into prominence the fact that *the speaking of language is part of an activity, or of a form of life* . . . .[94]

Given this warning, one should realize that the task must be
to find characterizations of language uses or forms of life that provide insight into the scope of first amendment protection, not to
develop a comprehensive catalogue. Two categories of use, self-
expressive and creative, cut across the communicative, noncommunicative dichotomy and closely correlate with the key first
amendment values of self-fulfillment and participation in change.

To engage voluntarily in a speech act is to engage in self-
definition or expression. A Vietnam war protestor may explain
that when she chants "Stop This War Now" at a demonstration,
she does so without any expectation that her speech will affect the
continuance of war or even that it will communicate anything to
people in power; rather, she participates and chants in order to
define herself publicly in opposition to the war. This war protestor provides a dramatic illustration of the importance of this self-
expressive use of speech, independent of any effective communication to others, for self-fulfillment or self-realization. Generally,
any individually chosen, meaningful conduct, whether public or
private, expresses and further defines the actor's nature and contributes to the actor's self-realization.

Speech is not merely communicative but also creative. The
Bible reports: "And God *said,* 'Let there be light;' and there was
light."[95] For six days God spoke and named things and by these
means created the world. Hannah Arendt reports that, to the ancient Greeks,

[T]hought was secondary to speech, but speech and action were considered coeval and coequal, of the same
rank and the same kind; and . . . finding the right words
at the right moment, *quite apart from the information or
communication they may convey,* is action. Only sheer

---

94. *Id.* at § 23 (emphasis added). After listing various uses, Wittgenstein continues: "It is interesting to compare the multiplicity of the tools in language and of the
ways they are used, the multiplicity of kinds of word and sentence, with what logi-
cians have said about the structure of language." *Id.*

95. *Genesis* 1:3 (emphasis added). *See also Psalms* 33:9 ("For he spoke, and it
came to be."); *Hebrews* 11:3 ("By faith we understand that the world was created by
the word of God."). Richardson explains that to the Hebrew mind: "Thought, word,
and deed are not three separate processes or acts but are organic elements of the same
single process, an act of volition." A THEOLOGICAL WORD BOOK OF THE BIBLE 232
(A. Richardson ed. 1950).

violence is mute, and for this reason violence alone can never be great.[96]

And, for Arendt, "to act . . . means to take an initiative, to begin."[97] Through speech and action new worlds are created—"new" because action, which "may proceed from nowhere," "acts upon beings who are capable of their own actions," and thus "action and reaction among men never move in a closed circle . . . ."[98] The practice of the poet parallels Arendt's description of the Greek emphasis on the creative use of speech. A poem, which "should not mean [b]ut be,"[99] requires no project but instead a "flicker of the soul."[100] Gaston Bachelard describes the poetic image as "a new being in our language, expressing us by making us what it expresses . . . . Here expression creates being . . . . Through this creativeness the imagining consciousness proves to be, very simply but very purely, an origin."[101]

More mundane practices may provide more convincing evidence of the creative use of language. For example, the creative use of language is particularly prominent in: 1) making up new rules for a game or practice, as well as the language embodying the new rules; 2) coining a word, forming a new verbal image; 3) writing a poem or a play; 4) verbally formulating an analysis in order to "discover" new relationships or possibilities, or a dialogue through which *both* participants gain insights which *neither* possessed before; 5) "creating" or planning a new strategy; 6) persuading another of something; 7) teaching or developing new capabilities in another. The creative aspect, the new aspect of the world which results, varies in these examples. But in each case either the speaker or the listener or both possess something new—new images, new capacities, new opportunities, new amusements—which did not exist before and which were created by people's speech activity. Often the new creation will influence behavior. And in each case the creation has changed the social world, the world of meanings, opportunities, and restraints, in which people live.

Self-expressive and creative uses of speech *more fully and uniformly* promote the two key first amendment values, self-fulfillment and participation in both societal decision making and culture building, than does speech which communicates propositions and attitudes. First, *solitary uses* of speech contribute to

96. H. ARENDT, THE HUMAN CONDITION 25-26 (1958) (emphasis added).
97. *Id.* at 177. *See also id.* at 175-81.
98. *Id.* at 190.
99. A. MACLEISH, POEMS, 1924-1933, 123 (1933)
100. G. BACHELARD, THE POETICS OF SPACE XVIII (1969).
101. *Id.* at XIX-XX. Compare Pierre-Jean Jouve's statement that "[T]here is no poetry without absolute creation." *Quoted in id.* at XXVIII.

self-fulfillment. Also, people's private analysis of their own character or of how to accomplish some goal, or people's practice of
singing or of creating or viewing obscenity for private entertainment or relaxation, are all private speech activities which, by
changing or defining people, change or modify the culture. Second, *communications* not intended to communicate propositions
or attitudes of the speaker—such as story telling intended merely
to entertain the listener, or singing intended merely to show the
accomplishments of the singer, or group singing or a verbal ritual
possibly intended to develop group solidarity—may both contribute to self-fulfillment and affect the culture. Third, self-expressive and creative uses properly exclude some uses that do not
promote the key first amendment values but that would be included in Scanlon's market place definition. At first, the broad
category of self-expressive acts might appear to include all speech
acts. Nevertheless, to the extent that speech is involuntary, is not
chosen by the speaker, the speech act does not involve the *self*-
realization or *self*-fulfillment of the speaker. Focusing on the
self-expressive uses of speech directs the inquiry toward the responsible source, not the content, of the speech. Thus, as I have
argued elsewhere, if in modern America commercial advertising
does not reflect anyone's voluntary or personal choice, this commercial speech should not be constitutionally protected.[102]

---

102. *Commercial Speech*, note 5 *supra*. My argument is that the market dictates
the content of commercial speech and, therefore, even if the speech happens to correspond to the speaker's values, the content is determined by the structure of the market
and is not chosen by the speaker. While not rejecting their prior commercial decisions, Justices White, Marshall and Brennan adopted the reasoning of this Article in
concluding that a corporation's political speech can be regulated. First Nat'l Bank v.
Bellotti, 98 S. Ct. 1407, 1430-39 (1978) (White, Marshall & Brennan, JJ., dissenting).
    Criticism of this argument focuses on other situations where "external" pressures
appear to control people's speech; for example, some politicians have told me that the
political speech of candidates does not represent the candidates' views but is "dictated" by the need of getting elected. Numerous distinctions make this analogy unacceptable. First, for many, if not most, political actors' political activity is not primarily
and, more importantly, is not necessarily determined by the need to maximize either
electoral support or economic profit. That is, the political realm resembles the "household" in being an arena where expenditures are made to promote one's substantive
values. *Commercial Speech, supra* note 5, at 12-14 (employing Max Weber's distinction of the "household" from the profit-oriented business enterprise). Thus, no structure requires that the speaker choose increased chances of election (which is not even
an option for minor parties) over increased advocacy of their values. Second, unlike
the economic sphere where efficiently fulfilling wealth-backed desires is considered
the most praiseworthy aspect of the enterprise's activity, many politicians and most
defenders of the political process argue that, here, it is highly praiseworthy to truth-
fully and forcefully state, explain, and advocate one's own visions or understanding of
the public good. In fact, such speech and advocacy may be an essential element in
"good" political leadership. I realize this may be less true in the type of interest group
politics that many pluralist political scientists presently defend than in a political
realm where the main activity is to participate in choosing and defining values. *See*
C. MACPHERSON, THE LIFE AND TIMES OF LIBERAL DEMOCRACY 77-115 (1977).
However, the fact that some politicians partially conform to external pressures or are

D. *How Speech Operates*

The first amendment could not possibly protect all the mani-fold activities, some of which involve violence or coercion, that further self-fulfillment or contribute to change. The logic of con-stitutionally protecting speech relates to the common sense per-ceptions both of the importance of speech for realizing certain values and of the method by which speech advances those values. In fact, in Part IV, I will argue that the first amendment protects non-verbal, creative and self-expressive activities when they ad-vance first amendment values in a manner relevantly similar to speech.[103] Here, the central problem is to determine what *methods* or *manner* of using speech deserve constitutional protection.

Speech, unlike other behavior, is seldom thought of as physi-cally violent or destructive[104]—the shrill voice breaking a glass is an aberrant example not typical of our normal notions of speech use. Similarly, using high decibel levels of sound to physically interfere with another's activities belies, rather than exemplifies, our characteristic image of speech; few urge constitutional protec-tion for sheer noise used to disrupt a meeting.[105] Speech may harm others; but normally, speech differs from most other harm-producing conduct in the way it causes the harm. Both the amia-ble interchange which leads to replacing old with new friendships (consider the tort of alienation of affection) and the destructive interchange well illustrated in Edward Albee's *Who's Afraid of Virginia Woolf* create an effect by influencing the mind—the per-ceptions, feelings, beliefs or understandings—of the listener (or the speaker).

Law is typically used to prohibit certain harmful actions. But if the Constitution limits the government's power to restrict people's liberty, then either some harms or some methods of caus-ing harms must not suffice to justify legal restrictions on behavior. This conclusion cannot be controversial. Under existing doctrine, harms caused by speech normally do not justify a restriction on speech, while harms that result from invading another's area of decision authority (*e.g.*, destruction of another's property or coerc-ing another's behavior) normally justify outlawing the invading

---

psychologically controlled by the combination of their desire to be elected and their assumptions concerning what speech will promote their election merely indicates one concept of self-interest that some political actors may adopt in choosing their speech; however, other choices are possible. My argument is that other choices are not permit-ted for economic enterprises operating in a profit-controlled competitive market. The above distinctions, I think, explain both the importance and the fact of greater free-dom in the political realm than in the market realm.

   103. *See* Part IV *infra*.
   104. Compare "sticks and stones may break my bones but names will never hurt me."
   105. *See* FREEDOM OF EXPRESSION, *supra* note 85, at 338.

conduct. The theoretical justification for this doctrine, as well as the explication of its scope, depends upon showing that the principle of respecting the equality and autonomy of individuals, which justifies limiting the collective's decision-making authority,[106] requires that people have the right to cause harms by certain means (speech caused harms) but not by others. This can be done. The key aspect distinguishing harms caused by protected speech acts from most other methods of causing harms is that speech harms occur only to the extent people "mentally" adopt perceptions or attitudes. Two factors deserve emphasis. First, the speech act does not interfere with another's legitimate decision authority, assuming that the other has no right to decide what the speaker should say or believe. This assumption is a necessary consequence of our respecting people's autonomy. Second, outlawing acts of the speaker in order to protect people from harms that result because the listener adopts certain perceptions or attitudes disrespects the responsibility and freedom of the listener. Both of these observations follow from our typical concept of the person which identifies a person, at least in part, with the person's perceptions and feelings; we hold a person responsible for actions that are based on the opinions or perceptions the person accepts. In fact, respecting the listener's integrity as an individual normally requires holding the listener responsible for her conduct unless she has been coerced or forced into the activity.

This explanation for protecting speech suggests the uses which do not merit protection. (Of course, one must be very careful not to find exceptions too easily—one must guard against the easy conclusion of those in authority that a particular "harmful" use of speech must fit into an exception.) The reasons why speech is protected do not apply if the speaker *coerces* the other or *physically interferes* with the other's rights. Respect for individual autonomy hardly requires protection of speech when the listener is coerced—"when [the listener] does something because of threats, the will of [the threatener] is operating or predominant."[107]

Thus, in order to determine what speech can be banned, one must be able to identify coercive speech.[108] Presumably, a major

---

106. *See* text accompanying notes 87-88 *supra*.

107. Nozick, *Coercion*, in PHILOSOPHY, SCIENCE, AND METHOD 440, 459 (S. Morgenbesser, P. Suppes & M. White eds. 1969).

108. In developing this description of threats, I am influenced by Nozick, note 107 *supra*. I deviate from Nozick in two important (and, probably, in other less important) respects. For reasons noted in the text, I think the benchmark position cannot be the "normal and expected course of events" but must be the events or options which the person has a moral or legitimate right to expect. (Of course, often the normal course of events contributes to what one has a right to expect.) Second, because in blackmail the threatener may have a right or duty to give information to others (*e.g.*, the police), Nozick viewed the blackmailer's statement that she would accept payment in return for making the disclosure to be an offer. *Id.* at 447. In consequence of

reason for a preferred status for freedom of speech is that speech behavior is normally noncoercive; instead, it depends for its power on increasing the speaker's own awareness or on the voluntary acceptance of listeners. Nevertheless, some speech may be coercive; the problem is that people sometimes invoke a carelessly formulated notion of coercion to justify regulation of behavior, or speech, of which they do not approve. A digression on the concept of coercion and of threats, an important subclass of coercive acts that must be distinguished from offers or warnings, will clarify the proper limits on protection of speech acts. A person coercively influences another if 1) she changes the other's options such that the other is worse off than he would be if he had the options that he had a moral (or legitimate) right to expect (*e.g.*, hijacking, threatened treason, or perjury) or 2) she employs means that she had no right to use for changing the threatened person's options (*e.g.*, blackmail).[109] An alternative formulation that I have rejected would use the "normal or expected course of events" or "options to which one has a legal right" rather than "options that one has a moral or legitimate right to expect" as the benchmark for determining whether the person has been made worse off. Three considerations indicate why normalcy or legality provide inappropriate benchmarks. First, particularly when used as a critical principle, for example, in evaluating a legal or social order, coercion refers to improper interferences with another's choices. If the normal conditions are morally objectionable, then one's (for example, the slave owner's) reliance on this state of affairs in influencing another's (the slave's) behavior can be coercive. Second, normality is not crucial if one has a right to change the normal order; for example, although in some contexts membership will involve continuing obligations, typically a member of a voluntary association is not being coercive when she states that she will change the existing situation (by dropping out of the association) unless certain conditions are met. Similarly, if the landlord normally has allowed the tenant to stay without paying rent, to demand that the tenant start paying is not coercive unless other special facts show that the tenant had a right to stay without paying or that the landlord did not have a right to demand rent. Third, reliance on law to specify the benchmark for when acts are coercive can be circular. Suppose Joe tells the Senator that he will continue his protests until the Senator supports the Equal Rights Amendment. To conclude that Joe has coerced the Sena-

---

looking not only at the opportunities to which the threatened person has a rightful expectation but also to the rights of the threatener, I conclude this involves a threat. *See* text accompanying note 112 *infra*.

109. The key problem in this second category is finding the theoretical limits on the extent to which the state can restrict the threatener's "rights."

tor because a law gives the Senator a right to be free from the protests is circular if Joe's protests can be legitimately outlawed only if the protests are coercive. If only coercive aspects of the speech can justify making the speech illegal, the speech's illegality cannot support the view that it is coercive. The prohibition cannot itself justify the prohibition. Clearly only an independent ethical defense of the legitimacy of the legal rule would suffice to show that its violation is coercive.

The reason for the special status of speech rights will clarify why speech is normally not coercive. Society can choose to create many different types of property rights, that is, can choose different ways to allocate decision-making authority. However, respect for the integrity and autonomy of the individual usually requires giving each person at least veto power over the use of her own body and, similarly, over her own speech. This respect implies that people should be viewed as responsible for and given maximal liberty in choosing how to use their bodies and minds to develop and express themselves and should be given an equal right to try to influence the nature of their collective worlds. Such respect is belied unless each person has a right to decide upon and employ speech—and possibily other non-coercive conduct—for realizing her substantive values and visions. The key ethical postulate is that respect for individual integrity and autonomy require the recognition that a person has the right to use speech to develop herself or to influence or interact with others. Granted this ethical postulate, and since the concept of coercion only has a place within some such ethical order, the use of speech (normally) ought not be viewed as coercive. These observations can be illustrated by seeing how they counter two arguments for regulating supposedly coercive speech.

First, often threats of certain acts—to throw a rock through another's window—are coercive only because the law happened to give the threatened person a particular right, the right to have others not to throw, intentionally and without permission, a rock through the window. Here, the particulars of the law determine whether an act is coercive and subject to prohibition. The parallel argument is that if the law gives a person a right to be free of certain speech, such as speech that undermines one's reputation, the other person illegally injures or coerces the person by making or threatening to make that speech. The circularity of this argument as a reason to outlaw the speech has already been noted. The key failure of the parallelism is that one's authority over windows is not a crucial aspect of one's integrity and autonomy as a person and, therefore, should be allocated or specified on the basis of collective, legal, choice while the authority to decide upon one's speech and to use speech to affect the world must be allocated to the speaker; these allocations are central to a respect for one's autonomy and integrity as a person.

Second, often one concludes that acts that result from and perpetuate an unjust order—for example, unconscionable contracts—are coercive, and, therefore, should be forbidden or can be voided. The parallel argument is that speech that arguably strengthens or embodies the structure or values of that unjust order can properly be regulated or prohibited. Radicals, for instance, might argue that existing inequalities justify stifling the speech of the rich; or possibly, that these inequalities justify expenditure limits on political speech. The parallelism is false. The type reference made to a just order when considering what rights can (or should) exist in the present social order differs in two cases. The unconscionable contract involves an instrumentally valued exchange that depends on the involvement of a person who, in a just social order, would be unwilling to enter into the agreement. (This fact is the basis for claiming the contract is unconscionable.) Since, in a just order, one would have no legitimate expectation of being able to find another with whom to enter into the agreement, one has no legitimate expectation of being able to form the agreement. Therefore, legally prohibiting the agreement does not disrespect the vendor's "rights," the vendor's autonomy. In contrast, in a just social order the law must respect one's choice of speech content. No reference to legitimate expectations, to a just order, can justify restricting one's present opportunities to speak. Since the law can eliminate this contract opportunity but not the speech opportunity without disrespecting people's autonomy, the contract but not the speech may be coercive. In other words, prohibiting the speech sacrifices the individual's autonomy in order to correct an evil for which the legal order (*e.g.*, property laws), not the individual right sacrificed, is responsible. Here, not the speech, but the restriction on the speech would be coercive.

Nevertheless, these observations do not preclude finding some speech to be coercive and, therefore, subject to prohibition. Both the concept of coercion and the rationale for protecting speech draw from the same ethical requirement that the integrity and autonomy of the individual moral agent must be respected. Coercive acts typically disregard the ethical principle that, in interactions with others, one must respect the other's autonomy and integrity as a person. When trying to influence another person, one must not disregard that person's will or the integrity of the other person's mental processes. The type of speech that manifestly disregards the other's will or the integrity of the other's mental processes is not protected. Thus, the political morality summed up by the first amendment requires protection for speech that manifests or contributes to the speaker's values or visions—speech which furthers the two key first amendment values of self-fulfillment and participation in change—as long as the speech does not involve violence to or coercion of another.[110] This leaves three types of speech properly subject to positive law control: 1) speech involved in an actual or attempted taking or physical injury to another's person or property; 2) speech designed to disrespect and distort the integrity of another's mental processes; 3) speech not chosen by the speaker and which, therefore, cannot be attributed to the speaker's manifestation of her substantive values.[111]

This abstract formulation must be tested in the context of concrete issues. The theory should explain why speech activities such as fraud,[112] perjury, blackmail, espionage, and treason are unprotected. Here, for illustrative purposes, I will focus on only two: 1) blackmail, because of its similarity to a presumably protected activity, whistle blowing (public exposure of other's misdeeds); and 2) espionage, because of its relation to frequently raised first amendment issues.

Consider two situations: First, Jane says to Dick, "I will tell the public what you did (or are about to do) unless you give me $1,000." Second, Lisa says to David, "I will tell the public (or the police) if you proceed." Both statements involved the speaker "warning" the listener that he will be harmed by public exposure unless he modifies his planned course of action. Moreover, in both cases the speaker may have a right to expose the other; she may have a right to "ruin" the other by informing the public that he is a robber, rapist, or Republican.

---

110. If one distinguishes the more positive, conventional rights—rights that typically control the instrumental aspects of one's acts—from those rights that are essential for one's autonomy, it seems autonomy rights must supersede (others') conventional rights. However, one's autonomy rights cannot override another's autonomy. In this second area, respect for one's autonomy, for one's speech rights, does not bar legal control of one's speech. Speech that invades another's area of autonomy is coercive and can be regulated. Note, however, that reputation, which depends on the precise form of the social order and the attitudes of other people, is clearly conventional or instrumental, not an autonomy right.

111. *See* text accompanying note 102 *supra*.

112. *Cf.* United States v. Ballard, 322 U.S. 78 (1944). The defendants were charged with obtaining money by false representations. Although the Court held the Constitution prevented conviction for making *false* religious claims—*i.e.*, the truth of the religious claims could not be submitted to a jury—it did not decide whether the defendants could be convicted for making religious claims which they believed to be false. In dissent, Justices Stone, Roberts and Frankfurter concluded the defendants could be and were properly convicted for making representations which they did not believe. *Id.* at 89-90. Note that although the effect on the listener would be the same whether or not the speakers believed their statements, the purpose or nature of the speaker's act would be different. In that context, to make false representations knowingly would be the type of speech that I have argued above to be coercive, hence unprotected.

The purpose of the "threat" as well as the latter public exposure, if it occurs, differs crucially in the two cases. In the blackmail situation, Jane attempts to make Dick a puppet of her will, while in the whistle blowing situation, Lisa does nothing more than attempt to make David bear responsibility for his act. In the first case, what Jane wants of Dick is unrelated to the facts that she might expose while, in the second situation, Lisa's precise concern is with the act that she might expose. In the first, the speaker attempts to transfer decision-making control to herself while, in the second, the speaker does not try to prevent the other from making his decision but merely forces him to take responsibility, an imposition that respects rather than subverts the other's integrity and autonomy. Since whistle blowing, but not blackmailing, involves using speech directly to make the world correspond to the speaker's substantive values rather than merely to increase the speaker's wealth (or area of decision-making domination) and does so without disrespecting the listener's integrity, it is not coercive; therefore, the first amendment should protect Lisa's speech acts. In contrast, blackmail disrespects the other's autonomy. And although Dick has no right to prevent the public exposure of the information, respecting Jane's integrity does not require that she be given an opportunity to subvert Dick's will; the state can protect people's autonomy by forbidding blackmail, a coercive use of speech.

The above example further illustrates the difference between a liberty theory of the first amendment and most marketplace theories. Marketplace theories typically focus on the content of the speech or on the effect of the speech on the social world. And in both whistle blowing and blackmailing, the content of the speech and its effect either on the person exposed or on the public could be the same. In each case, the speech could equally well serve the public's interest in or need for information. In contrast, the liberty model of the first amendment focuses on *the nature of the speaker's acts*, the purpose or method of having an effect on the world. To use a traditional example, the nature or purpose of the act is quite different when a person trips over, as opposed to when he kicks, a child. To conclude that the manner of acting is crucially different in these two cases does not require looking at the motives of the actor (although they may provide evidence as to which act was done) nor is the determination undermined by the fact that certain of the effects are the same. (The focus on "content" in the speech context resembles a focus on the physical act in the kicking or tripping case.) If the first amendment protects people's choices related to self-fulfillment and involvement in social, political, or cultural change, it must normally be agnostic in respect to content or effect. Instead, the identification of the coercive or noncoercive nature of the act, which one learns from context, is crucial for determining whether the first amendment protects the act.

The agnosticism in respect to content must also apply to evaluation of motives. The motive of both the blackmailer and whistle blower may be to achieve personal gain by her expected influence on another's behavior. In both cases, the speaker may have either "good" or "bad," public-spirited or selfish, motives. However, the first amendment protection of liberty means that, within the context of protected manners of acting, people can choose and attempt to advance their own ends. Whether a person acts coercively depends on the nature of the act; in characterizing the act, an analysis of purpose, not one of motive, is often relevant. In contrast to the concept of motive which applies exclusively to human actions, the concept of purpose is in addition applicable to laws and objects. The term "purpose" refers to the intended ends or results of particular actions or to the contemplated uses or effects of particular artifacts. When describing human conduct, purpose relates to intended effects while motive relates to the reasons for desiring those effects. Clearly, our ability to determine purpose depends on our common understanding of the conventional context. We attribute a purpose to an act on the basis of our common understanding of what consequences people think will follow. Given the distinctions we make and the practices we engage in, specific features of the context allow us to distinguish the purpose of forcing a person to take responsibility for her act—which does not disrespect the person's integrity—and the purpose of subordinating the other's will to one's own. And we normally recognize the purpose without any reference to the speaker's motives. Although knowledge of motives can be a contextual factor useful in determining purpose, it is a distinct concept and our awareness of motives will often be nonessential or even irrelevant for identifying a purpose.[113] Thus, if the first amendment protects a manner of acting, the nature or purpose of the act will be crucial, but normally the state may not justify regulation on the basis of content, effect, or motive.

Espionage—at least secret transmission to a foreign nation of information which relates to the security of this nation—presents, for me, a difficult issue. The speaker uses speech (or writing) to change the world in a desired fashion. Creative uses of speech are usually protected. Moreover, the effect of espionage may be the same as publishing classified, previously secret, information in a

---

113. I must leave for another time a discussion of the confusion, in which I think the Court has been embroiled, resulting from its failure to distinguish and explain the respective relevance of motive and purpose, particularly in its analysis of equal protection and first amendment issues.

newspaper.[114] The enemy may find the published information as useful as the information secretly delivered to its agents. And normally one's choice of audience, or its size, should not affect one's first amendment rights. Speech directed toward a large audience, no audience, or a carefully selected, exclusive audience may equally contribute to one's self-fulfillment or participation in change.

Emerson takes as a key reason for denying protection that "espionage [takes] place in the context of action"; that espionage usually "consists in conveying information concerning military secrets and would fall within the system of military operations" and always "involves aiding a foreign country." Therefore, he concludes, even if espionage is "expression," it "is not that form of domestic, civilian expression that is embraced within the system of freedom of expression."[115] I think Emerson is basically correct, but clarity requires an explanation of why the first amendment does not protect foreign-oriented, military-related expression.

An analogy will clarify the picture. Normally, the first amendment should protect publishing the layout and security system of a bank even though the publisher knows that a bank robber might use this information in a robbery attempt. Alternatively, in the context of carrying out a bank robbery, an individual's role might be to inform her associates about the bank's security and layout; this individual would be participating in an activity that used illegal force to invade and steal another's property. And, if a robbery or an attempted robbery resulted, the person who *participated* by contributing information would not be constitutionally protected.

Significant aspects of the relations between nations involve, unfortunately, both the actual and threatened use of violent force. First amendment liberty does not protect a person's knowing attempt to aid another person, or country, in the application of violent force. Engaging in espionage resembles supplying plans to fellow bank robbers. Neither the effect, which might also result from a newspaper article, nor even the motive, is crucial. Espionage is not protected only because, and only to the extent that, one's country can reasonably conclude that information gathered through espionage increases the coercive power of another country and because the purpose of the espionage activity is to have that effect. The first amendment extends protection until one's speech becomes merely one's method of involvement in a coercive or violent project.[116]

---

114. New York Times Co. v. United States, 403 U.S. 713 (1971).
115. FREEDOM OF EXPRESSION, *supra* note 85, at 58-59.
116. Still, one might adopt Emerson's approach and deny protection to espio-

Although my focus in this and other sections has been on the speaker, communications are also used for many diverse purposes by the listener. Without analyzing these uses, I merely assume for now that the broad categories of listener uses will resemble speaker's uses and will be protected to the same extent. Nevertheless, since each first amendment theory will have a characteristic justification for and interpretation of listener's rights, a brief digression on these interpretations may help clarify my analysis.

In the classic marketplace model, the listener's right is a correlate of the speaker's; the government must not interfere with communications between a willing speaker and willing listener. This conclusion, which corresponds to the case law holdings,[117] is also implied by the liberty theory. However, the classic market model, which gives protection so that people will have the information they need for thoughtful pursuit of truth or for intelligent decision making, easily collapses into a market failure version that would recognize affirmative claims to get "needed" information that otherwise would not be readily available. In the market failure version, listeners would have an independent right to know, which presumably could be asserted against an unwilling speaker, against the government, or against a government restraint of an unprotected speaker.[118] This market failure analysis will raise

---

nage because it falls in the "system of military operation," not "the system of freedom of expression," and merely rely on the argument in the text as a justification for the distinction. I do not wish to argue the point here. But note that Emerson's approach would allow greater restrictions, for example, where the espionage agent's acts are too far removed from any actual, attempted, or foreseen use of violence to justify prohibiting or punishing the speech act under my argument. However, if courts are going to allow this behavior to be sanctioned, Emerson's categorization might promote greater purity in overall doctrine, an important achievement.

117. In protecting the privacy of involuntary listeners, the government cannot regulate in a way that would prevent the speaker from communicating with willing listeners or burden the listener's receipt of desired communications. Erznoznik v. City of Jacksonville, 422 U.S. 205 (1975); Cohen v. California, 403 U.S. 15 (1971); Lamont v. Postmaster Gen., 381 U.S. 301 (1965); Saia v. New York, 334 U.S. 558 (1948); Martin v. City of Struthers, 319 U.S. 141 (1943). However, some content-neutral time, place, and manner regulations may be acceptable. Kovacs v. Cooper, 336 U.S. 77 (1949). And restraints that only prevent communications directed to unwilling listeners will be upheld. Rowan v. Post Office Dep't, 397 U.S. 728 (1970); Martin v. City of Struthers, 319 U.S. 141, 147-48 (1943) (dicta) (state can punish those who call on a home "in defiance of the previously expressed will of the occupant"). *See Commercial Speech, supra* note 5, at 8.

118. These cases are often cited to support an independent right to know: Virginia State Bd. of Pharmacy v. Virginia Citizens Consumer Council, Inc., 425 U.S. 748 (1976) (suit by consumers invalidated prohibition of pharmacist advertising drugs); Red Lion Broadcasting Co. v. FCC, 395 U.S. 367 (1969) (upheld fairness doctrine); and Lamont v. Postmaster Gen., 381 U.S. 301 (1965) (struck down regulation burdening receipt of communist political propaganda mailed from abroad). *See* L. TRIBE, *supra* note 89, at 675-76, 676 nn.7 & 8. Nevertheless, under *Virginia Board of Pharmacy*, once the Court concludes commercial speech is protected, presumably the pharmacist's speech is protected. *See* Bates v. State Bar of Arizona, 432 U.S. 350 (1977). In *Red Lion*, the permissibility of the government's regulation of broadcast

problems that are similar to those described earlier, problems that include court balancing and conflicts with liberty.

On the liberty theory, the purpose of the first amendment is not to guarantee adequate information. The liberty theory does, however, protect noncoercive methods of getting information. The listener uses speech for self-realization or change purposes and these uses provide the basis of the listener's constitutional right. But the listener does not have a general claim for societal (information) allocations—*e.g.*, for the wealth that comes if one has unencumbered access to any desired information.[119] To grant first amendment protection to an otherwise unprotected speaker is no more constitutionally justified as an aspect of the listener's liberty than are other claims of the listener for greater wealth allocations. The listener has a right to demand that the government not prohibit the listener from receiving or using information. Restrictions on the listener's receipt or use of information must be defended as not really interfering with the listener's self-realizing activities (beyond the fact that the limitation may have a wealth allocation effect) or justified by some special characteristic of the listener—for example, one could ask whether children or prisoners or soldiers have diminished constitutional rights. Thus, the constitutional analysis of any restriction must be in terms of who is restricted—the speaker or the listener. Both parties have separate constitutional claims. Only if the restricted party does not have a constitutional claim is the government restriction permissible. Press reporting of criminal trials provides an obvious context to apply the analysis. The press, as listener, may have no access right to restricted information. However, if the press "hears," the government cannot prohibit the speaker's use (the press's publication) of the restricted information.[120] Likewise, if commercial speech

---

media as a partial common carrier (or partial public forum), not a right to know, was the basis of the decision. *See* Columbia Broadcasting Sys. v. Democratic Nat'l Comm., 412 U.S. 94 (1973); *Commercial Speech, supra* note 5, at 41-42 & n.144. As for *Lamont*, it seems strange that the first amendment, which limits government power rather than giving individual rights, would permit the government to abridge the freedom of speech of foreigners. Clearly a willing speaker (with liberty interests) and a willing listener existed; moreover, unlike in Kleindienst v. Mandel, 408 U.S. 753 (1972), the legal burden was placed directly on listeners whose liberty interests were unquestionably involved. *See* text accompanying note 121 *infra*.

119.   Of course, increased access to information is normally a desirable societal policy. The general allocation effects of policies increasing access to governmental and corporate controlled information may be to increase the egalitarian and democratic nature of society. *See* Baker, *Posner's Privacy Mystery and the Failure of Economic Analysis of Law*, 12 GA. L. REV. 475 (1978).

120.   Nebraska Press Ass'n v. Stuart, 427 U.S. 539 (1976). *See* New York Times Co. v. United States, 403 U.S. 713 (1971). Of course, the argument in the text may have skipped a step. If the listener used illegal means to obtain the information, does that justify a limit on the listener's use of the information? Although the courts have not unambiguously answered this question, protecting the person's rights as a speaker would require that the state be permitted, but only permitted, to punish the illegal acts

were unprotected, the government could prohibit the druggist from publishing but, as Rehnquist pointed out, could not and did not prohibit the consumer from hearing or receiving price information; for example, the consumer could receive the information as a result of reporting by newspapers or consumer guides.[121] The speaker and listener have separate, although normally overlapping, liberty claims and the constitutional analysis of the restriction must always focus on the claim of the party who is restricted.

This focus on each participant's liberty interest and on the values of self-fulfillment and participation in cultural change alters, and sometimes simplifies, the analysis of some traditional first amendment issues. As noted earlier, the marketplace theories do not provide a convincing justification for protecting obscenity. Pornography has more to do with ribald entertainment than with robust debate. Nevertheless, pornographic communications, or even pornographic materials produced and pursued by a solitary individual, contribute to building the culture. Materials that most people view as pornographic, as Douglas pointed out, play an important role in some people's self-fulfillment and self-expression. Thus, even if obscene publications do not contribute to the marketplace of ideas, they promote these key first amendment values. Therefore, the first amendment should protect the listener's or reader's interest in obscenity.[122]

Complicated problems remain. However, the general approach to determining what and why speech is protected should be clear. And, one should find several striking differences in the practical applications of this "liberty" theory, as contrasted to the "marketplace of ideas" theories. Speech is protected because,

---

involved in obtaining the information, not its latter use. *See* Nebraska Press Ass'n v. Stuart, 427 U.S. at 598 (Brennan, Stewart & Marshall, JJ., concurring) (concluding that an injunction restraining publication would not be justified no matter how the information was obtained).

121. Virginia State Bd. of Pharmacy v. Virginia Citizens Consumer Council, Inc., 425 U.S. at 781-82 (Rehnquist, J., dissenting).

122. In Stanley v. Georgia, 394 U.S. 557 (1969), the Court apparently recognized the importance of the liberty interest of the reader. *Cf.* L. Tribe, *supra* note 89, at 676-77 (interpreting *American Mini Theatres* as involving only the lesser right of the listener if the commercial speaker had no personal first amendment claim). *But see* United States v. 12 200-Foot Reels of Film, 413 U.S. 123 (1973). As I have noted elsewhere, it may be difficult to determine whether the commercial publisher and distributor, the more typical defendant in an obscenity prosecution, manifests a liberty interest or a market-enforced profit motive. However, the first amendment protects one particular industry—the press—from regulations relating to its product on a fourth estate theory and on the basis of the conclusion that generally its product, print or speech, contributes importantly to its recipients' liberty while not itself being coercively or violently destructive. (Speech can, of course, destroy, but it destroys through the listener's choices respecting and responding to the message.) *Commercial Speech*, *supra* note 5, at 30-32. Thus, the liberty interest of the reader and the special constitutional status of the press combine to protect both parties in the distribution or communication of obscenity.

without disrespecting the autonomy of other persons, it promotes both the speaker's self-fulfillment and the speaker's ability to participate in change. This leads to the conclusion that, "[a]s long as speech represents the freely-chosen expression of the speaker while depending for its power on the free acceptance of the listener," and is not used in the context of a violent or coercive activity, "freedom of speech represents a charter of liberty for noncoercive action."[123] Now, I consider when the first amendment protects nonverbal actions.

IV. PROTECTION OF ACTION

If one concludes that the first amendment does not protect all speech, the literalist argument that all speech and *only* speech is protected loses force. Nevertheless, no accepted criteria exist to evaluate claims of first amendment protection for nonverbal conduct. I think, however, that a persuasive argument for protection of a particular type of conduct could be made by showing that: 1) the experience conduct furthers key first amendment values; 2) protection of this type of conduct is essential for an adequate realization of these values; 3) this conduct and protected verbal conduct promote first amendment values in a relevantly similar manner, and 4) principled lines can identify which conduct should be protected in what ways. My discussion will attempt to meet these four requirements.

A.   *The Inadequate Expression-Action Dichotomy*

Professor Emerson's approach to delineating the scope of protection relies on a fundamental distinction between "expression" and "action,"[124] a categorization which "must be guided by consideration of whether the conduct partakes of the essential qualities of expression or action, that is, whether expression or action is the dominant element."[125] Emerson explains how to make a determination of essential qualities: "The concept of expression *must be* related to the fundamental purposes of the system [of freedom of expression] and the dynamics of its operation."[126] If protection of such "expression" meets the four criteria I have suggested, and if "expression" can be successfully identified, my inquiry can come to an end.

---

123. *Commercial Speech, supra* note 5, at 7 (emphasis deleted).
124. This distinction between "expression" and "action" provides "the central idea . . . of freedom of expression;" that system "cannot exist effectively on any other foundation, and a decision to maintain such a system necessarily implies acceptance of this proposition." FREEDOM OF EXPRESSION, *supra* note 85, at 17.
125. *Id.* at 18.
126. *Id.* (emphasis added).

Unfortunately, neither identifying protected "expression" by determining the conduct's contribution to the purposes of the system nor by using common sense to distinguish between expression and action works. Clearly, the four central values of the first amendment found by Emerson, or the two key ones, self-fulfillment and participation in change, can be, and frequently are, furthered by many types of conduct—including violent, coercive action or other conduct generally thought properly subject to collective control. Thus, in themselves, these values cannot define or delineate spheres of protected expression and unprotected action.

The common sense distinction, relying on the essential qualities of expression and action, operates less to divide the world of behavior than to indicate the perspective of the person doing the dividing. If the distinction is between "expressing" and "doing," most conduct falls into both categories. Most consciously undertaken *actions* are at least self-expressive; and many—a political assassination, a hairstyle, a knife placed behind another's back—can be primarily intended to communicate something to others. Contrarily, people routinely use verbal conduct to do something—to write a poem, to command the troops, to test the student, to create a mood, to threaten an enemy, to make a promise.[127] In considering behavior, an observer can choose to focus on either what is done (other than expressing) or what is expressed. The choice of focus will be subjective: Either culture or personal idiosyncrasy, but not logical analysis, will determine the choice.[128] One might "give comfort" to a friend or to an enemy (of the state). If expression, but not action, is constitutionally protected, the determination of which element dominates in acts that "give comfort to an enemy" will likely depend on whether one believes the acts should be protected, not on the essential nature of the acts.

Not only does neither technique of distinguishing expression and action work, but since both verbal and nonverbal conduct advances first amendment values, the purpose of the distinction is unclear. Moreover, only an extremely crabbed reading of other clauses of the first amendment will be consistent with implementing an expression-action dichotomy. If religion plays a significant role in one's life, its *free exercise* normally will require doing or

---

127. *See* J. AUSTIN, HOW TO DO THINGS WITH WORDS (1962).

128. Or the choice might be "logical" if logic is seen as conventional. *See* C. MILLS, *supra* note 47, at 427-29. Mills quotes Ernest Nagel who said "the principles of logic are . . . conventional without being arbitrary . . . ." Mills then suggests that "laws of proof may be merely the conventional abstract rules governing what are accepted as valid conversational extensions." *Id.* at 428. In a separate essay Mills argues that "motives are the terms with which interpretation of conduct *by social actors* proceeds." *Id.* at 440 (emphasis original). Presumably, whether the motive was to do something or was to express something depends on the social context and on the needs of the interpreter.

abstaining from certain conduct. And people typically assemble and associate to multiply their power in order to do something.[129] Nevertheless, even if his "expression-action" dichotomy is not very helpful, Emerson consistently makes very perceptive analyses of concrete situations; and these analyses frequently appear to make a different distinction: whether or not the conduct is, or is intended to be, coercive or physically injurious to another. All Emerson's examples of unprotected conduct, "action," involve coercion or injury to or physical interference with another or damage to physical property. These acts cause harm in a manner quite different from the way protected conduct causes harm. In the case of protected conduct, the supposed harm results from the assimilation of messages by an independent agent, the listener, and from the acts of that independent agent.

In the case of meetings and assemblies, Emerson says:

> [A]ll nonverbal [as well as verbal] conduct that is an integral part of assembly would normally be considered "expression" . . . . On the other hand, the use of physical force or violence, against person or property, would be considered "action" . . . . Disruption of a meeting by moving about or making noise must also be counted as "action."[130]

This example illustrates that both speaking (if one includes chanting and yelling) and active conduct can be either "expression" or "action." The nonverbal conduct that Emerson would protect may well consist of doing things. The unprotected disruption of the meeting may further some people's self-fulfillment or may promote change. Neither the abstract character of the behavior nor the key first amendment values guide Emerson's categorization. Apparently, the essential distinction is solely that "action" involves coercive or physically interfering conduct.

Expressive political protests sometimes involve acts of physical obstruction like lying down in front of troop trains, blocking traffic in a city, or pouring blood over files. Emerson argues that these must be considered "action" and that to characterize them as "expression" would destroy the distinction between "expression" and "action."[131] Neither the physical activity nor the motives of the actor distinguish these "action" cases from draft card burning, which Emerson characterizes as expression. Rather, Emerson clas-

---

129. The size of a demonstration hardly affects the logic of a demonstrator's views. Rather, the existence and size of the assembly are important because they suggest the power and willingness of people to promote the position. Likewise, consider the way a group boycott both expresses ideas and exercises power. *See Commercial Speech, supra* note 5, at 54-56.

130. FREEDOM OF EXPRESSION, *supra* note 85, at 293.

131. *Id.* at 89.

sifies the first examples of civil disobedience "action" because the "[c]ivil disobedience attempts to achieve results through a kind of *coercion or pressure. . . .*"[132] However, burning a draft card, unlike failing to carry a draft card,[133] does not involve coercing or directly injuring or physically obstructing any person or government activity. This fact apparently explains why Emerson concludes that the expression element clearly predominates in draft card burning.[134]

Emerson finds "a fundamental difference between most labor picketing and most nonlabor picketing."[135] He points out that the "labor picket line is . . . not so much a rational appeal to persuasion as a signal for the application of immediate and enormous economic leverage, based upon an already prepared position."[136] Labor and nonlabor picketing may involve the same physical acts, but the context is dramatically different. Typically, nonlabor picketing is "directed much more to the general public than to their own members" and "is a call to reason, not the application of *economic coercion*, and as such must be classified as expression."[137] Although these distinctions deserve more careful analysis, clearly Emerson's approach is to determine whether and how the conduct is coercive. ("How" appears relevant. If nonlabor picketing changes the public's opinion, the public may bring pressure on someone to change her behavior. Even if the public pressure is very forceful, the first amendment clearly protects the speech and conduct that induces this public response.[138] This interpretation of Emerson's examples suggests a surprisingly broad scope of protection. Emerson's examples indicate that the relevant question is *how the conduct advances the key first amendment values*; the conduct that advances the actor's values should be protected unless it is "coercive" or physically injurious or intended to be improperly obstructionist. But a principled description of this distinction between protected and unprotected conduct must be developed.

---

132. *Id.* (emphasis added). Of course, those using coercion or pressure may believe that their acts will induce change by causing people to change their opinions; in fact, they may only want to stimulate discussion, *e.g.*, "raise consciousness," in these "action" cases.

133. Failing to carry a draft card presumably "interferes" or "obstructs" the working of the selective service system and apparently is classified as an "action" by Emerson. *Id.* at 86-87.

134. *Id.* at 84.

135. *Id.* at 445. This difference does not rely on Emerson's exclusion of commercial activities from the scope of the system of freedom of expression. *Id.* at 19-20, 447.

136. *Id.* at 445.

137. *Id.* (emphasis added).

138. *See* Organization for a Better Austin v. Keefe, 402 U.S. 415 (1971).

B.   *Interference with the Rights of Others*

The logic of Emerson's examples suggests John Stuart Mill's conclusions concerning liberty in general (as opposed to Mill's special defense of freedom of speech). Mill argued:

> [T]he sole end for which mankind are warranted, individually or collectively, in interfering with the liberty of action of any of their number is self-protection . . . . [T]he only purpose for which power can be rightfully exercised over any member of a civilized community, against his will, is to prevent *harm to others* . . . . The only part of the conduct of anyone for which he is amenable to society is that which *concerns others*.[139]

Unfortunately, the lack of criteria for determining when a person's behavior "harms" others or when a person's manner of acting "concerns others" prevents Mill's formulation from indicating when liberty should be protected. If "feeling harmed" or having one's interactions with others unfavorably "affected" count as criteria for "harm" or for being properly "concerned," then any action, no matter how privately undertaken, can be of concern to others, can harm others. Given that both one's public and private activities influence, develop, or "change" one's personality or capacities or inclinations, and since one's personality and capacities affect one's interactions with others, both one's private and public activities may cause frustration of others' desires (*i.e.*, may "harm" them). Even one's private yoga exercises or obscenity readings contribute to the culture and affect interpersonal relations in ways that may lessen some people's opportunities to realize their desires. Thus, harm to others can not be our touchstone. In order to preserve any area of liberty one must show that either certain harms or certain ways of causing harms cannot justify certain restrictions on liberty.

Just as neither law nor custom adequately defined the benchmark from which coercive threats could be identified, they do not provide an adequate guide to distinguish "improperly harming" from "permissibly offending" another. Law and convention are inadequate guides precisely because they provide no critical principle, sought by both Mill and Emerson, that can indicate limits on the proper use of law and can delineate a proper realm of protected liberty. In order to construct such a critical principle, two distinctions need development.[140]

Rules can directly prevent a person from fulfilling her desires in either of two ways.[141] First, some rules restrict a person's liberty

---

139. ON LIBERTY, *supra* note 1, at 13 (emphasis added).

140. This and the following paragraphs are based on Baker, note 51 *supra*.

141. The distinction in the text refers to how rules limit a person's authority to make a decision. In addition, the content of the rules will affect and reflect people's values; and by changing the costs and benefits of different activities, the rules will

by giving to another the opportunity or decision authority one wants for oneself. I will call these *allocation rules*. Second, other rules deny a certain decision authority or opportunity to all people. I will call these rules *general prohibitions*.

The liberty value embodied in the first amendment places few restrictions on the state's power to choose among allocation rules: The state can decide to give property or opportunities to one person rather than another and can determine the content of property, tort, or contract rules. The two main first amendment constraints on state choice of allocation rules are: 1) the state only rarely and in limited circumstances can give one person an original right to decide what another person must do or say or not say;[142] 2) sometimes the state may be obliged to respect some neutrality criteria[143] or guarantee some minimum level of opportunity

---

encourage or discourage different forms of social relations. Any evaluation of specific rules or systems of rules should consider these effects. However, these effects of the content of rules are not important for the present analysis.

142. *Cf.* New York Times v. Sullivan, 376 U.S. 254 (1964) (invalidating state libel law that gave a person authority to control—or sanction—certain speech of others). Constitutional requirements in various clauses, including the first amendment, the due process clause and the involuntary servitude clause, may limit the way government can allocate decision-making authority concerning a person's body. The government cannot give another, *e.g.*, a husband or parent, the right to prohibit or require a woman to have an abortion. *See* Planned Parenthood of Cent. Mo. v. Danforth, 428 U.S. 52 (1976). Possibly more is required. The concept of a person as someone whose dignity, integrity, and autonomy are respected generally requires that the person have decision authority over the purposes for which his or her body is used. One arguably has a right not to be required to use one's body over a long period of time to aid and support another, even though it is readily conceded that one may be required to forego claims to physical or economic resources needed to benefit another. This conclusion, of course, supports the second of two arguments commonly invoked to support the claimed right not to be prohibited from having an abortion. The two arguments are: 1) A fetus is not a person, an issue which has no clear resolution; and 2) one cannot be forced involuntarily to use one's body to support the existence of another. *See* Thompson, *A Defense of Abortion*, 1 PHILOSOPHY & PUB. AFF. 47 (1971).

143. Time, place, and manner regulations become obvious cases of prohibited censorship when they are not neutral in respect to content. *See, e.g.*, Police Dep't v. Mosley, 408 U.S. 92 (1972). However, the issue is more complicated if the regulation, neutral on its face and applied according to its terms, will necessarily limit some groups or some points of view more than others. *See, e.g.*, Kovacs v. Cooper, 336 U.S. 77, 102-03 (1949) (Black, Douglas & Rutledge, JJ., dissenting) (total ban on sound truck disadvantages poor and favors the views of those who own the dominant forms of media communication). In such cases of "facially neutral" regulation of time, place, and manner, "[w]hen a statute deals with conduct containing elements of both expression and action, the First Amendment issue turns in part upon the question whether the legislation is directed at the expression or action . . . ." FREEDOM OF EXPRESSION, *supra* note 85, at 85 (objecting to the Court's failure to do this in *O'Brien*). Invalidation only on evidence of a conscious desire to limit the expression of certain viewpoints provides insufficient protection if the first amendment requires the government to be careful not to restrict people's freedom of speech. This broader requirement explains the relevance of least restrictive means tests in the area of time, place, and manner regulations. The argument is that the failure to adopt a reasonable, but less restrictive, regulation is objective evidence of a purpose to ignore the first amendment mandate that the government be concerned with people's freedom of

in making allocations that promote private parties' opportunity or ability to express themselves. (Note, however, that the guarantee of some minimum level of opportunity, like most constraints placed on the state's choice among allocation rules, may be best derived from the fourteenth amendment notion that the state must treat and respect people as equals.[144])

General prohibitions do not allocate decision-making authority but deny authority to all individuals as individuals. General prohibitions say: "No one (or everyone) shall do X"—*e.g.*, read pornography, pollute the air, commit suicide, fix prices, create a fire hazard. A rule relating to intentional taking of life is an allocation rule if one can give another permission to take one's life but is a general prohibition if one cannot give another such permission. Forbidding theft is an allocation rule to the extent that the owner can permit the action by making a gift of the taken object.

Allocation rules either allow one to undertake the act or, to the extent that the activity involves another person or resources allocated to another, allocation rules allow one to undertake the act if one receives cooperation or authorization from another. Allocation rules can grant decision-making authority on numerous bases: to the person strong enough to undertake the act, on a first-come-first-serve basis, to the person with the greatest need, or as an exclusive right to make a large set of decisions relating to some object. Two people cannot simultaneously engage in mutually exclusive uses of space or objects. This natural possibility of conflict—a problem that is engendered by the inherent limit on available resources (scarcity)—creates the necessity of allocation rules or practices to determine where authority resides; *formally*, such allocation rules involve the *minimum possible limit* on individual liberty.[145]

---

speech. On this reasoning, *Kovacs*, which involved a complete ban on sound trucks, was decided incorrectly.

144. *But cf.* Karst, *Equality as a Central Principle in the First Amendment*, 43 U. CHI. L. REV. 20 (1975) (finding equality as a central value of the first amendment).

145. Since allocation of authority seems a logically necessary limit on individual liberty, I conclude that such allocation rules are *formally* the minimum limit on liberty. Put differently, allocation rules are a necessary part of the framework in which liberty can exist. If one had criteria or theory to distinguish the "amount of liberty" which possession of a specific decision-making authority gives different people, then different arrangements of allocation rules would provide different amounts of limits on liberty. For example, does control of a dollar's worth of food give a different amount of "liberty" to different people? Note, "liberty" here means relevant opportunity for self-realization, for self-determination, or for participation in group determination. This suggests liberty is a substantive matter—*i.e.*, liberty involves a person's opportunity to do or develop in the way she desires or in the way that most fully manifests or develops her potential. (Compare the popular distinction between positive and negative liberty.) Possibly, a specific combination of allocation rules and general prohibitions would be more successful in allowing everyone (or most people) to do or develop than would be possible with only allocation rules. I will argue that *sometimes* such a combination of allocation rules and general prohibitions, *e.g.*, of

1016   *UCLA LAW REVIEW*   [Vol. 25:964

General prohibitions restrict liberty in a different and frequently more objectionable manner than do allocation rules. By
excluding everyone from making certain decisions, they limit individual choice more than do allocation rules. General prohibitions let the majority directly control minorities; in contrast,
allocation rules allow both the majority and minority to use their
resources in ways they desire. Allocation rules define the context
for both egotistic projects and interpersonal cooperation while
general prohibitions unnecessarily restrict individual and cooperative initiatives. General prohibitions that prevent people from engaging in substantively valued behavior unnecessarily restrict
people's opportunity to engage in fulfilling activities. Moreover,
by completely denying the opportunity to engage in certain activities in which new logics or perspectives or values could gain coherence, general prohibitions drastically limit the possibility of
popular participation in change. For these reasons, I will conclude
that many general prohibitions violate the first amendment. To
reach this conclusion, I must first distinguish between two ways of
valuing behavior. Then, I will describe the first amendment restriction on the use of general prohibitions and defend this limit
against various objections, particularly "efficiency" or utility maximization arguments. Finally, I will note how this conclusion clarifies the structure of traditional first amendment arguments.[146]

An actor may or may not positively value a specific aspect of
her behavior that others find offensive. Presumably, the person
who chooses to read pornography, unless she happens to be a
Supreme Court Justice,[147] values this "polluting" activity. (The
term "polluting" will be used to refer to any activity that others
find offensive and that they would prefer to exclude from the

---

instrumentally valued behaviors, will be justified as proper means of promoting substantive liberty. *See* text accompanying notes 148-55 *infra.*

146. Note that rules governing transfer of rights, or rules prohibiting alienation,
are allocation rules in that they merely determine who has the decision-making authority. In discussing the notion of an "inalienable right of life," Professor Feinberg
apparently prefers the interpretation of the right that he attributes to our "founding
fathers." In effect, Feinberg suggests the inalienable right to life means that one cannot transfer the right to decide to take one's life to another, rather than that there is a
"general prohibition" on ending one's own life. Life is alienable but the right to life is
not. This rejection of the general prohibition mirrors the conclusions of this paper.
However, Feinberg does not determine whether the right to decide to take one's life
should be inalienable or non-transferable, that is, he does not decide what allocation
rule is best. Feinberg, *Voluntary Euthanasia and the Inalienable Right to Life,* 7 PHI-
LOSOPHY & PUB. AFF. 93 (1978). Although this alienation (transferability) question
should be analyzed in terms of what best indicates a respect for the autonomy and
integrity, of humans, in general, as Shelley v. Kraemer, 334 U.S. 1 (1948) graphically
illustrates, alienation rules raise allocation issues that involve both equality and liberty values.

147. "I can imagine no more distasteful, useless, and time-consuming task
. . . ." United States v. Thirty-Seven Photographs, 402 U.S. 363, 380 (1971) (Black &
Douglas, JJ., dissenting).

community.) Contrarily, owners of a steel plant or of an automobile that emits exhaust pollutants normally do not value polluting the air per se. Polluting the air is an undesired consequence, a subsidiary result, of their preferred behavior.

These two examples, pornography and air pollution, illustrate how the polluter can value a polluting activity either *substantively* or *instrumentally*. Since prohibiting the activity forecloses the possibility of anyone undertaking it, if the activity is substantively valued, the prohibition wholly prevents a specific form of self-fulfillment or self-realization. Contrarily, if the polluting activity is only instrumentally valued, prohibiting the pollution operates the same as an allocation rule. That is, the prohibition may affect an individual's wealth or the cost of a desired form of fulfillment, but the prohibition does not prevent one who has sufficient resources (or has the assistance of others who have rights to the needed resources) from undertaking the desired activity.

I am using "instrumentally" in a broader sense than seemed necessary in an earlier article, *Counting Preferences in Collective Choice Situations.*[148] Here, I use "instrumental" to refer to the value of distinguishable aspects of one's behavior as a means, even if this means for achieving one's aims is unrelated to the reaction of others. The auto owner can distinguish emitting pollutants and driving the car. Obviously, the aspects of the behavior that will be "distinguished" is culturally relative, dependent on how people perceive their world. In most cases, except where the actor substantively values publicity, acting in a manner that others can or will observe (*e.g.*, advocacy oriented speech), the aspects of the behavior that the actor substantively values will be distinct from the pollution aspects, but *despite* being distinguishable, if the only feasible way to engage in the substantively valued behavior is to engage also in the "polluting" behavior, a prohibition on the instrumentally valued aspects (the polluting aspects) may amount to a general prohibition on the substantively valued behavior. I tentatively conclude that in this situation equal respect for the autonomy and integrity of each individual permits the community to charge the "polluting" actor the cost (the negative value) of the pollution except that the community must not count as a cost the negatively valued aspects that the actor substantively values.

This principle will be difficult to apply in concrete contexts and will inevitably be reduced to various rule-of-thumb approximations. Sometimes, however, the application of the principle will be simple. In the context of sexual behavior between consenting adults, there will be few "pollutants" other than those aspects of the behavior that the participants specifically value; hence, neither

---

148. Baker, *supra* note 51, at 393-96.

general prohibitions nor charges are permitted. In the auto pollution situation, the rule of thumb must be that few people substantively value air pollutants. Then, if other feasible technologies exist, prohibiting the pollution only increases the "cost" of driving—an instrumental burden typical of many imposed by allocation rules. If no feasible alternative exists (the cost is infinity), the cost of these nonsubstantively valued, polluting aspects of the behavior can be charged to the auto owner. However, the substantively valued aspects cannot be viewed as a cost because that would violate the required respect for the individual chooser's autonomy.[149] A further example may help illustrate the importance of the substantive, instrumental distinction.

A rule prohibiting certain types of families from living together would prevent these families from realizing the substantive value they find in this family life.[150] In contrast, requirements that housing have a certain floor space per occupant, have adequate parking area, adequate fire protection services, etc., usually only impose added costs, impose instrumental burdens, on realizing substantive values relating to living arrangements.[151] Of course, even if this distinction between prohibiting realization of substantive values and imposing instrumental burdens is clear, its application may be difficult. Although a large group (a fraternity, a retirement community, etc.) may substantively value living together, their desire normally does not require living together at a particular place. And a geographic division of areas that only allows fraternities in certain areas might increase total community satisfaction while, at worst, only making it somewhat more expensive for particular groups to realize their values.[152] In this case, *assuming* housing opportunities for all groups are actually made available by the jurisdiction responsible for zoning, geographic limits on living arrangements would only instrumentally burden individuals—unless people not only substantively valued living together but also substantively valued living in a particular house

---

149. *See id.*
150. *See* Moore v. City of East Cleveland, 431 U.S. 494 (1977) (invalidating a zoning ordinance which prohibited such living arrangements). *But cf.* Village of Belle Terre v. Boraas, 416 U.S. 1 (1974) (upholding zoning ordinance prohibiting certain types of living arrangements).
151. Village of Euclid v. Ambler Realty Co., 272 U.S. 365 (1926).
152. *See* Mishan, *Pareto Optimality and the Law,* 19 OXFORD ECON. PAP. 255 (1967). *See also* Young v. American Mini Theatres, 427 U.S. 50 (1976) (upholding zoning ordinance regulating location of "adult" theatres). In *American Mini Theatres,* the regulation did not thwart or even greatly burden people in fulfilling their substantive desire to see adult films. *Id.* at 71-72 n.35. The case can be read to say that content restrictions in time, place, and manner regulations may be permissible *if* they do not limit the realization of the substantively valued aspects of the restricted activity. Thus, such a content based restriction would never justify limiting advocacy or propaganda but are proper in *American Mini Theatres.*

or community or type of community, *e.g.*, an integrated community. If they substantively valued the specific location, the geo-
graphical exclusion would thwart the group's substantive
values.[153] (Concern for such substantive values could provide ,a
partial explanation for pre-existing use exemptions or for prohibitions on legally enforced racial segregation.[154]) No matter how
one resolves these complexities, the distinction should be clear:
The implications of a general prohibition differ when it relates to
a substantively, as opposed to instrumentally, valued aspect of
one's behavior.

I conclude that if a general prohibition limits instrumentally
valued behavior, it operates like an allocation rule permissibly
used to implement the community's substantive and distributional
objectives. Also, if a few people, by engaging in a substantively
valued polluting activity, could nullify the consequences of the
choice of many people not to engage in such an activity, a general
prohibition may be appropriate as a means to prevent domination.[155] Generally, however, *when a general prohibition applies to
substantively valued behavior, it is an unconstitutional abridgement
of freedom of speech or expression.* This conclusion is based on the
following two observations: 1) substantively valued conduct is inherently expressive and clearly contributes to the two key first
amendment values of self-fulfillment and participation in change;
2) general prohibitions forbid behavior that promotes first amendment values in the same manner as protected speech—*i.e.*, in a
noncoercive manner. In fact, the evils of general prohibitions and
coerceive acts correspond. Like coercive acts, imposition of general prohibitions enables those who favor the rule to make use of
others (if the rule requires specified conduct) or to avoid the
bother of others (if it forbids specified activities) and, thereby, to
treat others as means. General prohibitions also unnecessarily restrict individual liberty, and thereby, like coercive acts, disrespect
individual autonomy. In contrast to the corresponding evils of co-

---

153. On this analysis, nudity could normally be prohibited in most public areas
on the assumption that the substantive expressive value of nudity does not require
exposure to those who find public nudity offensive. However, when nudity is a form
of expression, intended to confront the public and communicate a message, the argument for banning nudity from the public arena is weak. *But see* L. TRIBE, *supra* note
89, at 680-81 (1978).

154. When substantive values of two groups are involved, normally the proper
solution is to maximize realization of substantive values in choosing allocation rules.
But, as will be further argued below, promoting welfare maximization normally
would not justify general prohibitions, which would be required if one were to favor
those wanting over those opposing separation (segregation). Moreover, if maximizing
realization of substantive values involves the state distinguishing between people on
the basis of their inherent qualities and, then, limiting their liberty on this basis, the
state's rule may violate the constitutional requirement that the state treat people as
equals. *See* Baker, note 51 *supra*.

155. *See* Baker, note 51 *supra* (the determinative-additive distinction).

ercion and general prohibitions is the way that the notions of coercion and allocation rules intertwine. By defining and then forbidding invasions of a person's realm of decision-making authority, allocation rules provide the necessary context in which an act can be coercive; indeed, allocation rules are required by the grammer of coercion.

Like unconstitutional restrictions on verbal conduct, general prohibitions restrict expressive conduct that operates noncoercively to advance self-fulfillment and popular participation in change. But before accepting the conclusion that general prohibitions of substantively valued conduct are unconstitutional abridgements of first amendment rights, one must be convinced that the justifications typically offered for general prohibitions are unpersuasive—an issue to which I now turn.

Justifications for general prohibitions normally take one of three forms. General prohibitions are valuable because they: 1) define and help form a community; 2) result from a valuable group process of choice; 3) promote efficiency or welfare maximization. Although the first two are sometimes collapsed into the efficiency argument, they merit special attention because neither focuses on the *results* furthered by general prohibitions (results being the typical focus of efficiency arguments), but instead argue that people substantively value either the general prohibitions themselves or the process of generating them.

General prohibitions (or general requirements) sometimes help form or define a community valued by its members. A religious community may partially define itself by rules that prohibit smoking, drinking, working on certain days, or fighting in unjust wars or by rules that require praying or wearing certain clothes. A political association may require that all members do or believe certain things. The mores of a community may obligate a person to love one's brother or sister, or parents, or spouse, or neighbor. Moreover, the nature of the relationships among members of a particular community or family may be incompatible with even the most direct beneficiary of certain obligations having authority either to demand or to excuse compliance. One may be obligated to help or love one's sister even in times when she tells you that you need not do so. Or one may have a duty to follow the association's political line without anyone having the authority to excuse you. In other words, sometimes the obligations defining a family or voluntary association take the form of general prohibitions or requirements rather than allocation rules.

The clear importance of these definitions of community and of relationships must be recognized. Nevertheless, their value as well as legitimacy may relate to their origin in individuals' *voluntarily* adopted practices or *voluntarily* chosen allegiance to the group defined by these rules. By contrast, state-enforced obedience to rules that are valued precisely because of how they define both individuals and the community involve the state in attempting partially to define who a person is; such a practice clearly indicates disrespect for individual autonomy.[156] Since these self-defining obligations can and often do exist within the voluntary practices of people, state enforcement with the consequent disrespect for people's autonomy requires a justification beyond the mere observation that most people value these rules. The justification could be that state enforcement promotes efficiency, *i.e.*, that enforcement satisfies more desires, either due to a marginal reduction of deviation from the popularly favored practices or due to the symbol of state enforcement, than it thwarts. This efficiency argument will be evaluated below.[157]

Second, people may value the group process of formulating rules. Positive value may inhere in the process of identifying and understanding issues, in resolving or compromising conflicts, and, finally, in expressing group unity through group decisions. Moreover, the group process may improve the quality of the resulting decisions. However, the obvious importance of these process values does not provide an unambiguous justification for government decision making in respect to general prohibitions. Group decision making concerning general prohibitions or requirements, such as what books shall be read, may be a valuable exercise for a study group but not for a state. Only in the case of voluntary groups or relationships is the process a *noncoercive* method of individual or group self-definition. Social pluralism may require the existence of opportunities for voluntary associations to create general prohibitions or requirements;[158] but this pluralism could be coercively destroyed if the state could create general prohibitions or requirements.[159] And, of course, the principle of disallowing majority-imposed general prohibitions that outlaw some people's self-defining activities does not interfere with realizing whatever process value exists in the activity of choosing allocation rules and public programs, both of which involve the community determining what type of community will exist. Nevertheless, some positive process value may exist in community decision making concern-

---

156. *See, e.g.*, Wooley v. Maynard, 430 U.S. 705 (1977); Wisconsin v. Yoder, 406 U.S. 205 (1972); West Virginia State Bd. of Educ. v. Barnette, 319 U.S. 624 (1943).
157. *See* text accompanying notes 160-166 *infra*.
158. *See* Part V *infra*.
159. *See, e.g.*, Wisconsin v. Yoder, 406 U.S. 205 (1972). This case illustrates both the importance for social pluralism of the ability of voluntary groups to create general prohibitions or requirements and the possibility of the government using such prohibitions or requirements to destroy pluralism.

ing general prohibitions, and this value would contribute to utilitarian arguments for allowing such rules. Thus, these utilitarian or efficiency arguments must now be considered.

The efficiency argument notes that people who substantively desire to act in a manner others find offensive often would agree to abandon the offensive behavior and accept a restraint on their liberty if paid an amount that those offended would be willing to pay. For example, those opposed to air or pornographic pollution might be willing to pay the polluters an amount that the polluters would be willing to accept for ceasing their pollution. However, difficulties and expenses in negotiating and carrying out the transactions prevent them from occurring. In this situation, a general prohibition, although burdening some, may increase the general level of preference satisfaction, *i.e.*, may correct for the market failure and be efficient.

Three responses persuasively undermine the efficiency justification for general prohibitions. First, the dangers (or inefficiencies) of the predictable abuse by the majority of a power to adopt general prohibitions may significantly outweigh any efficiency gains that result from their use. An additional cost, the dissatisfaction generated among those who believe, and often *properly* believe, that the majority is imposing its values and increasing its own well-being by improperly restricting the liberty of minorities, reinforces this rule utilitarian conclusion.[160] Of course, this argument loses force if those who are restricted are adequately compensated (an unlikely event in the case of most general prohibitions). Also, this argument would not apply if those restricted favor the restriction and had engaged in the restricted conduct only in order to maximize their situation given their assumption that others would also engage in the behavior (that is, if the general prohibition is designed to avoid the typical prisoner's dilemma problem). Moreover, this rule utilitarian argument may only require care and circumspection in adopting general prohibitions.[161] Hence, this rule utilitarian analysis provides only weak support for a comprehensive constitutional ban on general prohibitions of substantively valued conduct; instead, because it

---

160. The arguments in this paragraph closely parallel some developed in Michelman, *Property, Utility and Fairness: Comment on the Ethical Foundations of "Just Compensation" Law*, 80 HARV. L. REV. 1165 (1967). The "takings" Michelman discussed primarily involved *resource allocations*, not liberty of action. And according to the analysis here, resource allocations are more legitimately subject to revision by majority decision.

161. Note that this rule utilitarian argument could be leveled against general prohibitions of both substantively and instrumentally valued behavior, although both abuses of the power and dissatisfaction caused by the abuses may be greater in respect to restrictions on substantively valued behavior. Carried to an extreme, this rule utilitarian argument could be applied to most cases of government decision making. *See* J. BUCHANAN, THE LIMITS OF LIBERTY (1975).

does not reject but only reinterprets the efficiency approach, it seems to suggest that balancing is appropriate in constitutional analysis.

Second, efficiency does not justify general prohibitions if such prohibitions violate people's rights.[162] To avoid circularity, however, one must establish that general prohibitions do violate rights; and, here, I can only sketch the argument for that view. A number of considerations provide at least a minimal argument. First, unlike allocation rules which necessarily exist and merely influence people's values and their opportunities to pursue their values, state-enforced general prohibitions of substantively valued behavior entirely prevent some people from acting in accord with their values. Second, unlike allocation rules, general prohibitions are adopted precisely in order to prevent people from living by those values. If, as argued earlier, state action must respect individual autonomy, general prohibitions of substantively valued behavior are objectionable because they violate this required respect. The majority employ general prohibitions to control and determine who other people can be. Third, these general prohibitions thwart people's self-expression and people's personal and social creativity; they directly impinge on realizing these two central values of the first amendment. Finally, although the distribution of wealth is not a central concern of the first amendment, freedom from general prohibitions provides a minimum guarantee of some "wealth" to each individual. If general prohibitions (or requirements) are permitted, except for the limitation inherent in the requirement that the rules be general in form, people could be stripped of virtually all wealth (*i.e.*, authority to make desired decisions about one's own or another's conduct) except for the value of one's political rights (*i.e.*, the right to participate in choosing general prohibitions); thus, permitting general prohibitions allows one's wealth to become even more dependent on whether one agrees with the majority.

Third, efficiency or welfare maximization may be a particularly incoherent justification for general prohibitions of substantively valued conduct. Certain activities that decrease the satisfaction of existing preferences may help create a better society where people will have "better" preferences than exist at present. Efficiency calculations must presuppose, but cannot justify, some particular, usually existing, tastes or desires as the ones to be satisfied.[163] Until some set of preferences is assumed, efficiency has no

---

162. *See* text accompanying notes 87-88 *supra*; R. DWORKIN, note 72 *supra*; *Economic Analysis, supra* note 5, at 32-41.

163. In fact, efficiency analysis must rely on both some assumed set of tastes and on some distribution of resources— and both assumptions bias the results of the calculations. *See* Baker, note 119 *supra*; *Economic Analysis*, note 5 *supra*; Tribe, *Tech-*

evaluative criteria. But if change is to be subject to human choice, if human self-determination is possible, then a central issue is determining what preferences are best. Thus, since efficiency analysis cannot justify its reliance on any set of preferences, it has no criteria with which to guide the choice. No intrinsic quality of *existing* tastes justifies their fulfillment always being the dominant concern. In fact, to paraphrase Mill's faith in people as progressive beings,[164] the merit of change must be evaluated not in terms of whether it fulfills existing tastes but in terms of whether it improves the type of people we are. And, as Professor Tribe has argued, the major choices facing us as a people are those that will determine who and what we will be.[165] If human integrity and responsibility require that people be free to decide (or participate in deciding) what or who they will be, then, when evaluating the process of change, it is a logical mistake to evaluate choices in terms of how well they satisfy existing preferences; rather, one must either evaluate change in terms of the legitimacy of the *process* or evaluate the political and ethical *content* of the change. This second type of evaluation corresponds to many people's practice of subjecting their attitudes and activities to ethical or political criticism. As for the legitimacy of the process, the irrelevance of an efficiency analysis that takes as given the key issue in dispute could explain why many intuitively conclude that the first amendment should (absolutely?) protect a process of change from limitations justified by mere utilitarian calculations (*i.e.*, balancing). This logical irrelevance of efficiency arguments for justifying general prohibitions should not be surprising if one accepts my earlier argument that the state is justified in adopting utility maximization as state policy only when necessary to carry out the state's obligation to treat all members as deserving equal respect as autonomous moral beings. Efficiency arguments must be irrelevant until the liberty rights of autonomous beings, particularly the right of self-determination, are assured protection.

One added argument suggests why general prohibitions are objectionable. The idea that we need, and sometimes have had, progressive change, suggests that the legal structuring of the process of change ought to protect those elements which could be progressive, and which, without protection, would be restricted. Identifying progressive elements is, of course, difficult. However, two factors indicate that barring general prohibitions of substantively valued conduct increases the chances of protecting progressive elements. Since a key aspect of general prohibitions is to

---

nology Assessment and the Fourth Discontinuity: The Limits of Instrumental Rationality, 46 SO. CAL. L. REV. 617, 635-41 (1973).
    164. ON LIBERTY, *supra* note 1, at 14.
    165. Tribe, *supra* note 163, at 640.

1978]   *FREEDOM OF SPEECH*   1025

suppress value realization that is contrary to majority or status quo values, one would expect popular support for precisely those general prohibitions that attempt to suppress those progressive practices which conflict with current regressive orientations. More important, our ethical and political judgments and concepts typically reflect presently shared values and logic. Theorists such as Robert Unger argue that the confidence we should have in our judgments depends on the extent to which these shared values are formed under circumstances of non-domination.[166] Since general prohibitions characteristically involve dominating minorities on the basis of current majority interests and values, they undermine the legitimacy of the very values they promote. Contrarily, by banning general prohibitions of substantively valued conduct, we decrease majority domination and increase the legitimacy of relying on the shared judgments that do exist. By allowing minorities to live their values even when the present majority finds the behavior offensive, society protects an important process for peaceful change of tastes and values while decreasing the conditions of domination.

These criticisms of efficiency justifications for general prohibitions complete the argument for barring the state from enforcing general prohibition of substantively valued expressive conduct. The above criticisms highlight many aspects of conventional first amendment analysis. Typical attempts to justify laws prohibiting specific expressive activity rely on: 1) predictions that the activity will lead to future violations of allocation rules—*e.g.*, the speech creates a clear and present danger to lawlessness, pornography leads to sex crimes; 2) predictions that the activity will affect the actors or observers in detrimental ways, thereby corrupting the cultural climate and negatively affecting friendships and interpersonal relations—*e.g.*, public sales or use of obscenity and public use of vulgar language undermines the desired moral tone of the community; 3) disapproval of the values or attitudes expressed by the activity—*e.g.*, flag burning, wearing long hair, draft card burning, representing unpatriotic attitudes.

Well developed defenses of free speech meet each claim. First, the classic objection to the bad tendency test for restricting speech is that the state can forbid the violation of the allocation rule but cannot prohibit the speech using a general prohibition. This objection parallels criminal law and due process notions which, except in exceptional circumstances, are offended by tak-

---

166. R. UNGER, *supra* note 42, at 242-45. "[T]he spiral of domination and community progresses through constant experiments in association. Unless emergent groups are free to develop and are not disadvantaged in relation to existing ones, there is the danger that a partial vision of the good will be petrified and the spiral arrested." *Id.* at 287.

ing away a person's liberty because of what a person might do in the future. Of course, like preventive detention, speech restrictions based on the bad tendency test may maximize preference satisfaction. The classic response relies on the same objections to efficiency as were developed above. It argues either that the bad tendency test will be abused or, like laws prohibiting obscenity or marijuana, cannot be effectively enforced and, thus, will not be efficient in practice; or more fundamentally, that speech restrictions based on the bad tendency test, even if efficient, violate individual rights that society must recognize.

Similarly, classic first amendment analyses reject the other two "efficiency" arguments for restricting people's noncoercive activities: Either the expressive activities will have a socially undesirable influence on people's personality and their behavior or the expression is itself offensive to the majority. These arguments are rejected on the ground that the majority must respect individuals' choices about their own values and not force them to falsify their values. This position is, of course, a straightforward application of the principle that the state must respect people's integrity and autonomy. Again, classic first amendment arguments repeat our objection to efficiency justifications for general prohibitions.

C. *The Market Place of Ideas Revisited*

One should not too quickly dismiss an analysis which has dominated informed opinion as completely as has the marketplace of ideas theory. I criticized the marketplace of ideas as a method of discovering truth or arriving at the "best" perceptions or values because its effectiveness for achieving these goals seemed dependent on several invalid assumptions. Here, my inquiry considers how protecting a broader range of expressive conduct, how forbidding general prohibitions of substantively valued conduct, blunts the criticism of the classic marketplace of ideas model. If interpreting the first amendment to include this broad protection of nonverbal conduct cures the defects of the marketplace theory, this fact would buttress the defense of this broad interpretation.

Protecting substantively valued conduct from abridgement by general prohibitions makes the hope that people will be able to make the "best" choices more plausible for at least four reasons. First, the classic model assumes that truth is discovered or found. To the extent that reality is created, the theory must be concerned with questions of who and how. Equality of opportunity to create reality provides a possible standard. However, since all conduct, not merely speech, contributes to this creation process, equality of opportunity would require a regime of *strict equality* of all resources *and skills*—a regime as unnecessary as it is inconceivable.

Lack of sufficient "wealth" is only one cause of the limits on people's opportunities. In addition, general prohibitions can be used by the majority to entirely suppress opportunities for certain choices. This use of majority power can be more oppressive, more totally limiting, and is usually less justified than are limits on opportunities due to inequality of resource distribution (at least, if the inequality is not too great or if a minimum level of opportunity is guaranteed). Clearly, barring state imposed prohibitions of substantively valued conduct greatly increases opportunities of minorities to develop new realities (this notion replaces objective truth). This broadened liberty eliminates a major method by which the choice process is often limited to prevent peaceful challenges to the existing orthodoxies. Thus, such a ban seems *necessary*, whether or not sufficient, to expand people's opportunities for creating new realities.

Second, the ban on general prohibitions makes the process of creating realities much more democratic. Many people may not have the resources, the skills, or the interest to participate in a rational or political search for the best societal decisions. Most people do have an interest in their own life and their relations with others; also, most have sufficient skill (and, in the liberty model, they also have the right) to pursue their own visions and values. Only by disallowing general prohibitions can everyone, by their choice of activities, participate in the debate and in building the culture.

Third, the liberty to live one's values provides for the possibility that at present, or always, pluralism best meets human needs and goals. Moreover, by allowing this pluralism, change can occur by people living, and finding others to join in living, a set of values. Thus, peaceful, gradual change will have space and opportunity to develop.

Fourth, protecting greater liberty of action breaches the status quo bias of the marketplace of ideas. Mass communications apparently are more effective in reinforcing the status quo than in stimulating criticism. Moreover, face-to-face verbal communication and existing forms of reason typically reflect people's experience of the existing order. Even if various economic or social groups experience the existing order from radically different perspectives and evaluate it differently, that existing order dominates people's logic and perceptions when considering alternatives. By discounting preferences of the majority for limiting conduct, the first amendment protects the possibility of developing new loci of experience which potentially can falsify the existing, dominant perspectives. Moreover, this method of change requires neither violence nor the approval of the dominant societal groups. Just as in the classic market model, the power of new perspectives depends on its voluntary acceptance by people; however, protection of new, nonverbal practices allows people to make a new perspective available in a form where its logic might be coherent, thereby overcoming the status quo bias of mere verbal debate.

This revised theory replaces both the doubtful assumptions of the classic marketplace of ideas theory and its hope for a basically rational discovery of timeless truth with a defense of the legitimacy of a social process of choice. The legitimacy must be defended on at least one of two grounds: Either all people have a right to participate in the individual and social processes of *self*-determination or a "better" individual and collective expression of humanity results from this social process because of the increased opportunity of each freely to participate. Either ground justifies protecting people's liberty to engage in substantively valued conduct. Moreover, both imply that eliminating or weakening existing structures of domination that influence or distort people's choices[167] improves the process of developing and expressing values. This concern with reducing domination was the one merit of the market failure version of first amendment theory. Unfortunately, that theory's focus on equality of *speech* opportunities—usually, equality of access to channels of mass communication—belies the fact that only general economic equality would suffice to validate the approach. Because of this theoretical confusion, the market failure theorists fail to realize that providing considerable equality of access to communication channels may be less central to dismantling the existing structures of domination than banning existing restrictions, general prohibitions, on liberty. This confusion illustrates the market failure theory's basic problem; it merges the concepts of equality and liberty which provide separate, although crucial, guidance for describing a just social order.

In addition to highlighting these mistakes of the market failure or equal access theory, the liberty approach avoids the problems which engulf that theory. The liberty model avoids offering the false hope that dissenting positions, even without a real basis in experience, can be shown to be best; instead, it provides for a more realistic method of change from "the bottom up." The liberty model, which protects noncoercive uses of speech and forbids enforcement of general prohibitions on substantively valued behavior, provides clearer, less subjective criteria for proper gov-

---

167. *Cf. Commercial Speech*, note 5 *supra* (where I argue that the market structure coerces or "dictates" the choice of speech messages by economic enterprises and, therefore, enterprise speech undermines the process of democratic decision making). Generally, a more thorough analysis of the influence of various power structures on people's expression is needed.

ernment action than the market failure model provides. Also, because it guarantees a realm of liberty rather than a properly functioning market, one can correct for perceived infringements of the guarantee by violating the "improper restriction" on liberty rather than taking the possibly violent action needed to get "proper results."

By protecting substantively valued conduct from abridgement by general prohibitions, the liberty model provides for a process of public decision making and a search for, or creation of, truth that avoids the problems and improper assumptions of both the market models. Thus, the liberty model better promotes the key value that justified the classic marketplace of ideas theory of freedom of speech: the value of furthering the search for truth or best premises, a value that, due to a failure of assumptions, the classic theory could not adequately serve. These observations provide convincing support for this liberty theory.

V. ASSEMBLY, ASSOCIATION, AND FREE EXERCISE OF RELIGION

The argument has been that the first amendment protection of freedom of speech should be interpreted to protect other expressive conduct that serves, in a similar manner, the same central purposes or functions as does verbal conduct. This method of interpretation, although it goes beyond one common reading of speech as referring only to verbal behavior, remains faithful to the constitutional text. Any textual interpretation requires a theory that explains why those particular words are used. The theory developed herein emphasizes that "speech" is chosen because it is a particularly good embodiment of a concern for expressive, nonviolent, noncoercive conduct that promotes self-realization and self-determination. This understanding of why the constitutional text uses the word "speech" guides the proper elaboration of what verbal and nonverbal conduct should be protected.

The other clauses of the first amendment, particularly the freedom to peaceably assemble and the right to the free exercise of religion, can be read either to bolster the broad liberty interpretation of speech or as alternative grounds for protecting this realm of liberty. One useful way of viewing these clauses is to see them as separate markers or strands of a single, but hard to verbalize, concept of the realm of individual freedom needed for individual self-development and democratic control of the common community. Under this view, if one completely grasped the meaning of any of the clauses, one would come close to grasping the comprehensive conception of the protected realm of liberty. However, each clause does have a different emphasis: Assembly emphasizes

plurality and action; religion emphasizes conscience. Still, the
Court may be right to think that speech is the most comprehensive
of the various clauses, although the Court is wrong to subsume the
other clauses in a crabbed, marketplace view of speech. In this
section, I claim that not only does a reasonable interpretation of
the assembly and free exercise clauses support recognizing the
breadth of the realm of liberty argued for herein, but also that the
liberty theory clarifies the meaning of these clauses and solves difficult problems in their elaboration. Nevertheless, these clauses
will be only briefly reviewed here.

A. *Assembly*

A typical Court treatment of assemblies, including parades,
pickets, or rallies, is to analyze them as speech plus.[168] Apparently
the Court's theory is that the function of assemblies is to aid in the
propagation of speech or ideas. This, however, is a limited function of subsidiary constitutional importance and, therefore, the
conduct aspects of assemblies are subject to regulation.[169] Nevertheless, the constitutional language that specifies "the right of the
people peaceably to assemble" hardly suggests that their central
purpose of the assembly must be speech. It certainly does not suggest that their purpose must be to disseminate or debate ideas. If
one takes any cue from the textual language, an alternative theory
would seem appropriate. People combine, assemble to do things;
they assemble for a wide variety of purposes: for celebrations, for
entertainment, for work, for generating or expressing power.
Many of these purposes, although important for people's lives and
although peaceable, fit poorly under any marketplace of ideas rubric. Of course, assemblies can be destructive and violate other's
rights. The obviousness of this fact suggests why the authors of the
constitutional text, who did not bother to write that only freedom
of "noncoercive speech" must not be abridged, specifically restricted the protection of assemblies to "peaceable assemblies."

---

168. For a discussion and criticism of the Court's approach, see FREEDOM OF
EXPRESSION, *supra* note 85, at 292-98. Kalven popularized and then criticized the
"speech plus" characterization of the Court's analysis. Kalven, *The Concept of the
Public Forum*: Cox v. Louisiana, 1965 SUP. CT. REV. 1, 21-25.
169. *See, e.g.*, Cox v. Louisiana, 379 U.S. 536, 555 (1965) ("We emphatically
reject the notion . . . that the First and Fourteenth Amendments afford the same
kind of freedom to those who would communicate ideas by conduct such as patrol-
ling, marching, and picketing on streets and highways, as these amendments afford to
those who communicate by pure speech."); International Brotherhood of Teamsters v.
Vogt, 354 U.S. 284 (1957). *But cf.* Brown v. Louisiana, 383 U.S. 131 (1966) (where
Justice Fortas argued that "these rights are not confined to verbal expression [but]
embrace appropriate types of action which certainly include the right in a peaceable
and orderly manner to protest by silent and reproachful presence, in a place where the
protestant has every right to be, the unconstitutional segregation of public facilities."
Id. at 141-42 (footnotes omitted)).

One cannot reasonably narrow the constitutional protection of assemblies to protection merely of an adjunct to speech or some marketplace of ideas. The logic of a broader, more adequate, theory can be discussed in conjunction with the theory of associations.

B.   *Associations*[170]

Although an independent first amendment right of association has been recognized,[171] the basis of this right is seldom articulated. Worse, when the Court tries to explain the scope of the right of association, it consistently sees it as derivative of the right of speech. Associations are protected as an instrument used to communicate in the marketplace of ideas.[172] This doctrinal sleight of hand severely limits the scope of the freedom of association.[173] And this narrowness has led at least one thoughtful commentator to argue for a nontextual, independent, constitutional right of association.[174] Despite this current fad of finding nontextual, nonconstitutional bases for constitutional decision making,[175] a better tack would be to recognize the first amendment right of assembly as the logical basis of the right of association.[176] This basis does provide for an expansive interpretation of the right.[177] In essence

---

170.   This discussion builds on remarks made in *Commercial Speech, supra* note 5, at 54-56.

171.   *See, e.g.*, NAACP v. Alabama *ex rel.* Patterson, 357 U.S. 449 (1958).

172.   *See, e.g.*, Bates v. City of Little Rock, 361 U.S. 516, 523 (1970) ("And it is now beyond dispute that freedom of association for the purpose of advancing ideas and airing grievances is protected. . ."). *See generally* Raggi, *An Independent Right to Freedom of Association*, 12 HARV. C.R.-C.L. L. REV. 1, 2-11 (1977). This same reduction of the right to assemble or associate to an appendage of the right of expression is evident in Note, *Political Boycott Activity and the First Amendment*, 91 HARV. L. REV. 659 (1978). This Note persuasively argues that some bans on some picketing—*e.g.*, to promote boycotts for political reasons—involve a state purpose to suppress expression in order to prevent conduct that may result from the expression and, therefore, that these bans violate the free speech provision. It assumes that although persuading another independently to refuse to deal is constitutionally protected, associating or combining to refuse to deal is not protected. *Id.* at 683-91. The greater power of concerted activity is obvious, but if assembly and association protect people's right to generate and apply power, the argument must show why this particular application of associational power can be banned, why it is coercive. For an attempt to analyze the problem in this way, see FREEDOM OF EXPRESSION, *supra* note 85, at 445-48.

173.   *See* Runyon v. McCrary, 427 U.S. 160, 175-76 (1976).

174.   *See* Raggi, note 172 *supra.*

175.   *See, e.g.*, Grey, *Do We Have an Unwritten Constitution?*, 27 STAN. L. REV. (1975).

176.   Apparently the Court, certainly Justices Black and Douglas, recognized this basis of the right of association in Bates v. City of Little Rock, 361 U.S. 516, 522-23 (opinion of the Court), 528 (Black & Douglas, JJ., concurring) (1960). In concurrence, Black and Douglas stated that "freedom of assembly, includes of course freedom of association." *Id.* at 528 (Black & Douglas, JJ., concurring).

177.   Raggi argued that freedom of speech and the right to petition could not support an adequately broad right of association. On this point, as long as speech is tied to a marketplace of ideas or advocacy model, she is clearly correct. However, she ignored the obvious first amendment basis of the right: the freedom of assembly.

an association is merely an assembly dispersed over time and space. The key aspect of both is that they are combinations, not mere aggregations, of people; and as combinations, they are a source of power. Both form relations between people that enable the group to do things—often to do things beyond merely reasoning together. People come together in assemblies or associations in order to pursue or fulfill their goals.

Clearly, the core first amendment values of self-fulfillment and popular participation in change are furthered not only by associations and assemblies designed to participate in the robust debate about truth or values or policies, but also by all associations and assemblies that people use to express, develop or implement their substantive values. As Justice Douglas pointed out in *Griswold v. Connecticut*,[178] many aspects of self-fulfillment require associations and the participation of more than one person.

Two interrelated aspects of assemblies and associations increase people's ability to participate in societal development and change. First, the interactions and relationships among people within these combinations provide the basis from which new logics, perceptions and values can grow and develop. Second, associations and assemblies generate the power needed to accomplish group goals.[179] This power-creating aspect of assemblies and associations requires close examination.

The importance of the right of association, and possibly a reason for the underdevelopment of implementing legal doctrine, derives from the fact that "[p]ower springs up whenever people get together and act in concert."[180] Often, power is incorrectly equated with violence or with the ability to employ violence.[181] This view is illustrated by the slogan that "power grows out of the

---

178. 381 U.S. 479, 486 (1965).

179. *See* McBride, *Voluntary Association: The Basis of an Ideal Model and the "Democratic" Failure*, in 11 NOMOS: VOLUNTARY ASSOCIATIONS 202, 214, 229-30 (J. Pennock & J. Chapman eds. 1969). McBride emphasizes the fact that voluntary associations can increase individual responsibility and the "member's role in the achievement of social change."

180. H. ARENDT, ON VIOLENCE 52 (1969); *See also id.* at 44. This paragraph and the next follow Arendt's reasoning.

181. *See* C. MILLS, THE POWER ELITE 171 (1956): "All politics is a struggle for power; the ultimate kind of power is violence." For a modern representative of this Hobbesian view in the legal community, see Leff, *Injury, Ignorance and Spite—the Dynamics of Coercive Collection*, 80 YALE L.J. 1, 8 (1970): "Behind every final judgment procured in any court in this country, stands, ultimately, the United States Army . . . ." H.L.A. Hart's recognition of the internal aspect of rules—that is, their existence in the forms of interaction or relations among people—parallels the distinction between power and violence, and his criticism of John Austin's equation of law and coercive threats amounts to a criticism of Austin for failing to see this distinction. H.L.A. HART, THE CONCEPT OF LAW (1961). Law also illustrates that power and violence are often found together and how, when this occurs, power is always in the dominant position. Consent, at least of the officials of the system, is necessary for law to operate.

barrel of a gun."[182] Because of this confused equation of power and violence, power must be distinguished from violence before one can offer a plausible interpretation of the first amendment as protecting people's right to create power.

Violence typically depends on implements, a fact which suggests the instrumental character of violence. In contrast, power is the strength and the capacity of people acting together to achieve their aims.[183] Power always involves an element of consent; it depends, at least in part, either on voluntary conformance to role positions or on accepted relationships among members of a group. Although power and violence are often found together, in these situations power will prevail since any coherent use of violence depends on the cooperative organization of the group; as long as the group exists, the violence of one person can be overpowered. Violence can be used to destroy power but not to create power. In contrast, power, people acting in concert, can be used to establish something new. Hannah Arendt uses these distinctions to show that the totalitarianism of Nazi Germany depended on a complete atomization or privatization of people's lives. Hitler used violence to destroy all dependable relations among people. This total destruction of power, destruction of the power existing in association, left only violence as means of control, a means that had to be constantly exercised to prevent associations and opposition power from developing.[184]

Once the distinction between power and violence is clear, the contribution of associations or assemblies as the embodiment of people's power to the first amendment values of self-fulfillment or participation in change should be obvious. Also, this power-creating aspect of voluntary associations may explain the fear of developing constitutional doctrine that would allow people's combinations to go unregulated. Early defenders of free speech, operating within the marketplace theory, were wary of the power aspects of association. William Godwin concluded "though association . . . must be granted to be an instrument of a very dangerous nature, . . . unreserved communication . . . , especially among persons who have already awakened to the pursuit of

---

182. *Honky Tonk Women*, in Weathermen 313, 314 (H. Jacobs ed. 1970); *National War Council, id.* 337, 337. *See also* Ashley, Ayers, Dohrn, Jacobs, Jones, Long, Machtinger, Meller, Robbins, Rudd & Tappis, *You Don't Need A Weatherman to Know Which Way the Wind Blows, id.* 51, 85; *Inside the Weather Machine, id.* 321, 326.

183. Arendt distinguishes strength from power in that strength is a capacity of the single individual while power is a capacity of the group. H. Arendt, *supra* note 180, at 44.

184. H. Arendt, Origins of Totalitarianism (2d ed. 1958).

truth, is of unquestionable advantage."[185] More recently, in his
criticism of the other Justices' analysis of a Smith Act prosecution
solely in terms of speech, Justice Jackson emphasized the power
aspect of association and viewed it as justifying regulation.[186] In
concluding that "there is no constitutional right to 'gang up' on
the government,"[187] thereby rejecting any significant theory of
freedom of assembly or association, Jackson explained:

> [A] combination of persons to commit a wrong, either as
> an ends or as a means to an end, is so much more dan-
> gerous [than an individual acting alone], because of its
> *increased power* to do wrong, because it is more difficult
> to guard against and prevent the evil designs of a group
> of persons than of a single person . . . .[188]

Once one rejects Jackson's premise that associations to create
power are not protected by the first amendment and instead recognizes that the rights of assembly and association must mean that
people have the constitutional right to join together to create the
power needed to realize their aims, first amendment protection
moves beyond a marketplace of ideas foundation. Constitutional
law must develop tools to protect associations from various forms
of governmental abridgements.

One possible direction of doctrinal development will be noted
here. The constitutional right to join together to create power suggests that the combination, like speech, cannot itself be prohibited. Of course, just as one can find examples of verbal behavior
that are not protected, some associations—agreements to monopo-
lize, for example—may likewise be unprotected.[189] Given, however, that the criminal law already forbids particular activities that
violate others' rights as well as aiding and abetting or attempting
to commit crimes, the only additional evil sought to be proscribed
by the law of conspiracy is the association itself. As Jackson argued, the association is defined as a separate offense because the
association itself is dangerous. But just as speech recommending
crime, in contrast to the acts carrying out the crime, should not be
punished,[190] a reasonable interpretation of people's right to join
together would suggest that the conspiracy, as opposed to the actual crime, should not be punished. Of course, this distinction be-

---

185. W. GODWIN, ENQUIRY CONCERNING POLITICAL JUSTICE 40-41 (abr. ed.
1971).
186. Dennis v. United States, 341, U.S. 494, 570-77 (1951) (Jackson, J., concurring).
187. *Id.* at 577.
188. *Id.* at 573-74 (citation omitted) (emphasis added).
189. I would argue that these are unprotected for the same reasons that commercial speech should be unprotected. *See Commercial Speech*, note 5 *supra*.
190. *See, e.g.*, Brandenburg v. Ohio, 395 U.S. 444 (1969).

tween what is and is not protected merely repeats the earlier distinction between general prohibitions and allocation rules. To construe the conspiracy as the crime, except in those few cases where the association itself is "coercive,"[191] amounts to a general prohibition on people's substantively valued behavior, and should not be permitted. Thus, the implication of this analysis of freedom of association duplicates the earlier conclusion about the proper scope of freedom of speech.

C. *Free Exercise of Religion*

The Supreme Court first considered, and improperly rejected, free exercise of religion claims in the context of tne government's prosecution (and persecution) of Mormons for practicing polygamy.[192] The polygamy cases illustrate the Court's dominant approach to the free exercise clause, an approach summed up by Justice Roberts for a unanimous Court: "[T]he Amendment embraces two concepts, freedom to believe and freedom to act. The first is absolute but, in the nature of things, the second cannot be. Conduct remains subject to regulation for the protection of society."[193]

To deny conduct any protection clearly would gut the meaning of "*free exercise.*" Religions demand more than holding beliefs; typically religions require the faithful to forbear or perform certain acts and to manifest certain values or principles in their conduct. In the recent conscientious objector cases, the Court recognized that conscience, ethics, or systems of value have taken the place of religion in the lives of many Americans.[194] Certainly, the free exercise of conscience, possibly the original[195] and certainly

---

191. "Coercive" includes situations in which the associations "determine" certain aspects of society such that choices of others, not members of the association, are made irrelevant. *See* Baker, note 51 *supra.* Although the application of the above limitation may be difficult and controversial, the possibility of associations exhibiting these coercive features can always be avoided if membership on an equal basis is available and if civil liberties of members are protected. However, it may be that the only constitutional basis on which the government can require the presence of either of these features of an association is if, in their absence, the association would be coercive. *See, e.g.,* Abood v. Detroit Bd. of Educ., 431 U.S. 209 (1977); Shelley v. Kraemer, 334 U.S. 1 (1948). *But see* Runyon v. McCrary, 427 U.S. 160 (1976).

192. Reynolds v. United States, 98 U.S. 145 (1878). *See generally* Linford, *The Mormans and the Law: The Polygamy Cases,* 9 UTAH L. REV. 308, 543 (1964-1965) (describing the vigor and violence of the United States government's attempt to destroy the Morman Church and its deviant life style).

193. Cantwell v. Connecticut, 310 U.S. 296, 303-04 (1940) (citations to polygamy omitted).

194. Of course, these cases involved an interpretation of statutory references to religion and not an interpretation of the constitutional meaning of religion. *See, e.g.,* United States v. Seeger, 380 U.S. 163 (1965).

195. One of the three parts of Madison's proposal, which became the first amendment, read: "The civil rights of none shall be abridged on account of religious belief or worship, nor shall any national religion be established, *nor shall the full and*

the most intelligible[196] meaning for the free exercise clause, involves people *acting* in accord with their concept of right and wrong. An adequate theory of the free exercise clause must be able to identify the actions and beliefs protected from governmental prohibition or burden.

The Court could protect conduct either by formulating a line distinguishing protected from unprotected conduct or by ad hoc "balancing" of religious claims against other societal interests. All the objections to balancing speech claims apply equally to balancing of free exercise claims. For example, if the Court decides not merely to defer to the legislature, one should expect its biases to control the balancing. The decision will embody the Court's present view of the societal importance of the particular interference with free exercise rights. It will also reflect the Court's biases for or against the particular religious group making the free exercise claim and the other groups who might have indistinguishable claims. *Wisconsin v. Yoder*[197] illustrates this tendency. There the Court emphasized that it would reach a different, nonprotective, result if the right not to attend school were claimed by a newly formed group trying to live and develop a better style of life.[198] Although this limitation might merely represent the Court's specification of its concept of religion for free exercise purposes,[199] I think, instead, it was a necessary concomitant of the Court's focused balancing. The limitation improperly allowed the Court's

---

equal rights of conscience be in any manner, or on any pretext, infringed." 1 ANNALS OF CONG. 451 (Gates ed. 1834) (emphasis added), *quoted in* N.Y. Times v. United States, 403 U.S. 713, 716 n.2 (1971) (Black & Douglas, JJ., concurring). Freeman argues that Congress intended the religion section of the first amendment to have the same meaning as it did when adopted by the House on August 24, 1789: "Congress shall make no law establishing religion or prohibiting the free exercise thereof, nor shall the rights of conscience be infringed." Freeman, *A Remonstrance for Conscience*, 106 U. PA. L. REV. 806, 812 (1958).

196. *See, e.g.*, Gillette v. United States, 401 U.S. 437, 465-66 (1971) (Douglas, J., dissenting).

197. 406 U.S. 205 (1972).

198. *Id.* at 235. The Court even noted that "few other religious groups or sects could make [the convincing showing made by the Amish]." *Id.* at 236.

199. *But see* text accompanying notes 194-96 *supra*. Although the point needs more elaborate development, it seems clear that the meaning of "religion" differs in the establishment and free exercise clauses. Both the historical concern and court cases emphasize, in the case of the establishment clause, the impermissibility of aid to religious sects or sponsorship of recognizably religious beliefs tied to traditional religious sects or groups. In free exercise situations, both history and court cases emphasize the individual's claims of conscience. That is, establishment relates to the sect and traditional religion, free exercise relates to the individual and conscience. Two paradoxes, otherwise unresolvable, are avoided by this interpretation. First, claims based on the free exercise and establishment claims will not conflict. *See* Welsh v. United States, 398 U.S. 333, 344-67 (1970) (Harlan, J., concurring). Second, the legitimacy of the government using its resources to promote ethical or social values is not undermined. The establishment clause is avoided because the government action is not tied to traditional sects while the free exercise clause only requires that the government not "coerce" individuals to adopt these values.

judgment to turn on its sympathy for the Amish, sympathy that was manifest in its emphasis on the desirable qualities of the Amish life style, particularly those aspects that allayed fears related to maintaining social control: The Amish did not commit crimes or go on welfare.[200] One wonders whether an unconscious belief that the Amish's deviation from the law posed no real threat to the values or practices of mainstream America influenced the Court's evaluation.

So far, the preferable approach of line drawing has been notably unsuccessful. Some Court decisions apparently distinguish active from passive conduct. The Court partially grounded the distinction between working on Sunday and not working on Saturday in that the first involved "overt acts" while the second "constitutes no conduct . . . of a kind within the reach of state legislation."[201] The Court has frequently rejected free exercise claims to engage in active conduct,[202] and, although the Court rejected the "passive" right not to fight in a war,[203] it has upheld other claims to refrain from action.[204]

The passive-active distinction might provide an expedient compromise position given that few positive commands of major Western religions require violations of existing state law and given that the modern state usually is more interested in preventing active disruptive conduct that offends or violates people's rights or challenges the status quo than it is in requiring conduct. Nevertheless, the distinction is misguided. It certainly does not embody a principled distinction between the importance or significance of a person's various religious or conscientious beliefs and practices. Most would concede that the first amendment protects some activities required by religions, for example, religious rituals that involve drinking small quantities of wine or eating bread. But protection of ritual is insufficient. Religion, as well as conscience, calls on people not merely to hold certain beliefs but also to act in accord with religious or ethical mandates.[205] It is irrational to

---

200. 406 U.S. at 222. *But see id.* at 247 n.5 (Douglas, J., dissenting in part).

201. Sherbert v. Verner, 374 U.S. 398, 403 (1963). Three judges, Harlan and White in dissent, *id.* at 421, and Stewart in concurrence, *id.* at 417-18, clearly reject the distinction. *See* note 212 *infra.*

202. Braunfeld v. Brown, 366 U.S. 599 (1961); Chatwin v. United States, 326 U.S. 455 (1946); Prince v. Massachusetts, 321 U.S. 158 (1944); Reynolds v. United States, 98 U.S. 145 (1878).

203. United States v. Seeger, 380 U.S. 163 (1965). Lower courts have typically rejected religious claims for exemption from public regulations whether or not the claimed exemption would involve passive or active conduct. *See* N. DORSEN, P. BENDER & R. NEUBORNE, 1 EMERSON, HABER & DORSEN'S POLITICAL AND CIVIL RIGHTS IN THE UNITED STATES 1257-64 (4th ed. 1976).

204. *See, e.g.,* Wisconsin v. Yoder, 406 U.S. 205 (1972); Sherbert v. Verner, 374 U.S. 398 (1963).

205. *See, e.g.,* Murdock v. Pennsylvania, 319 U.S. 105 (1943) (distributing religious pamphlets); Rex v. Singh, 39 A.I.R. 53 (Allahabad H.C. 1952) (carrying a sword).

deny protection to all conscientiously required practices merely because some free exercise claims—for example, conscientiously motivated kidnapping[206]—are unacceptable. From the perspective of the demands of religion or of conscience and from the perspective of the free exercise claimant, action and inaction are not intrinsically different.

Not only would using general prohibitions to ban active conduct negate reasonable free exercise claims of individuals, but also such regulations would enable the state to annul a major societal value of the constitutional guarantee. To protect religious freedom or freedom of conscience while prohibiting religious establishment amounts to a constitutional decision to protect people's right to maintain a pluralistic society.[207] This constitutional protection of pluralism in life styles is unacceptably shallow if it only protects groups in their differing inactions. Both moral and cultural pluralism require opportunities for different patterns of *active* conduct.

Some alternative to the passive-active distinction must be found. Justice Douglas suggested the line of criminal conduct.[208] Unfortunately, since the problem is to find limits on the state's authority to make acts criminal, Douglas' suggestion does not provide a solution unless one can establish definite limits to the scope of criminal law. Douglas' suggested limits—inherently "innocent" acts that "intrinsically are wholesome and not antisocial" cannot be prohibited[209]—are too vague and too much a matter of majority definition. Douglas argued that work, unlike polygamy, is not immoral;[210] but, of course, many Christians consider *Sunday* work immoral and, as Justice Murphy has pointed out, historically polygamy is the most common form of marriage and is firmly based on social and ethical principles subscribed to by many groups.[211]

A better solution would be to interpret the free exercise clause as protecting people's substantively valued conduct from general

---

One's religion may require engaging in polygamy, wearing certain clothing, avoiding public exhibition of certain parts of the body, as well as many other acts not normally prohibited by law.

206. *See* Chatwin v. United States, 326 U.S. 455 (1946). Murphy, for a unanimous court, stated that "bona fide religious beliefs cannot absolve one from liability under the Federal Kidnapping Act." *Id.* at 460.

207. Compare the speech parallel. Once one abandons the idea of objective truth, one finds that expression is important for self-improvement, not because it aids society in reaching universal agreement, but because it contributes to creating the possibly different environments best suited to different people's self-fulfillment. *See, e.g.*, Ginzberg v. United States, 383 U.S. 463, 489-91 (1966) (Douglas, J., dissenting).

208. McGowan v. Maryland, 366 U.S. 420, 575 (1961) (Douglas, J., dissenting).

209. *Id.*

210. *Id.* at 574-75. *See* Cleveland v. United States, 329 U.S. 14 (1946). *But see* Wisconsin v. Yoder, 406 U.S. 205, 247 (1972) (Douglas, J., dissenting in part) (indicating a hope that *Reynolds* will be overruled).

211. Cleveland v. United States, 329 U.S. 14, 26 (1946) (Murphy, J., dissenting).

prohibitions or from governmental decisions to penalize the valued conduct.[212] Under this interpretation, kidnapping, ritualistic assassination or torture and all other forms of active conduct that clearly ought to be subject to government control can be prohibited because they all involve violations of allocation rules. Because acting as required by conscience or religion is a form of self-expression or an attempt at self-realization it should not be surprising that this solution corresponds to the limits on government implied by the liberty interpretation of the free speech clause. Similarly, the free exercise clause's protection of pluralism in life styles parallels the speech clause's protection of expressive conduct involved in culture building and the process of change. Although the first amendment protection of speech, assembly and association, and religion and conscience describes a unified realm of liberty, this interpretation suggests that the free exercise clause should be read as emphasizing that a crucial aspect of this realm of constitutional liberty is the protection of conscience or substantively valued conduct. The free exercise clause thus supplements the role of the speech clause, which emphasizes the noncoercive and nonviolent character of expressive conduct as necessary prerequisites for first amendment protection.

CONCLUSION

Concluding that freedom of speech requires protecting self-chosen, nonverbal conduct from certain forms of government abridgement involves a considerable revision of first amendment theory. However, this conclusion appears to be the only principled interpretation of the first amendment once one demonstrates the

---

212. This approach would reconcile the generally thought unreconcilable decisions in Braunfeld v. Brown, 366 U.S. 599 (1961) (upholding prohibition on Sunday operation by certain businesses) and Sherbert v. Verner, 374 U.S. 398 (1963) (requiring the state to pay unemployment to a person who lost her job because she refused to work on Saturday). First, the state's general prohibition on certain businesses operating on Sunday decreased the instrumental value of the business for the Jewish merchant—the merchant would not be able to make as much money (possibly not enough to stay in business) as he otherwise would—but did not prohibit substantively valued behavior. It also must be shown that denial of unemployment benefits, but not forced Sunday closure, given the governmental programs involved, ought to be viewed as a penalty on the substantively valued activity rather than a resource allocation to promote proper state programs. *See* Sherbert v. Verner, 374 U.S. at 401-02 n.4. This argument can be made, although to be complete it would require a theory of unconstitutional conditions. Second, even if substantively valued, operating a business on Sunday could be prohibited. To the extent that opening on Sunday gives the merchant a significant economic advantage, if this practice is allowed, the market may force (or at least encourage) others to adopt this business practice, thereby forcing other people either to join the religion or to leave that realm of economic life to people of the given religion. In such a situation government regulation is appropriate. *See id.* at 409; *Commercial Speech*, note 5 *supra*.

inadequacy of both the classic marketplace of ideas theory and the market failure theory.

The argument for this liberty theory of freedom of speech involved, first, a review of the basic functions or values of the first amendment. The two key values were individual self-fulfillment and individual participation in public decision making. These values did not provide a coherent distinction between "expression," which Professor Emerson argued is protected, and "action," which he argued is not. Instead, the category of protected speech was better described as "noncoercive" expressive conduct. Neither the key first amendment values nor the noncoercive method by which clearly protected verbal conduct advances these values suggested any constitutionally relevant difference between verbal conduct and noncoercive, nonviolent, and expressive nonverbal conduct. This implies that both should be protected.

The state's authority to make allocation rules or decisions, limited mainly by equal protection notions and a required respect for people's autonomy, was assumed. However, a second category of laws, general prohibitions of substantively valued conduct, restricted conduct that, although typically not coercive of others, did advance first amendment functions in practically the same way as verbal conduct does. Thus, these general prohibitions appeared to be unconstitutional abridgements of expressive conduct. Finally, this extended scope of protection remedied the main inadequacies of the classic marketplace of ideas model for social decision making.

It seems only appropriate to note, in conclusion, a difficult problem that an adequate first amendment theory must resolve. In the modern welfare state, as Charles Reich pointed out over a decade ago,[213] how the government decides to allocate its wealth can greatly influence people's substantively valued behavior. As the country becomes increasingly socialized, the opportunity for the government unnecessarily to limit individual freedom by imposing conditions on the receipt of needed government "gratuities" increase. A method is sorely needed for determining when government-imposed conditions on the receipt of government allocations are proper means to advance the collective notion of the good and when, like general prohibitions, they are improper restraints on people's exercise of first amendment rights. This problem must be left for another paper.

---

213. Reich, *The New Property*, 73 YALE L.J. 733 (1964).

[5]

THE VALUE OF FREE SPEECH

Martin H. Redish †

Commentators and jurists have long searched for an explanation of the true value served by the first amendment's protection of free speech. This issue certainly has considerable intellectual appeal, and the practical stakes are also high. For the answer we give to the question what value does free speech serve may well determine the extent of constitutional protection to be given to such forms of expression as literature, art, science, commercial speech, and speech related to the political process.

There seems to be general agreement that the Supreme Court has failed in its attempts to devise a coherent theory of free expression.[1] These efforts have been characterized by "a pattern of aborted doctrines, shifting rationales, and frequent changes of position by individual Justices."[2] Commentators, by contrast, have been eager to elaborate upon their unified theories of the value of free speech. Professor Emerson, probably the leading modern theorist of free speech, has recognized four separate values served by the first amendment's protection of expression: (1) "assuring individual self-fulfillment;"[3] (2) "advancing knowledge and discovering truth;"[4] (3) "provid[ing] for participation in decisionmaking by all members of society;"[5] and (4) "achieving a more adaptable and hence a more stable community, . . . maintaining the precarious balance between healthy cleavage and necessary consensus."[6] Al-

---

† Professor of Law, Northwestern University. A.B. 1967, University of Pennsylvania; J.D. 1970, Harvard University. A modified version of this article will appear as part of the author's book *Freedom of Expression: A Critical Analysis,* forthcoming from the Bobbs-Merrill Co.

The author thanks Ms. Karen Zulauf (Northwestern University School of Law class of 1983) for her valuable research assistance.

[1] *See, e.g.,* T. EMERSON, THE SYSTEM OF FREEDOM OF EXPRESSION 15 (1970) ("The outstanding fact about the First Amendment today is that the Supreme Court has never developed any comprehensive theory of what that constitutional guarantee means and how it should be applied in concrete cases."); *see also* Bloustein, *The Origin, Validity, and Interrelationships of the Political Values Served by Freedom of Expression,* 33 RUTGERS L. REV. 372 (1981).

[2] Blasi, *The Checking Value in First Amendment Theory,* 1977 AM. B. FOUND. RESEARCH J. 521, 526.

[3] T. EMERSON, *supra* note 1, at 6.

[4] *Id.*

[5] *Id.* 7.

[6] *Id.*

592   UNIVERSITY OF PENNSYLVANIA LAW REVIEW   [Vol. 130:591

though Emerson sees these as distinct values, he believes that "[e]ach is necessary, but not in itself sufficient, for the four of them are interdependent."[7]

Other scholars have culled from the values suggested by Emerson, concluding either that the first amendment is designed to foster or protect only one of them, or that it protects a hierarchy of these different values, with the constitutional protection given to various forms of expression to be adjusted accordingly. Professor Meiklejohn, for example, spoke eloquently of the value of free speech to the political process.[8] In order to prevent the protection of such speech from being reduced to a matter of "proximity and degree,"[9] he urged exclusion from the first amendment guarantee of all speech that did not relate to this self-government value.[10]

Although Meiklejohn in later years appeared to soften the rigidity of his lines of demarcation by effectively extending his doctrine—in a somewhat less than persuasive manner—to many forms of apparently nonpolitical speech,[11] other commentators have adopted his initial premise and kept within its logical limits. Judge Bork, now the leading exponent of the government-process school of thought, has concluded that the sole purpose served by the constitutional guarantee is to aid the political process, and that absolutely no other form of expression can logically be considered to fall within it.[12] Professor Blasi, although not rejecting all other asserted values of free expression, has urged recognition of what he labels the "checking value" as the primary purpose of the first amendment.[13] Under this analysis, speech relating to official misconduct would receive the greatest degree of constitutional protection.[14] Other commentators have selected various forms of an "individual development" model as the touchstone of first amend-

---

[7] Emerson, *First Amendment Doctrine and the Burger Court*, 68 Calif. L. Rev 422, 423 (1980).

[8] *See* A. Meiklejohn, Political Freedom (1960) (expanded version of Meiklejohn's *Free Speech* (1948)).

[9] *Id.* 55.

[10] *See infra* notes 28-32 and accompanying text.

[11] Meiklejohn, *The First Amendment Is an Absolute*, 1961 Sup. Ct. Rev. 245; *see infra* text accompanying notes 32-33.

[12] Bork, *Neutral Principles and Some First Amendment Problems*, 47 Ind. L.J. 1 (1971); *see also* BeVier, *The First Amendment and Political Speech: An Inquiry Into the Substance and Limits of Principle*, 30 Stan. L. Rev. 299 (1978).

[13] Blasi, *supra* note 2.

[14] *See infra* notes 69-74 & 76 and accompanying text.

ment protection,[15] and have structured their constitutional interpretation accordingly. Finally, some scholars, of course, are committed to the "marketplace-of-ideas" approach (long associated with the famous dissent of Justice Holmes in *Abrams v. United States* [16]), which posits that the primary function of free speech is as a catalyst to the discovery of truth.[17]

Although many respected scholars have appraised this myriad of free speech theories, it is time for a major reassessment of the subject, for each of these theories is, I believe, flawed in result, or structure, or both. Many first amendment theorists have failed to return to first principles in determining the value served by free speech, whereas others who may well be approaching an analysis of true first principles have neglected to examine the logical implications flowing therefrom. The result in virtually all cases is an unduly narrow description of the category of communication that is deserving of full constitutional protection.

The position taken in this Article is that the constitutional guarantee of free speech ultimately serves only one true value, which I have labeled "individual self-realization." This term has been chosen largely because of its ambiguity: it can be interpreted to refer either to development of the individual's powers and abilities —an individual "realizes" his or her full potential—or to the individual's control of his or her own destiny through making life-affecting decisions—an individual "realizes" the goals in life that he or she has set. In using the term, I intend to include both interpretations. I have, therefore, chosen it instead of such other options as "liberty" or "autonomy," on the one hand, and "individual self-fulfillment" or "human development," on the other. The former pair of alternatives arguably may be limited to the decisionmaking value,[18]

---

[15] Baker, *Scope of the First Amendment Freedom of Speech*, 25 U.C.L.A. L. Rev. 964 (1978) ("liberty"); Scanlon, *A Theory of Freedom of Expression*, 1 Phil. & Pub. Aff. 204 (1972) ("autonomy").

[16] 250 U.S. 616, 630 (1919) (Holmes, J., dissenting).

[17] *See infra* text accompanying notes 88-90.

[18] One authority interprets "autonomy" to mean:

making one's own choices. A person is not autonomous whose choices are dictated 'from outside' at gunpoint or, perhaps, through hypnosis. . . . On the other hand, full deliberative rationality is not required for autonomy. Spontaneous or ill-considered decisions can be just as much *my* decisions, and that is the touchstone as I understand autonomy.

L. Crocker, Positive Liberty 114 (1980).

Professor Baker also adopts the term "liberty" to describe his operative model of free speech, yet appears to be referring to the concept of individual self-fulfillment. *See* Baker, *supra* note 15, at 990-96.

594   *UNIVERSITY OF PENNSYLVANIA LAW REVIEW*   [Vol. 130:591]

whereas the latter could be interpreted reasonably as confined to the individual development concept.

That the first amendment serves only one ultimate value, however, does not mean that the majority of values thought by others to be fostered by free speech—the "political process," "checking," and "marketplace-of-ideas" values—are invalid. I have not chosen from a list of mutually exclusive possibilities, nor do I argue that the value that I have selected supersedes these alternatives. My contention is that these other values, though perfectly legitimate, are in reality subvalues of self-realization. To the extent that they are legitimate, each can be explained by—and only by—reference to the primary value: individual self-realization. It thus is inaccurate to suggest that "the commitment to free expression embodie[s] a complex of values." [19]

This Article attempts to establish that this first principle—individual self-realization—can be proven, not merely by reference to some unsupportable, conclusory assertions of moral value,[20] but by reasoning from what we in this nation take as given: our democratic system of government.[21] It demonstrates that the moral norms inherent in the choice of our specific form of democracy logically imply the broader value, self-realization. It then concludes that all forms of expression that further the self-realization value,[22] which justifies the democratic system as well as free speech's role in it, are deserving of full constitutional protection.

An analysis of the self-realization value must avoid giving it an unduly restrictive interpretation.[23] Any external determination that certain expression fosters self-realization more than any other is itself a violation of the individual's free will, recognition of which

---

[19] Blasi, *supra* note 2, at 538.

[20] Professor Baker, for example, attempts to establish the correctness of his "liberty" model by reasoning in the following manner: "Obligation exists only in relationships of respect. To justify legal obligation, the community must respect individuals as equal, rational and autonomous moral beings. For the community legitimately to expect individuals to respect collective decisions, *i.e.*, legal rules, the community must respect the dignity and equal worth of its members." Baker, *supra* note 15, at 991. Although I personally might accept Professor Baker's moral assertion, I—and, I expect, Professor Baker—would have a difficult time responding to someone who denied that an individual's obligation to obey the law has anything to do with government's respect for the individual, other than to say, "Oh, yes it does."

[21] *See infra* text following note 48.

[22] For an analysis of exactly how expression may be thought to foster the self-realization value, see *infra* text following note 51.

[23] Professor Baker's analysis is flawed in this respect. *See infra* notes 101-06 and accompanying text.

is inherent in the self-realization principle. This Article therefore argues that the Supreme Court should not determine the level of constitutional protection by comparing the relative values of different types of speech,[24] as is the current practice.[25]

This Article then proceeds to discuss briefly the appropriate role of "balancing" in first amendment analysis. Although recognition of the self-realization value leads to the view that all forms of expression are equally valuable for constitutional purposes, this does not necessarily imply that all forms of expression must receive absolute, or even equal, protection in all cases. Protestations of a number of commentators to the contrary notwithstanding,[26] there is no inconsistency in recognizing that individual self-realization is the sole value furthered by free speech and simultaneously acknowledging that, at least in extreme cases, full constitutional protection of free expression may be forced to give way to competing social concerns.

In summary, then, this Article rejects those authorities (1) who believe that the first amendment is multivalued, whether they superimpose a hierarchy upon those values or recognize them as interdependent coequals; (2) who argue that the first amendment is single-valued, with that value being something other than individual self-realization; (3) who, although accepting the self-realization value or its rough equivalent as the sole determinant of free speech, refuse to acknowledge one or more of the various subvalues that derive from it; and (4) who believe that total reliance on something akin to the self-realization value is inconsistent with any form of constitutional balancing process with regard to free speech.

After detailing the sources and parameters of the self-realization value [27] and demonstrating how each legitimate subvalue is explain-

---

[24] See infra notes 119-202 and accompanying text.

[25] See, e.g., FCC v. Pacifica Found., 438 U.S. 726 (1978).

[26] See infra note 114.

[27] A word should be said at this point about the nature of my reasoning process. My argument is essentially a logical one, reasoning from what I take to be widely held premises. I make only brief and tangential reference to the history of the first amendment and the intent of the amendment's framers. See infra note 54. My theory therefore may be attacked by those who believe that historical analysis is the only appropriate method of constitutional interpretation.

Few, if any, of the commentators analyzing the value of free speech, however, place significant reliance on the intent of the framers. This is primarily because, as Judge Bork states, "[t]he framers seem to have had no coherent theory of free speech and appear not to have been overly concerned with the subject." Bork, supra note 12, at 22. To the extent that any consensus did exist, it appears to have been on an extremely narrow and technical conception of free expression. See generally L. Levy, Legacy of Suppression (1960). It is therefore not surprising that historical reference has been of limited value in first amendment analysis.

596   *UNIVERSITY OF PENNSYLVANIA LAW REVIEW*   [Vol. 130:591

able only as a manifestation of that principle, this Article considers how acceptance of these theoretical precepts would affect the level and form of constitutional protection given to three categories of expression: commercial speech, defamation, and obscenity.

I. Self-Realization and the Democratic Process: Ascertaining the Ultimate Value of Free Speech

A. *The "Democratic Process" Value*

An appropriate way to begin analysis of the self-realization value is, ironically, with a discussion of the theory of free speech perhaps farthest in practical result from that value: the view that the sole purpose of the free speech guarantee is to facilitate operation of the democratic process. Advocates of this position are logically required to establish two propositions: first, that the first amendment facilitates the political process, and second, that the first amendment does not foster any value other than conduct of the political process. Examination of the writings of those expounding this view reveals that they have established the former with considerably greater force than they have established the latter.

As already noted, the original exponent of such a theory was Professor Meiklejohn. He began with the premise that "[g]overnments . . . derive their just powers from the consent of the governed. If that consent be lacking, governments have no just powers." [28] Because government officials in a democracy are merely agents of the electorate, the electorate needs as much information as possible to aid it in performing its governing function in the voting booth.[29] Therefore, "[t]he principle of the freedom of speech springs from the necessities of the program of self-government. . . . It is a deduction from the basic American agreement that public issues shall be decided by universal suffrage." [30]

Few would argue with Meiklejohn's logic to this point. If the electoral decisions made by the voters are to be based on anything more than emotive hunches, they need a free flow of information that will inform them not only about the candidates but also about the day-to-day issues of government.[31] But what seemed counter-

---

[28] A. Meiklejohn, *supra* note 8, at 9.

[29] Meiklejohn, *supra* note 11, at 255.

[30] A. Meiklejohn, *supra* note 8, at 27.

[31] *Cf.* B. Berelson, P. Lazarsfeld & W. McPhee, Voting 307 (1954) ("If there is one characteristic for a democratic system (besides the ballot itself) that is theoretically required, it is the capacity for and the practice of discussion.").

intuitive to some was the apparent implication of Meiklejohn's theory that such "nonpolitical" forms of speech as art, literature, science, and education were not protected by the first amendment.[32] Meiklejohn himself ultimately concluded "that the people do need novels and dramas and paintings and poems, 'because they will be called upon to vote.'"[33] He thus included within the category of "political" speech numerous forms of expression that do not appear to have any direct—or arguably even indirect—impact upon the political process. He would presumably give full first amendment protection to both the author and the reader who profess absolutely no interest in the political system, and who have never voted and never will, but who simply enjoy writing or reading good fiction. For this extension of his theory, Meiklejohn has been attacked both by those who believe that the first amendment has no special political basis[34] and by political "purists" who accept Meiklejohn's initial premise about the relationship between the first amendment and the political process, but question the logic of his extension.[35]

Judge Bork begins his analysis with this same premise about the political process, but rigidly limits his conclusions to such speech, thus escaping the attack levelled at Professor Meiklejohn. Judge Bork, however, has great difficulty explaining why the first amendment should be read to protect *only* political expression.

Judge Bork's first amendment analysis flows from his concern that constitutional interpretation be premised on "neutral principles."[36] The decisions of the Supreme Court "must be controlled by principle,"[37] which may be defined as "'reasons with respect to all the issues in a case, reasons that in their generality and their neutrality transcend any immediate result that is involved.'"[38]

---

[32] *See* Kalven, *The Metaphysics of the Law of Obscenity*, 1960 Sup. Ct. Rev. 1, 15-16; Chafee, Book Review, 62 Harv. L. Rev. 891, 896 (1949).

[33] Meiklejohn, *supra* note 11, at 263.

[34] I include myself within this category. *See* Redish, *The First Amendment in the Marketplace: Commercial Speech and the Values of Free Expression*, 39 Geo. Wash. L. Rev. 429, 437-38 (1971).

[35] According to Professor BeVier, "[t]he essential problem with accepting Meiklejohn's analogies is that one cannot know in principle which forms of thought and expression contribute to 'the capacity for sure and objective judgment.'" BeVier, *supra* note 12, at 317.

[36] Bork, *supra* note 12, at 1-20. In so doing, he draws upon the famous work of Professor Wechsler. Wechsler, *Toward Neutral Principles of Constitutional Law*, 73 Harv. L. Rev. 1 (1959).

[37] Bork, *supra* note 12, at 2 (footnote omitted).

[38] *Id.* (quoting, with a minor error, Wechsler, *supra* note 36, at 19).

Judge Bork concludes that only speech serving the political process can be deemed "principled." [39]

The method by which Judge Bork reaches this conclusion may be described as a lesson in the limits of the "neutral principles" concept. It demonstrates all too clearly that if the selection of premises is flawed, "neutral principles" will not prevent a doctrine from being applied in a similarly flawed—albeit "principled" and consistent—manner. Judge Bork begins his analysis by quoting the well-known concurrence of Justice Brandeis in *Whitney v. California*.[40] Brandeis identified what Bork has distilled into four benefits provided by the free speech guarantee: "[t]he development of the faculties of the individual; [t]he happiness to be derived from engaging in the activity; [t]he provision of a safety value [sic] for society; and [t]he discovery and spread of political truth." [41] Bork then proceeds to explain why the first three values cannot be considered values of the first amendment under a "principled" analysis.

Since Justice Brandeis's first category is the closest to the concept of individual self-realization urged here, it is most relevant to determine why Judge Bork concludes that this value cannot be thought to lie behind the constitutional guarantee. Although Bork does not deny that free speech may develop individual faculties,[42] he nevertheless believes that the development of an individual's faculties and the happiness derived from engaging in speech

> do not distinguish speech from any other human activity. An individual may develop his faculties . . . from trading on the stock market, following his profession as a river-port pilot, working as a barmaid, engaging in sexual activity, playing tennis, rigging prices or in any of thousands of other endeavors. . . . These functions or benefits of speech are, therefore, to the principled judge, indistinguishable from the functions or benefits of all other human activity.[43]

Judge Bork ultimately concludes that Justice Brandeis's fourth category—the search for "political truth"—is the only legitimate ground of the first amendment. This conclusion in turn leads him to adopt a first amendment construction that is quite probably the

---

[39] Bork, *supra* note 12, at 26.

[40] 274 U.S. 357, 375 (1927) (Brandeis, J., concurring).

[41] Bork, *supra* note 12, at 25.

[42] *Id.*

[43] *Id.* A similar argument is fashioned by Professor BeVier. BeVier, *supra* note 12, at 313-14.

.most narrowly confined protection of speech ever supported by a modern jurist or academic: "Constitutional protection should be accorded only to speech that is explicitly political. There is no basis for judicial intervention to protect any other form of expression, be it scientific, literary or that variety of expression we call obscene or pornographic." [44]

Judge Bork's rationale for including political speech and excluding nonpolitical forms of expression, even if they further the value of self-fulfillment, is that it is logically possible to limit the value served by political speech to "speech." Self-fulfillment, on the other hand, cannot logically be limited to "speech," but must also be taken to include countless forms of action. Judge Bork's conclusion that political speech should be protected is, however, inconsistent with his belief that any acceptable rationale for free speech must be logically unique to speech. For there are countless actions—such as a bombing by the FALN to protest oppression of Puerto Rico, an assasination of a foreign political leader because of human rights violations in his country, and the breaking of windows at the Iranian Consulate to protest the treatment of Americans in Iran—that can be thought to convey very significant political messages. Those who undertake such activities could argue with a fair degree of persuasiveness that the public attention attracted to such acts is geometrically greater than that which would be received by public statements or pickets. Even if we rejected this argument, however, the issue for Judge Bork is not whether the value in question can be furthered by speech, as well as by conduct, but whether it can *only* be furthered by speech. Bork otherwise could not exclude nonpolitical speech that aids individual self-fulfillment on the ground that conduct may also aid such a goal. It is, therefore, difficult to understand how he can protect political speech, when countless forms of political action could achieve similar results.[45]

---

[44] Bork, *supra* note 12, at 20. "Moreover, within that category of speech we ordinarily call political, there should be no constitutional obstruction to laws making criminal any speech that advocates forcible overthrow of the government or the violation of any law." *Id.*

[45] One might argue that these actions standing alone do not effectively convey any message. Rather, there also must be some oral or written communication by the perpetrators of the act describing their motivation. Assuming this to be true, the point in no way undermines the conclusion that the act is an essential aspect of the attempt to convey political truth, since the statement of motivation would make little sense without performance of the act.

Professor BeVier, arguing in support of Judge Bork's position, reasons that "beliefs and opinions are often most effectively communicated by forms of conduct other than verbal expression." BeVier, *supra* note 12, at 319 (footnote omitted).

Political actions, unlike some of the faculty-developing activities referred to by Judge Bork, have as an essential part of their purpose a communicative aspect. But it is unlikely that Bork would be satisfied with a distinction based on communicative purpose, since he leaves little doubt that he would not choose to protect such actions. In any event, there are numerous noncommunicative, nonspeech activities that may be thought to aid in the attainment of political truth. For example, working as a farmer could help one understand the problems and benefits of farm price supports; working as a doctor could do the same with respect to socialized medicine; living in a large urban area and taking public transportation might convince one of the need for greater federal aid to cities and mass transit. Thus, nonspeech activities could aid attainment of knowledge of political truth as much as does any political discourse. Bork's logic therefore must be rejected, because it inescapably results in the content of speech protected by the first amendment being a null set: there is no category of expression that furthers a value or values unique to speech.

If one were to look for an appropriate basis for limiting the protection of the first amendment to "speech," the natural starting place would seem to be the language of the amendment itself, which says nothing about protecting only political speech.[46] What the language does refer to is "speech," and not action. Thus, we need not find a logical distinction between the value served by speech and the value served by conduct in order to justify protecting only speech, for the framers have already drawn the distinction. Whether or not the constitutional language must be read to provide absolute protection to speech,[47] there can be little doubt that it was intended to provide greater protection to speech than to conduct, which is relegated to the fifth amendment's protection against deprivation of "liberty" without "due process of law." Indeed, that the framers deemed it necessary to create a first amendment at all, rather than merely including speech within the other forms of liberty protected by the fifth amendment, indicates that speech is to receive a constitutional status above and beyond that given to conduct.

My point is, simply, that the exact same thing can be said about political speech, the only category of expression that Judge Bork and Professor BeVier believe deserves constitutional protection.

[46] One would think that any attempt to develop a "principled" interpretation of a constitutional provision would not begin by inserting limitations that are not even hinted at in the constitutional language, and that indeed appear to depart from a natural reading of the words. The first amendment refers simply to "the freedom of speech, and of the press."

[47] This issue has been the subject of endless debate. *See infra* notes 112-16.

It is not hard to understand why constitutional protection of speech would be greater than that of conduct. If we were to draw a rough distinction—the kind that must necessarily have been drawn by the framers—we could reasonably decide that speech is less likely to cause direct or immediate harm to the interests of others [48] and more likely to develop the individual's mental faculties, and that speech thus deserves a greater degree of constitutional protection than does conduct. Bork's assumption that any principled first amendment theory must rely solely on values that are *uniquely* protected by speech drastically undercuts this status by effectively removing all categories of speech from the amendment's protection.

B. *Deriving the Ultimate Value*

The primary flaw in the analysis of Bork and Meiklejohn is that they never attempt to ascertain what basic value or values the democratic process was designed to serve. Examination of the "process" values inherent in our nation's adoption of a democratic system reveals an implicit belief in the worth of the individual that has first amendment implications extending well beyond the borders of the political world. Indeed, political democracy is merely a means to—or, in another sense, a logical outgrowth of—the much broader value of individual self-realization. The mistake of Bork and Meiklejohn, then, is that they have confused one means of obtaining the ultimate value with the value itself.

The logic employed by Meiklejohn and Bork to reach their conclusion that the protection of speech was designed to aid the political process would have absolutely no relevance except in a democratic system. For a monarchy or dictatorship to function politically, it of course is not necessary that the general public be able to speak freely or receive information about pressing political

---

[48] Dean Wellington has correctly noted that "speech often hurts. It can offend, injure reputation, fan prejudice or passion, and ignite the world. Moreover, a great deal of other conduct that the state regulates has less harmful potential." Wellington, *On Freedom of Expression*, 88 YALE L.J. 1105, 1106-07 (1979) (footnote omitted). He cites, as one example of the latter, laws prohibiting certain forms of sexual relations between consenting adults. *Id.* 1107. But (as noted in the text), in establishing a constitutional rule that is to provide a guide for future generations, it is impossible to enumerate the specific instances that deserve a greater degree of protection and those that deserve a lesser degree. It is almost certainly true in the overwhelming majority of cases that speech is less immediately dangerous than conduct. In any event, I would argue, with respect to the example of laws regulating consensual sexual practices cited by Dean Wellington, that such conduct should (at least as a matter of logic and morals) be deemed fully protected by the self-realization principle. To the extent that it is not protected, it is probably because there is no constitutional provision giving it the high level of protection given speech by the first amendment.

602   UNIVERSITY OF PENNSYLVANIA LAW REVIEW   [Vol. 130:591

questions, because private individuals will have no say in decisions. Even a benevolent dictator would be more likely to allow free expression in traditionally nonpolitical areas such as art, literature, and music than in the political realm. The free speech value emphasized by Meiklejohn and Bork, then, is inherently linked to a democratic form of government.

Democracy is by no means the only system that could have been chosen when our nation was founded. Indeed, it is probably safe to say that the overwhelming majority of organized societies throughout history have not chosen it, even in its most diluted form. It would seem, then, that there must be some values that the founding fathers believed to be uniquely fostered by a democracy, values that succeeding generations of political leaders presumably have shared, since there has been little or no effort to alter substantially our system of government by constitutional processes.

One conceivable value is "consequentialist" in nature: efficiency. One could believe that the results of a democratic system are somehow better than any other system's. Such an argument, however, would be very difficult to prove, for several reasons. Initially, it would probably be difficult to obtain agreement on the criteria for measuring results. How are we to decide what is "better"? Higher gross national product? More international influence? And better for whom? Elites? A majority? Oppressed minorities? Secondly, it is doubtful that we could establish empirically that throughout history democracies have fared better than other forms of government. After all, we do know that the trains ran on time in Mussolini's Italy; can the Chicago Transit Authority make the same claim? Moreover, it may well be counter-intuitive to believe, especially in a modern, highly technological society, that decisions made by the masses or their elected representatives—who are rarely chosen because of any degree of real expertise—would be either the wisest or the most efficient. Finally, it is doubtful that many of us would be anxious to discard democracy even if it were established definitely that an alternative political system was more efficient. It is likely, then, that the values inherent in a democratic system are "process-oriented," rather than related to some objective standard of governmental efficiency.

These "process" values seem to translate into two forms: an "intrinsic" value and an "instrumental" value. The "intrinsic" value is one that is achieved by the very existence of a democratic system. It is the value of having individuals control their own destinies. For if one does not accept the morality of such a proposition, why bother to select a democratic system in the first place? As Meiklejohn said, "[i]f men are to be governed, we say, then that governing must be done, not by others, but by themselves. So far, therefore, as our own affairs are concerned, we refuse to submit to alien control." [49] The point is so obvious that it requires no further elaboration, except to say that the core concept of "self-rule" appears to have formed the cornerstone of every theory of democracy to date.[50] It would seem to be so as a matter of definition.

The second value of a democratic system is labeled "instrumental," because it is a goal to which a democratic system is designed to lead, rather than one that is attained definitionally by the adoption of a democratic system. It is a goal that is associated primarily with "classical" (fully participatory) democracy: development of the individual's human faculties. In the words of a leading authority:

> The most distinctive feature, and the principal orienting value, of classical democratic theory was its emphasis on individual participation in the development of public policy. . . . Although the classical theorists accepted the basic framework of Lockean democracy, with its emphasis on limited government, they were *not* primarily concerned with the *policies* which might be produced in a democracy; above all else they were concerned with *human development,* the opportunities which existed in political activity to realize the untapped potentials of men . . . .[51]

My thesis is that: (1) although the democratic process is a means of achieving both the intrinsic and instrumental values, it is only one means of doing so; (2) both values (which, as noted previously,[52] may be grouped under the broader heading of "self-realization")

---

[49] A. MEIKLEJOHN, *supra* note 8, at 9.

[50] In the words of Professor Bachrach, "[d]emocratic participation . . . is a process in which persons formulate, discuss, and decide public issues that are important to them and directly affect their lives." Bachrach, *Interest, Participation, and Democratic Theory,* in PARTICIPATION IN POLITICS: NOMOS XVI 39, 41 (J. Pennock & J. Chapman eds. 1975).

[51] Walker, *A Critique of the Elitist Theory of Democracy,* 60 AM. POL. SCI. REV. 285, 288 (1966) (emphasis in original); *see also* C. MACPHERSON, THE LIFE AND TIMES OF LIBERAL DEMOCRACY 51 (1977) ("[D]emocracy drew the people into the operations of government by giving them all a practical interest, an interest which could bring down a government. Democracy would thus make people more active, more energetic; it would advance them 'in intellect, in virtue, and in practical activity and efficiency'."). John Stuart Mill is often associated with this "developmental" value of democracy. *See* Walker, *supra,* at 285; *see also* J. MILL, ON LIBERTY (1947) (1st ed. London 1859).

[52] *See supra* text preceding note 18.

604   *UNIVERSITY OF PENNSYLVANIA LAW REVIEW*   [Vol. 130:591]

may be achieved by and for individuals in countless nonpolitical, and often wholly private, activities; and (3) the concept of free speech facilitates the development of these values by directly fostering the instrumental value and indirectly fostering the intrinsic value. Free speech fosters the former goal *directly* in that the very exercise of one's freedom to speak, write, create, appreciate, or learn represents a use, and therefore a development, of an individual's uniquely human faculties. It fosters the latter value *indirectly* because the very exercise of one's right of free speech does not in itself constitute an exercise of one's ability to make life-affecting decisions as much as it *facilitates* the making of such decisions.

This conceptual framework indicates that the appropriate scope of the first amendment protection is much broader than Bork or Meiklejohn would have it. Free speech aids all life-affecting decisionmaking, no matter how personally limited, in much the same manner in which it aids the political process. Just as individuals need an open flow of information and opinion to aid them in making their electoral and governmental decisions, they similarly need a free flow of information and opinion to guide them in making other life-affecting decisions. There thus is no logical basis for distinguishing the role speech plays in the political process. Although we definitely need protection of speech to aid us in making political judgments, we need it no less whenever free speech will aid development of the broader values than the democratic system is designed to foster.

Before this thesis can be accepted, however, each of its two prongs must confront significant counterarguments:

> (1) The moral value of "self-rule" intrinsic in the adoption of a democratic system is not transferable to the private sphere, because that we value society's collective ability to control its destiny does not necessarily imply that we place an equal value upon individuals' power to direct their personal lives. Individual and collective self-determination are very different conceptually, and indeed are often in conflict.

> (2) Although classical theorists of democracy may have believed that human development would result from mass political participation, modern theorists—the "elitists" or "revisionists"—have totally undermined the basis for this belief. Furthermore, that such human development could be gained from participation in the political process would not imply that similar benefits would derive from indi-

viduals' control over their private lives, because an essential premise of the classical theorists' belief was that this benefit stemmed from individuals extending themselves beyond narrow self-interest to concern about the common good.

Although each of these arguments deserves a detailed response, it is my contention that neither invalidates my thesis.

1. Collective Self-Rule and Individual Autonomy

One can argue that there is a conceptual difference between the value of collective self-rule and that of individual self-rule. In a democracy, numerous conflicts may develop between the majority's will and the desires of the individual. A "tyranny of the majority," under which there is little or no room for the exercise of individual autonomy, is readily imaginable.[53] But my purpose in this discussion is not to establish that the concept of collective self-rule necessarily implies an impenetrable sphere of individual autonomy (although the form of democracy established in this nation, both historically and morally, does include the existence of such a sphere).[54] My point, rather, concerns the level of constitu-

---

[53] *See generally* THE FEDERALIST Nos. 10 & 51 (J. Madison); 1 A. DE TOCQUE-VILLE, DEMOCRACY IN AMERICA 241-54 (1966) (1st ed. Bruxelles 1835); J. MILL, *supra* note 51, at 1-14.

[54] The ideological father of the American Revolution is generally thought to be John Locke. *See* L. LEVY, *supra* note 27, at 100; J. ROCHE, COURTS AND RIGHTS 9-10 (1961); *see also* G. WOOD, THE CREATION OF THE AMERICAN REPUBLIC, 1776-1787, at 14, 283-84 (1969). Locke is widely thought of as a libertarian who

> assumed . . . that there ought to exist a certain minimum area of personal freedom which must on no account be violated; for if it is overstepped, the individual will find himself in an area too narrow for even that minimum development of his natural faculties which alone makes it possible to pursue, and even to conceive, the various ends which men hold good or right or sacred.

I. BERLIN, FOUR ESSAYS ON LIBERTY 124 (1977); *see also* G. PARRY, JOHN LOCKE 158-60 (1978).

It may well be, as Professor Roche suggests, that only "[a] careless reading of Locke's *Second Treatise* suggests that he was a militant defender of the rights of the citizen against government in general." J. ROCHE, *supra*, at 9; *see also* L. LEVY, *supra* note 27, at 103-04. However, Locke was undoubtedly a libertarian relative to his contemporaries, *see id.* 100-01, and, as Roche acknowledges, the image (perhaps mythical) of Locke as a strong believer in individual rights "had an enormous impact, particularly in the American Colonies." J. ROCHE, *supra*, at 9. *See also* G. WOOD, *supra*, at 283-84. In any event, there can be little question that the form of democracy that we have adopted imposes constitutional enclaves to protect the individual's autonomy from majoritarian interference.

For an alternative interpretation of the ideological origins of the American Revolution—one that de-emphasizes the role of Locke and substantiates the influence of the moral-sense philosophy of the Enlightenment—see G. WILLS, INVENTING

tional protection to be given to speech that is related to whatever decisionmaking the collective society does allow the individual to make. I intend to show only that the logic employed by Meiklejohn and Bork to justify first amendment protection for speech relevant to political decisionmaking dictates a similar level of protection for speech related to whatever decisions actually are allowed to the individual.

Let us imagine a hypothetical democratic society premised solely on the utilitarian belief in the greatest good for the greatest number, and with no moral or political regard for the individual as such, except assurances that every individual will have a say (a vote) in decisionmaking. Assume further that in this society *every* decision affecting individuals—including decisions about dinner menus, hair styles, entertainment activities, and bedtimes—is made by a collective vote. Although in concept such a society is democratic, it of course removes from the individual more choices than does virtually any authoritarian regime. Nevertheless, the inherent value on which the system is premised is (collective) self-rule.

Under Meiklejohnian logic, debate and information about every one of these decisions, no matter how trivial, would presumably have to receive full constitutional protection, because the individuals that make up this society are in fact their own "governors," and therefore need open communication to aid them in their "political" decisionmaking. This logic applies to speech of the minority as well as the majority, because we presumably cannot determine before the actual vote who will be in each group. Therefore, every voter must have the right to hear and learn every factor that might influence the final vote.

Now assume a slight alteration in the arrangement of this society: instead of collectively voting on every conceivable life-affecting decision, the members of the society vote periodically for specific governors, who make each life-affecting decision for the entire society. Under Meiklejohnian logic, here, too, we need full protection of information for the society's members about each of the issues that the governors will decide, because the underlying moral precept of the society is still self-rule. The individuals therefore need to know how the competing candidates for office will decide these issues—for example, whether they will order chicken or steak for dinner—so that they can choose the governors whose

---

AMERICA (1978). Wills' interpretation provides a historical and intellectual background that is consistent with the theory of individual self-realization advanced in this Article.

views coincide most closely with the individuals' personal preferences.   Moreover, if the price of steak should rise during the governors' term of office, under Meiklejohnian logic the society's members would need the constitutional right to tell each other about
it, so that they might better judge the dinner choices made by
their governing agents.   Simply put, Meiklejohn and Bork would
protect all speech related to the political process, but the term
"political" does not include a set category of specific substantive
issues.   Rather, it applies to whatever issues a society decides collectively, whether by direct popular vote or through elected agents.

Now assume that, whether because of moral concern about individual autonomy or simply because it does not wish to be bothered
with so many decisions, the collective society cedes to each individual full decisionmaking power, much as our own democratic
society does, on such questions as what to eat for dinner, what com-
merical products to buy, whom and whether to marry, what career
to choose, and where and whether to go to college—decisions that
previously were made by the collective or its agents and that therefore were "political."   At this point, the individual has more than
an indirect say in how these decisions are to be made; he now has
full authority to make them, as well as commensurate responsibility
for their consequences.

Once these decisions have been removed from collective authority and completely given over to individual will, presumably
Meiklejohn and Bork would say that the individual no longer has
a constitutional right to information that will help him make them,
because they are no longer part of the political process.   Their
logic, however, leaves us with an untenable situation: when an individual only has an indirect say in governing his life, either by
voting on particular questions or by selecting governing agents who
will make the decisions, he has a right to information that will
enable him to exercise his power more effectively; but when the
individual has full and total authority to make the very same decisions, his right to the information mysteriously vanishes.   Reason
would seem to dictate, however, that the individual has at least as
great a need for a free flow of information and opinion related to
life-affecting decisions that he makes solely for himself.   For
whether the decisions are made collectively or by the individual,
in a democracy we assume the moral value of self-rule.   Thus, the
first amendment guarantee of free expression is designed to play
an important role in the exercise of that decisionmaking power at
either level.

2. The Impact of the Elitist Theorists and the Definition of "Political"

A critique based on the findings and conclusions of the so-called "elitist" [55] or "revisionist" [56] democratic theorists—who have come into prominence mostly within the last forty years [57]—is aimed at the "instrumental" value of a democratic system: the development of individual abilities and faculties thought by classical theorists to flow from participation in the political process. [58] The argument, put simply, is that it is today unrealistic to expect the common masses to gain such benefits, because it is unrealistic to expect them to have both the interests and the ability to involve themselves on a significant scale in day-to-day political affairs. The pulls of work and family, Professor Lipset tells us, are too great to expect the individual to bother with the complexities of political affairs, especially when he sees the impact of those matters on his life as remote. [59] Professor Dahl writes that "neither by instincts nor by learning is [man] necessarily a political animal." [60]

Well-known empirical studies describing the average American voter's shocking lack of knowledge underscore this judgment. [61]

---

[55] *See, e.g.,* P. BACHRACH, THE THEORY OF DEMOCRATIC ELITISM: A CRITIQUE (1967); Walker, *supra* note 51.

[56] Although the term "elitist" was apparently coined by one of the theory's proponents, *see* Lipset, *Introduction* to R. MICHELS, POLITICAL PARTIES 33 (1962), at least one of the theorists who is often thought to fall into this grouping rejects the term, because it is inaccurate and "even more so because in our language and in our society it is unavoidably . . . a pejorative, even a polemical epithet." Dahl, *Further Reflections on "The Elitist Theory of Democracy,"* 60 AM. POL. SCI. REV. 296, 297 n.7 (1966). The term "revisionism" is applied to this type of democratic theory in Keim, *Participation in Contemporary Democratic Theories,* in PARTICIPATION IN POLITICS: NOMOS XVI 1 (J. Pennock & R. Chapman eds. 1975).

[57] The origin of the theory of democratic elitism is contained in the later chapters of G. MOSCA, THE RULING CLASS (1939). *See* P. BACHRACH, *supra* note 55, at 10.

[58] *See supra* text preceding note 51.

[59] Lipset, *supra* note 56, at 17; *see also* P. BACHRACH, *supra* note 55.

[60] R. DAHL, MODERN POLITICAL ANALYSIS 55-56 (1963).

[61] *See, e.g.,* B. BERELSON, P. LAZARSFELD & W. McPHEE, VOTING (1954); A. CAMPBELL, P. CONVERSE, W. MILLER & D. STOKES, THE AMERICAN VOTER (1960). *But see* N. NIE, S. VERBA & J. PETROCIK, THE CHANGING AMERICAN VOTER 123-73, 319-44 (1979). This more recent analysis suggests that the indicia of voter awareness, issue consistency, and issue voting have demonstrated a marked increase in voter awareness between 1956 (the terminal year of the Campbell, Converse, Miller, and Stokes study) and 1976. However, Nie, Verba, and Petrocik add this cautionary note to their data: "This is not to say that the mass citizenry now has patterns of attitude consistency equal to that of a group of political Elites such as congressional candidates." *Id.* 137.

Note that these studies dealt only with the lack of knowledge of voters; the

Revisionists have therefore presented a vision of democracy in which more-involved elites compete for the allegiance of the masses at election time, but in which most individuals have no significant role beyond exercising a periodic choice through election, or occasionally through other formalized procedures.[62] Such data and theories may seem to make the instrumental value of classical democracy a museum piece. If so, it might be argued that the implications I have drawn from my theory about the broader value of individual self-realization are inaccurate. This, however, is not the case.

First, it should be noted that the impact of the elitists' argument goes at most to the instrumental value of democracy, and in no way challenges the *intrinsic* value of allowing individuals to maintain self-rule.[63] More importantly, the elitist theorists do not seem to question the *normative* imperative recognized by classical theorists, but rather only its attainability. Indeed, the impact of the elitist theorists is arguably to shift the emphasis from attaining this goal through the political process to its achievement through individual involvement in the private sector. Modern theorists have redefined the concept of the "political" to include decision-making within areas such as the work place, where decisions are likely to have a more immediately recognizable impact on the individual's daily life.[64] Therefore, the elitist theory can be seen as

---

implications about the many who do not even perform that minimal civic function are all too clear. Dahl has suggested an explanation for such behavior:

> The explanation, no doubt, lies in the fact that man is not by instinct a reasonable, reasoning, civic-minded being. Many of our most imperious desires and the source of many of our most powerful gratifications can be traced to ancient and persistent biological and physiological drives, needs, and wants. Organized political life arrived late in man's evolution; today man learns how to behave as a political participant with the aid, and often with the hindrance, of instinctive equipment that is the product of a long development. To avoid pain, discomfort, and hunger, to satisfy drives for sexual gratification, love, security, and respect are insistent and primordial needs. The means of satisfying them quickly and concretely generally lie outside political life.

R. DAHL, *supra* note 60, at 103-04. If Dahl is correct, the problem is not that the classical theories are outmoded in modern society, but rather that they were unrealistic from their inception. In any case, the problem remains with us.

[62] *See* Keim, *supra* note 56, at 7 ("[Under revisionist theory, h]omo *civicus* is constrained to a mode of participation characterized by the binomic 'yes' or 'no.' Participation is effectively reduced to the approval or disapproval of the performance of elected official and lobbyist.").

[63] *Id.*

[64] *See* P. BACHRACH, *supra* note 55, at 102-03. *See generally* R. PRANGER, THE ECLIPSE OF CITIZENSHIP (1968).

610   UNIVERSITY OF PENNSYLVANIA LAW REVIEW   [Vol. 130:591

being totally compatible with the thesis asserted here; democratic political control is only one means of achieving the values inherent in a democratic system, and it is therefore necessary to recognize that free speech may aid attainment of those values in nonpolitical settings.

Elitist thinking, then, does not undermine—indeed, it may facilitate—the extension of Meiklejohn's reasoning about the role of free speech to such nonpolitical activities as various kinds of community groups, as well as to the work place.[65]   What remains unclear, however, is whether this logic may be extended as well to such purely private decisions as commercial purchases or an individual's choice of friends.   The difficulty is that it has been generally assumed, since democracy's origins in ancient Athens, that the moral benefits to the individual derived from being forced to look beyond his or her own narrow interests and to work with others to attain the common good.[66]   It is perhaps for this reason that Professor Bachrach, the leading exponent of the redefined "political" sphere, believed it necessary to stay within the bounds of the "political," no matter how strained his definition of the term.[67] But whatever unique benefits one derives from involvement in organizations that look to the common, as opposed to the individual, good, it is impossible to deny that many of the developmental values—particularly the intellectual benefits—that are thought to result from participation in the political process also may be obtained from private self-government.   After all, the elitists tell us that "[p]olitical participation constitutes an effort to protect threatened interests," [68] and by adopting a democratic system we are expressing a belief that presumably individuals are capable of deciding what is best for them.   There is therefore no basis to believe that development can be derived solely from common, as opposed to individual, activity.

---

[65] *See* P. BACHRACH, *supra* note 55, at 96 & n.2; *see also* Mansbridge, *The Limits of Friendship,* in PARTICIPATION IN POLITICS: NOMOS XVI 246 (J. Pennock & J. Chapman eds. 1975).   Of course, the constitutional requirement of state or federal action would limit the first amendment's reach into these nonpolitical or private areas to restricting *governmental* interference with the exercise of free speech.

[66] *See* G. SABINE & T. THORSON, A HISTORY OF POLITICAL THEORY 64-66, 539-44 (4th ed. 1973).

[67] The political scientist must recognize, Bachrach says, "that large areas within existing so-called private centers of power are political and therefore potentially open to a wide and democratic sharing in decision-making." P. BACHRACH, *supra* note 55, at 102; *see also* Keim, *supra* note 56, at 13.

[68] Keim, supra note 56, at 7.

A final, related argument is that speech concerning the political process is simply more important than speech concerning private decisionmaking, because it affects many more lives. One may question, however, whether this is true of all activity within the political process; one can imagine town council elections in miniscule hamlets, which, I assume, both Meiklejohn and Bork would include in their definition of "political," even though relatively few people would be affected. In any event, the argument is misleading, because it fails to recognize that, when we value private decisionmaking, we are referring to such decisionmaking on the part of *all* individuals.

II. Separating Value from Subvalue: An Inquiry into the Alternative Goals of Free Speech

This Article so far has established at most that values inherent in the democratic process extend the benefit of free speech well beyond the confines of the "political." The original claim made in this Article, however, was considerably more ambitious: that all of the so-called "values" of free speech, to the extent that they are to be accepted, derive ultimately from the single value of self-realization. Such a demonstration would preclude future theorists from asserting that, although they believe in the concept of free speech, they will select a value other than self-realization as the guiding force. The argument here is that, to the extent you accept the value of free speech at all, you must necessarily accept the self-realization value, for there is no other. In addition, for the thesis to be complete, it must be established that those who do accept the self-realization value cannot logically escape acceptance of these "subvalues" as well. It is to these issues that we now turn.

A. *The Checking Function*

Perhaps the asserted value most closely analogous to the "democratic process" value is Professor Blasi's "checking function." Blasi believes that speech concerning misconduct by government officials deserves special constitutional protection.[69]

---

[69] In Blasi's words, "if one had to identify the single value that was uppermost in the minds of the persons who drafted and ratified the First Amendment, this checking value would be the most likely candidate." Blasi, *supra* note 2, at 527. Although Blasi at one point asserts that "the checking value is to be viewed as a possible supplement to, not a substitute for, the values that have been at the center of twentieth-century thinking about the First Amendment," *id.* 528, he later asserts that speech related to the checking function "should . . . be accorded a level of constitutional protection higher than that given any other type of communication," because "the particular evil of official misconduct is of a special order." *Id.* 558.

The first question about Blasi's checking function concerns the precise scope of the speech included within it. At different points, Blasi refers to speech concerning "abuse of power," the misuse of official power," and "breaches of trust by public officials," [70] implying that these are the operative terms. But the meaning of these terms is by no means self-evident. A natural starting point would seem to be illegal conduct on the part of public officials, such as taking bribes, and Blasi unquestionably intends to include such activity.[71] But he does not stop there, nor could he without all but trivializing the free speech guarantee. If we are to understand where his theory is to apply, we must know exactly what, in addition to illegal conduct, Blasi would include under the heading of "misconduct." In attempting to define "a viable concept of official 'misconduct' that does not simply collapse into 'unwisdom' or 'unpopularity,' " [72] Blasi provides some illustrations:

> Some governmental actions such as the deliberate bombing
> of civilians during wartime, the assassination of foreign
> political figures, or less extreme examples of improper in-
> volvement in the domestic affairs of another nation might
> also be regarded as so in violation of shared standards of
> morality as to fall within a distinctive concept of
> misconduct.[73]

So described, Blasi's first amendment theory degenerates into little more than a means of fostering one individual's—presumably Professor Blasi's—political philosophy and foreign policy.[74] What about the individual who believed that *not* bombing civilians in the Vietnam War would have been "misconduct"—someone who would assert that "if we are going to fight a war, let's win it; it's immoral to have our boys die in a limited war"—or who believes that assassinating certain foreign political figures—perhaps Castro or Hitler or Idi Amin—is morally dictated? Are only those who share the views on these issues described by Professor Blasi to receive the special pro-

---

[70] *Id.* 527.

[71] *See id.* 543 ("Behavior in violation of the applicable criminal code such as embezzlement or the acceptance of a bribe might provide a starting point for such a concept.").

[72] *Id.*

[73] *Id.*

[74] At the outset of his article, Professor Blasi notes the impact that public outcries had on limiting the Asian war policies of Presidents Johnson and Nixon. *Id.* 527; *see also id.* 640 ("[T]he communication achieved by the wave of draft-card burnings at the height of the United States involvement in Vietnam represents a paradigm example of the 'speech' with which the First Amendment is concerned.").

tection given speech concerning the checking function? Such a result-oriented, content-based approach to free speech must of course be rejected, yet it seems to be the implication of Professor Blasi's description of "official misconduct," for Professor Blasi's theory by its terms refers to conduct, rather than issues. Moreover, what about discussion of official conduct that, although perhaps not offensive to Professor Blasi, is considered by many to be so? Is it "misconduct" for the government to allow abortions? To pay welfare? Again, to deny the inclusion of speech concerning such official actions would constitute a wholly unacceptable interpretation of the first amendment on the basis of political or social viewpoint, for if the first amendment means anything it is that the level of constitutional protection cannot vary on the basis of differing viewpoints.[75]

Perhaps Professor Blasi did not intend to establish such a solipsistic view of the first amendment. At one point, he states that "[u]nder the checking value, that determination [of what actions can be considered misconduct] must be made by each citizen in deciding when the actions of government so transcend the bounds of decency that active opposition becomes a civic duty."[76] But Blasi's distinction of speech concerning official "misconduct" from speech about general governmental action collapses if the determination of what is official misconduct is to be left to the individual citizen. For how effective a limit would it be if any individual could render governmental action or inaction "misconduct" for first amendment purposes merely by characterizing it as such?

At least in a broad sense, however, it is accurate to recognize the value of speech, as Professor Blasi does, as a means of controlling governmental actions.[77] The question for discussion, then, is whether this value is independent of the self-realization value or, instead, as contended here, is merely derivative.

Professor Blasi describes the purposes thought to be served by the checking function. He argues primarily that "a proponent of

---

[75] I have argued elsewhere that it is improper to provide stricter constitutional scrutiny to regulation of expression based on content than to regulation that is imposed equally on all speech. Redish, *The Content Distinction in First Amendment Analysis*, 34 STAN. L. REV. 113 (1981). However, this was not intended to imply that *less* scrutiny should be given to viewpoint regulation, but rather that *greater* scrutiny should be given to neutral regulation.

[76] Blasi, *supra* note 2, at 543 (footnote omitted).

[77] As restructured, Professor Blasi's "checking function" appears strikingly similar to the "democratic process" value of Meiklejohn, notwithstanding Professor Blasi's statements to the contrary, *see id.* 558.

the checking value views speech of a certain content as important because of its *consequences*: alerting the polity to the facts or implications of official behavior, presumably triggering responses that will mitigate the ill effects of such behavior." [78]   If Blasi is correct in characterizing the checking function as fostering the consequential value of producing "good results," the value would in fact be distinct from the "process" goals inherent in the self-realization value.   But closer examination of the reasoning behind the checking function reveals that this value can be sustained only on the basis of process, rather, than consequential values.   To view the checking function as having a consequential value logically requires us to adopt the following reasoning: if government officials believe that it is correct to do "A"—a particular course of action or policy decision—and some or many members of the public believe that doing A would constitute "misconduct" and instead prefer that the officials do "B," we know that B will produce "better"—less evil or more beneficial—results than A will.   But this conclusion surely does not follow as a matter of logic, and may well be counter-intuitive in light of the empirical evidence obtained by elitist theorists of a tremendous lack of political interest and knowledge on the part of the large mass of private citizens. [79]

Of course, if we were to read Professor Blasi to suggest that there is a set category of political actions that are to be objectively deemed "misconduct," [80] then we would be able to conclude that speech by private citizens criticizing such activity would produce "better" results.   But, as already noted,[81] such an unprincipled construction of the first amendment, providing greater protection to speech urging results with which one agrees, is totally unacceptable.   Therefore, we must assume, as Blasi states at another point, that it is the individual citizen's subjective characterization of official action as "misconduct" that is determinative.[82]   Given

---

[78] *Id.* 546 (emphasis in original).   This emphasis on consequences is what Professor Blasi believes primarily distinguishes the checking function from what he describes as the "autonomy" value.   *Id.*   At another point, underscoring his "consequentialist" approach, he states that the evil of government misconduct "is so antithetical to the entire political arrangement, is so harmful to individual people, and also is so likely to occur, that its prevention and containment is a goal that takes precedence over all other goals of the political system."   *Id.* 558 (footnote omitted).

[79] *See supra* note 61 and accompanying text.   According to Professor Walker, "[a]t the heart of the elitist theory is a clear presumption of the average citizen's inadequacies."   Walker, *supra* note 51, at 286.

[80] *See supra* text accompanying notes 71-73.

[81] *See supra* text accompanying note 75.

[82] Blasi, *supra* note 2, at 543.

that premise, we cannot support the checking value on consequential grounds, for we cannot be sure that the official policies thought by particular individuals to constitute "misconduct" necessarily would be more evil than the alternative policies urged by the private individuals.

To the extent that there is an important value behind the checking function, then, it must be a process value. And it is not difficult to determine what that value is; it is the intrinsic democratic value that individuals should have a say in the policies of their government, because their government, in a democracy, is acting on their behalf. As democratic theorist Edmond Cahn has stated, democracy requires "examining, judging, and assuming responsibility for what our representatives do in our name and by our authority, the unjust and evil acts as well as the beneficent and good." [83]   Indeed, to the extent that Professor Blasi relies on the proposition that "the general populace must be the ultimate judge of the behavior of public officials," [84] he, too, is viewing the checking function as merely one manifestation of the intrinsic democratic value.[85]   Because the checking function ultimately derives

---

[83] E. CAHN, THE PREDICAMENT OF DEMOCRATIC MAN 29 (1961).

[84] Blasi, *supra* note 2, at 542.

[85] Blasi acknowledges that "the checking value grows out of democratic theory, but it is the democratic theory of John Locke and Joseph Schumpeter, not that of Alexander Meiklejohn." *Id.* His reference to Schumpeter, however, is puzzling. Blasi asserts that, under Schumpeter's view, "the role of the ordinary citizen is not so much to contribute on a continuing basis to the formation of public policy as to retain a veto power to be employed when the decisions of officials pass certain bounds." *Id.* (footnote omitted). However, Schumpeter actually raised serious doubts about the individual citizen's ability to question the specific policies of government. *See* J. SCHUMPETER, CAPITALISM, SOCIALISM AND DEMOCRACY 261 (3d ed. 1950); *see also* C. PATEMAN, PARTICIPATION AND DEMOCRATIC THEORY 3-4 (1970). Schumpeter urged an extremely limited role for private citizens, primarily that of "accepting or refusing the men who are to rule them." J. SCHUMPETER, *supra*, at 285. It is doubtful that this philosophy is consistent with Professor Blasi's view that private citizens have authority to determine for themselves what actions of public officials constitute misconduct. Blasi, *supra* note 2, at 543.

Blasi actually is probably much closer to Meiklejohn than he is to Schumpeter, for essential to Meiklejohn's philosophy was the belief that "[a] government of free men can properly be controlled only by itself. Who else could be trusted by us to hold our political institutions in check?" A. MEIKLEJOHN, *supra* note 8, at 16. Although Meiklejohn believed that the people were truly the "governors" and that elected officials were merely their agents, he did not advocate a system of direct democracy. Rather, he believed that citizens needed information and opinion, so that they could better perform their governing function *in the voting booth.* Meiklejohn, *supra* note 11, at 255-56.

Blasi asserts that "[t]he self-government value [of Meiklejohn] appears to place slightly more emphasis on argumentation (as contrasted with information) than does the checking value." Blasi, *supra* note 2, at 563. However, if Blasi believes that the activities of antiwar protestors (including draft card burning) constitutes a classic example of how the checking function operates, *see id.* 554, it is difficult

from the principle of democratic self-rule, and because that principle in turn follows from the self-realization value,[86] the checking function is merely one concrete manifestation of the much broader self-realization value.[87]

B. *The Marketplace-of-Ideas Concept*

"[T]he ultimate good desired," wrote Justice Holmes in his *Abrams* dissent, "is better reached by free trade in ideas—. . . the best test of truth is the power of the thought to get itself accepted in the competition of the market . . . . That at any rate is the theory of our Constitution." [88] The theory, derived originally from John Stuart Mill,[89] posits, in the accurate description of one of its critics, that:

> [C]ompetition among ideas strengthens the truth and roots out error; the repeated effort to defend one's convictions serves to keep their justification alive in our minds and guards against the twin dangers of falsehood and fanaticism; to stifle a voice is to deprive mankind of its message, which, we must acknowledge, might possibly be more true than our own deeply held convictions. . . . Just as an unfettered competition among commodities guarantees that the good products sell while the bad gather dust on the shelf, so in the intellectual marketplace the several competing ideas will be tested by us, the consumers, and the best of them will be purchased.[90]

The "marketplace-of-ideas" concept, in its use as a defense of free speech, has often been subjected to savage attack,[91] and to a

to accept his information-opinion distinction. For were not the primary activities of the antiwar movement more a matter of expressing opinion than of conveying information?

86 *See supra* text accompanying notes 49-50.

87 Blasi expends considerable effort in an attempt to establish a historical link between the checking value and the origins of the first amendment. Blasi, *supra* note 2, at 529-38. But most of the historical sources to which he refers were concerned primarily with ensuring the liberty of citizens—the intrinsic democratic value—and saw the checking of government not as an end in itself or as a means of assuring "better results," but as a means of assuring that government would not interfere with the individual's exercise of his liberty.

88 Abrams v. United States, 250 U.S. 616, 630 (1919) (Holmes, J., dissenting).

89 J. Mill, *supra* note 51. According to Professor Baker, Mill provides the "marketplace-of-ideas" theory's "best formulation." Baker, *supra* note 15, at 968 n.9; *see also* R. Wolff, The Poverty of Liberalism 11-12 (1968).

90 R. Wolff, *supra* note 89, at 11-12; *see also* Baker, *supra* note 15, at 967.

91 *See, e.g.*, R. Wolff, *supra* note 89, at 12-19; Baker, *supra* note 15, at 974-81. According to Professor Dworkin, "John Stuart Mill's famous essay *On Liberty* has on the whole served conservatives better than liberals. . . . [C]ritics

certain extent the attacks have been entirely valid. In one sense, the theory appears to suffer from an internal contradiction: the theory's goal is the attainment of truth, yet it posits that we can never really know the truth,[92] so we must keep looking. But, if we can never attain the truth, why bother to continue the fruitless search? More importantly, any theory positing that the value of free speech is the search for truth creates a great danger that someone will decide that he finally has attained knowledge of the truth. At that point, that individual (or society) may feel fully justified, as a matter of both morality and logic, in shutting off expression of any views that are contrary to this "truth." To be sure, Mill would not have accepted such reasoning. He believed that even views that we know to be false deserve protection, because their expression makes the truth appear even stronger by contrast.[93] But acceptance of Mill's initial premise that the goal of free speech is the ultimate attainment of truth does not necessitate acceptance of this second premise. For, as Dean Wellington has argued, "[i]t is naive to think that truth will *always* prevail over falsehood in a free and open encounter, for too many false ideas have captured the imagination of man."[94] Therefore, if the only value of free speech were the attainment of truth, we might persuasively argue that the view that the Earth is the center of the Universe does not deserve constitutional protection, because we know the truth to be different. Perhaps we could further conclude that constitutional protection should not be given to the assertion that cigarette smoking does not cause cancer, because the Surgeon General has already discovered the truth about this subject; the same could be said about the view that certain races are genetically inferior, since we know that all men are created equal. The danger—one that Mill would undoubtedly neither expect nor condone—should by now be clear.

It does not necessarily follow, however, that the marketplace-of-ideas concept must be discarded. To the contrary: if viewed as merely a means by which the ultimate value of self-realization is

---

of liberalism have been pleased to cite the essay as the most cogent philosophical defense of that theory, and then, by noticing the defects in its argument, argue that liberalism is flawed." R. DWORKIN, TAKING RIGHTS SERIOUSLY 259 (1977).

[92] *See* I. BERLIN, *supra* note 54, at 188 ("[Mill's] argument is plausible only on the assumption . . . that human knowledge was in principle never complete, and always fallible; that there was no single, universally visible, truth . . . .").

[93] J. MILL, *supra* note 51, at 34-45.

[94] Wellington, *supra* note 48, at 1130 (emphasis in original). *See also* I. BERLIN, *supra* note 54, at 187.

618   *UNIVERSITY OF PENNSYLVANIA LAW REVIEW*   [Vol. 130:591

facilitated, the concept may prove quite valuable in determining what speech is deserving of constitutional protection. In other words, it could be argued that, if the intrinsic aspect of the self-realization value [95] is to be maintained, the individual needs an un-inhibited flow of information and opinion to aid him or her in making life-affecting decisions, in governing his or her own life. Since the concept of self-realization by its very nature does not permit external forces to determine what is a wise decision for the individual to make, it is no more appropriate for external forces to censor what information or opinion the individual may receive in reaching those decisions. Thus, an individual presumably has the right [96] not to associate with people of different races in the privacy of his home, and may decide to exercise that right because he believes those who contend other races are genetically inferior.[97] That is his choice, and he may reach it on whatever basis he chooses, no matter how irrational it may seem to others. Because individuals constantly make life-affecting decisions—from the significant to the trivial—each day of their lives, there is probably no expression of opinion or information that would not potentially affect some such decision at some point in time. Therefore, the marketplace-of-ideas concept as a protector of all such expression makes perfect sense.[98]

So revised, the marketplace-of-ideas concept can be successfully defended against another attack: Baker's contentions that the theory "requires that people be able to use their rational capacities to eliminate distortion caused by the form and frequency of message presentation and to find the core of relevant information or argument," and that "[t]his assumption cannot be accepted [be-

---

[95] *See supra* text following note 49.

[96] In using the term "right" in this context, I do not intend to limit its meaning to a constitutional, or even a statutory, right, although in certain instances it could conceivably be either of these. I mean, rather, the absence of a governmental prohibition.

[97] An individual of course would not be allowed to decide on the basis of this information to kill members of these races, or to refuse to associate with them in public accommodations. These are situations in which society has decided to limit the individual's freedom of action.

[98] Although I will deal with the point in detail in subsequent discussion, *see infra* text accompanying notes 110-18, it is perhaps necessary to emphasize here that I am referring only to the issue of what speech rightfully belongs within the first amendment's umbrella of constitutional protection. Since I am not a believer in construing the first amendment to provide absolute protection to speech, the conclusion that speech falls within the first amendment does not necessarily imply that it will outbalance all competing social concerns.

cause e]motional or 'irrational' appeals have great impact." [99]   If we accepted the attainment of truth as the theory's goal, Professor Baker's point would be well taken.   But the point becomes irrelevant if we instead view the theory simply as a means of facilitating the value of self-realization.   For if an individual wishes to buy a car because he believes it will make him look masculine, or to vote for a candidate because the candidate looks good with his tie loosened and his jacket slung over his shoulder, who are we to tell him that these are improper acts?   We may prefer that he make his judgments (at least as to the candidate, if not the car) on more traditionally "rational" grounds, and hope that appeals made on such grounds will be heard.   But in these areas society has left the ultimate right to decide to the individual, and this would not be much of a right if we prescribed how it was to be used.[100]

C. *The "Liberty" Model*

Although Professor Baker's primary attack on the marketplace-of-ideas theory is premised on the inability of the system to produce rational results, the essential elements of his own theory of free expression, if accepted, logically lead to a rejection of even the revised version described here.   Professor Baker adopts as the center of his theory of free speech the "liberty model," [101] under which respect for individual autonomy leads us to protect communication

---

[99] Baker, *supra* note 15, at 976.   According to Baker, "[t]he assumptions on which the classic marketplace of ideas theory rests are almost universally rejected today."   *Id.* 974.   However, there may be some inconsistency in Baker's analysis. On the one hand, he attacks the marketplace-of-ideas concept because it is premised on a presumption of individual rationality that is unrealistic.   Yet Baker's own theory of free speech is based on the view that individuals must be respected as "equal, *rational* and autonomous moral beings."   *Id.* 991 (emphasis added).   He rejects limitations on free speech that are designed "to protect people from harms that result because the listener adopts certain perceptions or attitudes," because to do so "disrespects the responsibility and freedom of the listener."   *Id.* 998.

[100] It might be argued that the marketplace-of-ideas theory is unrealistic in assuming that, absent government regulation, individual decisionmakers will receive an unbiased flow of information because certain groups, holding particular viewpoints, control the media and exclude unpopular opinions from the information stream.   Many who have recognized this difficulty have urged increased right of access to the communications media.   *See, e.g.*, Red Lion Broadcasting Co. v. FCC, 395 U.S. 367 (1969); Barron, *Access to the Press—A New First Amendment Right*, 80 HARV. L. REV. 1641 (1967).   Such an access theory faces serious constitutional questions itself, *see* Miami Herald Publishing Co. v. Tornillo, 418 U.S. 241 (1974), but, at least under certain circumstances, provides an answer to this criticism.   In any event, even if this criticism were accepted, it does not imply that the marketplace-of-ideas theory is useless, but merely that it is not perfect.   Thus, this argument offers no support for any efforts to further impede the flow of information.

[101] Baker, *supra* note 15, at 990.

620   *UNIVERSITY OF PENNSYLVANIA LAW REVIEW*   [Vol. 130:591

that defines, develops, or expresses "the self." [102]   "[T]he values
supported or functions performed by protected speech," he writes,
"result from that speech being a manifestation of individual freedom and choice." [103]   Therefore, he concludes, speech that "does
not represent an attempt to create or affect the world in a way
which can be expected to represent anyone's private or personal
wishes" is not deserving of constitutional protection.[104]   It is for
this reason that Baker would give no constitutional protection to
commercial speech.[105]   Because there is presumably a considerable
amount of information or opinion flowing to individuals from corporations and others who are motivated by economic considerations,
Baker would not be likely to accept even the revised rationale for
the marketplace-of-ideas theory.   Although Baker correctly recognizes the self-realization value lying behind the protection given
free speech, he has so narrowly confined this concept that he has
effectively excluded significant amounts of expression that could
substantially foster the self-realization value.

Baker's adoption of an extremely narrow view of how the self-
realization value can be fostered apparently results from his acceptance of a truncated version of the value itself.   The form of
self-realization that he seems to be describing is limited to the
"instrumental" value referred to previously: the value of having
individuals develop their faculties.[106]   Even with this truncated
version, Baker has failed to acknowledge that individuals may develop their personal and intellectual faculties by *receiving,* as well
as by expressing.[107]   Once this is recognized, we can see that the

---

[102] *Id.* 992.

[103] Baker, *Commercial Speech: A Problem in the Theory of Freedom,* 62 Iowa
L. Rev. 1, 3 (1976) (footnote omitted).

[104] *Id.*   Baker elsewhere has argued that "if it is not a manifestation of the
speaker's values, even though the speech may cause change or advance knowledge,
it does not serve this liberty value and is not protected," Baker, *supra* note 15, at
991 n.86, and that "to the extent that speech is involuntary, is not chosen by the
speaker, the speech act does not involve the *self*-realization or *self*-fulfillment of the
speaker," *id.* 996 (emphasis in original).

[105] Baker, *supra* note 103, at 3.

[106] Baker notes that, "[o]n the liberty theory, the purpose of the first amendment is not to guarantee adequate information." Baker, *supra* note 15, at 1007.
He also writes, however, that "[s]elf-expressive and creative uses of speech more
fully and uniformly promote the two key first amendment values, self-fulfillment and
participation in both societal decisionmaking and culture building, than does speech
which communicates propositions and attitudes." *Id.* 995 (emphasis omitted).

[107] At one point, Baker acknowledges that "[t]he listener uses speech for self-
realization or change purposes and these uses provide the basis of the listener's
constitutional right." *Id.* 1007. He adds, however, that "the constitutional analysis
of any restriction must be in terms of who is restricted—the speaker or the listener.

motivation of the speaker may be irrelevant, as long as the individual's faculties are developed by the *receipt* of information whether it be opinion or fact. For example, that an author is writing primarily to make money, rather than to express his personality, does not diminish the potential development of the reader. More important, however, is Baker's refusal to recognize the correlative principle to self-fulfillment's instrumental value: the intrinsic value, self-rule. Thus, if an individual is given the opportunity to control his destiny, at least within certain bounds, he or she needs all possible information that might aid in making these life-affecting decisions. Because Baker fails to include this vital aspect of the self-realization concept, he develops a theory of free speech that is correspondingly incomplete.

Even if we were to accept Baker's unduly narrow conception of self-realization, his theory fails to deal adequately with the inseparability of the profit motive from the desire for self-expression. The problem arises because many people make a living by means of self-expressive work. Should the creative advertiser or commercial artist not be recognized for their "self-expression," merely because they are doing it to make money? Baker responds that "even if the speech happens to correspond to the speaker's values, the content is determined by the structure of the market and is not chosen by the speaker." [108] But surely within the dictates of the market structure the advertiser has a range of selection; there is never merely a single possible way to sell a product. Thus, can we not say that within that range the advertiser has exercised his or her self-expression? Moreover, if we accept Baker's analysis, what protection do we give to the political candidate who tailors his public positions to what he thinks will lead to his election, to the magazine or newspaper that chooses to publish what sells, or to the author who writes what he believes his audience will buy? Are *their* efforts not to receive first amendment protection? And what would Baker say about the level of first amendment protection to be given to welfare or social security recipients who picket to protest insufficient government aid? Is not *their* expression also dictated by the needs of the market?

Both parties have separate constitutional claims. Only if the restricted party does not have a constitutional claim is the government restriction permissible." *Id.* Thus, since Baker does not believe that those motivated by profit incentives, rather than self-expression, have a constitutional right, he must believe that these "speakers" can be constitutionally restricted, even though the listeners' ability to gain fulfillment may well suffer as a result.

[108] *Id.* 966 n.102.

622   *UNIVERSITY OF PENNSYLVANIA LAW REVIEW*   [Vol. 130:591]

Of all of these arguments, Baker attempts a response only to the question raised about political candidates. His answer is that:

> First, for many, if not most, political actors' [sic] political activity is not primarily and, more importantly, is not necessarily determined by the need to maximize either electoral support or economic profit. . . . Thus, no structure requires that the speaker choose increased chances of election (which is not even an option for minor parties) over increased advocacy of their values. Second, unlike the economic sphere . . . , many politicians and most defenders of the political process argue that, here, it is highly praiseworthy to truthfully and forcefully state, explain, and advocate one's own visions or understanding of the public good.[109]

Baker provides no statistical support for his first assertion, and it certainly seems counter-intuitive to me, at least, to think that most candidates for office do not have election as their primary goal. Nor am I convinced of the accuracy of his second assertion, but even if it were true it is irrelevant. That honesty may be "praiseworthy" does not mean that many candidates actually practice it, no matter how much they may purport to do so. Most importantly, what would Baker do if he could be convinced that ninety-nine percent of candidates were actually motivated more by the desire for election than by the desire to express their values? Would he urge no first amendment protection for their speeches? His logic would seem to lead to that conclusion. Baker's fundamental assumptions thus appear to be both pragmatically unrealistic and theoretically dubious.

III. The Self-Realization Value and the Balancing of First Amendment Interests

Professor Blasi writes that:

> The concept of human autonomy is largely irreducible. The libertarian argument from autonomy rests on the proposition that unless individuals retain a basic minimum of choice-making capability, they cease to be "individuals" at all. It is no accident, therefore, that claims based on the value of individual autonomy tend to be absolute in nature; they concern not interests to be promoted against competing regulatory interests but rather constitutive ele-

---

[109] *Id.*

ments the integrity of which must be respected if the whole edifice of constitutional limitations is to remain coherent.[110]

Professor Baker makes a similar point,[111] but it is difficult to understand. The concept of individual autonomy certainly has never been thought to lead to absolute protection for conduct, yet we may still maintain a belief in such an autonomy value. Why should our recognition of something akin to that value as the underlying force behind the protection of speech necessarily lead to any greater degree of absoluteness? There is, then, no logically necessary link between a belief in individual self-realization and a so-called "absolute" construction of the first amendment. In fact, the issue of absoluteness appears to present the same questions and to give rise to the same conflicting arguments whatever values are thought to be fostered by the free speech guarantee.

It is not the purpose of this Article to rehash the competing contentions on this issue, nor to consider the nuances of the various absolutist and balancing-test theories that have been suggested over the years. The primary goal, rather, has been to delimit the scope of the category of communication and expression that is to fall within the constitutional protection in the first place. But, in light of this suggested logical link, it is necessary to provide at least a brief explanation of why an absolute construction cannot be accepted, even if self-realization is recognized as the ultimate value underlying the first amendment.

The answer is simply that an absolute construction is (1) not required by the language of the amendment, (2) not dictated by the intent of the framers, and (3) impossible in practice. As to the issue of language, the phrase "freedom of speech" is not necessarily the same as "speech," and is certainly not self-defining. As to the intent of the framers, what little evidence there is suggests that, to the extent they thought about it at all, they intended an extremely narrow construction of the first amendment,[112] and certainly not an absolute construction. Finally, I simply refuse to believe that anything in first amendment language or policy requires us to protect the statement of a mob leader, outside a poorly defended prison,

---

[110] Blasi, *supra* note 2, at 547; *see also* BeVier, *supra* note 12, at 320.

[111] Baker, *supra* note 15, at 1009. Note, however, that Baker does not believe in "absolute" protection for speech (even though he does include certain types of conduct within the constitutional guarantee), since he excludes speech dictated by the market structure. *See id.* 996 & n.102.

[112] *See* L. LEVY, *supra* note 27, at 247-48.

urging his torch-carrying compatriots to lynch a prisoner inside.[113] Once it is acknowledged that the free speech interest must give way in such a situation to a competing social interest, acceptance of at least *some* form of balancing process is established. The question is simply where to draw the line.

The concept of balancing gained a bad name among civil libertarians during its heyday in the 1950's, because it was usually used simply as a code word for substituting legislative determinations for judicial review.[114] However, if we define "balancing" to include definitional balancing, as well as the *ad hoc* variety, we can see that the concept has gained wide acceptance,[115] for any general rule of first amendment interpretation that chooses not to afford absolute protection to speech because of competing social concerns is, in reality, a form of balancing. The point, however, is to balance with "a thumb on the scales" in favor of speech.[116] Although the first amendment cannot practically be interpreted to

---

[113] It appears that Professor Baker's construction of the first amendment would protect such expression. Although Baker believes that "[r]espect for individual autonomy hardly requires protection of speech when the listener is coerced," he also asserts that "outlawing acts of the speaker in order to protect people from harms that result because the listener adopts certain perceptions or attitudes disrespects the responsibility and freedom of the listener." Baker, *supra* note 15, at 998. Speech is protected because "it depends for its power on increasing the speaker's own awareness or on the voluntary acceptance of listeners." *Id.* 999. Because the harm in the lynching hypothetical results from "the voluntary acceptance of listeners," the conclusion seems inescapable that Baker would protect such speech.

[114] *See, e.g.,* Frantz, *The First Amendment in the Balance,* 71 YALE L.J. 1424, 1444 (1962) ("[I]t must be regarded as very nearly inevitable that a court which clings to the balancing test will sooner or later adopt a corollary that the balance struck by Congress is not only presumed correct, but is to be accorded extreme, almost total, judicial deference."); Mendelson, *On the Meaning of the First Amendment: Absolutes in the Balance,* 50 CALIF. L. REV. 821, 826 (1962) ("Above all, the open balancing technique is calculated to leave 'the sovereign prerogative of choice' to the people—with the least interference that is compatible with our tradition of judicial review."); *see also* Dennis v. United States, 341 U.S. 494, 525 (1951) (Frankfurter, J., concurring).

[115] It is not my purpose here to debate the relative merits of *ad hoc* and definitional balancing (also referred to as "categorization"). *See generally* Ely, *Flag Desecration: A Case Study in the Roles of Categorization and Balancing in First Amendment Analysis,* 88 HARV. L. REV. 1482 (1975); Nimmer, *The Right to Speak From Time to Time: First Amendment Theory Applied to Libel and Misapplied to Privacy,* 56 CALIF. L. REV. 935 (1968). My point is simply that one need not be an absolutist if one relies on self-realization as the ultimate value of free speech. What form of "balancing" one adopts at that stage is beyond this Article's scope. The only point to be underscored is that, in the broad sense of the term at least, the categorizers, too, are engaged in "balancing," in that they reject an absolutist approach in favor of an analysis that allows fully protected speech to be superseded by overriding social interests.

[116] Frantz acknowledges that "it is conceivable that a court might apply the balancing test, yet attach so high a value to freedom of speech that the balance would nearly always be struck in its favor." Frantz, *supra* note 114, at 1440.

provide absolute protection, the constitutional language and our political and social traditions dictate that the first amendment right must give way only in the presence of a truly compelling governmental interest.[117] To be sure, such an analysis places a good deal of faith in the ability of judges to exercise their authority with wisdom and discretion, both in establishing and applying general rules of first amendment construction and, where necessary,[118] in engaging in *ad hoc* balancing. But, after all, that is what they are there for, and in any event we appear to have little choice.

IV. Acceptance of the Self-Realization Value: Implications for Constitutional Construction

If the self-realization value were accepted as the guiding force behind constitutional protection of free speech, it is likely that the Court's approach to numerous issues of first amendment construction would have to change. The "two-level" concept of speech derived from *Chaplinsky v. New Hampshire*,[119] which recognizes a sublevel of speech that is unworthy of constitutional protection, would have to be abandoned. That doctrine posits that:

> There are certain well-defined and narrowly limited classes of speech, the prevention and punishment of which have never been thought to raise any Constitutional problem. These include the lewd and obscene, the profane, the libelous, and the insulting or "fighting" words—those which by their very utterance inflict injury or tend to incite an immediate breach of the peace. It has been well observed that such utterances are no essential part of any exposition of ideas, and are of such slight social value as a step to truth that any benefit that may be derived from them is clearly outweighed by the social interest in order and morality.[120]

The theoretical fallacy in the *Chaplinsky* doctrine is the assumption that the value of free speech is as a means to attain truth. Once one recognizes that the primary value of free speech is as a means of fostering individual development and aiding the making of life-affecting decisions, the inappropriateness of distinguishing between the value of different types of speech becomes clear. Al-

---

[117] I have discussed the application of a "compelling interest" test as a measure of free speech protection in Redish, *supra* note 75, at 142-50.

[118] *See id.* 150-51.

[119] 315 U.S. 568 (1942); *see also* Beuharnais v. Illinois, 343 U.S. 250 (1952).

[120] 315 U.S. at 571-72 (footnotes omitted).

though subsequent sections [121] deal explicitly with the categories of libel and obscenity to which the Court referred in *Chaplinsky,* the doctrine's problems can be seen clearly in its application to the type of speech actually at issue in that case: "fighting words."

In *Chaplinsky,* a Jehovah's Witness distributing literature was involved in a disturbance and was taken into police custody. On the way to the police station, he confronted the City Marshall and allegedly called him "a God damned racketeer" and "a damned Fascist." [122] He was convicted pursuant to a state statute that made it an offense to address "any offensive, derisive or annoying word to any other person who is lawfully in any street or other public place." [123] Why not view Chaplinsky's comments as a personal catharsis, as a means to vent his frustration at a system he deemed—whether rightly or wrongly—to be oppressive? Is it not a mark of individuality to be able to cry out at a society viewed as crushing the individual? Under this analysis, so-called "fighting words" represent a significant means of self-realization, whether or not they can be considered a means of attaining some elusive "truth."

This is not to suggest that fighting words should receive absolute protection, any more than any other form of expression deserves such a guarantee of freedom.[124] The point, rather, is that fighting words should not be deemed constitutionally regulable per se. If, in particular circumstances, such words are likely to have the effect of starting a riot or significantly and immediately disturbing the peace, their use can of course be subjected to penalty. But in *Chaplinsky* itself no such showing was even attempted, and, given the facts, it is unlikely that one could have been made. For the words were not spoken to militant armed opponents of Jehovah's Witnesses in the street, but to an apparently oversensitive city official on the way to the police station. Other than a slight ruffling of the official's feathers, Mr. Chaplinsky's colorful language did not cause any harm. Hence, if the Court had recognized the legitimate first amendment value in the use of such language, it would have been required to engage in a careful weighing of competing interests, an endeavor it seemingly found not to be worth the effort.

The discussion of the level of constitutional protection to be given so-called "fighting words" raises a broader issue: whether

---

[121] *See infra* text accompanying notes 158-202.

[122] 315 U.S. at 569.

[123] *Id.*

[124] *See supra* text accompanying notes 110-18.

there is *any* form of pure expression that does not foster self-realization, and that therefore is not worthy of first amendment protection.   In answering this question, it is necessary to recall the two different aspects of self-realization: self-governance and the development of one's human faculties.[125]   As to the former, there is clearly a wide variety of speech that is irrelevant, for this branch of the self-realization value is furthered only by expression that provides information or opinion that will aid an individual in making decisions about how his or her life will be conducted.   Thus, advocacy of unlawful conduct cannot be deemed relevant, because the individual is not allowed to undertake the conduct urged by that form of expression.   Nor is the dissemination of undisputedly false factual information a valid means of aiding private self-government, since such information cannot be thought to provide legitimate guidance to individual decisionmaking.[126]   A mere stream of obscenities must also be deemed irrelevant to the goal of private self-government.

There is more to self-realization, however, than private self-government.   For it is highly doubtful that fine art, ballet, or literature can be thought to aid one in making concrete life-affecting decisions, yet all three seem deserving of full first amendment protection.   This is because of the other branch of self-realization: the development of one's human faculties, recognized as an end in itself. Once this form of self-realization is acknowledged, it becomes significantly more difficult to exclude many of the categories of expression deemed irrelevant to the private self-government branch.

Of course, we might conclude that, whereas art, literature, and ballet are proper means of developing one's mental faculties, a mere stream of obscenities or advocacy of crime is not.   But, although it may well be appropriate to distinguish among different forms of expression on the ground that some of them present greater danger of harming society,[127] it is considerably more doubtful that an arm of the state should have the authority to decide for the individual that certain means of mental development are better than others.   If two consenting individuals wish to engage in a conversation consisting of little more than a stream of obscenities,

---

[125] *See supra* text accompanying notes 49-51.

[126] There may still be a problem about suppressing certain false factual assertions, because of the potential chilling effect on expression of true factual statements. *See* New York Times Co. v. Sullivan, 376 U.S. 254 (1964).

[127] *See supra* text accompanying notes 110-18.

628   *UNIVERSITY OF PENNSYLVANIA LAW REVIEW*   [Vol. 130:591

assuming no harm to others,[128] it is dangerous to provide the state
with the power to prohibit such activity on the ground that such
discourse is not "valuable." [129]   For, if the state can make that decision, what is logically to prevent it from deciding that the works
of Henry Miller are not "valuable" because of their constant use of
obscenities?   Or why could not the state similarly set up an administrative board to decide that certain works of literature, art,
dance, or music are not as "valuable" as others, and can therefore
be suppressed?   Most of us would no doubt find such a process
intuitively repugnant, presumably even if we agreed with the censor
about the lack of quality of a particular book, movie, or performance.   We would explain this feeling of repugnance, I suppose, by
reasoning that it is simply not the state's business to decide for
each individual what books, movies, or shows are "valuable"; that
is a decision for the individual to make for himself or herself.   But
once we have gone that far, how could we rationally distinguish
the stream of obscenities between consenting adults?   There, too, we
would have to reason that perhaps that particular form of discourse
is not our cup of tea, but that this gives the state no more inherent
right to suppress it than it would have to suppress a particular
book or movie we found distasteful.   A stream of obscenities may
not develop one's *intellectual* abilities (though it could conceivably
increase one's vocabulary), but neither does music, art, or dance.
An individual's "mental" processes cannot be limited to the receipt
and digestion of cold, hard theories and facts, for there is also an
emotional element that is uniquely human and that can be "developed" by such "non-rational" forms of communication.   Perhaps a libertarian reading this who still feels awkward about bringing the stream of obscenities within the bounds of the first
amendment should simply transform the hypothetical into a Lenny
Bruce- or George Carlin-type comedian,[130] who at various points
in his act employs a string of obscenities.   I would imagine that
a libertarian would be most uncomfortable in totally excluding such

---

[128] Even if a "stream of obscenities" were fully protected by the first amendment, legitimate "time, place, and manner" regulations could be imposed.   For
example, it would probably be legitimate to prohibit such a discussion on a public
street corner, unless the people talking could establish somehow that it was essential
that their discussion take place at that location.

[129] *Cf.* Cohen v. California, 403 U.S. 15 (1971) (state cannot prohibit display
of "Fuck the Draft" on a jacket, because it is the individual's choice how to convey
his substantive message).

[130] *Cf.* FCC v. Pacifica Found., 438 U.S. 726 (1978) (regulation of broadcast
of George Carlin's "Filthy Words" monologue).

expression from the first amendment. A conversation between consenting individuals composed exclusively of obscenities raises no additional problems.

There may, of course, be some forms of expression that could be thought to fall beyond the outer fringes of even this relaxed realm of faculty development. A "primal scream," at least if not used to communicate a need for help, might be thought to be so lacking in communicative value as to fall outside the range of self-realization in the sense contemplated by the first amendment. But such a purely academic question [131] need not detain us for long. For however the question is ultimately answered, both the courts and the commentators are a long way from the primal scream in their unduly narrow classification of expression deserving of full first amendment protection.[132]

Some might deem it the height of absurdity to equate the value of a stream of obscenities with great literature or eloquent political discourse. But, of course, not all literature or political discourse is of such a high order. There is much political speech that many of us find nonsensical, stupid, vile, and repulsive, yet we take it as given that we cannot gradate first amendment protection on the basis of how vile or stupid a court or legislature finds the particular political expression to be.[133] The same holds true for literature, at least outside of the realm of obscenity. Again, the reason presumably is that we have construed the first amendment to leave to the individual final say as to how valuable the particular expression is.

This broad discussion has been designed to demonstrate how constitutional analysis should be generally altered to reflect acceptance of the self-realization value as the guiding philosophy of the first amendment. The following discussions are designed to indicate the specific alterations needed in three important areas of first amendment application: commercial speech, obscenity, and defamation.

---

[131] The issue is largely academic, because it is difficult to conceive of a reason why the state would have an interest in regulating a primal scream other than in the form of traditionally accepted time, place, and manner regulations, which could be employed even if the actual speech were fully protected by the first amendment. *Cf.* Kovacs v. Cooper, 336 U.S. 77 (1949) (upholding neutral limits on the use of sound trucks).

[132] *See supra* text accompanying notes 1-17.

[133] *See* Police Dep't v. Mosley, 408 U.S. 92, 95 (1972) ("[A]bove all else, the First Amendment means that government has no power to restrict expression because of its message, its ideas, its subject matter, or its content.").

A. *Commercial Speech*

The impact of the self-realization value on the protection to be given commercial speech is not difficult to determine. My comment on the issue some eleven years ago is, I believe, equally applicable today:

> When the individual is presented with rational grounds for preferring one product or brand over another, he is encouraged to consider the competing information, weigh it mentally in the light of the goals of personal satisfaction he has set for himself, counter-balance his conclusions with possible price differentials, and in so doing exercise his abilities to reason and think; this aids him towards the intangible goal of rational self-fulfillment.[134]

To this should be added that information and opinion about competing commercial products and services undoubtedly aid the individual in making countless life-affecting decisions, and therefore can be seen as fostering both elements of the self-realization value.[135]

Although the Supreme Court for many years casually dismissed even the most minimal level of constitutional protection for commercial speech,[136] in 1976 the Court finally recognized this form of expression as falling within the constitutional guarantee, in *Virginia State Board of Pharmacy v. Virginia Citizens Consumer Council, Inc.*[137] The Court's analysis in reaching this conclusion, however, contained the seeds of its own destruction. It is therefore not surprising that six years later commercial speech is perhaps only marginally better off than it was in the years prior to *Virginia Board*.[138]

---

[134] Redish, *supra* note 34, at 443-44.

[135] In my earlier writing, I argued that commercial advertising that conveys significant factual information that will be of real service to the consumer should perhaps receive greater constitutional protection than its more "persuasional" counterpart. *Id.* 447. Under the analysis developed in this Article, however, such a distinction is unacceptable. Recognition of the individual's unencumbered right to make life-affecting decisions logically precludes the determination by external forces that certain grounds upon which to make such decisions are better than or preferable to others.

[136] *See, e.g.,* Valentine v. Chrestensen, 316 U.S. 52, 54 (1942). For a discussion of the early history of the commercial speech doctrine, see Rotunda, *The Commercial Speech Doctrine in the Supreme Court*, 1976 U. ILL. L.F. 1080; *see also* Redish, *supra* note 34, at 448-58.

[137] 425 U.S. 748 (1976).

[138] *See, e.g.,* Friedman v. Rogers, 440 U.S. 1 (1979); Ohralik v. Ohio State Bar Ass'n, 436 U.S. 447 (1978). Occasionally, however, the Court does still provide a significant degree of constitutional protection to commercial speech. *See* Carey v. Population Servs. Int'l, 431 U.S. 678 (1977); Linmark Assocs., Inc. v. Willingboro, 431 U.S. 85 (1977).

In *Virginia Board,* the Court advanced two grounds for providing constitutional protection to commercial speech, neither of
which represented recognition of a true first amendment value in
that form of expression. The first was more a concrete economic
consideration than a first amendment value. The case concerned a
prohibition on advertising of prescription drug prices, and the
Court noted that "[t]hose whom the suppression of prescription
drug price information hits the hardest are the poor, the sick, and
particularly the aged." [139] Information as to drug prices "could
mean the alleviation of physical pain or the enjoyment of basic
necessities." [140] Because of its focus on the immediate material
benefits that flow from commercial advertising and on how governmental regulation impedes such benefits, the Court's analysis
seems closer to the logic of the economic due process cases than it
does to traditional first amendment doctrine.[141]

The second ground recognized by the Court was an indirect
benefit of commercial speech: "Even an individual advertisement,
though entirely 'commercial,' may be of general public interest." [142]
The pharmacist affected by *Virginia Board,* for example, "could
cast himself as a commentator on store-to-store disparities in drug
prices, giving his own and those of a competitor as proof." [143]
Advertising might well be "indispensable to the formation of intelligent opinions as to how that system ought to be regulated." [144]
The primary first amendment value of commercial speech, in other

---

[139] 425 U.S. at 763.

[140] *Id.* 764. The Court stated also that:

Advertising, however tasteless and excessive it sometimes may seem, is
nonetheless dissemination of information as to who is producing and selling
what product, for what reason, and at what price. So long as we preserve
a predominantly free enterprise economy, the allocation of our resources in
large measure will be made through numerous private economic decisions.
It is a matter of public interest that those decisions, in the aggregate, be
intelligent and well informed.

Id. 765.

[141] *See* Comment, *First Amendment Protection for Commercial Advertising: The
New Constitutional Doctrine,* 44 U. Chi. L. Rev. 205, 216 n.75 (1976) ("The
Court's ruling that the microeconomic functions performed by commercial speech
constitute interests protected by the first amendment is a novel addition to the
list of interests traditionally thought to have first amendment protection. . . .
[T]he Court's recognition of resource allocation as a constitutionally protected interest, at least when 'speech' is involved, portends a partial return to *Lockner's* [sic]
substantive due process review of business regulation.").

[142] 425 U.S. at 764.

[143] *Id.* 764-65.

[144] *Id.* 765.

632   UNIVERSITY OF PENNSYLVANIA LAW REVIEW   [Vol. 130:591

words, is that it will lead individuals to think about not merely
what purchasing decisions are personally best for them, but also
about what level of political regulation of the economic system
would be appropriate. The Court appeared unwilling to acknowledge that commercial speech might benefit individuals in the exact
same ways that political speech does: by developing their individual
faculties and aiding them in making life-affecting decisions.

Because it selected indirect and diluted first amendment values
to rationalize protection of commercial speech in *Virginia Board*,
the Court was conveniently able in subsequent decisions to afford
"commercial speech a limited measure of protection, commensurate
with its subordinate position in the scale of First Amendment
values, while allowing modes of regulation that might be impermissible in the realm of noncommercial expression." [145] Thus,
the Court has felt free to allow regulation of commercial speech
when it is shown merely that damage "may" occur,[146] or that harm
is "likely," [147] or that there is a "possibility" of harm.[148] These
standards are clearly unacceptable in virtually any other area of
first amendment application. Recognition that protection of commercial and political speech derives from the same ultimate value—
as well as that they are equally capable of causing serious harm—
would have led the Court to provide them with a comparable level
of constitutional protection.

The difficulty that gave the Court the greatest trouble in providing even the slightest degree of protection to commercial speech
was the regulation of false and misleading advertising. The Court
in *Virginia Board* suggested two bases on which to distinguish
commercial speech from other forms of expression in order to validate such regulation: that "[t]he truth of commercial speech . . .
may be more easily verifiable by its disseminator than . . . news
reporting or political commentary," [149] and that, "[s]ince advertising is the *sine qua non* of commercial profits, there is little likelihood of its being chilled by proper regulation." [150] To these reasons, Justice Stewart, concurring, added that commercial advertisers
do not suffer from the burdens on "the press, which must often

---

[145] Ohralik v. Ohio State Bar Ass'n, 436 U.S. 447, 456 (1978).

[146] *Id.* 457.

[147] *Id.* 464.

[148] Friedman v. Rogers, 440 U.S. 1, 13 (1979). See also the diluted standard
of protection outlined in Central Hudson Gas & Elec. Corp. v. Public Serv. Comm'n,
447 U.S. 557, 564 (1980).

[149] 425 U.S. at 772 n.24.

[150] *Id.*

attempt to assemble the true facts from sketchy and sometimes conflicting sources under the pressure of publication deadlines."[151]

To the extent that these assertions are accurate, they may properly influence first amendment analysis under the theoretical constructs established in this Article. For they are distinctions premised not on difference in the relative values of different categories of expression, but rather on regulation's differing *effects* on these types of expression. There are serious reasons, though, for doubting the accuracy of the Court's suggested distinctions.

First, it is questionable whether, in general, the truth of commercial claims is more easily verifiable than the truth of political assertions. The Court's contention that "[u]nder the First Amendment there is no such thing as a false idea" [152] is correct if one is comparing statements of political ideology with commercial assertions. But many statements made in the course of political debate—particularly by the press—are simply assertions of fact, which are presumably verifiable. Moreover, it must be recalled that many claims about commercial products are, in reality, assertions of scientific fact, since many commercial products are chemical compounds that may or may not perform the functions or have the effects claimed for them by scientists If a consumer organization is constitutionally protected in asserting that a certain product does not do what is claimed, why should the product's manufacturer not be similarly protected in contending that it does? [153]

Second, it is also incorrect to distinguish commercial from political expression on the ground that the former is somehow hardier because of the inherent profit motive. It could just as easily be said that we need not fear that commercial magazines and newspapers will cease publication for fear of governmental regulation, because they are in business for profit. Of course, the proper response to this contention is that our concern is not *whether* they will publish, but *what* they will publish: fear of regulation might deter them from dealing with controversial subjects. But could not the same be said of the commercial advertiser? The possibility of regulation would not deter him entirely from advertising, but it might deter him from making certain controversial claims for his product.

---

[151] *Id.* 777 (Stewart, J., concurring).

[152] Gertz v. Robert Welch, Inc., 418 U.S. 323, 339 (1974).

[153] One possible distinction is the speaker's motivation, as in Professor Baker's theory; however, as noted previously, this argument does not hold up under proper analysis. *See supra* text accompanying notes 107-09.

Finally, the argument concerning deadline pressure is similarly not accurate in all cases. For stories of long-range interest or for some infrequently published journals, the deadline pressure is not great. For some advertisers who are attempting to defeat a competitor or to gain first entry into a new market, timing may be critical. Time pressure is relevant to deciding the reasonableness of an assertion that later proves to have been inaccurate, whether made by by an advertiser or by the press. It appears irrelevant, however, to a general attempt to distinguish the two.

It does not necessarily follow, however, that false or misleading advertising must go unregulated. Even in the area of commentary on the conduct of public officials, which is considered by many to be of central importance to first amendment values,[154] the Supreme Court has recognized that consciously false assertions may constitutionally be punished as libelous.[155] It would not undermine recognition of the full first amendment value of commercial speech, then, to allow regulation of consciously false or misleading assertions about commercial products or services. Of course, under this analysis, the infliction of a penalty could only be justified by a showing that such assertions were consciously false, but it is unlikely that this requirement would preclude the bulk of existing regulation. If the regulation were limited to a cessation of the advertising, rather than imposition of a penalty for past conduct, it is possible that the danger of a chilling effect would be sufficiently reduced to justify regulation even absent a showing of knowledge or intent.

It is even conceivable that differences would remain under this approach in the levels of constitutional protection given commercial and political speech. We might reject automatically the existence of a governmental board to review each political speech or newspaper article and to censor those found to be misleading. But, again, the difference appears to derive not from a difference in the relative values of the forms of expression, but from the relative dangers of regulation. We presumably find such regulation in the political process so abhorrent not because we wish to condone misleading political claims, but rather because of the dangers inherent in allowing the government to regulate on the basis of the misleading nature of assertions made in the political process. The

---

[154] *See* Kalven, *The New York Times Case: A Note on 'The Central Meaning of the First Amendment,'* 1964 SUP. CT. REV. 191; *see also supra* text accompanying notes 28-48.

[155] New York Times v. Sullivan, 376 U.S. 254, 279-80 (1964).

fear is that those in power will use such authority as a weapon with which to intimidate or defeat the political opposition, a result that has been all too common in our political history. For, in the words of the noted social commentator Bret Maverick, "the dealer always cheats." [156] In contrast, there is no reason to believe that much regulation of misleading advertising is similarly motivated.

Even though this analysis may justify many forms of governmental regulation of false and misleading advertising, it does not support attempts to draw additional distinctions between commercial and other forms of expression.[157] Although regulation and free expression must be carefully balanced, if balancing leads to different levels of regulation for different forms of speech, it cannot be because some forms are deemed to be more valuable than others.

B. *Obscenity*

In light of the significant amount of existing scholarship on the subject,[158] it is neither necessary nor advisable to engage in an extended commentary on the various doctrines of obscenity regulation that have pervaded Supreme Court opinions over the last twenty-five years.[159] Instead, this critique will examine the ration-

---

[156] J. ROCHE, *supra* note 54, at 130.

[157] *Compare* Ohralik v. Ohio State Bar Ass'n, 436 U.S. 447 (1978) *with In re* Primus, 436 U.S. 412 (1978).

Of course, it might be argued that the suspect nature of *any* regulation of political expression justifies providing greater protection to all political speech. But the suspect nature of the regulation of political speech is most acute when imposed during the course of a political campaign and on such vague grounds as the misleading nature of the expression. More importantly, whereas the presence of an improper legislative motive for a regulation of speech will justify a finding of unconstitutionality, it in no way follows that legislative or administrative good faith automatically justifies regulation of speech. *See generally* Redish, *supra* note 75.

[158] *See, e.g.,* J. NOWAK, R. ROTUNDA & J. YOUNG, HANDBOOK ON CONSTITUTIONAL LAW (1978); F. SCHAUER, THE LAW OF OBSCENITY (1976); Daniels, *The Supreme Court and Obscenity: An Exercise in Empirical Constitutional Policy-Making*, 17 SAN DIEGO L. REV. 757 (1980); Engdahl, *Requiem for Roth: Obscenity Doctrine is Changing*, 68 MICH. L. REV. 185 (1969); Henkin, *Morals and the Constitution: The Sin of Obscenity*, 63 COLUM. L. REV. 391 (1963); Kalven, *The Metaphysics of the Law of Obscenity*, 1960 SUP. CT. REV. 1; Katz, *Privacy and Pornography: Stanley v. Georgia*, 1969 SUP. CT. REV. 203; Lockhart & McClure, *Literature, the Law of Obscenity, and the Constitution*, 38 MINN. L. REV. 295 (1954); Richards, *Free Speech and Obscenity Law: Toward a Moral Theory of the First Amendment*, 123 U. PA. L. REV. 45 (1974); Schauer, *Response: Pornography and the First Amendment*, 40 U. PITT. L. REV. 605 (1979).

[159] Young v. American Mini Theatres, Inc., 427 U.S. 50 (1976) (holding zoning ordinances regulating locations of adult movie theatres permissible); Paris Adult Theatre I v. Slaton, 413 U.S. 49 (1973) (holding expert testimony on obscenity of films unnecessary when films available as evidence, and that states have legitimate interest in regulating use of obscene material in local commerce); Miller v. Cali-

ales offered for the Court's total exclusion of obscenity from the
first amendment in the light of the theoretical analysis of free
speech adopted in this Article. For whatever difficulties the Court
may face in defining obscenity, it continues to exclude obscenity
from any constitutional protection.

The Court's initial exposition of the rationale for excluding
obscenity from first amendment protection came in *Roth v. United
States*,[160] where Justice Brennan in part relied, unconvincingly,[161]
on historical considerations. More significant was his statement
that "[t]he protection given speech and press was fashioned to assure
unfettered interchange of ideas for the bringing about of political
and social changes desired by the people. . . . But implicit in the
history of the First Amendment is the rejection of obscenity as
utterly without redeeming social importance." [162] Justice Brennan
then made reference to *Chaplinsky's* "two-level" theory of free
speech.[163] Thus, the Court, employing a variation of the "search

---

fornia, 413 U.S. 15 (1973) (enumerating basic guidelines for triers of fact in
obscenity cases); United States v. Reidel, 402 U.S. 351 (1971) (holding statute
prohibiting distribution of obscene materials through the mail—even to willing
adult recipients—constitutional because commerce in obscene material is unprotected
by any constitutional doctrine of privacy); United States v. Thirty-Seven (37)
Photographs, 402 U.S. 363 (1971) (holding statute prohibiting importation of
obscene material constitutional on same grounds as in *Reidel*); Stanley v. Georgia,
394 U.S. 557 (1969) (holding individual has right to possess pornographic films
in privacy of home); A Book Named "John Cleland's Memoirs of a Woman of
Pleasure" v. Attorney Gen., 383 U.S. 413 (1966) (defining obscene material);
Roth v. United States, 354 U.S. 476 (1957) (holding obscenity not within the area
of constitutionally protected speech or press).

[160] 354 U.S. 476 (1957).

[161] Justice Brennan's historical evidence was that "[t]hirteen of the 14 States
[which had ratified the Constitution by 1792] provided for the prosecution of libel,
and all of those States made either blasphemy or profanity, or both, statutory crimes.
As early as 1712, Massachusetts made it criminal to publish any filthy, obscene, or
profane song, pamphlet, libel or mock sermon in imitation or mimicking of religious
services." *Id.* 482-83 (citations omitted). This is hardly strong support for a
historical obscenity doctrine. As Professor Richards has written:

> Colonial legislatures in America appear to have been either unprovoked
> by or indifferent to obscenity. Justice Brennan cited only one example of
> preconstitutional obscenity law: an early Massachusetts law forbidding
> obscene or profane mockery of religious services. This law, however, is
> more properly viewed as a religious establishment law than as a law
> against obscene literature or art in general . . . .

Richards, *supra* note 158, at 75 (footnotes omitted). Indeed, Justice Brennan's
historical reference to the Massachusetts law may prove too much, since there can
be little doubt that today such a law would be declared unconstitutional, regardless
of its historical status. Why, then, should obscenity's possible historical foundation
preclude it from receiving better modern treatment?

[162] 354 U.S. at 484.

[163] *Id.* 485.

for truth" analysis, concluded that on this subject at least, it had discovered the "truth" and knew that obscenity was not related to it.

Even under a "search for truth" analysis, the Court's conclusion in *Roth* is subject to criticism, for regulation of obscenity can be seen as a means of rejecting whatever life style such expression may implicitly urge.[164] But the Court's greater fallacy is to believe that the primary—or even secondary—purpose of the free speech guarantee is as a means of attaining truth. If the centrality of the self-realization value were recognized, the Court would necessarily acknowledge that it is not for external forces—Congress, state legislatures, or the Court itself—to determine what communications or forms of expression are of value to the individual; how the individual is to develop his faculties is a choice for the individual to make.

In more recent decisions, the Court has attempted to either expand upon or revise its rationale for excluding obscenity from the constitutional guarantees. In *Paris Adult Theatre I v. Slaton,*[165] Chief Justice Burger, speaking for the Court, reasoned:

> If we accept the unprovable assumption that a complete education requires the reading of certain books, . . . and the well nigh universal belief that good books, plays, and art lift the spirit, improve the mind, enrich the human personality, and develop character, can we then say that a state legislature may not act on the corollary assumption that commerce in obscene books, or public exhibitions focused on obscene conduct, have a tendency to exert a corrupting and debasing impact leading to antisocial behavior?[166]

Burger's logic fails. That we assume that good books are good for people does not necessitate our believing that bad books are bad for people.[167] Burger's erroneous reasoning may perhaps be

---

[164] *See* Richards, *supra* note 158, at 78-79.

[165] 413 U.S. 49 (1973).

[166] *Id.* 63 (citations omitted).

[167] The latter assertion is the inverse of the former. As a matter of pure logic, the inverse of a statement does not necessarily flow from acceptance of the statement itself, as Burger would have us believe. The *only* statement that does flow logically from acceptance of the statement itself is the contrapositive, the converse of the inverse. Thus, if we were to accept the primary statement, "if people read good books, they will become better people," the only other statement that is necessarily proven is that "if people have not become better people, they have not read good books." This has absolutely no relevance to the possible effect of so-called "bad" books.

forgiven, since he was apparently suffering from thinly-veiled irritation at those *literati* who readily assume—without any real empirical support—the practical value of good literature, yet denounce those who would restrict obscenity as harmful without any statistical foundation for their assertions. The Chief Justice failed to understand, however, that the former assertion does not need empirical support because no issue of constitutional interpretation turns on it. The same, of course, cannot be said of the latter. More importantly, the Chief Justice assumed that he, a state legislature, a city council, or a censor board is somehow morally entitled to determine for other individuals which movies and literary works are and are not "debasing."

Many of the arguments employed to justify regulation of obscenity are not confined to the worthlessness of the expression. Rather, it is contended that such speech, in addition to being worthless, is harmful in that it may lead to increases in the levels of sex-related crimes.[168] Under the first amendment analysis suggested here, regulation of speech may be justified, in rare cases, on a showing of harm to competing social interests.[169] But this argument cannot of its own weight justify an exclusion of obscenity from the scope of the first amendment. Initially, the harmful effect alleged is so speculative that in no area of protected speech would such a showing justify regulation.[170] If such a showing were sufficient, government could constitutionally regulate nonobscene movies or books that contained detailed depictions or even the slightest approval of violent acts, since these might result in some harm.[171] But this is clearly not the case,[172] so some other distinction must be thought to exist between obscenity and other forms of expression. This brings the analysis back full circle, to the contention that obscenity is inherently worthless. The argu-

---

[168] The Chief Justice's opinion in *Paris Theatre*, for example, noted that "[t]he Hill-Link Minority Report of the Commission on Obscenity and Pornography indicates that there is at least an arguable correlation between obscene material and crime." 413 U.S. at 58.

[169] *See supra* text accompanying notes 113-18.

[170] *See, e.g.*, Brandenburg v. Ohio, 395 U.S. 444 (1969). Even under the heavily criticized version of the "clear and present danger" test of Dennis v. United States, 341 U.S. 494, 505 (1951), the Court required a substantially greater showing before allowing regulation of speech advocating violence.

[171] In fact, much pornography may in no way directly encourage crime, as violent movies might be thought to, since it can consist of relations between fully consenting adults. *See* Yaffé, *The Law Relating to Pornography: A Psychological Overview*, 20 MED., SCI. & L. 20 (1980); *see also* Cochrane, *Sex Crimes and Pornography Revisited*, 6 INT'L J. CRIMINOLOGY & PENOLOGY 307 (1978).

[172] *See supra* note 170.

ment for excluding obscenity from the first amendment's scope therefore necessarily relies on its assumed lack of social value.

The final method that the Court has employed to justify the exclusion of obscenity is simply to resort to rhetorical devices. "[T]o equate the free and robust exchange of ideas and political debate with commercial exploitation of obscene material," wrote Chief Justice Burger in *Miller v. California*,[173] "demeans the grand conception of the First Amendment and its high purposes in the historic struggle for freedom."[174] In *Young v. American Mini Theatres, Inc.*, Justice Stevens, speaking for the Court, added that "few of us would march our sons and daughters off to war to preserve the citizen's right to see 'Specified Sexual Activities' exhibited in the theaters of our choice,"[175] and that "society's interest in protecting this type of expression is of a wholly different, and lesser, magnitude than the interest in untrammeled political debate."[176] By contrasting pornography in a demeaning or negative way with exalted political speech, the Court precludes, rather than contributes to debate. But, if we are to deal in such rhetorical terms, I suppose that the appropriate response to Justice Stevens is that we are willing to send our sons and daughters off to war, presumably to protect the right of each individual to decide what books he or she will read and what movies he or she will see, free from the state's power to determine that such forms of communication are "worthless." For such freedom is an important element of the freedoms of self-rule and self-fulfillment, the very same principles

---

[173] 413 U.S. 15 (1973).

[174] *Id.* 34.

[175] 427 U.S. 50, 70 (1976).

[176] *Id.* 70. Justice Stevens was not even referring to material that was legally defined as obscene. It was, rather, in a sort of constitutional twilight zone: not extreme enough to meet constitutional standards of obscenity, but nevertheless predominantly erotic in tone. *Id.*

The actual holding in *Young* may well have been correct. The Court held that zoning ordinances regulating the location of adult theatres were permissible:

> Since what is ultimately at stake is nothing more than a limitation on the place where adult films may be exhibited, even though the determination of whether a particular film fits that characterization turns on the nature of its content, we conclude that the city's interest in the present and future character of its neighborhoods adequately supports its classification of motion pictures.

Id. 71-72 (footnote omitted). In a footnote, the Court added: "The situation would be quite different if the ordinance had the effect of suppressing, or greatly restricting access to, lawful speech." *Id.* 71 n.35. In a decision last Term, the Court, in invalidating a local ordinance that excluded similar expression, distinguished *Young* on just such grounds. *See* Schad v. Borough of Mount Ephraim, 452 U.S. 61, 71 n.10 (1981).

640   *UNIVERSITY OF PENNSYLVANIA LAW REVIEW*   [Vol. 130:591

of autonomy from which ultimately derives the freedom to choose our political leaders.

C. Defamation

Professor Meiklejohn reportedly declared that the decision in *New York Times Co. v. Sullivan* [177] was an occasion for dancing in the streets.[178]   Such a reaction on his part is not difficult to understand.   In *New York Times,* the Court held that a state could impose penalties for libel of public officials only upon a showing of "actual malice," defined to include knowledge of falsity or reckless disregard for the truth.[179]   Although the Court declined to provide the absolute protection urged by Meiklejohn, and made no direct reference to his writings, his influence was clear.[180]   Indeed, that the Court limited its holding to protection of libels against public officials about their official conduct underscores the "political speech" influence of Meiklejohn.   For if the voters are the true "governors," they need an uninhibited flow of information and opinions about the conduct of their "agents."   As the Court stated in *Garrison v. Louisianna* [181] (another public official libel case) shortly after its decision in *New York Times,* "speech concerning public affairs is more than self-expression; it is the essence of self-government." [182]

In subsequent years, the Court came to face many of the logical difficulties encountered by Meiklejohn himself.[183]   In particular, the Court was not able to limit the special protection of the *New York Times* doctrine to public officials, since numerous technically private individuals might well have a significant impact upon the course of political decisionmaking.   Therefore, the doctrine was extended to apply also to "public figures." [184]   In the

---

[177] 376 U.S. 254 (1964).

[178] Kalven, *supra* note 154, at 221 n.125.

[179] 376 U.S. at 280.

[180] Justice Brennan, author of the Court's opinion in *New York Times,* is also the author of an article discussing Meiklejohn's philosophy of free speech.   Brennan, *The Supreme Court and the Meiklejohn Interpretation of the First Amendment,* 79 HARV. L. REV. 1 (1965).

[181] 379 U.S. 64 (1964).

[182] *Id.* 74-75.

[183] *See supra* text accompanying notes 31-35.

[184] Curtis Publishing Co. v. Butts, 388 U.S. 130 (1967).   Justice Harlan and three other Justices would have adopted a more easily met standard of liability in defamation cases involving public figures; under this standard, public figures could recover damages upon "a showing of highly unreasonable conduct constituting an

closely related area of privacy "false light" cases,[185] the Court applied logic similar to that of *New York Times* to suits both by a family that had been held hostage by escaped convicts and later made the subject of a fictionalized play,[186] and by a star baseball pitcher who was the subject of an unauthorized, fictionalized biography.[187]

One may question whether the apparent underlying premise of *New York Times*—that speech about the conduct of public officials is "the essence of self-government"—justifies the Court's extension of the doctrine to cases involving fictionalized stories about a family held captive or about baseball players. Apparently recognizing the logical difficulty of this extension, Justice Brennan's opinion for the Court in *Time, Inc. v. Hill* emphasized that:

> The guarantees for speech and press are not the preserve of political expression or comment upon public affairs, essential as those are to healthy government. One

extreme departure from the standards of investigation and reporting ordinarily adhered to by responsible publishers." *Id.* 155. However, Chief Justice Warren, joined by Justices Brennan and White, favored the *New York Times* standard, and Justices Black and Douglas argued for absolute protection, as they had done in *New York Times*. Thus, a majority of the Court desired to impose at least as stringent a protection as that imposed in *New York Times*. See Kalven, *The Reasonable Man and the First Amendment: Hill, Butts, and Walker*, 1967 Sup. Ct. Rev. 267.

As was the case with my discussion of obscenity, *see supra* notes 158-77 and accompanying text, this analysis of defamation is not intended to supply a detailed description of the relevant case law. The goal, rather, is to analyze the state of the law in terms of the theory of free speech described earlier. For a description of the case development, see J. Nowak, R. Rotunda & J. Young, *supra* note 158, at 781-89.

[185] According to Dean Prosser, the tort of invasion of privacy breaks down analytically into four categories: intrusion, revelation of private facts, commercial use of one's name or face, and holding someone up to the public eye in a "false light." W. Prosser, Handbook of the Law of Torts § 117 (4th ed. 1971). It is conceptually difficult to understand why the "false light" cases are part of the privacy tort. It appears that the doctrine actually arose indirectly. Under New York's statutory right against commercialization of name or face, the courts accepted as a defense (used primarily by newspapers and magazines) that the use was in the public interest. An exception to that defense then developed for fictionalized or false description. *See, e.g.,* Time, Inc. v. Hill, 15 N.Y.2d 986, 207 N.E.2d 604, 260 N.Y.S.2d 7 (1965), *rev'd*, 385 U.S. 374 (1967); Julian Messner, Inc. v. Spahn, 18 N.Y.2d 324, 221 N.E.2d 543, 274 N.Y.S.2d 877 (1966), *vacated*, 387 U.S. 239 (1967). From this background, Dean Prosser apparently conceived a separate category of the invasion-of-privacy tort.

[186] Time, Inc. v. Hill, 385 U.S. 374 (1967).

[187] Julian Messner, Inc. v. Spahn, 387 U.S. 239 (1967) (per curiam). The Court vacated and remanded the New York Court of Appeals judgment in Spahn v. Julian Messner, Inc., 18 N.Y.2d 324, 221 N.E.2d 543, 274 N.Y.S.2d 877 (1966), in light of the *Time* decision. The state court had granted damages for the unauthorized publication of a fictitious biography of a baseball player.

642   *UNIVERSITY OF PENNSYLVANIA LAW REVIEW*   [Vol. 130:591

need only pick up any newspaper or magazine to comprehend the vast range of published matter which exposes
persons to public view, both private citizens and public
officials. Exposure of the self to others in varying degrees
is a concomitant of life in a civilized community. The
risk of this exposure is an essential incident of life in a
society which places a primary value on freedom of speech
and of press. . . . We have no doubt that the subject of
the Life article, the opening of a new play linked to an
actual incident, is a matter of public interest.[188]

Justice Brennan's statement fails to explain either why our
society "places a primary value on freedom of speech," or what
limits, if any, remain on the extension of the *New York Times*
logic. Having begun in *New York Times* by justifying the potential imposition of significant harm to individuals on eloquently
described precepts derived from the concept of self-government, the
Court in *Time* retreated to some vague notion of "public interest."
And in doing so, the Court neglected to explain whether the "public interest" concept was a descriptive or normative principle. If
the latter, it remains unclear what that normative principle is,
what there is about particular stories such that the public will
benefit from reading them. If the former, it remains unclear why
the first amendment should be construed to allow the imposition
of harm on an individual merely to satisfy the public's idle curiosity.
What began as an attempt at a coherent theory of the value of free
speech thus rapidly dissipated into a collection of vague and unsupported assertions.

The absence of any coherent underlying first amendment
theory was even more evident in *Gertz v. Robert Welch, Inc.*[189] In
Gertz, the Court rejected the "public interest" concept [190] on two
grounds: that it "would abridge [a] legitimate state interest [191] to
a degree that we find unacceptable"; [192] and that "it would occasion the additional difficulty of forcing state and federal judges

---

[188] 385 U.S. at 388 (citations omitted).

[189] 418 U.S. 323 (1974).

[190] In Rosenbloom v. Metromedia, Inc., 403 U.S. 29 (1971), Justice Brennan's
plurality opinion had adopted a "public interest" test as the guiding principle for
determining application of the *New York Times* principle in defamation cases.

[191] This "legitimate state interest" reference is to the Court's conclusion "that
the States should retain substantial latitude in their efforts to enforce a legal remedy
for defamatory falsehood injurious to the reputation of a private individual." *Gertz*,
418 U.S. at 345-46.

[192] *Id.* 346.

to decide on an *ad hoc* basis which publications address issues of 'general or public interest' and which do not." [193] The *Gertz* majority instead applied the "actual malice" standard of liability only to suits by "public figures." The Court left to the states the task of defining the standard of liability for suits concerning "private" individuals involved in an issue of "public interest," but with the caveat that they "not impose liability without fault." [194] Two factors that were to influence the determination whether a defamation plaintiff is a "public figure" were "evidence of general fame or notoriety" and the extent to which the plaintiff had voluntarily thrust himself into the public eye.[195] The Court's emphasis on public officials' access to opportunities for effective rebuttal [196] indicates the importance of this factor in defining "public figure."

Although the Court thus has curtailed significantly the level of constitutional protection given to defamatory statements, it has also substantially expanded that protection in other respects. The Court held in *Gertz* that a state could not constitutionally impose a standard of absolute liability [197] or allow damages to be presumed [198] in defamation cases, even though both were well established practices at common law.[199] The Court was necessarily imposing these limitations under the first amendment; no other constitutional provision was mentioned, and certainly the Court has no authority to invalidate state common law or statutory practice without a finding of unconstitutionality. Yet the Court failed to point to any theory of free speech that justified imposing constitutional limitations on wholly private defamation.[200]

The Court was left, then, with a seemingly unprincipled crazy quilt of first amendment theory as it applied to defamation. On the one hand, the guiding principle of "public interest" was rejected, and the Court's emphasis on "voluntary" entry into the public eye was wholly irrelevant to the Meiklejohnian reasoning

---

[193] *Id.*

[194] *Id.* 347.

[195] *Id.* 351-52.

[196] *Id.* 344.

[197] *Id.* 347. *See supra* text accompanying note 194.

[198] *Id.* 349. The Court qualified this latter prohibition, however, by adding: "at least when liability is not based on a showing of knowledge of falsity or reckless disregard for the truth." *Id.*

[199] *See* W. PROSSER, *supra* note 185, § 113.

[200] Although a totally absolute interpretation of the first amendment would lead to this conclusion, the earlier portion of the Court's opinion made clear that it was not adopting such an interpretation. *See* 418 U.S. at 339-40.

644   UNIVERSITY OF PENNSYLVANIA LAW REVIEW   [Vol. 130:591

from which the Court had implicitly begun in *New York Times*. For, if the operative norm of the first amendment for Meiklejohn was the need for voters to receive information related to the political process, it would make no difference that that information concerned someone who had not voluntarily thrust himself into the public eye. The Court seemed to rely upon a tort concept rather than a theory of free speech. On the other hand, the Court was willing to use the first amendment as a means of limiting state choices in adjudicating private defamation suits.

Although it is almost certain that no member of the Court consciously applied the concept, it is quite possible to employ the self-realization principle developed here to rationalize many of the Court's conclusions in *Gertz*. First, under this rationale of the first amendment, it is not necessary to find a broad "public interest" in speech prior to providing it with significant constitutional protection: any speech that may aid in the making of private self-governance decisions is deserving of first amendment protection. Comments about a private individual may be relevant to numerous life-affecting decisions of others, such as whether they should deal with him socially, enter into a business arrangement with him, or buy in his store. And imposition of either a strict liability standard or presumed damages might well deter many defamatory comments. Thus, the self-realization principle allows us to fashion an arguable rationale for providing at least a certain level of first amendment protection even to wholly private defamations.

The self-realization principle cannot be employed so easily as a rationale for the remaining distinctions among public and private defamations drawn by the Court in *Gertz*. For it should be recalled that, although the Court gave a certain degree of constitutional protection to defamation about entirely private individuals, it retained use of *New York Times*' "actual malice" standard only for defamation of public officials and public figures. But, as noted previously,[201] recognition of the self-realization value does not preclude balancing the interest of free speech against competing social values. Under a balancing concept, we could accept on a theoretical level the equal value of different types of speech, yet still decide that the different areas of expression may be treated differently because of external considerations. Hence, the Court could arguably conclude that the social harm of defamation of an individual who has voluntarily entered the public arena is more tolerable than

---

[201] *See supra* text accompanying notes 113-18.

similar harm inflicted upon one who has assumed no risk, even though all types of defamation—at least in the absence of "actual malice"—may be thought to foster the self-realization value. Application of the theory developed here, combined with a form of categorical balancing,[202] thus could well lead to the complex structure of constitutional protection for defamatory statements adopted—albeit without much supporting explanation—in *Gertz*.

V. Conclusion

This Article has presented both a critique of preexisting first amendment theory and a new approach to the issue. Although each of the existing theories is correct as far as it goes, none sufficiently extends the scope of the constitutional protection. None of these theories recognizes that the values they advocate are manifestations of the broader principle of individual self-realization. Once this conclusion is reached, the values recognized in specific categories of expression will be seen to be no greater than the benefits of other forms of expression that in turn foster individual self-realization.

---

[202] Although the *Gertz* Court was undoubtedly engaged in a "balancing" process, in that it declined to give speech absolute protection, it was a form of categorical, rather than *ad hoc*, balancing.

[6]

INDIANA LAW JOURNAL

| Volume 47 | FALL 1971 | Number I |

NEUTRAL PRINCIPLES AND SOME FIRST AMENDMENT PROBLEMS*

Robert H. Bork†

A persistently disturbing aspect of constitutional law is its lack of theory, a lack which is manifest not merely in the work of the courts but in the public, professional and even scholarly discussion of the topic. The result, of course, is that courts are without effective criteria and, therefore we have come to expect that the nature of the Constitution will change, often quite dramatically, as the personnel of the Supreme Court changes. In the present state of affairs that expectation is inevitable, but it is nevertheless deplorable.

The remarks that follow do not, of course, offer a general theory of constitutional law. They are more properly viewed as ranging shots, an attempt to establish the necessity for theory and to take the argument of how constitutional doctrine should be evolved by courts a step or two farther. The first section centers upon the implications of Professor Wechsler's concept of "neutral principles," and the second attempts to apply those implications to some important and much-debated problems in the interpretation of the first amendment. The style is informal since these remarks were originally lectures and I have not thought it worthwhile to convert these speculations and arguments into a heavily researched, balanced and thorough presentation, for that would result in a book.

The Supreme Court and the Demand for Principle

The subject of the lengthy and often acrimonious debate about the proper role of the Supreme Court under the Constitution is one that preoccupies many people these days: when is authority legitimate? I find it convenient to discuss that question in the context of the Warren Court and its works simply because the Warren Court posed the issue in acute form. The issue did not disappear along with the era of the Warren Court

---

* The text of this article was delivered in the Spring of 1971 by Professor Bork at the Indiana University School of Law as part of the Addison C. Harriss lecture series.

† Professor of Law, Yale Law School.

2   *INDIANA LAW JOURNAL*

majorities, however. It arises when any court either exercises or declines
to exercise the power to invalidate any act of another branch of government. The Supreme Court is a major power center, and we must ask when
its power should be used and when it should be withheld.

Our starting place, inevitably, is Professor Herbert Wechsler's argument that the Court must not be merely a "naked power organ," which
means that its decisions must be controlled by principle.[1] "A principled
decision," according to Wechsler, "is one that rests on reasons with
respect to all the issues in a case, reasons that in their generality and their
neutrality transcend any immediate result that is involved."[2]

Wechsler chose the term "neutral principles" to capsulate his argument, though he recognizes that the legal principle to be applied is itself
never neutral because it embodies a choice of one value rather than
another. Wechsler asked for the neutral application of principles, which is
a requirement, as Professor Louis L. Jaffe puts it, that the judge
"sincerely believe in the principle upon which he purports to rest his decision." "The judge," says Jaffe, "must believe in the validity of the reasons
given for the decision at least in the sense that he is prepared to apply
them to a later case which he cannot honestly distinguish."[3] He must
not, that is, decide lawlessly. But is the demand for neutrality in judges
merely another value choice, one that is no more principled than any
other? I think not, but to prove it we must rehearse fundamentals. This
is familiar terrain but important and still debated.

The requirement that the Court be principled arises from the resolution of the seeming anomaly of judicial supremacy in a democratic society.
If the judiciary really is supreme, able to rule when and as it sees fit, the
society is not democratic. The anomaly is dissipated, however, by the
model of government embodied in the structure of the Constitution, a
model upon which popular consent to limited government by the Supreme
Court also rests. This model we may for convenience, though perhaps not
with total accuracy, call "Madisonian."[4]

A Madisonian system is not completely democratic, if by "democratic" we mean completely majoritarian. It assumes that in wide areas
of life majorities are entitled to rule for no better reason that they are
majorities. We need not pause here to examine the philosophical under-

---

1. H. WECHSLER, *Toward Neutral Principles of Constitutional Law,* in
PRINCIPLES, POLITICS, AND FUNDAMENTAL LAW 3, 27 (1961) [hereinafter cited as
WECHSLER].
2. *Id.*
3. L. JAFFE, ENGLISH AND AMERICAN JUDGES AS LAWMAKERS 38 (1969).
4. *See* R. DAHL, A PREFACE TO DEMOCRATIC THEORY 4-33 (1956).

pinnings of that assumption since it is a "given" in our society; nor need
we worry that "majority" is a term of art meaning often no more than the
shifting combinations of minorities that add up to temporary majorities in
the legislature. That majorities are so constituted is inevitable. In any
case, one essential premise of the Madisonian model is majoritarianism.
The model has also a counter-majoritarian premise, however, for it
assumes there are some areas of life a majority should not control. There
are some things a majority should not do to us no matter how democratically it decides to do them. These are areas properly left to individual
freedom, and coercion by the majority in these aspects of life is tyranny.

Some see the model as containing an inherent, perhaps an insoluble,
dilemma.[5] Majority tyranny occurs if legislation invades the areas properly left to individual freedom. Minority tyranny occurs if the majority is
prevented from ruling where its power is legitimate. Yet, quite obviously,
neither the majority nor the minority can be trusted to define the freedom
of the other. This dilemma is resolved in constitutional theory, and in
popular understanding, by the Supreme Court's power to define both
majority and minority freedom through the interpretation of the Constitution. Society consents to be ruled undemocratically within defined areas
by certain enduring principles believed to be stated in, and placed beyond
the reach of majorities by, the Constitution.

But this resolution of the dilemma imposes severe requirements upon
the Court. For it follows that the Court's power is legitimate only if it
has, and can demonstrate in reasoned opinions that it has, a valid theory,
derived from the Constitution, of the respective spheres of majority and
minority freedom. If it does not have such a theory but merely imposes
its own value choices, or worse if it pretends to have a theory but actually
follows its own predilections, the Court violates the postulates of the
Madisonian model that alone justifies its power. It then necessarily abets
the tyranny either of the majority or of the minority.

This argument is central to the issue of legitimate authority because
the Supreme Court's power to govern rests upon popular acceptance of
this model. Evidence that this is, in fact, the basis of the Court's power is
to be gleaned everywhere in our culture. We need not canvass here such
things as high school civics texts and newspaper commentary, for the most
telling evidence may be found in the U.S. Reports. The Supreme Court
regularly insists that its results, and most particularly its controversial
results, do not spring from the mere will of the Justices in the majority

5. *Id.* at 23-24.

4   *INDIANA LAW JOURNAL*

but are supported, indeed compelled, by a proper understanding of the Constitution of the United States. Value choices are attributed to the Founding Fathers, not to the Court. The way an institution advertises tells you what it thinks its customers demand.

This is, I think, the ultimate reason the Court must be principled. If it does not have and rigorously adhere to a valid and consistent theory of majority and minority freedoms based upon the Constitution, judicial supremacy, given the axioms of our system, is, precisely to that extent, illegitimate. The root of its illegitimacy is that it opens a chasm between the reality of the Court's performance and the constitutional and popular assumptions that give it power.

I do not mean to rest the argument entirely upon the popular under standing of the Court's function. Even if society generally should ultimately perceive what the Court is in fact doing and, having seen, prove content to have major policies determined by the unguided discretion of judges rather than by elected representatives, a principled judge would, I believe, continue to consider himself bound by an obligation to the document and to the structure of government that it prescribes. At least he would be bound so long as any litigant existed who demanded such adherence of him. I do not understand how, on any other theory of judicial obligation, the Court could, as it does now, protect voting rights if a large majority of the relevant constituency were willing to see some groups or individuals deprived of such rights. But even if I am wrong in that, at the very least an honest judge would owe it to the body politic to cease invoking the authority of the Constitution and to make explicit the imposition of his own will, for only then would we know whether the society understood enough of what is taking place to be said to have consented.

Judge J. Skelly Wright, in an argument resting on different premises, has severely criticized the advocates of principle. He defends the value-choosing role of the Warren Court, setting that Court in opposition to something he refers to as the "scholarly tradition," which criticizes that Court for its lack of principle.[6] A perceptive reader, sensitive to nuance, may suspect that the Judge is rather out of sympathy with that tradition from such hints as his reference to "self-appointed scholastic mandarins."[7]

The "mandarins" of the academy anger the Judge because they engage in "haughty derision of the Court's powers of analysis and reason-

---

6. Wright, *Professor Bickel, The Scholarly Tradition, and the Supreme Court*, 84 HARV. L. REV. 769 (1971) [hereinafter cited as Wright].
   7. *Id.* at 777.

ing."[8] Yet, curiously enough, Judge Wright makes no attempt to refute the charge but rather seems to adopt the technique of confession and avoidance. He seems to be arguing that a Court engaged in choosing fundamental values for society cannot be expected to produce principled decisions at the same time. Decisions first, principles later. One wonders, however, how the Court or the rest of us are to know that the decisions are correct or what they portend for the future if they are not accompained by the principles that explain and justify them. And it would not be amiss to point out that quite often the principles required of the Warren Court's decisions never did put in an appearance. But Judge Wright's main point appears to be that value choice is the most important function of the Supreme Court, so that if we must take one or the other, and apparently we must, we should prefer a process of selecting values to one of constructing and articulating principles. His argument, I believe, boils down to a syllogism. I. The Supreme Court should "protect our constitutional rights and liberties." II. The Supreme Court must "make fundamental value choices" in order to "protect our constitutional rights and liberties." III. Therefore, the Supreme Court should "make fundamental value choices."[9]

The argument displays an all too common confusion. If we have constitutional rights and liberties already, rights and liberties specified by the Constitution,[10] the Court need make no fundamental value choices in order to protect them, and it certainly need not have difficulty enunciating

---

8. *Id.* at 777-78.

9. This syllogism is implicit in much of Judge Wright's argument. *E.g.*, "If it is proper for the Court to make fundamental value choices to protect our constitutional rights and liberties, then it is self-defeating to say that if the Justices cannot come up with a perfectly reasoned and perfectly general opinion *now*, then they should abstain from decision altogether." *Id.* at 779. The first clause is the important one for present purposes; the others merely caricature the position of commentators who ask for principle.

10. A position Judge Wright also seems to take at times. "Constitutional choices are in fact different from ordinary decisions. The reason is simple: the most important value choices have already been made by the framers of the Constitution." *Id.* at 784. One wonders how the Judge squares this with his insistence upon the propriety of the judiciary making "fundamental value choices." One also wonders what degree of specificity is required before the framers may realistically be said to have made the "most important value choices." The Warren Court has chosen to expand the fourteenth amendment's theme of equality in ways certainly not foreseen by the framers of that provision. A prior Court expanded the amendment's theme of liberty. Are both Courts to be judged innocent of having made the most important value choices on the ground that the framers mentioned both liberty and equality? If so, the framers must be held to have delegated an almost complete power to govern to the Supreme Court, and it is untrue to say that a constitutional decision is any different from an ordinary governmental decision. Judge Wright simply never faces up to the problem he purports to address: how free is the Court to choose values that will override the values chosen by elected representatives?

6   *INDIANA LAW JOURNAL*

principles. If, on the other hand, "constitutional rights and liberties" are
not in some real sense specified by the Constitution but are the rights
and liberties the Court chooses, on the basis of its own values, to give to
us, then the conclusion was contained entirely in the major premise, and
the Judge's syllogism is no more than an assertion of what it purported
to prove.

If I am correct so far, no argument that is both coherent and respectable can be made supporting a Supreme Court that "chooses fundamental values" because a Court that makes rather than implements value
choices cannot be squared with the presuppositions of a democratic society.
The man who understands the issues and nevertheless insists upon the
rightness of the Warren Court's performance ought also, if he is candid,
to admit that he is prepared to sacrifice democratic process to his own
moral views. He claims for the Supreme Court an institutionalized role as
perpetrator of limited coups d'etat.

Such a man occupies an impossible philosophic position. What can he
say, for instance, of a Court that does not share his politics or his morality?
I can think of nothing except the assertion that he will ignore the Court
whenever he can get away with it and overthrow it if he can. In his view
the Court has no legitimacy, and there is no reason any of us should obey
it. And, this being the case, the advocate of a value-choosing Court must
answer another difficult question. Why should the Court, a committee of
nine lawyers, be the sole agent of change? The man who prefers results to
processes has no reason to say that the Court is more legitimate than any
other institution. If the Court will not listen, why not argue the case to
some other group, say the Joint Chiefs of Staff, a body with rather better
means for implementing its decisions?

We are driven to the conclusion that a legitimate Court must be controlled by principles exterior to the will of the Justices. As my colleague,
Professor Alexander Bickel, puts it, "The process of the coherent, analytically warranted, principled declaration of general norms alone
justifies the Court's function . . . ."[11] Recognition of the need for
principle is only the first step, but once that step is taken much more
follows. Logic has a life of its own, and devotion to principle requires that
we follow where logic leads.

Professor Bickel identifies Justice Frankfurter as the leading judicial
proponent of principle but concedes that even Frankfurther never found
a "rigorous general accord between judicial supremacy and democratic

---

11. A. Bickel, The Supreme Court and the Idea of Progress 96 (1970).

theory."[12] Judge Wright responds, "The leading commentators of the scholarly tradition have tried ever since to succeed where the Justice failed."[13] As Judge Wright quite accurately suggests, the commentators have so far had no better luck than the Justice.

On reason, I think, is clear. We have not carried the idea of neutrality far enough. We have been talking about neutrality in the *application* of principles. If judges are to avoid imposing their own values upon the rest of us, however, they must be neutral as well in the *definition* and the *derivation* of principles.

It is easy enough to meet the requirement of neutral application by stating a principle so narrowly that no embarrassment need arise in applying it to all cases it subsumes, a tactic often urged by proponents of "judicial restraint." But that solves very little. It cerainly does not protect the judge from the intrusion of his own values. The problem may be illustrated by *Griswold v. Connecticut*,[14] in many ways a typical decision of the Warren Court. *Griswold* struck down Connecticut's statute making it a crime, even for married couples, to use contraceptive devices. If we take the principle of the decision to be a statement that government may not interfere with any acts done in private, we need not even ask about the principle's dubious origin for we know at once that the Court will not apply it neutrally. The Court, we may confidently predict, is not going to throw constitutional protection around heroin use or sexual acts with a consenting minor. We can gain the possibility of neutral application by reframing the principle as a statement that government may not prohibit the use of contraceptives by married couples, but that is not enough. The question of neutral definition arises: Why does the principle extend only to married couples? Why, out of all forms of sexual behavior, only to the use of contraceptives? Why, out of all forms of behavior, only to sex? The question of neutral derivation also arises: What justifies any limitation upon legislatures in this area? What is the origin of any principle one may state?

To put the matter another way, if a neutral judge must demonstrate why principle X applies to cases A and B but not to case C (which is, I believe, the requirement laid down by Professors Wechsler and Jaffe), he must, by the same token, also explain why the principle is defined as X rather than as X *minus*, which would cover A but not cases B and C, or as X *plus*, which would cover all cases, A, B and C. Similarly, he must

---

12. *Id.* at 34.
13. Wright, *supra* note 6, at 775.
14. 381 U.S. 479 (1965).

explain why X is a proper principle of limitation on majority power at all. Why should he not choose *non-X*? If he may not choose lawlessly between cases in applying principle X, he may certainly not choose lawlessly in defining X or in choosing X, for principles are after all only organizations of cases into groups. To choose the principle and define it is to decide the cases.

It follows that the choice of "fundamental values" by the Court cannot be justified. Where constitutional materials do not clearly specify the value to be preferred, there is no principled way to prefer any claimed human value to any other. The judge must stick close to the text and the history, and their fair implications, and not construct new rights. The case just mentioned illustrates the point. The *Griswold* decision has been acclaimed by legal scholars as a major advance in constitutional law, a salutary demonstration of the Court's ability to protect fundamental human values. I regret to have to disagree, and my regret is all the more sincere because I once took the same position and did so in print.[15] In extenuation I can only say that at the time I thought, quite erroneously, that new basic rights could be derived logically by finding and extrapolating a more general principle of individual autonomy underlying the particular guarantees of the Bill of Rights.

The Court's *Griswold* opinion, by Justice Douglas, and the array of concurring opinions, by Justices Goldberg, White and Harlan, all failed to justify the derivation of any principle used to strike down the Connecticut anti-contraceptive statute or to define the scope of the principle. Justice Douglas, to whose opinion I must confine myself, began by pointing out that "specific guarantees in the Bill of Rights have penumbras, formed by emanations from those guarantees that help give them life and substance."[16] Nothing is exceptional there. In the case Justice Douglas cited, *NAACP v. Alabama*,[17] the State was held unable to force disclosure of membership lists because of the chilling effect upon the rights of assembly and political action of the NAACP's members. The penumbra was created solely to preserve a value central to the first amendment, applied in this case through the fourteenth amendment. It had no life of its own as a right independent of the value specified by the first amendment.

But Justice Douglas then performed a miracle of transubstantiation. He called the first amendment's penumbra a protection of "privacy" and

---

15. Bork, *The Supreme Court Needs a New Philosophy*, FORTUNE, Dec., 1968, at 170.
16. 381 U.S. at 484.
17. 357 U.S. 449 (1958).

NEUTRAL PRINCIPLES 9

then asserted that other amendments create "zones of privacy."[18] He had no better reason to use the word "privacy" than that the individual is free within these zones, free to act in public as well as in private. None of these penumbral zones—from the first, third, fourth or fifth amendments, all of which he cited, along with the ninth—covered the case before him. One more leap was required. Justice Douglas asserted that these various "zones of privacy" created an independent right of privacy,[19] a right not lying within the penumbra of any specific amendment. He did not disclose, however, how a series of specified rights combined to create a new and unspecified right.

The *Griswold* opinion fails every test of neutrality. The derivation of the principle was utterly specious, and so was its definition. In fact, we are left with no idea of what the principle really forbids. Derivation and definition are interrelated here. Justice Douglas called the amendments and their penumbras "zones of privacy," though of course they are not that at all. They protect both private and public behavior and so would more properly be labelled "zones of freedom." If we follow Justice Douglas in his next step, these zones would then add up to an independent right of freedom, which is to say, a general constitutional right to be free of legal coercion, a manifest impossibility in any imaginable society.

Griswold, then, is an unprincipled decision, both in the way in which it derives a new constitutional right and in the way it defines that right, or rather fails to define it. We are left with no idea of the sweep of the right of privacy and hence no notion of the cases to which it may or may not be applied in the future. The truth is that the Court could not reach its result in *Griswold* through principle. The reason is obvious. Every clash between a minority claiming freedom and a majority claiming power to regulate involves a choice between the gratifications of the two groups. When the Constitution has not spoken, the Court will be able to find no scale, other than its own value preferences, upon which to weigh the respective claims to pleasure. Compare the facts in *Griswold* with a hypothetical suit by an electric utility company and one of its customers to void a smoke pollution ordinance as unconstitutional. The cases are identical.

In *Griswold* a husband and wife assert that they wish to have sexual relations without fear of unwanted children. The law impairs their sexual gratifications. The State can assert, and at one stage in that litigation did assert, that the majority finds the use of contraceptives immoral. Knowl-

---

18. 381 U.S. at 484.
19. *Id.* at 485, 486.

edge that it takes place and that the State makes no effort to inhibit it causes the majority anguish, impairs their gratifications.

The electrical company asserts that it wishes to produce electricity at low cost in order to reach a wide market and make profits. Its customer asserts that he wants a lower cost so that prices can be held low. The smoke pollution regulation impairs his and the company's stockholders' economic gratifications. The State can assert not only that the majority prefer clean air to lower prices, but also that the absence of the regulation impairs the majority's physical and aesthetic gratifications.

Neither case is covered specifically or by obvious implication in the Constitution. Unless we can distinguish forms of gratification, the only course for a principled Court is to let the majority have its way in both cases. It is clear that the Court cannot make the necessary distinction. There is no principled way to decide that one man's gratifications are more deserving of respect than another's or that one form of gratification is more worthy than another.[20] Why is sexual gratification more worthy than moral gratification? Why is sexual gratification nobler than economic gratification? There is no way of deciding these matters other than by reference to some system of moral or ethical values that has no objective or intrinsic validity of its own and about which men can and do differ. Where the Constitution does not embody the moral or ethical choice, the judge has no basis other than his own values upon which to set aside the community judgment embodied in the statute. That, by definition, is an inadequate basis for judicial supremacy. The issue of the community's moral and ethical values, the issue of the degree of pain an activity causes, are matters concluded by the passage and enforcemment of the laws in question. The judiciary has no role to play other than that of applying the statutes in a fair and impartial manner.

One of my colleagues refers to this conclusion, not without sarcasm, as the "Equal Gratification Clause." The phrase is apt, and I accept it, though not the sarcasm. Equality of human gratifications, where the document does not impose a hierarchy, is an essential part of constitutional doctrine because of the necessity that judges be principled. To be perfectly clear on the subject, I repeat that the principle is not applicable to legislatures. Legislation requires value choice and cannot be principled in the sense under discussion. Courts must accept any value choice the legislature

---

20. The impossibility is related to that of making interpersonal comparisons of utilities. *See* L. ROBBINS, THE NATURE AND SIGNIFICANCE OF ECONOMIC SCIENCE, ch. 4 (2d ed. 1969) ; P. SAMUELSON, FOUNDATIONS OF ECONOMIC ANALYSIS 243-52 (1965).

NEUTRAL PRINCIPLES 11

makes unless it clearly runs contrary to a choice made in the framing of the Constitution.

It follows, of course, that broad areas of constitutional law ought to be reformulated. Most obviously, it follows that substantive due process, revived by the *Griswold* case, is and always has been an improper doctrine. Substantive due process requires the Court to say, without guidance from the Constitution, which liberties or gratifications may be infringed by majorities and which may not. This means that *Griswold's* antecedents were also wrongly decided, *e.g., Meyer v. Nebraska,*[21] which struck down a statute forbidding the teaching of subjects in any language other than English; *Pierce v. Society of Sisters,*[22] which set aside a statute compelling all Oregon school children to attend public schools; *Adkins v. Children's Hospital,*[23] which invalidated a statute of Congress authorizing a board to fix minimum wages for women and children in the District of Columbia; and *Lochner v. New York,*[24] which voided a statute fixing maximum hours of work for bakers. With some of these cases I am in political agreement, and perhaps *Pierce's* result could be reached on acceptable grounds, but there is no justification for the Court's methods. In *Lochner,* Justice Peckham, defending liberty from what he conceived as a mere meddlesome interference, asked, "[A]re we all . . . at the mercy of legislative majorities?"[25] The correct answer, where the Constitution does not speak, must be "yes."

The argument so far also indicates that most of substantive equal protection is also improper. The modern Court, we need hardly be reminded, used the equal protection clause the way the old Court used the due process clause. The only change was in the values chosen for protection and the frequency with which the Court struck down laws.

The equal protection clause has two legitimate meanings. It can require formal procedural equality, and, because of its historical origins, it does require that government not discriminate along racial lines. But much more than that cannot properly be read into the clause. The bare concept of equality provides no guide for courts. All law discriminates and thereby creates inequality. The Supreme Court has no principled way of saying which non-racial inequalities are impermissible. What it has done, therefore, is to appeal to simplistic notions of "fairness" or to what it regards as "fundamental" interests in order to demand equality in some

21. 262 U.S. 390 (1922).
22. 268 U.S. 510 (1925).
23. 261 U.S. 525 (1923).
24. 198 U.S. 45 (1905).
25. *Id.* at 59.

cases but not in others, thus choosing values and producing a line of cases as improper and as intellectually empty as *Griswold v. Connecticut.* Any casebook lists them, and the differing results cannot be explained on any ground other than the Court's preferences for particular values: *Skinner v. Oklahoma*[26] (a forbidden inequality exists when a state undertakes to sterilize robbers but not embezzlers) ; *Kotch v. Board of River Port Pilot Commissioners*[27] (no right to equality is infringed when a state grants pilots' licenses only to persons related by blood to existing pilots and denies licenses to persons otherwise as well qualified) ; *Goesaert v. Cleary*[28] (a state does not deny equality when it refuses to license women as bartenders unless they are the wives or daughters of male owners of licensed liquor establishments) ; *Railway Express Agency v. New York*[29] (a city may forbid truck owners to sell advertising space on their trucks as a distracting hazard to traffic safety though it permits owners to advertise their own business in that way) ; *Shapiro v. Thompson*[30] (a state denies equality if it pays welfare only to persons who have resided in the state for one year) ; *Levy v. Louisiana*[31] (a state may not limit actions for a parent's wrongful death to legitimate children and deny it to illegitimate children). The list could be extended, but the point is that the cases cannot be reconciled on any basis other than the Justices' personal beliefs about what interests or gratifications ought to be protected.

Professor Wechsler notes that Justice Frankfurther expressed "disquietude that the line is often very thin between the cases in which the Court felt compelled to abstain from adjudication because of their 'political' nature, and the cases that so frequently arise in applying the concepts of 'liberty' and 'equality'."[32] The line is not very thin; it is nonexistent. There is no principled way in which anyone can define the spheres in which liberty is required and the spheres in which equality is required. These are matters of morality, of judgment, of prudence. They belong, therefore, to the political community. In the fullest sense, these are political questions.

We may now be in a position to discuss certain of the problems of legitimacy raised by Professor Wechsler. Central to his worries was the

---

26. 316 U.S. 535 (1942).
27. 330 U.S. 552 (1947).
28. 335 U.S. 464 (1948).
29. 336 U.S. 106 (1949).
30. 394 U.S. 618 (1969).
31. 391 U.S. 68 (1968).
32. WECHSLER, *supra* note 1, at 11, *citing* Frankfurter, *John Marshall and the Judicial Function,* 69 HARV. L. REV. 217, 227-28 (1955).

NEUTRAL PRINCIPLES 13

Supreme Court's decision in *Brown v. Board of Education*.[33] Wechsler said he had great difficulty framing a neutral principle to support the *Brown* decision, though he thoroughly approved of its result on moral and political grounds. It has long been obvious that the case does not rest upon the grounds advanced in Chief Justice Warren's opinion, the specially harmful effects of enforced school segregation upon black children. That much, as Wechsler and others point out, is made plain by the per curiam decisions that followed outlawing segregated public beaches, public golf courses and the like. The principle in operation may be that government may not employ race as a classification. But the genesis of the principle is unclear.

Wechsler states that his problem with the segregation cases is not that:

> History does not confirm that an agreed purpose of the four-
> teenth amendment was to forbid separate schools or that there is
> important evidence that many thought the contrary; the words
> are general and leave room for expanding content as time passes
> and conditions change.[34]

The words are general but surely that would not permit us to escape the framers' intent if it were clear. If the legislative history revealed a consensus about segregation in schooling and all the other relations in life, I do not see how the Court could escape the choices revealed and substitute its own, even though the words are general and conditions have changed. It is the fact that history does not reveal detailed choices concerning such matters that permits, indeed requires, resort to other modes of interpretation.

Wechsler notes that *Brown* has to do with freedom to associate and freedom not to associate, and he thinks that a principle must be found that solves the following dilemma:

> [I]f the freedom of association is denied by segregation, in-
> tegration forces an association upon those for whom it is un-
> pleasant or repugnant. Is this not the heart of the issue involved,
> a conflict in human claims of high dimension. . . . Given a
> situation where the state must practically choose between
> denying the association to those individuals who wish it or
> imposing it on those who would avoid it, is there a basis in

---

33. 347 U.S. 483 (1954).
34. WECHSLER, *supra* note 1, at 43.

neutral principles for holding that the Constitution demands that the claims for association should prevail? I should like to think there is, but I confess that I have not yet written the opinion. To write it is for me the challenge of the school-segregation cases.[35]

It is extemely unlikely that Professor Wechsler ever will be able to write that opinion to his own satisfaction. He has framed the issue in insoluble terms by calling it a "conflict between human claims of high dimension," which is to say that it requires a judicial choice between rival gratifications in order to find a fundamental human right. So viewed it is the same case as *Griswold v. Connecticut* and not susceptible of principled resolution.

A resolution that seems to me more plausible is supported rather than troubled by the need for neutrality. A court required to decide *Brown* would perceive two crucial facts about the history of the fourteenth amendment. First, the men who put the amendment in the Constitution intended that the Supreme Court should secure against government action some large measure of racial equality. That is certainly the core meaning of the amendment. Second, those same men were not agreed about what the concept of racial equality requires. Many or most of them had not even thought the matter through. Almost certainly, even individuals among them held such views as that blacks were entitled to purchase property from any willing seller but not to attend integrated schools, or that they were entitled to serve on juries but not to intermarry with whites, or that they were entitled to equal physical facilities but that the facilities should be separate, and so on through the endless anomalies and inconsistencies with which moral positions so frequently abound. The Court cannot conceivably know how these long-dead men would have resolved these issues had they considered, debated and voted on each of them. Perhaps it was precisely because they could not resolve them that they took refuge in the majestic and ambiguous formula: the equal protection of the laws.

But one thing the Court does know: it was intended to enforce a core idea of black equality against governmental discrimination. And the Court, because it must be neutral, cannot pick and choose between competing gratifications and, likewise, cannot write the detailed code the framers omitted, requiring equality in this case but not in another. The Court must, for that reason, choose a general principle of equality that

---

35. Id. at 47.

applies to all cases. For the same reason, the Court cannot decide that physical equality is important but psychological equality is not. Thus, the no-state-enforced-discrimination rule of *Brown* must overturn and replace the separate-but-equal doctrine of *Plessy v. Ferguson.* The same result might be reached on an alternative ground. If the Court found that it was incapable as an institution of policing the issue of the physical equality of separate facilities, the variables being insufficiently comparable and the cases too many, it might fashion a no-segregation rule as the only feasible means of assuring even physical equality.

In either case, the value choice (or, perhaps more accurately, the value impulse) of the fourteenth amendment is fleshed out and made into a legal rule—not by moral precept, not by a determination that claims for association prevail over claims for separation as a general matter, still less by consideration of psychological test results, but on purely juridical grounds.

I doubt, however, that it is possible to find neutral principles capable of supporting some of the other decisions that trouble Professor Wechsler. An example is *Shelly v. Kraemer,*[36] which held that the fourteenth amendment forbids state court enforcement of a private, racially restrictive covenant. Although the amendment speaks only of denials of equal protection of the laws by the state, Chief Justice Vinson's opinion said that judicial enforcement of a private person's discriminatory choice constituted the requisite state action. The decision was, of course, not neutral in that the Court was most clearly not prepared to apply the principle to cases it could not honestly distinguish. Any dispute between private persons about absolutely any aspect of life can be brought to a court by one of the parties; and, if race is involved, the rule of *Shelley* would require the court to deny the freedom of any individual to discriminate in the conduct of any part of his affairs simply because the contrary result would be state enforcement of discrimination. The principle would apply not merely to the cases hypothesized by Professor Wechsler—the inability of the state to effectuate a will that draws a racial line or to vindicate the privacy of property against a trespasser excluded because of the homeowner's racial preferences—but to any situation in which the person claiming freedom in any relationship had a racial motivation.

That much is the common objection to *Shelley v. Kraemer,* but the trouble with the decision goes deeper. Professor Louis Henkin has suggested that we view the case as correctly decided, accept the principle

36. 334 U.S. 1 (1948).

that must necessarily underline it if it is respectable law and proceed
to apply that principle:

> Generally, the equal protection clause precludes state enforce-
> ment of private discrimination. There is, however, a small area
> of liberty favored by the Constitution even over claims to
> equality. Rights of liberty and property, of privacy and voluntary
> association, must be balanced in close cases, against the right
> not to have the state enforce discrimination against the victim.
> In the few instances in which the right to discriminate is pro-
> tected or perferred by the Constitution, the state may enforce
> it.[37]

This attempt to rehabilitate *Shelley* by applying its principle honestly
demonstrates rather clearly why neutrality in the application of principle
is not enough. Professor Henkin's proposal fails the test of the neutral
derivation of principle. It converts an amendment whose text and history
clearly show it to be aimed only at governmental discrimination into a
sweeping prohibition of private discrimination. There is no warrant
anywhere for that conversion. The judge's power to govern does not
become more legitimate if he is constrained to apply his principle to all
cases but is free to make up his own principles. Matters are only made
worse by Professor Henkin's suggestion that the judge introduce a
small number of exceptions for cases where liberty is more important
than equality, for now even the possibility of neutrality in the application
of principle is lost. The judge cannot find in the fourteenth amendment
or its history any choices between equality and freedom in private affairs.
The judge, if he were to undertake this task, would be choosing, as in
Griswold v. Connecticut, between competing gratifications without constitutional guidance. Indeed, Professor Henkin's description of the process
shows that the task he would assign is legislative:

> The balance may be struck differently at different times, re-
> flecting differences in prevailing philosophy and the continuing
> movement from *laissez-faire* government toward welfare and
> meliorism. The changes in prevailing philosophy themselves
> may sum up the judgment of judges as to how the conscience of
> our society weighs the competing needs and claims of liberty and
> equality in time and context—the adequacy of progress toward

---

37. Henkin, Shelley v. Kraemer: *Notes for a Revised Opinion,* 110 U. PA. L. REV.
473, 496 (1962).

equality as a result of social and economic forces, the effect of lack of progress on the life of the Negro and, perhaps, on the image of the United States, and the role of official state forces in advancing or retarding this progress.[38]

In short, after considering everything a legislator might consider, the judge is to write a detailed code of private race relations. Starting with an attempt to justify *Shelley* on grounds of neutral principle, the argument rather curiously arrives at a position in which neutrality in the derivation, definition and application of principle is impossible and the wrong institution is governing society.

The argument thus far claims that, cases of race discrimination aside, it is always a mistake for the Court to try to construct substantive individual rights under the due process or the equal protection clause. Such rights cannot be constructed without comparing the worth of individual gratifications, and that comparison cannot be principled. Unfortunately, the rhetoric of constitutional adjudication is increasingly a rhetoric about "fundamental" rights that inhere in humans. That focus does more than lead the Court to construct new rights without adequate guidance from constitutional materials. It also distorts the scope and definition of rights that have claim to protection.

There appear to be two proper methods of deriving rights from the Constitution. The first is to take from the document rather specific values that text or history show the framers actually to have intended and which are capable of being translated into principled rules. We may call these specified rights. The second method derives rights from governmental processes established by the Constitution. These are secondary or derived individual rights. This latter category is extraordinarily important. This method of derivation is essential to the interpretation of the first amendment, to voting rights, to criminal procedure and to much else.

Secondary or derivative rights are not possessed by the individual because the Constitution has made a value choice about individuals. Neither are they possessed because the Supreme Court thinks them fundamental to all humans. Rather, these rights are located in the individual for the sake of a governmental process that the Constitution outlines and that the Court should preserve. They are given to the individual because his enjoyment of them will lead him to defend them in court and thereby preserve the governmental process from legislative or executive deformation.

---

38. *Id.* at 494.

The distinction between rights that are inherent and rights that are derived from some other value is one that our society worked out long ago with respect to the economic market place, and precisely the same distinction holds and will prove an aid to clear thought with respect to the political market place. A right is a form of property, and our thinking about the category of constitutional property might usefully follow the progress of thought about economic property. We now regard it as thoroughly old hat, passe and in fact downright tiresome to hear rhetoric about an inherent right to economic freedom or to economic property. We no longer believe that economic rights inhere in the individual because he is an individual. The modern intellectual argues the proper location and definition of property rights according to judgments of utility—the capacity of such rights to forward some other value. We may, for example, wish to maximize the total wealth of society and define property rights in a way we think will advance that goal by making the economic process run more efficiently. As it is with economic property rights, so it should be with constitutional rights relating to governmental processes.

The derivation of rights from governmental processes is not an easy task, and I do not suggest that a shift in focus will make anything approaching a mechanical jurisprudence possible. I do suggest that, for the reasons already argued, no guidance whatever is available to a court that approaches, say, voting rights or criminal procedures through the concept of substantive equality.

The state legislative reapportionment cases were unsatisfactory precisely because the Court attempted to apply a substantive equal protection approach. Chief Justice Warren's opinions in this series of cases are remarkable for their inability to muster a single respectable supporting argument. The principle of one man, one vote was not neutrally derived: it runs counter to the text of the fourteenth amendment, the history surrounding its adoption and ratification and the political practice of Americans from colonial times up to the day the Court invented the new formula.[39] The principle was not neutrally defined: it presumably rests upon some theory of equal weight for all votes, and yet we have no explanation of why it does not call into question other devices that defeat the principle, such as the executive veto, the committee system, the filibuster, the requirement on some issues of two-thirds majorities and the practice

---

39. See the dissents of Justice Frankfurter in Baker v. Carr, 369 U.S. 186, 266 (1962) ; Justice Harlan in Reynolds v. Sims, 377 U.S. 533, 589 (1964) ; and Justice Stewart in Lucas v. Forty-Fourth Gen. Ass'y, 377 U.S. 713, 744 (1964).

of districting. And, as we all know now, the principle, even as stated, was not neutrally applied.[40]

To approach these cases as involving rights derived from the requirements of our form of government is, of course, to say that they involve guarantee clause claims. Justice Frankfurter opposed the Court's consideration of reapportionment precisely on the ground that the "case involves all the elements that have made the Guarantee Clause cases nonjusticiable," and was a "Guarantee Clause claim masquerading under a different label."[41] Of course, his characterization was accurate, but the same could be said of many voting rights cases he was willing to decide. The guarantee clause, along with the provisions and structure of the Constitution and our political history, at least provides some guidance for a Court. The concept of the primary right of the individual in this area provides none. Whether one chooses to use the guarantee of a republican form of government of article IV, § 4 as a peg or to proceed directly to considerations of constitutional structure and political practice probably makes little difference. Madison's writing on the republican form of government specified by the guarantee clause suggests that representative democracy may properly take many forms, so long as the forms do not become "aristocractic or monarchical."[42] That is certainly less easily translated into the rigid one person, one vote requirement, which rests on a concept of the right of the individual to equality, than into the requirement expressed by Justice Stewart in *Lucas v. Forty-Fourth General Assembly*[43] that a legislative apportionment need only be rational and "must be such as not to permit the systematic frustration of the will of a majority of the electorate of the State."[44] The latter is a standard derived from the requirements of a democratic process rather than from the rights of individuals. The topic of governmental processes and the rights that may be derived from them is so large that it is best left at this point. It has been raised only as a reminder that there is a legitimate mode of deriving and defining constitutional rights, however difficult intellectually, that is available to replace the present unsatisfactory focus.

At the outset I warned that I did not offer a complete theory of constitutional interpretation. My concern has been to attack a few points that may be regarded as salient in order to clear the way for such a theory. I

---

40. *See* Fortson v. Morris, 385 U.S. 231 (1966).
41. Baker v. Carr, 369 U.S. 186, 297 (1962).
42. THE FEDERALIST No. 43 (J. Madison).
43. 377 U.S. 713 (1964).
44. *Id.* at 753-54.

turn next to a suggestion of what neutrality, the decision of cases according to principle, may mean for certain first amendment problems.

SOME FIRST AMENDMENT PROBLEMS: THE SEARCH FOR THEORY

The law has settled upon no tenable, internally consistent theory of
the scope of the constitutional guarantee of free speech. Nor have many
such theories been urged upon the courts by lawyers or academicians.
Professor Harry Kalven, Jr., one whose work is informed by a search
for theory, has expressed wonder that we should feel the need for theory
in the area of free speech when we tolerate inconsistencies in other areas
of the law so calmly.[45] He answers himself:

> If my puzzle as to the First Amendment is not a true puzzle, it
> can only be for the congenial reason that free speech is so close
> to the heart of democratic organization that if we do not have
> an appropriate theory for our law here, we feel we really do not
> understand the society in which we live.[46]

Kalven is certainly correct in assigning the first amendment a central
place in our society, and he is also right in attributing that centrality to
the importance of speech to democratic organization. Since I share this
common ground with Professor Kalven, I find it interestng that my
conclusions differ so widely from his.

I am led by the logic of the requirement that judges be principled
to the following suggestions. Constitutional protection should be accorded
only to speech that is explicitly political. There is no basis for judicial
intervention to protect any other form of expression, be it scientific,
literary or that variety of expression we call obscene or pornographic.
Moreover, within that category of speech we ordinarily call political,
there should be no constitutional obstruction to laws making criminal
any speech that advocates forcible overthrow of the government or the
violation of any law.

I am, of course, aware that this theory departs drastically from
existing Court-made law, from the views of most academic specialists in
the field and that it may strike a chill into the hearts of some civil libertarians. But I would insist at the outset that constitutional law, viewed
as the set of rules a judge may properly derive from the document and its
history, is not an expression of our political sympathies or of our judg-

---

45. H. KALVEN, THE NEGRO AND THE FIRST AMENDMENT 4-5 (1966) [hereinafter
cited as KALVEN].
46. *Id.* at 6.

ments about what expediency and prudence require. When decision making its principled it has nothing to say about the speech we like or the speech we hate; it has a great deal to say about how far democratic discretion can govern without endangering the basis of democratic government. Nothing in my argument goes to the question of what laws should be enacted. I like the freedoms of the individual as well as most, and I would be appalled by many statutes that I am compelled to think would be constitutional if enacted. But I am also persuaded that my generally libertarian commitments have nothing to do with the behavior proper to the Supreme Court.

In framing a theory of free speech the first obstacle is the insistence of many very intelligent people that the "first amendment is an absolute." Devotees of this position insist, with a literal respect they do not accord other parts of the Constitution, that the Framers commanded complete freedom of expression without governmental regulation of any kind. The first amendment states: "Congress shall make no law . . . abridging the freedom of speech. . . ." Those who take that as an absolute must be reading "speech" to mean any form of verbal communication and "freedom" to mean total absence of governmental restraint.

Any such reading is, of course, impossible. Since it purports to be an absolute position we are entitled to test it with extreme hypotheticals. Is Congress forbidden to prohibit incitement to mutiny aboard a naval vessel engaged in action against an enemy, to prohibit shouted harangues from the visitors' gallery during its own deliberations or to provide any rules for decorum in federal courtrooms? Are the states forbidden, by the incorporation of the first amendment in the fourteenth, to punish the shouting of obscenities in the streets?

No one, not the most obsessed absolutist, takes any such position, but if one does not, the absolute position is abandoned, revealed as a play on words. Government cannot function if anyone can say anything anywhere at any time. And so we quickly come to the conclusion that lines must be drawn, differentiations made. Nor does that in any way involve us in a conflict with the wording of the first amendment. Laymen may perhaps be forgiven for thinking that the literal words of the amendment command complete absence of governmental inhibition upon verbal activity, but what can one say of lawyers who believe any such thing? Anyone skilled in reading language should know that the words are not necessarily absolute. "Freedom of speech" may very well be a term referring to a defined or assumed scope of liberty, and it may be this area of liberty that is not to be "abridged."

If we turn to history, we discover that our suspicions about the wording are correct, except that matters are even worse. The framers seem to have had no coherent theory of free speech and appear not to have been overly concerned with the subject. Professor Leonard Levy's, work, *Legacy of Suppression,*[47] demonstrates that the men who adopted the first amendment did not display a strong libertarian stance with respect to speech. Any such position would have been strikingly at odds with the American political tradition. Our forefathers were men accustomed to drawing a line, to us often invisible, between freedom and licentiousness. In colonial times and during and after the Revolution they displayed a determination to punish speech thought dangerous to government, much of it expression that we would think harmless and well within the bounds of legitimate discourse. Jeffersonians, threatened by the Federalist Sedition Act of 1798, undertook the first American elaboration of a libertarian position in an effort to stay out of jail. Professor Walter Berns offers evidence that even then the position was not widely held.[48] When Jefferson came to power it developed that he read the first amendment only to limit Congress and he believed suppression to be a proper function of the state governments. He appears to have instigated state prosecutions against Federalists for seditious libel. But these later developments do not tell us what the men who adopted the first amendment intended, and their discussions tell us very little either. The disagreements that certainly existed were not debated and resolved. The first amendment, like the rest of the Bill of Rights, appears to have been a hastily drafted document upon which little thought was expended. One reason, as Levy shows, is that the Anti-Federalists complained of the absence of a Bill of Rights less because they cared for individual freedoms than as a tactic to defeat the Constitution. The Federalists promised to submit one in order to get the Constitution ratified. The Bill of Rights was then drafted by Federalists, who had opposed it from the beginning; the Anti-Federalists, who were really more interested in preserving the rights of state governments against federal power, had by that time lost interest in the subject.[49]

We are, then, forced to construct our own theory of the constitutional protection of speech. We cannot solve our problems simply by reference to the text or to its history. But we are not without materials

---

47. L. LEVY, LEGACY OF SUPPRESSION (1960) [hereinafter cited as LEVY].
48. Berns, *Freedom of the Press and the Alien and Sedition Laws: A Reappraisal,* 1970 SUP. CT. REV. 109.
49. LEVY, *supra* note 47, at 224-33.

NEUTRAL PRINCIPLES   23

for building. The first amendment indicates that there is something special about speech. We would know that much even without a first amendment, for the entire structure of the Constitution creates a representative democracy, a form of government that would be meaningless without freedom to discuss government and its policies. Freedom for political speech could and should be inferred even if there were no first amendment. Further guidance can be gained from the fact that we are looking for a theory fit for enforcement by judges. The principles we seek must, therefore, be neutral in all three meanings of the word: they must be neutrally derived, defined and applied.

The law of free speech we know today grows out of the Supreme Court decisions following World War I—*Schenck v. United States*,[50] *Abrams v. United States*,[51] *Gitlow v. New York*,[52] *Whitney v. California*[53]—not out of the majority positions but rather from the opinions, mostly dissents or concurrences that were really dissents, of Justices Holmes and Brandeis. Professor Kalven remarks upon "the almost uncanny power" of these dissents. And it is uncanny, for they have prevailed despite the considerable handicap of being deficient in logic and analysis as well as in history. The great Smith Act cases of the 1950's, *Dennis v. United States*,[54] as modified by *Yates v. United States*,[55] and, more recently, in 1969, *Brandenburg v. Ohio*[56] (voiding the Ohio criminal syndicalism statute), mark the triumph of Holmes and Brandeis. And other cases, culminating perhaps in a modified version of *Roth v. United States*,[57] have pushed the protections of the first amendment outward from political speech all the way to the fields of literature, entertainment and what can only be called pornography. Because my concern is general theory I shall not attempt a comprehensive survey of the cases nor engage in theological disputation over current doctrinal niceties. I intend to take the position that the law should have been built on Justice Sanford's majority opinions in *Gitlow* and *Whitney*. These days such an argument has at least the charm of complete novelty, but I think it has other merits as well.

Before coming to the specific issues in *Gitlow* and *Whitney*, I wish

---

50. 249 U.S. 47 (1919).
51. 250 U.S. 616 (1919).
52. 268 U.S. 652 (1925).
53. 274 U.S. 357 (1927).
54. 341 U.S. 494 (1951).
55. 354 U.S. 298 (1957).
56. 395 U.S. 444 (1969).
57. 354 U.S. 476 (1957).

to begin the general discussion of first amendment theory with consideration of a passage from Justice Brandeis' concurring opinion in the latter case. His *Whitney* concurrence was Brandeis' first attempt to articulate a comprehensive theory of the constitutional protection of speech, and in that attempt he laid down premises which seem to me correct. But those premises seem also to lead to conclusions which Justice Brandeis would have disowned.

As a starting point Brandeis went to fundamentals and attempted to answer the question why speech is protected at all from governmental regulation. If we overlook his highly romanticized version of history and ignore merely rhetorical flourishes, we shall find Brandeis quite provocative.

> Those who won our independence believed that the final end of the state was to make men free to develop their faculties; and that in its government the deliberative forces should prevail over the arbitrary. They valued liberty both as an end and as a means. They believed liberty to be the secret of happiness and courage to be the secret of liberty. The belief that freedom to think as you will and to speak as you think are means indispensable to the discovery and spread of political truth; that without free speech and assembly discussion would be futile; that with them, discussion affords ordinarily adequate protection against, the dissemination of noxious doctrine. . . . They recognized the risks to which all human institutions are subject. But they knew . . . that it is hazardous to discourage thought, hope and imagination; that fear breeds repression; that repression breeds hate; that hate menaces stable government; that the path of safety lies in the opportunity to discuss freely supposed grievances and proposed remedies; and that the fitting remedy for evil counsels is good ones.[58]

We begin to see why the dissents of Brandeis and Holmes possessed the power to which Professor Kalven referred. They were rhetoricians of extraordinary potency, and their rhetoric retains the power, almost half a century latter, to swamp analysis, to persuade, almost to command assent.

But there is structure beneath the rhetoric, and Brandeis is asserting, though he attributes it all to the Founding Fathers, that there are four benefits to be derived from speech. These are:

---

58.   274 U.S. at 375.

NEUTRAL PRINCIPLES 25

1. The development of the faculties of the individual;
2. The happiness to be derived from engaging in the activity;
3. The provision of a safety value for society; and,
4. The discovery and spread of political truth.

We may accept these claims as true and as satisfactorily inclusive. When we come to analyze these benefits, however, we discover that in terms of constitutional law they are very different things.

The first two benefits—development of individual faculties and the achievement of pleasure—are or may be found, for both speaker and hearer, in all varieties of speech, from political discourse to shop talk to salacious literature. But the important point is that these benefits do not distinguish speech from any other human activity. An individual may develop his faculties or derive pleasure from trading on the stock market, following his profession as a river port pilot, working as a barmaid, engaging in sexual activity, playing tennis, rigging prices or in any of thousands of other endeavors. Speech with only the first two benefits can be preferred to other activities only by ranking forms of personal gratification. These functions or benefits of speech are, therefore, to the principled judge, indistinguishable from the functions or benefits of all other human activity. He cannot, on neutral grounds, choose to protect speech that has only these functions more than he protects any other claimed freedom.

The third benefit of speech mentioned by Brandeis—its safety valve function—is different from the first two. It relates not to the gratification of the individual, at least not directly, but to the welfare of society. The safety valve function raises only issues of expediency or prudence, and, therefore, raises issues to be determined solely by the legislature or, in some cases, by the executive. The legislature may decide not to repress speech advocating the forcible overthrow of the government in some classes of cases because it thinks repression would cause more trouble than it would prevent. Prosecuting attorneys, who must in any event pick and choose among cases, given their limited resources, may similarly decide that some such speech is trivial or that ignoring it would be wisest. But these decisions, involving only the issue of the expedient course, are indistinguishable from thousands of other managerial judgments governments must make daily, though in the extreme case the decision may involve the safety of the society just as surely as a decision whether or not to take a foreign policy stand that risks war. It seems

26   *INDIANA LAW JOURNAL*

plain that decisions involving only judgments of expediency are for the political branches and not for the judiciary.

This leaves the fourth function of speech—the "discovery and spread of political truth." This function of speech, its ability to deal explicitly, specifically and directly with politics and government, is different from any other form of human activity. But the difference exists only with respect to one kind of speech: explicitly and predominantly political speech. This seems to me the only form of speech that a principled judge can prefer to other claimed freedoms. All other forms of speech raise only issues of human gratification and their protection against legislative regulation involves the judge in making decisions of the sort made in *Griswold v. Connecticut*.

It is here that I begin to part company with Professor Kalven. Kalven argues that no society in which seditious libel, the criticism of public officials, is a crime can call itself free and democratic.[59] I agree, even though the framers of the first amendment probably had no clear view of that proposition. Yet they indicated a value when they said that speech in some sense was special and when they wrote a Constitution providing for representative democracy, a form of government that is meaningless without open and vigorous debate about officials and their policies. It is for this reason, the relation of speech to democratic organization, that Professor Alexander Meiklejohn seems correct when he says:

> The First Amendment does not protect a "freedom to speak." It protects the freedom of those activities of thought and communication by which we "govern." It is concerned, not with a private right, but with a public power, a governmental responsibility.[60]

But both Kalven and Meiklejohn go further and would extend the protection of the first amendment beyond speech that is explicitly political. Meiklejohn argues that the amendment protects:

> Forms of thought and expression within the range of human communications from which the voter derives the knowledge, intelligence, sensitivity to human values: the capacity for sane and objective judgment which, so far as possible, a ballot should express.

---

59. KALVEN, *supra* note 45, at 16.
60. Meiklejohn, *The First Amendment Is an Absolute*, 1961 SUP. CT. REV. 245, 255.

He lists four such thoughts and expressions:

> 1. Education, in all its phases. . . . 2. The achievements of philosophy and the sciences. . . . 3. Literature and the arts. . . . 4. Public discussions of public issues. . . .[61]

Kalven, following a similar line, states: "[T]he invitation to follow a dialectic progression from public official to government policy to public policy to matters in the public domain, like art, seems to me to be overwhelming."[62] It is an invitation, I wish to suggest, the principled judge must decline. A dialectic progression I take to be a progression by analogy from one case to the next, an indispensable but perilous method of legal reasoning. The length to which analogy is carried defines the principle, but neutral definition requires that, in terms of the rationale in play, those cases within the principle be more like each other than they are like cases left outside. The dialectical progression must have a principled stopping point. I agree that there is an analogy between criticism of official behavior and the publication of a novel like *Ulysses*, for the latter may form attitudes that ultimately affect politics. But it is an analogy, not an identity. Other human activities and experiences also form personality, teach and create attitudes just as much as does the novel, but no one would on that account, I take it, suggest that the first amendment strikes down regulations of economic activity, control of entry into a trade, laws about sexual behavior, marriage and the like. Yet these activities, in their capacity to create attitudes that ultimately impinge upon the political process, are more like literature and science than literature and science are like political speech. If the dialectical progression is not to become an analogical stampede, the protection of the first amendment amendment must be cut off when it reaches the outer limits of political speech.

Two types of problems may be supposed to arise with respect to this solution. The first is the difficulty of drawing a line between political and non-political speech. The second is that such a line will leave unprotected much speech that is essential to the life of a civilized community. Neither of these problems seems to me to raise crippling difficulties.

The category of protected speech should consist of speech concerned with governmental behavior, policy or personnel, whether the govern-

---

61. *Id.* at 256-57.
62. Kalven, *The New York Times Case: A Note on "The Central Meaning of the First Amendment,"* 1964 SUP. CT. REV. 191, 221.

mental unit involved is executive, legislative, judicial or administrative. Explicitly political speech is speech about how we are governed, and the category therefore includes a wide range of evaluation, criticism, election-eering and propaganda. It does not cover scientific, educational, commercial or literary expressions as such. A novel may have impact upon attitudes that affect politics, but it would not for that reason receive judicial protection. This is not anomalous, I have tried to suggest, since the rationale of the first amendment cannot be the protection of all things or activities that influence political attitudes. Any speech may do that, and we have seen that it is impossible to leave all speech unregulated. Moreover, any conduct may affect political attitudes as much as a novel, and we cannot view the first amendment as a broad denial of the power of government to regulate conduct. The line drawn must, therefore, lie between the explicitly political and all else. Not too much should be made of the undeniable fact that there will be hard cases. Any theory of the first amendment that does not accord absolute protection for all verbal expression, which is to say any theory worth discussing, will require that a spectrum be cut and the location of the cut will always be, arguably, arbitrary. The question is whether the general location of the cut is justified. The existence of close cases is not a reason to refuse to draw a line and so deny majorities the power to govern in areas where their power is legitimate.

The other objection—that the political-nonpolitical distinction will leave much valuable speech without constitutional protection—is no more troublesome. The notion that all valuable types of speech must be protected by the first amendment confuses the constitutionality of laws with their wisdom. Freedom of non-political speech rests, as does freedom for other valuable forms of behavior, upon the enlightenment of society and its elected representatives. That is hardly a terrible fate. At least a society like ours ought not to think it so.

The practical effect of confining constitutional protection to political speech would probably go no further than to introduce regulation or prohibition of pornography. The Court would be freed of the stultifying obligation to apply its self-inflicted criteria: whether "(a) the dominant theme of the material taken as a whole appeals to a prurient interest in sex; (b) the material is patently offensive because it affronts contemporary community standards relating to the description or representation of sexual matters: and (c) the material is utterly without redeeming social value."[63] To take only the last criterion, the determination of "social value" cannot be made in a principled way. Anything some people want has, to that degree, social value, but that cannot be the basis for constitutional protection since it would deny regulation of any human activity. The concept of social value necessarily incorporates a judgment about the net effect upon society. There is always the problem that what some people want some other people do not want, or wish actively to banish. A judgment about social value, whether the judges realize it or not, always involves a comparison of competing values and gratifications as well as competing predictions of the effects of the activity. Determination of "social value" is the same thing as determination of what human interests should be classed as "fundamental" and, therefore, cannot be principled or neutral.

To revert to a previous example, pornography is increasingly seen as a problem of pollution of the moral and aesthetic atmosphere precisely analogous to smoke pollution. A majority of the community may foresee that continued availability of pornography to those who want it will inevitably affect the quality of life for those who do not want it, altering, for example, attitudes toward love and sex, the tone of private and public discourse and views of social institutions such as marriage and the family. Such a majority surely has as much control over the moral and aesthetic environment as it does over the physical, for such matters may even more severely impinge upon their gratifications. That is why, constitutionally, art and pornography are on a par with industry and smoke pollution. As Professor Walter Berns says "[A] thoughtful judge is likely to ask how an artistic judgment that is wholly idiosyncratic can be capable of supporting an objection to the law. The objection, 'I like it,' is sufficiently rebutted by '*we* don't.' "[64]

We must now return to the core of the first amendment, speech that is explicitly political. I mean by that criticisms of public officials and policies, proposals for the adoption or repeal of legislation or constitutional provisions and speech addressed to the conduct of any governmental unit in the country.

A qualification is required, however. Political speech is not any speech that concerns government and law, for there is a category of such speech that must be excluded. This category consists of speech

---

63. A Book Named "John Clelend's Memoirs of a Woman of Pleasure" v. Attorney General, 383 U.S. 413, 418 (1966).
64. Berns, *Pornography vs. Democracy: The Case for Censorship*, THE PUB. INTEREST, Winter, 1971, at 23.

advocating forcible overthrow of the government or violation of law. The reason becomes clear when we return to Brandeis' discussion of the reasons for according constitutional protection to speech.

The fourth function of speech, the one that defines and sets apart political speech, is the "discovery and spread of political truth." To understand what the Court should protect, therefore, we must define "political truth." There seem to me three possible meanings to that term:

1. An absolute set of truths that exist independently of Constitution or statute.

2. A set of values that are protected by constitutional provision from the reach of legislative majorities.

3. Within that area of life which the majority is permitted to govern in accordance with the Madisonian model of representative government, whatever result the majority reaches and maintains at the moment.

The judge can have nothing to do with any absolute set of truths existing independently and depending upon God or the nature of the universe. If a judge should claim to have access to such a body of truths, to possess a volume of the annotated natural law, we would, quite justifiably, suspect that the source of the revelation was really no more exalted than the judge's viscera. In or system there is no absolute set of truths, to which the term "political truth" can refer.

Values protected by the Constitution are one type of political truth. They are, in fact, the highest type since they are placed beyond the reach of simple legislative majorities. They are primarily truths about the way government must operate, that is, procedural truths. But speech aimed at the discovery and spread of political truth is concerned with more than the desirability of constitutional provisions or the manner in which they should be interpreted.

The third meaning of "political truth" extends the category of protected speech. Truth is what the majority thinks it is at any given moment precisely because the majority is permitted to govern and to redefine its values constantly. "Political truth" in this sense must, therefore, be a term of art, a concept defined entirely from a consideration of the system of government which the judge is commissioned to operate and maintain. It has no unchanging content but refers to the temporary outcomes of the democratic process. Political truth is what the majority decides it wants today. It may be something entirely different tomorrow, as truth is rediscovered and the new concept spread.

Speech advocating forcible overthrow of the government contemplates a group less than a majority seizing control of the monopoly power of the state when it cannot gain its ends through speech and political activity. Speech advocating violent overthrow is thus not "political speech" as that term must be defined by a Madisonian system of government. It is not political speech because it violates constitutional truths about processes and because it is not aimed at a new definition of political truth by a legislative majority. Violent overthrow of government breaks the premises of our system concerning the ways in which truth is defined, and yet those premises are the only reasons for protecting political speech. It follows that there is no constitutional reason to protect speech advocating forcible overthrow.

A similar analysis suggests that advocacy of law violation does not qualify as political speech any more than advocacy of forcible overthrow of the government. Advocacy of law violation is a call to set aside the results that political speech has produced. The process of the "discovery and spread of political truth" is damaged or destroyed if the outcome is defeated by a minority that makes law enforcement, and hence the putting of political truth into practice, impossible or less effective. There should, therefore, be no constitutional protection for any speech advocating the violation of law.

I believe these are the only results that can be reached by a neutral judge who takes his values from the Constitution. If we take Brandeis' description of the benefits and functions of speech as our premise, logic and principle appear to drive us to the conclusion that Sanford rather than Brandeis or Holmes was correct in *Gitlow* and *Whitney*.

Benjamin Gitlow was convicted under New York's criminal anarchy statute which made criminal advocacy of the doctrine that organized government should be overthrown by force, violence or any unlawful means. Gitlow, a member of the Left Wing section of the Socialist party, had arranged the printing and distribution of a "Manifesto" deemed to call for violent action and revolution. "There was," Justice Sanford's opinion noted, "no evidence of any effect resulting from the publication and circulation of the Manifesto."[65] Anita Whitney was convicted under California's criminal syndicalism statute, which forbade advocacy of the commission of crime, sabotage, acts of force or violence or terrorism

---

65. 268 U.S. at 656.

"as a means of accomplishing a change in industrial ownership or control, or effecting any political change." Also made illegal were certain connections with groups advocating such doctrines. Miss Whitney was convicted of assisting in organizing the Communist Labor Party of California, of being a member of it and of assembling with it.[66] The evidence appears to have been meager, but our current concern is doctrinal.

Justice Sanford's opinions for the majorities in *Gitlow* and *Whitney* held essentially that the Court's function in speech cases was the limited but crucial one of determining whether the legislature had defined a category of forbidden speech which might constitutionally be suppressed.[67] The category might be defined by the nature of the speech and need not be limited in other ways. If the category was defined in a permissible way and the defenadant's speech or publication fell within the definition, the Court had, it would appear, no other issues to face in order to uphold the conviction. Questions of the fairness of the trial and the sufficiency of the evidence aside, this would appear to be the correct conclusion. The legislatures had struck at speech not aimed at the discovery and spread of political truth but aimed rather at destroying the premises of our political system and the means by which we define political truth. There is no value that judges can independently give such speech in opposition to a legislative determination.

Justice Holmes' dissent in *Gitlow* and Justice Brandeis' concurrence in *Whitney* insisted the Court must also find that, as Brandeis put it, the "speech would produce, or is intended to produce, a clear and imminent danger of some substantive evil which the state constitutionally may seek to prevent."[68] Neither of them explained why the danger must be "clear and imminent" or, as Holmes had put it in *Schenck,* "clear and present"[69] before a particular instance of speech could be punished. Neither of them made any attempt to answer Justice Sanford's argument on the point:

> [T]he immediate danger [created by advocacy of overthrow of the government] is none the less real and substantial, because the effect of a given utterance cannot be accurately foreseen. The state cannot reasonably be required to measure the danger from every such utterance in the nice balance of a

---

66. 274 U.S. at 372 (Brandeis, J., dissenting).
67. 268 U.S. at 668; 274 U.S. at 362-63.
68. 274 U.S. at 373.
69. 249 U.S. at 52.

jeweler's scale. A single revolutionary spark may kindle a fire that, smoldering for a time, may burst into a sweeping and destructive conflagration. It cannot be said that the state is acting arbitrarily or unreasonably when in the exercise of its judgment as to the measures necessary to protect the public peace and safety, it seeks to extinguish the spark without waiting until it has enkindled the flame or blazed into conflagration. It cannot reasonably be required to defer the adoption of measures for its own peace and safety until the revolutionary utterances lead to actual disturbances of the public peace or imminent and immediate danger of its own destruction; but it may, in the exercise of its judgment, suppress the threatened danger in its incipiency . . . .[70]

To his point that proof of the effect of speech is inherently unavailable and yet its impact may be real and dangerous, Sanford might have added that the legislature is not confined to consideration of a single instance of speech or a single speaker. It fashions a rule to dampen thousands of instances of forcible overthrow advocacy. Cumulatively these may have enormous influence, and yet it may well be impossible to show any effect from any single example. The "clear and present danger" requirement, which has had a long and uneven career in our law, is improper not, as many commentators have thought, because it provides a subjective and an inadequate safeguard against the regulation of speech, but rather because it erects a barrier to legislative rule where none should exist. The speech concerned has no political value within a republican system of government. Whether or not it is prudent to ban advocacy of forcible overthrow and law violation is a different question although. Because the judgment is tactical, implicating the safety of the nation, it resembles very closely the judgment that Congress and the President must make about the expediency of waging war, an issue that the Court has wisely thought not fit for judicial determination.

The legislature and the executive might find it wise to permit some rhetoric about law violation and forcible overthrow. I am certain that they would and that they should. Certain of the factors weighted in determining the constitutionality of the Smith Act prosecutions in *Dennis* would, for example, make intelligible statutory, though not constitutional, criteria: the high degree of organization of the Communist party, the

---

70. 268 U.S. at 669.

rigid discipline of its members and the party's ideological affinity to foreign powers.[71]

Similar objections apply to the other restrictions Brandeis attempted to impose upon government. I will mention but one more of these restrictions. Justice Brandeis argued that:

> Even imminent danger cannot justify resort to prohibition of these functions essential to effective democracy, unless the evil apprehended is relatively serious. . . . Thus, a state might, in the exercise of its police power, make any trespass upon the land of another a crime, regardless of the results or of the intent or purpose of the trespasser. It might, also, punish an attempt, a conspiracy, or an incitement to commit the trespass. But it is hardly conceivable that this court would hold constitutional a statute which punished as a felony the mere voluntary assembly with a society formed to teach that pedestrians had the moral right to cross unenclosed, unposted, waste lands and to advocate their doing so, even if there was imminent danger that advocacy would lead to a trespass. The fact that speech is likely to result in some violence or in destruction of property is not enough to justify its suppression. There must be the probability of serious injury to the state.[72]

It is difficult to see how a constitutional court could properly draw the distinction proposed. Brandeis offered no analysis to show that advocacy of law violation merited protection by the Court. Worse, the criterion he advanced is the importance, in the judge's eyes, of the law whose violation is urged.

Modern law has followed the general line and the spirit of Brandeis and Holmes rather than of Sanford, and it has become increasingly severe in its limitation of legislative power. *Brandenburg v. Ohio*, a 1969 per curiam decision by the Supreme Court, struck down the Ohio criminal syndicalism statute because it punished advocacy of violence, the opinion stating:

> . . . *Whitney* [the majority opinion] has been thoroughly discredited by later decisions. . . . These later decisions have fashioned the principle that the constitutional guarantees of free speech and free press do not permit a State to forbid or proscribe

---

71. 341 U.S. at 511.
72. 274 U.S. at 377-78.

NEUTRAL PRINCIPLES 35

advocacy of the use of force or of law violation except where such advocacy is directed to inciting or producing imminent lawless action and is likely to incite or produce such action.[73]

It is certainly true that Justice Sanford's position in *Whitney* and in *Gitlow* has been completely undercut, or rather abandoned, by later cases, but it is not true that his position has been discredited, or even met, on intellectual grounds. Justice Brandeis failed to accomplish that, and later Justices have not mounted a theoretical case comparable to Brandeis'.

*   *   *   *   *

These remarks are intended to be tentative and exploratory. Yet at this moment I do not see how I can avoid the conclusions stated. The Supreme Court's constitutional role appears to be justified only if the Court applies principles that are neutrally derived, defined and applied. And the requirement of neutrality in turn appears to indicate the results I have sketched here.

---

73.   395 U.S. at 447.

[7]

FREE SPEECH JUSTIFICATIONS*

*Kent Greenawalt***

INTRODUCTION

This Article sets out what I believe are the relevant justifications for free speech, the term "free speech" being meant to cover both freedom of speech and freedom of the press. These are the justifications one might use to assess whether communications fall within a political or judicial principle of free speech and how great the protection of the communications that are covered should be. Such assessments are undertaken in a longer study that is mainly about the ways in which different uses of language affect the application of principles of freedom of speech to the criminalization of behavior.[1] That study concentrates on the communicative acts that lie on the border of free speech, especially solicitations to crime and threats, in an attempt to examine the proper boundaries of free speech.[2]

My broader purpose illuminates the ambitions and limits of this Article. What follows is an attempt to set out the various justifications for free speech in a systematic way. This attempt should provide some antidote for confusion and for oversimplification, the main disease of legal and philosophical scholarship. The Article reveals the subtle plurality of values that does govern the practice of freedom of speech; and one can surmise that a similarly close investigation would reveal a plurality of values behind almost any important social practice. This Article also reflects my own sense that, whatever may be true at some ultimate level, human beings dealing with practical problems not only

---

   * Copyright © 1989 by Oxford University Press.
   ** Cardozo Professor of Jurisprudence, Columbia University. B.A. 1958, Swarthmore; B. Phil. 1960, Oxford; L.L.B. 1963, Columbia University.
   1. This broader effort is to appear as a book entitled *Speech, Crime, and the Uses of Language*, to be published in 1989 by Oxford University Press.
   2. The book considers both a "political principle of freedom of speech," relevant for liberal societies independent of whether they have written constitutions that yield judicial review protecting free speech, and the free speech and free press clauses of the United States Constitution. I contend that both political and judicial standards should be nuanced in response to how the justifications for free speech and free press reach variant uses of language. Some uses of language, words of agreement to rob a bank, for example, lie so far from the justifications for free expression that they should be regarded as wholly outside political and constitutional principles of free speech. "Wholly outside" means roughly that in practice legislatures may consider whether to penalize explicit agreements without worrying about free speech (although a principle of free speech does affect what counts as a serious agreement), and courts may sustain criminal sanctions without employing any first amendment test. I claim that some uses of language, particularly requests and encouragements that include neither threats nor inducements within the speaker's control, have enough expressive value to make free speech principles relevant, but that they may be suppressed in circumstances when straightforward claims of fact and value may not be suppressed.

do but should rely on a plurality of values. Rather than undertaking an exhaustive analysis of any individual justification, this Article attempts to set forth the relevant justifications for free speech as clearly, systematically and accurately as possible.

The main virtue of the following pages is that they provide a coherent and comprehensive overview of justifications for free speech, an overview that will enable the reader to see how one justification relates to others, to understand what may be left out if one or two justifications are portrayed as dominant, and to assess with a suitably critical eye claims about the content of particular justifications and why they should be given a central place or rejected.

Most of the Article is devoted to particular justifications for free speech, but first some preliminary matters are covered. Part I indicates why one can speak of a principle, or principles, of free speech only if there are bases for protecting speech that do not apply similarly to some substantially broader category of acts. Once Part I clarifies the idea of a principle of free speech, Part II examines the nature and classification of justifications. It maintains that efforts to arrive at any single unifying justification risk either simplifying or obscuring the complex values undergirding freedom of expression. This Part also suggests how the distinction between consequentialist and nonconsequentialist justifications usefully differentiates between reasons depending directly on empirical grounds and those resting on other normative claims. Parts III and IV then provide an account of multiple justifications divided along consequentialist and nonconsequentialist lines.

I. How a Genuine Principle of Freedom of Speech Compares with a Minimal Principle of Liberty and Broader Principles of Extra Protection

Given that various reasons for free speech apply unevenly to different sorts of communications, there is some question whether one should speak of "a principle" or "principles" of free speech. For simplicity's sake, the singular form is adopted here, but that form should not obscure the complexities of the subject.

A principle of freedom of speech asserts some range of protection for speech that goes beyond limitations on government interference with other activities. While a minimal principle of liberty maintains that government should not inhibit communications that pose no legitimate threat of harm, a distinctive principle of freedom of speech posits more robust constraints. Even if no rationale for liberty applies uniquely to speech, a distinctive principle of freedom of speech may yet be warranted, given that reasons of general applicability and various reasons in combination may apply to speech with special force.

A. *Beyond a Minimal Principle of Liberty*

A political principle of free speech is warranted only if reasons to protect speech go beyond the reasons for a minimal principle of liberty. According to a minimal principle of liberty, the government should not prohibit people from acting as they wish unless it has a positive reason to do so. The ordinary reason for prohibiting action is that the action is deemed harmful or potentially harmful in some respect; driving a car at 100 miles per hour is forbidden because people are likely to get hurt. Although sometimes the government may constrain behavior in order to compel some action that generates a benefit, or may potentially generate benefits,[3] that subtlety will be disregarded in order to concentrate on harm. What legitimately counts as "harm" is an important and controversial aspect of political theory,[4] but here the term is meant in an inclusive, nonrestrictive sense, including indirect harms, psychological harms, harms to the actor, and even harms to the natural order. Thus, sexual intercourse between human beings and animals might be prohibited on the ground that it has deleterious indirect effects on family life, is psychologically bad for the people involved, or is intrinsically unnatural.

Since governments have little apparent reason to prohibit action other than to prevent harm the action may cause, an assumption that people should otherwise be left free comes very close to being a principle of rationality for governance. A challenge to the principle is imaginable, but the theory of human nature and government it would represent would be most unattractive. Government control of perfectly harmless actions like whistling in one's room might be a technique to induce unquestioning obedience to government authority. In that event, the prohibition would be designed to prevent some harm, such as "unhealthy" independent civic attitudes, but the harm would be unrelated to acts of whistling or their effects.[5] Conceivably, such control of "neutral" matters may have a place in training techniques for highly

---

3. This subject is complicated in ways that would demand examination were this not a preface to a discussion of free speech. Parents may be directly compelled to confer benefits, such as food and clothing, on their children. One argument for forbidding adultery is that it threatens families and less tangible benefits, such as loving companionship, that many children receive. Other acts might be compelled or forbidden in order that people develop regular habits of doing those acts that will lead overall to benefits for others. How far the last justification for control of adults is acceptable is something that may separate "liberal" societies from many others. Since any failure to receive a benefit may be understood as a harm, the line between actions that confer benefits and those that prevent harm is thin; but performing compulsory jury service, for example, may be viewed as a required conferral of a benefit, as may food and clothing for one's children.

4. See generally J. Feinberg, Harm to Others (1984) (developing a principle of harm that applies when harm includes both a setback of an interest as well as a violation of a person's rights).

5. This is what differentiates stopping whistling from stopping acts that themselves threaten harm over the long run.

disciplined subgroups, such as monastic orders or military personnel, but accepting its appropriateness for regulating the general class of citizens would be to embrace the kind of extreme totalitarianism suggested by fantasies like George Orwell's *Nineteen Eighty Four*.[6] The alternative—the "minimal principle of liberty"—is a fundamental premise of all "Western" governments, and in this modest form, is probably accepted as well by almost all authoritarian or dictatorial governments, whether of the right or the left.[7]

As far as speech is concerned, the minimal principle of liberty establishes that the government should not interfere with communication that has no poten,tial for harm. To be significant, a principle of freedom of speech must go beyond this,[8] positing constraints on the regulation of speech that are more robust than constraints on the regulation of other matters. A principle of free speech could establish more stringent constraints than the minimal principle of liberty either by barring certain possible reasons for prohibition or by establishing a special value for speech. The latter way is the easier to understand. If some human activities have special value, a good government will need stronger reasons to prohibit them than to prohibit other activities. If speech has more positive value than acts of physical aggression, for example, more powerful reasons will be needed to warrant its suppression. A related but more subtle point is that legislatures or other political actors may be prone in particular instances to undervalue certain kinds of acts; were that true about speech, a principle of free speech might compensate for that tendency. In effect, the principle would tell those involved in government that acts of speech should be assumed to have a higher value than they seem to have in the immediate context.

The second way in which a principle might give special protection to speech is by positing that the government is barred from employing certain reasons for prohibiting speech. Such a constraint might derive from a notion that particular reasons for prohibitions are at odds with how human beings should be regarded or with the proper role of government. Thus, it might be claimed that because an aspect of the autonomy of human beings is that people should discover for themselves what is true, suppressing speech to prevent contamination by false ideas is impermissible. Or, it might be said that the government cannot suppress political ideas that pose challenges to it, because one aspect of a legitimate government is that criticism of those presently in power may be entertained. The import of a "disqualifying" principle might not warrant total exclusion of a reason for prohibition. A reason might

---

6. G. Orwell, Nineteen Eighty Four (I. Howe 2d ed. 1982).

7. But the "nonliberal" government may be much more willing to forestall perceived indirect harms and to promote virtuous habits than a liberal government. See supra note 3.

8. See F. Schauer, Free Speech: A Philosophical Enquiry 5–12 (1982).

be viewed with great suspicion, but treated as a legitimate basis for prohibition if the case were sufficiently compelling.[9] Building on these arguments, a principle or theory of freedom of speech would claim that expression cannot be regulated on every basis that could surmount the minimal principle of liberty and satisfy ordinary prudential considerations regarding effective legislation.[10]

Some claims about the value of speech or about the inappropriateness of certain reasons for prohibition could be thought to be largely independent of wider assertions of political ideology, but many claims bear a distinctive relation to liberal political theory. A proponent of claims that involve a controverted liberal view of human autonomy and government might assert that the liberal view is fundamentally correct, and should be embraced by all peoples, or all peoples at a certain stage of economic and social development; in that event, a complete defense of the claims about free speech would require argument for the superiority of the liberal perspective. Alternatively, one who advances liberal claims might assert that since a particular society is grounded on liberal ideas, that society should act on their implications, at least absent opposed premises for social life that are clearly preferable and attainable.

Because the aim here is to elucidate standards that could be endorsed by people who disagree about many fundamental matters, the following account does not depend on a single systematic version of liberal political theory. But doubting whether there is a better form of government for large developed countries and strongly believing that no other form is clearly preferable and attainable, I assume in this study that conclusions about freedom of speech that can be drawn from basic premises of liberal democracy are sound, without examining possible competing premises.[11] Reliance on these basic premises does not mean uncritical acceptance of every liberal idea; rather, discrete arguments having to do with freedom of speech are scrutinized carefully in turn.

---

9. One might say, to illustrate with an example not involving speech, that any government justification for enforced segregation based on violence that might flow from hostility between members of different racial groups should be viewed with extreme suspicion, but that temporary racial segregation in a prison might be warranted following an extensive race riot in which prisoners have been killed.

10. Prudential considerations, such as the costs of administration, might make it unwise to forbid much behavior that could be forbidden under a minimal principle of liberty.

11. The discussion that follows suggests the basic premises of liberal democracy. My views on that subject are developed in K. Greenawalt, Religious Convictions and Political Choice 14–29 (1988). I do not think that the basic premises of liberal democracy include extreme rationalism, extreme individualism, neutrality among ideas of the good, or exclusive reliance for political choice on shared premises and publicly accessible grounds for determining truth.

B. *Is There a Distinctive Principle of Free Speech?*

A principle of freedom of speech does not itself flow from the conclusion that the minimal principle of liberty inadequately protects some
liberties. The question remains why, and whether, freedom of speech
should be singled out, since a sound principle more robust than that of
minimal liberty might apply to matters other than speech. Only the
analysis of the justifications for speech reveals the full response to this
query, but that analysis can be clarified by a number of preliminary
points.

First, a principle of freedom of speech is certainly compatible with
other principles that are more protective of liberty than the minimal
principle. One might defend, for example, a distinctive principle of
religious liberty or of family liberty. The scope of another liberty can
overlap with liberty of speech; for example, assertions of propositions
about religion are covered both by religious liberty and by freedom of
speech.

Second, a principle that covers most speech may or may not cover
all speech and it may or may not cover only speech. Although it would
be misleading to refer to any distinctive principle of free speech if a
principle covered such wide areas that speech was only one small subcategory, or if a principle covered only a little of speech, someone
might talk roughly about a principle of free speech if the principle
reached a few other activities besides speech or failed to cover all
speech. Another conceptual approach, the one mainly employed here,
is to understand "speech" as including only, and all of, what is actually
covered by a proper principle of freedom of speech, using some other
term, like communication, to cover the broader class of activities that
may superficially resemble what is covered by the principle.[12]

Contrary to what has sometimes been supposed,[13] a distinctive
principle of freedom of speech may be maintainable even if no reasons
for liberty uniquely apply to speech.[14] An insistence on unique reasons
disregards the possible complexity of justifications. Reasons of more

---

12. This is a fairly common approach, followed by F. Schauer, supra note 8, at
89–92, among others. The sentence in the text, however, requires an important qualification, or clarification. A government might prohibit acts, such as the sale of toy guns,
that are not designed to communicate messages because it fears what observers will take
as implicit messages, e.g., that shooting guns is fine. In such cases, a principle of free
speech may affect the legitimacy of the prohibition although the acts viewed by themselves may not be speech. From this perspective, an activity may be affected by the free
speech principle either becaue it qualifies directly as "speech" or because it is regulated
on the basis of the government's view about appropriate messages.

13. See, e.g., Bork, Neutral Principles and Some First Amendment Problems, 47
Ind. L.J. 1, 25–27 (1971) (arguing that speech which merely develops human faculties
and furthers happiness is indistinguishable from other human activity, and that a principled judge "cannot, on neutral grounds, choose to protect speech that has only those
functions more than he protects any other claimed freedoms").

14. See generally M. Redish, Freedom of Expression 1 n.1, 40 (1984) (fact that a

general applicability may have special strength as to speech, and various reasons in combination may apply to speech in a way that is not true of other activities. In either event speech might warrant unique protection, though no single reason for protection uniquely applied to speech. However, should the only good reason for liberty of speech apply in the same strength to a much broader range of activities, any claim for a distinctive principle of free speech would be undercut.

Some aspects of a principle of free speech may lie closer to more general claims of liberty than do others. The reasons for protecting speech apply with variant strength to different sorts of speech. Even within the domain of what counts as speech, some communications may deserve more protection, or protection for different reasons or protection against different bases for suppression, than do other communications. A political principle of free speech need not, and should not, amount to a single rigid principle, having the same import for all kinds of speech. Indeed, a more precise portrayal might show a loose constellation of reasons, subjects, and subprinciples governing the protection of speech.[15] Some of these subprinciples might lie particularly close to principles governing certain nonexpressive activities. For example, as to communication whose main justification is that it provides an outlet for emotional release, the reasons behind its protection might cover other activities by which people vent emotions, such as vigorous athletic activities. Yet other reasons covering other forms of speech might have no bearing for athletic endeavors.

II. THE RELEVANCE OF MULTIPLE JUSTIFICATIONS AND THE CONSEQUENTIALIST-NONCONSEQUENTIALIST DISTINCTION

What sorts of reasons justify acceptance of a principle that protects speech even when speech seems to carry a potential for harm that would warrant prohibition if all that were at stake were the minimal principle of liberty and ordinary canons of prudent legislation? Although their importance varies generally, and particularly in respect to discrete classes of communications, many reasons have substantial force that justifies protection for much speech. Since there is no single unifying justification for a principle of free speech, a problem arises as to how the various justifications should be classified. While no single categorization is uniquely correct, a division between consequentialist and nonconsequentialist reasons is the most useful for my purposes here.

A. *Multiple Reasons or a Single Unifying Justification?*

Some have suggested in recent years that there is a single unifying

---

conglomeration of traditionally accepted values is served by the protection of free speech does not disqualify them as rationales for free speech).

15. See F. Schauer, *supra* note 8, at 14.

justification for freedom of speech, at least as far as the law of the first amendment is concerned.[16] One of two unpersuasive strategies is followed to give credence to this initially implausible proposal.

The first strategy is elimination. Various reasons for free speech are found to be applicable to things other than speech and therefore are presumed to be nonsupportive of a distinctive principle of free speech, whatever their relevance for some more general theory of liberty.[17] A single reason for free speech is left, and that is said to be the reason behind a principle protecting speech. (Were no reason left over, the assumption is that no principle of freedom of speech would be warranted.)

Such efforts must be viewed with great skepticism. A reason that applies to other subjects may apply with special intensity to speech; various reasons may coalesce in a unique way with respect to speech. The idea that any justification with broader relevance may be written off as not bearing on a principle of freedom of speech is thus erroneous and must be strongly resisted.

The second strategy for arriving at a single principle is inclusion.[18] A number of reasons are taken as having some merit, but this merit is then shown as contributing to some yet larger value. Suppose, for example, that maximizing individual fulfillment is taken as the overriding value behind freedom of speech, and one considers the claim that speech also promotes scrutiny of government misdoing. The linkage is that government wrongdoing interferes with human fulfillment, and the seemingly independent reason is then swallowed up in the broader reason.

The strategy of inclusion suffers some basic defects. One is that any reason broad enough to yield a plausible claim that it includes everything else is bound to be extremely general and vague. Such a reason will not provide a very helpful starting point for dealing with many actual social problems if citizens, legislators, and judges must descend quickly to the more specific "subsidiary" reasons whose implications are clearer. And a reason broad enough to swallow up all

---

16. See, e.g., M. Redish, supra note 14, at 1–86; Baker, Scope of the First Amendment Freedom of Speech, 25 UCLA L. Rev. 964–90 (1978); Bork, supra note 13, at 20–26. Since Redish includes within the broad value of self-realization both "the inherent value in allowing individuals to control their own destiny, and the instrumental value in developing individuals' mental faculties," M. Redish, supra note 14, at 30, it may be argued whether he settles finally on one or two values. A similar question may be raised about Baker, who talks of individual self-fulfillment and participation in change as key first amendment values. Baker, supra, at 991. And because Bork is concentrating on an appropriate principle of constitutional law for the courts and rejects the "safety valve" function of speech because it raises issues of prudence inappropriate for the judiciary, Bork, supra note 13, at 25–26, he might consider a safety-valve reason for free speech as having a place in a justification of a political principle of free speech.

17. See, e.g., Bork, supra note 13, at 25.

18. See, e.g., M. Redish, supra note 14, at 11–12.

narrower reasons for free speech is unlikely to apply uniquely to speech; further exploration will be needed of why the reason undergirds a principle of freedom of speech rather than some wider robust principle of liberty.[19]

Another defect of the inclusive strategy involves an error that creeps in during the process by which narrower reasons are subsumed. No doubt, holding the government to account contributes to individual human fulfillment, but there may be other reasons, such as social justice, for responsible government. The value of free speech for accountable government may be underestimated if only the relationship to individual fulfillment is addressed. Putting the point more abstractly, the process of inclusion may distort the significance of more discrete reasons whose importance lies partly, but only partly, in what they contribute to the most general value. This distortion often occurs when people seek to bring multiple and diverse considerations within some large umbrella value. For practical thought about most social practices, the distortion is best avoided by acknowledging a plurality of values.

B. Consequentialist and Nonconsequentialist Reasons

There is no single correct way of presenting the justifications that matter for a principle of freedom of speech. One can distinguish, for example, between reasons that focus on individuals and those that focus on society at large, between reasons that relate to speakers and those that relate to listeners or a broader public, between reasons that relate to the form of government and those that do not, between reasons that reflect optimism about human capacities and those that reflect pessimism, between reasons that concentrate on the positive value of speech and those that emphasize the untrustworthiness of government. Because the reasons for free speech are based on complex and somewhat overlapping elements, no basic division or multiple categorization can be wholly satisfactory.

This analysis of free speech justifications distinguishes between consequentialist and nonconsequentialist reasons. This division too has its drawbacks, requiring, among other things, a somewhat strained breaking down of arguments concerning individual autonomy and of arguments concerning democracy. Nonetheless, this familiar way of distinguishing reasons for action is useful here, because it differentiates claimed reasons that are to be viewed in light of factual evidence and claimed reasons that rest more purely on normative claims.[20]

---

19. Redish acknowledges that his overall principle of individual self-realization covers more than speech, but he argues that communicative activities are especially likely to develop individuals' mental faculties, are less likely to be harmful than other courses of conduct, and, in any event, received special protection by the adopters of the Bill of Rights. See Redish, Self-Realization, Democracy and Freedom of Expression: A Reply to Professor Baker, 130 U. Pa. L. Rev. 678, 684 (1982).

20. It is likely that many nonconsequentialist claims rest on deep factual assump-

COLUMBIA LAW REVIEW   [Vol. 89:119

A practice has value from a consequentialist point of view if it contributes to some desirable state of affairs. Thus, to say that free speech contributes to honest government is to advance a consequentialist reason for free speech. The force of a consequentialist reason is dependent on the factual connection between a practice and the supposed results of the practice. A nonconsequentialist reason is one which claims that something about a particular practice is right or wrong independent of the consequences. Notable among reasons of this sort are reasons cast in terms of present rights or claims of justice: "Suppressing Joan's ideas is wrong because it violates rights or is unjust."

The relation between consequentialist and nonconsequentialist reasons is an enduring problem for moral philosophy. One philosophical position is to suppose that nonconsequentialist arguments are in some sense reducible to consequentialist considerations, that the only really good practices are those that produce desirable states of affairs broadly understood and that the better practice is one that produces better effects. On this view, it becomes an open question whether it is desirable that people should actually think in terms of effects. According to the most unqualified consequentialist position, citizens ideally would conceive moral problems in terms of consequences. But it is possible that overall better effects will occur if ordinary people accept some nonconsequential norms; for example, perhaps the most wholesome effects of truth-telling will be produced if people think it is always inherently wrong to tell a lie.

What matters for the purposes of practical thought about a particular social practice are the critical perspectives that members of a society would best adopt. Even if an outsider might rightly say that the best practice produces the best effects, even if in some ultimate sense nonconsequentialist reasons can be reduced to some form of consequentialist evaluation, a reason counts as nonconsequentialist here if it is the sort of reason to which citizens should give weight and it is best cast for them in nonconsequentialist terms. In our culture many nonconsequentialist claims are conceived as having force, and few are confident that it would be helpful to banish those claims from practical discussion. Nonconsequentialist reasons do have force for normative issues in moral and political philosophy.

On the opposite end of the spectrum from unmitigated consequentialism is the view that nonconsequential claims should dominate political and moral thinking, that what mainly is involved is according people rights and justice and that calculations of consequences should play a decidedly secondary role. Whether any such priority can be es-

----

tions about human nature, so in this respect the distinction between consequentialist and nonconsequentialist reasons is less sharp than the text indicates. This problem is addressed in relation to a "natural duty" to obey the law in K. Greenawalt, Conflicts of Law and Morality 159–86 (1987).

tablished is highly questionable,[21] and freedom of speech affords an apt illustration of why such a priority is dubious in the evaluation of social practices. In any event, both consequentialist and nonconsequentialist considerations count and count significantly, and no collapse of one to the other or priority of one over the other works at the level of practical thought.

The line between consequentialist and nonconsequentialist claims, however, is not always clear. Part of the problem is deciding where the intrinsic nature of the act stops and consequences begin. Is the fact that a listener will be misled an aspect of the nature of lying (there are unsuccessful lies, so not every lie actually misleads), or is the likelihood of someone's being misled to count as a common consequence of lying? A second concern is the kinds of consequences that matter for a consequentialist justification. Although consequentialist reasons are often linked to claims about overall welfare or satisfying people's preferences or desires, this analysis counts as consequentialist any claim resting on the production of future consequences, including a claim, say, that the recognition of rights or justice will be promoted in the future if particular practices are engaged in for the present.[22] A third difficulty, which emerges as more serious in the context of free speech, is the status of certain reasons that are cast rather vaguely. Suppose it is said that free speech conforms with a view that people should be rational. If the idea is that free speech actually helps make people more rational, it is consequentialist. If the idea is that a principle of free speech treats people as rational, and that that is intrinsically appropriate, the reason is nonconsequentialist. Claimed justifications for free speech, then, may straddle consequentialist and nonconsequentialist reasons.

Closely related to this third difficulty for classification is another: how to treat coherence arguments for free speech. Suppose it is argued that given certain institutions or practices, having freedom of speech is required, or at least is positively indicated. A full defense of such an argument requires reasons why the underlying institutions may be taken as starting points and reasons why free speech connects to the underlying institutions. Roughly, the reasons for the institutions might be cast in terms of justice or fairness ("only democratic forms of government are just"), in terms of consequences ("democracy better serves human welfare than other forms of government"), or in terms of social acceptance ("whether better or not, liberal democracy is our form of government and should be taken as a starting point for evaluation of practices like free speech"). The coherence reasons for free speech might be cast in terms of what the underlying institutions some-

---

21. An attempt to show the implausibility of any clear priority in one context is provided in id. at 207–25.

22. See id. at 213–20 (discussing in more detail claims based on effects on future compliance with rights and justice).

130   *COLUMBIA LAW REVIEW*   [Vol. 89:119

how imply ("to deny free speech is to refuse to treat people as democratic citizens"), or in terms of how free speech serves objectives of the institutions ("representatives will make better decisions if speech is free"). The complexity here is that the reasons supporting the connection of free speech to the more underlying institutions may or may not be of the same kind as the reasons why the institutions may be taken as starting points for evaluation. The classification that follows concentrates on the distinctive reasons for free speech. Since the purpose is not to develop a general theory of government, justifications for democracy are not explored. What is examined is how free speech connects to basic premises of democratic government.

III. Consequentialist Justifications

During most of the twentieth century, consequentialist arguments have dominated the discussion of freedom of speech, although the last two decades have seen a resurgence of nonconsequentialist arguments cast in terms of basic human rights and dignity.[23] This section examines the major consequentialist arguments: truth discovery, interest accommodation and social stability, exposure and deterrence of abuses of authority, autonomy and personality development, and liberal democracy. Consequentialist arguments reach public and private life; they reach governmental and nongovernmental matters; they reach speakers, listeners, and others who are indirectly affected.

A. *"Truth" Discovery*

1. *The Basic Justification.* — The most familiar argument for freedom of speech is that speech promotes the discovery of truth. Found in Milton's *Areopagitica*[24] and in eloquent opinions by Holmes[25] and Brandeis,[26] the argument is the core of John Stuart Mill's defense of freedom of speech in *On Liberty*.[27] Mill says that if the government suppresses communications, it may suppress ideas that are true or partly true. Moreover, even if an idea is wholly false, its challenge to received understanding promotes a reexamination that vitalizes truth.[28] Mill's assertion that government suppression of ideas rests necessarily

---

23. For excellent modern discussions, see Emerson, Towards a General Theory of the First Amendment, 72 Yale L.J. 877, 877–86 (1963); Feinberg, Limits to the Free Expression of Opinion, in Philosophy of Law 217–32 (J. Feinberg & H. Gross 3d ed. 1986); Scanlon, Freedom of Expression and Categories of Expression, 40 U. Pitt. L. Rev. 519 (1979).

24. J. Milton, Areopagitica (London 1819).

25. Abrams v. United States, 250 U.S. 616, 624, 630 (1919) (Holmes, J., dissenting).

26. Whitney v. California, 274 U.S. 357, 372, 377 (1927) (Brandeis, J., concurring).

27. J.S. Mill, On Liberty, in Selected Writings of John Stuart Mill 121 (M. Cowling ed. 1968) (1st ed. 1859).

28. Id. at 136, 152–62.

on a false assumption of infallibility,[29] however, overstates his case. Suppression might correspond with a cynical skepticism about any truth, with a belief that, fallible as it is, government is likely to judge more accurately than a dissident minority, or with a conviction that true or not, some ideas are too destructive of a social order to be tolerated. But Mill's basic point that speech contributes greatly to the search for truth does not depend on whether suppression always represents a claim of infallibility. Mill's sense of truth is broad, covering correct judgments about issues of value as well as ordinary empirical facts and embracing knowledge conducive to a satisfactory personal life as well as facts of general social importance.

Although he does not assume that people will grasp the truth whenever it appears, Mill believes that if voice is given to a wide variety of views over the long run, true views are more likely to emerge than if the government suppresses what it deems false.[30] In this standard form, the truth-discovery justification combines a contained optimism that people have some ability over time to sort out true ideas from false ones with a realism that governments, which reflect presently dominant assumptions and have narrow interests of their own to protect, will not exhibit exquisite sensitivity if they get in the business of settling what is true.

Often taken as an axiom in liberal societies, the truth-discovery justification is subject to a number of possible challenges: that objective truth does not exist; that if truth does exist, human beings cannot identify it, or the conditions under which it is discovered; that if human beings can identify truth sometimes, free discussion does not evidently contribute to their capacity to do so; and that the way free discussion works in practice contravenes the open market of ideas that the truth-discovery justification assumes.[31] A searching answer to these doubts would require a systematic examination of notions of truth and evidences of truth and of human learning. Although such an exploration lies beyond the scope of the present investigation, the ensuing discussion of truth discovery is nonetheless much longer than the treatment of other justifications of free speech. This indulgence seems warranted by the need to understand how far these sweeping challenges really do threaten this most commonly offered rationale for free expression. Each of the four challenges is examined in turn, the one that is the most troublesome for a principle of free speech reserved for last: the doubt that free discussion contributes to the discovery of truth.

---

29. Id. at 136.

30. Id. at 164–65.

31. See Baker, supra note 16, at 965–81; see also DuVal, Free Communication of Ideas and the Quest for Truth: Toward a Teleological Approach to First Amendment Adjudication, 41 Geo. Wash. L. Rev. 161, 190–94 (1972) (arguing that no good reason exists to suppose that freedom of expression will result in either greater or lesser understanding).

2. *Does Truth Exist?* — Contrary to the blithe assertion that "the assumption of the existence of objective truth is crucial to classic marketplace theory, [and] almost no one believes in objective truth today,"[32] the truth-discovery argument can survive a substantial dose of skepticism about objective truth.[33] This is most obvious with respect to factual matters. Suppose no objective truth exists outside human experience or that the only truth for human beings is the set of propositions that serves them best or most fully conforms with their experiences at a given stage in history. These positions about truth do not deny that people can learn from evidence and argument or that in some sense they can be closer or farther from understanding what is true. Given all the ways in which available evidence suggests that the earth is round rather than flat and the usefulness of people's operating on that assumption, we can say that someone who believes that the earth is round is closer to the truth than the person who believes it to be flat. Similarly, the person who thinks that many Jews were killed in Nazi concentration camps in World War II is closer to the truth than the person who denies that such events took place. Whatever the ultimate status of the propositions that the earth is approximately a sphere and that many Jews were exterminated, virtually everyone accepts some notion of empirical truth that renders claims of truth something other than wholly subjective or relative.[34] That is a sufficient beginning for the truth-discovery theory.[35]

Claims of values pose somewhat greater difficulties, since the assertion that they are wholly subjective is not so plainly fallacious. I shall not pause here to defend my own belief that rational discourse can say a good deal about ultimate values,[36] but whether or not this is so, such discourse certainly can test the coherence of value claims, and can elucidate and clarify the values of a culture and of individuals. Thus,

---

32. Ingber, The Marketplace of Ideas: A Legitimizing Myth, 1984 Duke L.J. 1, 25.

33. See Emerson, Colonial Intentions and Current Realities of the First Amendment, 125 U. Pa. L. Rev. 737, 741 (1977) ("The essential point is that the process is necessary for reaching the best social decision, regardless of whether ultimate values are conceived in absolute or relative terms."); see also F. Schauer, supra note 8, at 18–26 (argument from truth does not require accepting the possibility of acquiring knowledge with certainty).

34. In T. Kuhn, The Structure of Scientific Revolutions 35–51 (2d ed. 1970), Thomas Kuhn takes a relatively skeptical position about the nature of scientific theories, but he does not deny that within a given paradigm answers to "puzzles" are correct or incorrect; that in choosing among possible paradigms, observations and experimental conclusions are highly important, if not completely determinative; and that later theories are generally better at solving puzzles than the earlier theories they replace. On Kuhn's view of science, there are more than sufficient indicia of objective judgment to make justifications for free speech relevant.

35. See Wellington, On Freedom of Expression, 88 Yale L.J. 1105, 1130–31 (1979).

36. Although rational discourse can say much about ultimate values, many fundamental conflicts in values are not finally resolvable on rational grounds. K. Greenawalt, supra note 11, gives a fairly comprehensive account of my sense of the limits of reason.

for example, an American might have said during the 1950s: "Given the social history and racial attitudes of this country, acceptance of racial segregation in public facilities is in severe tension with a belief that people should be treated as morally equal." Propositions like these can be extremely important for how people try to resolve social problems, and one can say that such propositions may be true or sound without invoking an objective status for ultimate values. If the idea of truth is broadened a bit further to include people's understanding of the claims of value that best suit them personally, one could speak of truth discovery even in respect to claims of value and other matters as to which one doubted whether there was any interpersonal truth.

3. *Can People Identify Truth and Regimes That Promote It?* — These examples demonstrate that significant domains of truth exist even on relatively skeptical premises; the examples also show that many truths are accessible to people and that most people are somewhat open to evidence and argument about those truths. This is not to say that people can ever be completely sure of anything, but it is nonetheless reasonable for them to have a high degree of confidence about some propositions, for example, that "in the northern latitudes, January is usually colder on the average than July," or that "people who are deprived of what they value the most often resent those who they think have deprived them." Even when a dominant theory is understood to be provisional, as is the case with many abstract scientific theories, there may be a high degree of confidence that certain conceivable competitors are false.

If so much is granted, any idea that people are wholly incapable of evaluating what sorts of social practices promote discovery of truth is untenable. If truth is a meaningful concept and people are capable of asserting many propositions of fact and value with confidence, they must have some basis for recognizing what social practices promote the discovery of truth. One approach is to look at various societies and historical periods to see when the discovery of truth has prospered. That method obviously is most practical for questions of undisputed interpersonal truth; we can examine whether belief in the earth's roundness happened more quickly where discourse was relatively free. Assessing degrees of coherence about values or whether the values people accepted were personally suited to them, however, is a daunting task in respect to other historical eras and cultures. The needed judgments are incredibly complex and we are hard put to make the imaginative leap from our experience and values to those of other societies. In respect to values, personal experience may be of some help. Of course, experience is inevitably limited and people are notoriously incapable of assessing much of their own experience objectively; moreover, they can barely guess what their own internal life would be like in a society with very different social practices. Still, they can ask themselves whether open discussion has enlightened or confused them, helped them to achieve a more coherent and personally satisfactory set of values or not. They can try to imagine what life would be like if certain ideas were not available, and they can draw from the experience of acquaintances who have been brought up in very different cultures, a rich source of enlightenment in a society with as many immigrants as the United States.

People can reasonably differ over the persuasiveness of available evidence connecting free speech to truth discovery. Judgments are undoubtedly subject to many of the uncertainties that infect psychology and the social sciences; and certainly few judgments about the effects of social practices on the fate of truth can have the degree of confidence attainable about propositions like the roundness of the earth. Any sensible position probably must distinguish among kinds of truths, among communities in which discussion is free, and among degrees of suppression. But what is important here is that all the uncertainties and needed qualifications do not show that the question of whether free speech promotes truth is somehow beyond our capacities to consider. Relevant evidence and arguments do exist.

4. *The Significance of Inequality in the Marketplace.* — Acquiring confidence that truth will advance in a regime of freedom would be simple if people rather quickly understood the truth when it was presented to them and if competing ideas had an equal claim on people's attention. Two claims undermine such confidence: the gross inequality among communicators in the marketplace of ideas and the inclination of people to believe messages that are already dominant socially or that serve unconscious, irrational needs.

Standing alone, the inequality of those who seek to communicate supports a particular understanding of freedom of speech rather than a rejection of the entire concept.[37] If people are reasonably competent to sift claims of truth, then a process in which all relevant claims are provided with a fair hearing is plainly preferable to government suppression of apparent falsehood. If the problem with present social arrangements is that an aggregation of economic and social power so largely determines what the public hears that unfavored ideas have no chance to gain a foothold, the government might make available new channels of communication or regulate existing channels to assure more equal access. Conceivably the latter approach would include restricting the frequency with which some kinds of messages were presented, but no message would be denied an outlet altogether. Such an approach to speech would emphasize fairness in the dissemination of messages rather than the unrestricted liberty of those who want to communicate and hear, and movement toward that approach might drastically alter the freedom some media presently enjoy to present what they choose. There is a conceivable equality-based argument that

---

37. See D. Richards, Toleration and the Constitution 216–24 (1986) (suggesting a more equality-focussed approach to the first amendment); L. Tribe, Constitutional Choices 194–98 (1985) (same).

government is unable in practice to regulate the presentation of ideas in the interests of fairness and that the realistic alternatives are government suppression of ideas or domination by private centers. But given government's power to circulate ideas itself or make forums available, using the more drastic remedy of prohibiting the expression of some ideas altogether would clearly be unwarranted.[38]

5. *Free Speech and Capacities to Discover Truth.* — The claim that people are persuaded to believe what is already dominant or what fits their irrational needs is a much more serious challenge to the truth-discovery justification for free speech. If people were incapable of assessing claims of truth, then Mill's argument for free speech would falter at a critical point. People are able to learn some things from experience; if they find that each time they take the bus the trip takes over an hour and each subway trip to the same spot takes only twenty minutes, they come to realize they should take the subway when they are in a hurry. People also learn from communications of the experiences of others; out-of-towners told of the trips of residents will also understand that the subway is faster than the bus. But perhaps on deeper questions, people do not make reasoned judgments about competing positions but merely acquire reinforcement of views that conform with social conventions or serve their particular interests or unconscious desires. In that event, the "marketplace of ideas" of which Holmes speaks gives little promise of yielding truth even in the long run, particularly if the disproportionate influence of a few centers of private power over what gets communicated is likely to be exercised in favor of dominant and comforting views.[39]

The critical question is not how well truth will advance absolutely in conditions of freedom but how well it will advance in conditions of freedom as compared with some alternative set of conditions.[40] Suppose one were highly pessimistic about the capacity of people to ascertain important kinds of truths, but believed that governments that suppress ideas almost always manage to promote falsehoods, and, further, that the propensity of officials to support falsehoods flows from the nature of government and is not corrigible. One might then support freedom of speech as less damaging to truth than an alternative

---

38. It may, of course, be argued that a principle of freedom of speech largely denies government the power to tell private media what to communicate. The point here, however, is that if the unfairness of the marketplace is raised as an objection to free speech altogether, accepting a version of free speech that allows such regulation makes much more sense than assuming that there is no principled barrier to complete suppression of some ideas. For a critique of a "market failure" model, see Baker, supra note 16, at 981–90.

39. See id. at 976–80; Ingber, supra note 32, at 26.

40. This claim is true at least if some minimum threshold of truth discovery is exceeded. If truth advanced terribly under any conditions but slightly better under freedom, perhaps it would be all right to forget about truth and concentrate on other objectives.

social practice. One's overall judgment on this subject must depend on a delicate judgment about people's responses to claimed truth, about the effects of inequality of private power over what is communicated, and about the soundness of government determinations about valid ideas.

A sensitive assessment requires subcategorization among domains of truth and audiences, and recognition of degrees of possible interference. For example, freedom of speech almost certainly contributes to the understanding of truth in the physical sciences. Although some broad scientific questions are not now answerable with confidence, and although most dominant theories are provisional and will probably not be accepted in some distant future, many important questions have fairly definite answers about which there exists a wide range of agreement.[41] There is also wide agreement that advancement in understanding among persons capable of assessing scientific claims is promoted by freedom of communication within the scientific community, that government intervention to suppress some scientific ideas in favor of others would not promote scientific truth.

For most scientific truths, ordinary people accept as accurate a view that is widely agreed upon among scientists. As to many subjects, people have no psychological investment in one account rather than another. Even when the dominant appraisal is unsettling, the general public is likely to accept it so long as the subject is widely understood to be scientific, the virtually unanimous judgment of scientists is well publicized, and the judgment matters to citizens. This generalization is supported by opinions about the dangers of smoking. Though much uncertainty remains about causes and effects, disinterested experts now agree that substantial smoking poses a serious risk to health and life. This message is one confirmed smokers were psychologically disinclined to accept, but nearly all smokers, in the United States at least, now believe it,[42] although the government has never forbidden communication of the competing message.[43]

Before a general lesson can be drawn about freedom of speech for scientific matters, we need to consider the possibility that broad freedom is unnecessary, only freedom within the scientific community. When the scientific community is relatively united behind judgments, it might make sense to allow contrary views to be presented to scientists but not to the general public, which would only be confused by opposing claims on matters it does not understand. But such a proposal

41. See T. Kuhn, supra note 34.
42. At least they believe it on the general and abstract level. Quite possibly, many smokers do have a hunch that is not rationally based that they will not be seriously hurt by smoking.
43. The example is a less-than-perfect illustration because the government does restrict cigarette advertising on television and radio and requires the printing of a warning on advertisements and on packages of cigarettes.

would be very difficult to carry out within a generally open society. Many scientists teach at universities. Would they have to withhold dissident theories and the evidence for them from students in classes and from graduate students who help with research? Would students who have access be forbidden to disclose to other students? How would the government decide whether a view had become unanimous enough to warrant suppression of competitors? Who would decide exactly which expressions of views fell afoul of restrictions on broad publication? At the least, such a regime would be extremely unwieldy and would require setting up formal channels of communication among scientists not accessible to the general public. By far the simplest way to assure freedom of scientific communication within the community of experts is to have a general regime of free speech for science.

In domains other than the physical sciences, the grasp of truth is much less secure. For many value judgments, no one is a real expert, and for many interpretive judgments about complex historical and psychological questions, experts disagree about many fundamental questions. For subjects like these, confidence in any advance of truth needs to be highly qualified, but these are also the subjects in which judgments by governments are least to be trusted. Accepting of dominant opinion and desirous of preserving its own power, a government deciding what historical, political, and moral ideas to suppress is bound to be affected by aims other than the disinterested pursuit of truth.

Owners and editors of newspapers and television stations and other private individuals with huge influence over the dissemination of ideas will also have their own objectives to pursue; but private influence is a far cry from outright suppression. No private enterprise can prevent others from speaking. On many points, those with private power will have different visions of the truth or will have reasons to present competing claims. Even when that is not the case, competing ideas may gain some access, say through radical professors writing in academic journals, to some part of the public. Furthermore, if government intervention of some sort is warranted to redress an imbalance, regulation, as by the fairness doctrine for television and radio,[44] or government presentation of a competing point of view, is less drastic than outright suppression. One could sensibly support extensive suppression only if one were very skeptical of the ability of people to deal with claims of

---

44. According to the fairness doctrine developed by the Federal Communications Commission, broadcasters had to present sides of a topic fairly. An adjunct of the doctrine granted people attacked a right to respond, and a parallel provision required equality of time for political candidates. The Supreme Court upheld aspects of the fairness doctrine against a first amendment challenge in Red Lion Broadcasting Co. v. F.C.C., 395 U.S. 367 (1969), but in the second Reagan Administration, the Commission decided to drop the requirements imposed by the doctrine. See 52 Fed. Reg. 31,768 (1987); Syracuse Peace Council v. Television Station WTVH, 63 Rad. Reg. 2d (P & F) 541, 543 (F.C.C. 87–266, released Aug. 6, 1987).

138   COLUMBIA LAW REVIEW   [Vol. 89:119

truth and had a great deal more confidence in government than in private institutions.

Given important matters of degree, a comparison between a regime of free speech and one of suppression is overly simple. Indeed, one might look at the question as being how far constraints on conversation[45] imposed by the government will serve the truth. For the government to promote particular messages, as the United States government has done with advertising of the dangers of smoking, is already to depart from a pure marketplace approach to speech. And, if government prohibits some messages in some contexts, as it has done with broadcast advertising for cigarettes, and requires warnings of danger for advertising that is permitted, government is going further and restricting speech. If one concludes that free speech generally is better than suppression for discovering truth, it does not follow that every kind of government restriction on speech will be harmful to understanding truth. Suppose it were proposed that government suppression of scientific ideas is appropriate if, and only if, the following conditions are met: 1) there is virtual unanimity among scientists that the contrary ideas are correct; 2) the subject is one as to which government officials can be relatively dispassionate; 3) public misjudgments are likely; 4) public misjudgments will cause serious harm; and 5) suppression will extend only to communicators who have a dominantly commercial motive. It is at least possible that this and perhaps other modest limits on maximum freedom of speech will contribute to the promotion of truth.

6. *The Scope of the Truth-Discovery Justification.* — A final objection to truth discovery as a justification for free speech requires consideration, as does the appropriate political force of the justification if its intrinsic validity is in doubt. The objection is that even if the truth-discovery argument for liberty has some force, it has no special application to speech. Crudely put, the contention is that the discovery of truth comes from experience as well as speech and that, if valid, the reason should protect all forms of liberty, or many forms of liberty other than speech. The wider applicability of a reason for protecting liberty would not necessarily undercut its relevance for a distinctive free speech principle; the reason might have a special intensity for speech or coalesce in a special way with other reasons in respect to speech. But since truth discovery has traditionally been regarded as such an important support for free speech, it would be troubling if that support applies with equal force to many other activities.

To evaluate the claim that any truth-discovery rationale applies much more broadly, that claim must first be put in a reasonably precise

---

45. There is a big step from believing in "constrained conversation"—in the sense of thinking that citizens and officials dealing with public matters in a liberal society should not rely on certain kinds of arguments such as personal superiority or religious insight—to believing that the government should mandate constraints.

and plausible form. Occasional intimations that experience and communication may be substitutable, that one can learn from either,[46] are at most true only at the margins. Experience and communication are both necessary conditions of understanding. Without communicating in language to their fellows, men and women would be incapable of understanding much more than nonhuman animals; without some personal experience of life besides cognitive thought, most ideas would have no reality for people. Only for people who have already received substantial amounts of communication and had substantial experience apart from communication could more of one be a good substitute for less of the other. And even this proposition about substitutability requires substantial qualification. Any sensible thought about communication and experience must recognize that as to some domains of truth personal experience has little to contribute and that for others communication can supply only a pale shadow of understanding; relatedly, though some forms of noncommunicative experience are highly valuable for understanding, other forms teach little about truth in any significant sense.

There are whole domains of knowledge that ordinary living hardly touches. An increase or decrease in my personal noncommunicative liberty will hardly affect my understanding of math or many aspects of the physical sciences. Although scientific experiments involve a kind of experience, and experiments may be indispensable to the learning of some scientific truths,[47] no one individual can perform many complex experiments. For learning the fruits of experiments, even a scientist's overwhelming reliance will have to be on communications about experiments performed by others. In respect to matters like history and politics, the role of personal experience is more complex. One's personal life provides a perspective against which to evaluate competing historical claims, but there are few pieces of ordinary living one can do to increase the ability to assess claims about particular historical events. Active involvement in local affairs may teach a good bit about contemporary political life. Travel can contribute to a grasp of both historical and political truth. A trip to the ruins of Athens can enrich one's appreciation of the ancient Athenian civilization, and a trip to Nicaragua could enlighten perspectives on the revolutionary government there. It would be odd to think that either of these experiences would have much truth value without extensive communication as well, but if travel were forbidden, important sources for truth discovery would be foreclosed.

For some forms of understanding, particular personal experience

---

46. See, e.g., F. Schauer, *supra* note 8, at 57 (doubting that communication is a necessary condition for intellectual self-fulfillment); see also Baker, *supra* note 16, at 975 ("the individual is as likely to find needed information in experiences as in speech").

47. An outright ban on experiments with human embryos, for example, would impede discovery of some scientific truths.

is indispensable. If the truth in question is how one feels when one falls in love, has an orgasm, or drinks a lot of alcohol, no amount of reading or discussing can make up for a lack of experience. If the government were capable of foreclosing a kind of experience and did so,[48] it would sharply inhibit appreciation of particular truths of that sort.

Other limitations on liberty touch experiences that have little to do with the discovery of truth in any significant sense. Suppose the government is considering regulating the sale of alcohol, forbidding sales below and above certain prices. The experience of charging a certain price is not a significant avenue toward truth, and a truth-discovery rationale is no reason against the regulation.[49]

The following conclusions may be drawn. There are some basic aspects of human understanding, or understanding within a certain culture, that cannot be fully appreciated without immediate experience. Some particular kinds of experience, such as experiments and travel, may either be indispensable or a substitute for listening to communications. Other liberties of action bear only a remote relation to discovering truth, and for many truths the acquisition of much learning depends almost entirely on communication.

The truth-discovery reason is widely understood to reach activities like experiments and travel, which are properly seen as closely related to liberty of speech. It also underlies solid arguments against forbidding highly significant forms of experience, as Mill recognized in his claim that the interests of human beings as progressive beings were served by acquaintance with a wide diversity of styles of life.[50] Still, the truth-discovery reason has little to do with many liberties, and the connection between understanding and communication is powerful enough to warrant the conclusion that truth discovery is a very important reason for a distinctive principle of freedom of speech.

7. *Acting in Conditions of Uncertainty.* — If the challenges to the truth-discovery justification for free speech are largely misconceived, continued reliance on the justification is clearly proper; but suppose someone entertains much more skepticism about truth discovery than the discussion here reflects. What would be the appropriate practical place of the justification in the face of significant uncertainties about its force? One might say that no justification can stand unless supported by convincing evidence, but a different, more conservative, position values cultural

---

48. Governments can forbid drinking alcohol but they cannot forbid falling in love (though they might create conditions that would make falling in love less common).

49. Knowing how it feels to break the law may be a significant experience, but that experience can occur only if liberty is curtailed and is thus not a reason against regulation. Knowing how it feels to set one's own price rather than be restricted may be a significant experience, but a person can have both experiences only if there is both regulation and liberty; so the experience of liberty cannot underlie a truth-discovery argument against any particular regulation, unless regulation is otherwise pervasive.

50. See J.S. Mill, supra note 27, at 171-89.

continuity and is modest about powers of rational understanding. If a justification that remains coherent in its premises has long been assumed to support a settled social practice, the justification is entitled to continued weight until the case against it becomes very strong. Since legal interpretation rightly gives effect to the justifications that lay behind the framing of legal norms, that conservative principle is certainly correct for reasoning within the law. Given the desirability of continuity of political institutions, discourse, and values, the principle is also appropriate for nonlegal political assessments. At a minimum the truth-discovery reason for free speech is neither incoherent nor evidently fallacious. This showing is sufficient to warrant continued reliance on the justification in our culture.

B. *Interest Accommodation and Social Stability*

A good answer to many social problems depends not so much on the discovery of "true principles" as on an accommodation of competing interests and desires. Of course, no sharp line demarcates truth discovery from interest accommodation. Learning someone else's desires is discovery of one kind of truth, and even determining an optimal, or acceptable, accommodation of competing desires or interests can be seen as understanding a mix of relevant facts and values. And when social action (say, abolition of capital punishment) is based on an assessment of empirical information (that capital punishment does not uniquely deter) and a sound resolution of value questions (that retribution is an unacceptable basis for punishment), the decision may still work some kind of accommodation among affected interests. Still, a significant difference in approach remains between seeking to find true principles to resolve troubling issues like capital punishment and seeking to strike a sort of balance among conflicting desires, as in working out a schedule of household responsibilities.

Appropriate accommodations are more likely if those making decisions can assess desires and interests accurately, and communication serves this purpose. Few societies bar the expression of personal feelings and attitudes that contribute to acceptable accommodations in families and other small social units, but many societies proscribe public discussion of significant points of view, and they pay some price in their ability to estimate relevant sentiments within the community.

The interest-accommodation reason for free expression can be challenged on grounds similar to those advanced in respect to truth discovery. It may be said that free expression does not produce an adequate reflection of the spectrum of desires and interests. Because the desires of the rich, powerful, and articulate are given more voice than those of the poor, powerless, and inarticulate, decisionmakers, themselves mostly members of the favored group, get a false picture of what people generally want. The difficulty in respect to "real" interests goes deeper; so great is the control of culture by the privileged that the dispossessed lack even the ability to understand what their real interests are; even the expression of their desires is not a reflection of what they genuinely need.

No doubt this picture has much truth. In no society are desires and interests[51] assessed without distortion, and the distortion almost always favors the privileged classes to some degree. But what is the remedy, if any? Would matters be improved if the government suppressed the expression of certain desires and interests? For reasons indicated in connection with truth discovery, it seems highly unlikely that outright government prohibitions would produce a more accurate account of the desires and interests of citizens.

Failures of accommodation are often a source of social instability. Those who are resentful because their interests are not accorded fair weight are likely to be doubly resentful if they have been denied the opportunity to present those interests in the political process. If sufficiently frustrated, they may seek to attain by radical changes in existing structures what they have failed to get from officials within those structures. Though liberty of speech can often be divisive, it can, by forestalling this sort of frustration, also contribute to a needed degree of social stability.[52]

C. *Exposure and Deterrence of Abuses of Authority*

Closely linked to truth discovery and interest accommodation is a consequentialist justification that warrants separate mention because of its historical significance and central importance: free speech as a check on abuse of authority, especially government authority. The idea, powerfully developed by Vincent Blasi in a well-known article,[53] is that if those in power are subject to public exposure for their wrongs in the manner exemplified by journalists' accounts of the Watergate scandal, corrective action can be taken. And if public officials know they are subject to such scrutiny, they will be much less likely to yield to the inevitable temptation presented to those with power to act in corrupt and arbitrary ways.

In major part, the justification based on exposure and deterrence of government abuse can be seen as a subcategory of the truth-discovery justification. When truths about abuse of authority are revealed, citizens or other officials can take corrective action. But an extra dimension of truth discovery is important here. In areas of human life

---

51. I accept the basic premise that real interests may differ from desires; but that premise is not defended here nor is attention paid as to how the two things may diverge.

52. Since too much stability is undesirable, especially in the face of serious injustice or outmoded practices, it is very hard to estimate any ideal mix of stability and ferment or to say exactly how free speech affects an existing mix.

53. Blasi, The Checking Value in First Amendment Theory, 1977 Am. B. Found. Res. J. 521 (providing both an account of this rationale for free speech and an argument about its implications).

involving choice, what people do is partly dependent on what they think will become known. Most particularly, persons are less likely to perform acts that are widely regarded as wrong and that commonly trigger some sanction if they are not confident they can keep the acts secret. Thus, the prospect of truth being discovered influences what happens; public scrutiny deters. Viewed from the perspective of interest accommodation, a free press that exposes wrongs affects the balance of sensitivity to the interests of ordinary citizens as compared with the interests of the officials themselves and of those to whom they feel especially aligned by mutual advantage or common feeling. Perhaps the benefits of exposure and deterrence reach beyond anything neatly captured by truth discovery or interest accommodation. Apart from truths it actually reveals, and even when what its claims turns out to be inaccurate, a critical press affects how officials and citizens regard the exercise of government power, subtly supporting the notion that government service is a responsibility, not an opportunity for personal advantage.

The ways in which exposures of abuse contribute to healthy government are not limited to liberal democracies. Even for relatively authoritarian regimes in which ordinary citizens have little say about who makes up the government, the threat of exposure can restrain officials from personal abuses of office. In fact, in some countries, such as Yugoslavia, where selection for office remains largely the responsibility of a single party and proposals for complete change of that social system are beyond bounds, press criticism of official inadequacies can be quite sharp.

D. *Autonomy and Personality Development*

By affording people an opportunity to hear and digest competing positions and to explore options in conversations with others, freedom of discussion is thought to promote independent judgment and considerate decision, what might be characterized as autonomy.[54] This consequentialist argument connecting free speech to autonomy is not true by definition. Freedom of speech would not promote autonomy in this sense if it failed to bring the range of relevant considerations as effectively before people as would a structure of discourse controlled by government, or if, despite opportunities to converse and exposure to more of the relevant points of view, people in a regime of free speech passively followed the opinions of persons in authority or decided on the basis of irrational passions. The factual premises of the claim about autonomous decisions are that when all ideas can be expressed, people

---

54. See D. Richards, *supra* note 37, at 167; see also S. Shiffrin, The First Amendment, Democracy and Romance (forthcoming) (stressing the role of free speech in protecting those who "speak out against . . . existing institutions, habits, customs, and traditions").

will be less subject in their decisions to the dictates of others and will be encouraged to exercise this independence in a considerate manner that reflects their fullest selves. The supposition is not that freedom of speech will actually produce fully autonomous persons, or even that by some measure it will produce people who are more autonomous than not; the claim is only that people will be more autonomous under a regime of free speech than under a regime of substantial suppression.

Any attempt to establish the claimed factual links convincingly faces severe difficulties. It is very hard to compare degrees of autonomy among citizens of different societies, and whether a country enjoys free speech is only one of many relevant cultural factors. Moreover, it is possible that a certain kind of freedom lulls people into a passive acceptance of things as they are, whereas stark suppression forces them to focus on their values. As evidence of the dangers of the "repressive tolerance" of freedom, it is sometimes remarked that political discussions at the dinner table in countries tending toward totalitarianism have a liveliness that is lacking in liberal democracies. Yet lively conversation is sometimes an outlet for those incapable of making choices that influence events; and the liveliness of ordinary conversation under the most oppressive regimes, such as Nazi Germany, was certainly not great. Matters of degree are important here, and confidence in generalizations must be modest; but we are warranted in believing that government control of communication usually tends to induce unreflective reliance on authority and that, if one regards societies in history, comparative autonomy of individuals is linked to relative freedom of opinion.

If one grants that free speech contributes to autonomy, there is still the question why independence of judgment and considerate decision are good. It may be believed that those who decide for themselves and in a rational manner are acting in a more distinctly human, and intrinsically better, way than those who passively submit to authority; then these personal qualities will be valued for their own sakes. The qualities may also be sources of achieving other values. For example, despite the burden of anxiety that often accompanies serious personal choice, many people can work out for themselves a style of life that is more fulfilling than what they could achieve by simply conforming to standards set by others. Both the valuation of autonomy for its own sake and the belief that it contributes to other satisfactions are aspects of traditional liberal theory.

The practice of free speech enhances the lives of those who seek to communicate in various other ways. For the speaker, communication is a crucial way to relate to others; it is also an indispensable outlet for emotional feelings and a vital aspect of the development of one's personality and ideas.[55] The willingness of others to listen to what one has

---

55. See M. Redish, *supra* note 14, at 20–30 (arguing that free speech fosters the

to say generates self-respect. Limits on what people can say curtail all these benefits. If the government declares out of bounds social opinions that a person firmly holds or wishes to explore, he is likely to suffer frustration and affront to his sense of dignity.

Because communication is so closely tied to our thoughts and feelings, suppression of communication is a more serious impingement on our personalities than many other restraints of liberty, but some noncommunicative restraints, for example, those relating to sexual involvements or drug use, may equally impair personal self-expression in a broad sense. An argument based on the value of liberty as an emotional outlet and means of personal development is not restricted to speech alone. Indeed, it may reach widely and strongly enough to some other matters so that alone it would not warrant anything properly identified as a distinctive principle of free speech. But if a principle of free speech is supportable on other grounds, this justification does provide an extra reason why speech should not be prohibited and may help determine what the boundaries of protected speech should be.

E. *Liberal Democracy*

Arguments from democracy have been said in a comparative study to be the "most influential . . . in the development of twentieth-century free speech law."[56] The claim that free speech contributes importantly to the functioning of liberal democracy and to the values it serves is largely reducible to the reasons already discussed as they apply to political discourse and decisions and to the participation of people in the political process. A liberal democracy rests ultimately on the choices of its citizens. Free speech can contribute to the possibility that they, and their representatives, can grasp truths that are significant for political life; it can enhance identification and accommodation of interests; and it can support wholesome attitudes about the relations of officials and citizens.[57] Government officials are especially to be distrusted in deciding what political messages may be heard because of their interest in staying in office and in promoting the political ideas in which they believe. And government suppression of political messages is particularly dangerous because it can subvert the proper functioning of ordinary

development of the individual's human faculties and facilitates the making of life-affecting decisions); Baker, supra note 16, at 966, 990–96 (self-expressive and creative uses of speech more fully and uniformly promote the key first amendment values, self-fulfillment and participation in change, than do other forms of speech); Emerson, supra note 23, at 879–80 (right to freedom of expression is justified first of all as the right of the individual to realize his character and potentialities through forming his own beliefs and opinions). As these writings reflect, consequentialist arguments in respect to personality development and autonomy are not sharply distinct.

56. E. Barendt, Freedom of Speech 23 (1985).

57. See generally A. Meiklejohn, Political Freedom 115–24 (1960) (revolutionary self-governing principles of constitution, exercised through a free vote, must be protected by absolute first amendment rights).

political processes that might serve as a check on other unwarranted suppression.[58] Unrestrained speech serves as a check on abuse of office; since citizens' votes matter so much in a liberal democracy, the importance of their being informed of government misconduct is particularly great under that form of government. It has long been assumed, though perhaps hard to prove, that a better informed citizenry will yield a better government and better political decisions.[59]

Whether participation in the political order is deemed uniquely important for people or one of many opportunities for realizing participatory values, that participation can be more autonomous if relevant information and arguments are available; and a regime of free speech may help develop the kinds of self-reliant, courageous citizens that Justice Brandeis holds up as an ideal in his opinion in *Whitney v. California*.[60] Finally, the healthy sense that one is participating as an equal citizen is enhanced if what one believes about politics can be communicated, and speech about injustice can help relieve frustration about an undesired course of political events.

Because a decent political process and informed decision making by citizens are such critical aspects of a model of liberal democracy, and because government suppression of political ideas is so likely to be misguided, the application of a principle of freedom of speech to political affairs is centrally important. The sorts of underlying consequentialist reasons for freedom are not radically different for political speech than for speech about nonpolitical facts and values, but these reasons take on extra weight when political matters are involved.

F. *Promoting Tolerance*

It has been suggested in a thoughtful recent book by Lee Bollinger that the main modern justification for a principle of free speech is its capacity to promote tolerance.[61] The basic idea is that if we are forced to acknowledge the right of detested groups to speak, we are taught the

---

58. This, it seems, is the main reason why the fact of a majority vote to suppress is not sufficient. Even a majority should not be able to undermine the conditions for a fair political process. See J. Ely, Democracy and Distrust 135–36 (1980).

59. This conclusion does not itself depend on a presumed equality of all citizens. Even if some citizens could not vote, as women in the past could not, or citizens had weighted votes, there would still be strong reasons for each citizen to be as fully informed as possible. People whose votes count less than others need to be informed, as do nonvoters who talk with voters about public matters.

60. 274 U.S. 357, 375–77 (1927) (Brandeis, J., concurring); see Blasi, The First Amendment and the Ideal of Civic Courage: The Brandeis Opinion in *Whitney v. California*, 29 Wm. & Mary L. Rev. 653, 679–83 (1988).

61. L. Bollinger, The Tolerant Society (1986). The book leaves some doubt how far more traditional justifications that lie in the background still have force and how far the tolerance justification applies to matters other than dissenting and extremist speech. For a thorough and perceptive review of the book, see Blasi, The Teaching Function of the First Amendment (Book Review), 87 Colum. L. Rev. 387 (1987).

lesson that we should be tolerant of the opinions and behavior of those who are not like us. Almost certainly the core of Bollinger's claim is true; living in a regime of free speech helps teach tolerance of many differences, just as living in a regime of religious liberty helps teach tolerance of religious diversity. But it does not follow either that promoting tolerance is now the primary justification for free speech or that attention to tolerance should play the critical role in decisions whether to restrict speech.

If it is true that people in liberal societies have so internalized a norm of free speech that traditional justifications are no longer extensively argued, and the potential acts of suppression these justifications cover most strongly are not even attempted, that does not mean these justifications have somehow been supplanted by the aim of promoting toleration. And, even if Dean Bollinger is right that the tolerance justification has more force than any other for the extremist destructive speech of the Nazis,[62] it is not the main justification for many other forms of speech. Given the assumption that broad tolerance of how others live can be encouraged in different ways, it is doubtful that one would introduce and defend a principle of freedom of speech absent other more basic justifications, and it is questionable whether a persuasive argument against particular suppression can be grounded mainly in the tolerance justification.[63]

IV. Nonconsequentialist Justifications

Not all arguments for free expression rest on desirable consequences; some liberal conceptions of the relationship between state and citizen may suggest a liberty of citizens to express opinions that is independent of the likely consequences of prohibition. As the phrase "liberal conceptions" implies, these justifications draw more distinctly on characteristic value premises of liberal theory than do the consequentialist justifications, though embedded in many of the latter are common liberal assumptions about facts and values.

A. *Social Contract Theory: Consent and the Private Domain*

The Anglo-American tradition of liberal democracy has historically been linked to a theory of social contract, which grounds the legitimacy of the state in the consent of the governed and establishes significant limits on the authority of government. According to John Locke, whose views greatly influenced the revolutionary generation of Americans, the

---

62. L. Bollinger, supra note 61, at 126–30.
63. See Schlag, Freedom of Speech as Therapy (Book Review), 34 UCLA L. Rev. 265, 281–82 (1986). One of the great strengths of Bollinger's book is its illuminating analysis of dimensions of tolerance. Since too much tolerance, as he recognizes, itself presents social dangers, notably passive acceptance of injustice, the use of tolerance to decide whether to suppress is troublesome. See L. Bollinger, supra note 61, at 140–44.

legitimate authority of government is based on consent and is limited
to the protection of rights and interests that individuals could not adequately safeguard.[64] Individuals entering into a social contract consent
to government power to secure their lives, liberty, and property; but
they do not give the state authority to interfere in other domains. In his
Letter Concerning Toleration,[65] Locke employs this analysis to put control
of religious beliefs and expressions outside the ambit of secular authority, but his conclusions have broader implications, reaching all states of
mind and activities that do not threaten interference with the limited
aims a government may permissibly have.

Locke apparently supposed that at some early stage in history people actually entered into a social contract. That is implausible, but his
theory can be interpreted in a hypothetical way, as indicating the form
and purposes of government to which individuals leaving a state of nature would consent. To be morally legitimate a government needs to
take this limited form and pursue only the prescribed purposes. Even
in this hypothetical version, the theory is now highly controversial, because it posits individuals outside of organized society with needs,
desires, talents, and property. Such an approach pays insufficient regard to the extent to which human nature and human purposes are
themselves determined by organized society, and it underestimates the
positive contributions that society and government can make to human
flourishing. Still, the ideas that government should take a form to
which people do or would consent and should do only those things that
people need it to do (or that it is uniquely suited to accomplish) retain a
powerful appeal in liberal societies.

The implications of these ideas, the conditions of consent and the
concept of limited government, reach far beyond speech but they have
considerable relevance for it as well. No doubt valid consent to something can often be based on less than full information, but a problem
arises when the authority that seeks consent also controls available information. If someone asks my agreement to a course of action and
then actively conceals much relevant information that would affect my
judgment, my "consent" is of lessened or no effect. Under social contract theory, a government is legitimate only if it receives or warrants
consent from the people under it. It may be debated exactly what conditions are required for valid actual consent, or for the hypothetical
consent of persons whose natures and social conditions fit some
model.[66] However, a claim of actual consent would certainly be under-

---

64. J. Locke, [Second] Treatise of Civil Government, *in* 5 The Works of John Locke
§§ 123–131 (1963) (1st ed. London 1690). But see G. Wills, Inventing America 167–74
(1978) (suggesting that the influence of the less individualist Scottish "common-sense"
philosophy was greater than has been commonly realized).

65. See J. Locke, A Letter Concerning Toleration, *in* 6 Works of John Locke passim
(1963) (1st ed. London 1689).

66. See the original-position analysis of J. Rawls, A Theory of Justice 136–42

mined if information highly relevant to evaluation of the government was systematically suppressed; rational actors in some idealized setting could not be expected to give valid consent in such circumstances and would be unlikely to approve in advance a regime that would conceal such information from actual citizens.[67] Thus, the idea that government should be of a kind that people would consent to, and the idea that actual citizens should have the opportunity to consent to the legitimacy of their governments, underlie a substantial argument against the suppression of political ideas and facts, even when a present majority approves that suppression.

The notion of limited government most obviously constrains what can count as harms and proper purposes for a liberal society. Suppressing expressions of belief simply to prevent mistakes about religion or aesthetics would not, for example, constitute a proper purpose. And the propriety of suppressing obscenity because it tends to make those who look at it unhappy would be doubtful, since liberal governments should not often be protecting individuals against themselves.

Most claims in favor of prohibiting speech in modern Western societies do not rest on asserted harms that are controversial in this way, perhaps partly because critical assumptions about the limits of government are deeply entrenched. Usually the harm that is to be avoided by prohibiting speech is a harm that a liberal government undoubtedly can try to prevent. But questions about limits on government power may remain—more subtle questions about the remoteness of the prohibited speech from the asserted harm and the extent to which the government may interfere in a normally private realm to accomplish concededly valid objectives. To take an extreme case, imagine a proposal that, because the attitude of racial prejudice generates the social harm of racial discrimination, the government should undertake compulsory psychological conditioning to erase that attitude from individuals who have

---

(1971), which contemplates rational actors knowledgeable about general facts but ignorant about their own characteristics making a self-interested choice about principles of justice.

67. In considering possible hypothetical consent one needs to think of two stages or aspects. The first involves the conditions under which the hypothetical actors consent. As to these, it is hard to imagine any model that permits actively misleading the actors about true facts (although they may be in ignorance of certain facts, especially relating to their own personal talents and position). The second stage involves the conditions of consent for an actual society that the hypothetical actors would choose. It is conceivable that actors deciding in hypothetical "presocial" conditions might knowingly consent to live in a political regime that would then engage in active suppression of important political ideas, so that consent in the regime would be given in conditions of substantial ignorance. They might do so, for example, if their judgment (as hypothetical rational beings) was that actual people are so irrational and destructive that necessary social solidarity can only be achieved by the government rigidly controlling opinion. The sentence in the text assumes that the factual judgment of the hypothetical actors would not lead them to confer such unbounded power over ideas to the government.

150   *COLUMBIA LAW REVIEW*   [Vol. 89:119

it.[68] Almost everyone would agree that such an interference with the private domain would be unacceptable,[69] and many would say that the connection between private thought and harmful act is too remote or indirect to warrant social control, even though the government's ultimate objective is appropriate.[70] Similar concerns would be raised if instead of trying to control thoughts themselves, the government forbade all expressions of racial prejudice. The communication of attitudes would be regarded as closer to the private domain of having the attitudes than to the public domain of acting upon the attitudes in a socially unacceptable way.

In summary, the traditional idea of limited government operates at two levels with respect to free speech, setting some constraints on appropriate government objectives and requiring that the connection between prohibited speech and social harm be reasonably direct. Although social contract theory cannot plausibly be thought to yield the conclusion that all communication must be left untouched by government prohibition, the theory may illuminate some inhibitions on government interference with private individuals.

B. *Recognition of Autonomy and Rationality*

Respect for individual autonomy may curb interference with expression. Whether or not speech actually contributes to the development of autonomy in citizens, there are two related nonconsequentialist arguments that the government should treat people as it would treat autonomous persons. Of course, every government prohibition of action interferes with free choice, and therefore with the exercise of autonomy. If autonomy is to undergird a principle of freedom of speech, a notion of autonomy is required that has some special relation to communication and that helps draw lines between permissible and impermissible regulation.[71]

The most straightforward claim is that the government should always treat people as if they were rational and autonomous by allowing them all the information and advocacy that might be helpful to a rational, autonomous person making a choice. This claim focuses on the autonomy of the recipient of communication. As Thomas Scanlon has

---

68. This example assumes what not everyone accepts, that a liberal government can properly prevent "private" racial discrimination in housing and employment.

69. To be more precise, one would need to distinguish children from adults and coercive from educational efforts to influence thoughts. The government's latitude with respect to school children is greater in some ways than its latitude with respect to adults. Even as to adults, education to influence thoughts may be warranted. What are objectionable are coercive efforts to invade the private domain.

70. Edwin Baker's "liberty model" for free speech, Baker, supra note 16, at 990–1009, might be regarded as in part an elaboration of an idea of limited government, although Baker does not subscribe to social contract theory.

71. Two writers who place great emphasis on respect for autonomy are D. Richards, supra note 37, at 85, 167–69, 183; and Baker, supra note 16, at 991–92, 998.

put it, "[a]n autonomous person cannot accept without independent consideration the judgment of others as to what he should believe or what he should do."[72] A principle that the government should always treat its citizens as autonomous would not necessarily lead to freedom for every kind of communication—outright lies and subliminal manipulation may not contribute to autonomous choice and might be restricted. But a strong version of a principle that the government must always treat citizens as autonomous by maximizing opportunities for informed choice would be powerfully protective of many kinds of speech.

The difficulty with the principle in this strong form lies in its implausibility. The government must protect citizens from social harms, and many fellow citizens do not act in a rational and autonomous way. If some communications are especially likely to lead irrational people to do harmful things, why must the government permit them access to those communications as if they were rational and autonomous, rather than protecting potential victims of their irrational actions? Few suppose that compulsory commitment of insane people who are demonstrably dangerous to others is a violation of liberal government; we cannot rule out in advance the possibility that government may regulate communications in a manner that takes account of frequent deviations from an ideal of autonomy.

Furthermore, a critical ambiguity lurks in the concept of rationality and autonomy. Does a rational and autonomous person always act with appropriate regard for the interests of others, or might such a person pursue his own interests unjustly at the expense of others? If it is supposed that the rational, autonomous person always acts morally, then such a person can be trusted with as complete information and advocacy as is possible. In that event the only worry about treating actual people as rational and autonomous is how far short people fall of being rational and autonomous. Matters are more complicated if it is supposed, to the contrary, that rational, autonomous people may freely choose to pursue their own interests immorally. In that case, were rational, autonomous people given full information about how to engage in undeterrable cheating on their income taxes, many would take advantage of the information by cheating. A principle ensuring full freedom of speech might thus lead to social harms that could be avoided if some information were suppressed. One might contend that the government's treating people as autonomous is more important than preventing the social harms that would result from full information, but a defense of that position would then be needed.

---

72. Scanlon, A Theory of Freedom of Expression, 1 Phil. & Pub. Aff. 216 (1972).

In an article[73] whose major thesis he no longer defends,[74] Thomas Scanlon develops a somewhat more complex claim about autonomy and expression. He takes as a standard for the limits of legitimate government "the powers of a state . . . that citizens could recognize while still regarding themselves as equal, autonomous, rational agents."[75] In this form the claim in favor of treating people as autonomous is grounded in a version of social contract theory that asks what rational, autonomous people would agree to. This extra step actually eliminates assurance that the government should treat people as autonomous and rational on every occasion. For the reasons that have just been rehearsed, rational, autonomous people deciding on the general limits of government interference would want to protect themselves from harms wrought by irrational people and by rational, immoral people (Scanlon is quite clear that his notion of autonomy and rationality does not guarantee moral action).[76] To protect themselves from those harms, rational, autonomous people might agree to constraints that would inhibit to some degree the extent to which all citizens, including themselves, would have available information and advocacy that would maximally serve rational and autonomous choice.

In brief, rational, autonomous people setting limits on government might well conclude that the government should not always allow people everything a rational, autonomous person would want to have in making a particular choice.[77] And if one simply asserts a principle that the government should never act to inhibit conditions for rational, autonomous choice, it is hard to see how that principle could be supported.

What may remain is a less rigorous standard, namely a premise of liberal democracy that human beings are largely rational and autonomous and should be treated in that way. That a proposed prohibition would not treat people in this manner counts against it, and prohibitions that do not respect autonomy may call for especially careful review of possible justifications.

C. *Dignity and Equality*

A justification for free speech that is closely related to the points just made but that focuses on the speaker more than his listeners is the

---

73. Id. The article and its claimed connection between freedom of speech and autonomy are perceptively criticized in Amdur, Scanlon on Freedom of Expression, 9 Phil. & Pub. Aff. 287 (1980).

74. See Scanlon, supra note 23, at 533–34.

75. Scanlon, supra note 72, at 215.

76. Id. at 215–22.

77. See id. Scanlon suggests that an autonomous decision permitting the government prospectively to disallow harmful expression would not jeopardize autonomy as long as the actor retained the freedom to judge independently whether the government's assessment was correct; for Scanlon it is the absence of valid information on which to base this judgment that constrains autonomy.

idea that the government should treat people with dignity and equality. As a matter of basic human respect we may owe it to each other to listen to what each of us has to say, or at least not to foreclose the opportunity to speak and to listen. Under this view, suppression represents a kind of contempt for citizens that is objectionable independent of its consequences; and when suppression favors some points of view over others, it may be regarded as failing to treat citizens equally.

How to take this argument depends on whether any infringement of liberty impairs dignity and any infringement that is significantly selective impairs equality. Many actions that people would like to engage in must be restricted, and some of these restrictions, for example, denying the right to practice medicine to those not certified in a prescribed way, are bound to be "selective." The concerns about dignity and equality may seem not to be specially related to speech but to be arguments, perhaps rather weak ones, in favor of liberty generally.

There may, however, be a tighter connection between restrictions on communications and affronts to dignity and equality. Expressions of beliefs and feelings lie closer to the core of our persons than do most actions we perform; restrictions of expressions may offend dignity to a greater degree than most other restrictions; and selective restrictions based on the content of our ideas may imply a specially significant inequality. So put, the notions of affront to dignity and equality bear a plausible relationship to free speech, though they also reach other forms of liberty, such as liberty of sexual involvement and liberty of personal appearance, that lie close to how we conceive ourselves.

D. *The Marketplace of Ideas*

One mistaken or incomplete argument for free speech claims that suppression is wrong because truth should not be impaired and that what emerges from the marketplace of ideas simply counts as the truth under a liberal government. The marketplace of ideas approach, so conceived, is either unpersuasive or must rest on some further unexpressed premises. Holmes's notion that the best test of truth is what is produced from the marketplace of ideas[78] is sometimes taken as a version of the truth-discovery theory already discussed—namely, that there are things that count independently as the truth and that the chances of those being accepted by people are enhanced by a marketplace of ideas. On that account, whether free speech contributes to truth is a factual question, however hard to answer. The alternative way of regarding what Holmes said is that there really is no test of truth except what comes out of the marketplace, because there is no independent truth. On that interpretation, a normative claim is made that people should accept as decisive the results of a marketplace of ideas rather than the results of some other process. But once the claim

---

78. Abrams v. United States, 250 U.S. 616, 630 (1919) (Holmes, J., dissenting).

154   COLUMBIA LAW REVIEW   [Vol. 89:119]

is so understood, the question arises why people should accept those particular results. If the answer is "Because we live in a liberal democracy," the next question is why liberal democracy commits us to the results of a marketplace of ideas rather than, say, the results of democratically determined suppression. An attempt to answer that question returns us to the various justifications already considered. Unless an independent notion of truth is supposed, an argument that truth is what emerges from the marketplace of ideas does not yield distinctive support for a free speech principle.

CONCLUSION: THE IMPORT OF THE JUSTIFICATIONS

The nonconsequential justifications, like the consequentialist ones, fall short of setting clear principles that can be confidently applied to decide what practices of suppression are unwarranted. What all these perspectives do provide, however, is a set of considerations, a set of standards for the relation of government to citizens, that helps delineate what interferences with expression are most worrisome and that operate as counters, sometimes powerful ones, in favor of freedom.

Assertions of fact and value come to mind immediately as communications evidently covered by the justifications for freedom of speech. Claims about general facts are critical for people's understanding of the world they inhabit, for their choices about how to live, and for their decisions on public issues. The truth-discovery justification applies strongly to general factual statements, and suppression of such statements would undermine independence of judgment and personal development. Many general claims about facts are important to the considered appraisal of government on which consent must rest; a government that recognizes autonomy and dignity will allow speakers to express and listeners to hear such claims about facts.

The reasons for protecting claims of value look similar to those applying to factual assertions, if one believes that all or many value statements are in some sense true or false. But even if one is radically skeptical about the truth or falsity of claims of value, strong reasons exist for extending protection to them. As far as personal dignity and emotional release are concerned, freedom to express one's judgments of value is as important to speakers as freedom to indicate views about facts. Government suppression of talk about values circumscribes the process of self-development, perpetuates institutions that would no longer win knowing acceptance, and frustrates the desire of people to converse with others about matters that concern them deeply.

Claims to coverage become less secure, however, when assertions of fact and value are dominantly aimed at producing specific, often immediate action, and when utterances are primarily something other than statements of fact and value. Requests and encouragements are not such statements, but they are commonly intertwined with claims of fact and value. When a speaker tells young men not to volunteer for the armed services because the country is fighting an immoral war, she has shown with clarity the practical consequences of her moral beliefs and she has evidenced their intensity. She might be able to indicate those specific consequences and her own intensity while falling short of actually encouraging a course of behavior, but pushing people to communicate in this manner creates certain difficulties. As the speaker comes closer to communicating all the beliefs about fact and value that would be contained in an encouragement, she comes closer to making that encouragement. And speech that matters is less free if ordinary persons must pick their words with exquisite care. If communications had to meet strict standards of correct formulation, people would be hesitant to speak their minds and what they did say would be less an expression of their personality, less an emotional release, than utterances that would come to them more naturally in the absence of constraint. Because requests and encouragements are designed to induce action and because much of what they implicitly communicate about facts and values could be otherwise communicated, they lie at the margin of a principle of free speech; but such a principle cannot disregard them altogether.

With considerations like these in mind, one is ready to move forward and grope with other elements in a theory about free speech and with the fascinating, intricate, and varied questions of how far speech should be left unrestricted in our liberal democratic polity.

[8]

THE JOURNAL OF PHILOSOPHY
VOLUME LXXXVIII, NO. 3, MARCH 1991

EPISTEMIC PATERNALISM: COMMUNICATION CONTROL IN LAW AND SOCIETY*

A popular principle in epistemology and the philosophy of science is the requirement of total evidence (RTE). A weak version of this principle may be stated as follows:

(W-RTE) A cognitive agent X should always fix his beliefs or subjective probabilities in accordance with the total evidence in his possession at the time.[1]

This version says nothing about acquiring or collecting evidence, only about the use of evidence already in one's possession. A stronger version of RTE, however, addresses evidence gathering as well:

(S-RTE) A cognitive agent X should collect and use all available evidence that can be collected and used (at negligible cost).[2]

This principle had best be understood in purely epistemic terms, rather than moral or legal terms. Some evidence collection might

---

* For valuable comments and advice, I am grateful to Holly Smith, Allen Buchanan, Henning Jensen, Joel Feinberg, Richard Lempert, and the members of the 1989 Dubrovnik conference on epistemology and philosophy of mind.

[1] See Rudolf Carnap, *Logical Foundations of Probability* (Chicago: University Press, 1950), p. 211; and Carl G. Hempel, "Inductive Inconsistencies," in *Aspects of Scientific Explanation* (New York: Free Press, 1965), pp. 64–7.

[2] See I. J. Good, "On the Principle of Total Evidence," in *Good Thinking* (Minneapolis: Minnesota UP, 1983); and Paul Horwich, *Probability and Evidence* (Cambridge: MIT, 1982), ch. 6. Good's argument for the strong version of RTE appeals to the criterion of maximizing expected utility, so it seems more pragmatic than purely epistemic. Horwich's argument, however, is purely epistemic. He shows that the *expected error* in one's probability judgment vis-à-vis some hypothesis H is minimized by the acquisition of any new evidence E (as long as $0 < \text{prob}(E) < 1$, and $\text{prob}(H/E) \neq \text{prob}(H/-E)$). I shall not discuss these arguments in detail because I am not so much interested in S-RTE as in the two-agent "control" version of RTE. In fact, I am not even primarily interested in the control version of RTE. I really use it as an expository heuristic to introduce the topic of epistemic paternalism, and the topic of communication control more generally.

0022-362X/91/8803/113–31
© 1991 The Journal of Philosophy, Inc.

involve invasion of privacy or harmful experimentation on human subjects, which would be objectionable on moral and/or legal grounds. But if we abstract from these factors and restrict attention to epistemic considerations, the principle has initial intuitive appeal.

A plausible-seeming corollary, or extension, of S-RTE is a principle governing the practices of a second agent, Y, who is in a position to control the evidence made available to X. This interpersonal principle would say that Y should make available to X all evidence that is subject to his (Y's) control. Of course, like S-RTE itself, the envisaged extension or corollary of S-RTE must be restricted to epistemic contexts or concerns. Thus, we might formulate the "control" version of RTE roughly as follows:

> (C-RTE) If agent X is going to make a doxastic decision concerning question Q, and agent Y has control over the evidence that is provided to X, then, from a purely epistemic point of view, Y should make available to X all of the evidence relevant to Q which is (at negligible cost) within Y's control.

The restriction to the epistemic viewpoint is again important. In legal settings, for example, there are many nonepistemic reasons for refusing to provide relevant evidence to jurors. Available evidence may have been illegally obtained. Relevant evidence may be obtainable from the defendant, but the Fifth Amendment forbids his being compelled to testify against himself. Or the defendant may have testified elsewhere under a grant of limited immunity, providing that his testimony would not subsequently be used against him. In these cases, the judge (Y) is obliged not to provide the jurors (X) with all available evidence logically relevant to the question of guilt. These constraints, though, are not of an epistemic nature. Thus, the stated version of C-RTE may still be defensible. Indeed, anyone persuaded by John Stuart Mill's[3] famous thesis that, if we are interested in having truth prevail, we should allow all available arguments to be heard, should be attracted to C-RTE.

I shall argue, nonetheless, that C-RTE is unacceptable. More cautiously, I shall show that existing provisions and practices, both in the law and elsewhere in society, contravene C-RTE. Although I shall not defend each provision and practice in detail, many of them seem to be quite reasonable. This raises some interesting questions for a branch of epistemology that I have elsewhere called *social epistemics*.[4] The aim of this paper is to formulate these questions in a general way and to undertake a preliminary exploration of them.

[3] *On Liberty*, ch. 2.
[4] See *Epistemology and Cognition* (Cambridge: Harvard, 1986), pp. 1, 5–9, 136–8; "Foundations of Social Epistemics," *Synthese*, LXXIII, 1 (1987): 109–44;

I

The American legal system has a set of explicitly formulated rules of evidence for the federal courts. These and other trial-related procedures are substantially dedicated to the goal of getting the truth about the issues under litigation (in a criminal trial, the guilt or innocence of the accused). Since the aim of these rules is, accordingly, heavily or predominantly epistemic, they provide excellent examples for our scrutiny.

The Federal Rules of Evidence[5] resulted from proposals by an Advisory Committee appointed by the Supreme Court, which were passed into law (with some revisions) by Congress in 1975. Although the rules do not, in general, bind judges on the admission or exclusion of evidence, they provide guidelines that should be followed if decisions are not to be overturned. Rule 102 declares their purpose: "These rules shall be construed to secure fairness in administration, elimination of unjustifiable expense and delay, and promotion of growth and development of the law of evidence *to the end that the truth may be ascertained* and proceedings justly determined" (emphasis added). The truth goal is implicit in the declaration (Rule 602) that witnesses may only testify to a matter of which they have "personal" (especially perceptual) knowledge, and in the general exclusion of hearsay evidence (Rule 801). Such rules codify what McCormick calls a "most pervasive manifestation" of the common law, viz., insistence upon "the most reliable sources of information."[6] Reliance on reliable sources, clearly, is more likely to produce accurate (i.e., truthful) judgments. The admission of testimony by experts (Rule 702) also exemplifies a dedication to truth, since experts are people presumed to know relevant truths. The requirement of witnesses to make an oath or affirmation before testifying is still another device calculated to secure truthful evidence (Rule 603), as are statutory provisions of penalties for perjury. The entire procedure of cross-examination, which holds an exalted place in the Anglo-American trial system, is similarly rationalizable by reference to the truth goal. Since it is impossible to prevent false evidence from ever being introduced, at least there should be ample opportunity to contravert it, to reduce the likelihood of its being believed by the fact finder and thereby promoting a false verdict.

What is interesting in the present context is that the rules of

---

and "The Cognitive and Social Sides of Epistemology," in A. Fine and P. Machamer, eds., *PSA 1986*, II (East Lansing: Philosophy of Science Association, 1987), pp. 295–311.

[5] See *Federal Rules of Evidence for United States Courts and Magistrates* (St. Paul: West, 1989).

[6] In E. Cleary, ed., *McCormick on Evidence*, 3rd ed. (St. Paul: West, 1984), p. 23.

evidence frequently foster the exclusion of evidence from the jurors, in conflict with principle C-RTE. On the matter of admission or exclusion of evidence, one governing provision is that *relevant* evidence is generally admissible, but *irrelevant* evidence is not admissible (Rule 402).[7] In the matter of hearsay evidence, the basis for exclusion ostensibly falls under a different principle, not irrelevance but unreliability or doubtful veracity. Still other rules promote exclusion even when the evidence is both relevant and presumptively true. Evidence about the character of an accused is not admissible for the purpose of proving that he acted according to character on the occasion in question (Rule 404). In particular, evidence of previous *crimes* by the accused is not admissible to help prove that he committed the present crime. Also, evidence that the defendant initially entered a guilty plea on the present charge, and then withdrew it, is inadmissible (Rule 410). Here we have examples of a particularly interesting kind, in which judges are allowed or enjoined to exclude presumptively true and relevant evidence. Can these be rationalized on epistemic grounds?

The general rationale is given in Rule 403, which states in part: "Although relevant, evidence may be excluded if its probative value is substantially outweighed by the danger of unfair prejudice, confusion of the issues, or misleading the jury, ..." The phrase 'misleading the jury' apparently refers to the jury's being led into making an incorrect judgment, and the language of 'prejudice' and 'confusion' can also be readily interpreted this way. It appears, then, that the Federal Rules of Evidence provide an *epistemic* rationale for excluding various types of evidence from doxastic decision makers (jurors), contrary to what C-RTE enjoins.

II

A better understanding of the underlying rationale for the relevance rules can be gleaned from a theoretical reconstruction by a legal scholar, Richard Lempert.[8] Lempert offers several reconstructive suggestions, but I shall present just the one employing a Bayesian interpretation. The discussion assumes that the fact finder is a jury and the issue to be resolved is a defendant's guilt.

One form of Bayes' Theorem, suitable to the present case, is formulated as follows:

$$O(G/E) = \frac{P(E/G)}{P(E/\text{not-}G)} \cdot O(G)$$

---

[7] Relevant evidence is characterized as "evidence having any tendency to make the existence of any fact that is of consequence to the determination of the action more probable or less probable than it would be without the evidence" (Rule 401).

[8] "Modeling Relevance," *Michigan Law Review*, LXXV (1977): 1021–57.

This formula describes the way that a new item of evidence (*E*) should influence a rational agent's odds (*O*) that a defendant is guilty (*G*).[9] It says that the posterior odds of the defendant's guilt is equal to (1) the probability that the evidence would obtain if the defendant is in fact guilty, (2) divided by the probability that that evidence would obtain if the defendant is in fact not guilty, (3) multiplied by the prior odds on the defendant's guilt. The ratio of items (1) and (2) is conventionally called the *likelihood ratio*. On Lempert's reconstruction, a necessary and sufficient condition for evidence to be logically *irrelevant* to the defendant's guilt is that the likelihood ratio be 1:1 (or close to 1:1). This holds when the evidence in question would be just as likely to arise if the defendant were not guilty as if he were guilty, i.e., if $P(E/G) = P(E/\text{not-}G)$. Evidence of this sort has no "probative" value, that is, warrants no change in the posterior odds of guilt. Such evidence is unhelpful and therefore should not be admitted. Logically *relevant* evidence is evidence whose likelihood ratio departs (substantially) from 1:1.

Why should courts declare even relevant evidence inadmissible? Lempert expresses this in terms of the danger that the fact finder will misestimate the probabilities that comprise the likelihood ratio, and hence assign excessive (or insufficient) weight to the evidence. Overestimating the numerator or underestimating the denominator makes the conclusion sought by the proponent of the evidence appear more probable than it actually is; underestimating the numerator or overestimating the denominator has the opposite result. For example, suppose that in an assault case it can be shown that the defendant is a heroin addict, and also that one out of 500 criminal assailants are heroin addicts, whereas of the people who never engage in criminal assault only one in 1,000 are heroin addicts. Then knowledge that the defendant is an addict should result in a doubling of the prior odds that the defendant was the assailant. Suppose further that the fact finder (mistakenly) thinks that the probability that a nonassailant would be a heroin addict was one in 10,000 rather than one in 1,000. This misestimation of the denominator by a factor of ten leads to a twentyfold increase in the odds of guilt rather than a twofold increase. It is precisely this sort of danger which concerns the courts. Rule 403, excluding character evidence, is partly justified

---

[9] I do not mean to endorse the Bayesian analysis for all purposes, including legal purposes. I am merely expositing Lempert's reconstruction. The same morals could well be drawn without commitment to Bayesianism. For an alternative account of reasoning principles for the law, see L. Jonathan Cohen, *The Probable and the Provable* (New York: Oxford, 1977) (which I also do not mean to endorse).

on this ground, says Lempert. Jurors are likely to magnify the import of character traits, or past criminal record;[10] and similarly for withdrawn guilty pleas. When courts or the codified rules speak of the problem as one of juror "prejudice," or when they speak of "confusing" or "misleading" the jury, this should be understood, according to Lempert, in terms of the jury's being prone to such misestimations.[11]

III

Whether or not Lempert's Bayesian reconstruction is wholly faithful to the intent of the rules, it is apparent that the framers of the rules, and judges themselves, often wish to *protect* jurors in their search for truth. If, in the framers' opinion, jurors are likely to be misled by a certain category of evidence, they are sometimes prepared to require or allow such evidence to be kept from the jurors. This is an example of what I shall call *epistemic paternalism*. The general idea is that the indicated rules of evidence are designed to protect jurors from their own "folly," just as parents might keep dangerous toys or other articles away from children, or might not expose them to certain facts. I do not wish to quibble here over precise definitions of the term 'paternalism'. My usage, however, has much in common with H. L. A. Hart's characterization of paternalism as "the protection of people from themselves," and with Joel Feinberg's emphasis on the analogy to parental relations with children.[12] Jurors may have flaws in their background beliefs, or in their ability to draw apt conclusions from evidence. If so, the courts are prepared to protect them against these information-processing deficiencies in order to get truthful judgments on the issues at hand. Admittedly, in the judicial case, the prime objects of "protection" are plausibly the parties to the litiga-

---

[10] In defending the rule against character evidence, the Advisory Committee for the Federal Rules of Evidence quotes the California Law Revision Commission with approval: "Character evidence is of slight probative value and may be very prejudicial. It tends to distract the trier of fact from the main question of what actually happened on the particular occasion. It subtly permits the trier of fact to reward the good man and to punish the bad man because of their respective characters despite what the evidence in the case shows actually happened" (*op. cit.*, p. 31).

[11] In Horwich's terms (see fn. 2 above), we might express the court's fear of jurors being misled by E as an assessment that the result of their getting E would be an *increase* in the probability of their making an error rather than a reduction. The crucial point, of course, is that the court substitutes its *own* expectation of juror error for that of the jurors themselves, who perhaps would welcome information about the accused's character, criminal record, or withdrawn guilty pleas as likely to reduce their probability of error.

[12] Hart, *Law, Liberty, and Morality* (New York: Vintage, 1966), p. 31; and Feinberg, *Harm to Self* (New York: Oxford, 1986), pp. 3–8. For other discussions of the definition of paternalism, see Rolf Sartorius, ed., *Paternalism* (Minneapolis: Minnesota UP, 1983); and Donald Van DeVeer, *Paternalistic Intervention* (Princeton: University Press, 1986), pp. 16–24.

tion, or perhaps society at large, not the jurors. So the present use of the term 'paternalism' may extend a bit beyond its standard usage. The indicated parties are protected, however, by getting jurors to make accurate judgments. Protection of the *jurors'* epistemic ends therefore assumes derivative importance.

In any event, I shall construe epistemic paternalism in a broad sense. I shall think of communication controllers as exercising epistemic paternalism whenever they interpose their own judgment rather than allow the audience to exercise theirs (all with an eye to the audience's epistemic prospects). Thus, the exclusion of evidence of doubtful veracity (e.g., hearsay evidence) also qualifies as epistemic paternalism. The courts apparently feel that jurors cannot be counted on to discount hearsay testimony adequately. So they substitute their own wisdom for that of the jurors. Similarly, when judges exclude evidence as irrelevant, they must use *their* assessment of whether the evidence affects the probabilities of the propositions in question (the jurors' assessments might have been different). When these categories of exclusion are added, it is clear that courts engage in a substantial amount of epistemic paternalism.

Is such paternalism really warranted? Are these rules *good* rules from an epistemic point of view? This is open to dispute. Lempert contends that evidence should not be excluded when the probative value is substantial, i.e., when the likelihood ratio deviates markedly from 1:1. The preferred solution, he says, is to provide the jury with the information needed to assess accurately the probative value of the offered evidence.

There are general problems with this solution, though. For one thing (as Lempert notes), there may not be hard data that indicate just how heavily a piece of evidence should be weighted. There may be no well-researched (base rate) "facts" to give to the jury. Nonetheless, people with judicial experience may have good reasons to suspect that juries would exaggerate the import of that type of evidence. Second, there is a question of whether statistical information, even if it were available, would psychologically displace or override jurors' prior prejudices.[13] Third, there is a question of whether *all* the relevant considerations that bear on the import of the evidence

---

[13] Studies by Lee Ross and colleagues give evidence of a "perseveration" phenomenon, in which previously acquired beliefs are not eradicated even by new evidence showing that the original basis of those beliefs was ill-founded. See Richard Nisbett and Lee Ross, *Human Inference: Strategies and Shortcomings of Social Judgment* (Englewood Cliffs, NJ: Prentice-Hall, 1980), ch. 8. I have suggested more generally that beliefs can never be "erased," but at best only "overridden." This allows for the presence of *credal residues*. See *Epistemology and Cognition*, pp. 223–6.

should be given to the jurors. Should they be presented with the
Bayesian framework in terms of which the evidence may be interpreted? Should they be informed of theoretical disputes over the
correctness of Bayesianism, or the potential for its misapplication?
Much of this material would surely confuse most jurors. The dangers
of introducing mathematical techniques into the fact-finding process
have been emphasized by Laurence Tribe.[14]

I am inclined to think that *some* paternalism is appropriate in this
arena, although I shall not take a firm stand on specific policies.
What I want to do is identify the questions clearly, and put them in
the framework of a wider set of questions. What we have here is a set
of rules or practices whose adoption has an impact on the truth
values of the doxastic decisions that cognizers make. One question is:
For each such rule, how good is its impact from a *veritistic* point of
view, that is, in terms of the likelihood of getting truth and avoiding
error? Would alternative rules or practices have better veritistic
properties?

This type of question falls under what I call *social epistemics*.
Epistemics generally is my (partly "reforming") conception of epistemology, with three main divisions: primary individual epistemics,
secondary individual epistemics, and social epistemics. All three divisions seek to make evaluations in terms of veritistic ends, i.e., in
terms of the effect on people's getting truths and avoiding errors.
The objects or targets of evaluation, however, differ from division to
division. Primary epistemics studies the veritistic properties of basic
psychological processes. Secondary epistemics assesses the veritistic
properties of learnable problem-solving methods, such as mathematical proof techniques, carbon-dating procedures, and the like. Social
epistemics studies the veritistic properties of social practices, or institutional rules that directly or indirectly govern communication
and doxastic decision. Judicial rules of evidence clearly fall in this last
category.[15] The focus of the present paper is the class of institutional
rules or practices that have a flavor of epistemic paternalism, e.g.,
those which weed out some possible communications that might be
directed to a cognitive agent, by appeal to that agent's own veritistic
ends. Are such rules and practices defensible, and, if so, which ones?

---

[14] "Trial by Mathematics: Precision and Ritual in the Legal Process," *Harvard
Law Review*, LXXXIV, 6 (1971): 1329–93.

[15] For further discussion of the divisions of epistemics, and the rationale for
them, see "Foundations of Social Epistemics" and "The Cognitive and Social Sides
of Epistemology." For another treatment of judicial rules of evidence in the context
of social epistemics, see Keith Burgess-Jackson, "An Epistemic Approach to Legal
Relevance," *St. Mary's Law Journal*, XVIII, 2 (1986): 463–80. I thank Burgess-
Jackson for helping draw my attention to relevance rules.

Although social epistemics could content itself with the separate evaluation of individual practices, it seems more advisable to address whole classes of practices. What one wants is a general assessment of paternalistic control practices, first in terms of purely epistemic considerations and second on more inclusive grounds. Before turning to general principles, however, let us examine some additional cases of paternalistic practices.

IV

Start with curriculum selection in education, especially in primary and secondary schools. School personnel at various levels—boards of education, principals, and teachers—select curricular materials in the form of textbooks, course syllabi, and so forth. (When teachers do it, they assume something of a dual role: both controller and speaker.) In the nature of this business, some points of view and supporting argumentation are left out. Students are not exposed to all possible ideas on a given subject. Is this objectionable? Set aside highly publicized examples of book banning based on obscenity, profanity, or offensiveness. Think instead of simply ignoring opinions that have (or once had) their exponents, but are regarded by current authorities as palpably false or indefensible. Mathematics classes do not present alternative (crackpot) mathematics. Science classes do not (often) present the flat-earth viewpoint, Ptolemaic astronomy, or astrology. Schools rarely if ever invite Jeane Dixon or her ilk to give guest lectures, or recount as serious alternatives the theories of Velikovsky. Classes in health education do not give "equal time" to drug pushers to defend the safety of drug use, or to quacks to present and defend their cures. These omissions probably have veritistically good consequences. Of course, it might also be appropriate to have classes sample and compare "bad" and "bogus" science along with the good.[16] But this kind of course might be advantageous only for high-school students, not for younger pupils, who would only be confused.

The most public controversy surrounds the question of "equal time" for creationism in biology classes. Here, too, paternalism seems to be warranted on epistemic grounds. Experts on science should be allowed to decide that creationism is not a scientifically viable or serious contender, and hence should not be taught in the classroom.[17] What about the teaching of creationism in nonscience

[16] The phraseology is borrowed from the title of Martin Gardner's book, *Science: Good, Bad, and Bogus* (Buffalo: Prometheus, 1981).
[17] This is not to dispute Paul Feyerabend's point [*Science in a Free Society* (London: Verso, 1978)] that the expertise of science and scientists must ultimately be judged by laymen. The thesis that laymen can assess the credentials of putative experts is discussed below in sect. VIII.

classes? Is it legitimate for a local community to require this in their schools? Here extra-epistemic issues intrude. Creationism is presumably a religious doctrine, so that constitutional issues arise about its being taught in public schools. What about the putative right of parents to control their children's education? If such an alleged right is supposed to rest on purely epistemic considerations, it would be very hard to defend. If it is based on nonepistemic considerations of an ethical or sociopolitical nature, it goes beyond the main focus of our discussion, although I shall briefly return to it in section VII.[18]

Turn next to the sphere of commercial advertising, where the Federal Trade Commission has authority to take actions against false or deceptive advertising. This exemplifies epistemic paternalism because it prevents some potential messages from being conveyed to an audience, and it does so with veritistic ends in mind: to keep them from believing untruths about commercial products. The FTC has four types of remedies for inhibiting false and deceptive advertisements, or even requiring truthful disclosures that the "speakers" would not independently make.[19] First, it can issue *cease and desist* orders. Second, it can seek to obtain *affirmative disclosure*, forcing a manufacturer to disclose by mark or label material facts concerning the merchandise. The most familiar such example is the requirement of warning labels on cigarette packages (although this is under the jurisdiction of the Food and Drug Administration, rather than the FTC). A third remedy is *corrective advertising*. When consumer misconceptions about a product have resulted from past advertising, the FTC has sometimes forced the manufacturer to devote 25% of its advertising budget for one year to corrections of past inaccuracies. In this arena, then, communication control sometimes takes a stronger form than the one considered thus far: not excluding messages, but mandating messages of a specified kind or content. A fourth remedy is the FTC's advertisement *substantiation* program. This forbids manufacturers to make certain advertising claims unless they have done competent scientific tests that substantiate their claims. This piece of epistemic paternalism has been rationalized by appeal to the relatively poor opportunity of consumers to obtain accurate information themselves.[20]

---

[18] On issues of educational philosophy and the control of educational policy, see Amy Gutmann, *Democratic Education* (Princeton: University Press, 1987).

[19] On these topics see Donald Gillmor and Jerome Barron, *Mass Communication Law*, 4th ed. (St. Paul: West, 1984), ch. 8; and Daniel Rohrer, *Mass Media, Free Speech, and Advertising* (Dubuque, IA: Kendall/Hunt, 1979), ch. 3.

[20] FTC Chairman Miles Kirkpatrick wrote: "The manufacturer has the ability, the knowhow, the equipment, the time and the resources to undertake such information by testing or otherwise—the consumer usually does not" (quoted in Gillmor and Barron, pp. 618–9).

Another class of examples involves television and radio news. Generally speaking, American network news broadcasts offer a relatively limited variety of interpretations of each news event; nor do they detail the evidence for each of the possible interpretations. This is partly due, no doubt, to severe time constraints. But there is also the deliberate attempt to simplify, to make the news understandable and digestible to a large audience. Certainly this must be included under the rubric of epistemic paternalism. There is room for debate over how acceptable this practice is, and doubtless different programs and newscasters deserve different ratings on this dimension. But it is hard to deny the need for some degree of simplification, especially on technical topics. If this is at all legitimate, some degree of epistemic paternalism again seems inevitable and unobjectionable.

Simplification involves the omission of some truths. So paternalism in this form reduces the number of truths an audience has an opportunity to acquire. Nonetheless, the trade off of error avoidance, or confusion avoidance, may compensate for this loss (depending partly on how different segments of the audience are affected).

A further element in the trade off is that simplification can increase the audience size. This may mean that more true beliefs (i.e., belief tokens) are acquired through the simplified set of messages than would otherwise be the case. Although members of the media may care about this chiefly because of Nielsen ratings, and their consequent attractiveness to advertisers, the number of people acquiring true beliefs is a genuinely epistemic value, which I elsewhere call *fecundity*.[21]

The epistemic consequences of an institutional policy are often difficult to anticipate. The Federal Communication Commission's "Fairness Doctrine" is a good case in point. Since holders of its broadcast licenses are supposed to operate in the public interest, the FCC has required licensees to devote a reasonable amount of time to issues of public importance. Moreover, if a station presents one side of a controversial issue of public importance, it must afford reasonable opportunity for presentation of contrasting views. This policy was intended to promote veritistic outcomes by exposing the public to a wide diversity of opinion. It has been argued, however, that its actual result is opposite to its intent. The threat of incurring FCC suits has allegedly discouraged stations from airing controversial material. This "chilling" effect has tended to guarantee blandness, and to retard rather than enhance a free marketplace of ideas. This is a

---

[21] See "Foundations of Social Epistemics" and "The Cognitive and Social Sides of Epistemology."

good example of how a policy's epistemic consequences (historical or prospective) can be a complex empirical question. This is why empirical sciences have a role to play in social epistemics.

V

Let us now inquire into the general circumstances in which epistemic paternalism, and other communication control policies, have good or bad epistemic consequences, i.e., good *veritistic* outcomes. A number of variables are relevant, especially: (1) the characteristics of the *controller* (or "gatekeeper"), (2) the characteristics of the *speakers* who wish to send messages via the communication channel, (3) the controller's *criterion of selection* among speakers or messages, (4) the characteristics of the *audience,* and (5) the availability of *alternate channels* that address the same topic.

Epistemic outcomes obviously depend heavily on the (epistemically) good judgment of the message controller. If the controller accurately distinguishes true and false claims, and/or true and false pieces of evidence for claims (and their relevance), then the choice of included and excluded messages may well promote truth acquisition on the part of the audience. This brings us immediately to variable (3): the criterion of selection. Does the controller select among candidate messages by reference to (A) their specific content, or (B) the characteristics of the speaker (or a combination of the two)? If the messages directly attempt to answer primary questions in the domain, and the controller himself has expertise on these questions, then a selection based on message content may positively contribute to veritistic outcomes. The controller may not purport to know answers to the primary questions in the domain, however. He may only select messages on the basis of prospective speakers' "credentials." Was the speaker an eyewitness to the putative events he wants to describe, or does he have some other access to, or authority about, the facts in question? If the controller is to make veritistically good selections, he must at least have expertise on the question of speaker credentials. (We might call this *secondary,* as opposed to *primary,* expertise.) This is what judges or rule framers claim to have in the field of legal evidence.

Selection criteria do not always involve purely veritistic considerations. A network may shy away from certain political interpretations because of prospective sponsor or audience disapproval. Since this is not a truth-oriented selection rationale, it raises doubts about the epistemic optimality of the control process.

Speaker characteristics are equally critical to (audience) veritistic outcomes. We have already mentioned the "access" or authority of speakers on the matters whereof they speak. Of almost comparable importance are the speakers' motivational properties. Do prospective speakers have an incentive for accuracy, or do they have incentives for deception and misrepresentation, as in the case of manufacturers, partisan witnesses, and perhaps even research scientists? If there are incentives for deception, does the *controller* know or suspect them, and does he use them in his selection policy?

Turning to audience characteristics, how informed, sophisticated, rational, etc., are the audience members who are likely to receive the channel's messages? How good are they at weighing competing views or complex chains of evidence? How good are they at assessing the reliability of various speakers or sources of evidence? Clearly, all these traits are crucial to veritistic outcomes. Furthermore, to the extent that the controller takes account of audience characteristics in selecting messages, the controller's knowledge (or true belief) about their characteristics is critical. If the controller has an accurate assessment of the audience's cognitive limits or shortcomings, a paternalistic choice of messages to include (or to *mandate*) may avert potential audience error. Or his policy of selection may avert potential *confusion*, which can lead to doxastic indecision or simple incomprehension of the truth (either of which is a comparatively bad veritistic outcome).

Finally, the availability of alternate communication channels can influence veritistic outcomes. If one channel deploys restrictive selection policies, that does not necessarily mean that the audience is confined to those messages. There may be other potential sources of information.

These are some of the salient factors which bear on the epistemic success of various alternative institutions of communication control. They are the sorts of factors to which social epistemics should appeal in evaluating existing or prospective institutions. As the discussion indicates, institutions or policies of these sorts cannot be rated in the *abstract*, apart from the properties of the individuals who occupy, or are likely to occupy, the different institutional roles. The same institution or policy might work well if the controller has considerable expertise, but poorly if he does not. In any case, when the cited variables or parameters take on appropriate values, epistemic paternalism will be justified. My previous examples are, quite plausibly, instances of this sort. So C-RTE must be rejected as a universal principle.

VI

I have been equating epistemically valuable outcomes with true belief and error avoidance. Are there additional epistemic values that this ignores? What about Mill's value of a "clearer perception and livelier impression of truth," produced by its collision with error (*op. cit.*, ch. 2)? And what about the skills to be learned from the process of wrestling with competing doctrines? I suspect that the livelier impression of truth, of which Mill speaks, can be cashed out in terms of a grasp of a larger number of related truths. One learns not simply that answer A_1 to question Q is correct, but that certain other answers, A_2, A_3, etc., have been offered to Q, what the arguments for and against these alternative answers are, and why these alternatives are mistaken. Learning these things doubtless has epistemic value, but it is not an additional *kind* of value. Similarly, the value of argumentative skills can be cashed out in terms of their instrumental value for discovering further truths on one's own, when no instructor is available.

Thomas Scanlon[22] has expressed doubts about epistemic protectionism by appeal to the value of autonomy, which consists in a person seeing himself as sovereign in deciding what to believe and in weighing reasons for action. Is autonomy an epistemic value of which a person is deprived by epistemic paternalism? If sovereignty is a matter of reserving the final doxastic choice to oneself, as some of Scanlon's passages suggest, this is not compromised by epistemic paternalism. The juror who did not hear certain excluded evidence still has to decide whether to believe what was presented. Perhaps the point, however, is that, whenever a cognitive agent is deprived of some doxastic alternative, or some evidence relevant to that alternative, some degree of sovereignty is reduced. This may be granted, but does this reduction constitute a diminution in *epistemic* value (especially *intrinsic* epistemic value)? I doubt it, though the matter is not wholly clear. An analogous case involves "practical" value, and the range of alternatives actually scanned by a deliberating agent. Suppose agent S wishes to select a plan of action designed to achieve goal G. If an assistant fails to call S's attention to some unnoticed alternative plan which is in fact worthless (it would not achieve G at all, or would be much too costly), S's planning sovereignty has been reduced; he loses an opportunity to deliberate about the unpresented alternative. But is this a loss in "practical" value? Again, I am doubtful.

Even if we concede a measure of (intrinsic) epistemic value to autonomy, a value compromised in epistemic paternalism, it is questionable whether the loss always outweighs the gains. As John Hardwig[23] has stressed, we live in an epistemically complex world, where each of us cannot reasonably hope to assess all evidence for all theses personally. We often have to depend on the authority of others.

---

[22] "A Theory of Freedom of Expression," *Philosophy and Public Affairs*, I, 2 (1972): 204–26.
[23] "Epistemic Dependence," this JOURNAL, LXXXII, 7 (July 1985): 335–49.

Given this situation, it seems likely that epistemic paternalism will frequently be necessary, and sometimes epistemically desirable.

VII

The burden of the preceding sections is that epistemic paternalism can sometimes be warranted on *epistemic* grounds. Extra-epistemic considerations, however, should unquestionably enter into overall assessments of communication control policy. What are these other considerations?

Let me briefly suggest five additional factors that ought to be considered. First is the *practical significance* factor. Some communications induce audience beliefs that are likely to produce immediate actions with serious outcomes, including harms either to themselves or to other agents. (This is similar to the "clear and present danger" idea.) Direct and serious outcomes are salient in a trial, where juror beliefs dictate court sanctions that directly affect the defendant's welfare (and the welfare, one might say, of society).[24] Similarly, consumer beliefs about commercial products standardly lead to consumption choices, which may directly affect health or safety. These are the cases where epistemic paternalism seems most appropriate. Consumers' welfare, for example, seems to outweigh any presumed right of manufacturers to send any message they like.[25]

A second factor is the *power of the controlling agent*. Epistemic paternalism on the part of isolated individuals is quite a different matter from paternalism exercised by the state, or any other powerful organ of society. There are historical reasons for being very cautious about state control of information.

Closely related to this is the third factor: the *scope* of control. The greater the breadth, the greater the dangers of communicational restriction. This was already mentioned in section V, but is worth repeating here. The exclusion of certain viewpoints from school curricula seems more defensible when it is recalled that students have other communication channels available. They can be taught things (e.g., religion) outside of school. In the case of broadcast news, the public is free to select among numerous stations, and to read newspapers, books, and magazines as well. Thus, the extent of

---

[24] Of course, where the defendant is in fact guilty, his welfare is not served by finding the truth. Presumably, however, society's utility is increased by accurate verdicts.

[25] There is ongoing debate, however, over the extent to which commercial speech is protected under First Amendment guarantees of freedom of speech. Not everyone agrees that regulation of advertising is legally defensible, or a good idea. See, for example, R. H. Coase, "Advertising and Free Speech," *Journal of Legal Studies*, VI, 1 (1977): 1–34.

control of any single news outlet is *partial* (and small). The chief objection to state censorship, by contrast, is that it is *total*. This is a very different kettle of fish. My condoning of local epistemic paternalisms should not be taken as an endorsement of global state censorship, especially on topics like news, politics, and public affairs.

This brings me to a fourth factor: the *topic* of the messages being controlled. It has been contended—quite plausibly, in my opinion —that an unregulated marketplace of ideas seems essential for political speech but not commercial speech. Thus, policies should differ for different subjects. I mention this here under nonepistemic factors; but actually it *may* be explainable by reference to epistemic ones. Perhaps we feel comfortable with a mathematics or science authority omitting nonstandard treatments from the curriculum because we acknowledge their expertise in their subjects. By contrast, in matters of (normative) politics and religion, we have no analogous conviction—as a society, at any rate—that there are any experts, and certainly no societal consensus on who the experts are (if any).

A fifth factor (or group of factors) concerns the putative *rights* of concerned agents: a speaker's right to freedom of speech, a communication channel owner's right to run his own station or publication, a parent's right or a community's right to predispose their children toward certain values or heritages, and so on. As indicated, some of these (putative) rights may be rationalized by epistemic factors, but others may be independent. In each case, moreover, the right may not be unconditional, but must be balanced by other rights or interests.[26]

How these nonepistemic factors should be balanced along with the (purely) epistemic ones is a complex matter, and I have no formula to offer. The variability of situations along these dimensions, however, makes it reasonable to expect epistemic paternalism to be appropriate (all things considered) in some contexts though inappropriate in many others.

VIII

Since expertise is a prime epistemic factor in the defense of epistemic paternalism, more should be said about it. To justify any particular instance of such paternalism, involving a particular controller, we must have grounds for taking that agent to be an expert. But how, it

---

[26] Scanlon has emphasized that issues in the freedom of expression hinge on the interests of three parties: participants (speakers), audiences, and bystanders. See "Freedom of Expression and Categories of Expression," reprinted in David Copp and Susan Wendell, eds., *Pornography and Censorship* (Buffalo: Prometheus, 1983). In cases of communication control, however, the interested parties are even more numerous. And in the case of children, some sort of special status (not merely "bystander") seems appropriate for parents and community.

may be asked, are people supposed to *tell* who (if anyone) has expertise? In particular, if (primary) expertise is defined in terms of believing domain-relevant truths, how can people lacking expertise —novices—identify an expert? Furthermore, when different people hold conflicting views and each claims to be an expert, how can the issue be resolved to their mutual satisfaction?

The problem of *expert identifiability* involves large epistemological issues that can only be addressed here partially, not fully. First, let us define an expert as someone who either (1) *has* true answers to core questions in the domain (i.e., believes or assigns high probability to these answers), or (2) has the *capacity* (usually through the possession of learned methods) to acquire true answers to core questions when they arise. Degree of expertise, then, is primarily a function of the candidate's question-answering *power*, i.e., how often he can form a belief in a correct answer as opposed to having either no opinion or an incorrect opinion.[27] Expertise can also be understood in either a *comparative* or an *absolute* sense. Someone is comparatively expert if his question-answering power ranks high compared with others; absolutely expert if his power ranks high in absolute terms.

The crucial requirement for expert identifiability is that, once candidate experts have produced their answers to target questions, there are "truth-revealing" situations in which novices and rivals can recognize which answers (if any) are correct. With enough such cases, the genuine experts can be identified. In fact, there are many domains in which such truth-revealing situations exist. Let me catalogue four homely domains of this sort: (1) *prediction* domains, (2) *factual-record* domains, (3) *repair* domains, and (4) *design* domains.

Prediction domains are ones in which the core questions are questions about future events, e.g., the weather, the economy, the stock market, or an upcoming election. When the events actually occur, the correct answers to the questions are revealed.

Factual-record domains can be illustrated with baseball and opera. An expert in these fields can correctly answer (from memory) questions about baseball or opera facts, e.g., who stole the most bases in 1973, which arias are from which operas, and so forth. Here there are undisputed records to which novices and rivals can appeal to verify correctness.

[27] The epistemic importance of question-answering power is emphasized in my *Epistemology and Cognition*, ch. 6. A further dimension in the definition of expertise should probably be added: the ability to recognize *wrong* answers as wrong (or assign them a low probability). Even if nobody has a correct answer to question Q, someone who knows (or truly believes) that each of the available answers is wrong is better off, epistemically, than someone who mistakenly believes (or assigns high probability to) wrong answers.

System-repair cases are more interesting. Whether a system (e.g., an air conditioner, an automobile, or a human body) is functioning properly or malfunctioning is frequently an uncontested, novice-detectable affair. Suppose system S is malfunctioning, so the question arises: "What techniques, steps, operations, or therapies would be followed by S returning to proper functioning?" A novice will typically have no answer at all. An expert, by contrast, can often answer correctly. The expert electrician, mechanic, or physician commonly proceeds as follows. First, he tries to find a system component that is causing the malfunction, using gauges, instruments, or other diagnostic techniques. Second, having diagnosed the cause, he decides what part replacements, alterations, adjustments, or medications would correct the malfunction. He thereby arrives at an answer to the target question. Can the truth of his answer be checked? Often it can. If and when the prescribed measures are executed, it will be novice-detectable whether the system resumes normal operation.

The fourth category of domains—design domains—is a fairly heterogeneous lot. Here the core question is: "What specific design or performance features would produce a certain desired effect, or meet certain standards or specifications?" This is the sort of question that sundry artists, designers, product engineers, or even mathematicians might be asked. The engineer might be asked for a blueprint of a dam that will meet certain specifications. A mathematician might be asked for a sequence of steps that would comprise a proof of a given theorem (according to understood constraints on the nature of proof).[28] In each of these cases, novices could not answer such questions correctly very often; but an expert could. (At least he could indicate correctly which answers are erroneous.) Is the correctness of an answer novice-detectable? Often the answer is 'yes'. Unable to produce a proof himself, the novice mathematician may nonetheless be able to verify whether someone else's proposal constitutes a proof. Whereas it may be difficult to design a theater set or choreograph a sequence that produces a desired effect, it may be palpable and uncontroversial that a certain design or sequence *does* (or does not) achieve that effect.

The moral is that, in many familiar cases, it is relatively easy, even for novices or rivals, to identify expertise. Needless to say, not all cases are straightforward. There is no necessary 'paradox', however, or impossibility in principle, of expert identification. There is no theoretical objection, then, to invoking the notion of expertise, construed veritistically, in the evaluation of communication practices.

[28] Even certain questions of theoretical science might be construed in this fashion, namely, "What is a theory in domain D that meets all the known empirical and conceptual constraints?"

IX

Let me return to the theme of epistemic paternalism, first illustrated with the rejection of C-RTE. To the extent that traditional epistemology has been attentive to the existence of multiple agents, it has generally assumed an idealized setting, in which all agents have the same cognitive resources, skills, and opportunities, where there are no time constraints, and so forth. In that sort of setting, a communication control principle like C-RTE might make sense. But in settings marked by different levels of expertise, by different opportunities for information gathering, by different levels of cognitive maturity and training, and by severe time constraints, idealized principles of communication do not plausibly apply. A social epistemology for the real world needs to take these constraints into account.[29]

The very question of communication control policy is relatively neglected in philosophy,[30] perhaps because the topic has been so thoroughly dominated by the Millian dedication to a free market of ideas. Interestingly, though, organized science and scholarship are very far from laissez-faire marketplaces. On the contrary, professional journals rely heavily on (putatively) expert referees and editors to weed out inferior contributions. Only offerings that are judged methodologically sound, well-informed, and possibly in the direction of truth are accepted for publication (or, in a related arena, given research funding). Thus, even in the purely intellectual sphere, laissez faire is not the de facto policy. More precisely, there is a complex layering of institutions. In free societies, governments pursue the laissez-faire policy of allowing private information channels to proliferate. But these information channels may themselves be highly restrictive in the messages they transmit. It could be argued that successful pursuit of epistemic ends depends not only on "deregulation" at the highest level, but on wise regulation at lower levels. This problem needs a more subtle and systematic examination than it has hitherto received. The present paper is intended to help motivate such an examination.

ALVIN I. GOLDMAN

University of Arizona

---

[29] I stress a similar theme of psychological realism in *Epistemology and Cognition*. Issues raised for moral theory by cognitive limits are stressed by Holly M. Smith in "Making Moral Decisions," *Nous*, XXI (1988): 89–108, and "Two-Tier Moral Codes," *Social Philosophy and Policy*, VII, 1 (1989): 112–32.

[30] One author who stresses the role of communication in a theory of rationality, however, is Jürgen Habermas, *The Theory of Communicative Action, vol. 1, Reason and the Rationalization of Society*, Thomas McCarthy, trans. (Boston: Beacon, 1981).

[9]

Copyright 1984 by Northwestern University School of Law
Northwestern University Law Review

Printed in U.S.A.
Vol. 78, No. 5

REVIEW ESSAY

THE IMPOSSIBILITY OF A FREE SPEECH PRINCIPLE*

Lawrence Alexander**
Paul Horton***

Philosopher: I search for a Free Speech Principle, a principle (or particular, idiosyncratic conflux of principles) that serves to make "freedom of speech" (or "freedom of speech and press") into a concept that understandably is to be distinguished from other concepts, principles, or confluences of principles.

Bystander: I guess that's a worthwhile undertaking. But what do you mean by "speech" and by "freedom of speech," and why are you engaged in such a search?

Philosopher: We will get to these matters down the line. In the interim, what do you mean by "mean"?

The topic of "freedom of speech" historically has invited considerable attention from professional philosophers and philosophically oriented lawyers. Thus approached, the topic has entailed a search for underlying principles or values that might be found to identify—and then to support—"speech" and "press" as independent freedoms.[1]

Several reasons may be proffered for the special philosophical popularity enjoyed by theories of "freedom of speech."[2] One reason is

---

* We dedicate this essay to Nat Nathanson, superb colleague and dear friend.

** Professor of Law, University of San Diego. B.A. 1965, Williams College; LL.B. 1968, Yale University.

*** Professor of Law, University of San Diego. A.B. 1965, Occidental College; J.D. 1968, University of Southern California; LL.M. 1969, Yale University.

[1] We view "freedom of the press" as totally encompassed within and redundant of "freedom of speech," and thus will use the latter phrase to embody both concepts. Our view— the orthodox view of both the Supreme Court and legal scholars—has evoked some notable dissent. *See, e.g.*, Nimmer, *Introduction—Is Freedom of the Press a Redundancy: What Does It Add to Freedom of Speech?*, 26 HASTINGS L.J. 639 (1975); Stewart, *"Or of the Press*," 26 HASTINGS L.J. 639 (1975); *But see* Lange, *The Speech and Press Clauses*, 23 UCLA L. REV. 77 (1975).

[2] Similar philosophical searches have been conducted for the underlying principles and values that identify and support "privacy," "basic lifestyle choices," "religion," "property," "equal protection," and "procedural fairness" as independent freedoms or rights. *See, e.g.*, B. ACKERMAN, PRIVATE PROPERTY AND THE CONSTITUTION (1977) (property); D. RICHARDS, SEX, DRUGS, DEATH, AND THE LAW (1982) (basic lifestyle choices); Perry, *Modern Equal Protection: A Concep-*

NORTHWESTERN UNIVERSITY LAW REVIEW

that philosophers have had considerable influence on the lawyers and judges who have fashioned the constitutional doctrines of freedom of speech. Mill and Meiklejohn immediately come to mind.[3] Contemporary philosophers Thomas Scanlon, Ronald Dworkin, David Richards, and Joel Feinberg also are likely to have lasting influence on the development of free speech principles.[4] Surely professional philosophers must find especially attractive an area in which their efforts are eagerly perused by important societal policy makers.

Another reason is that we have a pre-legal concept of "free speech." This pre-legal concept produces clear intuitions in some cases but cloudy or conflicting intuitions in others, thus leading us to search for philosophical clarification. Philosophers have tended to begin with the clear intuitions, to attempt to construct a theory that accounts for them, and then to revise both the theory and the intuitions until "reflective equilibrium" is achieved.[5] The lawyers then attempt to employ this philosophically articulated intuition in order to reach one conclusion or another in the cases in which pre-legal intuition has proved to be cloudy or conflicting.

Other reasons can be adduced to explain why philosophical treatment of freedom of speech concepts might prove especially influential with American lawyers and judges. Our federal and state constitutions announce specific protections for speech and press. A judge or constitutional lawyer might adhere to a theory of constitutional language that identifies certain words and phrases, such as "freedom of speech" or "freedom of press," as especially "theory-laden."[6] Alternatively, he or she might adhere to a theory of the Constitution that requires the construction of the best political or moral theory that would account for its

---

tualization and Appraisal, 79 COLUM. L. REV. 1023 (1979) (equal protection). Often, however, these searches have concluded with a denial that the particular freedom or right in question is supported by its own independent principle or value. *See, e.g.*, Alexander, *Modern Equal Protection Theories: A Metatheoretical Taxonomy and Critique*, 42 OHIO ST. L.J. 3 (1981) (equal protection); Alexander & Horton, Ingraham v. Wright: *A Primer for Cruel and Unusual Jurisprudence*, 52 S. CAL. L. REV. 1305 (1979) (procedural fairness); Westen, *The Empty Idea of Equality*, 95 HARV. L. REV. 537 (1982) (equal protection).

[3] J.S. MILL, ON LIBERTY (D. Spitz ed. 1975); Meiklejohn, *Free Speech and its Relation to Self-Government*, in POLITICAL FREEDOM: THE CONSTITUTIONAL POWERS OF THE PEOPLE (1965).

[4] The pertinent works of Scanlon, Dworkin, and Richards are cited *infra* notes 43, 35, 7, & 93. Professor Feinberg has devoted most of his considerable philosophical attention in the area of freedom of speech to offensive and obscene speech. *See, e.g.*, Feinberg, *Harmless Immoralities and Offensive Nuisances*, in ISSUES IN LAW AND MORALITY 83 (N. Care & T. Trelogan eds. 1973); Feinberg, *Pornography and the Criminal Law*, 40 U. PITT. L. REV. 567 (1979). Occasionally, however, he has dealt with other free speech topics. *See, e.g.*, Feinberg, *Limits to the Free Expression of Opinion*, in PHILOSOPHY OF LAW 191 (J. Feinberg & H. Gross eds. 2d ed. 1980).

[5] *See* J. RAWLS, A THEORY OF JUSTICE 48-51 (1971); Daniels, *Wide Reflective Equilibrium and Theory Acceptance*, 76 J. PHIL. 256 (1979).

[6] *See* Schauer, *An Essay on Constitutional Language*, 29 UCLA L. REV. 797, 824-28 (1982).

78:1319 (1983) *Essay*

language.[7] In either event, interpretation of the Constitution's words and phrases would require us to go outside the language of ordinary legal discourse and into the domain of political and moral theory for explanations of the constitutional text.

For these and other reasons, freedom of speech is, and probably will remain, a favorite topic for philosophers. In this essay, we will examine in some detail an important recent philosophical contribution—the work of Frederick Schauer, a philosophically oriented lawyer—to the topic of freedom of speech and its underlying principles.[8]

Schauer is a philosophical pluralist, at least when it comes to constitutional interpretation.[9] Thus, he sets out to formulate a theory of freedom of speech as an *independent* political/moral principle of general application, rather than as a principle that is derived from some more general principle of liberty.[10] Both the structure of our federal Constitution, with its separate free speech and free press clauses, and our ordinary, pre-legal discourse about free speech appear to presuppose that free speech is an independent concept supported by an independent principle or special conflux of principles.[11]

The burden of our essay is to demonstrate that Schauer's attempt to formulate cogently and to justify an independent Free Speech Principle is a failure. We believe this failure is an inevitable result of Schauer's conception of his project, which is to uncover an independent principle for something called "speech." In focusing on Schauer's theory, we do not intend to take him specially to task; rather, we believe his powerful effort exemplifies both the strengths and the weaknesses of all attempts to make free speech into an independent value or principle. For these reasons, we believe the use of Schauer's work as our foil will serve us well in our larger project, which is to demonstrate that "freedom of speech" is not an independent concept with a supporting principle, or idiosyncratic conflux of principles, all its own.

Basically, we contend that within any plausible deontological theory—any theory that treats certain acts, such as infringements of individual autonomy, as forbidden regardless of their consequences—"freedom of speech" will not have its own principle, but instead will be part of a more general liberty. And the same will be true for "freedom

---

[7] Ronald Dworkin and David Richards are two philosophers of the United States Constitution who take such a tack. *See* R. DWORKIN, TAKING RIGHTS SERIOUSLY 81-130 (1977); D. RICHARDS, THE MORAL CRITICISM OF LAW 51-54 (1977); Dworkin, *No Right Answer?*, in LAW, MORALITY, AND SOCIETY 58 (P. Hacker & J. Raz eds. 1977). This approach has been criticized vigorously. *See, e.g.*, Alexander & Bayles, *Hercules or Proteus? The Many Theses of Ronald Dworkin*, 5 SOC. THEORY & PRAC. 267 (1980); Schauer, *supra* note 6, at 814-21.

[8] F. SCHAUER, FREE SPEECH: A PHILOSOPHICAL ENQUIRY (1982).

[9] *See* Schauer, *Codifying the First Amendment*: New York v. Ferber, 1982 SUP. CT. REV. 285, 310-13; Schauer, *supra* note 6, at 820-21.

[10] F. SCHAUER, *supra* note 8, at 4-7.

[11] *Id.* at 6.

NORTHWESTERN UNIVERSITY LAW REVIEW

of speech" within any plausible consequentialist theory of general application that attempts to achieve a certain level or distribution of some value such as "utility," "autonomy" (as a condition to be achieved), or "truth."[12]

"Speech," we contend, does not denote any particular set of phenomena. Everything, including all human activities, can "express" or "communicate," and an audience can derive meaning from all sorts of human and natural events. Moreover, "speech" is regulated and affected by regulation in a multitude of different ways and for a multitude of different reasons. Finally, with respect to any value, "speech" both serves and disserves that value in an indefinite variety of ways and degrees. Considering these points, it would be truly amazing if "freedom of speech" really did have a coherent and independently justifiable principle all its own.

The demonstration of these matters proceeds along the following course. First, relying heavily on Schauer's work, we review the main "positive" theories for an independent Free Speech Principle of general application and expose their weaknesses. Then we take up Schauer's "negative" Free Speech Principle and demonstrate its deficiencies. Finally, we identify the criteria that we think any coherent and general theory of freedom of speech must fulfill, and we embellish our doubts that any theory could successfully establish and justify free speech as an independent value or principle of general application.

SCHAUER'S CRITIQUE OF OTHER FREE SPEECH THEORIES

Schauer begins his search for a Free Speech Principle by clarifying the form that such a principle must take. Then, in what may be his most valuable contribution to free speech theory, Schauer proceeds to canvass all of the major theories that have been offered to justify and delimit a Free Speech Principle. With one possible exception, we concur with Schauer's treatment of these matters; his canvass serves our purposes well, and we summarize it here.

---

[12] We are not entirely happy dividing moral theories into the categories of deontological and consequentialist (teleological), and we are acutely aware of the notorious difficulties that are entailed in making the distinction between them. If the notion of "consequences" is expansive enough, there obviously is a sense in which all theories are consequentialist. Nevertheless, we think a useful line can be drawn between those theories that begin with values and then characterize acts as right or wrong depending upon the effects of those acts in terms of promoting those values, and perhaps promoting a particular distribution of those values, and those theories that characterize acts as right or wrong regardless of their effects on the sum and distribution of values. *See* J. KUPPERMAN, THE FOUNDATIONS OF MORALITY (1983); S. SCHEFFLER, THE REJECTION OF CONSEQUENTIALISM (1982). Thus, Nozick, for example, is a paradigmatic deontologist because he disallows, except in catastrophic circumstances, all nonconsensual appropriations of others' bodies, labor, or talents, including even those appropriations that ultimately reduce the total number of such appropriations. R. NOZICK, ANARCHY, STATE, AND UTOPIA 28-33 (1974). There is no easy way to translate a deontologist's criteria of right and wrong into a calculus of value.

78:1319 (1983) *Essay*

Schauer posits that any independent Free Speech Principle will entail the demand that government must justify any restriction of speech covered by that Principle with reasons that are weightier than those we ordinarily accept as justifying governmental restrictions of our conduct.[13] Any Free Speech Principle is a side-constraint, not necessarily absolute in form or effect, on governmental policies that are otherwise justifiable under whatever political theory we may accept.[14] Thus, for example, if one generally accepts a slight gain in total societal welfare as a justification for governmental regulation of individual activity, then the existence of a Free Speech Principle would require, at a minimum, a greater-than-slight gain in welfare to justify regulation of speech covered by the Principle. In this essay, we do not quarrel with Schauer's requirements for an independent Principle.

Schauer's canvass of other free speech theories may be divided into three parts. First, he critiques theories that view freedom of speech primarily as a socially useful device. Next, he critiques a variety of "individualistic" theories. Finally, he concludes his survey with a discussion of the disutility of governmental suppression of speech.

"Freedom of Speech" and Social Utility

Schauer identifies two theories that view freedom of speech primarily in terms of a socially useful device. The first such theory is the "argument from truth," and the second is the "argument from democracy."

The argument from truth posits that unrestricted speech is essential to the quest for knowledge and the discovery of error. Schauer, like many others, points out two major flaws in such an argument. First, there is no empirical support for the notions that reason prevails in society, or that truth has the inherent power to defeat error.[15] Second, the quest for knowledge is not a value that has clear priority over many other values that might be disserved by free speech.[16] Speech, Schauer observes, is not self-regarding conduct. Rather, speech frequently can cause harm to others' interests, some of which are at least as important as the quest for, and possession of, knowledge.[17]

Schauer does extract a useful notion from the argument from truth: Because persons in government are fallible in their judgments and rarely are pure in their motives, there is considerable danger in entrusting government with the authority to determine what is true and false, or what is right and wrong.[18] This notion provides Schauer with

---

[13] F. SCHAUER, *supra* note 8, at 7-8.

[14] *Id*. at 8.

[15] *Id*. at 33.

[16] *Id*.

[17] *Id*. at 10-12.

[18] *Id*. at 34.

NORTHWESTERN UNIVERSITY LAW REVIEW

a bridge to the second social-good argument.

The argument from democracy has two strands. The first strand is the requirement that citizens, for intelligent self-government, must have the fullest possible information about every subject of democratic decisionmaking.[19] The second strand is that democratic theory posits "the people" as masters and "government" as servant, a relation that renders anomalous any attempt at governmental censorship.[20]

Although he does not totally reject the argument from democracy, Schauer does find this argument to be incomplete as a broad principle. The argument from democracy, Schauer argues, is most plausible as a justification for treating a narrow category of speech—"political speech"—as especially important.[21] Accordingly, Schauer notes that free speech is a problematic derivative of the concept of popular sovereignty, because it represents a limit on popular sovereignty itself. There is nothing "undemocratic" about censorship that is directed or ratified by majority vote.[22]

If free speech is a part of democratic theory, it must be because its restriction is an affront to more basic principles that underlie representative government, such as equality of respect for individuals.[23] If such a principle as "equality of respect for individuals" is what justifies freedom of speech—an idea Schauer examines later in his critique[24]—then freedom of speech is not an independent principle.

Moreover, the "full information" aspect of the argument from democracy tends to presuppose a "town meeting" model of self-government. To the extent it is based on this presupposition, the argument is weakened considerably by the failure of politics in modern western democracies to function like a town meeting.[25]

"Freedom of Speech" and Individualism

Schauer next turns to individualistic theories that have been advanced to support freedom of speech as an independent principle. These theories justify freedom of speech by resort to its contribution to the good of individuals or to respect for individual worth. We follow

---

[19] *Id.* at 38.

[20] *Id.* at 38-39.

[21] *Id.* at 45-46.

[22] *Id.* at 41.

[23] *Id.* at 41-42.

[24] *Id.* at 61-66.

[25] *Id.* at 43. As support for an independent Free Speech Principle, the argument from democracy largely dovetails with the argument from truth in producing a special distrust of the judgment and motives of governmental censors, though the former argument adds the point that censorship of political speech is particularly dangerous because of free speech's "checking" value. *Id.* at 44-46.

78:1319 (1983)   *Essay*

Schauer's critique here in all respects save one, and divide our discussion accordingly.

Stock Theories. —First, Schauer examines the theory that freedom of speech is justified by its contribution to the good of individual self-expression. He correctly observes that all conduct, not merely speech, can be self-expression. Thus, "freedom of speech as freedom of self-expression" collapses into a general principle of freedom of action, and fails to support freedom of speech as an independent principle.[26]

The same objection may be lodged against theories that link freedom of speech with the individual good of diverse lifestyle choices. These theories posit that a society that promotes free speech is much more likely than a society that suppresses speech to present an individual with a smorgasbord of possible values from which to choose. Schauer correctly responds that, to the extent such a theory does not overlap with the "argument from truth" (in which diversity is instrumental to the quest for knowledge), it supports a general principle of freedom of action, not an independent Free Speech Principle.[27]

Next, Schauer examines the theory that freedom of speech is justified by its contribution to individual self-development. The emphasis of such a theory is on the listener—the recipient of ideas—rather than on the speaker. Schauer agrees that freedom of speech—here, freedom of communication—is important to individual fulfillment.[28] He correctly argues, however, that the importance of free speech in this regard fails to generate an independent Free Speech Principle for two reasons. First, other interests besides the intellectual interests in communicating are just as important for self-fulfillment; yet not all of those equally important interests can be side-constraints.[29] Second, even if the intellectual development fostered by free speech has primacy among basic needs, *experiences* can be just as important as speech in fostering that development; yet there can be no "freedom to experience" principle.[30]

Next, Schauer examines theories positing that suppression of speech violates the right of individuals to equal respect. According to these theories, suppression of speech shows lack of respect for the speaker and his or her ideas, and thus affronts the speaker's dignity. Schauer first points out that only the most extreme skeptic would deny that some people's ideas *are* better than others',[31] and that equality of respect does not require equality of treatment in the realm of ideas any

---

[26] *Id.* at 52, 93.

[27] *Id.* at 67.

[28] *Id.* at 55.

[29] "The Free Speech Principle, if it exists, operates as a side constraint, or trump. But if all of the suits are trumps, we are in effect playing at no trumps." *Id.* at 55-56.

[30] *Id.* at 56-57.

[31] *Id.* at 62.

NORTHWESTERN UNIVERSITY LAW REVIEW

more than elsewhere.[32] Schauer then observes that proponents of these theories link freedom of speech with freedom from paternalistic regulation of self-regarding behavior;[33] thus, these theories suffer not only because speech is *not* self-regarding behavior, but also because the Free Speech Principle is not then independent but rather is linked with a broader principle of freedom from paternalistic intervention.[34]

Scanlon's Theory.—The final individualistic theory is associated with Thomas Scanlon's first article on free expression.[35] Scanlon's argument is that autonomous individuals, in something like a Rawlsian "original position," would refuse to cede authority to government either to decide what the individual should believe or to prevent the individual from weighing reasons for action. Accordingly, even when government has legitimately prohibited a course of conduct, government may not interdict communication that urges disobedience to the prohibition, because the individual retains the right to decide whether disobedience is justified.[36]

In our opinion, Schauer's response to Scanlon is the weakest part of his critique of major free speech theories. He argues that Scanlon's position implies a right to disobey even good and just laws.[37] Scanlon's principle of autonomy, however, does not entail a right, even a moral right, to disobey. A right to make up one's own mind regarding whether there are persuasive reasons for disobedience does not entail a right to disobey.[38] Perhaps there is something paradoxical about a legal right to communicate reasons to disobey laws, but there is nothing illogical about such a right.[39]

Instead of entailing a right to disobey, Scanlon's principle rests on something like the moral autonomy of the individual that is reflected in the Publicity Principle. The Publicity Principle, which many philosophers claim is a metaethical requirement for any valid normative system,[40] rules out of bounds any set of normative principles that cannot

---

[32] *Id.* at 63.

[33] *Id.* at 65.

[34] *Id.*

[35] Scanlon, *A Theory of Freedom of Expression*, 1 PHIL. & PUB. AFF. 204 (1972).

[36] F. SCHAUER, *supra* note 8, at 69-70.

[37] *Id.* at 70.

[38] One might as well argue that because no legal regime could ever recognize a right to disobey valid laws, the whole topic of disobedience could be banned from the classroom and parlor as well as from the streets.

[39] Moreover, the paradox really is part of the paradoxical nature of legal authority—the authority, perhaps morally justified, to exclude from consideration all non-legally recognized reasons for action. *See* J. RAZ, THE AUTHORITY OF LAW 21-33 (1979).

[40] *See* J. RAWLS, *supra* note 5, at 133. *See also* Alexander, *supra* note 2, at 13 n.41; Alexander, *Painting Without The Numbers: Noninterpretive Judicial Review*, 8 U. DAYTON L. REV. 447, 460 n.52 (1983).

78:1319 (1983) *Essay*

be publicized without thereby becoming self-defeating.[41]

It is possible that a morally proper law might justifiably punish conduct that itself was morally justifiable.[42] According to Scanlon, however, no morally proper law can deny individuals the right to decide that disobedience is justifiable. *A fortiori*, no legal system legitimately can preclude individuals from assessing the reasons for disobeying laws that may not be morally justifiable, even though, from the legal system's point of view, every valid law is justifiably to be enforced.

Thus, Schauer has not effectively challenged Scanlon's theory of freedom of speech. Scanlon himself, however, has identified some of the problems with that theory.[43] Moreover, as we point out later in this essay, deontological theories like Scanlon's must meet formidable challenges other than the challenge Schauer has offered.

On the other hand, Schauer also runs into trouble when he comments that Scanlon's theory, as contrasted with the other individualistic theories, has the advantage of dealing specifically with speech rather than with a broader range of conduct.[44] Although Schauer is technically correct here—in that Scanlon deals exclusively with speech—Scanlon's theory cannot be divorced meaningfully from a more general theory of individual autonomy that entails principles going beyond freedom of speech. The same view that deems it wrong to conceal from an individual arguments or principles that he or she might misuse strongly suggests a more general anti-legal-moralism and anti-paternalism. These matters will be embellished later in our essay.

The Disutility of Governmental Suppression of Speech

Schauer concludes his survey of freedom of speech theories with a discussion of the disutility of governmental suppression of speech. Here he identifies the argument, traceable to Mill, that the challenge of false doctrine aids the intellectual development of individuals. (Previously Schauer had accepted the notion that free communication about political matters may be useful as a means of keeping government responsive and responsible, of checking governmental abuses and ineptitude.[45]) Schauer observes that this argument largely dovetails with the

---

[41] For example, if by publicly proclaiming that act-utilitarianism is the proper principle for everyone to follow, we would produce less utility than if we were publicly to proclaim that some other principle was correct; and if act-utilitarianism thereby requires that we *not* publicly proclaim its correctness, then act-utilitarianism cannot be a proper normative principle according to the metaethical Publicity Principle.

[42] *See* R. SARTORIUS, INDIVIDUAL CONDUCT AND SOCIAL NORMS 51-80 (1975).

[43] Scanlon, *Freedom of Expression and Categories of Expression*, 40 U. PITT. L. REV. 519, 532-34 (1979).

[44] F. SCHAUER, *supra* note 8, at 71.

[45] *Id*. at 44.

NORTHWESTERN UNIVERSITY LAW REVIEW

"argument from truth," and correctly concludes that it suffers from the same problems as that argument—namely, that the benefits of the quest for truth may be outweighed by its dangers.[46]

Another argument examined by Schauer is that suppression of false doctrine is counter-productive because suppression actually produces more interest in and support for the false doctrine than would the free promulgation of the doctrine.[47] After recognizing that this argument has some plausibility based on human experience, Schauer concludes that empirical support for the argument is too uncertain to support the generation of a Free Speech Principle.[48] He reaches the same conclusion with respect to the theory that nonsuppression of speech allows "letting off steam" and thus provides a safety valve for the energies of opposition that otherwise would produce violence and instability.[49]

As previously stated, we concur almost entirely with Schauer's survey and critique of the major theories that attempt to support "freedom of speech" as an independent principle. Our only significant disagreement is with Schauer's treatment of Scanlon's theory—a theory that we find to be deficient for reasons other than those that lead Schauer to reject it. What, then, remains to support an independent Free Speech Principle? Schauer finds that something still remains. We now turn to an examination of Schauer's attempt to construct a new Free Speech Principle.

SCHAUER'S "NEGATIVE FREE SPEECH PRINCIPLE" (AND A THIRD-PARTY REJOINDER)

Schauer's powerful critique—the first section of his book—is addressed to "positive theories" that purport to justify an independent Free Speech Principle. These positive theories attempt to identify some individual or collective good that free speech uniquely facilitates, or some individual or collective harm that suppression of free speech uniquely produces.

The final theory that Schauer turns to—and endorses—is what he calls "the argument from governmental incompetence."[50] The argument from governmental incompetence is a negative theory: it purports to justify an independent Free Speech Principle not based *per se* on the positive good of free speech or the positive harm of its denial, but rather on the unique inability of government officials to weigh properly the costs and benefits of suppressed speech.[51]

---

46 *Id.* at 74-75.
47 *Id.* at 75-78.
48 *Id.* at 77.
49 *Id.* at 78-80.
50 *Id.* at 86.
51 *Id.* at 80-86.

78:1319 (1983) *Essay*

Schauer's Theory

As Schauer puts it, "[f]reedom of speech is based in large part on a distrust of the ability of . . . governmental determinations of truth and falsity, an appreciation of the fallibilty of political leaders, and a somewhat deeper distrust of governmental power in a more general sense."[52] Already the question is presented: How can such an "argument from governmental incompetence" be used to support "freedom of speech" as an *independent* principle, rather than as merely a part of a broader principle of "distrust of governmental power in a more general sense"?

Schauer's answer to this queston is that governmental officials tend to engage in over-suppression of speech because of self-interest and the slippery-slope quality of attempts to regulate and distinguish among types of speech.[53] To Schauer, a negative justification for the Free Speech Principle operates to ensure that speech is given its proper weight in government policy; speech receives special protection in order to counteract the government's tendency to over-suppress speech relative to other activities.[54]

How would such a negative Free Speech Principle work? Schauer, in a section of his book called "Explication," attempts to describe its operation. The description, even on its own terms, is not problem-free.

Schauer first discusses the meaning of "speech." He concludes that "speech," for purposes of his Free Speech Principle, must be equated with "communication" generally, rather than with some more restricted and artificial category like "written words" or "phonemes."[55] We are fully prepared to accept such a broad domain for "speech." Our question then becomes: How can we differentiate this "speech"— "communication," or perhaps *the* "communication"—from the rest of individual or collective activities in a way that permits *any* Free Speech Principle to have a discrete area of application?

Schauer's response to this important question is difficult to discern. In one place he asserts that the Free Speech Principle should not apply without "communicative intent, a communicated message, and a recipient of the communication."[56] Once the superficial plausibility of such an assertion is dissected, several problems appear.

One formidable problem lies in determining the meanings to be attributed to the three components that Schauer identifies. What is meant by "communicative intent"? For example, does "communicative intent" belong to the "speaker," or does it belong to the "recipient" as well? Suppose the "speaker" had "communicative intent" but

---

[52] *Id.* at 86.
[53] *Id.* at 82-85.
[54] *Id.* at 80-81.
[55] *Id.* at 91-101.
[56] *Id.* at 98.

NORTHWESTERN UNIVERSITY LAW REVIEW

the "recipient" did not; or suppose the "recipient" had "communicative intent," but the "speaker" did not; what then? What if the "communicated message" was X from the speaker's point of view, but was Y (or $X + 3$ or $X - 3$) from the recipient's point of view? What is the meaning, or character, or range of meanings and characters, to be attributed to "communication," "intent," "message," and "recipient," for purposes of ascertaining the ambit of a Free Speech Principle's operation?

Another formidable problem, at least for purposes of understanding Schauer's exegesis of his Free Speech Principle, is whether the three components of "communication" that he identifies are necessary for operation of the Principle. Does the Principle apply only to speech that includes, or but for governmental intervention would or could include, *all three* of these components: (1) "communicative intent," (2) "a communicated message," and (3) "a recipient of the communication"? Or would the Principle apply to speech that includes, or but for governmental intervention would or could include, fewer than all three?

Apparently Schauer's main response, at least to the latter problem, is to settle upon two targets for his Free Speech Principle and its operation. The Principle's target for protection seems to be the "recipient of the communication," while its primary target for interdiction seems to be government's motive for regulating activities. Thus, Schauer recognizes that freedom of speech is implicated under his negative Principle whenever government attempts to regulate the communicative impact of an activity, regardless of whether communication is the purpose of the activity.[57] If government forbade Schauer to view the Matterhorn in order to prevent him from being awed by it (rather than, for example, in order to effectuate environmental concerns), then this government regulation would fall within the jurisdiction of his Free Speech Principle.[58]

Thus, to Schauer, it is irrelevant whether a "message" is produced by a human author ("intending," for example, to reveal truth) or whether it is produced by the random banging of monkeys on typewriter keys. Government's motive to suppress speech—apparently, the reception of speech (at least predominantly)—is the key to Schauer's theory. When government is concerned with the communicative impact of the message on the audience, the message should be treated as "speech" for purposes of Schauer's Free Speech Principle.[59] (The point here has obvious importance for the debate over the free speech rights of corporate speakers.[60])

---

[57] *Id*. at 111. *See also id*. at 159.

[58] *Id*. at 98.

[59] *Id*. at 100, 159.

[60] *See* First National Bank of Boston v. Bellotti, 435 U.S. 765 (1978); Redish, *The Value of Free Speech*, 130 U. PA. L. REV. 591 (1982); Baker, *Realizing Self-Realization: Corporate Political Expenditures and Redish's* The Value of Free Speech, 130 U. PA. L. REV. 646 (1982); Redish, *Self-Realization, Democracy, and Freedom of Expression:*

78:1319 (1983) *Essay*

Defining "speech" by resort to government's motive for regulating, rather than by resort to the activity being regulated, does eliminate a major problem in defining "speech." That problem, of course, is that (1) all speech is symbolic conduct, (2) all conduct can be used by the actor to communicate meaning, and (3) from the point of view of those who "receive"—or "perceive"—conduct, all conduct does, in part, communicate meaning. The elimination of this problem, however, does not eliminate all problems in defining speech.

We will illustrate the problems that remain by employing one of Schauer's favorite topics, the governmental regulation of "hardcore pornography." Is hardcore pornography "speech" (and thus subject to the Free Speech Principle)? "No," Schauer answers. Hardcore pornography is merely a "sex aid"—like a vibrator, or like having two prostitutes engage in sex acts in front of a customer who has requested this method of arousal[61]—and a governmental motive to regulate "sex aids" does not implicate the Free Speech Principle.

Schauer's argument here moves much too quickly. In the first place, hardcore pornography, even to its recipients, is not always a sex aid; to some it communicates the potentiality and poses of the human body, and to others it communicates attitudes about women and children.[62] Put differently, hardcore pornography is, at best, a sex aid only from the point of view of *most* of its recipients.

Democracy, and Freedom of Expression: A Reply to Professor Baker, 130 U. Pa. L. Rev. 678 (1982).

[61] F. Schauer, *supra* note 8, at 181-82.

[62] Consider, for example, David Richards' suggestion:

[T]here is today in America substantial and growing disagreement regarding many questions of sexual and personal morality, a few of which have already surfaced dramatically in major constitutional adjudications. Part of this disagreement is over notions of proper sexual function, with serious arguments being proposed for major constitutional attacks on various statutes regulating sexual function. The revaluation of the obscene is one aspect of this debate. In this context, pornography can be seen as the unique medium of a vision of sexuality, a "pornotopia"—a view of sensual delight in the erotic celebration of the body, a concept of easy freedom without consequences, a fantasy of timelessly repetitive indulgence. In opposition to the Victorian view that narrowly defines proper sexual function in a rigid way that is analogous to ideas of excremental regularity and moderation, pornography builds a model of plastic variety and joyful excess in sexuality. In opposition to the sorrowing Catholic dismissal of sexuality as an unfortunate and spiritually superficial concomitant of propagation, pornography affords the alternative idea of the independent status of sexuality as a profound and shattering ecstacy.

D. Richards, The Moral Criticism of Law 71 (1977) (footnotes omitted). For a different view, see Bryant, *Sexual Display of Women's Bodies—A Violation of Privacy*, 10 Golden Gate 1211, 1224-27 (1980). The point made in the text, of course, may be carried far afield from pornography into the functions, meaning levels, and interpretative malleability of virtually all perceptive experiences. After all, we suspect that voyeurs in search of sex aids peruse medical texts—or legal scholarship about pornography that contains examples of the topic; why would they do so? (And why do we suspect that they do so?) *Cf.* L. Wittgenstein, Philosophical Investigations 11e (1953) ("Imagine a picture representing a boxer in a particular stance. Now, this picture can be used to tell someone how he should stand, should hold himself; or how he should not hold himself; or how a particular man did stand in such-and-such a place; and so on.").

NORTHWESTERN UNIVERSITY LAW REVIEW

Then does government's ability to regulate an activity (hardcore pornography) without implicating the Free Speech Principle now depend on the activity's "primary" use? Suppose there are more voyeurs who use the pictures in medical texts for sex aids than there are medical students who use the pictures for information relevant to the practice of medicine. Can the medical-text pictures be banned without implicating the Free Speech Principle? Or does the Principle force government to focus its regulations on particular uses, rather than on the items used?

The correct answer to these questions, according to Schauer's model, appears to be that government may regulate *any* activity without implicating the Free Speech Principle if its motive is anything other than the interdiction of communicative impact. In other words, the reasons why most people engage in the activity would not matter; rather, the government's motives for regulating would be the determinative factor. Thus, even medical texts that are used primarily by medical students rather than by voyeurs could be banned—at least without violating freedom of speech—if government's motive is to prevent their noncommunicative uses.[63]

The implications of Schauer's approach to the question "What is speech?" are sweeping. Those implications are that any communicative activity may be banned—at least without offending the Free Speech Principle—so long as government is concerned solely with the noncommunicative impact of the activity.[64] We are left to watch helplessly—again, so far as the Free Speech Principle is concerned—as government, acting in good faith, clears medical texts from the shelves.

In order to avoid this helplessness, Schauer would have to extend the Free Speech Principle to cover the impact on communication resulting from government regulations that concededly were directed at noncommunicative impact. *All* regulations, however, have communicative impact, whether or not they affect obvious "communication." Therefore, the Free Speech Principle could not function as an independent political/moral principle, demanding a weightier than normal justification for governmental regulation; if it did function as such an independent principle, either the phrase "weightier than normal justification" would have to become meaningless lip-service, or government would become an exercise in futility. For these reasons, Schauer must stick to his approach of defining speech in terms of government's reasons for regulating rather than in terms of the potential communica-

---

[63] Indeed, use of the word "mother" can be banned without violating freedom of speech if, for example, the word itself, or perhaps the letter "m," is owned by someone. *Cf.* Ely, *Flag Desecration: A Case Study in the Roles of Categorization and Balancing in First Amendment Analysis*, 88 HARV. L. REV. 1482, 1503-04 (1975).

[64] Of course, principles and constitutional norms other than freedom of speech might be implicated. But insofar as free speech is concerned, the absence of an overt or covert governmental concern with communicative impact would be dispositive.

78:1319 (1983)   *Essay*

tive uses of the activity regulated. Once more the spectre appears of government clearing medical texts off the shelves while concededly and meticulously following Schauer's Free Speech Principle.

Schauer's analysis of hardcore pornography regulation raises another tough problem. Assume that government bans hardcore pornography in order to prevent its use as a sex aid, and not for any other reason. Schauer says that such a ban, for such a motive, would not implicate his Free Speech Principle. But *why does government's banning the use of sex aids not implicate freedom of speech?*

After all, the harm that the government seeks to prevent by banning "hardcore pornography, a sex aid" is not masturbation, rape, or teenage pregnancy. The *communication* in hardcore pornography, not hardcore pornography itself, is what might lead to these other harms. The recipient of hardcore pornography receives a communication that produces a mental effect; the mental effect then may be translated by the recipient—now the actor—into unwanted activity. Put differently, the harm depends on the mental effect—the communication—that the sex aid produces in its user. If the physical effects of a sex aid are themselves produced by its recipient's mental experiences, or if government's true concern is with the mental states produced by the physical effects of sex, then government regulation of hardcore pornography surely invades the domain of Schauer's Free Speech Principle. At least, government regulation invades the Principle's domain if Schauer's theory is to be rendered internally consistent.[65]

We do not believe, at this level of analysis, that our illustrative critique of Schauer's discussion of hardcore pornography necessarily destroys the viability of his Free Speech Principle. Schauer's discussion of hardcore pornography, not his Free Speech Principle, may be the source of his difficulties. He is still free to revise, or perhaps to strengthen, his analysis of governmental interdiction of hardcore pornography without abandoning his Principle.

---

[65] Indeed, government's decision to ban "hard-core pornography, a sex aid" itself has communicative impact that, according to Schauer's Free Speech Principle, government would seem required to take into account. The government's ban tells potential hard-core pornography recipients that government considers (1) hard-core pornography to be primarily a sex aid, (2) use of sex aids is wrong, and (3) use of hard-core pornography for purposes other than as a sex aid are less important—less worthwhile; less necessary to be taken into account—than its use as a sex aid. Similarly, government's interdiction of Schauer's visit to the Matterhorn for motives of environmental protection communicates to Schauer that "environmental protection" is a more worthy value than "inspiring awe." These communicative impacts of governmental regulation clearly seem to fall within the ambit of Schauer's Free Speech Principle. *See infra* text accompanying note 105.

The point carries over into numerous other areas, including the debate over whether video games and other similar forms of entertainment are "speech." *See* Ziegler, *Trouble in Outer Galactica: The Police Power, Zoning, and Coin-operated Videogames*, 34 SYRACUSE L. REV. 453 (1983).

NORTHWESTERN UNIVERSITY LAW REVIEW

Schauer also fails to analyze carefully another problem involving the definition of "speech." Consider government actions that have as their motive the protection of people from communications that those people do not want to receive. Into this category fall laws banning offensive speech, the tort of intentional infliction of emotional distress, and even laws banning conduct, such as public nudity or fornication, that "communicates" unwanted messages to a nonconsenting audience. Do these governmental actions implicate Schauer's Free Speech Principle?

Schauer clearly believes that laws banning offensive speech do implicate his Principle.[66] Consistency would require Schauer to adopt the same stance regarding all of the examples mentioned in the previous paragraph. After all, by banning public nudity, government is attempting to interdict the same kind of communicative impact that results from offensive speech. Indeed, aesthetic regulations—and some bans on hardcore pornography—also may fall into the same category.[67]

A counterargument is available, however, to meet the contention that all these laws fall within the ambit of protected speech. This counterargument is at least consistent with Schauer's justification for his Free Speech Principle. In all of these examples, government is attempting to protect the recipient of the message in accordance with the recipient's own values and conceptions of truth. In other words, in none of these examples is government interdicting a communication because *government* believes the communication is untrue or because *government's* values differ from the recipient's values. In the paradigmatic instances of government violation of freedom of speech, however, government *does* attempt to prescribe for the recipients either what is true or what is important or safe to know. Thus, according to this counterargument, governmental regulations of offensive speech and its analogues do not fall within the ambit of the Free Speech Principle—an interesting and perhaps, to Schauer, unsettling point.[68]

---

[66] F. Schauer, *supra* note 8, at 147-48.

[67] *See* J. Hodson, The Ethics of Legal Coercion 140-50 (1983); Alexander, *Introduction: Motivation and Constitutionality*, 15 San Diego L. Rev. 925, 946-47 (1978) [hereinafter cited as Alexander, *Introduction*]; Alexander, *Liberalism as Neutral Dialogue: Man and Manna in the Liberal State*, 28 UCLA L. Rev. 816, 846-47 (1981); Dworkin, *Is There a Right to Pornography?*, 1 Oxford J. Leg. Stud. 177 (1981).

[68] At a still deeper level of analysis, however, regulations of offensive behavior arguably *do* implicate the Free Speech Principle. Why is certain behavior "offensive" to us? In many cases it is offensive because it suggests values and ideas that we strongly disagree with and, most important, that we do not wish others to hold. Public fornication, for example, may offend us because we fervently desire that others not hold certain values regarding sexual relations. In other words, the fact that we take offense is at some deep level a reflection of a censorial disposition that we possess. Regulation premised on offense of that nature represents what Dworkin calls the imposition of "external preferences," preferences about what others should do or believe. *See supra* note 67. On the other hand, if our interest in not being offended does not spring ultimately from censorial motives, the paragraph in accompanying text suggests that regulation to protect that

78:1319 (1983)   *Essay*

Again, we suspect that these matters are little more than important quibbles with the margins of Schauer's Free Speech Principle that go primarily to the way the "speech" that falls within the Principle's ambit of operation is defined. After discussing the meaning of "speech"—the scope of his Free Speech Principle—Schauer reaches a critical section of his argument, however, in which he attempts to describe how his Principle would deal with regulations of whatever "speech" falls within its ambit. It is here that our rejoinder turns from quibbling to full-fledged attack.

The model Schauer employs for handling free speech claims is that of a "thumb on the scales": a balancing-of-interests model in which speech is given a certain constant weight that, although unspecified, is equal to important or compelling government objectives. Schauer draws an analogy between this thumb-on-the-scales approach for speech and the approach of imposing a very severe burden of proof on government in order to avoid the conviction of innocent criminal defendants. According to Schauer, just as we consider one erroneous conviction to be as serious as, say, ten erroneous acquittals, so too do we consider a suppression of non-harmful speech to be much more serious than the non-suppression of harmful speech.[69]

Accordingly, Schauer proposes that we construct a balance on which to weigh—either on a case by case basis, or through the development of general categories and rules[70]—speech interests against governmental interests supporting suppression. In Schauer's view, we should construct this balance so that speech is weightier than other interests that are not the subjects of special anti-governmental political/moral principles.[71]

In short, Schauer's Free Speech Principle requires no more than a cost-benefit analysis, except that suppression of speech, when given its proper weight in that analysis, always requires a very high offsetting benefit. This cost-benefit model, Schauer contends, supports a Free Speech Principle that functions as an independent political/moral principle.

---

interest does not implicate freedom of speech. *See* Ellis, *Offense and the Liberty Conception of the Law*, 13 PHIL. & PUB. AFF. 3 (1984).

This last conclusion regarding offensive speech is somewhat reinforced by Schauer's discussion, following his discussion of the meaning of "speech," of speech whose context is excluded from the special protection of the Free Speech Principle precisely because the distrust of government premise that provides the negative justification for the Principle is inapplicable to such content. F. SCHAUER, *supra* note 8, at 101-02. Performative uses of speech ("I promise," "I give," etc.) are excluded. So, too, are some propositional uses, such as those that amount to fraud or perjury. *Id.* at 102-03. Schauer's treatment of the content boundaries of freedom of speech in this section of his book is generally incisive, though brief.

[69] F. SCHAUER, *supra* note 8, at 136-39, 141-44, 192.

[70] *Id.* at 135, 142-43.

[71] *Id.* at 133.

NORTHWESTERN UNIVERSITY LAW REVIEW

The Deficiencies of Schauer's Free Speech Principle

The time has come to assess Schauer's negative Free Speech Principle, rather than to skirmish around it. In order to do so we shall present four different models of that Principle. Schauer does not tell us which of these four models he has in mind. Each of these models is supported by some of Schauer's arguments, but none of them is consistent with all that Schauer claims. And each of these models requires a more general, positive theory of free speech—a positive theory that Schauer does not provide.

Two of these models of the Free Speech Principle focus on government's motives; two of them focus on the effects of government action. Two of these models are "judicial review" models, and two are not. We divide the four models, and analyze them, accordingly.

Model 1: Judicial Review for Improper Motivation of the Primary Governmental Decisionmaker: "Suspect Classifications" and "Compelling Interests."—The first way of conceptualizing Schauer's Principle is by analogy to judicial review of "suspect classifications" under the equal protecton clause of the United States Constitution. When government employs a particular form of regulation—one that contains "suspect classifications," such as classifications based on race or alienage—the courts demand the showing that a "compellng interest" supports government's employment of that form of regulation.

At first blush, the "compelling interest" model for judicial review of "suspect classifications" appears to be an appropriate model of Schauer's Principle. Schauer characterizes his Principle as being based upon a negative, distrust-of-government rationale. Most commentators maintain that courts demand a showing of compelling interest because, in the absence of such a showing, the probabilities are high that government has employed a suspect classification for forbidden reasons (such as reasons that reflect racial prejudice).[72] Proof of a compelling interest lowers the probability of forbidden reasons sufficiently to warrant judicial validation of the regulation.

Suppose that most instances of suppression of speech ostensibly based solely on ordinary governmental objectives, like most instances of suspect classifications, in fact result from improper governmental motives. Suppose further that most instances of suppression of speech ostensibly supported by very important governmental objectives in fact do not result from improper governmental motives. Then a test that requires an important governmental objective to justify a suppression of speech is a good evidentiary test for a court to employ.

Of course, if the "suspect classification" model is appropriate for his Free Speech Principle, then Schauer needs to tell us the meaning of

---

[72] *See* J. ELY, DEMOCRACY AND DISTRUST 145-70 (1980); Alexander, *supra* note 2, at 58-60.

78:1319 (1983)

"speech," or at least "suppression of speech," for purposes of the model. Put differently, Schauer must tell us what kinds of laws are "suppression of speech" laws, and thus are analogous to suspect classifications that trigger compelling-interest judicial review. The problem here is that all laws—and thus all possible sets of laws—"suppress" some speech; yet one cannot demand a compelling interest for everything government does or does not do.

Thus, in order to make the Free Speech Principle workable under this model, Schauer would have to pick out a particular category or categories of regulations as the focus of compelling interest review. Some of Schauer's discussion of the defamation and privacy torts could be developed into a general theory of "free speech suspect classifications,"[73] but that theory surely is not developed as yet.

If this first model is what Schauer has in mind for his Free Speech Principle, then some of his claims for the Principle are rather straightforwardly mistaken. For instance, his discussion of governmental advocacy and public education[74] seems insensitive to the close connection between the governmental motives behind indoctrination and the governmental motives behind suppression. After all, if suppression of speech without a compelling governmental interest violates the Free Speech Principle because of the likelihood of improper governmental motives and biased governmental judgments, then it appears that governmental advocacy should be held to violate the Principle for the same reasons.[75]

It is also important to note that this model of Schauer's Principle sets forth an evidentiary test, not a substantive test. Nevertheless, Schauer implies that his Free Speech Principle operates independently of judicial review: that is, that the Principle can be employed by the

---

[73] *See* F. Schauer, *supra* note 8, at 174-75.

[74] *Id.* at 155-56. *See also* Schauer, *Is Government Speech a Problem?* (Book Review), 35 Stan. L. Rev. 373 (1983).

[75] Moreover, Schauer's discussion of governmental advocacy and public education here seems inconsistent in tone if not content with his earlier discussion of the allocation of "privileges" on the basis of views expressed or held. In that earlier discussion, Schauer takes a more hostile attitude toward governmental attempts to influence opinion through rewards rather than punishments. F. Schauer, *supra* note 8, at 116-19. Government speech and the award of governmental largess to favored speakers surely are closely related issues.

One advantage that Schauer claims for his Principle is that it does not require special treatment of governmental regulations that are aimed at the noncommunicative impact of speech. *Id.* at 100-01, 204. Schauer surely would be mistaken if his model were intended as an implementation model for the primary governmental decisionmaker rather than as an evidentiary test for the courts that is based on the probability of improper motives. After all, speech, or speech with a specific content, can be suppressed as easily and as severely by regulations aimed at noncommunicative impact as by regulations aimed at communicative impact. If, however, we are concerned with government's motives, and not with the quantity or quality of speech that government's regulations permit, then Schauer's claim for his principle is more plausible, though, as we shall demonstrate, it is ultimately erroneous. *See infra* text accompanying notes 68-71.

NORTHWESTERN UNIVERSITY LAW REVIEW

primary governmental decisionmaker.[76] If, however, his Principle were modeled along the lines of compelling interest review of suspect classifications, Schauer's implication—that the Principle operates independently of judicial review—would be wrong unless the primary governmental decisionmaker were required to distrust its own motives. Unless the courts were to convert this evidentiary test into something else—a *per se* rule—the primary governmental decisionmaker would not be obligated to refrain from suppressing speech for ordinary governmental objectives, so long as it believed it was acting with proper motives.

When a court confronts a racial classification that is not supported by a compelling interest, it strikes down the classification. But the primary governmental decisionmaker may have employed the racial classification for proper, albeit not compelling, reasons.[77] In such a situation, it is accurate to assert that government acted constitutionally, but that its action was properly, though erroneously, held to be unconstitutional by the courts.

Conversely, when government acts for improper reasons but does not employ a suspect classification, the courts will uphold the action as "not unconstitutional" so long as some ostensible, legitimate interest for the action can be adduced, even though the action really is unconstitutional.[78] The courts cannot demand the showing of a compelling interest for all neutral classifications that have some disproportionate impact on groups that might be the targets of improper governmental motives. To do so would entail intolerable social costs.[79] Accordingly, the courts are put to upholding many laws that in fact were the products of an unconstitutional motivation, and hence are unconstitutional.

Thus, if Schauer's Free Speech Principle is understood to be analogous to compelling interest review of suspect classifications, the Principle speaks to reviewing courts, not to primary decisionmakers.

---

[76] F. Schauer, *supra* note 8, at 129-30.

[77] For example, a legislature may require blacks, but not whites, to be screened for genetic diseases, such as sickle-cell anemia. The legislature may have a non-prejudiced, rational, legitimate reason for the discrimination. Perhaps blacks are more subject to genetic diseases, or detectable genetic diseases, than whites. If equal protection forbids only irrational or prejudiced legislative action, the legislature has not violated equal protection. But unless its reason for discriminating can be deemed compelling, strict judicial scrutiny will result in judicial invalidation of the discriminatory requirement.

[78] For example, a legislature may require all applicants for a civil service position to take and pass a certain aptitude test, not because the test is the most job-related test available, but simply because the legislature predicts and hopes that blacks will fail the test—but not a more job-related test— in disproportionately high numbers. Because the test on its face is colorblind, the courts will review its use under a very lenient standard that the legislature surely can meet. The test will be upheld in court against a constitutional challenge despite its inherent unconstitutionality. *See* Brest, *The Conscientious Legislator's Guide to Constitutional Interpretation*, 27 Stan. L. Rev. 585 (1975).

[79] *See* Washington v. Davis, 426 U.S. 229, 248 (1976).

78:1319 (1983) *Essay*

Primary decisionmakers need only act with proper motives, not with compelling interests, even if their actions also suppress speech. Because Schauer denies that his Principle requires judicial review for its operation, there is good reason to doubt that the "compelling interests" model of the Principle is the model Schauer has in mind.

Moreover, Schauer's analogy to the thumb-on-the-scales approach in criminal trials furnishes another reason for doubting that he would adopt this "compelling interests" model for his Free Speech Principle. The thumb-on-the-scales approach in criminal trials is inapposite to compelling interests judicial review.

In criminal trials, our allocation of burdens of persuasion represents a balancing of the respective interests in convicting the guilty and acquitting the innocent. "Proof beyond reasonable doubt" represents neither a procedure for flushing out improper motives nor a procedure for reviewing the actions of the primary decisionmaker. Rather, this form of thumb-on-the-scales approach reflects the values that the primary decisionmaker itself—in criminal prosecutions, a jury or judge— must assign to particular outcomes. This approach thus requires a positive theory of values.

The analogy that Schauer draws between his Free Speech Principle and the allocation of burdens of persuasion in criminal trials, then, suggests that his conception of the Principle rests on a positive theory of the value of speech. Such a theory would construct a balance on which the primary decisionmaker could weigh speech against other interests. The analogy to criminal trials does not fit easily with a conception of the Free Speech Principle that focuses on judicial review for improper motives, as opposed to assessment by the primary decisionmaker of untoward effects.

This critique of Schauer's analogy to criminal trials brings us to the fundamental weakness of the first model for Schauer's Principle that we have been considering. This weakness is inherent in any negative theory of rights that is based on fear of improper governmental motives. Such theories ultimately must always be parasitic on positive theories: that is, we cannot know which governmental motives regarding speech are improper, or why they are improper, unless we first know which motives *are* proper, and why they are proper.

If Schauer's Free Speech Principle is modeled on compelling interest review of suspect classifications, then Schauer must identify both the motives that are improper and the theory that tells us why those motives are improper. However, Schauer clearly has not identified improper motives or the theory that proves their impropriety.[80] Thus

---

80 Such theories usually are deontological, like Scanlon's, though they can be consequentialist. (A consequentialist will absolutely forbid actions where based on particular motives when the consequences of such an absolute prohibition are better than the consequences of any alternative.) *See* Alexander, *Introduction, supra* note 67, at 934-35. In any event, Schauer has presented no

NORTHWESTERN UNIVERSITY LAW REVIEW

Schauer has presented no positive theory from which a theory of improper motives can be derived. The absence of such a presentation furnishes more evidence that Schauer would not endorse this "compelling interests" model for his Principle.

In sum, the model of the Free Speech Principle that compares it to compelling interest review of suspect classifications (1) requires a fuller elaboration of the indicia of "suspectness" than Schauer gives, (2) clashes with Schauer's claim that his Principle is not a principle of judicial review, (3) bears no resemblance to the allocation of burdens of persuasion in criminal trials, and (4) requires a positive theory, nowhere suggested by Schauer, for identifying proper and improper governmental motives. Hence, we believe it fair to conclude that this model is not what Schauer has in mind for his Free Speech Principle.

Model 2: Compelling Interests as Ingredients of Proper Motives. — The second model takes seriously Schauer's claim that his Free Speech Principle does not entail judicial review. According to this model, certain motives of the primary governmental decisionmaker underlying the suppression of speech—call them motives of suppression—are improper unless the decisionmaker is motivated not only by them but also by compelling interests. In other words, this model of the Free Speech Principle builds the compelling interests test into the concept of improper motive.

This model potentially does provide a Free Speech Principle that the primary decisionmaker can employ. Certain governmental motives for regulating speech are given weight (equal to compelling interests), but speech itself is not given weight. Moreover, this model fits better, though not with complete comfort, with Schauer's analogy to the criminal trial model; the analogy would fit if we were to view "punishing a person without proof of guilt beyond a reasonable doubt" as an act that is wrong without regard to further consequences.

What is missing from Schauer's work, however, is any elaboration and justification of this model or its underlying theory. Without such elaboration and justification, the assertion is pure *ipse dixit* that suppression of speech without a compelling interest is wrong without regard to any further consequences. The implicit theory for this model is similar to the theory of the first model we discussed, except that this second model does not absolutely proscribe the motives in question.[81]

In any event, there is good reason to doubt that Schauer embraces this model as the one that characterizes his Free Speech Principle, because Schauer repeatedly suggests that his Principle is based on distrust

---

positive theory from which a theory of improper motives can be derived, more evidence that the conception of his Principle under consideration is not his conception.

[81] *See supra* note 80.

78:1319 (1983)   *Essay*

of the primary governmental decisionmaker.[82] How would "distrust of the decisionmaker" fit into this model? Such distrust would have to be translated into "distrust by the decisionmaker of its own decisions." In order to make such a notion of distrust coherent, the decisionmaker would have to distrust its own assessment of the consequences of suppressing speech—for example, the consequences associated with the lost value of the speech suppressed versus the likelihood and importance of the goals served by its suppression.

This type of "distrust," however, differs from the categorical impropriety of speech-suppressing motives that characterizes this model. Put differently, this second model for the Free Speech Principle assumes, contrary to Schauer's basis for his Principle, that the primary governmental decisionmaker can be trusted to take speech and suppression-of-speech values into account. The model merely proscribes certain value rankings without regard to notions of trust or distrust.

Model 3: Judicial Review for Erroneous Assessments of Consequences by the Primary Decisionmaker: "Compelling Interests" as an Actuarial Gauge of the Primary Decisionmaker's Balancing of Effects, Their Value, and Their Probability.—A third model of Schauer's Free Speech Principle, like the first model we have identified, would view the Principle as one of judicial review. Unlike the first model, which was premised on a categorical assessment of motives underlying the regulation of speech, this model would be premised upon an underlying consequentialist theory. This model is based upon the following propositions:

(a) Both speech and suppression of speech have values.

(b) In order to make a correct decision regarding the regulation of speech, the primary decisionmaker must accurately assess the lost value of the speech suppressed and then weigh that value against the values served by its suppression, factored by the probability that the regulation will achieve the values of suppression.

(c) Certain types of regulations, because of the likelihood of bias or incompetency on the part of the primary decisionmaker, contain a high antecedent probability that either the value of suppression has been overestimated or the value of the speech regulated has been underestimated.

(d) The probability of miscalculation on the part of the primary decisionmaker is sufficiently reduced to justify a reviewing court in upholding the regulation only if the primary deci-

---

[82] F. SCHAUER, *supra* note 8, at 80-81, 86, 100-01, 105, 111, 124-25, 155, 162, 175, 177, 196, 204.

sionmaker proves that the regulation in fact serves a compelling interest.

The problem with this model for the Free Speech Principle—as Schauer recognizes[83]—is that a theory is inadequate that speaks only to judicial review of the primary governmental decisionmaker. This model takes the position that government should *not* be trusted to regulate speech as opposed to other activities (or to regulate some speech but not other speech), but should be trusted if it demonstrates a compelling interest. The question then goes beyond why such a position should be taken, to how such a position *could* be taken.

In order to implement such a position, the elaboration of a positive theory of speech is required. This positive theory would assign values to various types of speech, values that in turn could be weighed against the values underlying regulation of such speech. Without such a positive theory to refer to, the negative theory of distrust of the primary governmental decisionmaker can never satisfactorily establish free speech as an independent principle. Again, Schauer has not even attempted to provide a positive theory of freedom of speech; instead, he has seriously, and successfully, called into question all extant positive theories.

Thus, Model 3 leaves stringent judicial review of speech regulations unjustified and the primary governmental decisionmaker totally without guidance, beyond doing whatever comes naturally, concerning speech regulation.

Model 4: The Compelling Interest Test as the Primary Decisionmaker's Check on Its Own Assessments of Value. —The final model is the one that is most consistent with what Schauer has to say. According to this model, the Free Speech Principle is designed to tell the primary governmental decisionmaker to distrust its own assessments of the values at stake in certain types of speech regulation. That is, without a compelling interest, the primary decisionmaker's distrust of itself should lead it to forgo regulation.

True, government often operates under conditions of uncertainty. Will speech, if unsuppressed, lead to harm? Can that harm be averted through other means? These and similar questions often will be answerable only by resort to highly fallible legislative guesses. Those guesses can be "distrusted" for either of two reasons: (1) because they are guesses; (2) because they are the primary decisionmaker's guesses. The primary decisionmaker can engage in the first form of distrust with respect to any kind of regulation, not just regulation that suppresses speech. The second form of distrust perhaps is more applicable to spe-

---

[83] *Id.* at 129-30.

78:1319 (1983) *Essay*

cific types of regulation, such as regulation of speech. Schauer's theory points to the second form of distrust.

Once again, however, the principal difficulty with this model for the Free Speech Principle—and hence the inconsistency with Schauer's theory—is the absence of a positive theory that assigns values to speech. Unless we have such a theory, we cannot know what regulations of speech a trustworthy primary decisionmaker would enact; unless we know what regulations a trustworthy decisionmaker would enact, we cannot justify our distrust of actual primary decisionmakers. At least we cannot justify the compelling interest test as the measure of distrust.

With respect to regulation aimed at communicative impact, consider what would be needed under this model in order to answer questions such as these:

(a) If the primary governmental decisionmaker is reponsible for constructing the proper balance on which to weigh speech against other interests, how much weight should it assign to speech?

(b) What weight should be attached to advocacy that threatens to incite others to crime? What weight should be attached to speech that threatens to provoke a hostile audience? What weight should be attached to speech that threatens to reveal confidential information, or to infringe a copyright, or to deceive consumers?

Unless it is never proper to suppress activity because of its communicative impact, the primary decisionmaker, acting properly, will assign a finite weight to "communicative impact," and will employ that weight in the balance that this model requires the decisionmaker to construct. Nevertheless, the decisionmaker is left with more questions:

(c) What is that weight?

(d) How was that weight selected?

(e) Why was that weight, as opposed to a greater or lesser weight, selected?

(f) Should the weight accorded to communicative impact be a constant one, or should it vary with the subject matter of the speech?

(g) Should the weight assigned to communicative impact vary with its specific viewpoint, its probable truth, or the frequency with which it has been or likely will be aired?

According to the model presently before us, all these questions must be answered. These questions will be answered, somehow, by the responsible primary governmental decisionmaker when it considers regulation aimed at the communicative impact—the "speech component"—of an activity. Sometimes these questions will be answered in favor of "freedom of speech"; other times they will be answered in favor of "suppression of speech." Without a positive theory of speech to guide its processes, however, the answers to these questions will lack

NORTHWESTERN UNIVERSITY LAW REVIEW

cogency and trustworthiness even to the primary governmental decisionmaker.

Schauer might attempt to avoid the need for a positive theory of speech by arguing that, with respect to regulations of communicative impact, government should never assess the truth or importance of speech, or of certain categories of speech. The most plausible interpretation of such a position would be that government must treat all speech as infinitely important. If accepted, this extreme position would disable government from ever regulating the communicative impact of an activity (or of an activity with a communicative impact that fell into specified categories) no matter how grave the harm threatened by that activity.

Even such an extreme position fails to escape the need for a positive theory of speech. That is so because *all* governmental action (or inaction) affects to some degree, often greatly, what is said, by whom, to whom, how often, and how effectively. In addition, the value of what is said, by whom, to whom, how often, and how effectively, remains the same regardless of whether the government action (or inaction) that affects it is aimed at communicative impact.

This observation surely is accurate with respect to the myriad of so-called "time, place, and manner" restrictions. For example, banning all leafletting in airports will disproportionately affect the dissemination of the views of Hare Krishnas and Jehovah's Witnesses. This observation also is accurate, however, with respect to the general laws of property, contract, torts, taxation, and regulation generally—all laws that, for example, determine the distribution of wealth, which in turn is a major determinant of what is said by whom and to whom and with what effect. Although some laws may affect speech less obviously, or less directly, than other laws, all laws affect speech.

Moreover, Schauer surely has not justified the extreme position that all speech content should be assigned an infinite value by the primary governmental decisionmaker. Indeed, he has not justified the less extreme position that all speech content should be assigned a value equal to a compelling governmental interest. To the contrary: throughout his book Schauer asserts, sometimes almost casually, that some types of speech content are different in value from other types.[84]

Nevertheless, if this model for the Free Speech Principle is still to be followed, then the primary governmental decisionmaker is faced with two alternatives. The first alternative is to disregard totally the effects that government regulation may have on speech. The second alternative is to assign some value to those effects.

The approach signaled by the first alternative is irrational. That approach, for example, would preclude government from building

---

[84] F. SCHAUER, *supra* note 8, at 101-12, 169, 173-77, 181-84.

more auditoriums or libraries rather than playgrounds if government's reasons were produced to any degree by a desire to encourage speech activities more than volleyball. That approach also would preclude government from refusing to enact stringent bans on making noise through talking, or bans on cutting down trees for newspapers, because there would be no speech interest that government could place in the balance to offset the aesthetic and other interests in having such regulations.

When confronted with the implications of this approach, Schauer might respond that government is not precluded from giving speech in general a value, but rather is precluded from varying its value based on viewpoint. Nevertheless, the slope surely is slippery between the peak (assigning no positive or negative value to speech as an activity) and the abyss (assigning varying values to viewpoints).[85] Must government treat all subjects and viewpoints, the trivial and patently absurd as well as the significant and serious, as having equal weight? Is it likely that whatever positive theory is used to assign a weight to speech—or, say, to "political speech" as a special category—in government's balance will prove to be silent when it comes to distinctions among subjects and viewpoints? Must the flat-earth theories receive the same allocation of societal resources as are allocated to astro-physics theories?

The approach signaled by the second alternative—assignment of some value to the effects on speech of governmental regulation—leads immediately back to the essential question: What value must government assign to speech that is affected by regulation of noncommunicative impact? Assignment of infinite value surely is out of the question, because many other values outweigh speech in many contexts. Should speech then be assigned a value representing, say, the utility that various persons attach to it, so that assessing a soundtruck ordinance would require totalling up the positive and negative utilities that speakers and listeners assign to speech and to noise? We need some positive theory to answer this question.

In sum, whether or not it distrusts itself, the primary governmental decisionmaker cannot avoid assessing the importance of speech. That is so because speech is affected by all regulations—regulations aimed at noncommunicative impact as well as those aimed at communicative impact. A negative, distrust-based theory such as Schauer's might stand by itself in a very narrow range of cases, such as those that involve suppression of direct criticisms of government policies and officials. It is clear, however, that we need a positive theory of speech—

---

[85] It is notoriously difficult, for example, to distinguish viewpoint discrimination from subject matter—"thematic" (*See* P. BREST & S. LEVINSON, PROCESSES OF CONSTITUTIONAL DECISION-MAKING 1223 (2d ed. 1983))—discrimination. *See* Stone, *Restrictions of Speech Because of Its Content: The Peculiar Case of Subject-Matter Restrictions*, 46 U. CHI. L. REV. 81 (1978).

NORTHWESTERN UNIVERSITY LAW REVIEW

deontological or consequentialist—if we are to have a Free Speech Principle that is truly both significant and independent.

THE IMPOSSIBILITY OF A FREE SPEECH PRINCIPLE THAT IS BOTH GENERAL AND INDEPENDENT

We have examined Schauer's "negative" theory for an independent Free Speech Principle that is meant to have general application to the domain we associate with "speech" and "freedom of speech." Like other "negative" theories that purport to have general application, Schauer's theory leaves us with important, unresolved problems. Most of these problems are traceable to the absence of a background "positive" theory that buttresses the "negative" theory.

The problems caused by the absence of a positive theory of free speech lead us to return, once again, to the positive theories that Schauer has canvassed. We believe that Schauer has played the craftsman in identifying their difficulties. The major positive theories that have been proposed for a general and independent Free Speech Principle rest upon either (1) dubious empirical assumptions (such as the assumption that truth is best attained by leaving speech unregulated), (2) dubious value judgments (such as the belief that the search for truth transcends all other individual and social interests), or (3) broader theories of liberty of action that do not justify the independence of free speech from, not to mention the primacy of free speech over, other liberties.

The most influential positive theories for a Free Speech Principle may be divided roughly into those that are consequentialist/balancing in character and those that are deontological in character. Examples of theories in the former category include the theories recently proposed by Martin Redish,[86] Michael Perry,[87] and the more recent work of Thomas Scanlon.[88] Examples of theories in the latter category are the theories of Rawls,[89] Nozick,[90] Ackerman,[91] Dworkin,[92] Richards,[93] the earlier work of Scanlon,[94] Haiman,[95] and Baker.[96]

---

[86] Redish, *Advocacy of Unlawful Conduct and the First Amendment: In Defense of Clear and Present Danger*, 70 CALIF. L. REV. 1159 (1982); Redish, *The Content Distinction in First Amendment Analysis*, 34 STAN. L. REV. 113 (1981); Redish, *The Value of Free Speech*, 130 U. PA. L. REV. 591 (1982).

[87] Perry, *Freedom of Expression: An Essay on Theory and Doctrine*, 78 NW. U.L. REV. 1137 (1983).

[88] Scanlon, *supra* note 43.

[89] J. RAWLS, *supra* note 5, at 201-28.

[90] R. NOZICK, *supra* note 12, at 129-30.

[91] B. ACKERMAN, SOCIAL JUSTICE IN THE LIBERAL STATE 177-80 (1980).

[92] R. DWORKIN, *supra* note 7, at 266-78.

[93] D. RICHARDS, THE MORAL CRITICISM OF LAW 39-59 (1977).

[94] Scanlon, *supra* note 35, at 204.

[95] F. HAIMAN, SPEECH AND LAW IN A FREE SOCIETY (1981). Haiman's approach to freedom

78:1319 (1983)   *Essay*

The consequentialist/balancing theories to which we have referred
are consequentialist, but not utilitarian. These theories seek to maxi-

---

of speech is not philosophical; and while he proffers four basic principles for the legal regulation
of speech, it would be excessively generous to label these principles a "theory." Nonetheless, we
cite Haiman here because of the comprehensiveness of his treatment of speech, and its nonconsequentialist character. For Schauer's views on Haiman's approach, and his trenchant critique of
Haiman's general denial of speaker responsibility for speaker-induced harm, see Schauer, *Free
Speech and the Assumption of Rationality* (Book Review), 36 VAND. L. REV. 199 (1983).

[96] Baker, *Scope of the First Amendment Freedom of Speech*, 25 UCLA L. REV. 964 (1978).

In another recent philosophical contribution to free speech theory, Robert Ladenson presents
a theory of free speech that is a vague amalgalm of Rawlsian methodology—rational contractors
behind their veil of ignorance—and Millian arguments regarding the values of individuality and
the attainment of truth that depend on free speech. R. LADENSON, A PHILOSOPHY OF FREE EX-
PRESSION 37-39 (1983).

Thomas Scanlon, of course, also blended Rawls and Mill to arrive at his "Millian Principle":
There are certain harms which, although they would not occur but for certain acts of expression, nonetheless cannot be taken as part of a justification for legal restrictions on these acts.
These harms are: (a) harms to certain individuals which consist in their coming to have false
beliefs as a result of those acts of expression; (b) harmful consequences of acts performed as a
result of those acts of expression, where the connection between the acts of expression and the
subsequent harmful acts consists merely in the fact that the act of expression led the agents to
believe (or increased their tendency to believe) these acts to be worth performing.
Scanlon, *supra* note 35, at 213, *quoted in* R. LADENSON, *supra*, at 40.

Ladenson, however, rejects Scanlon's "Millian Principle" for several cogent reasons that
Scanlon himself had recognized earlier. For instance, Scanlon's principle apparently would allow
suppression of speech with a content that is offensive or embarrassing, a sign that the principle is
in some respect too narrow as a principle of free speech. R. LADENSON, *supra*, at 40. On the other
hand, the principle would ban all causes of action premised on deceit, even intentional deceit, a
sign that the principle is too broad. *Id.* at 40-41.

If Scanlon did not get things quite right, Ladenson's own set of seven "per se" categories of
violations of free speech, which he derives from Rawls plus Mill, is a vague, confusing, unparallel,
and entirely unhelpful concoction of armchair empiricism and loose casuistry. Ladenson's categories of *per se* violations are: (1) sedition laws—because government is fallible and untrustworthy;
(2) obscenity laws—because government is fallible in predicting anti-social effects and cannot
protect public morality without thwarting individuality; (3) censorship—which Ladenson defines
eccentrically narrowly to encompass only the proscription of "precisely identified acts of expression" (without this narrow definition, censorship would include not only sedition and obscenity
laws, but the various deceit torts and crimes that Ladenson wishes to preserve); (4) prior restraints—a category that Ladenson also defines eccentrically as consisting of literal gags and
seizures rather than injunctions and other orders backed by some sort of collateral bar doctrine;
(5) penalization (noncriminal sanctions); (6) regimentation (forced expression); and (7) vagueness
and overbreadth.

Ladenson has nothing much or new to say about sedition, obscenity, regimentation, and
vagueness/overbreadth. The other categories—censorship, prior restraints, and penalization—focus upon the form of regulation rather than the content of what is regulated or government's
reasons for the regulation. Nevertheless, Ladenson has told us nothing about why, if those forms
include *all* regulations of content, all content regulation is a *per se* violation of freedom of speech.
Surely intentional misrepresentation and malicious defamation can be "censored" and "penal-
ized." Nor has Ladenson told us, if those forms do not include all regulations of content, what
forms of regulation are not *per se* violations, or why.

Once Ladenson identifies his seven categories of *per se* violations of free speech, he moves
into a discussion of "hard cases"—a motley collection including dangerous information, commercial speech, public school curricula, and symbolic speech. He then concludes the book with
lengthy discourses on the press and on speech in the private workplace. The arguments here are

NORTHWESTERN UNIVERSITY LAW REVIEW

mize, within limits imposed by other values, some specific values served by speech. These values are various; they include individual self-rule, individual self-development, and political self-rule. To the extent that we can characterize these theories as based on the general value of autonomy, they seek to maximize autonomy rather than to treat it as some absolute or near-absolute side-constraint.[97]

The autonomy these theories seek to maximize, however, is not affected only by regulations aimed at communicative impact. Autonomy also is affected as well by any regulation that affects the information and opinions one receives—that is, by all governmental regulations. All of government's regulations—those affecting access to information; access to the indefinite diversity of the media of communication; access to private property in others' possession that may be useful for communicating generally, or communicating certain ideas, or communicating in a particular form—affect the ideas that individuals receive. Hence, all government regulations influence individuals' self-rule and self-development.[98] And, of course, the interests that government balances against speech—such as security of person, security of property, protection of privacy—all affect autonomy values.

Thus, these consequentialist positive theories all require some sort of balancing mechanism. Balancing is required so that government can, for example, decide whether allowing Able to burn Baker's dollar bill without Baker's consent (in order, say, to protest inflation in front of a particular audience and with a particular communicative effect) advances autonomy more than not allowing Able to do so (with the resulting benefits of protecting security of property while permitting

---

either correct but commonplace, unsupported, or confused. The *per se* categories—the centerpiece—are almost totally ignored as soon as they are introduced.

What is really appalling about the book, aside from the absence of the order and rigor that one would expect from a philosopher of Ladenson's caliber, is that its most provocative and original claim, found in the opening chapter, if valid, completely undermines the remainder of the book. Ladenson's claim is that only those moral principles whose violation can be relatively uncontroversially asserted should be considered fundamental legal rights, enforceable by courts against legislatures. *Id.* at 16-18. The claim is worth considering in the current debate over interpretivism and noninterpretivism. It is clear, however, that Ladenson himself has provided us with very few instances in which regulations of speech constitute uncontroversial violations of moral principles, even if we accept as valid those moral principle derivable by Rawls's methodology. Much of the current free speech doctrine may qualify as a fundamental right in Ladenson's sense, and Rawls's principles of justice may be correct, but Ladenson has nowhere shown the uncontroversial linkage that he views as necessary.

[97] A parallel comparison can be drawn between theories regarding paternalism that allow interference with autonomous choice in order to maximize autonomy, and deontological theories that preclude any interference with truly autonomous choices, no matter how demeaning and destructive of long-term autonomy. *See* J. CHILDRESS, WHO SHOULD DECIDE? 64-66 (1982).

[98] Schauer recognizes the communicative effects of regulations not aimed at communicative impact. F. SCHAUER, *supra* note 8, at 100, 124-26, 204.

78:1319 (1983)   *Essay*

whatever speech would result if property allocations were undisturbed, and so forth).

Positive consequentialist theories require that speech be assigned a "proper value" in furthering autonomy. They likewise require that other values be assigned "proper weights" relative to autonomy. Surely "speech" has some value; and surely the value of "speech" varies with its truth, its importance, and so forth. Therefore, these theories require some government agency—ultimately courts or legislatures—to assess speech for its truth, importance, and so forth, as well as to balance the value of "speech" against other values.

None of these theories justifies the special treatment of "speech" as distinguished from other activities that contribute to autonomy. None of them justifies distinguishing courts from primary governmental decisionmakers, either by treating courts as more trustworthy balancers or by recognizing a special need for a second opinion from the courts with respect to "speech" but not with respect to other activities. None of these theories even presents a comprehensive scheme for balancing speech against other activities that contribute to autonomy. None of them, indeed, presents a comprehensive scheme for balancing "autonomy" against other values.

Of course, the perennial favorite among consequentialists is the theory that relates free speech to the pursuit of truth. That theory is inadequate, however, for reasons that Schauer either mentions or implies.[99] There is no *single thing* called "Truth" that we can approach obtaining, either absolutely or in varying degrees. To ask whether a regulation promotes or impedes Truth is to ask a question that is essentially meaningless, like asking how many individual things there are in the universe. All regulations, and all failures to regulate, produce different environments; and each environment reveals some truths and obscures others.

Of course, the truthseekers might want to see the question posed differently. Instead of posing the question in a way that invokes Truth, we may pose a specific truthseeking question: whether a regulation promotes or impedes a specific truth.

We are prepared to concede that there are specific truths—"right answers" to specific truthseeking questions. We also are prepared to concede that some of those specific truths can be viewed as particularly important to obtain. These concessions having been made, it would follow that if (1) a governmental regulation interferes with the search for the answer to a particular question—a particular truth—and if (2) obtaining the answer to that particular question is viewed as very important, then (3) the regulation is unjustified unless (4) the other val-

---

[99] *Id.* at 15-34.

ues served, or "truths" revealed, by the regulation are equally as important as obtaining the answer to that particular question.

For example, we may believe that forbidding the publication of the *Pentagon Papers* substantially obstructs the search for the truth about our involvement in Viet Nam, and that the "truths" and other values served by keeping the *Pentagon Papers* secret are less important than the truth about that involvement.[100] If we subscribe to this belief, then we will condemn any attempt to restrain the publication of the *Pentagon Papers*, even though, because of other values that would be implicated, we might not allow citizens to search the Pentagon looking for those papers, or we might punish those whose thievery was responsible for their publication.

The problem with the "quest for truth" as a theory of free speech in the "specific truths" sense is that one cannot extrapolate from the quest for specific truths to any recognizable general theory of free speech. The quest for specific truths demonstrates only that some speech does help answer some questions that are relatively important, and that regulation of speech sometimes will be unjustified. Other speech contributes little toward answering some questions; some activities other than speech contribute a great deal toward answering some questions; and answering some questions is less important than, and occasionally is downright destructive of, other values that even avid specific-truthseekers would want to protect or maximize.

So where are we with respect to the stock consequentialist theories that purport to establish and justify an independent Free Speech Principle? Any truly independent Principle turns out to establish and justify an area of free speech, or perhaps a few pockets of speech, that is entirely too narrow to satisfy the demands of a general theory.

The positive deontological theories are more promising than the consequentialist theories in their attempts to justify a Free Speech Principle. These deontological theories hold that certain restrictions on speech violate absolute or near-absolute moral side-constraints on government's power to regulate. In one form or another, these theories posit that government violates the listeners' right to autonomy when it regulates speech because of its communicative impact, even if government's justification is that regulation will increase the listeners' autonomy in the long run.[101]

Promising though these deontological theories may be, they still

---

[100] *See* New York Times Co. v. United States, 403 U.S. 715 (1971).

[101] Again, the analogous deontological-consequentialist rift is over what paternalistic interventions are and are not justifiable. Consequentialists look to the long-term autonomy of the individual, deontologists to the voluntariness of the action that is restrained. *See supra* note 97. "Original position" derivations of principles can lead both ways, as Scanlon's switch between positions illustrates. Under the veil of ignorance we are concerned both with long-range *and* short-range autonomy.

78:1319 (1983) *Essay*

have major difficulties when it comes to establishing a Free Speech Principle. We identify four such difficulties here, believing that they are sufficient to put the deontological theories back on the drawing boards so far as freedom of speech is concerned.

First, the deontological theories do not treat freedom of speech distinctively. Rather, they are addressed to all paternalistic, moralistic, and censorial governmental interventions. Of course, this observation is not intended as an attack on these theories, but only as an attack on attempts to use them in order to establish an independent Free Speech Principle. The failure of these theories to treat speech distinctively is a difficulty in only some conceptions of the enterprise of constructing a theory of free speech—conceptions that assume the accuracy of our pretheoretical intuitions that free speech is an independent value. Other conceptions would view the collapse of free speech into more comprehensive values to be a theoretical advantage.[102]

Second, the deontological theories, at least those unveiled so far, lead to rather extreme views with respect to governmental restrictions based on the communicative impact of activities. According to these theories, listener autonomy is the dispositive criterion that distinguishes appropriate from inappropriate governmental regulation. Thus, although speakers may bear moral responsibility for the acts of others that their speech induces, the listeners' autonomy requires that the speaker be immunized from legal sanctions.

Thus, restrictions aimed at false and deceptive speech, or coercive speech, might be acceptable—on grounds that listeners' autonomy is not impaired—under most of these theories.[103] Nevertheless, any restrictions seem impossible to justify if they are aimed at those who incite crime, provoke hostile audiences, solicit criminal acts, misuse secret or dangerous information, or engage in similar activities. Under the deontological theories, these latter restrictions are forbidden because they all seek to prevent fully responsible listeners from hearing certain reasons for action.[104]

Third, deontological theories do not treat distinctively—perhaps, do not treat at all—the related issues of government speech and governmental favoritism toward certain private speech. These theories stand firm against most forms of censorship because censorship violates individual autonomy. But how is our autonomy violated, if at all, by

---

[102] *See infra* text accompanying note 109.

[103] *But see* Scanlon, *supra* note 35. Scanlon's earlier position is criticized sharply by Robert Ladenson, *see* R. LADENSON, *supra* note 96, at 40-41, as well as by Scanlon himself in a later article. *See* Scanlon, *supra* note 43, at 532-34.

[104] The most successful attempt to square a deontological approach that focuses on responsible listeners with some limitations on incitement and solicitation is that of Sheldon Leader. *See* Leader, *Free Speech and the Advocacy of Illegal Action in Law and Political Theory*, 82 COLUM. L. REV. 412 (1982).

NORTHWESTERN UNIVERSITY LAW REVIEW

government propaganda in favor of measures that government constitutionally could enact? How is our autonomy violated if, for instance, government bans the communication of some ideas or subjects at certain times or places, or in certain manners, when government constitutionally could have banned all communication at those times or places, or in those manners?

The deontologist could, of course, deny that these government actions are problematic; but that denial would seriously undermine efforts to achieve a *general* theory of freedom of speech.[105] More plausibly, the deontologist could talk about the negative effect that taxation has on autonomy and about the costs imposed by exempting governmentally favored speech from regulation. Still, the deontologist will have a long and complicated tale to tell about these issues—if she has any tale to tell at all—in order to incorporate and resolve these issues within a general deontological Free Speech Principle.

Finally, the deontological theories still need to develop some method of valuing speech in those situations in which government affects speech through regulations and allocations that are not themselves aimed at communicative impact. Even a deontological theory of free speech must answer questions like these: If some of us value serenity in our surroundings and others value communication and its attendant noise, how should government choose between these values? In making the choice, can government look to "importance" or "truth" in attaching value to communication? Must government treat communication as having no value, positive or negative, beyond the utility that speakers and listeners attach to it? Would this latter approach tend to favor widely held orthodox views over other views in the competition for resources and rights between communication and other activities?

So again, where are we with respect to our quest for a Free Speech Principle? The extant positive theories, consequentialist or deontological, are either (1) wrong, (2) too narrow in their theoretical ambit or practical application to support a Principle of general application, or (3) not about "speech" or "freedom of speech" as an independent Principle at all, but rather about concepts or activities in which speech or freedom of speech is only a lesser and completely included subcategory. The extant negative, distrust-of-government theories, like Schauer's, are either (1) wrong, (2) not supportive of an independent Free Speech Principle, or (3) dependent on the construction, as yet not even in blueprint form, of a supporting positive theory of general application.

---

[105] Government speech is widely thought to implicate freedom of speech concerns. See M. YUDOFF, WHEN GOVERNMENT SPEAKS (1983); Kamenshine, *The First Amendment's Implied Political Establishment Clause*, 67 CALIF. L. REV. 1104 (1979); Shiffrin, *Government Speech*, 27 UCLA L. REV. 565 (1980). *But see supra* note 74 and sources cited therein.

78:1319 (1983)

CONCLUSION

True it is that our Constitution sets forth explicit guarantees for "freedom of speech" and "freedom of press." True it may be that most Americans, if not most people everywhere, have the intuitive sense that "freedom of speech" is traceable to an underlying principle or theory of "speech" and of the relationship of government to "speech." That unarticulated principle or theory likely is intuited to be wide-ranging in application and to set "freedom of speech" apart as an independent value among many other values we hold dear. And it may well be true that our intuitions, more frequently than not, prove to be trustworthy companions.

Intuition, however, is simply not enough for philosophers or lawyers. The job of philosophers and lawyers is to follow common intuitions into the articulation of the principle or theory that underlies and justifies them. And, for centuries, philosophers have attempted to articulate a Free Speech Principle that is both independent and appropriately general in character.

These attempts have failed. Their failure should not be greeted with chagrin. Consider instead what would be needed for success. Any comprehensive theory of free speech must in some way deal satisfactorily with all of the following issues:

(1) *Definitions*. The theory should tell us what "speech" is and what "speech" is not. Included within this exercise would be provision of a mechanism for differentiating activities that are "speech" from activities that are not "speech."

(2) *Moral Foundations*. What are the ultimate values that underlie free speech? Are those values justifiably held? How are those values arranged among themselves? What is the linkage, if any, between those values and other values that do not underlie free speech? Theoretically, the answers to these questions might lead us to an independent and general *moral* Free Speech Principle.

(3) *Legal Foundations*. To what extent, and with what justification, is any *moral* Free Speech Principle—derived from the processes identified in issue (2)—transformable into a *legal* (or United States constitutional) Free Speech Principle? How is this legal Free Speech Principle to be positioned within the arrangement of other legal principles like "liberty," "autonomy," "equality," "property," "contract," and "authority of government"?

(4) *Institutional Enforcement*. How should any legal Free Speech Principle—derived from the processes identified in issue (3)—be implemented by the societal institutions that are concerned with it? For instance, should there be judicial review? If so, how stringent?

(5) *Doctrinal Elaboration*. How should any legal Free Speech Principle—derived from the processes identified in issues (3) and (4)—

NORTHWESTERN UNIVERSITY LAW REVIEW

be translated into legal doctrine? A comprehensive theory of free speech should give us an approach to the following categories of doctrines:

(a) *Regulation of Communicative Impact*. The theory should treat those situations in which communicative impact ultimately results from a responsible, proscribable act of the audience, such as matters of "incitement," "solicitation," and "dangerous information." Equally important, the theory should treat situations in which communicative impact is more direct, such as "defamation," "invasion of privacy," "breach of confidence," "offense," "infringement of copyright," "coercion," and "prejudice of judical proceedings."

(b) *Regulation of Noncommunicative Impact*. The theory should provide an approach to situations in which governmental regulation, ostensibly for "other purposes," has a positive or negative impact on freedom of speech. These situations include "time, place, and manner" regulations of speech, as well as more general regulations that affect the distribution of wealth and influence, or intrude into the privacy of beliefs, and in turn affect speech in various ways.

(c) *Government as Communicator*. The theory should tell us what to do when government takes an active role as speaker or audience in communication. Situations in which government is "speaker" include governmental advocacy, governmental subsidy of particular views, public education, and exemption from regulation of particular subjects of speech. Situations in which government is "audience" include various information-gathering activities, such as legislative hearings, police investigations, and demands by administrators for information from those they are charged with regulating.

(d) *Diversity of Communication*. As an aspect of (a), (b), and (c), the theory should display the relevance of the balance and diversity of views that are expressed in the marketplace of ideas, and should provide an approach by which the diversity of media within that general marketplace may be assessed in terms of the balance and diversity of views.

(e) *Form and Procedure of Regulation.* The theory should offer an approach to the various potential forms of governmental regulation of speech, such as "prior restraints," "overbreadth," "vagueness," and *per se*, prophylactic rules.

It is thus a tall order to design any comprehensive theory of "freedom of speech," or for that matter, to design any comprehensive theory of any intuitively basic human value. Frederick Schauer's theory—the proposed Free Speech Principle that we have used as our main foil in this essay—omits issue (3). We do not fault this omission, because he

78:1319 (1983) *Essay*

intends his theory to be applicable outside the United States and the jurisdiction of our Constitution. Nevertheless, the omission of issue (3) necessarily calls into question the validity of his treatment of issues (4) and (5), because their treatment depends in part on the articulation of *Legal Foundations*. Surely one still would need to forge the link between his theory and the first amendment, or at least with some other United States constitutional provision, in order for his theory to be useful in United States constitutional law.[106]

More seriously, Schauer's theory fails with respect to issue (1), *Definitions*. Schauer does attempt to give us a picture of what "speech" is; but his definition of "speech" is so inclusive that the picture dissolves into ambiguity and even self-contradiction. Given the inclusive character of his definition of "speech," we are entitled to demand a clear picture of "what 'speech' is not," and Schauer does not provide us with that picture.

Schauer's response to this latter observation may be that he does not care about the distinction between "speech" and other activities that are not "speech." That is, he may intend his Free Speech Principle to operate with respect to any such distinctions within a wide range of potentially acceptable definitional frameworks. If that is Schauer's response, then surely we must pause before accepting his Principle. The definitions chosen for "speech" and "not speech" will have a great deal to say about the way his Principle will operate, the way it will interface with other values and their supporting principles, and the range of appropriate governmental regulation.

Even if we are able to accept the absence of a clear definitional framework for Schauer's theory, however, we still are left with issue (2), *Moral Foundations*. Here we find the primary source of failure in Schauer's quest for a general, independent Free Speech Principle. Schauer's negative, distrust-of-government justification for his Principle is incomplete. Speech, however generally defined, must be regulated by government, regardless of whether or how much government is to be distrusted. Yet Schauer has not told us how government should regulate, or why it should do so. Without an adequate moral foundation for free speech, we cannot begin to construct a cogent legal foundation. The inevitable result is that Schauer's discussions of institutions and doctrines are both incomplete and unconvincing.

We also should observe that Schauer, in his Free Speech Principle, goes further than merely to tell us what free speech *is*. Schauer pursues the larger, more important project of attempting to *justify* free speech as an independent principle. The process of justification, however, necessarily entails the linkage of speech and free speech with more basic

---

[106] Schauer has disclosed the type of arguments *he* would make for such a link in a recent article on constitutional language. Schauer, *supra* note 6.

NORTHWESTERN UNIVERSITY LAW REVIEW

values. "Free speech is justified because . . ."—what comes after the "because" inevitably will link free speech with something else, usually more basic, and thus will destroy free speech's independence. Put differently, any attempt to *justify*, rather than merely to identify, a Free Speech Principle will require acceptance of principles that are broader than the Free Speech Principle itself, with respect to which the Free Speech Principle is not independent.[107]

Any negative justification for free speech—like Schauer's distrust-of-government justification for his Free Speech Principle—will entail some positive theory and its articulation. That positive theory will cover an area that is broader than the subject of speech. Once the positive theory is articulated, the negative Free Speech Principle may prove to be of general application, but it will not prove to make free speech into an independent value or principle.

Consequentialist theories of free speech—whether directed toward attaining truth, facilitating political decisionmaking, maximizing autonomy, or maximizing utility—inevitably require the construction of a balancing mechanism, by which free speech may be weighed against other values.[108] Balancing mechanisms, however, like the more plausible versions of Schauer's Free Speech Principle, require a positive theory for constructing and using the mechanism.

Again, Schauer's balancing model renders problematic his claim that his Free Speech Principle establishes free speech as an independent principle. Balancing models all employ forms of cost-benefit analysis. If freedom of speech is no more than ordinary cost-benefit analysis—with "speech" receiving its proper weight in that analysis—then "freedom of speech" is no more governed by an independent principle than is any other interest of great weight.

Deontological theories are perhaps most successful in justifying the bulk of our pretheoretical intuitions regarding freedom of speech. They prove superior to consequentialist theories in treating "speech" as different in kind from many other, though by no means all other, activities regulated by government. Nevertheless, these theories encounter major difficulties because of their rigidity, and because of their inattention to regulation not directed at communicative impact, even when they otherwise offer cogent theoretical bases for freedom of speech. Ultimately, however, the categories of activities dealt with by deontologi-

---

107 Pluralistic theories thus cannot respond to demands for justification of their basic normative principles. Hence the recently proposed pluralistic theories of John Finnis and Michael Walzer, J. FINNIS, NATURAL LAW AND NATURAL RIGHTS (1980); M. WALZER, SPHERES OF JUSTICE (1983), have been strongly attacked for their failure to justify their prescriptions. *See, e.g.*, Wilcox, Book Review, 68 CORNELL L. REV. 408 (1983)(review of J. FINNIS, *supra*); Dworkin, *To Each His Own*, N.Y. REV. BOOKS, April 14, 1983, at 4 (review of M. WALZER, *supra*).

108 They also require, as theories of the American constitutional right of free speech, a theory of judicial review of legislative action and its rationale and operation with respect to free speech.

cal theories are not coextensive with "speech" no matter how broadly or narrowly "speech" is defined. Most deontological theories do not even pretend to treat free speech as an independent value or principle, and the theories that make such pretensions fail in their efforts.

The point that emerges here is that quests like Schauer's for an independent Free Speech Principle of general application probably are doomed to failure. Descriptively, it may be accurate to assert that pluralism of moral-political values is the true regime. Normatively, however, the attempt to justify discrete principles and values—especially when they are to have a general application—inevitably links them with more basic, overarching, and less numerous values.[109] Thus, unless one is ideologically wedded to moral pluralism, or unless one sees moral pluralism as a reflection of the constraint of constitutional pluralism on the development of more monolithic theories, it is probably best to search for more basic values than freedom of speech.

Indeed, in an article published after his book, Schauer suggests that free speech might represent several distinct values, whose linkage consists in the fact that each is implicated by some form of government regulation of communication.[110] If such a suggestion is accurate, then there is no Free Speech Principle. Instead, there are merely some improper government regulations of speech, just as there are some improper government regulations of other activities. And we may put our pretheoretical intuitions aside, to await a narrower articulation of free speech principles in the specific contexts in which specific governmental regulations of specific communicative activity are brought to our attention.

---

[109] *See supra* note 107.
[110] Schauer, *Codifying the First Amendment: New York v. Ferber*, 1982 Sup. Ct. Rev. 285, 313.

[10]

Copyright 1984 by Northwestern University School of Law
Northwestern University Law Review

Printed in U.S.A.
Vol. 78, No. 5

MUST SPEECH BE SPECIAL?

Frederick Schauer *

    Academic and judicial thinking about freedom of speech seems to have entered a new phase, one that might be called the "reemergence of theory." We are now experiencing an attention to the underlying premises of the principle of freedom of speech that is both more conscious and more sustained than at any time in the past. In order to explain this development, it is necessary to take a brief look at the phases that have preceded the current one. Obviously these phases overlap, and my characterizations represent rough generalizations rather than inviolate truths. Indeed, any such characterization is little more than the identification of one interesting feature from among a morass cf interconnected similarities and differences. Thus, like most attempts to put the phenomena of the world into large generalizations, drawing these distinctions says much more about the draftsman than about the world. I plead guilty to the charge, but the contrasts seem nevertheless worthy of exploration.

    From 1919 until about twenty years ago, discussion about freedom of speech in the context of the first amendment took place largely in the "How much?" mode. The courts and first amendment theorists commonly acknowledged, as Holmes put it, that the first amendment was not "intended to give immunity for every possible use of language."[1] Thus, the various exceptions to the coverage[2] of the first amendment—

---

    * Cutler Professor of Law, College of William and Mary. Visiting Professor of Law (1983-1984), University of Michigan. A.B., M.B.A., Dartmouth College; J.D., Harvard University. Although this Article deals with a theme similar to that of the Review Essay by Professors Alexander and Horton that appears in this issue, Alexander & Horton, *The Impossibility of a Free Speech Principle*, 78 Nw. U.L. REV. 1319 (1983), I had not seen their review when this Article was written. I plan to respond to Professors Alexander and Horton at some later date.

    [1] Frohwerk v. United States, 249 U.S. 204, 206 (1919).

    [2] I use the word "coverage" to refer to those activities the regulation of which is to be measured against the standards of the first amendment. It is quite possible that certain conduct, even when measured against the standards of the first amendment, will remain unprotected. Yet the distinction between coverage and protection is designed to point out that there is a big difference between those activities (some of which are verbal) that have nothing to do with the first amendment, and those that at least require that governmental action be tested against relatively stringent first amendment standards. I have dealt with this distinction at great length elsewhere. F. SCHAUER, FREE SPEECH: A PHILOSOPHICAL ENQUIRY 89-92, 134-35 (1982); Schauer, *Can Rights Be Abused?*, 31 PHIL. Q. 225 (1981); Schauer, *"Private" Speech and the "Private" Forum: Givhan v. Western Line School District*, 1979 SUP. CT. REV. 217, 227-29 [hereinafter cited as Schauer, *Private*

78:1284 (1983)   *Special Speech*

commercial advertising,[3] defamation,[4] obscenity,[5] and fighting words[6]—were rarely called into serious question. Moreover, even with respect to political and other speech that the first amendment plainly covered, the battle lines were narrowly drawn. No one doubted that free speech was a good thing, at least in the abstract, and consequently there was little concern for *why* free speech was valued. Instead the problems centered around the weight to be given freedom of speech when it conflicted with other universally acknowledged values, most commonly national security and public order.[7] Although in retrospect it seems that this debate could have been illuminated by closer attention to the philosophical foundations of the principles of free speech, that was not the course taken. Rather, the tired metaphors of the marketplace of ideas and the search for truth served as stage props for a debate over how much the values of free speech would have to yield in the face of exigent public concerns.[8]

This is not to say that the issues present in this phase were easy. On the contrary, the judicial and academic divisions during this period of growth of free speech doctrine—roughly from 1919 to the mid-1960's—were as sharp as they have ever been.[9] But the combatants

---

Speech]; Schauer, *Categories and the First Amendment: A Play in Three Acts*, 34 VAND. L. REV. 265, 267-82 (1981) [hereinafter cited as Schauer, *Categories*].

[3] Valentine v. Chrestensen, 316 U.S. 52 (1942).

[4] Beauharnais v. Illinois, 343 U.S. 250 (1952).

[5] Roth v. United States, 354 U.S. 476 (1957).

[6] Chaplinsky v. New Hampshire, 315 U.S. 568 (1942).

[7] *E.g.*, Dennis v. United States, 341 U.S. 494 (1951); Cox v. New Hampshire, 312 U.S. 569 (1941).

[8] *E.g.*, Dennis v. United States, 341 U.S. 494 (1951); Schneider v. State, 308 U.S. 147 (1939).

[9] Many of these debates took place between the so-called "absolutists" and the so-called "balancers." *E.g.*, Barenblatt v. United States, 360 U.S. 109 (1959); Sweezy v. New Hampshire, 354 U.S. 234 (1957); Frantz, *The First Amendment in the Balance*, 71 YALE L.J. 1424 (1962); Mendelsohn, *On the Meaning of the First Amendment: Absolutes in the Balance*, 50 CALIF. L. REV. 821 (1962); Meiklejohn, *The Balancing of Self-Preservation Against Political Freedom*, 49 CALIF. L. REV. 4 (1961).

I suppose that characterizing an enormously complex range of issues in terms of a simple dichotomy between balancing and absolutism served a purpose in its time, but it has had the unfortunate consequence of continuing to channel debate about important first amendment issues into a preconceived mold of balancing versus absolutism, even among those who ought to know better. *E.g.*, Baker, *Unreasoned Reasonableness: Mandatory Parade Permits and Time, Place, and Manner Regulations*, 78 Nw. U. L. REV. 937 (1983); Shiffrin, *The First Amendment and Economic Regulation: Away From a General Theory of the First Amendment*, 78 Nw. U.L. REV. 1212 (1983). For example, the simple designation of "balancing" masks questions about *who* should weigh competing values, the extent to which balancing should take place in more or less rigid rules or in the circumstances of the individual case (and that is a continuum and not a dichotomy), and the level of abstraction at which the competing values should be described and weighed. Similarly, absolutism may be taken to entail a narrowly circumscribed first amendment within which direct restrictions are prohibited, or it may be taken instead as a desire to formulate specific first amendment rules of adjudication that grant little if any power to the judge in the individual case to examine the state's particular reasons for restricting in that case, or to examine the extent to which

NORTHWESTERN UNIVERSITY LAW REVIEW

seemed relatively unconcerned with the deeper meaning of free speech. First amendment partisans took it as a given that maximum protection of free speech was a good thing,[10] and devoted their efforts to arguing that the perceived dangers of speech were not nearly as great as was often assumed. And those who were wary of excess protection of speech were similarly unconcerned with the deep theory of the first amendment. They saw no reason to doubt the value of free speech in the abstract, but were unwilling in real cases to sacrifice many of their fears about dangers to security, order, and the stability of the state.[11]

The 1960's and 1970's brought a new phase to free speech theory, a phase that substituted for the question "How much?" the seemingly simpler question of "How?" This was, of course, a period of intense solicitude for individual rights, and free speech was no exception. There was no call to examine the reasons for accepting the principle of free speech, for everyone agreed without question that maximum freedom of speech (and most other things as well) was desirable. As a result, most disputes focused on the strategies for achieving maximum protection.[12] This search for how to attain optimal free speech protection pervaded not only the academic commentary, but the work of the courts as well. For it was during this phase that those studying the first amendment witnessed the judicial creation of the various devices that have now become acknowledged weapons in the first amendment arsenal—vagueness,[13] overbreadth,[14] the chilling effect,[15] special proce-

---

a particular speaker or speech is important in light of the principles of freedom of speech. This latter version of absolutism, focusing on restricting judicial power, is implicit in Baker's argument, and is quite different from the former version, which partially characterizes Meiklejohn's special concern with restricting legislative power.

That an absolutist-balancer dichotomy obscures important problems and variations is only part of the problem. Equally troublesome is the extent to which language from a former and largely different war is used to describe the battles of today. The language has acquired so much baggage from its previous usage that it blocks us from appreciating the ways in which today is different from yesterday. *Cf.* Holmes, *The Path of the Law*, 10 HARV. L. REV. 457, 464 (1897) (deploring the confusion caused when terms with ethical associations are used in legal discourse).

[10] Indeed, for some the refusal to consider first principles was part of a belief that the first amendment itself had already resolved the question. *E.g.*, Konigsberg v. State Bar of Cal., 366 U.S. 36, 56 (1961) (Black, J., dissenting).

[11] *E.g.*, Dennis v. United States, 341 U.S. 494, 561 (1951) (Jackson, J., concurring); Feiner v. New York, 340 U.S. 315 (1951); Wigmore, Abrams v. U.S.: *Freedom of Speech and Freedom of Thuggery in War-Time and Peace-Time*, 14 ILL. L. REV. 539 (1920). The tendency to accentuate dangers is somewhat related to another problem, that of being most willing to support freedom of speech as long as it takes place Somewhere Else. This view is not surprising, for in most of the interesting free speech disputes of recent times the litigants have been quite unpleasant people carrying equally unpleasant messages. *See* Schauer, *Codifying the First Amendment:* New York v. Ferber, 1982 SUP. CT. REV. 285, 286-87, 315-16.

[12] *E.g.*, T. EMERSON, THE SYSTEM OF FREEDOM OF EXPRESSION (1970); Kalven, *"Uninhibited, Robust, and Wide-Open"—A Note on Free Speech and the Warren Court*, 67 MICH. L. REV. 289 (1968); Nimmer, *The Right to Speak from Time to Time: First Amendment Theory Applied to Libel and Misapplied to Privacy*, 56 CALIF. L. REV. 935 (1968).

[13] *E.g.*, Smith v. Goguen, 415 U.S. 566 (1974); Keyishian v. Board of Regents, 385 U.S. 589

78:1284 (1983)   *Special Speech*

dural protection,[16] and many others. With free speech once again taken as a given in this search for methods of protecting it, there was, as in the previous phase, little occasion for concentrated attention on the "Why?" rather than the "How?" or the "How much?" of the first amendment.

From the foregoing two phases, a first amendment emerged that was, at its core, quite strong. Although perhaps it was not strong enough to satisfy those who exalt free speech above all other values, there is little doubt that *Brandenburg v. Ohio*,[17] *New York Times Co. v. Sullivan*,[18] and *Cohen v. California*[19] represent a profound commitment to virtually unlimited discussion of political, moral, and social questions of all types.[20] Moreover, this strong core was well guarded by a host of procedural and subsidiary doctrines that seem to make it relatively safe from erosion.

From this secure core, arguments in the current phase of free speech theory have centered around the *broadening* of the first amendment. The most prominent example of the broadening of the first amendment is of course commercial advertising,[21] but the same phenomenon exists with respect to campaign contributions,[22] speech by public employees during working hours,[23] nude dancing,[24] and the choice by government of the books or entertainment that it will offer in

---

(1967). The vagueness doctrine, of course, is of rather more ancient lineage, *e.g.*, Winters v. New York, 333 U.S. 507 (1948), thus making it an especially available tool somewhat later.

[14] *E.g.*, Zwickler v. Koota, 389 U.S. 241 (1967); NAACP v. Alabama *ex rel*. Flowers, 377 U.S. 288 (1964).

[15] *E.g.*, Dombrowski v. Pfister, 380 U.S. 479 (1965); Freedman v. Maryland, 380 U.S. 51 (1965).

[16] *E.g.*, Monitor Patriot Co. v. Roy, 401 U.S. 265, 275 (1971) (burden of proof); Freedman v. Maryland, 380 U.S. 51 (1965) (burden of proof; promptness; availability of appeal); New York Times Co. v. Sullivan, 376 U.S. 254 (1964) (burden of proof).

[17] 395 U.S. 444 (1969) (per curiam). *Brandenburg*'s strength is best appreciated if assessed in light of Hess v. Indiana, 414 U.S. 105 (1973).

[18] 376 U.S. 254 (1964).

[19] 403 U.S. 15 (1971).

[20] The clearest indicator of the strength of the core of the first amendment today is the ease with which the Supreme Court has overturned content-based restrictions of speech that are related to public issues. *E.g.*, NAACP v. Claiborne Hardware Co., 458 U.S. 886 (1982); Consolidated Edison v. Public Serv. Comm'n, 447 U.S. 530 (1980); Landmark Communications, Inc. v. Virginia, 435 U.S. 829 (1978). Indeed, the importance of discussion of "matters of public concern" is underscored by the Court's recent protection of the right to discuss those matters by an employee on a government employer's premises and time. Connick v. Myers, 103 S. Ct. 1684 (1983).

[21] Virginia Bd. of Pharmacy v. Virginia Citizens Consumer Council, 425 U.S. 748 (1976). On what counts as commercial speech, see Bolger v. Youngs Drug Prods. Corp., 103 S. Ct. 2875 (1983).

[22] Buckley v. Valeo, 424 U.S. 1 (1976).

[23] Connick v. Myers, 103 S. Ct. 1684 (1983). *See also* Givhan v. Western Line Consol. School Dist., 439 U.S. 410 (1979).

[24] Schad v. Mt. Ephraim, 452 U.S. 61 (1981). *See also* Doran v. Salem Inn, Inc., 422 U.S. 922 (1975).

NORTHWESTERN UNIVERSITY LAW REVIEW

its facilities.[25] In each of these areas, recent developments have made first amendment considerations applicable to issues that in the recent past were considered well without the boundaries of the first amendment. Moreover, for every instance of judicial broadening of the first amendment, there seem to be at least ten attempts in the academic literature to have the first amendment swallow up one more segment of society or of governmental action.[26]

With this process of broadening, or at least arguing about broadening, has come the reemergence of theory. For although the accepted assumptions, traditional metaphors, and standard platitudes about the value of free speech might have been largely sufficient to deal with the issues of the past, they are clearly inadequate to confront the questions we must ask when trying to determine the extent to which, if at all, the courts should broaden the coverage of the first amendment to encompass a wide range of activities seemingly so far from the comprehension of the classical free speech theorists that the relevance of classical theory has become attenuated. In the place of the classical theories have come new attempts to ask about the "Why?" of the first amendment, in the hope of developing a theory that will explain the values that the concept of free speech is designed to serve. With such a theory in place, of course, it becomes much easier to confront the questions raised by the broadening of the first amendment. For if we know *why* we have the principles of free speech, then we can determine in the new case whether that class of activities is the type that the first amendment is designed to promote.

Would that it be so easy! The problem, of course, is that there are numerous candidates for the appropriate underlying theory of the free speech and free press clauses of the first amendment. Indeed, the concentration in this Symposium on deep theory, either explicitly or implicitly, is strong evidence of the way that debate about freedom of speech has shifted. In order to shed some light on the debate about the philosophical/sociological/political/historical foundations of free speech, it seems appropriate to set some ground rules, or at least some standards that an adequate theory must satisfy. Surprisingly, hardly any attention has been devoted to this task.[27] On second thought, it probably is not so surprising. Almost everyone would prefer being the star quarterback to being the referee or a member of the rules commit-

---

25 Board of Educ., Island Trees Free Union School Dist. v. Pico, 457 U.S. 853 (1982) (plurality opinion); Southeastern Promotions, Ltd. v. Conrad, 420 U.S. 546 (1975).

26 *E.g.*, Kamenshine, *The First Amendment's Implied Political Establishment Clause*, 67 CALIF. L. REV. 1104 (1979); Morgan, *The Constitutional Right to Know Why*, 17 HARV. C.R.-C.L. L. REV. 297 (1982). See also the fascinating analysis of sleeping as speech in Community for Creative Non-Violence v. Watt, 703 F.2d 586 (D.C. Cir. 1983).

27 The most notable exception is Tribe, *Toward a Metatheory of Free Speech*, 10 SW. U.L. REV. 237 (1978).

tee. Yet if there were no rules, and no referees, there would be no star quarterbacks, so someone has to do the job, and that is part of what I want to accomplish here. But it is also too large a task to complete in this forum, so I want to concentrate on only part of it. I want to deal with the question of whether, and if so to what extent, an adequate theory of free speech must explain the way in which the activities encompassed by the first amendment are importantly distinct from activities that do not receive such uniquely cherished protection. In other words, must speech be special?

I

In asking whether speech is or must be special, we must start by clarifying the nature of the question. That is, no one could plausibly claim that the activities covered by the first amendment share no characteristics whatsoever with activities not covered by the first amendment. Rather, the claim I want to consider is more modest. Do the activities covered by the first amendment[28] possess at least one and maybe more theoretically relevant differences from those activities not so covered? If they do, then we can say that the activities covered by the first amendment are in some sense special. But if they do not—if they are an analytically indistinguishable subset of a larger category, not all of which is protected by the first amendment—then we can say that speech is not special.

The question of whether speech is special has a descriptive side and a normative side. On the descriptive side, the question is whether one can identify relevant differences between speech and activities not covered by the first amendment. But on the normative side, the question is whether such a difference is necessary for a satisfactory underlying theory of the first amendment. For it is by no means inconceivable, and indeed may very well be the case, that what is analytically necessary for a satisfactory theory of the first amendment is unattainable given the existing state of the world. Yet that is getting ahead of things. For the moment, it is sufficient to note that the question "Must speech be special?" is analytically distinct from the question "Is speech special?".

In dealing with these issues, I want to discuss one particular strand of free speech theory that presents the problems most starkly. This strand I will call the "self-development" theory, and I use that designation precisely because it is different from the titles of the various theories that I believe comprise it. I mean to include within the category

---

[28] Whether the "activities covered by the first amendment" are all "speech" in a non-technical sense is a crucially important question, but not germane to the instant discussion. The reader may assume that "activities covered by the first amendment" and "speech" in a technical sense are here used synonymously. *See* Schauer, *Speech and "Speech"—Obscenity and "Obscenity": An Exercise in the Interpretation of Constitutional Language*, 67 GEO. L.J. 899 (1979).

NORTHWESTERN UNIVERSITY LAW REVIEW

those theories relying variously on self-realization,[29] self-fulfillment,[30] self-expression,[31] and variants on the individual liberty core of all of these theories. Conversely, I mean to exclude from the category the leading consequentialist justifications for a principle of freedom of speech, including most prominently the search for truth/marketplace of ideas theories,[32] the popular sovereignty/democratic process theories,[33] and the distrust of government theories.[34]

There are important differences among the various theories that are components of the self-development strand of first amendment theory, and I do not want to suggest that they are little more than minor variations of each other. For present purposes, however, they do share significant similarities. One is that they are all based on the value to the individual of a regime in which free speech flourishes, and that this value to the individual is taken as an end in itself. These theories, therefore, although perhaps consequentialist with respect to the individual, are not premised on the value to society of permitting free speech. Rather the focus is on what free speech can do for the individual, either as speaker,[35] or as listener,[36] or both.

But the most striking feature of all of these self-development theories is that they identify as the value underlying the principle of freedom of speech a value that is not peculiar to speech. In every variant at issue the value that self-development theorists urge is a value that can undoubtedly be promoted by speech. Nevertheless, that same value can also be promoted by other activities that do not involve communication, and self-development theorists offer no particular reason why

---

29 *E.g.*, Redish, *The Value of Free Speech*, 130 U. PA. L. REV. 591 (1982) [hereinafter cited as Redish, *Free Speech*]; Baker, *Realizing Self-Realization: Corporate Political Expenditures and Redish's The Value of Free Speech*, 130 U. PA. L. REV. 646 (1982); Redish, *Self-Realization, Democracy, and Freedom of Expression: A Reply to Professor Baker*, 130 U. PA. L. REV. 678 (1982).

30 *E.g.*, T. EMERSON, *supra* note 12, at 6-7; L. TRIBE, AMERICAN CONSTITUTIONAL LAW 578-79 (1978).

31 For a fuller description and critique of this whole range of theories, see F. SCHAUER, *supra* note 2, at 47-67.

32 *E.g.*, J.S. MILL, ON LIBERTY ch. 2, in ESSENTIAL WORKS OF JOHN STUART MILL 268-304 (M. Lerner ed. 1961); J. MILTON, AREOPAGITICA (J.C. Suffolk ed. 1968). The leading judicial embodiments are Abrams v. United States, 250 U.S. 616, 630 (1919) (Holmes, J., dissenting); IBEW Local 501 v. NLRB, 181 F.2d 34, 40 (2d Cir. 1950), *aff'd*, 341 U.S. 694 (1951) (L. Hand, J.).

33 *E.g.*, A. MEIKLEJOHN, FREE SPEECH AND ITS RELATION TO SELF-GOVERNMENT (1948); BeVier, *The First Amendment and Political Speech: An Inquiry into the Substance and Limits of Principle*, 30 STAN. L. REV. 299 (1978); Bork, *Neutral Principles and Some First Amendment Problems*, 47 IND. L.J. 1 (1971). *See also* H. KALVEN, THE NEGRO AND THE FIRST AMENDMENT (1966); M. YUDOF, WHEN GOVERNMENT SPEAKS: POLITICS, LAW, AND GOVERNMENT EXPRESSION IN AMERICA (1983).

34 *E.g.*, F. SCHAUER, *supra* note 2, at 73-86; Blasi, *The Checking Value in First Amendment Theory*, 1977 AM. B. FOUND. RESEARCH J. 521.

35 *E.g.*, Baker, *supra* note 29; Baker, *Scope of the First Amendment Freedom of Speech*, 25 UCLA L. REV. 964 (1978).

36 *E.g.*, Redish, *supra* note 29.

communicative activities can serve the goal more completely or more frequently than other activities that are not in any significant sense communicative.[37]

I want to illustrate this point from two different perspectives. First, we can look at those theories emphasizing in some way or another the self-expressive aspects of communicating.[38] Each of these theories relies on the fact that expressing one's self is an important component of individual liberty, and if we do not allow channels of self-expression then we will suffer accordingly. Now this is of course true, but the question is whether communicating serves any particularly special function in terms of self-expression.[39] I can also express myself in my attire, my occupation, my sexual activity and preferences, my residence, my hobbies and other recreations, and so on. The list is virtually endless, and that is exactly the point. Communicating is obviously a form of self-expression, but it is by no means the only form of self-expression, and it is by no means the form of self-expression that is most important to everyone. Thus, the argument from self-expression leads to the conclusion that all forms of self-expression are worthy of equivalent protection. As a result, it is impossible to distinguish an argument from self-expression as an argument for freedom of speech from an argument from self-expression as an argument for liberty in general.

The same conclusion follows if we focus not on the self-expression of the speaker, but rather on the self-fulfillment or self-realization of the speaker or listener—on the ways that speaking or listening to speech makes one a better, or fuller, or more satisfied, or more perfect person.[40] Again, I have no doubt that speech does indeed serve all of these functions. Yet once again there seems no reason to believe that communication serves these functions any better or more often than do non-communicative activities. For some people, self-realization lies in their occupation, their travels, their inner contemplation, or their family life. Communication, whether one is speaker or listener, is merely one of a myriad of activities that in some way promotes self-fulfillment or self-realization.

In the form just presented, therefore, the theories under discussion

---

[37] In one sense, of course, all actions are communicative, or at least those actions that are in one way or another perceived by someone else. But in this sense Pike's Peak, the Empire State Building, and a 1957 Ford are all communicative, for all can inspire thoughts in a viewer. But comprehending the notion of free speech will be even more hopeless than it already is unless we assume a specific intention by a human being to communicate some message to another human being. Even this may not help very much, but that is probably because of the pervasive difficulty that I suggest at the very end of this Article.

[38] *E.g.*, Baker, *supra* note 35; Richards, *Free Speech and Obscenity Law: Toward a Moral Theory of the First Amendment*, 123 U. PA. L. REV. 45 (1974).

[39] For a fuller elaboration of this point, see F. SCHAUER, *supra* note 2, at 50-52.

[40] *E.g.*, T. EMERSON, *supra* note 12, at 6-7; Redish, *supra* note 29.

NORTHWESTERN UNIVERSITY LAW REVIEW

provide the ideal vehicle for discussing whether it is necessary for a satisfactory theory of the first amendment that speech be in some way special. For under these theories and their variants, speech is not claimed to be special, or significantly distinguishable from the other activities that may also contribute to the value that provides the basis of the theory. If it is necessary to a satisfactory theory of the first amendment that some such distinguishing feature be provided, then all of these theories must be considered to be failures.

II

The *locus classicus* of objections to self-development theories is a paragraph in an article by Robert Bork[41] in which Bork scrutinizes the claimed benefits from speech of "development of individual faculties and the achievement of pleasure."[42] He finds both of these justifications wanting for precisely the reason that I am discussing here:

[T]he important point is that these benefits do not distinguish speech from any other human activity. An individual may develop his faculties or derive pleasure from trading on the stock market, following his profession as a river port pilot, working as a barmaid, engaging in sexual activity, playing tennis, rigging prices or in any of thousands of other endeavors. Speech with only the first two benefits can be preferred to other activities only by ranking forms of personal gratification. These functions or benefits of speech are, therefore, to the principled judge, indistinguishable from the functions or benefits of all other human activity. He cannot, on neutral grounds, choose to protect speech that has only these functions more than he protects any other claimed freedom.[43]

This argument draws its significance from the fact that the first amendment protects speech more than it protects non-speech conduct.[44] Without this contrast the first amendment serves no function. To the extent that the argument from self-development in all of its

---

41 Bork, *supra* note 33. Expressing sympathy with part of Bork's article, as I am about to do in the text, runs a great risk of confusion, owing to the fact that Bork's article contains an enormous number of highly contested points of constitutional theory. For a taste of the dispute, see, *e.g.*, Brest, *The Fundamental Rights Controversy: The Essential Contradictions of Normative Constitutional Scholarship*, 90 YALE L.J. 1063 (1981). I find guilt by association quite deplorable in academic discourse, but let me make it clear that I do not mean to be taken as dealing with or expressing sympathy with any of Bork's theory except the particular point quoted below.

42 Bork, *supra* note 33, at 25. This is Bork's characterization of the first two of the four values underlying free speech as set forth by Justice Brandeis in Whitney v. California, 274 U.S. 357, 375 (1927) (Brandeis, J., concurring) (*Whitney* was later overruled in Brandenburg v. Ohio, 395 U.S. 444, 449 (1969).

43 Bork, *supra* note 33, at 25. The references to the "principled judge" and "neutral grounds" relate to Bork's full theory of constitutional adjudication and are not under discussion here. *See supra* note 41.

44 I use "non-speech conduct" to refer to activities not covered by the first amendment. The contrast between the amount of protection given within the first amendment and that given outside it is nowhere presented more clearly than in Paris Adult Theatre I v. Slaton, 413 U.S. 49 (1973).

forms collapses into an argument for general liberty, then no argument has been presented for a principle of free speech that is stronger than a general principle of personal liberty. Because in American constitutional doctrine we protect personal liberty only by application of the minimal scrutiny of the rational basis standard,[45] a justification that fails to distinguish the activities protected by the stringent standard of the first amendment from the activities protected by the minimal scrutiny of the rational basis test has failed in its task of explaining the protection of freedom of speech under the first amendment.

III

Now that I have presented the issue, I want to step away from the Constitution for a moment. Thus, I will first consider the argument against self-development as a question of social and political philosophy, completely divorced from any questions about American law in general or the first amendment in particular. This will provide the appropriate background for then turning to the argument as a question under the first amendment. I consider the two questions to be separate, and therefore consider them separately, because there is a point in having a written, authoritative constitution. Moreover, the authoritative nature of a written constitution makes it possible that an answer generated by ideal political theory will be unsupportable in the constitutional text, and indeed possibly even inconsistent with it.[46] In these cases, it is the duty of the judge to refrain from doing what is foreclosed by the text, even if that judge's own view of ideal political theory might lead to the opposite result.[47]

As a question of social and political philosophy, the argument against the adoption of the self-development principle is premised on a point about the nature of moral and practical reason. If a specific principle is generated by a broader principle, and if we accept the broader principle, then we must, at the risk of self-contradiction, accept every other specific principle also generated by the broader principle, unless we can give particular and articulated reasons for drawing a distinction.[48] If we accept X, and if X generates a, b, and c, then we must be

---

[45] *E.g.*, Doe v. Commonwealth's Attorney, 425 U.S. 901 (1976) (per curiam); Hollenbaugh v. Carnegie Free Library, 439 U.S. 1052 (1978); Kelley v. Johnson, 425 U.S. 238 (1976); Ferguson v. Skrupa, 372 U.S. 726 (1963); Williamson v. Lee Optical Co., 348 U.S. 483 (1955).

[46] I am here presupposing a by no means uncontroversial point of constitutional theory, but this is not the place to present a full theory of constitutional adjudication. For the constitutional theory that (in part) undergirds the views presented here, see Schauer, *An Essay on Constitutional Language*, 29 UCLA L. REV. 797 (1982).

[47] *See* Monaghan, *Our Perfect Constitution*, 56 N.Y.U. L. Rev. 353 (1981). *See also* J. ELY, DEMOCRACY AND DISTRUST (1980).

[48] For a more extensive discussion, see F. SCHAUER, *supra* note 2, at 3-12.

NORTHWESTERN UNIVERSITY LAW REVIEW

willing, if we are to act rationally, to accept a, b, and c, and not just the one or two of those that happen to strike our fancy at the moment.

In the context of the principle of freedom of speech, then, if we say that we value free speech because it is a form of self-development, and if we accept self-development as a given, then, if we have not justified any qualification, we must be willing to protect every form of self-development as much as we protect speech. Yet many forms of self-development, as I am using that term, can cause harm to other individuals or to society in general. It would be implausible to suppose that the state is or could be significantly disabled to prevent harms merely because the cause of those harms was, in the process, engaged in self-expression, self-fulfillment, or self-realization. Thus we acknowledge that, in general, the prevention of harm is a proper function of the state, regardless of how nice the causing of harm may make someone feel.

But if speech is merely one category within the larger universe of self-developing actions, then it would seem, again to be consistent, that we would have to accept the principle that speech may be restricted when it causes harm to others. Yet then what is the point of a principle of free speech? Many communicative acts, including many that our pre-theoretical understanding of the nature of free speech would lead us to want to protect, have the capacity for causing significant harm to others or to society in general. Indeed, if I may return to American constitutional law for a moment, it is hard to think of any first amendment case in which the communicative acts at issue did not cause some degree of harm, or at least offense.[49] The anguish caused by the Nazis in Skokie,[50] the offense and annoyance of Cohen's jacket[51] and Cantwell's phonograph,[52] the damage to Damron's reputation and career,[53] the economic losses of even the innocent merchants of Claiborne

---

[49] Offense now seems to have settled in as a recognized harm under the first amendment. *E.g.*, FCC v. Pacifica Found., 438 U.S. 726 (1978); Young v. American Mini Theatres, Inc., 427 U.S. 50 (1976). Nevertheless, the question of whether offense should be treated as a cognizable harm under the first amendment is by no means beyond dispute. *Compare* Feinberg, *Pornography and the Criminal Law*, 40 U. PITT. L. REV. 567 (1979) *with* Schauer, *Response: Pornography and the First Amendment*, 40 U. PITT. L. REV. 605 (1979).

The very fact that we can still debate about offense in the first amendment context underscores the point in the text, because there is no question that, outside of the first amendment context, a large variety of actions that are merely offensive can be controlled by government. Even though some may argue that offense is still far too often used as an improper basis for governmental regulation, *e.g.*, D. RICHARDS, SEX, DRUGS, DEATH, AND THE LAW (1982), there is still no question that offensive smells can be regulated, and so too in general can unsightly buildings, etc. *See* Metromedia, Inc. v. San Diego, 453 U.S. 490 (1981).

[50] Collin v. Smith, 578 F.2d 1197 (7th Cir.), *stay denied*, 436 U.S. 953, *cert. denied*, 439 U.S. 916 (1978).

[51] Cohen v. California, 403 U.S. 15 (1971).

[52] Cantwell v. Connecticut, 310 U.S. 296 (1940).

[53] Ocala Star-Banner Co. v. Damron, 401 U.S. 295 (1971).

County,[54] the distortion of the election process by money or misleading promises,[55] and the humiliation caused by publicity about the victim of a sex offense[56] are but a small sample of instances in which the principle of freedom of speech is understood to prevent the government from intervening to deal with the kinds of harm that are normally taken to be sufficient to justify use of the state's coercive powers.

Thus, we want to protect speech not because it causes no harm, but *despite* the harm it may cause.[57] Our search for a justification, therefore, is a search for a reason to distinguish speech from the entire range of intentional actions. This is exactly the distinction that the various arguments from self-development fail to provide. As a result, these arguments tell us why we should protect liberty in general, but in the process they also become arguments for giving speech no greater protection than that given to the full range of other intentional actions. As a question of social and political theory, therefore, the arguments from self-development fail to provide a reason for recognizing a principle that grants greater protection for speech against state intervention than it grants to anything else the individual might wish to do.

IV

Let us now turn from abstract political theory, and attempt to look at this question as one arising in the attempt to formulate a theory of *this*[58] Constitution's first amendment. In order to do this, we must rely on the notion of principled adjudication. Unfortunately, however, the idea of principled adjudication, or of neutral principles,[59] has been the subject of so much redefinition and misinterpretation that I would like to use an alternative term, confessing in the process that this term merely reflects an idea already well-established in the literature,[60] if only one is willing to wade through all the drivel.[61]

---

[54] NAACP v. Claiborne Hardware Co., 458 U.S. 886 (1982).

[55] Brown v. Hartlage, 456 U.S. 45 (1982); Citizens Against Rent Control v. Berkeley, 454 U.S. 290 (1981).

[56] Globe Newspaper Co. v. Superior Court, 457 U.S. 596 (1982).

[57] *See* Schauer, *supra* note 49.

[58] *See* Van Alstyne, *Interpreting This Constitution: The Unhelpful Contributions of Special Theories of Judicial Review*, 35 U. FLA. L. REV. 209 (1983).

[59] Wechsler, *Toward Neutral Principles of Constitutional Law*, 73 HARV. L. REV. 1 (1959). *See also* Bork, *supra* note 33. The notion, in some form or another, has made its way into the jargon of the Supreme Court. *E.g.*, Akron v. Akron Center for Reproductive Health, 103 S. Ct. 2481, (1983) (O'Connor, J., dissenting). For a broadside attack, see Tushnet, *Following the Rules Laid Down: A Critique of Interpretivism and Neutral Principles*, 96 HARV. L. REV. 781 (1983).

[60] *See* Golding, *Principled Decision-Making and the Supreme Court*, 63 COLUM. L. REV. 35 (1963); Greenawalt, *The Enduring Significance of Neutral Principles*, 78 COLUM. L. REV. 982 (1978).

[61] Unfortunately, I do not have the nerve to supply references for the characterization made in the text.

NORTHWESTERN UNIVERSITY LAW REVIEW

Thus, I want to refer to the notion of *articulate consistency*.[62] This term is designed to emphasize that we are dealing with a question of consistency and not of the rightness or wrongness of principles, and that the particular notion at issue is largely controlled by the way that a court chooses to articulate its reasons for a decision. The constraint of articulate consistency suggests that when we justify a decision by reference to a principle (or a reason, rule, standard, justification, or theory) we must be willing to apply the principle, as articulated in the first decision, to all cases coming within the verbal description of that principle. When a court provides, without qualification, a reason for its decision, it must be willing to apply that reason in future cases, absent particularly strong reasons to the contrary.[63] The key feature of articulate consistency is the way in which it is normatively neutral, or procedural. The requirements of articulate consistency can apply to good reasons, bad reasons, or reasons totally unjustified by the judicial role. If a court sticks to what it says, if it is willing to take seriously its own statements,[64] then it has satisfied the requirements of articulate consistency. And this is no less true if the original reasons or justifications are wrong, outrageous, or whatever.

We can see, therefore, that the court in the first case has a great deal of control over how much of a constraint the notion of articulate consistency is going to be. If the court in the first case justifies its decision by a very narrow principle, festooned with caveats, qualifications, and exceptions, then it is unlikely that the constraint of articulate consistency will be a significant barrier to what the court decides to do in the next case.[65] On the other hand, if the court in the first case justifies its decision by a broad and generally unqualified principle, then the

---

62 After imagining that I was the first to use this term, I discovered that it had been used previously by Ronald Dworkin. R. DWORKIN, TAKING RIGHTS SERIOUSLY 88 (1977). My use is quite similar to his, and I have been unable to come up with an acceptable alternative, so I will forfeit my claim to originality, if not to independent creation.

63 That is, most of the constraints on adjudication, including this one, are presumptive rather than absolute. Yet the creation of a presumption in place of a clean slate is still a significant change. On the less than absolute nature of the neutral principles constraint, see Greenawalt, *supra* note 60, at 1007-08. *Cf.* R. DWORKIN, *supra* note 62, at 110-15 ("gravitational force" of precedent).

64 *See* Monaghan, *Taking Supreme Court Opinions Seriously*, 39 MD. L. REV. 1 (1979). *See also* Maltz, *Some Thoughts on the Death of Stare Decisis in Constitutional Law*, 1980 WIS. L. REV. 467; Monaghan, *supra* note 47, at 387-91; Munzer & Nickel, *Does the Constitution Mean What It Always Meant?*, 77 COLUM. L. REV. 1029 (1977); Schauer, *supra* note 46, at 829. For the Supreme Court's most recent dispute about the weight to be given to its precedents, see the various opinions in City of Akron v. Akron Center for Reproductive Health, Inc., 103 S. Ct. 2481 (1983).

65 The difficulty, of course, is that a highly qualified opinion will provide little if any guidance to lower courts as they attempt to follow the Supreme Court. One wonders at times whether the Court does not pay too little attention to this "guidance" function. *See* Corr, *Retroactivity: A Study in Supreme Court Doctrine "As Applied,"* 61 N.C.L. REV. 745 (1983); Easterbrook, *Ways of Criticizing the Court*, 95 HARV. L. REV. 802, 807-11 (1982); Schauer, *Private Speech*, *supra* note 2, at 217-18.

necessity of remaining faithful to this principle will exercise a substantial constraint on future decisions. Thus, the extent to which a principle applies in future cases is controlled by the justification that the court has provided in the first case.

We can now return to the principle of free speech, for it is the notion of articulate consistency that provides the link between the points made in the previous section and the same issue in the context of constitutional law. If a court says that it is protecting act x under the first amendment because x is an instance of self-expression, self-fulfillment, or self-realization, and the first amendment protects self-expression, self-fulfillment, or self-realization, then the court must be willing to apply that same principle in future cases. But since any intentional action can and usually is an instance of self-expression, self-fulfillment, or self-realization, then the constraints of articulate consistency would require the court to protect all intentional actions under the first amendment. The court, to be consistent, must be willing to apply the reason given in the first case to subsequent cases fitting within the description of the principle. If the principle is described merely as self-expression, then the first amendment must protect all self-expressive actions. Yet of course it is not true that all self-expressive actions are protected by the first amendment,[66] or even by any other part of the Constitution.[67] Thus, the problem with the entire range of self-development justifications for the first amendment is that they fail the test of articulate consistency. Without more, they offer a rationale that is far broader than we are willing to accept, which if consistently applied would protect almost all activities to the same extent that we protect certain communicative activities. Because we are unwilling to do this, these justifications might just as well not have been mentioned at all. A reason we are not willing to follow is no reason at all.

V

I noted in Section III that there was a point in having written and authoritative constitutions, or at least that an authoritative constitution must be taken as such. In order to be faithful to this conviction, I must deal with the textual response to the arguments I have just presented.[68] Thus, it is freedom of speech and press, and not freedom of liberty in general, that is specifically set forth in the text for special protection. Even if the justification would, to be fully consistent, have to be applied to a far wider range of cases, only part of this range is picked out by the constitutional text for special attention. The reason we do not apply the self-development arguments to their full reach is that we lack the

---

[66] *See* Paris Adult Theatre I v. Slaton, 413 U.S. 49 (1973).

[67] Kelley v. Johnson, 425 U.S. 238 (1976).

[68] *See especially* Redish, *The Value of Free Speech*, 130 U. PA. L. REV. 591 (1982).

constitutional mandate for so doing. Because we have that mandate in the case of speech, we can proceed to apply that justification in speech cases. The relevant distinction under this argument—what makes speech special—is the very fact that the constitutional text says it is.

One might call this the argument from coincidence. Even if there is no good reason for treating speech specially, the text says we must, and that is sufficient to justify the special protection for speech. And to the extent that the text is clear, we cannot legitimately avoid it. Thus, there may be no completely justifiable reason for limiting the presidency to those thirty-five years old or older,[69] or for giving equal representation in the Senate to Delaware and California,[70] but these are the mandates from the text, so we follow them. And so too, picking out speech for special treatment is the mandate from the text, and that's that. Speech is special by stipulation, even though now the stipulation may seem a bit odd.

But this loses sight of why we are looking at justifications at all. The very reason we are concerned about the underlying theoretical justification for the principle of freedom of speech, in a way that we are not with respect to the age of the presidency and equal representation in the Senate,[71] is that the text is not clear,[72] and we are therefore required to work out a theory of free speech so that we can intelligently apply the vague words of the document.[73] The argument from coincidence is therefore circular. It calls upon us to note the presence of speech and not action in general in the text, but it is the very unclarity of the text that is the impetus for the entire enterprise. If we assume we cannot have a literal interpretation of the first amendment,[74] then we

---

69 U.S. CONST. art. II, § 1, cl. 6.

70 U.S. CONST. art. I, § 3, cl. 1; U.S. CONST. art. 5.

71 It is incorrect to say that we are not concerned about justifications for, say, the age requirement because the issues do not arise. The very reason they do not arise is that the text is clear. If article II specified merely that the President had to be of "sufficient maturity", there would be frequently litigated controversies over that phrase (unless it was deemed a political question), and consequent great concern with underlying purpose and theory.

72 For many years those sympathetic to a strong first amendment were influenced by the view of Justice Black that the first amendment was plain and unequivocal. *See, e.g.*, Barenblatt v. United States, 360 U.S. 109, 134 (Black, J., dissenting); Smith v. California, 361 U.S. 147, 155 (1959) (Black, J., concurring); Street v. New York, 394 U.S. 576, 609 (1969) (Black, J., dissenting). Fortunately, we have now been released from the shackles of literalism, and we understand the way in which the text of the first amendment is importantly vague. *See, e.g.*, Greenawalt, *Speech and Crime*, 1980 AM. B. FOUND. RESEARCH J. 645, 731; Van Alstyne, *A Graphic Review of the Free Speech Clause*, 70 CALIF. L. REV. 107, 110-28 (1982). *See also* Schauer, *Categories, supra* note 2, at 267-68; Schauer, *supra* note 28, at 902-05. An intriguing analysis is found in Note, *The Speech and Press Clauses of the First Amendment as Ordinary Language*, 87 HARV. L. REV. 374 (1973).

73 Obviously, my reference to "working out a theory" presupposes an approach that treats the free speech and other similar constitutional clauses as more or less discrete units of analysis, and, more importantly, places no great weight on the specific or general intentions of the drafters. *See* Schauer, *supra* note 46.

74 This assumption can take two forms. First, it can be a conclusion from the vague and

must interpret it in light of some underlying purpose or theory. But if that underlying theory says nothing in particular about speech, if it does not set speech apart from a vast range of other conduct, then there is no principled stopping point after we leave the domain of what is very specifically and unequivocally mentioned in the text. To put it bluntly, the argument from coincidence might support applying the first amendment to all self-expressive or self-fulfilling instances of *speech* (taken literally) or press (taken literally), but the argument is of no assistance if we are trying to figure out why or how to apply the first amendment to oil paintings and handwritten manuscripts but not to nude bathing or riding a motorcycle without a safety helmet.[75]

VI

I now want to consider an alternative response to the argument

---

equivocal language of the text. *See supra* note 72. *See also* J. ELY, *supra* note 47, at 105; Mendelson, *supra* note 9, at 821. On the other hand, it can also flow from what Professor Van Alstyne calls the "irresistable counterexample." Van Alstyne, *supra* note 72, at 113. Even if the language were both literal and absolute, which it clearly is not, it is inconceivable that certain "speech" activities, whether perjury, price-fixing, extortion, ordinary solicitation to ordinary crimes, face-to-face fraud, or the making of representations about securities, could be considered exempt from governmental regulation. This latter approach can be characterized as "The Constitution does not mean what it says." The former can be characterized as "The Constitution means what it says, but it says less than you think." In terms of general fidelity to the notion of a written, authoritative, constitution, this last-mentioned approach has significant advantages. Fortunately, it is also justified by the text.

[75] Another possibility, of course, is to take the references to "speech" and "press" as little more than quaint anachronisms, and then proceed to use the first amendment as the vehicle for protecting an enormous range of individual, non-communicative conduct. *See* Baker, *supra* note 35, at 964. Less explicit hints at the same perspective are in L. TRIBE, *supra* note 30, at 938-90. Tribe refers to the first amendment throughout his discussion of various forms of expression of "personhood," but he is rarely explicit about which constitutional provision protects which activity.

Apart from the difficulties I have with treating the constitutional text so casually, there is still the more important problem of justifying an exemption for speech in those circumstances in which it causes a clear harm. Suppose we change the facts of New York Times v. Sullivan, 376 U.S. 254 (1964), slightly. That is, suppose that the authors of the advertisement, negligently and erroneously but in good faith, charged in the advertisement that Sullivan had served two years in jail for embezzlement. Suppose as well that as a result of this Sullivan loses the next election, cannot get another job, and winds up on the steps of the Salvation Army as a derelict. Clearly there are some intervening causes here, but it is also plain that the negligent and erroneous but not intentional falsity has served as a "but for" cause of Sullivan's downfall. In these circumstances the New York Times and the authors of the advertisement would still prevail under the rule of *New York Times*. But would we be comfortable if someone's non-communicative and non-political but self-expressive embodiment of their personhood negligently caused an equivalent harm? I think not, and I think we would have no problem in wanting to impose liability. I would imagine, for example, that many motorcyclists not only feel that they can better express their personhood without a helmet than with one, but also that they can better express their personhood at eighty miles an hour than at fifty-five. Are they responsible for the harms they negligently cause when riding at eighty? I hope so. Are newspapers responsible for negligently causing harms of the same magnitude? No. *See* Ocala Star-Banner v. Damron, 401 U.S. 295 (1971).

NORTHWESTERN UNIVERSITY LAW REVIEW

that we must reject self-development justifications for freedom of speech because they do not set speech apart from the entire range of intentional actions. Under this alternative response, presented at one time or another by several of the participants in this Symposium,[76] there might be reasons why *speech* relating to or causing self-expression, self-fulfillment, or self-realization might be more important than other forms of conduct relating to or causing self-expression, self-fulfillment, or self-realization.[77] Alternatively, there might be greater danger in regulating the communicative aspects of, say, self-expression than in regulating the non-communicative aspects of self-expression.[78]

I have no desire whatsoever to refute any of these arguments, because these arguments, unlike the argument from coincidence, acknowledge the very point at issue. Indeed, they do more than acknowledge it, they concede it; for the qualifications about speech being a more important form of self-expression, or about the regulation of speech-related self-expression being particularly dangerous, are concessions of the very point under dispute. If there is some reason to treat self-expressive speech differently from other forms of self-expressive activities (and the same would apply to activities that foster self-fulfillment or self-realization), then that reason becomes part of the underlying theoretical justification for the first amendment. In other words, a reason has just been given for treating speech specially.

When we combine a general justification, such as self-expression, with a specifically articulated qualification, as in the arguments now being discussed, the underlying justification for the principle of freedom of speech might be complex rather than simple. This, of course, is not in itself a problem. Indeed, general justifications are likely to become so general that they are of little if any assistance in helping us to decide actual cases.[79] Nevertheless, if we are to use this more complex underlying theory to help us reach a decision in a hard case, we must use the entire justification and not only part of it. That is, we would have to look not only for the presence or absence of self-development factors, but also for the presence or absence of those factors that lead us to treat speech as a particularly important and special subset of self-development in general.

For my own part, I happen to believe that if we look closely at these distinguishing factors, we will find sufficient dangers in govern-

---

[76] Greenawalt, *supra* note 72, at 734 n.344; Perry, *Freedom of Expression: An Essay on Theory and Doctrine*, 78 Nw. U.L. Rev. 1137, 1154 (1983); Shiffrin, *supra* note 9, at 1238-39. Perry's "epistemic value" seems responsive to some of the concerns I am expressing, but I question whether the response is successful. In other words, is the epistemic value sufficiently different from or narrower than the various self-realization values so that it does not present the same problems I am raising here?

[77] Greenawalt, *supra* note 72, at 734 n.344.

[78] *Id.*

[79] For a fuller discussion, see Schauer, *supra* note 11, at 311-12.

ment regulation of a wide range of communication—dangers different in kind and degree from government regulation of other activities—to justify a principle of freedom of speech without having to resort to notions of self-expression, self-fulfillment, or self-realization. To me the dangers of excess governmental regulation are a self-sufficient justification.[80] I may be wrong in this. The point, however, is that if some such reason is either self-sufficient or supplementary, it is still a reason for treating speech specially.

VII

Although the foregoing discussion has taken place in the context of self-development values that are argued to provide the foundations for the principle of free speech, the self-development justification is offered merely as an example of the larger question of the extent to which speech is or must be special. When I claim that a principle of free speech is "independent,"[81] therefore, I am not claiming that the principle is or can be entirely self-standing. Nor do I claim that free speech is an end in itself,[82] or an ultimate, irreducible value, although I do believe that ultimate irreducible values exist.[83] Thus, free speech, perhaps because it is so counter-intuitive[84] in protecting a wide panoply of

---

[80] F. SCHAUER, *supra* note 2, at 80-86.

[81] *Id.* at 3-7. *See* Perry, *supra* note 76, at 1154 n.72.

[82] *See* Emerson, *Toward a General Theory of the First Amendment*, 72 YALE L.J. 877, 880 (1963). There is an unfortunate tendency to say that everything that is valued for non-utilitarian or anti-utilitarian reasons is a "good in itself." Yet such a statement confuses utilitarianism with any talk of causes and conditions. That is, there may be certain primary personal goods, perhaps such as autonomy and liberty. It may also be that a certain deontological, anti-utilitarian theory holds that individual liberty and autonomy should be protected even at the expense of the general public welfare. It also may be that certain conditions, such as freedom of speech, are *conducive* to autonomy and liberty. In these circumstances it would be erroneous to say that free speech is a "good in itself," because it is good for what it does, or what it leads to, and not what it is. It is possible that free speech may under some theories be a component of a primary good such as liberty or autonomy, and in this case we would be more warranted in saying that it was a good in itself. Nevertheless, the point is that speech or free speech can be merely instrumental with respect to certain individual primary goods, and still be a component of an anti-utilitarian theory.

[83] *See* I. BERLIN, CONCEPTS AND CATEGORIES: PHILOSOPHICAL ESSAYS (1978); Williams, *Ethical Consistency*, in PROBLEMS OF THE SELF 166 (1973). Thus, I have considerable sympathy for what Rawls refers to as "intuitionism." J. RAWLS, A THEORY OF JUSTICE 34 (1971). *See* Feinberg, *Rawls and Intuitionism*, in READING RAWLS: CRITICAL STUDIES ON RAWLS' A THEORY OF JUSTICE 108 (N. Daniels ed. 1975).

[84] *See* Emerson, *supra* note 82, at 887-900. Because Emerson's distinction between expression and action has not stood the tests of either time or close scrutiny, *see, e.g.*, L. TRIBE, *supra* note 30, at 579, 598-601; Ely, *Flag Desecration: A Case Study in the Roles of Categorization and Balancing in First Amendment Analysis*, 88 HARV. L. REV. 1482 (1975); Yacavone, *Emerson's Distinction*, 6 CONN. L. REV. 49 (1973), there is an unfortunate tendency to discount the remainder of his contributions to free speech theory. But we should not allow the sneers of the contemporary cognoscente to distract us from recognizing Emerson's profoundly important insights regarding the counter-intuitive nature of the principles of free speech, and the importance of designing not only principles, but institutions, to accomodate and compensate for this factor. Unless we recognize, as

harmful and obnoxious activities, must especially be justified by reference to some other, presumably more fundamental, principle or principles.

When we engage in the process of searching for these more fundamental principles, we must, as I have argued,[85] be willing to accept all of the conclusions that follow from acceptance of the more fundamental principle, or provide some distinction between speech and the other activities generated by the principle. If we justify free speech by reference to a principle of democracy,[86] or some broader principle or scheme of political liberty,[87] for example, then we must be willing to accept not only a principle of free speech, but also those other more specific principles that follow from a general principle of democracy or political liberty. In fact we do precisely that, because we protect voting and other activities related to the process of government as strongly as we protect freedom of speech,[88] albeit in different ways and with different doctrines. An argument based on democracy, therefore, even without any further qualifications, satisfies the constraint of articulate consistency in a way that an argument from self-expression *simpliciter* does not.

Thus, we cannot distinguish free speech, or speech itself, from all other activities. That is undoubtedly impossible.[89] It nevertheless remains crucial that we treat freedom of speech as being independent from general liberty, because of two interrelated problems. First, we want to protect speech *more* than we protect many other activities that are part of some conception of general liberty. For example, we want to protect speech more than we protect economic activity, although under some theories economic activity is an important and perhaps even central part of liberty in general.[90] We also want to protect free speech more than we want to protect a wide range of non-communica-

---

Emerson has forced us to do, that freedom of speech is a fragile value, and one whose protection is likely to focus on the crackpots and ideological dregs who are the most common litigants in first amendment cases, we will make little progress in designing doctrines and institutions sufficient to the task.

[85] *See supra* text accompanying notes 46-47.

[86] *E.g.*, A. MEIKLEJOHN, *supra* note 33; Kalven, *The* New York Times *Case: A Note on "The Central Meaning of the First Amendment,"* 1964 SUP. CT. REV. 191. *See also* Brennan, *The Supreme Court and the Meiklejohn Interpretation of the First Amendment*, 79 HARV. L. REV. 1 (1965).

[87] *See* Rawls, *The Basic Liberties and Their Priority*, in 3 THE TANNER LECTURES ON HUMAN VALUES 1 (S. McMurrin ed. 1982).

[88] In some instances we do so by explicit textual commitment. *E.g.*, U.S. CONST. amends. XV, XVII, XIX, XXIV, XXVI. In other instances we use interpretation of broader constitutional provisions. *E.g.*, Reynolds v. Sims, 377 U.S. 533 (1964). At times we construct entire theories. *E.g.*, J. ELY, *supra* note 47.

[89] *See* Perry, *supra* note 76, at 1185.

[90] *E.g.*, F. HAYEK, THE CONSTITUTION OF LIBERTY (1960); R. NOZICK, ANARCHY, STATE, AND UTOPIA (1974).

tive lifestyle choices, although once again these choices are to some an important component of liberty in general.[91] The second point, inseparable from the first, is that we are unwilling to disable ourselves from dealing with harmful, offensive, obnoxious, dangerous behavior in general in the way that we are with reference to speech.

Thus there exists in current free speech doctrine a difference in both the type and probability of harms that will justify government intervention. Harms that are sufficient outside the coverage of the first amendment are non-cognizable within the coverage of the first amendment; and even with respect to harms that are entitled to consideration both inside and outside the first amendment, the first amendment requires a likelihood of harm much higher than we otherwise require.[92] It is this difference that is in need of theoretical justification, at least as we continue to contemplate broadening the first amendment, and thus it is important to see why speech might be special with respect to general liberty. Fortunately, this is an easier task than trying to see if speech is special *simpliciter*, but that does not mean that we have already achieved success.

VIII

In searching for an underlying theoretical justification for the principle of freedom of speech, it is possible that we will find a number of different justifications. Although some theories are indeed unitary,[93] and although there need not be anything inherently wrong with a unitary theory, so, too, there need not be anything wrong with a multi-valued theory.

When I refer to a multi-valued theory of the first amendment, I am actually including two different types of multi-valued theories. One type views the language of the free speech and free press clauses of the first amendment as the umbrella under which are located a number of more or less distinct separate principles, each with its own justification, and each directed towards a separate group of problems. Under such a view, for which I acknowledge considerable sympathy,[94] we might in fact have several first amendments. We might have one first amendment directed primarily to the problem of government suppression of its critics. The justifications for this first amendment might be largely of the democratic theory[95] and abuse of governmental power[96] vari-

---

[91] *See* Dworkin, *Liberalism*, in PUBLIC AND PRIVATE MORALITY 113 (S. Hampshire ed. 1978).

[92] Compare the standard of likelihood in Brandenburg v. Ohio, 395 U.S. 444 (1969)(per curiam), with the "unprovable assumption" theme in Paris Adult Theatre I v. Slaton, 413 U.S. 49 (1973).

[93] *E.g.*, Perry, *supra* note 76; Redish, *Free Speech*, *supra* note 29.

[94] *See* Schauer, *supra* note 11, at 313.

[95] *See supra* note 33.

[96] *See supra* note 34.

NORTHWESTERN UNIVERSITY LAW REVIEW

eties, and this first amendment might be the one that is most applicable to cases such as *New York Times Co. v. Sullivan*,[97] *NAACP v. Claiborne Hardware Co.*,[98] and *United States v. Grace*,[99] just to take one famous and two recent examples. Another first amendment might be directed primarily towards the problem of open inquiry in the sciences and at academic institutions, being based primarily on the heritage of Galileo and the search for truth/marketplace of ideas justifications for the principle of free speech.[100] Perhaps this is the first amendment, albeit with some overlap with the one mentioned previously, that lurks around cases such as *Sweezy v. New Hampshire*[101] and *Board of Education, Island Trees Free Union School District v. Pico*.[102] A third first amendment might be a reaction to an excess of historical censorship of the arts,[103] leading to cases such as *Southeastern Promotions, Ltd. v. Conrad*[104] and *Jenkins v. Georgia*,[105] and perhaps even based in part on notions of self-realization. This list of possible first amendments is of course representative rather than exhaustive, but I think I have made the point.

Alternatively, the other variety of multi-valued theory might say that speech represents a unique mix of various different characteristics, not duplicated in other human endeavors.[106] This unique mix of self-expression, self-realization, capacity for influencing political change, and so on, is then said to justify special protection for speech. This is by no means an implausible view, but it seems somewhat sticky in application, at least at the margin. That is, what do we do when we are unsure of first amendment coverage in a close case? I suspect that here it would be futile to inquire into whether this instance presents the same kind of unique mix of characteristics that justifies the special pro-

---

[97] 376 U.S. 254 (1964).

[98] 458 U.S. 886 (1982).

[99] 103 S. Ct. 1702 (1983).

[100] *See supra* note 32.

[101] 354 U.S. 234 (1957). I pick *Sweezy* because it concerns speech *in the classroom*, albeit indirectly, but still in contrast with all of the supposed "academic freedom" cases that in fact involve merely the free speech rights of public employees, on their own time, some of whom coincidentally happen to be teachers. *See* Schauer, *Private Speech*, *supra* note 2, at 242-49. These issues were raised but ultimately not decided in Princeton Univ. v. Schmid, 455 U.S. 100 (1982) (per curiam) (dismissing appeal for mootness, lack of standing, and absence of article III jurisdiction).

[102] 457 U.S. 853 (1982) (plurality opinion).

[103] I use "historical" not in the sense of a problem that was perceived as significant by the framers, or even at that time, but rather in the sense of a problem that the Court has perceived as having been a problem in the past. Thus, the rigidity of current standards for obscenity, Miller v. California, 413 U.S. 15 (1973); Jenkins v. Georgia, 418 U.S. 153 (1974); Pinkus v. United States, 436 U.S. 293 (1978), is likely a reaction to the extremes of the nineteenth and first half of the twentieth centuries, and not to problems identified as such, or even existing, in the eighteenth century.

[104] 420 U.S. 546 (1975).

[105] 418 U.S. 153 (1974).

[106] *E.g.*, Shiffrin, *supra* note 9, at 1238-39.

tection of speech.[107] Rather, we would look at the particular components of that mix that were present in the case at hand, and when that happens this second type of multi-valued theory collapses into the first.

IX

Earlier I drew the distinction between abstract political theory and constitutional interpretation.[108] Although it is a hotly contested point of constitutional theory,[109] at least all of the participants in this Symposium subscribe to the view that the development of constitutional principles need not be based solely on the dictionary definition of the words in the text,[110] nor on the specific understandings of those who drafted the provisions at issue. Thus, the task of the courts, in attempting to interpret the open-ended and morally loaded constitutional provisions—freedom of speech, equal protection, cruel and unusual punishment, and so on—is to develop a theory of these clauses, a theory that will be significantly philosophical but will include a large dose of precedent.[111]

When we are engaged in theory construction in this sense, we can proceed in alternative ways. One approach is to attempt to work out an ideal political theory independent of the particular constitutional provision at issue, such as freedom of speech, and then proceed to apply that clause to the extent that it supports that theory. I have little sympathy for this approach, in large part because its chief analytical tool seems to be the shoehorn. To the extent that the text does not fit the preconceived theory, then a little pushing and pulling, huffing and puffing, bending and slicing, and—*voila*—one's preconstructed political theory just happens to be embodied in the Constitution, with nothing left out.[112]

An alternative approach, and one much more consistent with my vision of constitutionalism, is one that starts with the particular clause as the mandate for building a narrow theory *of that clause*. We start with freedom of speech, for example, because freedom of speech is

---

[107] It is possible, of course, that we might create a rule based on a certain general mix of characteristics, and then, like most rules, apply it more or less mechanically without determining whether this particular instance does or does not fit the underlying theory of the rule. That perception, however, does not apply to this inquiry, in which, by stipulation, we are dealing with those close instances that require that we go beneath the surface of the rule.

[108] *See supra* text accompanying notes 46-47.

[109] *See Constitutional Adjudication and Democratic Theory*, 56 N.Y.U. L. Rev. 259 (1981); *Judicial Review versus Democracy*, 42 Ohio St. L.J. 1 (1981); *Judicial Review and the Constitution The Text and Beyond*, 8 U. Dayton L. Rev. 443 (1983).

[110] I use "dictionary definition" to make the statement non-trivial. Everyone purports to be defining the terms in the Constitution. The dispute is about where the definition comes from. *See* Schauer, *supra* note 28.

[111] *See* Schauer, *supra* note 46. *See also supra* note 64 and accompanying text.

[112] For more extensive criticism of this approach, see Monaghan, *supra* note 47.

NORTHWESTERN UNIVERSITY LAW REVIEW

written down in the authoritative document, and then proceed to work out a theory of freedom of speech. Under this approach we accept the presupposition that speech is special, because the text imposes that presupposition on us. Then we try as hard as we can to derive an underlying theory that is consistent with the textual presupposition. It is this process that I have implicitly described throughout this Article. We are required to accept the view that the Constitution gives speech and press special protection, that in close cases we must develop an underlying theory of the first amendment, and that this underlying theory must be consistent with, and preferably supportive of, the special protection for speech given by the document. It is in this sense that I maintain that speech must be special.

X

There is an intellectual ache in all of this, and it may be shared by many people now engaged in the process of trying to explore the theoretical foundations of the principle of freedom of speech. As we reject many of the classical platitudes about freedom of speech and engage in somewhat more rigorous analysis, trying to discover why speech—potentially harmful and dangerous, often offensive, and the instrument of evil as often as of good—should be treated as it is, our intuitions about the value of free speech, solid as they may be, are difficult to reconcile with this analysis. The ache, it seems to me, is caused by the fact that although the answer to "Must speech be special?" is probably "Yes," the answer to *"Is* speech special?" is probably "No." Reconciling this inconsistency is the agenda we cannot avoid.

Copyright 1984 by Northwestern University School of Law
Northwestern University Law Review

Printed in U.S.A.
Vol. 78, No. 5

COMMENTARY

> *The following Commentary is exerpted from the Symposium discussion held following the presentation of Professor Michael J. Perry's paper* Freedom of Expression: An Essay on Theory and Doctrine, *the final version of which appears on pages 1137-1211 of this issue, Professor Steven Shiffrin's paper* The First Amendment and Economic Regulation: Away from a General Theory of the First Amendment, *the final version of which appears on pages 1212-83 of this issue, and Professor Frederick F. Schauer's paper* Must Speech Be Special?, *the final version of which appears on pages 1284-1306 of this issue.*

Professor Nathanson: Perhaps I may depart just slightly from my role as impartial moderator to say a word in defense of the title, for which I am not responsible. I started with a criticism of the last part of the title, because it referred only to theoretical perspectives, and not realistic or surrealistic perspectives. Now, Professor Schauer has attacked the *first* part of the title, because, he says, the amendment says freedom of speech, and not freedom of expression. But surely, he has to admit that the first amendment also refers to freedom of assembly and freedom of the press. And now I think we've reached the point of open house, and I suppose I ought to turn first to the panel to say whether anyone wants to say a word in defense or offense. I must say that while I was listening to Professor Schauer, I kept thinking on 'he one hand of Moses, and Einstein. Weren't they looking for the one principle—did he find it?

Professor Schauer: I think not.

Professor Redish: Fred, I've looked at your book, I looked at your paper before you delivered it today, and I listened to you today. And, in all three instances, you argue, as does Judge Bork, that the only satisfactory approach to the first amendment is to find some value distinct, or above and beyond, the broader liberty value. Maybe it's my fault—I'll be damned if I can figure out what that is, from either what you've written or what you've said. And this is basically what my criticism of Judge Bork was. To argue that the only category of speech that can be protected is that which fosters a unique value to speech leaves protected speech as a null set. As I commented in my article on this issue, I think Judge Bork is simply incorrect when he argues that political truth is the only type of speech that fosters a unique value to speech. There are numerous activities, wholly non-communicative, that can help you attain knowledge of political truth. Being a doctor can help you figure out whether socialized medicine is a good idea. Riding on the CTA can help you figure out whether aid to mass transit is necessary. So not even the one category Judge Bork suggests fosters a value unique to speech. I think Fred's characterization of my criticism of Bork was a little misleading, although true, as far as it went. I did say that a natural starting place, if we're going to look for a response to Bork, is the language of the first amendment. And I argued there that if one is to be truly principled, as Judge Bork is suggesting you must be, one would not start inserting limits on otherwise unlimited language in the first amendment. The amendment says nothing about only protecting political speech. It says "speech."

Yet I think that my argument went further than merely an argument from coincidence. I added that had the framers thought about whether they should provide special protection to speech rather than conduct, they had some very good reasons for doing so. The first amendment protection of communicative activities can be seen as a recognition of the value of development of the intellect, development of the mind, and not just self-realization of your talent as a tennis player, or as a barmaid, as Judge Bork says, but of the development of the unique qualities of a human being—the ability to reason, to think, to appreciate. Now it is true that sometimes conduct can do this, indirectly. It is also true that sometimes speech can cause significant harm. But in drafting a constitution, the framers cannot articulate individual instances deserving of protection and those not deserving of protection. They have to generalize. And it seems to me that in generalizing, they can appropriately say that, more often than not—in fact, *much* more often than not—communicative activities are likely to develop the intellect and again, much more often than not, the dangers of these communicative activities are not likely to be as harmful, or certainly as acute or immediate, as conduct or action. So it seems to me that that explains why speech is given such special protection, rather than pure liberty, which of course is relegated to the lesser protection of the fifth amendment. The people who characterize my theory as fostering only one value have not been technically incorrect, but have certainly been incomplete in describing what I say. When I say in my earlier writings that self-realization is the only value ultimately fostered by free speech, I argue that the other values that people have suggested, such as the marketplace of ideas, or the democratic process value, or the checking function, are simply sub-values of the broader goals of self-realization. I don't think that extension necessarily means that the self-realization characterization is unhelpful, as I gather that Professor Shiffrin was implying. It seems to me that the failure to recognize that all of these

78:1307 (1983)   *Commentary*

values which people have argued that the first amendment fosters ultimately derive from what I call self-realization prevents us from seeing that *all* subjects of expression are equally worthy of protection. Thus, acceptance of my theory establishes that there is no justification for giving greater protection to political expression than to commercial advertising, or obscenity, or literature, or art. The example that I usually give to show the absurdity of protecting political expression more than other forms, such as commercial expression, is to assume a hypothetical society in which all decisions are made by the electorate—what kind of toothpaste you'll use, what kind of television set you'll buy. Presumably, Bork, Meiklejohn, and the other "political process" free speech theorists would say that speech relating to those decisions is part of the political process and therefore is protected by the first amendment. Meiklejohn says this is so because the people are ultimately the governors and they need this information to help them govern their lives better. If we then change the hypothesis and cede to the individual full responsibility for each of these decisions—the decision of what toothpaste to buy, where to go to college, whom to marry, what television set to buy—now the individual's influence in governing his or her life is not diluted, it is not indirect; it is total, it is 100 percent, as are the consequences. Now the logic of Bork's division, of Meiklejohn's division, and I suppose of your's, Fred, although I'm not clear on what your's is, exactly, would be to say that all of a sudden, the interest in free speech, the interest in providing information to the individual so he or she could govern his or her life, disappears. To me that is, at best, counterintuitive, and that is why I think it is a necessary and important task to figure out why we are protecting speech related to the political process, why we want to protect speech related to literature. If the value we find there is really fostered also by protecting obscenity, by protecting private defamation, by protecting commercial speech, we can see that any hierachy in those values in really irrational. That's really where I set out to go, and I guess I remain unconvinced that I was wrong.

Professor Greenawalt: Well, what I want to say is not directly in response to anything that anybody said, although I think it's an objection to Bork's position. It does suggest that Michael Perry may be struggling to accomplish something that could be accomplished more easily in another way. The point is this: there is a free exercise clause in the Constitution. When that was adopted, it clearly protected prosyletizing and talk about religious matters. Most talk or a lot of talk about moral questions would then have been regarded as closely linked to or as being an aspect of talk about religious matters. So I think that it is a ludicrous position that talk about moral questions and so on would be talk outside the first amendment, and it is therefore a ludicrous position

NORTHWESTERN UNIVERSITY LAW REVIEW

that the first amendment could somehow single out political speech. That clearly is an independent objection to Bork's theory different from others that have been raised here today. I think this blindness in people who write about the first amendment—I don't know what they have against the free exercise clause insofar as it relates to free expression about religion, but it is very rarely mentioned—is both troubling and important.

Professor Shiffrin: I share Professor Schauer's point that there is a disagreement among members of this panel in terms of whether or not political systems or moral systems are derivative of first principles or whether or not there is a plurality of irreducible, irreconcilable principles. I think in philosophy we are beginning to see a movement away from what was the trend in the '70's, which was Rawls, Dworkin, Ackerman, Richards, Freed, and others, attempting to justify liberalism by resort to very thin conceptions about human beings and to derive sweeping conclusions on the basis of a Kantian-oriented style of argument. I am committed to attacking that view and defending a different form of liberalism, a form of liberalism which I argue is derivative of John Stuart Mill and which builds on a plurality of principles. I have two fundamental objections to the system builders. The first objection is that society is simply too complex and human beings are too complex with too many conflicting values to assume that deductive modes of argument from their premises about human beings are promising argumentative strategies. Secondly, I think the system builders implicitly emphasize the intelligent side of human beings, the reasoning side, while diminishing the passionate side. That problem inheres in the Kantian tradition. By leaving out the passionate side of human beings, by regarding legal, moral, and political problems as logical puzzles to be "solved," system builders too often ignore strongly held values. They produce systems far too removed from human communities to be considered attractive.

The system building controversy is obviously alive in first amendment theory. The need for attempting to develop systems to avoid ambiguity, to try to say that there's this principle out there that is dictating what we are doing seems strongly evident in Professor Baker's writing and in Professor Redish's writing. I've not read Professor Perry's article with care, but I think he may also be a card-carrying system builder.

Two final comments. With respect to Professor Redish's emphasis on self-realization, his claim is that all worthy first amendment values are captured in the self-realization concept. But one important first amendment value is not captured by self-realization. It is the idea that a system of freedom of speech helps to prevent abuses of power. Professor Redish says that he doesn't think the case has been made in support of that value. We could have an argument about it, but his self-realization does not embrace a first amendment value that has long been considered important. There is also an emphasis on *self* in self-realization. It seems to ignore collective values. It seems to ignore associational values. Ignore is too strong, because self can be realized through associations. But one can start from a conception of communication which is less rigidly individualistic and more social in character. Finally—I may be totally off base here—with respect to Professor Perry's piece, to focus on information and opinion in the first amendment is to focus on the content of speech. And it seems to me that one can look at speech as a process, as interaction, as a relationship, and that a focus on content obscures those dimensions. A focus on information and opinion seems to downplay the importance of relational values. I don't know whether that is a legitimate objection.

Professor Baker: I want to talk about balancing versus absolutism, something that hasn't really been a theme in my writing, partly because I view that as one of the simpler of the first amendment issues. But the issue relates to comments I have about some of the papers presented today. But first, let me make a different point.

An account of the value or values with which the first amendment is concerned, I would assume, is only an initial aspect of a first amendment theory. And as I've developed the theory in the article, *Scope of the First Amendment* in *UCLA*, I try to develop the needed additional aspect, an aspect which I argue relates to how protected conduct promotes the relevant value or values. This aspect of the theory responds to Professor Schuaer's well-taken point that the value itself may overprotect, may protect virtually everything. For example, my self-expression might be forcefully and meaningfully embodied in my shooting a couple of our political leaders. That expressive conduct also might be politically expressive and, thus, promote the central value in the political conception of the first amendment. I would not claim however, that either the self-expression or the political expression justification for the first amendment then ought to lead to protection of the assassinations. The key—and most difficult—problem of an adequate theory of the first amendment is figuring out in what ways the first amendment protects the values that justify the first amendment—that is, what individual conduct is protected or what government practices are required or prohibited and in what way, to what extent, and in what circumstances is the conduct protected or the practice required or prohibited. As to these issues the language of the first amendment may be quite suggestive—the focus on things like speech, assembly, and religion seems to suggest protection of the type of activity where people are trying to realize themselves in ways that, although the activity may harm others, are typically noncoercive and are not physically injurious—activities that can harm a person only because of that person's or another's acceptance of values or information. If this quality is typical of conduct named by the first amendment, the key to what is protected may be conduct that operates in this manner—conduct in which you're realizing your liberty or autonomy in ways that aren't coercive upon other people. Of course, this opens up a new can of worms in trying to deal with concepts with which philosophers have had a lot of trouble, concepts like violence or coercion. I thought that Professor Greenawalt's piece this morning did a good job elaborating some of these issues.

Once you look at the first amendment this way, as including both central values and as protecting certain ways of promoting those values, then I would argue that Professor Perry is wrong in his conclusion that the process-democratic theory notion as well as the epistemic notion, at least if it is not supplemental and dominated by self-realization, self-expression, autonomy values, leads to the same results. First of all, I have problems with any postulate of the primacy of democratic process in that, by itself, this notion doesn't have any particular content. So many different practices could amount to a democratic process that the concept at least by itself and without a value-based interpretation, is inadequate to lead to any conclusion about the scope of the first amendment. Now, in fact, I've ended up agreeing with Professor Perry, in an article I did for *Southern Cal*, that a properly devised first amendment theory based on the idea of individual liberty or autonomy would in fact protect a process that we could both call democratic and that we could have some confidence would progressively lead to an ever more democratic and more just society. But that result follows only because the notion of autonomy or liberty gives, I think, some content to what an appropriate, or desirable democratic process is. Only when the democratic process is congruent with these values can one expect that it would lead to good results.

To the extent, for instance, that you are only concerned with process, Professor Redish's early paper on commercial speech was persuasive. Commercial speech may very well be useful not only to individual self-realization, but may provide information that is relevant to the political marketplace. The Court's decision in *Virginia Board of Pharmacy*, it seems to me, took all of the best analysis in Redish's article and put it into constitutional law. And given a particular notion of the way the first amendment promotes or protects a democratic process or individual autonomy, that decision would be the natural result. In a less positive way, that is, with a view of the first amendment as a constraint on certain types of interferences with or abridgements of liberty, I have argued for a different way of protecting or promoting autonomy, a way that I've argued reaches a result diametrically opposed to that of the Court and Professor Redish. The key issue is how you determine and elaborate what the protective nature of the first amendment is.

78:1307 (1983)   *Commentary*

At that point, we might return to Professor Shiffrin's comment about clear truth. We know that there are pharmacists, drugs, and drug prices, and can, with little controversy, check the accuracy of many statements about drug prices. A lot of other corporate speech is clearly going to be accurate. This speech is also, as the Court in *Pharmacy* recognized, going to have political implications. It's going to have re- source-allocation implications. Although a lot of people are not very persuaded by my argument for this conclusion, if, for whatever reason, given one's notion of autonomy, one is convinced that corporate actors are not appropriate agents in the political process, then protecting their speech would not lead to a better realization of autonomy. The influ- ence that even accurate advertising will have on people's values, the way it will lead to particular decisions about resource allocation, means that to protect this commercial speech is to give the corporate enter- prise—and, arguably, the market structure itself—the power to influ- ence the political process. That result is not so obviously correct. So at that point the notion of clear truth does not so obviously point to any conclusion. The *distortion* that corporate advertising causes in the political arena is one aspect of what this *accurate* advertising might do.

At this point, I want to say just a couple of things about the issue of balancing. And I'll have to admit to not being completely convinced on my own position, particularly vis a vis the position that Professor Shiffrin describes in terms of multiplicity of principles. I'm even more troubled by my position because it seems to me that intellectual catego- ries that humans develop are inevitably going to be makeshift and rough. To accord these categories or concepts or values some absolute status seems to me to be just like reifying their inevitable ad hocness. Despite that, I would argue that a more absolutist, non-balancing ap- proach is appropriate for a number of reasons. I argue that balancing is generally conservatively biased, although I accept Professors Perry's and Shiffrin's point that theoretically a person could only try to place true human interests into the balance rather than rely on existing pref- erences. Many people would find this enlightened form of balancing even more troublesome and dangerous than the conservative version. Herbert Marcuse advocates that notion of freedom of speech when he argues that we should supress various viewpoints or the speech of vari- ous people or groups in society, the capitalist group, for example. Not all of us would want to go along with someone else's conclusions as to what our true interests are. Identification of our true interests is also quite obviously difficult at the present time, given that our present in- terests are presumably distorted. Despite these doubts about our abil- ity fully to recognize and, thus, to balance our true interests, I would also argue that there is a sense in which a thin Kantian notion of auton- omy does lead to an appropriate constitutional standard—not for eval- uating the whole human world, but for prescribing the degree to which we ought want to constrain the political process, constrain collective freedom of choice; I would argue that there is some relevance in elaborating an idea of both individual autonomy and the quality of respect; and that we would want the content of this elaboration to be constitutive aspects of, to be constitutive rules for, our political society in which we would argue as Professor Shiffrin argues about the more specific aspects of what it is to be a human. The notion of a basic constitutive framework for further political choice embodies the first reason to adopt an absolutist approach. There are at least three other pragmatic reasons. One is as an intellectual tool: an absolutist approach would arguably force us to examine and reexamine our instincts with greater care. And it would require us to engage in a more tightly-knit analysis that often would lead us to conclusions that we weren't previously ready to accept. In this way, absolutism provides an effective tool to force us to consider new possibilities and to break the hold of conventionality. It's a method of moving us to Rawl's reflective equilibrium. Finally, there are two systemic arguments for a more absolutist approach. One was developed by Justice Linde, namely that in contrast to balancing, an absolutist or rule-based interpretation gives much more reality to the Constitution; this approach will provide much better direction to the lawyers and lawmakers, who initially will be making the constitutional decisions and would at least be able to rely on some concrete principles. Second, there is Professor Emerson's point, also a systemic point—his book is called *The System of Freedom of Expression*—that we need to think about what doctrinal approaches will be applied in ways that give adequate protection in times of hysteria or social conflict to speech that in calmer times we'd all agree ought to be protected. It may be that, in times of calmness, Justice Powell will typically come up with relatively mainstream, liberal, protective results. The danger is that in times of tension, or in respect to issues that threaten conventional values, the balancing type of approach doesn't give the Court or the individual Justices guidance or a doctrinal basis to support taking a position that is likely to be unpopular. And so, as a matter of how the system is likely to operate, there is this practical interest in a more absolutist approach.

Professor Redish: I wanted to say a few words about Professor Baker's summation of the view of balancing and absolutism. The first point may be a little unfair, because I'm not sure if this was a conscious choice on your part, or just a matter of semantics. But throughout the day, you've referred to to the concept of being *more* absolute. That sounds to me like being slightly dead. Either you give absolute protection or you don't. I'm not sure how you can be *more* absolute than somebody else. But what this implies to me is that perhaps you are subliminally acknowledging that what you are doing is really engaging

78:1307 (1983)   *Commentary*

in an extremely protective form of balancing, which you label absolutism. I find this a little misleading. I don't think you're anything approaching an absolutist; I don't accept Professor Schauer's first, second, third generation concepts. I think perhaps you lose some credibility in the debate when you label yourself absolutist; I think that turns a lot of people off who won't listen beyond that. I think if they listen, what they'll find is that you're setting up some very carefully, well thought-out, structured balancing. My second point concerns your argument that one of the systemic justifications for this so-called absolutism is as a protection against the Court getting caught up in the paranoia of the age, the concern Professor Ely has suggested as a basis for strict categorization rather than balancing. The way I see it, you can make your categorization as strict as you want, but if the Court wants to get caught up in the paranoia of the age, it will chuck those categorizations. The *Dennis* case in 1951 is a classic illustration. I have no doubt that if the Court in *Dennis* did what it claimed it was doing, which was applying the Holmes-Brandeis version of clear and present danger, there's absolutely no way they could have upheld the conviction there. But because that Court actually had gotten caught up in the nation's paranoia, the majority twisted and manipulated the language of at least a somewhat more categorical rule beyond all recognition, and the more candid Justices, in concurring, suggested that the Court discard the clear and present danger test, because that test would prevent the Court from sufficiently protecting society. So if there is to be any protection against the Court's getting caught up in the paranoia of the age, I think that it is our long tradition of judicial independence, and the Court's own recognition of its role as a buffer, to protect the minority in such times. But if the Court is unwilling to recognize its role, no absolute statement, no categorical statement is going to avoid that.

Professor Shiffrin: Professor Baker made a point which was that one of the reasons he favored more absolutist approaches was that he thought it would lead to better results. It seems to me that that is the real point. When we create either a balancing approach or an absolutist approach, we do it with an eye toward what the results for human beings are going to be. And as commentators, we are certainly no different than the Court in that respect. You notice in the fourth amendment area— in one compartment of the fourth amendment—it is the conservatives who want to break down the categories and who have a more open-ended view. They want to break down probable cause and start having a sliding scale of reasonableness. They want to take all of the factors into account. And they want to do it because of what the results would be. It would give law enforcement greater flexibility and discretion. And the liberals have opposed balancing in that area simply because they want to protect rights of individuals from invasions of privacy,

NORTHWESTERN UNIVERSITY LAW REVIEW

and the like. In the equal protection area, it is the liberals who want to break down the categories. They want to say, we've only got a couple of suspect classes here, and we want to expand them. We only have a couple of fundamental rights and we want to expand them. It's the conservatives who there say, we can't balance at all; it would be bad. It's very clear why that debate is taking place: it's because of what the consequences will be. I agree that the question of whether or not we should be balancing or creating rules is in part dependent upon—in large part dependent upon—what the outcome is going to be. But this whole dispute we're having over whether we should have balancing is collapsing two different questions. One is the extent to which we can have rules. The other is the question of how much we value speech. And that in turn is related to the coverage question. The more speech the first amendment covers (my view is that at a minimum all ordinary language is covered) then the more you are going to want to balance, because the more that's swept in, the more likely a lot of it is not going to be terribly important. And if you are weighing speech against reputation or privacy or security, there is no particular reason to think that speech is more important at the outset. That forces one into a balancing methodology. So it seems to me that these things are complex and interrelated. The question of coverage is related to the question of whether one balances. Finally, I'd like to associate myself with Marty Redish's point, which is that we can certainly exaggerate the extent to which rules will bind judges. It seems to me that whether we have a rule approach or a more flexible approach, the cases like *Dennis* are going to recur.

Professor Baker: A response to Professor Redish's and Professor Shiffrin's comments would require a lot in the way of empirical arguments about the likely results of the different approaches. I would argue, although for somewhat different reasons, that in the equal protection area, as well as in the first amendment area, that we need an adequate elaboration of a normative theory of what the equal protection clause is about; and that an absolute application of that theory is more appropriate and would be more liberal, more progressive, than what the Court is presently doing. I have argued in my articles that this is the case. I would, however, certainly admit that judges are not bound by their approaches. Still I would want to argue that to some extent one can be convinced of, and then committed to, an approach. If I accept an approach that gives me guidance, if it gives me help, something that I can rely upon, then the approach will tend to lead to particular results. Thus, it should be no surprise that absolutism is associated with Douglas, who tended to be pro-first amendment expression. I would also characterize Brennan, in many aspects of his analysis, as being more a categorizer, absolutist-oriented Justice than a balancer. It seems to me

78:1307 (1983) *Commentary*

that where Brennan, who is another Justice for whom I have the very highest respect, deviates from an absolutist first amendment approach is where to some extent he gives play to the marketplace of ideas theory as well as an individual liberty theory. He balances only when he relies on the marketplace theory, which I think is almost necessary because here without balancing competing instrumental concerns you get bad results. Thus, Brennan balances in some areas and is an absolutist in others, a result that follows because of his particular commitment both to a constitutive individual liberty notion and an instrumental marketplace of ideas or political process conception.

But as a general matter, I would not want to rely on empirical claims that in fact an absolutist approach would work out better. In the end, I believe that there are several fundamental values that are not in conflict and ought to be bases for organizating human society—notions of individual autonomy and of quality of respect, and that these values can be developed by a relatively abstract, universalist theory and implemented as relatively absolute, constitutive constraints on or requirements for the legal or political organization of society. These values lead both to limits on our political process and they, at the same time, also justify the political process. And so, therefore, it's appropriate to conclude that the political process ought to dominate within certain realms, and it ought to have either no room or a theoretically restricted role in certain realms.

Professor Schauer: I want to say one more thing about rules. We can all come up with examples like *Dennis*, where rules break down in times of extreme panic. *Korematsu* is another example. But it is also important to realize that in the non-extreme cases, rules may serve a much more important function in channelling behavior, including judicial behavior, and we should be wary of focusing only on the extreme, war-time panic kinds of cases. Take for example *Jenkins v. Georgia*. The Supreme Court in 1974 decided nine to nothing, with Justice Rehnquist writing the opinion, that *Carnal Knowledge* was not obscene regardless of what the State of Georgia thought. I have grave doubts that Justice Rehnquist thought that *Carnal Knowledge* was a good movie. I have grave doubts as to whether Justice Rehnquist, as a matter of abstract political theory, would think that *Carnal Knowledge* ought to be protected and much in Justice Rehnquist's philosophy would support deference to state judgments about such matters. But the rules have become relatively settled, at least as applied to that kind of case, and the Court, barring wartime situations, seems to me to be significantly channelled, and appropriately so, by the gradual evolution of rules. The rules channel the decisions away from pre-legal instincts in many cases, and it is a mistake to take the occasional aberration as a mandate for discounting the importance of rules.

NORTHWESTERN UNIVERSITY LAW REVIEW

Finally, Ed Baker mentioned a few minutes ago something about speech being inherently, or in most cases, less coercive. Maybe the appropriate way to end, or at least for me to end, is to suggest that this is something that divides many of us and that's worth thinking about. Implicit in what Professors Perry, Baker and Haiman have said is the idea that speech is, in many ways, different from other forms of conduct. It is in most cases inherently less coercive, they argue; it operates much more on the mind; it is a fundamentally different form of behavior. But, it can be argued, as I have argued, that speech can cause the same kinds of consequences and the same kinds of harms as the full range of other behavior. Speech can hurt people; it can embarass them; it can humiliate them; it can cause them financial harm and it can do many other things normally taken as sufficient to justify government intervention. It seems to me that it is artificial to say that speech is totally different in kind or even largely different in kind from other forms of human behavior. Speech, or language, is part and parcel of what we are, and the task of justifying carving speech out for special solicitude is not nearly as easy as is often assumed.

Part III
Focus: Action Regulated or Government Reason?

[11]

COMMENT

FLAG DESECRATION: A CASE STUDY
IN THE ROLES OF CATEGORIZATION
AND BALANCING
IN FIRST AMENDMENT ANALYSIS

John Hart Ely [*]

*Since 1969, the Supreme Court has three times reversed the con-
victions of persons who "desecrated" the American flag as a symbolic
means of political protest. But each time the Court avoided a broad
holding that flag desecration for symbolic purposes is constitutionally protected under the first amendment. In this Comment, Professor Ely describes a doctrinal framework for first amendment
analysis originally developed by the Supreme Court of the late
Warren era. This framework, he argues, not only provides a stable
basis for judicial resolution of free expression questions generally,
but also suggests both the immediate difficulty and the ultimate
resolution of the flag desecration problem.*

O N three occasions over the past few years the Supreme Court, on one narrow ground or another, has avoided definitively ruling on the constitutionality of convictions for politically inspired destruction or alteration of the American flag.[1] The most recent decision, *Spence v. Washington*,[2] does seem to approach such a ruling, at least if one ignores the various irrelevancies with which the Court hedged its opinion.[3] But logical or not, the qualifications are part of the opinion, and one must assume that the Court finds the issue troubling. At first glance, however, it is hard to see why. Laws prohibiting flag desecration [4] quite obviously inhibit political

---

* Professor of Law, Harvard University. A.B., Princeton, 1960; LL.B., Yale, 1963.

[1] *See* Spence v. Washington, 418 U.S. 405 (1974) (per curiam); Smith v. Goguen, 415 U.S. 566 (1974); Street v. New York, 394 U.S. 576 (1969).

[2] 418 U.S. 405 (1974) (per curiam).

[3] *See id.* at 413–15 (relying on facts that Spence's disfigurement was temporary, and unlikely to lead viewers to conclude that the government agreed with his views). One also hopes that the Court is not prepared to distinguish among future cases on the basis of its characterization of Spence's behavior as "a pointed expression of anguish" rather than "an act of mindless nihilism." *Id.* at 410. *See also id.* at 414–15 n.10. It could happen, though. *Cf.* Wisconsin v. Yoder, 406 U.S. 205, 216–17, 222–23 n.11, 235–36 (1972) (distinguishing Amish, who are nice people not on welfare, from other groups who might seek to keep their children out of school).

[4] "Desecration" and "improper use" provisions are commonly distinguished. *See*

expression,[5] and the state's interest in doing so — at least when
the flag is owned by the person doing the disfiguring, and that is
how these cases come up — seems scarcely articulable, let alone
strong. The Court's hesitancy, one gathers, stems at least in part
from its 1968 decision in *United States* v. *O'Brien*,[6] upholding a
conviction for draft card burning.[7] And indeed the act of burning a
flag does look a lot like the act of burning a draft card, which
makes it difficult to deny the surface plausibility of the inference
that the former can also be proscribed. The plausibility is mostly
on the surface, however. Indeed, once certain ambiguities in
the test *O'Brien* set forth are resolved — in the only way that is
defensible or even remotely consistent with other, virtually con-
temporaneous decisions — the case will be seen to argue rather
strongly *against* the constitutionality of such laws.[8]

I

The "crux of the Court's opinion"[9] in *O'Brien* was that:[10]

> [A] governmental regulation is sufficiently justified . . . [1] if it
> furthers an important or substantial governmental interest; [2] if the

---

pp. 1502, 1503 *infra*. Until we reach section VI of this Comment, at which point
the distinction will become relevant, I shall use "desecration" to encompass all
alterations.

[5] Property rights would also seem to be involved. Believers in substantive due
process — and I do not so count myself — might well question whether the state
can constitutionally prohibit the destruction of one's own personal property unless
it is unique (a Rembrandt) or scarce (uranium). The point is not pursued, however, since a governmental justification that would answer the first amendment
objection would seem a fortiori to dispose of this one.

[6] 391 U.S. 367 (1968).

[7] *See, e.g.*, Smith v. Goguen, 415 U.S. 566, 589–90 (1974) (White, J., concurring); *id.* at 599–600 (Rehnquist, J., dissenting); Street v. New York, 394 U.S. 576,
616 (1969) (Fortas, J., dissenting).

[8] This Comment makes no attempt to synthesize or even to describe the first
amendment thinking of the present Supreme Court. It suggests, rather, that there
was a period of several years, spanning the end of Earl Warren's Chief Justiceship
and the beginning of Warren Burger's, when the Court (with important, though
by no means exclusive, input from Justice Harlan) began to describe a general
theory of the first amendment that assigned distinct and quite sensible roles to the
two general techniques of evaluation — categorization and balancing — that had
theretofore been regarded as mutually exclusive approaches to all free expression
problems. *See generally* pp. 1500–02 *infra*. The record of the Court more recently
is by no means uniformly negative: much that was good in the period I have mentioned has been preserved. *See* note 32 *infra*. But the effort at explicit system-
atization seems to have been suspended, and the more recent decisions therefore
do not figure importantly in this discussion.

[9] This is Justice Harlan's characterization. *See* 391 U.S. at 388 (Harlan, J.,
concurring).

[10] *Id.* at 377 (bracketed numbers added). The requirement that the regulation
be "within the constitutional power of the Government," *id.*, is omitted on the

governmental interest is unrelated to the suppression of free expression; and [3] if the incidental restriction on alleged First Amendment freedoms is no greater than is essential to the furtherance of that interest.

Whatever *O'Brien*'s other merits or demerits, the Court is surely to be commended for here attempting something it attempts too seldom, the statement of a coherent and applicable test. The test is not limited to cases involving so-called "symbolic speech." [11] (One conclusion that should emerge from this Comment is that that is one of its virtues.) The test is, however, limited in the sense that it is incomplete. The fact that a regulation does not satisfy criterion [2] does not necessarily mean that it is unconstitutional. It means "only" that the case is switched onto another track and an approach other than that indicated in criterion [3] will be employed,[12] a categorizing approach elaborated in other decisions of the late Warren period, which is in fact substantially more demanding than the approach indicated by criterion [3]. Criterion [3] is also incomplete as described in *O'Brien*. In practice its application involves a choice between different conceptions of its standard, a choice made by reference to factors neither *O'Brien* nor any other Supreme Court decision has yet made explicit. This variability in the content of criterion [3] is important: it reduces the reliability of what at first might seem to be the most restrictive element of *O'Brien*'s test, and thus highlights the significance of what is in fact critical — the "switching function" performed by criterion [2]. It is to criterion [3] that we first look.

II

Criterion [3]'s requirement that the inhibition of expression be no greater than is essential to the furtherance of the state's interest strikes a familiar chord: "less restrictive alternative" analysis is common in constitutional law generally and in first amendment cases in particular. But there is always a latent ambiguity in the analysis, and *O'Brien* brought it to the surface. Weakly construed, it could require only that there be no less

---

ground that it is superfluous in light of the most natural reading of what is designated criterion [1]. (Accepted notions of what is within the constitutional power of government have, in any event, become extremely broad.)

[11] Earlier in the paragraph in which the Court stated its test, there is reference to cases in which "'speech' and 'nonspeech' elements are combined in the same course of conduct." *See id.* at 376. But the decisions cited in connection with that passage concern forms of expression that transcend narrowly defined "symbolic speech." *See id.* at 376–77 & nn.22–27. *See also* p. 1494 *infra*.

[12] *See also* Spence v. Washington, 418 U.S. 405, 414 n.8 (1974).

restrictive alternative capable of serving the state's interest *as efficiently as it is served by the regulation under attack*.[13] But as I have noted elsewhere, in virtually every case involving real legislation, a more perfect fit involves some added cost.[14] In effect, therefore, this weak formulation would reach only laws that engage in the gratuitous inhibition of expression, requiring only that a prohibition not outrun the interest it is designed to serve.

Further language in the *O'Brien* opinion,[15] and the holding of the case, indicate that this is the strongest form of less restrictive alternative analysis in which, under the circumstances, the Court was prepared to engage.[16] Coupled with the trivial func-

---

[13] *See, e.g.,* Struve, *The Less-Restrictive-Alternative Principle and Economic Due Process,* 80 HARV. L. REV. 1463, 1463 (1967) (footnotes omitted):

> The principle [endorsed by the author] is this: an economic regulation violates due process if the government . . . can achieve the purposes of the challenged regulation equally effectively by one or more narrower regulations. The term "equally effective" is meant literally: a regulation should not be invalidated because of an alternative that is "nearly as effective" or "tolerably effective."

[14] *See* Ely, *The Constitutionality of Reverse Racial Discrimination,* 41 U. CHI. L. REV. 723, 729 (1974). *See also* note 16 *infra.*

[15]

> The 1965 Amendment prohibits such conduct and does nothing more. In other words, both the governmental interest and the operation of the 1965 Amendment are limited to the noncommunicative aspect of O'Brien's conduct. The governmental interest and the scope of the 1965 Amendment are limited to preventing harm to the smooth and efficient functioning of the Selective Service System.

391 U.S. at 381–82.

> In conclusion, we find that . . . because amended § 462(b) is an appropriately narrow means of protecting this interest and condemns only the independent noncommunicative impact of conduct within its reach . . . a sufficient governmental interest has been shown to justify O'Brien's conviction.

Id. at 382.

[16] *See* Ely, *Legislative and Administrative Motivation in Constitutional Law,* 79 YALE L.J. 1205, 1340 (1970). In his opinion for the Court in United States v. Robel, 389 U.S. 258 (1967), decided a year before *O'Brien*, Chief Justice Warren had insisted in a footnote that less drastic means analysis involves no balancing of interests whatever, but rather an almost mechanical pruning of superfluous restraints:

> It has been suggested that this case should be decided by "balancing" the governmental interests expressed in [the statute] against the First Amendment rights asserted by the appellee. This we decline to do. . . . We have ruled only that the Constitution requires that the conflict between congressional power and individual rights be accommodated by legislation drawn more narrowly to avoid the conflict.

Id. at 268 n.20. That is good propaganda, but it does not accurately reflect what was going on in *Robel* and similar cases. *See* H. WELLINGTON & R. WINTER, THE UNIONS AND THE CITIES 79 (1971); Note, *Less Drastic Means and the First Amendment,* 78 YALE L.J. 464 (1969). Of course the balancing is "at the margin," comparing the incremental promotion of the interest on which the government relies with the incremental threat to free expression. *See id* .at 467–48; *cf.* Note, *The First Amendment Overbreadth Doctrine,* 83 HARV. L. REV. 844, 914–15 (1970). *See*

tional significance the Court attached to criterion [1]'s critical
word "substantial," [17] however, this turned out to be no protection
at all: [18] legislatures simply do not enact wholly useless provisions.[19] It is therefore no surprise to discover that earlier cases
protecting more traditional forms of expression (such as the distribution of handbills [20]), although they too purported to apply a
sort of less restrictive alternative test, gave it a significantly
stronger meaning. The point of these cases, in contradistinction to
O'Brien, was that the absence of gratuitous inhibition is *not*
enough. For in banning the distribution of handbills, municipali-
ties pursue a goal unconnected with the inhibition of expression,
the reduction of litter, and they do so without placing any gratuitous limits on expression: the entirety of an anti-handbill ordinance
serves the goal of reducing litter. Such cases thus suggest that the
existence of possible alternative approaches — such as more trash
cans and an anti-littering ordinance — triggers a serious balancing
of interests: the question is whether the marginally greater effectiveness of an anti-handbill ordinance relative to alternative means

---

also United States v. Robel, 389 U.S. 258, 266 (1967) (stressing the nonsensitive
nature of many of the positions from which Communists were barred). Thus a
more manageable, indeed more intelligible, sort of balancing is involved, but it
remains balancing nonetheless. But although *Robel*'s footnote did not accurately
describe what was happening in *Robel*, it seems to have been taken seriously in
O'Brien.

[17] *See* Smith v. Goguen, 415 U.S. 566, 599 (1974) (Rehnquist, J., dissenting)
(requirement of substantial government interest not easily severed from requirement
that restriction on expression be no greater than essential). The interests served
by protecting draft cards from destruction are listed by the Court, *see* 391 U.S.
at 378–80: they are plausible but little more. Should it be answered that that is the
wrong level at which to view the government's interests — that the interests really
involved are the draft, thus the armed forces and the very security of the nation —
one can only respond that that move is always available. (An anti-handbill ordinance, for example, does not simply reduce littering, it guards against urban de-
terioration and preserves the ecological balance, thereby safeguarding the very
quality of life and even the survival of the planet.) There is, to repeat, nothing in
O'Brien's response to its requirement of "substantiality" that suggests that the requirement will not always be satisfiable.

[18] In fact, the protection *O'Brien* ended up extending to the expression there involved is the precise equivalent of the protection that has been extended, since the
mid-1930's, to economic activity by the so-called "minimum rationality" test. The
question is whether there is any restriction that does not to some extent serve the
state's goals, and the answer, provided the test is candidly applied, must inevitably
be no.

[19] *See, e.g.,* Tribe, *The Supreme Court, 1972 Term — Foreword: Toward a
Model of Roles in the Due Process of Life and Law*, 87 HARV. L. REV. 1, 5–6
(1973); Note, *Legislative Purpose, Rationality, and Equal Protection*, 82 YALE
L.J. 123 (1972). *See generally* Linde, *Without "Due Process": Unconstitutional
Law in Oregon*, 49 ORE. L. REV. 125 (1970).

[20] *See, e.g.,* Schneider v. State, 308 U.S. 147, 162 (1939). For a listing of cases,
see Ely, *supra* note 16, at 1335 n.412.

of litter control justifies the greater burden on communication. In order to clear room for effective expression, the Court was saying, cities will simply have to put up with some litter, to be satisfied with less than optimal vindication of the interest they are pursuing, unconnected with expression though it is.[21]

It is not entirely clear what the Court will do, or indeed what it should do, about resolving this apparent discontinuity in its approach to the less restrictive alternative analysis. Bringing the handbill and kindred cases into line with *O'Brien* would go a long way toward eviscerating the first amendment. Given the state's perfectly legitimate and expression-unconnected interests in keeping thoroughfares clear and controlling crowds, noise and litter, an approach that rejected only the gratuitous inhibition of expression could effectively close altogether such traditional channels of communication as pamphleteering, picketing and public speaking. But bringing *O'Brien* into line with the handbill cases' balancing version of the less restrictive alternative analysis has a parade of horribles all its own. Suppose O'Brien had convinced the Court to void his draft card burning conviction on the ground that the government's interest could be fairly well, if not quite as well, served by some alternative means. (The alternative most often suggested by critics of the decision is enforcement of the regulation requiring continued possession of one's draft card.[22]) But then suppose that O'Brien or someone else chose symbolically to flout *the possession requirement*. (The most dramatic way of doing this would probably be by publicly burning one's draft card.) It is difficult to see why he could not successfully defend this case on the theory of the prior one, namely that his expression is being inhibited for no very good reason, in that the interests served by the possession requirement too can be fairly well, if not quite as well, served by alternative means. (Governmental maintenance of several sets of records and the increased use of mailings and television reminders like those used for alien registration suggest themselves.) That case having been won, someone turning eighteen might make a public point of refusing to register for the draft in the first place, arguing in his defense that the system can get along fairly well (if not quite as well) without his contacting his draft board, since the information the board needs is all readily available without his sending it to

[21] *Id.* at 1335, 1340.

[22] *See, e.g.,* T. EMERSON, THE SYSTEM OF FREEDOM OF EXPRESSION 84–85 (1970). *See also* O'Brien v. United States, 376 F.2d 538, 540 & n.6 (1st Cir. 1967), *vacated,* 391 U.S. 367 (1968). It is difficult to understand the respect in which this regulation is "narrower" or "less drastic." (The penalties for violation are precisely the same.) It seems, if anything, broader, in that it would cover all persons who had destroyed their draft cards and all other nonpossessors as well.

them. The point by now is clear, and it is, of course, a point that
is not limited to the context of the draft: universalizing the balancing approach of the handbill cases would seem at least potentially [23] to establish the constitutional right symbolically to
break any law, or perhaps it is only any "little" law, so long as its
purposes can be fairly well served, as of course they almost always
can, by alternative means.[24]

Assimilation in either direction thus appearing unlikely, the
time will come when a new set of facts will force the Court to
acknowledge that indeed a distinction was drawn between the
O'Brien situation and the handbill and similar early cases, and
to turn to the task of giving that distinction determinate content.[25] One approach, and I suspect this in fact was what was
unconsciously going on in *O'Brien*, would be to reserve the earlier
cases' serious balancing version of less restrictive alternative
analysis for relatively familiar or traditional means of expression,[26] such as pamphlets, pickets, public speeches and rallies —
thereby affirmatively obliging the state to free up certain forums,
even at some sacrifice of its legitimate expression-unconnected
interests [27] — and to relegate other, less orthodox modes of communication to the weak, nay useless, "no gratuitous inhibition"

---

[23] The qualification is necessitated by the inherent unpredictability of balancing
tests.

[24] One might argue that that is a result the first amendment requires us to put
up with: most of us would not rush out and "jaywalk against police brutality,"
even given the assurance of ultimate acquittal. One conclusion seems quite clear,
however: the Supreme Court of the United States is not about to go this route.
Chaos is not part of its constitutional order.

[25] I refer here to the two distinct approaches the Court has taken to the issue
covered by *O'Brien's* criterion [3]. A more important distinction, which is the
major concern of this Comment, was drawn by criterion [2]. *See* pp. 1496–1500,
1506–08 *infra*.

[26] Both of the accounts of the apparent bifurcation of criterion [3] discussed
here are geared to the *medium* of communication employed. Surely O'Brien's message, opposition to the draft, was comfortably within anyone's notion of what
messages the first amendment protects. It is, therefore, the medium, not the
message, that can fairly be labeled untraditional and thus arguably not entitled to
protection as strong as other media would be accorded. (Similarly, it is the
medium — draft card burning — to which one would have reference in suggesting
that a weaker form of protection may be appropriate because communicative
effectiveness is largely a function of illegality.) On the other hand, the categorization
approach to which regulations that "fail" criterion [2] are properly subjected is
one that is geared solely to the message being expressed, and not to the medium by
which it is conveyed. Thus when the state's regulation is related to the suppression
of expression — when it intervenes because it thinks the message conveyed is dangerous — the constitutionality of the regulation is entirely a function of what is
being said and is unconcerned with how it is being said.

[27] *See generally* G. GUNTHER & N. DOWLING, CASES AND MATERIALS ON CON-
STITUTIONAL LAW 1140–42 (8th ed. 1970).

approach that sustained the draft card burning law.[28] The distinction is its own objection, however: only orthodox modes of expression will be protected. There's truth in the old saw that familiarity breeds contempt: nobody goes to Speakers' Corner to listen.

An alternative line of distinction, one that at least on its face would seem to promise a similar avoidance of illimitability without at the same time officially limiting protection to the traditional and therefore relatively humdrum, is suggested by the fact that much of the effectiveness of O'Brien's communication, unlike the others we have been discussing, derived precisely from the fact that it was illegal.[29] Had there been no law prohibiting draft card burning (or requiring the continued possession of one's draft card), he might have attracted no more attention than he

---

[28] This distinction between familiar and unfamiliar modes of expression rose to the surface in Justice Blackmun's plurality opinion in Lehman v. City of Shaker Heights, 418 U.S. 298 (1974):

> These situations [involving political advertising on public transit vehicles] are different from the traditional settings where First Amendment values inalterably prevail. . . .

> . . . .

> Here, we have no open space, no meeting hall, park, street corner, or other public thoroughfare. . . .

> . . . .

> No First Amendment forum is here to be found.

Id. at 302-04. *Cf.* United States v. O'Brien, 391 U.S. 367, 388-89 (1968) (Harlan, J., concurring) (availability of familiar forms of communication cited as reason for denying protection to unfamiliar).

[29] This suggests another sort of *reductio* of O'Brien's argument. Since the expressive impact of the act derives largely from its illegality, that suggests that someone burning his draft card after O'Brien had won his case should lose. For the fact that O'Brien had won would probably mean that draft card burning would attract less attention, and that would make the first amendment balance, necessarily at the heart of every burner's case, look very different. (O'Brien's challenge, of course, was only to the statute as applied. 391 U.S. at 376.) But that would seem to imply that the third burner — draft card burning again apparently being illegal — should win: he is back in O'Brien's position so far as the first amendment balance is concerned. This would seem to generate a pattern of alternating constitutionality, with only the even-numbered burners — O'Brien being burner #1 — going to jail. But people might soon catch on to the pattern, and start paying attention only to the even-numbered burners, since they are the only ones that are in any real sense risking imprisonment. That would imply that the even-numbered burners *shouldn't* go to jail, since burning greatly enhances their expressive ability and tips the first amendment balance in their favor. So maybe it is the *odd*-numbered burners who should go to jail after all, since people will anticipate their winning and thus pay no attention. Or maybe only the burner immediately succeeding O'Brien should be punished, since he is the only one people will assume (albeit wrongly) is taking no risk and therefore ignore in sufficient numbers to blunt his first amendment claim. You may have detected an element of frivolity in all this, but it does underscore the oddity of extending first amendment protection to an act whose effectiveness as expression derives largely from it illegality.

would have by swallowing a goldfish. That devious "might" points up the problem with the distinction thus suggested: there will be no bright-line test distinguishing situations where the act's communicative impact results largely from its illegality from those where it does not. But at least the question is intelligible, and it does not seem much harder than others courts answer in this or other contexts. For one prepared to balance reductions in communicative effectiveness against incremental additions to other societal costs — and the approach of the handbill and other early cases has to come to that [30] — this would seem just one of a series of nonquantifiable steps.

But perhaps because of such difficulties of application, and probably more because the Court, like most of the rest of us, first learned to think about the first amendment in more traditional contexts, it seems likely that the Court will continue, either explicitly or implicitly, to distinguish between familiar and unorthodox modes of communication in deciding whether genuinely to balance in evaluating less restrictive alternatives or rather simply to assure itself, as it will always be able to, that no gratuitous inhibition of expression has been effected. In any event, the question of how to accommodate freedom of expression with the state's various expression-unconnected interests is, and will remain, an extremely difficult one. As I hope to demonstrate, however, the question posed by flag desecration laws is not that question, but one a good deal easier.

III

The two sorts of review we have been discussing — the "no gratuitous inhibition" approach that upheld the draft card burning law, and the balancing approach that has been employed in cases involving more familiar forms of expression — do differ significantly. That is not, however, because the latter is especially protective of expression (in fact it is notoriously unreliable) but rather because the former, honestly applied, will invalidate nothing. There was, of course, a time when balancing was sufficient to satisfy a majority of the Court as a general approach to the first amendment.[31] But that was hardly the attitude of the Warren Court, at least in its later years.[32] During the very period

---

[30] *See also* Cox v. Louisiana, 379 U.S. 536, 554–55 (1965).

[31] *See, e.g.,* Communist Party v. Subversive Activities Control Bd., 367 U.S. 1, 91 (1961); Barenblatt v. United States, 360 U.S. 109, 126 (1959). *See also* Dennis v. United States, 341 U.S. 494, 510 (1951).

[32] The recent restriction of the overbreadth doctrine, *see* Parker v. Levy, 417 U.S. 733, 760–61 (1974); Broadrick v. Oklahoma, 413 U.S. 601, 615 (1973), to the contrary notwithstanding, the Burger Court has kept alive many of the protec-

when *O'Brien* was decided, the Court was making clear its dissatisfaction with a general balancing approach, indicating that only expression fairly assignable to one of an increasingly limited set of narrowly defined categories could be denied constitutional protection. Thus in *Brandenburg v. Ohio*,[33] decided a year after *O'Brien*, a unanimous Court, invalidating the Ohio Criminal Syndicalism Act, indicated that:[34]

> [T]he constitutional guarantees of free speech and free press do not permit a State to forbid or proscribe advocacy of the use of force or of law violation except where such advocacy is directed to inciting or producing imminent lawless action and is likely to incite or produce such action.

There is in *Brandenburg* no talk of balancing, let alone of a simple prohibition of gratuitous suppression: the expression involved in a given case either does or does not fall within the described category, and if it does not it is protected.[35] (O'Brien's expression, it is hardly necessary to add, did not fall within the described category, and no one claimed it did.) Quite obviously the Court of the late Warren period had two radically different first amendment approaches for what it saw as two significantly different sets of problems. Something about O'Brien's case caused the Court to adopt an approach much less protective of first amendment interests than that put forth in *Brandenburg*.

The explanation for this difference is not that Brandenburg was actually talking — moving his mouth and uttering words — whereas O'Brien was expressing himself nonverbally. *Tinker v. Des Moines School District*,[36] decided nine months after *O'Brien*,

---

tions devised by the Warren Court to safeguard first amendment values. *Brandenburg*, in particular, survives. *See* Hess v. Indiana, 414 U.S. 105, 108 (1973) (per curiam).

[33] 395 U.S. 444 (1969) (per curiam).

[34] *Id.* at 447.

[35] By indicating that a speech, to be punishable, must not only advocate immediate lawless action but also be likely to produce it, the Court supplements its categorization test with a reference to likely effect. The two elements are not stated in the alternative; both are plainly required. *See* Gunther, *Learned Hand and the Origins of Modern First Amendment Doctrine: Some Fragments of History*, 27 STAN. L. REV. 719, 722, 754 (1975). Thus in *Brandenburg* the danger question never had to be reached, since the speech itself did not fit within the category described by the Court. *See also* Cohen v. California, 403 U.S. 15, 19-22, 24 (1971), *discussed* pp. 1492-93 *infra*; Yates v. United States, 354 U.S. 298, 325-25 (1957). *Cf.* Street v. New York, 394 U.S. 576, 591-93 (1969). On the difference between categorization on the one hand, and "clear and present danger," balancing and other approaches that are geared to the effects of the speech on the other, *see also* Gunther, *supra;* Linde, *"Clear and Present Danger" Reexamined: Dissonance in the* Brandenburg *Concerto*, 22 STAN. L. REV. 1163, 1168-69 (1970); note 44 *infra*.

[36] 393 U.S. 503 (1969).

involved the suspension of school children for wearing black armbands to protest the Vietnam War. The protest's target was very
much the same as that in *O'Brien*; the setting, the classroom rather
than the post office steps, was if anything more fragile; the
penalty was milder; and most important for present purposes,
the communication was, again, entirely nonverbal. Yet the Court
did not hesitate a moment: this was, it announced — without
supporting argument or any attempt to distinguish *O'Brien* —
"the type of symbolic act that is within the Free Speech Clause
of the First Amendment . . . . It was closely akin to 'pure
speech' which, we have repeatedly held, is entitled to comprehensive protection . . . ."[37] Comprehensive protection is certainly what it was given, and the suspensions were reversed. The
Court is still unable to account very convincingly for the difference between *O'Brien* and *Tinker*,[38] but the contrast in tone between the two opinions, to say nothing of the results, could hardly
be starker.[39] Similarly, in *Cohen v. California*,[40] decided in 1971,
the Court reversed the conviction of a young man, obviously a
latter day Billy Budd, who found he could adequately convey his
feelings only by parading about in a jacket that said "Fuck the
Draft." Rejecting the dissenters' claim that "Cohen's absurd and
immature antic" — so far one must assume no disagreement —
"was mainly conduct and little speech,"[41] the Court employed,
and in the process importantly clarified, the categorization approach it had adopted in *Brandenburg*.[42] The dangers of censorship of both emotive and cognitive content, Justice Harlan sug-

---

[37] *Id.* at 505–06.

[38] *See* Spence v. Washington, 418 U.S. 405, 409–10 (1974) (per curiam). *See
also* note 53 *infra*.

[39] *Tinker*, like *O'Brien*, does not employ a categorization approach. However,
quite unlike *O'Brien*, it starts with an unmistakable presumption that the regulation involved is unconstitutional and sticks with it despite some far from trivial
arguments on the other side. Nor is the difference attributable to a "swing vote" or
two. Only Justices Black and Harlan dissented in *Tinker*, and only Justice Douglas
in *O'Brien*.

[40] 403 U.S. 15 (1971).

[41] *Id.* at 27 (Blackmun, J., dissenting). *But see* p. 1495 *infra*.

[42]
> [T]his case cannot be said to fall within those relatively few categories of
> instances where prior decisions have established the power of government to
> deal more comprehensively with certain forms of individual expression simply
> upon a showing that such a form was employed.

403 U.S. at 19–20.

> [W]e cannot overemphasize that . . . most situations where the State has a
> justifiable interest in regulating speech will fall within one or more of the
> various established exceptions, discussed above but not applicable here, to the
> usual rule that governmental bodies may not prescribe the form or content
> of individual expression.

Id. at 24.

gested for the majority, must lead us to reject attempts to punish "offensive language";[43] "fighting words" are unprotected, but that category is no longer to be understood as a euphemism for either controversial or dirty talk but requires instead an unambiguous invitation to a brawl;[44] and anyone who finds Cohen's jacket "obscene" or erotic had better have his valves checked.[45] There is little trace of balancing here, and surely not simply a search for gratuitous inhibition.

IV

The distinction between cases like *O'Brien* on the one hand and cases like *Tinker* and *Cohen* on the other can, in fact, be

---

[43] *Id.* at 23–26.

[44] *Id.* at 20, 23. *But see* Feiner v. New York, 340 U.S. 315 (1951).

As Justice Harlan suggests, the context in which a message is communicated may have to be considered in determining its meaning and thereby whether it falls within one of the unprotected categories of speech. 403 U.S. at 20, 23. (The less verbal the communication, the more necessary such a reference will be: an armband, for example, might convey a variety of messages or even no message at all.) What distinguishes a categorization approach from "clear and present danger" and similar tests is that context is considered only to determine the message the defendant was transmitting and not to estimate the danger that the audience would react to the message by antisocial conduct. Of course such considerations figure in the initial definition of the unprotected categories. *See, e.g.,* Chaplinsky v. New Hampshire, 315 U.S. 568, 571–72 (1942). But once they are defined, a categorization approach, in determining the constitutionality of a given restriction of expression, asks only "What was he saying?"—though admittedly a reference to context may be needed to answer that question. A clear and present danger or ad hoc balancing approach, in contrast, would regard that question as nondispositive: a given message will be sometimes protected and sometimes not, depending on the actual or projected behavior of the audience in response to it. *See also* Linde, *supra* note 35, at 1169.

Of course, the two kinds of reference to context will on occasion, particularly when nonverbal communication is involved, come so close to converging that it will be difficult to argue that the two general approaches in which they figure are importantly different. And none of us is so naive as to be unaware that any verbal formula is subject to conscious or unconscious manipulation. Perhaps, therefore, the wisest course is that recommended at various times (though not in precisely these terms) by Justices Black and Douglas: a total refusal to allow the inhibition of expression for reasons having to do with the actual or expected audience reaction to the message communicated. Although that is in fact my inclination (subject to a limited exception for demonstrable falsehoods regarding people or products), a majority of the Court has never endorsed such a view. And within the range of realistic alternatives, a categorization approach, which looks only to the message conveyed, does seem to me significantly preferable to one that would guess about dangers case by case. It cannot guarantee fair warning, nor is it a sure barrier against judicial capitulation in times of national hysteria. But in both regards it seems the best we are likely to be able to do: words may let us down from time to time, but they are all we have to work with. *See also* pp. 1500–02 *infra.*

[45] *See* 403 U.S. at 20.

found in the *O'Brien* opinion itself, but you have to hunt around a bit to find it. The Court gives us at least one false lead [46] — suggesting early on that perhaps O'Brien's act was not "speech" at all and therefore simply not covered by the first amendment: [47]

> We cannot accept the view that an apparently limitless variety of conduct can be labeled "speech" whenever the person engaging in the conduct intends thereby to express an idea.

Although the Court did not ultimately rely on this distinction, it nonetheless deserves some attention. It has received the endorsement of scholars who must command respect, and the fallacy that underlies it is one that has similarly infected other, apparently more subtle, approaches to the problem of "symbolic speech."

It is, of course, undeniable that O'Brien's burning of his draft card involved conduct as well as expression. As Professor Emerson, the foremost advocate of an "expression-action" distinction, points out: [48]

> To some extent expression and action are always mingled: most conduct includes elements of both. Even the clearest manifestations of expression involve some action, as in the case of holding a meeting, publishing a newspaper, or merely talking. At the other extreme, a political assassination includes a substantial measure of expression.

He nonetheless maintains that the "predominant element" in a course of conduct can be identified, and first amendment protection thereby determined. [49] The results of this process can be quite striking. In the first place *O'Brien* was wrongly decided: [50]

> The burning of a draft card is, of course, conduct that involves both communication and physical acts. Yet it seems quite clear that the predominant element in such conduct is expression (opposition to the draft) rather than action (destruction of a piece of cardboard).

The same analysis applies to the turning in of draft cards — "[i]n making this gesture the quality of expression clearly prevails

---

[46] Thus Professor Henkin cites only this passage and proceeds to criticize the Court on that basis. *See* Henkin, *The Supreme Court, 1967 Term — Foreword: On Drawing Lines*, 82 HARV. L. REV. 63, 77–80 (1968).

[47] 391 U.S. at 376. *Compare* Cohen v. California, 403 U.S. 15, 27 (1971) (Blackmun, J., dissenting) (distinction drawn to exclude conduct from first amendment protection), *with* Spence v. Washington, 418 U.S. 405, 409–10 (1974) (per curiam) (distinction drawn to include conduct within scope of first amendment protection).

[48] *See* T. EMERSON, *supra* note 22, at 80.

[49] *Id.*

[50] *Id.* at 84.

over the element of action" [51] — but not to the consequent condition of being without one's card: [52]

> The separation of expression and action under these circumstances involves some difficulties, but they are not insuperable. The failure to keep a draft card in one's possession would seem to be conduct classifiable as action, not expression. Though the initial destruction or return of the card may have been expression protected by the First Amendment, the consequent failure to carry the draft card is conduct in which the action (or inaction) element predominates.

But burning a draft card to express opposition to the draft is an undifferentiated whole, 100% action and 100% expression. It involves no conduct that is not at the same time communication, and no communication that does not result from conduct. Attempts to determine which element "predominates" will therefore inevitably degenerate into question-begging judgments about whether the activity should be protected. [53]

The *O'Brien* Court thus quite wisely dropped the "speech-conduct" distinction as quickly as it had picked it up. [54] In *Cohen*, however, Justice Harlan resurrected the distinction, albeit with a somewhat different twist: [55]

> The only "conduct" which the state sought to punish is the fact of communication. Thus, we deal here with a conviction resting solely upon "speech," . . . not upon any separately identifiable conduct . . . . Cf. *United States v. O'Brien* . . . .

An act like O'Brien's or Cohen's, the Court now seems to be suggesting, is neither entirely speech nor entirely conduct: it has

---

[51] *Id.* at 86.

[52] *Id.* For Professor Emerson, the pouring of blood on selective service files would also be unprotected: "To attempt to bring such forms of protest within the expression category would rob the distinction between expression and action of all meaning . . . ." *Id.* at 89.

[53] *See also* Scanlon, *A Theory of Freedom of Expression*, 1 PHIL. & PUB. AFF. 204, 207–08 (1972). The expression-action distinction is by no means all there is to Professor Emerson's theory of the first amendment. His sensitive explication of the values underlying that amendment cannot be ignored by anyone who would try to understand it. The impulse to define clear categories, and thus better to safeguard freedom of expression in times of national panic, is also one I share. *See* pp. 1500–02 *infra.* I simply do not think this distinction can be made to work.

Nor will the cases be helpfully distinguished by asking whether the act involved is intended as political expression and/or likely to be perceived as such, *see, e.g.,* Spence v. Washington, 418 U.S. 405, 410–11 (1974) (per curiam); Cohen v. California, 403 U.S. 15, 18 (1971); Note, *Symbolic Conduct*, 68 COLUM. L. REV. 1091, 1109 (1968). The firebombing of an induction center, or the assassination of a President, can obviously be both.

[54] *See* 391 U.S. at 376.

[55] 403 U.S. at 18 (citation omitted).

elements of both, and the trick is to look closely and see which element it is the state is regulating. Unfortunately, this is not different enough, for it engages in the same ontological fallacy. Burning a draft card to express one's opposition to the draft is an undifferentiated whole, 100% action and 100% expression, and to outlaw the act is therefore necessarily to regulate both elements.

V

When the Court in *O'Brien* gets around to what is obviously intended as the definitive statement of its test — specifically in what I have designated criterion [2] — it gives us something substantially more helpful: [56]

> [A] governmental regulation is sufficiently justified . . . if it furthers an important or substantial governmental *interest* [*that*] *is unrelated to the suppression of free expression* . . . .

Here the Court shifts from ontology to teleology. It abandons its earlier suggestion that the constitutional answer can be found by examining O'Brien's act — either to determine whether it is really expression or conduct, for of course it is both, or to identify which aspect of the act is being regulated, for of course they both are — and suggests instead an inquiry into whether the governmental interest or interests that support the regulation are related to the suppression of expression.[57]

Obviously this approach is not self-defining: it can, for one thing, be interpreted in a way that will guarantee that its demand can always be satisfied.[58] Restrictions on free expression are rarely defended on the ground that the state simply didn't like what the defendant was saying; reference will generally be made to some danger beyond the message, such as a danger of riot, unlawful action or violent overthrow of the government. Thus in *Brandenburg* the state's defense was not that the speech in question was distasteful, though it surely was, but rather that speeches of that sort were likely to induce people to take the law into their

---

[56] 391 U.S. at 377 (emphasis added).

[57] The Court here means to include any interest that reasonably supports the regulation involved, and not to limit its consideration to those that "really" influenced the legislative decision. *See* 391 U.S. at 382–85. I shall suggest that this is the preferable approach. *See* note 98 *infra*.

[58] *See, e.g.*, Feiner v. New York, 340 U.S. 315, 319–20 (1951) ("Petitioner was thus neither arrested nor convicted for the making or the content of his speech. Rather, it was the reaction which it actually engendered."). *See also* Tinker v. Des Moines Indep. Community School District, 393 U.S. 503, 526 (1969) (Harlan, J., dissenting).

own hands. The reference of *O'Brien*'s second criterion is therefore not to the ultimate interest to which the state is able to point,
for that will always be unrelated to expression, but rather to the
causal connection the state asserts. If, for example, the state
asserts an interest in discouraging riots, the Court will ask why
that interest is implicated in the case at bar. If the answer is (as
in such cases it will likely have to be) that the danger was created
by what the defendant was saying, the state's interest is not unrelated to the suppression of free expression within the meaning
of *O'Brien*'s criterion [2]. The categorization approach of cases
like *Brandenburg* and *Cohen*, rather than (either variant of)
O'Brien's criterion [3] is therefore in order, and the regulation
will very likely be invalidated.[59] The critical question would
therefore seem to be whether the harm that the state is seeking
to avert is one that grows out of the fact that the defendant is
communicating, and more particularly out of the way people can
be expected to react to his message, or rather would arise even
if the defendant's conduct had no communicative significance
whatever.[60]

There may be a temptation to conclude that one has seen all
this before, or at least its functional equivalent, in the shopworn
distinction between "regulation of content" and "regulation of

---

[59] Conceivably, the government might assert that two interests justify its action, one related to expression, the other not. For example, a municipality might
attempt to enjoin the operations of a new drive-in theater both because the theatre
plans to specialize in films the officials regard as obscene and because public showing of films at the theater will create a traffic hazard. (The theory here would be
that any configuration of lights on the screen, communicative or not, would distract
drivers.) On review, the first justification would "fail" criterion [2] and would
be invalid unless the films were in fact obscene under the prevailing standard.
However, the second justification would "pass" criterion [2] and its validity
would be judged under criterion [3]. At this point, the outcome would depend
upon the particular less restrictive alternative test used by the court. *See* pp. 1485–
90 *supra*. If the second justification satisfies criterion [3], the regulation would
be valid even if the first justification failed to survive the categorization analysis.

[60] The *O'Brien* opinion itself suggests this definition of its test, in distinguishing
the earlier — and in terms of the conduct regulated, disturbingly similar — case
of Stromberg v. California, 283 U.S. 359 (1931):

> The case at bar is therefore unlike one where the alleged governmental interest
> in regulating conduct arises in some measure because the communication al-
> legedly integral to the conduct is itself thought to be harmful. In *Stromberg
> v. California* . . . , for example, this Court struck down a statutory phrase
> which punished people who expressed their "opposition to organized govern-
> ment" by displaying "any flag, badge, banner, or device."

391 U.S. at 382. *See also* Cohen v. California, 403 U.S. 15, 18 (1971). *But cf.* pp.
1495–96 *supra*. *See generally* A. MEIKLEJOHN, POLITICAL FREEDOM 27 (1960);
Scanlon, *supra* note 53, at 209, 222–23. I shall suggest later that this specification of
O'Brien's criterion [2], though correct and helpful as far as it goes, is incomplete.
See pp. 1507–08 *infra*.

time, place and manner." [61] That would be a mistaken equation, however, and one with severe costs for free expression. For the state obviously can move, and often does, "simply" to control the time, place or manner of communication out of a concern for the likely effect of the communication on its audience. Thus in *Tinker* the state regulated only the place and manner of expression — no armbands in school — but it did so, or at least this is the account most favorable to the state, because it feared the effect that the message those armbands conveyed would have on the other children.[62] (Had the armbands lacked communicative significance, there would have been no way to defend or even account for the regulation.[63]) The regulation at issue in *Cohen* might well be styled by a resourceful prosecutor as simply a restriction on the manner of expression, but perhaps it can also be regarded as a restriction on content.[64] But this brand of ontology, like the others we have seen, is as irrelevant as it is unintelligible. *O'Brien*'s second criterion is no more concerned with "what sort of regulation it really is" than with "what it is that is really being regulated"; the critical point in *Cohen*, as in *Tinker*, is that the dangers on which the state relied were dangers that flowed entirely from the communicative content of Cohen's behavior. Had his audience been unable to read English, there would have been no occasion for the regulation.

O'Brien was different. The interests upon which the government relied were interests, having mainly to do with the preservation of selective service records, that would have been equally threatened had O'Brien's destruction of his draft card totally lacked communicative significance — had he, for example, used it to start a campfire for a solitary cookout or dropped it in his garbage disposal for a lark. (The law prohibited all knowing

---

[61] *See generally* Kalven, *The Concept of the Public Forum:* Cox v. Louisiana, 1965 SUP. CT. REV. 1; G. GUNTHER & N. DOWLING, *supra* note 27, at 1137-42.

[62] Had armbands been banned simply because the school board favored the war, the case would have been still easier. *See* Tinker v. Des Moines Indep. Community School District, 393 U.S. 503, 526 (1969) (Harlan, J., dissenting). However, given that the state's alternative account — a fear of disruption and distraction — plausibly fit the regulation, the Court was quite correct in refusing to assume the less admirable motivation. But that turns out not to matter greatly, since the state's account too was geared to the communicative nature of the armbands. *See* Ely, *supra* note 16, at 1338.

[63] *Tinker* would have been a quite different case had it arisen, for example, in the context of a school regulation banning armbands in woodworking class along with all other sartorial embellishments liable to become safety hazards.

[64] *See* 403 U.S. at 26 ("words are often chosen as much for their emotive as their cognitive force").

destructions, public or private.[65]) Perhaps the Court should have engaged in some serious balancing,[66] but its refusal even to consider the categorization approach appropriate to cases like *Brandenburg* and *Cohen* was quite correct. *O'Brien* is more like *Prince* v. *Massachusetts*,[67] in which the Court upheld the application of the state's child labor law to a child distributing Jehovah's Witness literature. Obviously the state was thereby regulating expressive activity, but the evil it was trying to avert was one that would have been equally implicated had the child been engaged in work with no communicative component whatever.[68] Similarly, by employing what amounts to a balancing test to permit some municipal regulation of sound-trucks, the Court surely permits some restriction of expression.[69] But again, the values the state seeks to promote by such regulation, values of quiet and repose, would be threatened as much by meaningless moans and static (which is usually how it comes out anyway) as by a political message. And although I am not aware that the Court has ever decided such a case,[70] it seems clear that it would refuse to extend constitutional protection to the right to interrupt a public speaker, even by the most coherent and trenchant of political commentary.[71] For the values the state seeks to protect by forbidding interruption, the right of the originally scheduled speaker to have his say and of his audience to listen, are not geared to the message of the interrupter or even to the fact that he has a message. Interruption that expresses disagreement with the speaker threatens those values, to be sure, but no more than

---

[65] *See* 50 U.S.C. § 462(b)(3) (Appendix) (1970). *But cf.* T. EMERSON, *supra* note 22, at 85:

> Certainly it would make no sense for Congress to prohibit loss of possession *by reason of burning*, rather than loss of possession generally. What Congress did, in short, was simply to punish a form of expressing opposition to the draft . . . .

[66] *See* pp. 1485–90 *supra*.

[67] 321 U.S. 158 (1944).

[68] I am disregarding for purposes of this analysis the fact that religious literature was involved. In fact I would argue that it should be disregarded even for purposes of a "free exercise" analysis, since the regulation did not single out religious expression for inhibition. *See* Ely, *supra* note 16, at 1315–24. The Court has not always agreed, however. *Compare* Martin v. City of Struthers, 319 U.S. 141 (1943), *with* Breard v. Alexandria, 341 U.S. 622 (1951).

[69] *See* Kovacs v. Cooper, 336 U.S. 77 (1949).

[70] The Court has had an opportunity to review a somewhat similar situation. *See* Reynolds v. Tennessee, 414 U.S. 1163 (1974) (refusing to review conviction, under statute prohibiting disturbance of religious assemblies, for chanting during President Nixon's speech at the Reverend Billy Graham's East Tennessee Crusade, held in a football stadium in Knoxville).

[71] Of course, it may prove difficult to frame such a statute in language not vulnerable to charges of vagueness, particularly if one does not wish to outlaw applause.

they would be threatened by a chant of "Chocolate Mousse" or a chorus of *South Side Shuffle* on the slide trombone.[72]

Sorting out free speech issues along these lines should have salutary consequences for freedom of expression. The debate on the first amendment has traditionally proceeded on the assumption that categorization and balancing — and I am using this as a generic term, to encompass all approaches (including "clear and present danger") that consider the likely effect of the communication — are mutually exclusive approaches to the various problems that arise under the first amendment.[73] The categorizers, or "absolutists," [74] were surely right that theirs was the approach more likely to protect expression in crisis times.[75] But just as

---

[72] The Court's reaction to disorderly conduct convictions would also quite obviously vary significantly according to whether or not the theory of the arrest and conviction was that the disorder arose in response to what the defendant was saying. A loud and incoherent drunk is one thing, a "provocative" speaker another.

[73] *See* Gunther, *supra* note 35.

[74] "Absolutism" is a term that has been used inconsistently by both friend and foe. The only clear core meaning it carries is that *something* is "absolutely" required, forbidden or protected, regardless of context: thus certain restrictions may be absolutely proscribed, certain categories of speech absolutely sheltered. *See also* Linde, *supra* note 35, at 1183 n.66. Any categorization approach, therefore, can quite properly be labeled absolutist. The term has often been identified, usually by foes, with the view that all expression is to be absolutely protected. However, I am aware of no one who has been seriously prepared so to define it and at the same time endorse it. *See, e.g.,* pp. 1494–95 *supra* (views of Professor Emerson). *But cf.* note 44 *supra* (suggesting that it may ultimately be wisest course to disallow any justification that is geared to the feared effect of the message being regulated). *See also* Linde, *supra,* at 1183 (arguing that "any law directed in terms against some communicative content of speech" should be declared unconstitutional, provided that "the proscribed content is of a kind which falls under any circumstances within the meaning of the first amendment"). Professor Linde's approach has obvious similarities to that suggested in the text of this Comment — surely the animating instincts are related — but there is at least one clear and important difference. I do not refer to my recognition that some categories of speech can be proscribed because of their content, for Linde's proviso has precisely the same effect. (Indeed, it appears he may be willing to exclude from the coverage of his principle certain *modes* of communication on the ground that they are not protected "speech". *See id.* at 1183 n.66 (flagging the possibility that cases like *Tinker* and *Street* may fall outside his principle).) The important difference, and perhaps this is the ground on which Professor Linde would prefer to distinguish *Tinker* and *Street,* is that I would treat as properly subject to the stronger categorization approach any restriction that is justified by reference to the message the defendant is communicating, irrespective of whether the law authorizing the restriction is in terms directed to the restriction of expression. Where the authorizing law is not so directed on its face, Linde is prepared to test the restriction by clear and present danger or another approach that considers the likely effect of the communication. *See id.* at 1174, 1185.

[75] It is true that even the clearest principle can be manipulated — but only up

surely, an all-encompassing categorization approach could be made to look awfully silly, indeed to confess error, by demonstrations that there were contexts in which a refusal to admit the possibility of balancing was simply untenable. The sound-truck cases furnished a familiar example: "I understand that you would protect sound-trucks. But what about a hospital zone? What about the middle of the night? Surely you wouldn't let a mayoral candidate aim a bullhorn at your window at three in the morning. Surely you have to balance, or employ a clear and present danger test, at *some* point." [76]

The argument is convincing — in context. But what the decisions of the late Warren era began to recognize is that categorization and balancing need not be regarded as competing general theories of the first amendment, but are more helpfully employed in tandem, each with its own legitimate and indispensable role in protecting expression. The fact that one would balance where the evil the state would avert does not grow out of the message being communicated — thereby balancing away the right to use a bullhorn at three in the morning, to shout "Boo!" at a cardiac patient, or to firebomb the induction center in protest against the draft — does not, the Court began to understand, commit him to a balancing approach to the constitutionality of a Criminal Syndicalism Law.

The categorizers were right: where messages are proscribed because they are dangerous, balancing tests inevitably become intertwined with the ideological predispositions of those doing the balancing — or if not that, at least with the relative confidence or paranoia of the age in which they are doing it — and we must build barriers as secure as words are able to make them. That means rigorous definition of the limited categories of expression that are unprotected by the first amendment. But in order thus to protect what really is in need of and amenable to such protection, we must first set to one side, by determinate principle rather than hunch, those situations to which such a categorization approach

---

to a point. Thus while such principles cannot guarantee liberty — nothing can — they are the surest hedge against judicial capitulation that is available:

> [E]ven their Ineffabilities, the Nine Elder Statesmen, have not shown themselves wholly immune from the "herd instinct" . . . . I own I should prefer a qualitative formula, hard, conventional, difficult to evade. If it could become sacred by the incrustations of time and precedent it might be made to serve just a little to withhold the torrents of passion to which . . . democracies [are] subject . . . .

Letter from Learned Hand to Zechariah Chafee, Jr., Jan. 2, 1921, *quoted* in Gunther, *supra* note 35, at 749–50. (Hand's views obviously changed as he grew older. *See generally* L. HAND, THE BILL OF RIGHTS (1958).) *See also* Frantz, *The First Amendment in the Balance*, 71 YALE L.J. 1424 (1962); Linde, *supra* note 35.

[76] *See, e.g.*, Henkin, *supra* note 46, at 80–81.

will inevitably prove unsuited. The Court has made a clear start in this direction, and it is a good one.

VI

State laws typically extend American flags two separate sorts of protection.[77] One provision, and it is this that is generally referred to as the "desecration" provision,[78] is likely to provide that "[n]o person shall publicly mutilate, deface, defile, defy, trample upon, or by word or act cast contempt upon any such flag . . . ."[79] The language outlawing contemptuous *words* was declared unconstitutional in 1969, in *Street v. New York*,[80] and that prohibiting the casting of contempt was held void for vagueness (even as applied to nonverbal expression) in 1974, in *Smith v. Goguen*.[81] Some of the statutory language that is left ("defile," "defy") is unmistakably limited to hostile treatment of the flag, and even language that in isolation might boldly be characterized as neutral ("mutilate," "deface," "trample upon") would doubtless receive a similar construction, given surrounding language and the obvious legislative intent.[82] Thus such statutes proscribe

---

[77] *See generally* Rosenblatt, *Flag Desecration Statutes: History and Analysis*, 1972 WASH. U. L.Q. 193, 195–98 & nn.17 & 22. One might wonder whether the protection of the American flag is not a matter of exclusively federal concern. This argument was rejected in Halter v. Nebraska, 205 U.S. 34 (1907). The Court rested its decision in part upon the questionable conclusion that no federal statute then enacted was relevant. *Id.* at 41–42. *But see id.* at 39. There is one now, however, *see* 18 U.S.C. § 700(a) (1970), *quoted* note 82 *infra*, but Congress has expressly provided that the statute not be construed to preempt state laws, *see* 18 U.S.C. § 700(c) (1970).

[78] *See* Spence v. Washington, 418 U.S. 405, 406 (1974) (per curiam). However, the Uniform Flag Act, 9B UNIFORM LAWS ANN. 48 (1966), which has been adopted in a number of states, *see* Rosenblatt, *supra* note 77, at 196–97, entitles this the "mutilation" provision, reserving "desecration" for another purpose. *See* Uniform Flag Act §§ 2, 3, *supra*. *See also* note 86 *infra*.

[79] Uniform Flag Act § 3, *supra* note 78. *See also* note 82 *infra*.

[80] 394 U.S. 576 (1969). Actually the holding was that the law's application to verbal expression was unconstitutional in all but the most unusual circumstances — as where the defendant incited immediate lawless action or directly invited physical retaliation. *See id.* at 591–92. *See also* pp. 1491, 1493 *supra*. Since Street did neither, the Court was not confronted with, and did not comment on, the question whether the preponderance of possible unconstitutional applications rendered the provision relating to words void for overbreadth. The provision is unconstitutional on its face for reasons other than overbreadth, however, in that its application is limited to "unpatriotic" expression. Thus even if its overinclusiveness is not fatal, its underinclusiveness is. *See* note 85 *infra*.

[81] 415 U.S. 566 (1974). The language actually at issue — "treats contemptuously" rather than "cast contempt upon" — was obviously so close that distinction is impossible.

[82] Were these words to be construed otherwise, they would raise the problem discussed at pp. 1503–08 *infra*. The federal statute, 18 U.S.C. § 700(a) (1970),

only ideologically charged acts, and beyond that, only acts charged with a particular set of ideological outlooks. The state's defense, consequently, must be geared to the unusual danger of that set of sentiments; such a defense will of necessity relate to the suppression of expression within the meaning of *O'Brien*'s second criterion.[83] That in turn implies that the categorization approach of *Brandenburg* and *Cohen* is appropriate. Since such laws obviously are not tailored to reach only expressions of incitement to immediate lawless action, or any other presently recognized category of unprotected expression,[84] they must fall.[85]

The other sort of provision typically employed, sometimes called an "improper use" provision,[86] outlaws affixing to the flag any "word, figure, mark, picture, design, drawing or advertisement of any nature," or publicly displaying any flag so embellished.[87] The law is thus ideologically neutral on its face,[88] and

---

leaves no doubt about its lack of neutrality:

> Whoever knowingly casts contempt upon any flag of the United States by publicly mutilating, defacing, defiling, burning, or trampling upon it shall be fined not more than $1,000 or imprisoned for not more than one year, or both.

[83] Justice Fortas' suggestion that because the state can generally prohibit burning on public thoroughfares it necessarily can prohibit the contemptuous burning of flags there, *see* Street v. New York, 394 U.S. 576, 616 (1969) (Fortas, J., dissenting), is a classic example of the "greater includes the lesser" fallacy. The old saw that the government can "deal with one part of a problem at a time" surely has no application in first amendment cases. *See, e.g.,* Police Dep't v. Mosley, 408 U.S. 92 (1972). Had Street in fact been charged under a general no burning ordinance, his prosecution would have raised the sort of problem considered at pp. 1485–90 *supra*.

[84] *See* Street v. New York, 394 U.S. 576, 591–92 (1969). *See generally* Cohen v. California, 403 U.S. 15, 19–22 (1971).

[85] Virtually all prosecutions authorized by such laws would be unconstitutional under *Brandenburg* and *Cohen*. The likelihood that the laws would be invalid on their face as overbroad has been diminishing in recent years. *See, e.g.,* Broadrick v. Oklahoma, 413 U.S. 601 (1973). But even if such statutes were judicially or legislatively limited to the categories approved by *Brandenburg* and *Cohen* — and thus outlawed only those hostile alterations or destructions of the flag that (as by a prearranged signal) either directly incited immediate lawless action or explicitly invited retaliation — they would still be invalid on their face for limiting their coverage to contemptuous treatment of the flag. *See* Smith v. Goguen, 415 U.S. 566, 588 (1974) (White, J., concurring in the judgment); *cf.* Police Dep't v. Mosley, 408 U.S. 92, 96 (1972) (law allowing labor picketers but not others to demonstrate in front of schools unconstitutional); Schacht v. United States, 398 U.S. 58, 62–63 (1970) (law denying actors use of military uniforms if their theatrical production would "tend to discredit" the military unconstitutional). *See also* Stromberg v. California, 283 U.S. 359, 369–70 (1931).

[86] *See* Spence v. Washington, 418 U.S. 405, 406–07 (1974) (per curiam). Somewhat perversely, the Uniform Flag Act entitles this the "desecration" provision. *See* Uniform Flag Act § 2, *supra* note 78.

[87] Uniform Flag Act § 2, *supra* note 78.

[88] Neutral, that is, as respects the message the defendant is conveying. *But cf.* p. 1506 *infra*.

would proscribe the superimposition of "Buy Mother Fletcher's Ambulance Paint" [89] or even "It's a Grand Old Flag" as fully as it would the addition of a swastika.[90] Such "improper use" provisions are more complicated constitutionally than the ideologically tilted "desecration" provisions. The difficulty arises not from the suggestion of Justices White [91] and Rehnquist [92] that altering a flag is like painting up a public building (where, it is quite true, even the most patriotic of graffiti are disallowed). For there a governmental interest quite obviously unrelated to the suppression of expression is implicated, namely the cost and trouble of sandblasting. The case the Justices suggest is akin to one involving the alteration of a publicly owned flag, where no one suggests that the state may not protect its own property from defacement.[93] However, the state may assert an interest — which justifies control over even privately owned flags — similar to that asserted in the case of the interrupting audience. The state's interest in both of these cases might be characterized as an interest in preventing the jamming of signals, an interest not in preventing the defendant from expressing himself but rather in keeping him from interfering with the expression of others. Thus we do not care what the interrupter is saying: all that matters is that he is interrupting another's expression. The flag too is the embodiment of a set of ideas — surely no one defending against a charge of disfigurement is in a position to deny *that* — and our case can therefore be seen in much the same light. The state does not care what message the defendant is conveying by altering the flag: all that matters is that he is interrupting the message conveyed by the flag.[94]

---

[89] The constitutionality of banning this sort of embellishment might be thought to depend on the question whether "commercial speech" will remain an unprotected category of expression. *See* Spence v. Washington, 418 U.S. 405, 413 n.7 (1974) (per curiam). *See generally* Pittsburgh Press Co. v. Pittsburgh Comm'n on Human Relations, 413 U.S. 376, 388 (1973). *But see* note 103 *infra.*

[90] A similar approach of ideological neutrality might be employed in an attempt to save certain aspects of the "desecration" provisions discussed above. For example, a state might without qualification simply outlaw intentionally stepping on the flag. It seems unlikely that any such "neutral" approach to flag burning would be practicable, however, at least so long as the Boy Scouts continue to insist that that is the only appropriate way to dispose of one.

[91] Smith v. Goguen, 415 U.S. 566, 587 (1974) (White, J., concurring in the judgment).

[92] Spence v. Washington, 418 U.S. 405, 417 (1974) (Rehnquist, J., dissenting).

[93] *See id.* at 409 ("We have no doubt that the state or national governments constitutionally may forbid anyone from mishandling in any manner a flag that is public property").

[94] The fact that such laws typically prohibit the public display of altered flags does not, of course, imply that the state is concerned only with censoring the al-

Although the analogy may suggest that improper use provisions — like restrictions on audience interruption — satisfy *O'Brien's* criterion [2], the analogy seems uneasy under criterion [3], in that the balance looks very different. Acknowledging that the state's interests in the two cases are of similar contour — that each is concerned only with preventing the interruption of a message emanating from another source and not with the content of the interrupter's message — need not commit one to the view that they are of equal weight. In the interrupting audience case, one of the weightiest interests imaginable, namely the first amendment rights of the speaker, supports the state's intervention. That analysis will not fit the flag disfigurement situation, however. Even granting, as I think we must, the legitimacy of the government's interest in the flag's symbolic value,[95] it plainly is not a first amendment interest, for the simple reason that the government or polity — and in the case of a privately owned flag I don't know who else's rights could be invoked on the prosecution's side — has no first amendment rights.[96] The cloth, in such a case, is surely the disfigurer's alone. And while the ideas it represents just as surely are not, neither are they the exclusive property of the government.

This distinction, in terms of the relative strength of the governmental interests involved, is less than wholly reassuring, for

---

terer's expression: it is entirely consistent with an intention only to prevent interference with the ideas the flag conveys.

In a footnote in *Spence* the Court stated:

If this interest [prevention of interference] is valid, we note that it is directly related to expression in the context of activity like that undertaken by appellant. For that reason and because no other governmental interest unrelated to expression has been advanced or can be supported on this record, the . . . analysis of United States v. O'Brien . . . is inapplicable.

418 U.S. at 414 n.8. Of course expression is involved, namely the expression of the ideas the flag conveys; what the Court apparently fails to take into account is the fact that the state interest is one that is unconcerned with what ideas, if any, the defendant is expressing. However, there may have been more analysis in the Court's footnote than meets the eye. I shall argue later that the Court's conclusion was correct, that indeed this should be regarded as an interest that is related to the suppression of expression within the meaning of *O'Brien's* second criterion. *See* pp. 1506–08 *infra*.

[95] Otherwise, the official endorsement of the flag as a national symbol would seem to be unconstitutional. West Virginia Bd. of Educ. v. Barnette, 319 U.S. 624 (1943), is not authority to the contrary: a declaration that people cannot be compelled to affirm their patriotism by saluting the flag is not the same as a declaration that the government has no interest whatever in encouraging patriotism by such a symbol. *Barnette* is, however, a precedent most relevant to the problem posed by improper use statutes. *See* p. 1507 & note 100 *infra*.

[96] An individual can obviously employ his flag in the exercise of his first amendment freedoms: indeed he does so every time he flies it. By interfering with that expression, whether or not I actually destroyed his physical property, I would be subjecting myself to quite justifiable punishment by the state: *that* seems the case that is analogous to the interrupting audience.

two reasons. The first is the obvious one, that balancing tests are simply not the stuff on which reassurance can confidently be built. The second is that it is far from clear that the Court would even be prepared to employ the serious balancing version of criterion [3] in either of these cases. Both interrupting and flag disfigurement would, it is true, attract considerable attention even if they were legal. But although I have suggested that this consideration should trigger a serious balance, this seems unlikely, for reasons we have canvassed above, to be the approach the Court will follow in deciding whether such a balance, as opposed to the virtually automatic validation of the "no gratuitous inhibition" approach, is the appropriate specification of *O'Brien*'s criterion [3]. More likely, the Court will extend the stronger brand of protection only to what it is prepared to regard as orthodox modes of expression.[97] And while flag desecration (and interruption of speakers as well) can undoubtedly claim a lengthy historical lineage, the only "tradition" with which the Court is likely to associate them is a tradition of rowdyism. It thus seems highly questionable that a Court proceeding on the assumption that a less restrictive alternative analysis is all that is required would employ a version of that analysis sufficiently serious to invalidate improper use statutes. More likely, it would employ a weak version of criterion [3], akin to that invoked in *O'Brien* itself, and thereby uphold such laws.

If, therefore, the flag alteration and audience interruption cases are to be confidently distinguished, the distinction must be in other than balancing terms. Such a distinction is available. A deeper analysis of "improper use" statutes will reveal that they must after all be regarded as relating to "the suppression of free expression" within the meaning of *O'Brien*'s criterion [2], and that they therefore should be analyzed (and invalidated) under the categorization approach rather than being approached in terms of either version of criterion [3].

What has not yet been sufficiently noted is that although improper use statutes do not single out certain messages for proscription, they *do* single out one set of messages, namely the set of messages conveyed by the American flag, for protection. That, of course, is not true of a law that generally prohibits the interruption of speakers: such a law is neutral not only respecting the content of the interruption but also respecting the content of the message interrupted.[98] The distinction seems a critical one, and

---

[97] *See* pp. 1488–90 *supra*.

[98] One might attempt to use this distinction as the basis of an argument sounding in legislative motivation. The legislature undoubtedly expects that the majority of messages conveyed by disfiguring the flag — and certainly the vast majority of

suggests that the definition we have thus far given *O'Brien*'s
second criterion, as referring to situations where the harm the
state seeks to avert is one that arises from the defendant's communication, may have been incomplete. An adjustment of our
earlier elaboration of that criterion so as to encompass the case in
which the government singles out a specific message or set of
messages for protection would fit the cases more comfortably —
and in particular, would provide firmer ground for the decision in
Spence.[99] That it is also required by the sense of the criterion
seems clear too, given the functional similarity, in terms of
"the free marketplace of ideas," between singling certain messages out for prohibition and singling certain messages out
for protection.[100] Orthodoxy of thought can be fostered not
simply by placing unusual restrictions on "deviant" expression
but also by granting unusual protection to expression that is officially acceptable. An "improper use" statute, neutral respecting
the messages it would inhibit though it may be, is not analogous
to a law prohibiting the interruption of speeches.[101] It is, at best,

---

those that will be prosecuted — will be unfriendly to the government or at least
to one or more of its policies. Thus, although such laws are facially neutral with
respect to the sentiments they proscribe, their underlying motivation, the argument
would run, is in fact identical to that which appears on the face of "defacement"
laws, namely the stilling of antipatriotic expression. To translate the argument
into the terms of *O'Brien*'s criterion [2], the government's "real" interest, as opposed to the interest the state attorney general will argue to the Court, is quite
directly related to the suppression of expression. This argument raises a question
that pervades much of constitutional law and, indeed, legal "interest analysis"
generally — whether the relevant interests are those that are reasonably ascribable
to the rule under consideration or only those that "really" influenced its enact-
ment. For reasons I have already elaborated at inordinate length, I would reject
the latter approach in a context like this, and would argue that no rational explanation capable of accounting for the law in issue can confidently be rejected
by the Court as not "truly" having influenced the legislative decision. *See generally*
Ely, *supra* note 16 (the approach suggested there is nonetheless one that leaves
substantial room for the consideration of legislative motivation in constitutional
adjudication).

    If a pattern of enforcing an improper use statute only against "antipatriotic"
expression could be demonstrated, a defendant could gain relief without referring to
the legislature's motivation. *See id.* at 1235 n.98. But although one must suspect
that such a criterion is often employed by enforcement agencies, it would obviously be very difficult to prove.

    [99] *See* note 3 *supra. See also* note 94 *supra.*

    [100] *Cf.* West Virginia Bd. of Educ. v. Barnette, 319 U.S. 624 (1943) (mandatory
flag salutes held unconstitutional).

    [101] A ban on the intentional alteration of any privately owned symbol would
present a different case, one that in my opinion should be subjected to (and invalidated under) a balancing analysis of the sort suggested at p. 1505 *supra.* (If
the material altered is government property or belongs to someone else, there is no
problem in justifying regulation. *See* p. 1504 *supra.*) But the very idea of such a

analogous to a law prohibiting the interruption of patriotic speeches,[102] and that is a law that is hardly "unrelated to the suppression of free expression." [103]

---

statute is bizarre: it is hard to see how it could be other than void for vagueness, and it is, in any event, politically unthinkable.

[102] *But see* p. 1505 *supra.*

[103] Since improper use statutes single out a particular political symbol for protection, they too are unconstitutional on their face. *See* note 85 *supra.* Protection for a defendant therefore should not require the conclusion that his disfigurement was itself protected expression.

[12]

Trouble on Track Two: Incidental Regulations of Speech and Free Speech Theory

by
LARRY A. ALEXANDER*

I. Introduction: Track One and Track Two First Amendment Analyses

Standard First Amendment free speech analysis divides cases into two major groups. One group consists of those cases that Laurence Tribe has labeled "track one" cases.[1] In track one cases, the government's concern expressed in the challenged regulation is the communicative impact of speech, the messages that the audience for the speech will receive. Those messages may be objectionable from the government's standpoint for many reasons, some legitimate, others not. First, the messages may induce the audience to violate the law. Second, the messages may create in the audience's mind false and derogatory impressions of other people, reveal private and embarrassing facts about them, disclose confidential or classified information, or represent appropriations of others' creative endeavors. Third, the government may be concerned that the audience, through the messages, will learn the truth about the government's own misfeasance or nonfeasance. Finally, the government may be interested in preventing the audience from having false beliefs about certain subjects, not for the sake of some further harms to which those beliefs might lead, but because of a concern with truth for its own sake.[2]

Track one analysis, inquiring what governmental purposes are legitimate bases for interdicting the receipt of messages, and what means the government may employ to accomplish those purposes, is difficult, com-

* Professor of Law, University of San Diego. I would like to thank Robert Post, Fred Schauer, Chris Wonnell, Fred Zacharias, and those colleagues who attended the work-in-progress workshop at University of San Diego at which I presented the initial outline of this article. I am also heavily indebted to Scott Oliver for his able research assistance.
1. LAURENCE H. TRIBE, AMERICAN CONSTITUTIONAL LAW § 12-2, at 791 (2d ed. 1988).
2. This is less likely to be advanced as a reason for restricting speech in a secular era.

plex, and controversial. It divides both courts and commentators along many lines. Yet despite its difficulty, complexity, and controversiality, track one analysis is relatively stable doctrinally if not theoretically. While courts and commentators may disagree over the outcomes of many of those cases that because of their difficulty actually get litigated or over the theoretical bases for the decisions, the courts and commentators do agree on the outcomes in the vast majority of *possible* cases. Moreover, almost all observers would agree that track one analysis is extremely speech protective. The government is rarely successful in meeting track one's relatively settled tests for when it may legitimately interdict receipt of a message based upon a concern with the message's effect on the audience. Courts have protected speech that advocates crime, defames, discloses secrets or private matters, threatens fair trials, offends, threatens, or insults.[3] Speech can be regulated on track one only when it falls within a few narrow categories.[4] Indeed, most liberal commentary today concerning track one urges less rather than more free

---

3. *See, e.g.*, R.A.V. v. City of St. Paul, 112 S. Ct. 2538 (1992) (threatening speech); Gentile v. State Bar of Nevada, 111 S. Ct. 2720 (1991) (speech threatening fair trial); Florida Star v. B.J.F., 491 U.S. 524 (1989) (speech threatening privacy); Texas v. Johnson, 491 U.S. 397 (1989) (offensive speech); Hustler Magazine, Inc. v. Falwell, 485 U.S. 46 (1988) (insulting speech); Landmark Communications, Inc. v. Virginia, 435 U.S. 829 (1978) (confidential communications); Nebraska Press Ass'n v. Stuart, 427 U.S. 539 (1976) (speech threatening fair trial); Cox Broadcasting Corp. v. Cohn, 420 U.S. 469 (1975) (speech threatening privacy); Cohen v. California, 403 U.S. 15 (1971) (offensive speech); Brandenburg v. Ohio, 395 U.S. 444 (1969) (advocacy of illegal action); New York Times Co. v. Sullivan, 376 U.S. 254 (1964) (defamation).

4. Cases in which the Supreme Court has allowed, or said it would allow, regulation of track one speech include those in which the speech constitutes: incitement, *see Brandenburg*, 395 U.S. 444, fighting words, *see* Chaplinsky v. New Hampshire, 315 U.S. 568 (1942), obscenity, *see* Miller v. California, 413 U.S. 15 (1973), confidential communications (in some instances), *see Landmark Communications*, 435 U.S. at 45, defamation (in some instances), *see* Gertz v. Robert Welch, Inc., 418 U.S. 323 (1974), invasion of privacy (in some instances), *see Cox*, 420 U.S. at 491, *Florida Star*, 491 U.S. at 532-33; Globe Newspaper Co. v. Superior Court, 457 U.S. 596, 606-07 (1982), revelation of secret information (in some instances), *see* New York Times Co. v. United States, 403 U.S. 713, 725-27 (1971), false or deceptive advertising, *see* Friedman v. Rogers, 440 U.S. 1 (1979), advertising of harmful or illegal products or transactions, *see* Posadas de P.R. Assoc. v. Tourism Co., 478 U.S. 328 (1986); Pittsburgh Press Co. v. Pittsburgh Comm'n on Human Relations, 413 U.S. 376 (1973), coercion (in some instances), *see* International Longshoremen's Ass'n v. Allied Int'l, 456 U.S. 212 (1982); Ohralik v. Ohio State Bar Ass'n, 436 U.S. 447 (1978); International Bhd. of Teamsters v. Vogt, Inc., 354 U.S. 284 (1975), and speech internal to the workplace (in some instances), *see* N.L.R.B. v. Gissel, 395 U.S. 575 (1969). The Court would undoubtedly affirm, in the face of free speech challenges, convictions for perjury, criminal solicitation, criminal conspiracy, and misrepresentation. *See* KENT GREENAWALT, SPEECH, CRIME, AND THE USES OF LANGUAGE 132, 239-80, 315-21 (1989).

speech protection, particularly with respect to pornography, hate speech, harassing speech, defamation, invasion of privacy, and corporate speech.[5]

The other major group of First Amendment free speech cases consists of Tribe's "track two" cases.[6] Here, government is concerned with the noncommunicative impact of speech, not the message that is being conveyed.[7]

Track two cases have traditionally been broken into two subcategories: the public forum cases and the symbolic speech cases. The former concern access of private speakers to governmental or quasi-governmental facilities, and in some cases to private facilities that the speaker seeks to have treated like governmental facilities.[8] Current First Amendment jurisprudence distinguishes among traditional public fora, such as streets, sidewalks, and parks, public fora created by government designation, and nonpublic fora.[9] The conventional doctrine in public forum cases is that the government may impose narrowly drawn regulations of the time, place, and manner of speech in traditional public fora and designated public fora in order to serve significant governmental objectives unrelated to the speaker's message. The government may not, however, bar speech

---

5. *See, e.g.,* Kingsley R. Browne, *Title VII on Censorship: Hostile-Environment Harassment and the First Amendment,* 52 OHIO ST. L.J. 481 (1991) (harassing speech); Richard Delgado, *Words That Wound: A Tort Action for Racial Insults, Epithets, and Name-Calling,* 17 HARV. C.R.-C.L. L. REV. 133 (1982) (hate speech); Marc A. Franklin, *Constitutional Libel Law: The Role of Content,* 34 UCLA L. REV. 1657 (1987) (defamation); Thomas C. Grey, *Civil Rights vs. Civil Liberties: The Case of Discriminatory Verbal Harassment,* 8 SOC. PHIL. & POL'Y 81 (1991) (hate speech); Charles R. Lawrence III, *If He Hollers Let Him Go: Regulating Racist Speech on Campus,* 1990 DUKE L.J. 431 (hate speech); Frederick Schauer, *Reflections on the Value of Truth,* 41 CASE W. RES. L. REV. 699 (1991) (defamation and privacy); Cass R. Sunstein, *Pornography and the First Amendment,* 1986 DUKE L.J. 589 (pornography).

6. TRIBE, *supra* note 1, § 12-2, at 792.

7. The Court has sometimes treated as track two cases those that, properly analyzed, belong on track one. For example, in the adult entertainment cases—City of Renton v. Playtime Theatres, Inc., 475 U.S. 41 (1991), and Young v. American Mini-Theatres, Inc., 427 U.S. 50 (1976)—the harms the cities were attempting to prevent were traceable to the communicative impact of the adult entertainment, yet the Court treated the regulations as though they were dealing with noncommunicative impact. In the recently decided case of Barnes v. Glen Theatre, Inc., 111 S. Ct. 2456 (1991), the Court treated the regulation of public nudity as a track two regulation, though careful analysis would suggest that the harms about which the government was concerned depended upon the message conveyed by the nudity.

8. *Compare* Marsh v. Alabama, 326 U.S. 501 (1946) (proscribing regulation of speech in a company town) *with* Hudgens v. NLRB, 424 U.S. 507 (1976) (allowing ban on picketers at privately owned shopping center).

9. Cornelius v. NAACP Legal Defense & Educ. Fund, Inc., 473 U.S. 788, 802 (1985); G. Sidney Buchanan, *The Case of the Vanishing Public Forum,* 1991 U. ILL. L. REV. 949, 954. In International Society for Krishna Consciousness, Inc. v. Lee, 112 S. Ct. 2701 (1992), four Justices, Kennedy, Souter, Blackmun, and Stevens, would have held that airports, as well as other facilities, were public fora. *Id.* at 2715-20 (Kennedy, J., concurring in Judgment); *id.* at 2724 (Souter, J., concurring in judgment and dissenting).

924   HASTINGS LAW JOURNAL   [Vol. 44

entirely from such public fora and must leave adequate alternative channels of communication available.[10] On the other hand, if a facility is a nonpublic forum, the government may bar speech entirely or selectively, so long as it does not discriminate according to viewpoint.[11]

Public forum cases are more complicated, however, than the preceding account indicates. First, alternative channels of communication are never entirely adequate. Thus, all regulations of the public fora will entirely suppress speech with respect to some potential audience and with a particular cognitive and emotive impact. Second, the analysis leaves unresolved whether the government must make a certain quantum of traditional public fora available, whether it must construct such fora if few are available or be prevented from razing those that are available, or whether it need only maintain those available as of a certain date or those of a certain vintage.[12] Lastly, the Court has recognized that, with respect to designated public fora, the government may and often has opened fora to speech on a limited basis. The Court has found no First Amendment violation where the government creates fora for speech of all kinds but for only certain speakers.[13] It has similarly found no violation where the government creates fora for speech on some subjects but not others.[14] Lastly, it has upheld the government's creation of fora for only those viewpoints the government favors, as when it runs public schools.[15] This offends the asserted doctrine that even in nonpublic fora, government may not engage in viewpoint discrimination.

The other subcategory of track two cases consists of the symbolic speech cases.[16] Here, the government forbids certain conduct irrespec-

---

10. Ward v. Rock Against Racism, 491 U.S. 781, 796-802 (1989); Buchanan, *supra* note 9, at 954. It need not, however, choose the least restrictive means available. *See Ward*, 491 U.S. at 796-802; Buchanan, *supra* note 9, at 954.

11. Perry Educ. Ass'n v. Perry Local Educators' Ass'n, 460 U.S. 37, 46 (1983).

12. The Court in *Lee*, 112 S. Ct. 2701, suggests in dicta that the government may fail to construct public fora and may convert public fora into other facilities; the only restrictions track two analysis imposes upon the government in this regard concern public fora that are currently in existence. *Id.* at 2706-07; *see also supra* note 9 and accompanying text.

13. *See* Minnesota State Bd. for Community Colleges v. Knight, 465 U.S. 271 (1984); Buchanan, *supra* note 9, at 959-60. *But see* Widmar v. Vincent, 454 U.S. 263 (1981) (university cannot bar religious speech from university facilities).

14. A public hospital's bulletin board can be limited to posting notices concerning hospital business; and a public school classroom discussion can be restricted to subjects in the curriculum. *See* Stephen R. Goldstein, *The Asserted Constitutional Right of Public School Teachers to Determine What They Teach*, 124 U. PA. L. REV. 1293 (1976) (public school newspaper is part of curriculum).

15. *See* Hazelwood Sch. Dist. v. Kuhlmeier, 484 U.S. 260 (1988); Board of Educ. v. Pico, 457 U.S. 853 (1982); Goldstein, *supra* note 14.

16. Given that all speech employs symbols and is thus symbolic, the area should perhaps be redescribed.

tive of whether those who would otherwise engage in that conduct intend their engaging in it to symbolize and communicate some idea to others. The free speech issue arises when someone in fact wishes to engage in that conduct to symbolize and communicate an idea. The accepted doctrine is that government may regulate the symbol on the same grounds and with the same restrictions as it may regulate the time, place, and manner of speech in a public forum. That is, it may do so if it is advancing a significant interest unrelated to the communicative impact of the conduct, if its statute is narrowly tailored, and if adequate alternative means exist for the speaker to convey his message.[17]

Unlike track one analysis, track two analysis has not proven to be speech protective, at least not as we normally think of speech protective doctrines. The government has always won track two cases, with two clear and two less clear exceptions.[18] The clear exceptions are the decisions in *Schneider v. State*,[19] which struck down anti-littering ordinances as applied to the passing out of pamphlets,[20] and *International Society for Krishna Consciousness, Inc. v. Lee*,[21] which upheld the right to distribute literature in an airport terminal.[22] The less clear exceptions are the Court's decisions in *Hague v. CIO*,[23] which established the speech easement over public streets, sidewalks, and parks,[24] and *Schad v. Borough of Mount Ephraim*,[25] which overturned a complete ban of live entertainment.[26]

---

17. *See* United States v. O'Brien, 391 U.S. 367 (1968); Buchanan, *supra* note 9, at 953.

18. In addition to the exceptions discussed in the text, the government has also lost those cases challenging licensing schemes, which have constitutional defects related to the track one fear of message censorship. *See* Poulos v. New Hampshire, 345 U.S. 395 (1953).

19. 308 U.S. 147 (1939).

20. *Id.* at 162.

21. 112 S. Ct. 2701 (1992).

22. *Id.* at 2713-14.

23. 307 U.S. 496 (1939).

24. *Id.* at 514-15.

25. 452 U.S. 61 (1981).

26. *Id.* at 67-77. Arguably, *Schad* is a track one case, since the effects with which *Mount Ephraim* was concerned were not unrelated to the fact that messages were being conveyed. (Consider what "entertainment" is.) *Schad* is what *Schneider* would have been had the ordinances in the latter banned distributing pamphlets but not distributing blank sheets of paper, equally litterable but not message-bearing.

Lee could have struck down the airport authority's ban on the sale and distribution of literature on the ground that the sale and distribution *of literature* caused no more congestion than the sale and distribution of other items, rendering the ordinance underinclusive and hence discriminatory against communication as an activity. The Court's actual analysis implies, however, that a broader ban on all potentially congesting sales and distributions of items would have been unconstitutional as applied to the sale and distribution of literature, making *Lee* analogous in that regard to *Schneider*.

Moreover, recent case developments have perhaps eviscerated whatever little speech-protective force track two might have had. *United States v. Kokinda*,[27] upholding the Postal Service's banning of petition signature gatherers from sidewalks on postal service property,[28] coupled with the Court's prior approval of noise restrictions on city streets,[29] trespass laws' application to speakers on shopping center property,[30] and bans on residential picketing,[31] leaves almost nothing to *Hague's* speech easement over streets, sidewalks, and parks. *O'Brien's*[32] promise of a free speech exemption from regulations of conduct in circumstances where the conduct conveys a symbolic message may have been nipped in its latency by *Barnes v. Glen Theatres*.[33] And *Schneider's* future force was rendered doubtful by *City Council v. Taxpayers for Vincent*,[34] though revived to some extent by *Lee*.[35]

Although Tribe does not describe it as such, there is actually a track three in free speech jurisprudence. On this track are the cases where government is using the mechanisms of the affirmative state, not to censor others' messages, but to communicate its own messages, either directly, as when it runs public schools,[36] libraries,[37] or theatres,[38] or by subsidizing private parties who agree to promote its messages.[39] Track Three cases, like other "unconstitutional conditions" cases,[40] involve the intersection of constitutionally optional benefits characteristic of the modern affirmative state—for example, public schools and libraries—and constitutional liberties established against the background of the very

27. 497 U.S. 720 (1990).
28. *Id.* at 731-37.
29. *See* Kovacs v. Cooper, 336 U.S. 77, 78-79 (1949).
30. *See* Hudgens v. N.L.R.B., 424 U.S. 507 (1976).
31. *See* Frisby v. Schultz, 487 U.S. 474 (1988).
32. United States v. O'Brien, 391 U.S. 367 (1968).
33. 111 S.Ct. 2456, 2457 (1991).
34. 466 U.S. 789 (1984) (upholding ordinance banning posters from utility poles).
35. In International Society for Krishna Consciousness, Inc. v. Lee, 112 S.Ct. 2701 (1992), five justices, Blackmun, Kennedy, O'Connor, Souter, and Stevens, were willing to impose some inconveniences—congestion and potential littering—on the operators of airports and their customers so as to allow the Hare Krishnas and others to get their messages to whatever audience they could gather in the airports. *Id.* at 2715-16. The other justices, Rehnquist, White, Scalia, and Thomas, did not regard the airports as public fora like streets, sidewalks, and parks, and thus did not express an opinion on the current status of *Schneider* and restrictions on speech in public fora. *Id.* at 2710 (Rehnquist, C.J., dissenting).
36. *See* Hazelwood Sch. Dist. v. Kuhlmeier, 484 U.S. 260 (1988).
37. *See* Board of Educ. v. Pico, 457 U.S. 853 (1982).
38. *See* Southeastern Promotions, Ltd. v. Conrad, 420 U.S. 546 (1975).
39. *See* Rust v. Sullivan, 111 S. Ct. 1759, 1762-63 (1991).
40. *See Unconstitutional Conditions Symposium*, 26 SAN DIEGO L. REV. 175 (1989).

minimal state.[41] Track three is perhaps more accurately described as track one and one-half, because it involves a blend of track one's concern with government's control of messages and track two's concern with government's allocation of resources.

My principal focus in this Essay will be on track two. In the next Part, I intend to show that track two is much more expansive than is realized, and is central to the quantity and quality of available information and to the quality of public debate and discourse.

In Part III, I intend to show that the failure of track two analysis to be speech protective was inevitable. Track two analysis must of necessity involve some kind of balancing. But speech interests cannot be balanced against those the government is attempting to foster through its track two regulations because balancing involves someone's prejudging the outcome that the First Amendment demands not be prejudged. In a sense, and somewhat counterintuitively, the First Amendment dictates that speech *not* be treated as important (or as unimportant).

Finally, in Part IV, I examine somewhat more speculatively the implications the track two analysis proposed in Part III carries for track one and track three cases, and for First Amendment theory generally.

II. The Entire Corpus Juris as Track Two

I will establish two propositions in this Part. The first, and easier to establish, is that the public forum cases and the symbolic speech cases have been, and should be, treated under the same standards. The second is that track two analysis potentially covers challenges to any law. In other words, the entire body of laws is subject to track two First Amendment analysis.

An examination of both the phrasing and application of the Supreme Court's time, place, and manner test for public forum speech and its test for regulation of symbolic speech reveals that they are essentially the same test. Both tests, as stated, require that the regulation in question be narrowly tailored but not that it be the least restrictive alternative.[42] Moreover, in both tests the government's objectives must be significant, and the government must leave the speaker adequate alternative means to convey the message.[43]

---

41. I address the general topic in a forthcoming piece on constitutionally optional benefits.

42. *See supra* notes 10, 17 and accompanying text.

43. *Id.* The Supreme Court itself has recently recognized the similarity of its time, place, and manner test and its symbolic speech test. *See* Ward v. Rock Against Racism, 491 U.S. 781, 798 (1989); Clark v. Community for Creative Non-Violence, 468 U.S. 288, 298-99 (1984).

Regardless of the test it employs, the Court is correct, from a theoretical standpoint, in employing the *same* test for both areas. Whenever government is regulating conduct that is being engaged in as a symbol, it is regulating the "time, place, and manner" of speech. It is easy enough to see that, for example, burning a draft card or dancing in the nude is employing a particular manner of expression to symbolize a message. However, the time of a speech or demonstration or the place in which it occurs may also be employed symbolically.

Susan Williams has recently noted the Supreme Court's erosion of any distinction between its time, place, and manner and symbolic speech tests.[44] She nonetheless urges that a distinction should be maintained between regulations that affect those aspects of time, place, and manner that are merely "facilitative" of speech—that affect the speaker's ability to convey his message to a particular audience—and regulations that affect those aspects of time, place, and manner that are themselves "expressive" (communicative)—that are part of the message itself.[45] She argues that there is never an adequate alternative available to the speaker when the regulation affects the communicative aspect of speech and thus what gets said.[46] Therefore, she would require regulations of that type to meet a higher standard of validity.[47]

Nonetheless, it is both theoretically difficult and practically impossible to separate the uniqueness of a particular message from the uniqueness of a particular audience at a particular time and place.[48] The Supreme Court has recognized how the choice between words having the same denotative meaning can affect the emotive and ultimately the cognitive significance to the audience,[49] and how the choice between verbal and nonverbal symbols can do the same.[50] Surely, the choice between audiences and times affects not only the impact of a message, but also how that message will be translated and understood. To illustrate this, imagine delivering a talk on a given subject first to teenagers and then to senior citizens, or first at 5 a.m. and then at 8 p.m. The facilitative and the expressive, the media and the message, are ultimately inseparable.

---

44. Susan H. Williams, *Content Discrimination and the First Amendment*, 139 U. PA. L. REV. 615, 644-45, 653-54 (1991).

45. *Id.* at 659-63.

46. *Id.* at 706.

47. *Id.* at 707-19.

48. Williams herself comes close to recognizing this proposition. *Id.* at 715-16.

49. *See* Cohen v. California, 403 U.S. 15, 25-26 (1971) ("one man's vulgarity is another's lyric").

50. *See* Texas v. Johnson, 109 S.Ct. 2533, 2538-40 (1989) (burning a flag carries a message subtly different from verbal denunciation).

The second proposition I want to establish is that, just as there should be no distinction between track two regulations affecting the facilitative aspects of speech and those affecting the expressive aspects, so too should there be no distinction between track two laws directly regulating speech activities and all other laws. All track two laws regulate speech only indirectly in this sense: In a track two case, government's interest is not in what is being communicated but in the communication's effects on values unrelated to communication, such as noise, congestion, property, aesthetics, or privacy. Track two regulations are of First Amendment concern because they affect what gets said, by whom, to whom, and with what effect even though the regulations are not intended to affect such matters. Nevertheless, *all laws affect what gets said, by whom, to whom, and with what effect*. In short, all laws have information effects. Therefore, all laws, the entire corpus juris, should be subject to track two analysis.

Track two includes not only restrictions on obstructing traffic while speaking or demonstrating, using amplifying devices in residential neighborhoods, posting signs on utility poles, burning draft cards, or sleeping in parks, but also includes tort, contract, and property law, the tax code, and the multitude of criminal and regulatory laws and administrative regulations. For example, laws determining who owns what property under what restrictions or the price and availability of various resources will also determine what gets said, by whom, to whom, and with what effect—that is, the laws will have information effects. A change in the laws of any region of the corpus juris will have information effects. Laws equalizing income would surely have dramatic information effects. Elimination of the law against battery would produce a new form of symbolic speech as well as information—for example, what it is like to batter and be battered—and concerns that do not exist while the law against battery is on the books.

The ubiquity of potential track two cases has been noted.[51] Susan Williams, for example, notes that "[t]here is . . . no clear dividing line between facilitative aspects of speech and other activities. Instead, there is a continuum . . . ."[52] Yet she believes that a line must be drawn.

> The task is required . . . because the alternatives are simply unacceptable. Some activities or resources that are not themselves a part of the act of speaking are, nonetheless, so closely related to speech that it would be absurd not to recognize that regulating them raises first amendment issues. Access to paper or typewriters might be a good

---

51. *See* Cass R. Sunstein, *Free Speech Now*, 59 U. Chi. L. Rev. 255, 273-77, 296 (1992); Williams, *supra* note 44, at 658-59, 722-25.
52. Williams, *supra* note 44, at 724.

example. On the other hand, without some limit, the free speech guarantee would be transformed into an invitation for all speakers to violate any generally applicable law if the violation contributes in any way, no matter how indirect, to their ability to speak. The constitutional solicitude for free speech demands that speakers receive special protection from regulations (even generally applicable ones) that affect either a communicative or a directly facilitative aspect of their speech activity. Nonetheless, at some point the connection to speech becomes so attenuated that the protection must disappear.[53]

Although Williams's concern is well-founded, the "direct-indirect" imagery on which she relies misses the fundamental point that the most profound information effects are produced by laws she would place on the indirect side of the divide. Cass Sunstein, on the other hand, is quite anxious to exploit precisely this point:

> [T]here may be no neutrality in use of the market status quo when the available opportunities are heavily dependent on wealth, on the common law framework of entitlements, and on the sorts of outlets for speech that are made available, and to whom. In other words, the very notions "content-neutral" and "content-based" seem to depend on taking the status quo as if it were preregulatory and unobjectionable.
>
> At least two things follow. The first is that many content-neutral laws have content-differential effects. They do so because they operate against a backdrop that is not prepolitical or just. In light of an unjust status quo, rules that are content-neutral can have severe adverse effects on some forms of speech. Greater scrutiny of content-neutral restrictions is therefore appropriate. Above all, courts should attend to the possibility that seemingly neutral restrictions will have content-based effects.[54]

As Williams recognizes, however, and Sunstein does not, the courts cannot apply the ordinary track two test to all laws, even though all laws are logically subject to track two analysis. For example, the setting of the marginal tax rate affects my income, which, if greater, I might devote to increased speaking. Under the current track two test, if the government's interest in the present rate is not significant, and the rate adversely affects my speech, the government would be required to abandon that rate in favor of another rate. But any other rate the government chooses will affect somebody's speech—it may result in lower transfer payments, adversely affecting the communication between poorer speakers and their audience—and, thus, *it* will have to serve a significant interest as well.[55] Therefore, the track two test cannot be applied universally,

---

53. *Id.*

54. Sunstein, *supra* note 51, at 296 (footnotes omitted).

55. Moreover, all laws curtail the symbolic expression of opposition to the laws themselves through violations, a point that by itself undermines the possibility of requiring a significant interest in order to restrict symbolic speech.

unless the requirement of a significant government interest is trivialized either by finding almost any interest to be significant or by being made synonymous with "the entire corpus juris is what it should be." (The latter trivializes because it tautologizes: track two laws are constitutional if they are constitutional.)

This leaves the following problems. First, track two covers all laws since all laws have information effects—they affect what gets said, by whom, to whom, and with what effect. Second, a track two First Amendment challenge to a law or group of laws is a demand that the laws be changed; but every change in the laws will have information effects, so that track two First Amendment claims are always aligned against each other. Thus, testing challenged laws by the significant government interest test will entail testing all of their alternatives by that test. Finally, the universal application of track two analysis would result in the elimination of all sets of laws except those serving significant interests (as compared to all possible alternative sets). Because of this difficulty, the universal application of track two analysis would most likely result in complete abandonment of track two protection, with all asserted interests deemed "significant" so long as they are not concealing track one, message-related, governmental concerns.[56]

III. The Inevitable Failure of Track Two Analysis

Track two laws have much greater information effects than track one laws (if the concept of greater effects is meaningful in this context). Yet, while track one analysis has been quite speech protective, at least superficially, track two analysis has been anything but speech protective.

The preceding Part demonstrated that track two covers all laws that incidentally affect speech—that is, *all* laws—and for that reason, the significant government interest test is unworkable. The significant government interest test treats all speakers, messages, and audiences as equally important, of a constant weight in the constitutional balance equal to that of significant government interests.

---

56. I treat the government's decision to ban conduct *because* it is message-bearing as a track one decision, even if the government is not concerned with the content of the message. In other words, government's concerns with paper-as-litter, book-as-merchandise, or newspaper-as-high-revenue-business are track two concerns when the government bans dispensing paper on the streets, bans sales in airports, or imposes sales taxes. The government crosses over to track one, however, when it singles out "pamphlets," "literature," or "newspapers." *See* Frank I. Michelman, *Property and the Politics of Distrust: Liberties, Fair Values, and Constitutional Method*, 59 U. CHI. L. REV. 91, 108 n.56 (1992) (discussing discrimination against speech as an activity and citing Minneapolis Star & Tribune Co. v. Minnesota Comm'r of Revenue, 460 U.S. 575 (1983)).

What happens if instead of treating all speech interests as having a constant and significant weight, the particular value of the intended speech, given its intended audience, is weighed against the values the particular laws serve? This is the heart of my critique of track two analysis. In this Part, I propose that the value of speech cannot be balanced against the government's track two interests in any way that is principled and that respects the very freedom of thought that the First Amendment itself protects.

To make track two analysis work, we must assign a value to the audience's loss of information due to incidental restrictions on speech. That value in turn must be weighed against the values furthered by the incidental regulations at issue, values such as freedom from noise, litter, congestion, and taxes. Moreover, that value must also be weighed against the information lost to that and other audiences if the incidental regulations are struck down. (Each alternative set of regulations produces a different state of the world, which in turn makes available different information and/or different audiences for the same information. A trivial example: a world without an anti-litter law lacks the information "what a world with an anti-litter law is like." A less trivial example: a world in which extra police must be assigned to monitor and control street demonstrations and reroute traffic has less tax money available to hire teachers in public schools than a world in which street demonstrations are prohibited.[57])

In addition to the theoretical difficulties of the balancing process, the track two analysis also poses the theoretical problem of placing a value on the information at stake. On the one hand, if we evaluate the information at stake from the position of not knowing yet what it is, we face the theoretically impossible task of placing a specific value on unknown information. On the other hand, if we evaluate the information at stake from the position of knowing or imagining what it is, we risk imposing our evaluation on others through the striking down of the existing set of incidental regulations, and, thereby preempting the very freedom

---

57. It is bootless to attempt to tote up the information gained and lost under alternative sets of incidental restrictions. Information does not come in discrete units such that it would be meaningful to compare states of the world in terms of which state has more information. We can count up the number of television channels, the amount of time spent viewing television, the number of magazines and books purchased, or the number of words in each; but talking of the amount of information is meaningless. This point is frequently ignored. One student note speaks of "a concern for maximizing information" and "concern for a laws' effect on the net stock of information." *The Supreme Court, 1990 Term—Leading Cases*, 105 HARV. L. REV. 177, 284-85 (1991). Maximizing the net stock of information in the global sense used by the note is quite meaningless. All laws have information effects, but that is all one can say.

of evaluation of others that is central to the First Amendment. In the name of the First Amendment we are imposing an evaluative framework on others and arguably violating the First Amendment. Put differently, the First Amendment is supposed to protect a realm of pure process, the substantive results of which are legitimate only because that process is pure; once substantive results begin guiding the construction of the process itself, the legitimacy of the results of that process is compromised.[58]

The above argument is not one directed exclusively at courts. It applies to all coercive impositions of such valuations of information and thus suggests that legislative evaluation of information gains and losses is equally problematic. It suggests that legislatures should perhaps measure only the strength of the constituents' preferences in deciding, for instance, between open space suitable for speech and alternative land uses. And it suggests that taxing one group because of another group's preference for speech activities—for example, in building a town meeting hall—is illegitimate to the extent its justification depends upon public good derived from the speech. (Building a meeting hall, an auditorium, or a library is non-problematic to the extent it reflects the majority's private good preference for information of a certain type rather than, say, more tennis courts.) Finally, when government itself speaks with taxpayers' resources, it is evaluating specific information—the most problematic of all government activities from a First Amendment standpoint. Public schools and universities, public grants and subsidies for research, public broadcasting, public financing of election campaigns, and a variety of other activities, rather than being extensions of the animating spirit of the First Amendment, are in tension with it.

I will discuss each of these points at greater length.

A. Balancing Speech Interests Against Non-Speech Values Served by Incidental Regulations

The entire corpus juris, from the general common law of contracts, property, and torts to the most particular tax regulation, affects what gets said, by whom, to whom, and to what effect. Speech and listening

---

58. *See* Robert C. Post, *Managing Deliberation: The Quandary of Democratic Dialogue,* 103 ETHICS (forthcoming July 1993) [hereinafter Post, *Managing Deliberation*]; Robert C. Post, *Racist Speech, Democracy, and the First Amendment,* 32 WM. & MARY L. REV. 267, 282-83, 290, 293 (1990) [hereinafter Post, *Racist Speech*]; Robert C. Post, *The Constitutional Concept of Public Discourse: Outrageous Opinion, Democratic Deliberation, and* Hustler Magazine v. Falwell, 103 HARV. L. REV. 601, 670 (1990) [hereinafter Post, *Public Discourse*] ("[T]he normative conception of public concern, insofar as it is used to exclude speech from public discourse, is . . . incompatible with the very democratic self-governance it seeks to facilitate.").

are costly activities. They use resources such as space, newsprint, radio frequencies, presses, and police protection, and impose other costs—noise, litter, and clutter. *Schneider*, for example, imposed the costs of litter or, alternatively, the costs in excess of the state's next best alternative for eliminating litter. (If a less restrictive alternative is on the order of a Pareto superior move—the alternative does all the good at no greater cost and without affecting speech—then less restrictive alternatives are unlikely to exist; all alternatives will have greater costs in some respects.)

Thus, the Court's decision in *Schneider* constitutionally mandated what can be viewed as a subsidy of pamphleteers. But why such a subsidy of pamphleteers?[59]

Consider Jane, who complains about the high costs of *The New Republic*, cable television, books from Oxford Press, and a college education. Those costs result from laws—laws regarding property rights, laws conserving trees, laws affecting labor costs, laws regarding tax liability, and many other laws. Jane's receipt of speech—which is, after all, what the First Amendment is really about—is adversely affected by those laws. Why should her attempt to receive this speech not be subsidized? (Alternatively, if one resists the notion that listeners' rights are central to the First Amendment, why should *The New Republic* and Oxford Press, for example, not receive subsidies or relief from various laws in order to communicate with a wider audience?)

Next, consider John, who wishes to demonstrate on Main Street, which will tie up traffic and require police presence. If, against the city's wishes, a court mandates that he be allowed to demonstrate, then the decision can be viewed as a forced subsidy of John and correlatively a forced imposition of costs on others.

Next, consider Joan, who is denied several outlets for her message that, given her limited resources, would be the most effective: putting graffiti on the side of city hall, using a loudspeaker at night in a residential neighborhood, or putting up a pamphlet stand on land that, due to various zoning laws, is currently unaffordable for her. Why should Schneider but not Joan get a First Amendment subsidy here?

Finally, consider Jason, who wants the city to build an auditorium suitable for public lectures and rallies, but who is opposed by Jean, who would like the city to build more tennis courts because she and others prefer playing and discussing tennis to attending public lectures, and Jerry, who wants lower taxes so that he can afford to go to night school.

---

59. If one objects that the term "subsidy" is rhetorically loaded in favor of the existing set of entitlements, we can more neutrally ask why we should give the entitlement to the pamphleteer.

The *O'Brien* line of cases raises the same questions. If a medium is being regulated for non-censorial reasons, then striking down the regulation under the First Amendment imposes a costly First Amendment easement on others. If Jake wishes to protest inflation by burning an inexpensive work of art in the lobby of the Treasury Building, presumably a court will not protect him, even though he has cost each taxpayer an insignificant amount. Yet, how is Jake different from any other user of a tangible medium that the government wishes to regulate to avoid costs to a variety of values? This question is especially relevant since those values might always be translated into amounts of money that the taxpayers would pay to preserve them.

Track two also includes such obviously important-to-speech governmental decisions as what resources should be dedicated to the police and courts, and as a component of that decision, to protecting speakers from hostile audiences beyond those dedicated to protecting persons from assault and battery generally. Resources that go to protecting speakers are, of course, unavailable for other public projects, which include such things as public schools and libraries and the ideas they would otherwise communicate. Since track two includes *all* laws and governmental decisions, however, it includes these allocations of resources decisions.

Without a theory of proper information effects, non-content-related regulations cannot be evaluated under the First Amendment, except in an arbitrary manner. Schneider did win, of course, and so did the Hare Krishnas in *Lee*. But why they and not O'Brien, the sleep-in protesters in *Clark v. Community for Creative Non-Violence*,[60] or the many other actual losers? And if Schneider and the Krishnas, why not my hypothetical Jane, John, Joan, and Jason?

As discussed above, assigning the speech value a constant weight in the calculus—for instance, equal to a significant governmental interest—does not help. Without a theory regarding information effects—what gets said, by whom, to whom, and with what effect—assigning any weight will be arbitrary. More importantly, because speech interests are affected regardless of what set of track two laws are chosen, the speech "constant" appears on both sides of the equation and does not produce a winner.

An alternative that might be considered would be straightforward balancing rather than assigning speech an arbitrary constant value. Under this approach, all of the information at stake under all alternative

---

60.   468 U.S. 288 (1984).

936   HASTINGS LAW JOURNAL   [Vol. 44

sets of laws would be examined, as well as all the non-speech values, and a determination would be made as to which set of laws is superior.

There are obvious practical and institutional objections to such a balancing proposal. Given that this approach would involve nothing less than a comparison of all possible entire sets of laws, both for their information effects and for their effects on all the non-speech values, the proposal is a practical impossibility for a legislature and surely for a court.

This practical objection should by itself be sufficient to undermine all track two judicial decisions and to dictate complete judicial withdrawal from track two. There remains, however, a theoretical objection to the enterprise as well. In principle, we cannot evaluate the information effects of track two laws: Either we assume the viewpoint of one who does not know what the information at issue will be, in which case we cannot evaluate it at all, or we assume the viewpoint of one who does know what the information will turn out to be, in which case we can evaluate it, but only from a partisan perspective inconsistent with the First Amendment itself. These two points are discussed below.

(1) Assume Ignorance of What Information Will Turn Out to Be

Information is in some respects a commodity just like toothbrushes, automobiles, and bananas. We buy it and sell it. When we buy it we place a value on it in the sense that we decide to pay a particular price for it. Nevertheless, information is unique as a commodity in this crucial respect: The value of information, and therefore the price we should pay for it, is generally unascertainable until it has been purchased and received.[61]

For example, the fifty-dollar medical book at the bookstore may contain information that will save my life or my loved ones' lives. Then again, it may not. Should I pay the fifty dollars and find out? Similarly, in deciding whether to buy a seventy-five-dollar electric razor, should I purchase the issue of *Consumer Reports* that evaluates it? The magazine

---

61. *See* KENNETH J. ARROW, THE ECONOMICS OF INFORMATION 137, 160, 171 (1984); KENNETH J. ARROW, ESSAYS IN THE THEORY OF RISK-BEARING 151-52 (1971); F. KNIGHT, RISK, UNCERTAINTY, AND PROFIT 348 (1921); J. Hirshleifer & John G. Riley, *The Analytics of Uncertainty and Information—An Expository Survey*, 17 J. ECON. LITERATURE 1375, 1395 (1979); *see also* James Boyle, *A Theory of Law and Information: Copyright, Spleens, Blackmail, and Insider Trading*, 80 CAL. L. REV. 1413, 1438, 1443-44, 1448-50 (1992) (pointing out the paradox resulting from regarding information both as a conceptual precondition for analyzing markets and as a commodity to be traded in markets); *cf.* Guido Calabresi, *The Pointlessness of Pareto: Carrying Coase Further*, 100 YALE L.J. 1211, 1212 (1991) (arguing that if transaction costs are taken seriously, including the costs of obtaining new information, we are always at a Pareto optimal point).

may save me some money, perhaps an amount greater than the magazine's cost. But I will not know that until I pay the price to get the magazine.

Interestingly, economic theory is mute here. It cannot tell me whether information is worth its price, except when I have good actuarial information about the information itself, such as that there is a one-in-three chance that *Consumer Reports* will save me ten dollars on a seventy-five-dollar purchase, which makes it worth a $2.00 asking price. Economic theory itself normally assumes full or adequate information, or at least actuarial information about information,[62] which makes economic theory largely irrelevant to purchases of information itself.

Economic theory does tell us, however, that the enterprise of producing information for sale—for example, what newspapers do—suffers from a public goods problem. Because information, once purchased, will be disseminated by the original purchaser for free[63] or at nominal charge, the producer cannot capture the full public benefit of the information in the price charged. As a result, if the cost of production is greater than the price purchasers will pay, though less than the total public benefit of the information, the information will not be produced even though it would have been socially beneficial to produce it.[64]

In view of this inability of producers to recapture the full public value of the information in the price charged and the resulting underproduction of information, one might argue that we subsidize the production of information for distribution.[65] There are, however, several difficulties with this conclusion.

First, there are an indefinite number of activities that might produce—or might produce if subsidized—information of public benefit. Without knowing what information would be produced that is not produced now, how can we determine which information's production costs should be subsidized?[66]

---

62. *Cf.* Randy E. Barnett, *The Function of Several Property and Freedom of Contract*, 9 SOC. PHIL. & POL'Y 62, 69-70 (1992) (arguing, based on knowledge of who is most likely to have the knowledge necessary for efficient allocations of resources, for a centralized structuring of a decentralized market).

63. Information is never consumed at no cost to the consumer; there are always at least the costs of time and attention. *See* ANTHONY DOWNS, AN ECONOMIC THEORY OF DEMOCRACY 209-73 (1957). These costs, however, do not involve payment to the producer.

64. *See* Daniel A. Farber, *Free Speech Without Romance: Public Choice and the First Amendment*, 105 HARV. L. REV. 554, 558-68 (1991).

65. *Id.* at 570-79.

66. Interestingly, in Minneapolis Star & Tribune Co. v. Minnesota Commission of Revenue, 460 U.S. 575 (1983), the Supreme Court held a special tax subsidy for the press to be unconstitutional because of the dangers of covert viewpoint discrimination inherent in the gov-

There are several layers to this problem. Because we cannot know what information will be produced by any information producer if we subsidize its production, we cannot know whether the information's total social value—the public's willingness to pay for the information if free-riding were precluded—will equal its social cost. In turn, this means we cannot determine which of the many producers to subsidize or at what level.[67] Moreover, there are other public goods that require protection or subsidization apart from information, some of them in direct opposition to information production. In addition, both the content of information and its production also produce *negative* externalities not reflected in the costs because of collective action problems. For example, those who don't like the noise and congestion of demonstrations, the scandal-mongering of the tabloids, or the eyesores of campaign posters might, but for collective action problems, pay off the information producers in question to eliminate the negative externalities.

The second general problem with this public goods argument for subsidizing information production is that its own logic renders it impotent as a track two tool. It highlights a problem information producers face—they cannot recapture in their price the public value of the information they produce. But defining who is a "producer of information" and what is a "subsidy" requires analytically privileging a certain set of entitlements and background laws; for it is only against that background that we identify who is producing information and what is a subsidy. A track two challenge, however, is a challenge to precisely that set of background entitlements and laws on First Amendment grounds. With a different set of background entitlements and laws, there would be different information producers producing—or potentially producing—different information, who would face the recapture (of costs of production) problem.[68] Paradoxically, the public goods argument works as a potential track two First Amendment argument only if we first decide on First Amendment grounds which set of entitlements and background laws to

---

ernment's singling out the press for special treatment. The Court, however, has been quite schizophrenic in this regard, hardly blinking at the subsidies of particular viewpoints inherent in such things as public education, publicly funded research, publicly funded arts, and public libraries. For example, in Leathers v. Medlock, 111 S. Ct. 1438, 1442-43 (1991), the Court upheld a subsidy for the press broader than the one in *Minneapolis Star*.

67. Indeed, because information is a byproduct of the production of other items, any producer may claim that he cannot recapture full social value of his product and therefore should be subsidized.

68. Consider whether we should subsidize those who already produce information for public distribution or those who would do so if they received a subsidy. Consider further those who would produce information for public distribution if they did not have to incur the costs of such subsidies to others?

privilege; but once that is decided, everything is decided, leaving nothing for the public goods argument to do. In short, the public goods argument has no force as a track two First Amendment argument because it provides no grounds for criticizing the background entitlements and laws that determine who the information producers will be.

(2) *Assume Knowledge of What Information Will Turn Out to Be*

The previous Part raised the difficulties that arise for any track two First Amendment enterprise if we do not know what information will be gained and what information will be lost under alternative sets of laws. The difficulties stem from two fundamental points. First, we cannot evaluate information and whether it is worth the costs required to obtain it until we actually have it; therefore, because different information will be gained and lost under every alternative set of track two laws, we have no way of assessing which of those sets of laws is preferable. Second, the fact that we will tend to underproduce information as a commodity because of the opportunity to free-ride is no grounds for making a track two attack, because each alternative set of track two laws produces its own distinct set of information that is underproduced.

If now we make the heroic assumption that we know what specific information will be gained and lost under each alternative set of entitlements and background laws, are we in a better position to evaluate the information effects of alternative sets of laws?

Yes and no. Yes in the obvious sense that we can and do evaluate information's importance once we have it. No, however, in the most crucial sense for First Amendment analysis. That is because the First Amendment expresses as its primary value that government not preempt individuals' evaluations of information.[69] Put differently, the First Amendment protects a process of citizens' evaluations of information and forbids governmental preemption of that process by privileging certain evaluations.

Al believes that knowing intimate facts about Bill Clinton's life is more important than knowing how Clinton's tax policy will affect the economy. Barbara believes the opposite. And Charles believes that knowing how many blades of grass there are in his lawn is more important than either Clinton's private life or tax policy. There may be a point of view from which it is possible to say whether Al or the others are

---

69. I am using information throughout this Essay in a broad sense, including not just items of data, but, for example, arguments, and ways of seeing and categorizing.

correct or incorrect in their evaluations, but whose point of view is it?[70] Each person—you, I, Al, Barbara, and Charles—will believe his or her point of view to be the correct one; that is why he or she holds that point of view.

The Krishnas in *Lee* no doubt believed the information about religion that they wished to distribute to airport patrons was more important than the information conveyed by an airport uncongested and uncluttered by solicitors and proselytizers and their litter or the information that would be produced by the resources used to police and clean up after the Krishnas. Is it? What if the religious teachings are false or sinister? What if an uncluttered environment heightens valuable aesthetic sensibility?

The point is not that an individual cannot have a point of view about the values of the competing types of information, or that one point of view cannot be correct. The point is, rather, that the First Amendment requires government to treat any point of view on these matters as just one point of view among many.[71] The only point of view it privileges is its own—namely, that no particular point of view shall be privileged.[72]

Of course, this view of the First Amendment's central value is contestable and contested. For example, some argue that the First Amendment requires only that no "political" position be privileged, and that only "political" speech and information are protected.[73] This position,

---

70. Of course, for much information, its value will be purely agent-relative. *See* Schauer, *supra* note 5, at 706-13.

71. *See* West Virginia State Bd. of Educ. v. Barnette, 319 U.S. 624, 642 (1943) ("If there is any fixed star in our constitutional constellation, it is that no official, high or petty, can prescribe what shall be orthodox in . . . matters of opinion . . . ."); Susan M. Gilles, *All Truths Are Equal, But Are Some Truths More Equal Than Others?*, 41 CASE W. RES. L. REV. 725, 726, 740-41 (1991); *cf.* David A. Strauss, *Persuasion, Autonomy, and Freedom of Expression*, 91 COLUM. L. REV. 334, 370 (1991).

> Indeed, the liberal ideal observer construct I have described may not even be coherent. Real individuals have more than a bare desire to decide correctly what candidates they should vote for, or what views to hold about others in society, or what occupation they should pursue, or what products they should buy. They have concrete desires and views about products and candidates and occupations. It is possible that unless one knows what those concrete desires are, one cannot make sense of the question: what information would this person want in circulation? The bare desire to reach a correct decision may leave that question unanswerable in principle.

Id.

72. This is paradoxical. Indeed, the First Amendment has been held to protect anti-First Amendment views, which is also paradoxical. *See* Carl A. Auerbach, *The Communist Control Act of 1954: A Proposed Legal-Political Theory of Free Speech*, 23 U. CHI. L. REV. 173 (1956); *see also* Post, *Racist Speech*, *supra* note 58, at 303-04 (discussing the paradox of public discourse exemplified by tolerating the intolerant).

73. *See, e.g.*, Lillian R. BeVier, *The First Amendment and Political Speech—An Inquiry into the Substance and Limits of Principle*, 30 STAN. L. REV. 299, 300 (1978) (proposing that

however, is, for related reasons, both unhelpful for track two analysis and also wrong. Regardless of what alternative sets of laws we compare in assessing track two challenges, political information will be lost and gained under each.[74] Furthermore, the evaluation of the political information at stake surely will be political in the sense that requires governmental nonpartisanship. More fundamentally, the question of what information has political relevance is itself political.[75] If that is true, the position that the First Amendment protects only political speech devours itself.

Would track two analysis avoid the "point of view" problem if it sought "balance" or "representation" or "adequate airing" of points of view? This tack is equally unavailing. First, how many issues are there, and how many points of view are there on each? Second, whose position "represents" a point of view? Third, when has that position been "adequately aired"? The first question, if it is a meaningful one, is not a metaphysical one but one itself referable to points of view. Moreover, the number of points of view per issue is not determinable, since any answer depends on how the "issue" is described and what information and state of the argument is posited.[76] As for representation and adequacy of airing, no one can represent my point of view except me; and that point of view has not been adequately aired until it is universally accepted. To illustrate, if people disagree with me, they obviously have not listened or understood, or they are intellectually deficient. How else can I explain their disagreement if I still hold my point of view to be correct?

This discussion reveals a deep paradox in First Amendment theory. There are those, like Owen Fiss and Jürgen Habermas, who want the realm of speech to be a realm of pure process, the substantive results of which are correct because of the purity of the process from which they emerge.[77] Yet, to make the process "fair," they would build in substan-

---

in principle the First Amendment protects only "political" speech); Robert H. Bork, *Neutral Principles and Some First Amendment Problems*, 47 IND. L.J. 1 (1971) (proposing that the categories of protected speech should consist of speech concerned with governmental behavior, policy, or personnel).

74. Consider the effect of Schneider v. State, 308 U.S. 147 (1939), and International Society for Krishna Consciousness, Inc. v. Lee, 112 S.Ct. 2701 (1992), on the political proposition that "streets and airports should be free of pamphleteers," a proposition communicated symbolically by the presence of the laws struck down in those cases.

75. Ninety-nine percent of us would agree that the *MacNeil/Lehrer News Hour* has more relevance to political choices than do re-runs of *Gilligan's Island*. Yet, how do we convince the remaining one percent while remaining politically "neutral"?

76. *See* Strauss, *supra* note 71, at 349.

77. *See* JÜRGEN HABERMAS, COMMUNICATION AND THE EVOLUTION OF SOCIETY (1979); JÜRGEN HABERMAS, LEGITIMATION CRISIS (Thomas McCarthy trans., 1973); Owen

942   HASTINGS LAW JOURNAL   [Vol. 44

tive constraints. Fiss wants more diversity, more balance. Habermas wants to build in the various conditions that define his "ideal speech situation." Any conception of diversity and balance, however, will be the product of, and will privilege, particular points of view. Balance and diversity can only be ascertained relative to an opinion of what points of view are plausible or sound.[78] Fiss's version of a fair process will be partisan, and the partisanship deprives any outcome of pure procedural legitimacy.[79] Similarly, Habermas's conditions for the ideal speech situation build partisan positions on all the major substantive issues into his

---

M. Fiss, *Why the State?*, 100 HARV. L. REV. 781 (1987); Owen M. Fiss, *Free Speech and Social Structure*, 71 IOWA L. REV. 1405 (1986).

78. *See* Post, *Managing Deliberation, supra* note 58; Kenneth L. Karst, *Equality as a Central Principle in the First Amendment*, 43 U. CHI. L. REV. 20, 40 (1975); *cf.* Michelman, *supra* note 56, at 103-04 n.47.

> There are other arguable cases of unfair impairment by some people's speech of the value of other people's speech that a committedly liberal constitutional-legal order may have little choice but to disregard. It may happen that less meritorious arguments backed by an individual speaker's superior personal endowment of wit, chutzpah, eloquence, or charisma gain undue advantage in the speech market over more meritorious insights that a slower-witted, duller-spoken person has trouble articulating. However, personal handicapping in such circumstances seems not a liberally entertainable possibility. Again, it may happen that what an audience experiences as comparative cogency and soundness of argument is just a reflex of the comparative familiarity or conventionality of the ideas being urged. If this is at all a frequent occurrence, then public-forum doctrines of content-neutral order-maintenance and equal access may be a recipe for ensuring that currently prevalent views and perspectives will continue to prevail regardless of their responsiveness to the interests and values of the audience. But by what standard can liberals deal out 'deviance' or 'dissidence' subsidies?

Id. (citations omitted).

79. *See* Charles Fried, *The New First Amendment Jurisprudence: A Threat to Liberty*, 59 U. CHI. L. REV. 225, 251 (1992).

> To be sure, if government controlled all the resources, then very little would be left of the value of free speech. There are two responses, however, to this concern. First, as classic liberals have always known but socialists have forgotten, a limited government and a vigorous private sector firmly beyond government's reach are crucial to freedom of the spirit as well as to economic liberty. This is the basis of the old saying that liberty is indivisible. Since community control over resources is the light that beckons on the left, the left—to the extent it cares about freedom of the spirit—must seek out devices that will discipline the government's monopoly in the realm of ideas. But any such device must consist of an official arbiter (that is, a government arbiter) to attempt to distribute access to the public forum. And that device cannot be content-neutral. It must decide which views have been heard too much, which not enough, and which should not be heard at all. The only content-neutral device turns out to be a society in which a significant portion of the resources are in private hands and beyond the reach of government altogether.

Id.

procedural conditions. What comes out of the process will be predetermined by what went into setting it up.[80]

In short, a pure free speech process is a vacuous concept. There are just different background conditions for speech, each of which will lead to different substantive outcomes.

Post understands the legitimacy difficulty faced by those who, like Fiss and Habermas, seek to manage free speech. On the other hand, Post fully appreciates the other side of this paradoxical predicament.[81] For Fiss, Habermas, and others with similar views are correct that the set of background entitlements and laws will affect the outcomes of the free speech process.[82] Yet, one such set must always be in place. If we cannot evaluate that set and compare it with other possible sets in terms of information effects, we cannot evaluate the most important determinants of outcomes of free speech, at least not on free speech grounds.

This is the paradox. Track two laws are extremely important in determining the quality of public debate. Indeed, track two laws have a much greater effect on speech than track one laws, if relative effects can be meaningfully measured. Nevertheless, the core First Amendment value that no partisan point of view be privileged precludes government from evaluating information gains and losses, which, in turn, means that track two analysis is precluded by the First Amendment itself.

Again, the point is not just an institutional one about the limits of courts. It applies to any governmental institution. Legislative evaluations of information, though democratic (unlike judicial evaluations), are themselves antithetical to the core First Amendment value.[83]

Finally, one might argue that adopting a comprehensive normative theory—such as Rawlsianism, utilitarianism, or libertarianism—as the vantage point for First Amendment analysis provides a basis for evaluating information gains and losses and thus for evaluating track two laws. The rejoinder to this position is that although comprehensive normative theories are in one sense the proper bases for evaluating track two laws,

---

80. *See* Strauss, *supra* note 71, at 352-53; Michael Walzer, *Moral Minimalism, in* FROM THE TWILIGHT OF PROBABILITY 3, 3-14 (William R. Shea & Antonio Spadafora eds., 1992).

81. *See* Post, *Managing Deliberation, supra* note 58, at 37-38; Post, *Racist Speech, supra* note 58, at 287-88; Post, *Public Discourse, supra* note 58, at 683-85.

82. *See* Sunstein, *supra* note 51, at 262, 271-77, 294-97; *see also* Julian N. Eule, *Promoting Speaker Diversity:* Austin *and* Metro Broadcasting, 1990 SUP. CT. REV. 105, 111-16.

83. Thus, a decision that there shall be public libraries, not public tennis courts, if it is a decision about the relative values of the information provided by libraries and tennis (and not just a weighing up of constituents' preferences qua preferences), represents government's endorsement of a partisan political view inconsistent with the First Amendment. *See supra* text accompanying notes 57-58.

944   HASTINGS LAW JOURNAL   [Vol. 44

they are the proper bases only insofar as they are not distinctly related to free speech. Rawlsianism, utilitarianism, and libertarianism are frameworks for assessing the entire corpus juris—to see if it maximizes liberties and wealth, maximizes aggregate or average welfare, or reflects libertarian rights—and in that sense they are important to track two analysis. In that same sense, however, they have nothing to do with speech or relative information value as distinct issues apart from liberties, welfare, and libertarian rights. Usually a comprehensive normative theory assumes full information of whatever type the theory makes relevant and then directs that that information be deployed to produce the results the theory dictates. Nevertheless, even if we assume the lack of full information, information effects can only be relevant to the choice of track two laws in a very restricted way. We would have to assume that the choice among track two laws was entirely neutral with regard to all values made relevant by the theory in question, and that relative information effects was the only ground for choice. The theory would then dictate that we choose that set of laws most likely to lead to the information upon which the theory itself places the higher value.

Yet, even in this extremely restricted way in which comprehensive normative theories would be relevant to track two analysis, such laws pose a First Amendment problem. Presumably the First Amendment, even if its ultimate justification rests on a comprehensive normative theory, forbids imposing such a comprehensive normative theory on citizens' evaluative decisions. Further, since imposition of a single comprehensive normative theory is the strongest of all governmental intrusions on the citizens' evaluative processes, it is the most antithetical to the First Amendment.

(3) Summary

If we assume the position of ignorance regarding information effects—what would get said, to whom, by whom, and to what effect—under alternative sets of track two laws, then we can make no evaluation of those sets in terms of information gains and losses. At most we can assume that under each such set, the deliberate production of information will face a recapture problem, a point that is normatively impotent because it applies to all alternative sets of laws.

On the other hand, if we assume the position of knowing the information effects under each alternative set of track two laws, we then face the problem that all evaluations of such information are positional and partisan and may not be endorsed by government. Even a comprehensive normative theory underlying the First Amendment will be too strong to be a track two tool, since it will usually endorse a set of track two laws on grounds independent of information gain and loss. Moreover, comprehensive theories are nothing more than partisan positions that the government may not endorse in attempting to structure public debate, even if, paradoxically, they themselves provide the justification for the First Amendment and its proscription of their own endorsement.

B. The Implication of the Failure of Balancing

Track two First Amendment analysis requires that we balance information gains and losses and all other values furthered by the entire set of laws in question against the information gains and losses and all other values furthered by all the alternative entire sets of laws. We cannot do this as a practical matter. Perhaps more importantly, we cannot do this as a theoretical matter. Even if we knew what information each alternative set of laws would generate, the First Amendment itself forbids government to act on an evaluation of that information. Track two analysis is not an extension of the First Amendment but a violation of it. Track Two laws can be evaluated on many grounds—but not on First Amendment ones.

There are two major implications for the First Amendment to be drawn from this conclusion. Most obviously, the courts should no longer hear track two challenges to laws. This would not have a great impact because track two challenges, as discussed earlier, almost never succeed.

The second implication, however, is directed at legislation, not adjudication, and is quite far-reaching. For if my analysis is correct, the legislature violates the First Amendment if it adopts and imposes through law any partisan evaluation of information, which is any evaluation. Essentially, while the government may enact laws based on a variety of values, it may not constitutionally rely on the value of information gained or lost in choosing which laws to enact or repeal.

This, in turn, suggests that the government's decisions whether to build an auditorium to provide a forum for public debates, to fund election campaigns, to expand public education, to fund research, and a multitude of other track two and track three decisions resting wholly or in part on government's evaluation of information rather than its aggregation of private preferences, are constitutionally problematic.

This implication, however, appears to offend common sense. Do we not need more fora for public debate, more public funding of elections, more broadcasting options, more education, and more research? Should government not support such endeavors?[84] Yet, how can I answer those who disagree without presupposing what information such endeavors would produce and without evaluating that information and its opportunity costs by reference to a controverted, partisan point of view?

Ultimately, track two analysis reveals not only its own First Amendment illicitness, but also the illicitness of all information-conscious legislative decisions regarding the quality and quantity of public discourse. Consider a legislative debate, such as might have occurred within the New York City Port Authority prior to *Lee*, over whether to allow the sale and distribution of literature inside the airport terminals and thereby incur the costs of congestion, annoyance, extra policing, clean-up, and so forth. The legislative body will be aware that if sale and distribution are not allowed, some passengers will not receive some messages, usually religious or political, and usually not mainstream. On the other hand, a clean, uncongested airport, aside from being valuable in itself, also communicates various messages to its patrons. Furthermore, the money saved on clean-up can be used to provide other services—including perhaps schools and libraries—or can be put in the pockets of taxpayers who might spend it on information. How is the choice to be made? The legislative body might disregard remote, uncertain, or amorphous information effects and focus only on the most direct, certain, and specific effects, such as the effects on the Hare Krishnas or the LaRoucheites. Even so, what should it do? Should it count these effects as outweighing the non-speech costs? Why? Because it sympathizes with the Hare Krishnas and LaRoucheites and believes others should hear their messages at the cost of other values and messages? Alternatively, should it count these effects as outweighed by the costs? Again, why? Legislative evaluation of the Hare Krishnas' and LaRoucheites' messages seems inevitable if speech effects are to be taken into account, but such evaluation on closer examination appears quite illicit.

Alternatively, consider a debate within Congress or the FCC over whether the broadcast media are sufficiently "diverse" or "balanced" in the array of information they provide the listeners and viewers in their markets. This debate can be meaningful only if there are criteria for identifying degrees of importance of information,[85] criteria for diver-

---

84. *See* BENJAMIN BARBER, STRONG DEMOCRACY 267-68, 305-07 (1984); Curtis J. Berger, Pruneyard *Revisited: Political Activity on Private Lands*, 66 N.Y.U. L. REV. 633, 646-47 (1991).

85. For example, diversity of political information is more important than diversity of music formats.

sity,[86] and criteria for balance.[87] The choice of such criteria is deeply evaluative and partisan.

Current Supreme Court track two jurisprudence seems most consistent with the following position: The legislative bodies may enact or modify track two laws explicitly in order to facilitate speech activities or to promote balance and diversity so long as the legislature is presumed to have had no clear impression of what information would be favored and disfavored, or no particular sympathy for the messages likely to be favored. Governmental decisions to allow demonstrations, to open facilities for pamphleteering, to build public auditoria and other communicative fora, to break-up media monopolies, and to subsidize broad categories of information media will uniformly be upheld, even if those decisions were premised on some estimate of the relative value of information lost and gained.[88] Because the content of the information gained in these cases cannot be known with any certainty when the decisions are made, the decisions are no more arbitrary than had they been made without regard to information gains and losses. So long as the legislative body is operating in the dark, the Court will not care that concern for information effects was what determined the outcome of the legislative balance.

This analysis explains as well why the Court often strikes down obviously content-based regulations of time, place, and manner. If, for example, the legislative body has taken a partisan position in favor of speech related to labor disputes and against all other speech,[89] or in favor of non-religious speech and against religious speech,[90] the Court will strike down the time, place, and manner regulation.

---

86. For example, how many positions are there on labor policy, is a novel free market position on world trade more or less diverse than a tired Marxist view, and is the latter more "diverse" relative to mainstream political programming than is religious programming or farm reports?

87. For example, does a strong speech by Cuomo balance three speeches by Quayle?

88. It is difficult to come up with unambiguous support for this statement because governmental decisions are almost always challenged on First Amendment grounds when they obviously restrict speech or obviously favor some subjects or viewpoints, and not when they subsidize speech in an apparently nonpartisan manner. Nonetheless, the Supreme Court has occasionally faced First Amendment challenges to governmental speech subsidies. *See, e.g.,* Buckley v. Valeo, 424 U.S. 1, 92-108 (1976) (holding federal subsidy of election campaigns constitutional); Red Lion Broadcasting, Co. v. FCC, 395 U.S. 367 (1969) (holding fairness doctrine in broadcasting constitutional); *cf.* Metro Broadcasting Inc. v. FCC, 110 S. Ct. 2997, 3025-26 (1990) (allowing preference for minority ownership in awarding broadcasting licenses).

89. *See* Carey v. Brown, 447 U.S. 455 (1980); Police Dept. v. Mosley, 408 U.S. 92 (1972).

90. *See* Widmar v. Vincent, 454 U.S. 263 (1981).

Thus, when the government makes a track two decision based on information effects, the Court will sustain the decision if it believes that the legislature could not have evaluated information effects in a partisan manner. Where the legislative decision appears to be partisan, however, the Court will invalidate it.

Track two First Amendment jurisprudence is destined to fail because no track two theory is available that is consistent with the core value of the First Amendment—citizen autonomy regarding the evaluation of information. The courts can strike down and, as in *Schneider* and *Lee*, have struck down laws in track two cases. Nonetheless, track two judicial decisions can only be arbitrary or illicit.

IV. Implications for Track One and Track Three Jurisprudence

A. Track One

The foregoing analysis of track two jurisprudence has profound implications for track one and track three. Essentially, its lesson is that track one and track three decisions cannot be justified by reference to the value of information at stake.

The content of speech—its message—has enormous capacity to inflict harm on values that government may legitimately seek to protect.[91] Yet the courts have consistently struck down attempts to interdict the receipt of such harmful messages unless the messages fall within a few unprotected categories.[92] The courts frequently justify this protection by reference to the value of the message.

Consider the following examples of track one jurisprudence. Defendant publishes a false and defamatory statement about a public figure plaintiff or satirizes a public figure plaintiff in an offensive manner that causes emotional distress.[93] Alternatively, plaintiff public employee makes a public criticism of defendant public employer that might adversely affect office morale.[94] The Supreme Court protects the speaker against sanctions in these cases and justifies protection on the ground that not protecting the speech would deter speech, the value of which is

---

91. *See* Frederick Schauer, *The Phenomenology of Speech and Harm*, 103 Ethics (forthcoming 1993); Frederick Schauer, *Uncoupling Free Speech*, 92 Colum. L. Rev. 1321 (1992) [hereinafter Schauer, *Uncoupling Free Speech*].

92. *See supra* text accompanying notes 3-4.

93. *See* Hustler Magazine, Inc. v. Falwell, 485 U.S. 46 (1988); New York Times Co. v. Sullivan, 376 U.S. 254 (1964).

94. *See* Pickering v. Board of Educ., 391 U.S. 563 (1968).

expected to outweigh the harm prevented by deterrence.[95] If the previous Part's argument is correct, however, the Court cannot make the judgment of relative value for two reasons: it cannot know what information will be lost or who will lose it through deterrence; and it cannot place a value on that information such that its value can be compared with the values the government is seeking to protect.[96]

Consider the protection tort law provides against revelation of private and embarrassing information. Should that protection withstand a track one First Amendment challenge? If so, then certain information will be lost to certain audiences. We do not know, however, what that information will be. Moreover, although any one of us may place a value on that information if we discover it, we have only our plural individual vantage points from which to assign a value to it.

On the other hand, consider the multitude of other track one First Amendment doctrines that purport to protect speech because of its information value despite the real and tangible harms it causes. The First Amendment law regarding defamation, regarding speech that induces others to engage in harmful conduct, and regarding pornography can be viewed as resting on the fear of "chilling" the communication of valuable information.[97] Frederick Schauer convincingly makes the point that our decision not to chill defamatory, inciting, or (soft-core) pornographic speech does not require that we allow the harm from some speech to remain on its immediate victims.[98] For example, we can shift its costs to the public through some sort of social insurance mechanism so that those costs truly are the costs we bear as the price of freedom of speech. Both Schauer and the Supreme Court fail to address, however, the loss of in-

---

95. See, e.g., id. at 571-75 (holding that a teacher's exercise of his right to speak on issues of public importance many not be the basis for his dismissal from public employment); New York Times Co. v. Sullivan, 376 U.S. 254, 271-83 (1964) (holding that the public interest in having free and unhindered debate on matters of public importance precludes a public official from receiving damages for defamation unless the statements were made with reckless disregard for the truth or with knowledge of their falsity).

96. This last statement needs to be qualified in this respect: Sometimes the information that is suppressed by censorship bears on the same value that government is seeking to further through censorship and thus reveals the censorship's self-defeating nature. In such a case the valuation of the information is no less legitimate than the valuation on which its suppression is premised. For instance, if the suppression of speech in the name of copyright and patent laws is meant to produce a net increase in ideas that can be copyrighted or patented by giving authors and inventors the incentive of legal monopoly, then that justification for suppression would be undermined by a showing that copyright and patent laws lead to fewer ideas that can be copyrighted or patented than would exist in their absence.

97. Although these aspects of First Amendment law might rest on other grounds, such as some conception of the right to autonomy. See infra Part IV.C.

98. See Schauer, Uncoupling Free Speech, supra note 91.

950 HASTINGS LAW JOURNAL [Vol. 44

formation that any method of allocating the costs of harms entails. Every possible legal regime—the law of defamation prior to *New York Times v. Sullivan*, the *Sullivan* regime itself,[99] or Schauer's social insurance system[100]—will produce its own distinctive supply and type of information. An information effects approach to track one jurisprudence is unavailing.

Other track one maneuvers, such as denying value to certain speech, are equally unavailing. Consider, for example, the categories of hate speech and pornography. While they undoubtedly cause harm, are they valuable? Alon Harel argues that they are not.[101] Harel places hate speech and pornography in a category called "abhorrent speech." Abhorrent speech lacks value, not because it communicates no ideas, and not because its ideas are not important or political in some sense, but because its ideas do not make up part of our political discourse, a discourse that extends only to those values and ideas capable of generating legitimate political obligations.[102] In other words, because we cannot legitimately act on racist or sexist values, we cannot assign First Amendment value to speech supporting such values.

Harel's position can be viewed as an outright denial of my contention in the previous Part that the core First Amendment principle is preventing any institution from assigning values to messages. Harel asserts that "[t]here are some values and ideas that are so abhorrent that they are not part of political discourse. The test is the degree to which values and ideas that purport to shape the nature of our political obligations can succeed in doing so."[103]

Harel recognizes that courts have consistently granted First Amendment protection to what he labels abhorrent speech, but argues that such protection is a mistake. He rejects, quite correctly, any notion that all political messages are equally valuable:

> Any participant in political discourse believes that her or his idea is more valuable than others; indeed, the reason why the participant holds a particular political position is precisely because he or she believes that this political idea is more valuable than the alternatives. If no political idea were more valuable than any other, we could arbitrarily choose any political view and govern our lives in accordance with it. The claim that all political ideas are equally valuable is inconsistent with the basic assumptions of participants in political discourse. The

---

99. *Sullivan*, 376 U.S. at 282-84.
100. *See* Schauer, *Uncoupling Free Speech*, *supra* note 91, at 1338-55.
101. Alon Harel, *Bigotry, Pornography, and the First Amendment: A Theory of Unprotected Speech*, 65 S. CAL. L. REV. 1887 (1992).
102. *Id.* at 1889.
103. *Id.* at 1889-90.

> equal protection principle applies not because all political ideas are
> equal but *in spite of* the unequal value of political statements.[104]

He then goes on to consider various theories that might nonetheless support First Amendment protection for abhorrent speech and finds them all wanting.

Most significantly for my purposes, Harel rejects institutional justifications for protecting abhorrent speech.[105] He does so for two reasons. First, he says that institutional incompetence is inconsistent with actual First Amendment decisionmaking. For example, courts assess the value of particular instances of political discourse when they ask whether obscene speech meets the *Miller* test[106] for unprotected status.[107] The courts also assess its value when they declare it to be more valuable—and thus subject to greater protection—than commercial speech.[108] Second, the incompetence argument is circular in that courts can become good at assessing the value of speech if First Amendment doctrine is changed to allow them to do so.[109]

Harel is responding here to an argument that all governmental institutions should be deemed incompetent to assess the value of speech. Yet his response is limited to courts. Moreover, his response misses the particular type of governmental incompetence at the core of the First Amendment. First Amendment concerns are not implicated if a court or a legislature assesses the value of arguments and information worse than you, I, or anyone else would. The concern is that a court's or legislature's assessment—like yours, mine, or anyone else's—will be in an important sense just another point of view that should not be privileged by government. You, I, and most other people believe—no, we know—that bigotry is wrong. We also know that the First Amendment is a good thing. Further, what we know the government is quite likely to know as well. Nevertheless, the government is forbidden by the First Amendment to interdict ideas it believes to be false, including, not just the idea that bigotry is good, but, paradoxically, the idea the First Amendment is bad.

Harel, in fact, believes that in arguing for nonprotection for abhorrent speech, he is arguing for a minor amendment of First Amendment jurisprudence. The ideas expressed by abhorrent speech are not just wrong, says Harel, they are ideas that cannot provide the basis for legiti-

---

104. *Id.* at 1914.
105. *Id.* at 1915-16.
106. *See* Miller v. California, 413 U.S. 15, 24 (1973).
107. Harel, *supra* note 101, at 1917.
108. *Id.*
109. *Id.*

mate political obligation. Harel contrasts abhorrent speech, such as hate speech and pornography, with pro-life and pro-choice speech regarding abortion. Pro-lifers regard the pro-choicers as advocating murder. The latter regard the former as advocating subordination of women. Neither murder nor subordination are acceptable political values, so it might seem that Harel would allow the silencing of one group by the other. Harel denies this consequence of his position. He says that the underlying values of the pro-life and pro-choice positions—protection of life and equality—are values that can sustain legitimate political obligations, even if, from the point of view of the other side, these values have been misapplied.[110]

This maneuver leads Harel into an impossible dilemma. All proponents of abhorrent speech are expressing, at some level of generality, perfectly legitimate political values. As Harel notes, Nazis can argue that their speech conveys ideals of patriotism.[111] Likewise, racists and sexists can talk about respecting a natural moral order. Harel's response is weak:

> A judgment must be made in each case as to the prominence of the abhorrent values and that of the legitimate ones. Speech should be denied or granted protection only after careful examination of the complex of values the speech conveys and reinforces. *All* discourse conveys a variety of different and contradictory values. Identifying the primary values and ideas conveyed by a particular form of discourse requires more than the identification of the explicit agenda advocated by the participants.[112]

There is no way in principle for a court, or anyone else, to disentangle the question of whether a political position is wrong from the question of whether a political position expresses legitimate political values. At some level of generality, almost any political position, including "abhorrent" ones, expresses legitimate political values. Yet, at another level of generality, any political question expresses legitimate political values only if it is correct.

Harel's argument purports to be critical, and not descriptive, of track one jurisprudence. He is seeking to reform, not legitimize, the jurisprudential status quo. I am also critical of many First Amendment precedents. My argument against Harel is not that he is at odds with First Amendment jurisprudence, but that he is more fundamentally at odds with a central value underlying the First Amendment. Whether an idea can form the basis for political obligations cannot be disentangled

---

110. *Id.* at 1925-26.
111. *Id.* at 1926.
112. *Id.*

from the question of whether the idea is correct. Furthermore, if the correctness of an idea is the touchstone for its track one protectability, the First Amendment is not merely drained of its central meaning but is turned inside out.

Nonetheless, Harel and I agree on one thing: track one First Amendment jurisprudence protects more speech than it can justify protecting. Harel's point is that some speech that is currently protected is valueless. My point is that placing a positive value on speech—as track one jurisprudence currently does in dealing with contending values of privacy, confidentiality, property, and sensibility—is itself problematic.

B. Track Three

If my arguments are correct, they reveal a major problem with what I have called track three governmental decisions, decisions by the government to promote its own views. These would seem to be the most suspect according to the analysis I have applied to the other tracks, yet the Court treats them quite deferentially. There are, of course, a number of track three decisions that deal with speech appurtenant to government enterprises that are not principally information oriented. For example, when the government runs the military, the police, public hospitals, the welfare department, and other enterprises, it has a concern with what gets said that is no different from the concern a private enterprise would have. It wants its welfare workers to give clients advice about welfare, not politics or religion. It wants the police department's bulletin board to be used for notices of seminars, union meetings, and shift information. In short, the government wants to make sure that the information necessary for the success of its enterprises be conveyed, and that it not be drowned out by extraneous information.[113] If government's enterprises

---

113. Several cases fall into this realm. *See, e.g.,* Minnesota State Bd. for Community Colleges v. Knight, 465 U.S. 271 (1984) (restrictions on who could participate in college governance institutions); Perry Educ. Ass'n v. Perry Local Educators' Ass'n, 460 U.S. 37 (1983) (restrictions on who could communicate through teachers' mail system). More problematic, because they disclose the lack of a clear boundary between government's legitimate concern for its own enterprises and its more suspect concern with public debate over its effectiveness, are cases in which employee speech is suppressed because of morale effects. *See* Rankin v. McPherson, 483 U.S. 378 (1987) (balancing potential value of speech by public employee against potential for undermining her effectiveness); Connick v. Myers, 461 U.S. 138 (1983) (upholding dismissal based upon speech by public employee affecting office morale and undermining employer's authority); Pickering v. Board of Educ., 391 U.S. 563 (1968) (holding employee's speech on matters of public importance cannot be a basis of dismissal); Robert C. Post, *Between Governance and Management: The History and Theory of the Public Forum,* 34 UCLA L. REV. 1713, 1812-16 (1987). Ironically, the concern for morale is less problematic the broader the muzzling that occurs. *See, e.g.,* Greer v. Spock, 424 U.S. 828 (1976) (upholding

Freedom of Speech I

are legitimate, then so too is its concern with speech that interferes with those enterprises.

When government becomes an educator or patron of scholarship, research, and the arts, the tension with the First Amendment's central values is most acute. If the government may not establish an evaluative orthodoxy regarding citizens' exchanges of information, why may it do so when it speaks itself, as it does through public education, the funding of research, scholarship, the arts, public broadcasting, family planning counseling, and myriad other enterprises? Does the First Amendment speak differently to government's evaluation of information when it is using citizens' tax monies as opposed to censoring citizens' speech or manipulating time, place, and manner regulations in order to favor and disfavor certain subjects and viewpoints?

I cannot square the Court's general concern with content discrimination and its currently quite permissive attitude toward track three governmental speech. Why the government may monetarily subsidize speech that promotes live birth over abortion but may not subsidize labor speech by granting an exemption from a general ban on demonstrations near schools is a theoretical mystery. Perhaps the Court believes that partisan use of resources is more of a threat to the First Amendment when the resources are parks, streets, sidewalks, and perhaps airports than when the resources are tax monies. Nevertheless, current track three jurisprudence is surely in need of a theoretical reconciliation with the principle of governmental evaluative neutrality that underlies the First Amendment.[114]

---

regulation banning political speech from military base); Lehman v. City of Shaker Heights, 418 U.S. 298 (1974) (upholding regulation banning political advertisements from public transport).

114. For scholarly commentary on track three First Amendment jurisprudence, see generally MARK G. YUDOF, WHEN GOVERNMENT SPEAKS: POLITICS, LAW, AND GOVERNMENT EXPRESSION IN AMERICA (1983), Stanley Ingber, *Socialization, Indoctrination, and the 'Pall of Orthodoxy': Value Training in the Public Schools*, 1987 U. ILL. L. REV. 15, Robert D. Kamenshine, *The First Amendment's Implied Political Establishment Clause*, 67 CAL. L. REV. 1104 (1979), Steven Shiffrin, *Government Speech*, 27 UCLA L. REV. 565 (1980), Cass R. Sunstein, *Government Control of Information*, 74 CAL. L. REV. 889 (1986), and Edward H. Ziegler, Jr., *Government Speech and the Constitution: The Limits of Official Partnership*, 20 B.C. L. REV. 578 (1980).

My fanatical conclusion regarding track three jurisprudence could be softened somewhat if the legislature were allowed to act on premises on which there were a broadbased consensus. Thus, the schools could teach that the earth is round, that America was discovered by Columbus in 1492, and that $2 \times 2 = 4$. The legislature could fund medical research and basic physics but not astrology. *See infra* text accompanying notes 122-124. It could also decide that public libraries and public theaters were more valuable than more shopping malls. Moreover, the courts could develop a track three jurisprudence that would focus on structural issues, such as how decisions about curricula, collections, or research, for example, are made within track three governmental entities, with a First Amendment preference for decentraliza-

C. Autonomy and First Amendment Jurisprudence

This Essay has asked the reader to accept the proposition that a central principle underlying the First Amendment is that the government is forbidden to impose on citizens a particular evaluation of information, ideas, and arguments. This proposition entails that any governmental decision, whether on track one, two, or three, is illegitimate if premised upon the government's evaluation of the decision's information effects, even if government's ultimate aim is to prevent some harm more tangible than ignorance or falsehood.[115] Government must act for reasons that do not require citizens to believe, or be ignorant of, certain things.

While there are many theories of freedom of speech and the First Amendment, I will not attempt to canvass them, much less recite the problems internal to each.[116] What is important is that those theories generally do not dispute the central principle upon which I have been relying, but rather, attempt to justify that principle by reference to a still broader aim, such as pursuit of truth, democratic self-governance, self-realization, or distrust of government.

The major competitor to consequentialist theories of freedom of speech, those that depend upon evaluating information differentially, are those deontological theories that are based upon some conception of individual autonomy.[117] According to these theories, the paradigmatic violation of freedom of speech is an attempt to penalize or interdict the sending or receipt of a message because of the fear that the audience will, on account of the message, believe things to be true and good that are not and, as a result of that belief, act to its or others' detriment. If someone

---

tion and professionalism. The legislature, however, could not take sides on widely disputed issues. Moreover, this concession to legislative assessments of the value of information would not entail any judicial track two role (unless one took the position that the First Amendment was an *affirmative* command to produce a certain level of education and a certain kind of public discourse).

For a more permissive view of track three government action, see David A. Strauss, *The Liberal Virtues, in* VIRTUE 197, 202 (John W. Chapman & W. Galston eds., 1992) (arguing that the government should be able to teach "liberal virtues," presumably even if liberal virtues include the unwillingness to force others to accept those virtues).

115. Government must, of course, evaluate information and find facts for its own purposes. It must decide questions of adjudicative fact (Did Mary rob John?) and questions of legislative fact (Will clearcutting in national forests worsen erosion?). The question is not whether government may evaluate information for its purposes but whether its purposes may legitimately include concern that citizens receive information government deems valuable.

116. For a discussion of theories of freedom of speech and their problems, see Lawrence Alexander & Paul Horton, *The Impossibility of a Free Speech Principle*, 78 Nw. U. L. REV. 1319 (1983).

117. *See* Thomas Scanlon, *A Theory of Freedom of Expression*, 1 PHIL. & PUB. AFF. 204 (1972); Strauss, *supra* note 71, at 356-57.

wishes to convince me that socialism is the best governmental program, then according to autonomy theories of freedom of speech, government cannot attempt to prevent me from hearing these arguments, even if government is convinced that the arguments are wrong and afraid that if I hear them, I will cast a misguided vote for a catastrophic socialism.

Autonomy theories lead to a First Amendment that is narrower than current doctrine in some respects, but broader in others. Most important for my purposes, autonomy theories eliminate track two from the First Amendment altogether.[118] Autonomy theories also revise track one in several respects. They arguably expand protection for commercial, pornographic, and other forms of speech that receive no, or reduced, track one protection where the government's concern is that the audience will be persuaded of error in action or belief.[119] On the other hand, First Amendment protection of speech invasive of privacy might not be granted to the same extent as at present, since limiting access to private information for the victim's sake does not, at least arguably, infringe on the audience's deliberative autonomy. The precise implications of autonomy theories for track one will, of course, depend upon the particular conception of autonomy they embrace, but there is no doubt that all of them will be revisionary to some extent.[120]

---

118. This is not true when a content-neutral law is enacted *because* of its content effects, a case that has always been rightly considered to be on track one.

119. A classic example is Posadas de Puerto Rico Associates v. Tourism Co., 478 U.S. 328 (1986), in which the Court upheld Puerto Rico's ban on casino advertising in Puerto Rico, a ban premised on a fear that the audience would be persuaded to gamble, to its and Puerto Rico's detriment.

120. Autonomy theories have difficulty dealing with false statements of facts upon which the audience might detrimentally rely. Scanlon believed his conception of autonomy prevented government from penalizing such statements, a result that led him to abandon his autonomy theory of freedom of expression. *See* T.M. Scanlon, Jr., *Freedom of Expression and Categories of Expression*, 40 U. PITT. L. REV. 519, 532 (1979). Strauss believes that his autonomy theory can distinguish between false statements of fact, which government may regulate without violating the First Amendment, and actions of government which violate the First Amendment because they manipulate audience deliberation. *See* Strauss, *supra* note 71, at 357, 366-68. He also believes that his theory can maintain the distinction between private and governmental attempts to manipulate audiences, with the latter forbidden by the theory and the former protected against governmental restriction. *Id*. at 362-63. I believe both of Strauss's distinctions are problematic. Both depend upon the existence of a distinction between false or misleading statements of fact and false or misleading statements of some other kind. (The private manipulation Strauss *would* permit government to restrict is manipulation through false statements of fact.) But as Strauss himself acknowledges, the line between statements of fact and First-Amendment-protected political statements is difficult to maintain because the latter, to the extent one thinks they are wrong, usually are wrong in some factual aspect. *Id*. at 366 n.76. Whether lowering taxes will increase the deficit is a factual question. Government might believe that my position, that it will, is incorrect because my predictive models, my information, or my inferences are flawed *as a matter of fact*. The same criticism can be levelled at the

Autonomy theories of freedom of speech, as opposed to consequentialist theories, are quite consistent with the core First Amendment principle of governmental neutrality in evaluating ideas. Indeed, that core principle derives from and is an expression of the value of autonomy. Of course, the value of autonomy has implications far beyond speech and government neutrality regarding ideas. In that sense, autonomy theories do not specially justify freedom of speech.[121]

D. Categories of Speech and the First Amendment

One approach to free speech and the First Amendment limits the protection to certain categories of information, such as political and religious information. Any of the First Amendment theories discussed

---

distinction in the realm of professional ethics between misstating in one's brief the record or the courts' holdings in the area and making an argument that one believes will sound persuasive but that one also believes is logically fallacious. *Cf.* Fried, *supra* note 79, at 239-41 (asking whom could we trust to ferret out falsehood). In general, much more needs to be said about the ethics of conveying and withholding information, including when we must publicize the full bases of our actions, when we may withhold information in the hope others will be deceived, and when we can use bad arguments to corrupt others for good ends. *See* Larry Alexander, *Pursuing the Good—Indirectly*, 95 ETHICS 315, 325-29 (1985).

Strauss proposes the following test for when government may restrict private manipulative statements: Government may restrict private manipulative statements whenever a hypothetical individual with no desire other than reaching the best decision would want the speech restricted. Strauss, *supra* note 71, at 369. The problem with the test is that it depends on the level of generality at which the manipulation is described and thus yields no determinate answers. *But see* Fried, *supra* note 79, at 236-37 (arguing that audience has no right not to receive unwanted messages).

Interestingly, autonomy theories of freedom of speech do not appear to protect statements that the audience does not wish to hear, such as statements designed solely to insult the audience but not to persuade others. Indeed, autonomy theories may not even protect speech meant to persuade others if the government's purpose in forbidding the speech is not to prevent the persuasion but is instead to protect other values, such as privacy, confidentiality, property (in ideas), sensibility (from insult and offense), and equal opportunity (from harassment, assuming the sense of harassment is not merely concern about others' being persuaded). Perhaps we can say that the rightful sphere of autonomy of a speaker and his willing audience is infringed whenever government acts to interdict speech because the speech insults, offends, or distresses third parties or an unwilling audience if the harms to the third parties are caused by their beliefs about what others believe. *See* Larry Alexander, *Harm, Offense, and Morality, in* READING FEINBERG (Howard McGary ed., forthcoming) (manuscript at 34-37, on file with author); *see also* JUDITH JARVIS THOMSON, THE REALM OF RIGHTS 253-57 (1990) (causing belief-mediated distress to another does not infringe that person's rights). *But see id.* at 354-56 (discussing legislative ability to prohibit behavior causing belief-mediated distress). It is not clear whether autonomy theories can be extended to invalidate governmental interdiction of insulting or offending speech, or extended even further to invalidate protections of privacy or reputation. If not, then perhaps very few governmental track one laws infringe the rightful sphere of speaker or audience autonomy. In other words, autonomy theories may lead to a much, much narrower track one First Amendment than we currently have.

121. *See* Alexander & Horton, *supra* note 116, at 1356-57.

958   HASTINGS LAW JOURNAL   [Vol. 44

above can be applied broadly so as to include all information or applied more narrowly so as to include only a subset of information. Likewise, the central principle upon which I have been relying can be limited to only certain categories of information.

A "categories" approach to free speech and its jurisprudence has powerful proponents in the literature,[122] as well as considerable precedential support.[123] It also has a powerful appeal. Most of us believe that government should not make retail decisions—censorial or advocative—about the value of specific items of information, such as that the teachings of the Hare Krishnas are false or wicked, that socialism is not worthy of consideration, or that feminist legal theory is muddled. Moreover, most of us believe that government should not be authorized to censor "unreasonable" views or to advocate "reasonable" ones because we do not trust the government's ability to distinguish what it believes to be unreasonable from what it believes to be incorrect.[124] On the other hand, most of us think it reasonable to believe that political and religious information is, on average, more valuable than other kinds of information, for example, backyard gossip, the common fare of supermarket tabloids, or "trivia."

So long as the common consensus is that some categories of information are on average more valuable than others, we might believe that government may legitimately distinguish *among* the categories but not *within* them. Of course, we would also have to believe that government is capable of determining in most cases the category into which various information falls.[125] This does not mean that the line between, say, political speech and commercial speech must be bright and susceptible to formalistic application. It does mean, however, that the line cannot be so

---

122. The most powerful proponent is Frederick Schauer. *See* Frederick Schauer, *Categories and the First Amendment: A Play in Three Acts*, 34 VAND. L. REV. 265 (1981).

123. The Supreme Court has treated adult movies and books and commercial speech as "low value" speech, and has treated pornography and other types of speech as having no value. *See, e.g.,* Central Hudson Gas & Elec. Corp. v. Public Serv. Comm'n, 447 U.S. 557, 562-63 (1980) (commercial speech); Young v. American Mini-Theatres, Inc., 424 U.S. 50, 70 (1976) (adult movies and books); Miller v. California, 413 U.S. 15 (1973) (pornography); *see also* Larry Alexander, *Low Value Speech*, 83 NW. U. L. REV. 547 (1989) (discussing the division of speech into categories according to value). Within the defamation area, the Court has distinguished speech about matters of "public concern" from purely private speech. *See* Dun & Bradstreet, Inc. v. Greenmoss Builders, Inc., 472 U.S. 749, 758-59 (1985).

124. All views that we believe to be incorrect we believe to be unreasonable given the information we possess.

125. To take an oft-cited example, does an advertisement urging lifting of restrictions on domestic oil production count as "political speech" or "commercial speech," and is the answer dependent on whether it is paid for by Common Cause or Mobil Oil? *See* David F. McGowan, Comment, *A Critical Analysis of Commercial Speech*, 78 CAL. L. REV. 359 (1990).

vague that the majority of cases are incapable of principled categorization. If the latter were true, then not only would the categories be manipulable, but the judgments of higher and lower average value would look insupportable.

This categorical approach helps to justify those aspects of track one and track three jurisprudence that I found troubling. Speech about public officials, public figures, or matters of public concern receives protection in the defamation and privacy contexts that purely private speech does not. The public schools' choice to teach American history, or certain topics within it, rather than to count blades of grass or memorize the phone book is justifiable, though teaching the superiority of Democrats over Republicans is not.

Nonetheless, a categorical approach does nothing to justify track two decisionmaking. No matter what track two laws the government adopts, information will be lost, and information in each category will be lost. Change the laws, and you change what gets said, by whom, to whom, and to what effect with respect to politics, religion, commerce, and every other possible category.[126]

More importantly perhaps, a categorical approach relies on the reasonableness of imposing an evaluative ranking on everyone. You and I may agree that political speech is more valuable than the typical contents of the *National Enquirer*. Indeed, almost everyone would agree with us, including almost every reader of the *National Enquirer*. Yet, what makes our judgment reasonable, such that we may legitimately impose it on a solitary dissenter, that does not make my judgment that Bill Clinton is superior to George Bush, or that most multi-culturalist apologia are rubbish, "reasonable" as well? Controversiality surely does not determine reasonableness as a matter of legitimate governmental action. As an epistemic matter, we can be more confident of judgments with which most others would concur. Nevertheless, if that is what is at stake, freedom of speech looks less like a protection of the lonely dissenter and more like a crude and costly bulwark against entrenching error. Furthermore, a noncontroversiality approach to the relative value of categories of speech does not, in principle, prevent categorization *within* categories such as political or religious speech that would cordon from protection political or religious views that almost all of us believe are worthless.

Robert Post adopts something akin to a categorical approach in track one analysis. He asks whether particular speech is part of "public

---

126. *See supra* text accompanying notes 57 and 74.

discourse."[127] If so, it receives First Amendment protection, though perhaps not absolute protection. The question whether speech is part of public discourse is, as Post admits, a deeply evaluative one regarding the relation of the speech to a proper conception of democratic decisionmaking.[128] The problem is that any conception of the autonomy required by democracy will be based on an evaluation regarding autonomy's requisite knowledge, skill, and character that, from another angle, can be viewed as a heteronymous imposition. Post argues that this paradox of the heteronymous construction of autonomy is, like other antinomies such as that of free will and determinism, unavoidable, and should therefore be embraced. If Post is correct, something like a categorical approach is perhaps inevitable, with only judgment and not algorithms available for drawing lines.[129]

V. Conclusion

One of the clearest expressions of the core principle of the First Amendment, an expression that reveals the value of autonomy underlying that principle, is Charles Fried's:

---

127. *See* Robert Post, Personal Correspondence with Author, Nov. 23, 1992 (on file with the *Hastings Law Journal*) [hereinafter Post, Personal Correspondence]; Post, *Racist Speech, supra* note 58, at 279-85; *see also* Calvin R. Massey, *Hate Speech, Cultural Diversity, and the Foundational Paradigms of Free Expression,* 40 UCLA L. REV. 103, 116-18, 151-52 (1992) (distinguishing public discourse, which government may not coerce, from utterances outside the scope of public discourse).

128. *See* Post, Personal Correspondence, *supra* note 127.

129. Post believes, contrary to my position, that there is a tenable track two jurisprudence. *Id.* Post would not conflate, as I have done, public forum analysis and symbolic speech analysis. His focus would be on the former, which he would recast as an analysis of the health of media of communication. The question of what is a medium of communication, like a newspaper, as opposed to an expressive act, like burning a draft card, would be a sociological one addressed to how we, as a society, understand such things. The First Amendment analysis would ask how a time, place, or manner regulation affects a medium of communication's health.

I am generally less sanguine than Post about entrusting courts with deciding subtle questions of sociology such as whether and when "we" understand an activity to be a medium of communication. Even if I were perfectly happy with entrusting the courts with that question, however, I cannot imagine on what ground they would assess a regulation's effect on a medium's "health." The latter assessment assumes a normative baseline regarding well-functioning media of communication, and no judgment about that baseline can be divorced from judgments of the baseline's information effects. Are newspapers "healthy"? Is television? Has placing graffiti on others' property become a medium of expression, and, if so, is it "healthy"? Post criticizes Owen Fiss's and Cass Sunstein's urge to manage democratic deliberation, but his approach to public forum analysis commits him to precisely the same evaluative judgments with which he saddles Fiss and Sunstein. *See* Post, *Managing Deliberation, supra* note 58, at 29-38.

There are famous difficulties in defining these spheres of liberty against encroachment by the actions of others—one man's liberty is another's constraint—and many have despaired of deriving any practical conclusions from this principle as it relates to laws bearing on conduct. But the way is much clearer with respect to thought, expression and persuasion. There the claim to liberty runs directly to the foundational. Our ability to deliberate, to reach conclusions about our good, and to act on those conclusions is the foundation of our status as free and rational persons. No conviction forced upon us can really be ours at all. Limits may be put on my actions insofar as my actions impinge on others, but my status as a rational sovereign requires that I be free to judge for myself what is good and how I shall arrange my life in the sphere of liberty that the similar spheres of others leave me. I cede authority to the state to draw the necessary concrete boundaries between our respective spheres of action. But no such necessity requires, indeed self-respect forbids, that I cede to the state the authority to limit my use of my rational powers. That is why lying, while not the most damaging offense to another's moral right, is one of the clearest. It is also why the state has no claim to dominion over our minds: what we believe, what we are persuaded to believe, and (derivatively) what others may try to persuade us to believe.[130]

It should be obvious that if Fried is correct, there is no place for a track two jurisprudence in the First Amendment. However, track one and track three jurisprudence remain. The government actions that invoke track three are quite problematic; the shape of track one is difficult to discern, though autonomy theories would undoubtedly require some changes in current track one doctrine. In a true track two case, however, there is no toehold for finding government's actions or laws to violate the First Amendment.

This conclusion is, of course, deeply paradoxical. Track two laws have profound effects on what gets said, by whom, and to what effect, and they thus have a profound effect on what we believe and value. Yet because the First Amendment's core principle enjoins government—including the courts—from deciding what we should believe and value, the First Amendment disables government from dealing with the belief and value effects of its track two laws.

This paradox, of course, extends beyond track two. The absence of education surely undermines our autonomy, but government-run schools, which must decide what shall be taught and what shall not, raise a profound track three First Amendment problem.[131] And track one

---

130. Fried, *supra* note 79, at 233 (footnotes omitted).

131. *See* Larry Alexander, *Liberalism as Neutral Dialogue: Man and Manna in the Liberal State*, 28 UCLA L. Rev. 816, 853-58 (1981).

962   HASTINGS LAW JOURNAL   [Vol. 44

analysis paradoxically disables government from protecting our autonomy from private manipulative and deceptive speech.[132]

That the First Amendment contains paradoxes should not be surprising. The First Amendment is a feature of liberalism, which gives pride of place to individual autonomy. Autonomy, however, is a paradoxical value. Enshrined in the First Amendment, it tells us that even when we are convinced we know what is correct and wish to keep others from falling into errors of belief and value, we may do so only with our own private resources and acting within our own private domain. We are forbidden to enlist the weapons of the state, even to save others' autonomy and the First Amendment itself.[133]

---

132. *See* Strauss, *supra* note 71, at 362-65.
133. *See* Larry Alexander, *Liberalism, Religion, and the Unity of Epistemology*, 30 SAN DIEGO L. REV. (forthcoming November 1993).

[13]

Copyright 1989 by Northwestern University, School of Law
Northwestern University Law Review

Printed in U.S.A.
Vol. 83, No. 3

LEGAL THEORY

LOW VALUE SPEECH

Larry Alexander *

Several theories of freedom of speech divide speech into the categories of "high value," "low value," and "no value."[1] For example, Cass Sunstein has recently argued for increased governmental authority to ban pornography (as defined by him) on the ground that, in addition to being speech that produces harms that government should seek to prevent, it is "low value" speech.[2] The United States Supreme Court has deemed pornography (as defined by it) to be "no value" speech, thus subject to a complete ban; and it has deemed adult books and movies and commercial speech to be "low value" speech, thus subject to regulation beyond that to which "high value" speech is subject.[3]

Dividing the realm of speech into "high value," "low value," and "no value" is quite problematic, however, and for a reason that is very seldom addressed. Such division assumes that, for purposes of "freedom of speech" values, "speech" resides in an object, such as a printed page, a frame of film, or a series of sounds, rather than in the derivation of meaning from the object by the audience or in the intended meaning of the speaker. But that assumption is erroneous. The statement, "Subjugate women!," appearing on a political pamphlet, may convey exactly the same meaning to its audience as a pornographic picture of a woman in bondage. That is, the viewers of the pornographic picture may react to the picture by forming the idea of subjugating women, the same idea that they derive from the pamphlet. If that is the case, then there seems to be

---

* Professor of Law, University of San Diego. I gratefully acknowledge the excellent suggestions I have received from Carl Auerbach, Kevin Cole, Paul Horton, Richard Saphire, Fred Schauer, and Chris Wonnell.

[1] *See, e.g.,* Farber, *Commercial Speech and First Amendment Theory,* 74 Nw. U.L. Rev. 372 (1979); Franklin, *Constitutional Libel Law: The Role of Content,* 34 UCLA L. Rev. 1657 (1987); Perry, *Freedom of Expression: An Essay on Theory and Doctrine,* 78 Nw. U. L. Rev. 1137 (1983); Wright, *A Rationale from J.S. Mill for the Free Speech Clause,* 1985 Sup. Ct. Rev. 149. *See generally* L. Tribe, American Constitutional Law 920-44 (2d ed. 1988).

[2] Sunstein, *Pornography and the First Amendment,* 1986 Duke L.J. 589.

[3] *See* Central Hudson Gas Elec. Corp. v. Public Serv. Comm. of New York, 447 U.S. 557 (1980) (commercial speech); Young v. American Mini Theaters, 427 U.S. 50 (1976) (adult books and movies); Miller v. California, 413 U.S. 15 (1973) (pornography).

547

NORTHWESTERN UNIVERSITY LAW REVIEW

a good argument for regarding the pamphlet and the picture as having the same value as speech. If the pamphlet is "high value" speech, then so too it would appear is the pornographic picture. Conversely, if the latter is "low" or "no value" speech, then so is the pamphlet.

What are the arguments available for distinguishing these two types of speech in terms of their value?

It is important to point out that one cannot create a distinction between the pamphlet and the picture by reference to the government's reasons for banning the picture, at least if the reasons are those advanced by Sunstein and others.[4] If the government is banning the pornographic picture because viewing such pictures leads people to form the idea of subjugating women, which idea then leads some of them to commit acts of violence and discrimination against women, the government has an equal interest in banning the pamphlet.

How else might the Court, Sunstein, and others defend their distinctions? Not by pointing out that only a few viewers of the pornographic picture will derive the loathsome message from it, whereas almost all readers of the pamphlet will derive its literal message from it. If true, that fact cuts exactly the wrong way, for it makes the government's concern with the pamphlet greater than its concern with the picture. Moreover, I doubt that the proponents of making value distinctions among types of speech would ban National Geographic, medical textbooks, or paintings of nudes even if it turned out to be the case that the most numerous viewers of those items were voyeurs.[5]

Nor would distinctions work that were based on the speaker's intent. The problem with focusing on the speaker's intent is not just that the pornographic picture may have been intended to be a political statement, and the "political" pamphlet may have been written by one who sells S & M paraphernalia. The fundamental problem is that under the most plausible theories regarding the justification of freedom of speech, the "value" of speech resides in the derivation of meaning by its audience and not in the intended meaning, *if any*, of the speaker. I shall return to this point later.[6] It is sufficient at this juncture to point out, by way of an example drawn from commercial speech (another category of speech dubiously considered to be "low value"[7]), that the "value" of "buy a Chrysler" does not decline when its author is Lee Iacocca rather than

---

[4] Sunstein supports bans on pornography because pornography can be linked to violence and discrimination against women. Sunstein, *supra* note 2, at 594-602.

[5] *See* Alexander & Horton, *The Impossibility of a Free Speech Principle*, 78 Nw. U.L. Rev. 1319, 1331-32 (1983).

[6] *See infra* text accompanying notes 19-21 and note 19 *infra*.

[7] *See generally* L. Tribe, *supra* note 1, at 931-34. For attacks on the relegation of commercial speech to "low value" status, see Redish, *The Value of Free Speech*, 130 U. Pa. L. Rev. 591 (1982); Wolfson, *The First Amendment and the SEC*, 20 Conn. L. Rev. 265 (1988).

83:547 (1989)

Ralph Nader.[8]

Another basis for a distinction between picture and pamphlet that might be offered is the distinction between verbal and nonverbal media. "Low value" or "no value" speech may be meaning transmitted by and/or derived from nonverbal media.

There are three problems with this focus on verbal content. First, many may derive a meaning from the picture that they consciously verbalize, a meaning that is as fully cognitive for them as the meaning they derive from the pamphlet. Second, the noncognitive "meanings" conveyed by nonverbal media may also be conveyable by verbal media.[9] Third, and most important, there is no question that the proponents of the distinction in question would treat many dangerous messages as "high value" speech even if communicated through nonverbal media. A Diego Rivera mural that clearly "advocates" violent revolution would undoubtedly be treated by almost everyone as "high value" political speech,[10] and given the same protection as a political tract verbally advocating violent revolution (assuming no imminent danger).[11] But how then can the case for banning the pornographic picture be distinguished?

There is still another case that might be offered for dividing speech into "value" categories and distinguishing the pornographic picture from the pamphlet. One might argue that there is a free speech distinction between messages delivered in propositional form and messages delivered in nonpropositional form. This distinction is different from the verbal-nonverbal distinction; much verbal expression is nonpropositional. Literature is one example since, although novels and poems contain propositions, their "meaning" cannot be fully captured by only some of their propositions or by alternative propositions.

The distinction is relevant in two ways. On the one hand, nonpropositional messages may never become consciously propositional for the audience, but may instead affect behavior only subliminally. Dangerous nonpropositional messages are therefore more threatening than their equivalent propositional messages because the audience, not being di-

---

8 Though, of course, its credibility might. *See* Alexander, *Speech in the Local Marketplace: Implications of* Virginia State Bd. of Pharmacy v. Virginia Citizens Consumer Council, Inc. *for Local Regulatory Power*, 14 SAN DIEGO L. REV. 357, 374 (1977); Shiffrin, *The First Amendment and Economic Regulation: Away From a General Theory of the First Amendment*, 78 NW. U.L. REV. 1212, 1257-58 (1983).

9 Consider, for example, Cohen v. California, 403 U.S. 15 (1971) (expression "Fuck the Draft" is constitutionally protected because it has an emotive force and hence a "meaning" different from alternative verbal formulations of the abstract idea).

10 First amendment protection of expression through nonverbal media is well entrenched in Court doctrine. *See, e.g.,* Schad v. Borough of Mount Ephraim, 452 U.S. 61 (1981); Winters v. New York, 333 U.S. 507 (1948). There is some dissent, however, from this position. *See, e.g.,* E. WOLGAST, THE GRAMMAR OF JUSTICE 122-24 (1987); Wright, *supra* note 1, at 169-71.

11 *See* Brandenburg v. Ohio, 395 U.S. 444 (1969) (advocacy of violence must amount to incitement of imminent lawless action to lose its constitutional protection).

NORTHWESTERN UNIVERSITY LAW REVIEW

rectly aware of them, cannot reject them through rational consideration of their merits.[12] On the other hand, in terms of positive freedom of speech values, nonpropositional communications have little weight. That is, or so the argument goes, freedom of speech exists primarily to protect the full consideration of propositions. Therefore, if the government is dealing with a nonpropositional form of expression, and it believes the audience will receive a dangerous message in nonpropositional, subliminal form from the expression, it may regulate the expression without offending free speech values.

This distinction between propositional and nonpropositional expression is a distinction that may have some intuitive appeal, but is it a distinction that we wish the courts to make under the first amendment? The distinction not only places the Diego Rivera mural on the wrong side of the line, leaving it unprotected under the first amendment; the distinction also reads out of the first amendment everything that is nonpropositional: literature, art, movies, dance, and so on. For although such forms of nonpropositional expression may convey ideas that can be stated propositionally, they themselves, viewed as wholes, are nonpropositional. Mountains of Supreme Court precedents protecting such items would have to be overturned to limit the first amendment to the protection of propositions.[13] Moreover, even propositional speech has nonpropositional emotive (and even subliminal) qualities that the government might wish to regulate.[14] In the absence of such a diminished role for the first amendment, the propositional-nonpropositional distinction cannot serve as the basis for dividing up types of speech according to their value.

Even if one does not view the wholesale overturning of precedent as too high a price to pay in order to purify first amendment doctrine and relegate protection only to propositions (on the theory that the first amendment is concerned with rational debate rather than with communication of ideas per se), the problem of drawing the line between propositional and nonpropositional speech should give one pause. A string of propositions can convey a message that is found in none of the propositions taken singly nor in all of them construed as an argument, but that is instead located in the nonpropositional, emotive "spin" or affect that the proposition generates for its audience. Is such a string "propositional" or "nonpropositional"? I'm relatively sure that there is no principled way of answering that question. I'm even more certain that most of us don't want the courts to be in the business of deciding whether an expression is sufficiently "propositional" to warrant protection from regulation motivated by legitimate governmental concern with the expression's nonpropositional spin.

---

[12] *See* Sunstein, *supra* note 3, at 606; E. WOLGAST, *supra* note 10, at 122-24.

[13] *See supra* note 10.

[14] *See, e.g.*, Cohen v. California, 403 U.S. 15 (1971).

Moreover, the attempt to distinguish speech of different value leads to intractable difficulties of classification. The attempt to distinguish commercial from other speech has already spawned several examples of these difficulties in the case law.[15] But pornography is just as rife with examples. What if our pornographer puts a typed political statement underneath the picture? What if the political pamphleteer puts an otherwise pornographic picture on his pamphlet? Why look at *Ulysses* as a whole rather than at particular "pornographic" words or sentences? And what if a pornographic work is of great value in a social science class or research project? Is it still "low" or "no value" speech? Or is the "whole" work the item plus the class or research project that incorporates it? The point here is not the usual one about the difficulty of drawing lines among categories that are hard to distinguish at their margins but easy to distinguish at their cores. The point is rather that "pornography" cannot be distinguished from "other speech" except in terms of the ideas it conveys or the uses to which it is put.

None of these puzzles can be solved, I believe, because they are all based on an assumption that is mistaken, namely, the coherence for freedom of speech purposes of the "value" taxonomy when applied to various forms of communication.

If, taken singly, neither nonpropositional form, authors' intentions, audience interests, nor linkage to harms distinguish pornography from other, fully protected speech, then perhaps it is the combination of these characteristics that does. That is, in fact, Sunstein's position on what distinguishes "low value" from "high value" speech:

[I]n determining whether speech qualifies as low value, the cases suggest that four factors are relevant.

First, the speech must be far afield from the central concern of the first amendment, which, broadly speaking, is effective popular control of public affairs. Speech that concerns governmental processes is entitled to the highest level of protection; speech that has little or nothing to do with public affairs may be accorded less protection. Second, a distinction is drawn between cognitive and noncognitive aspects of speech. Speech that has purely noncognitive appeal will be entitled to less constitutional protection. Third, the purpose of the speaker is relevant: if the speaker is seeking to communicate a message, he will be treated more favorably than if he is not. Fourth, the various classes of low-value speech reflect judgments that in certain areas, government is unlikely to be acting for constitutionally impermissible reasons or producing constitutionally troublesome harms. In the cases of commercial speech, private libel, and fighting words, for example, government regulation is particularly likely to be based on legitimate reasons. Judicial scrutiny is therefore more deferential in these areas.[16]

Sunstein adverts to the problems with each of the criteria he men-

---

15 *See* L. TRIBE, *supra* note 1, at 896-98.
16 Sunstein, *supra* note 2, at 603-04.

NORTHWESTERN UNIVERSITY LAW REVIEW

tions.[17] But he believes the enterprise of dividing the realm of speech into "high value," "low value," and "no value" speech to be necessary in order to make the kinds of distinctions—say, between a political stump speech and a bribe—any sensible system of free expression must make.[18]

Sunstein is correct that we must be able to distinguish among bans on various types of speech. In my opinion, however, the "high value," "low value," "no value" taxonomy is completely wrongheaded, if not incoherent. I have already stated why I do not think that speaker's intent, typical audience reaction, or nonpropositional form can individually demarcate a special category of "low value" speech, at least without overturning a good deal of established precedent.[19] I will add now that I

---

[17] *Id.* at 604-05.

[18] *Id.* at 605.

[19] Sunstein's difficulties with these factors are instructive. For example, when discussing the distinction between cognitive and noncognitive "speech," which he concedes is a difficult distinction to draw, Sunstein says that speech that is not intended to communicate a substantive message, or that is directed solely to noncognitive capacities, may be wholly or largely without the properties that give speech its special status. *Id.* at 606. Subliminal advertising and hypnosis, for example, are entitled to less than full first amendment protection. Listeners or observers will frequently draw messages from speech or conduct whether or not it has communicative intent. The fact that a message may be drawn does not mean that the speech in question has the usual constitutional value. For this, Sunstein cites U.S. v. O'Brien, 391 U.S. 367 (1968), the case in which the Supreme Court upheld the prosecution of draft card burners who intended to communicate opposition to the draft through the forbidden conduct.

But *O'Brien* didn't hold that the speech—the communicative aspect of what was going on in burning draft cards—had low value. Quite the contrary. The communicative aspect of the speech had quite high value, and everyone recognized that fact. Rather, it was the fact that the noncommunicative aspect of the medium of expression, namely, the loss of the draft card, was harmful independently of its communicative aspect, not the fact that the speech was "low value" as speech, that legitimated the government's prosecution of O'Brien.

Sunstein goes on to repeat Fred Schauer's equation of hard core pornography and sexual paraphernalia. Sunstein, *supra* note 2, at 606-07. *See* F. SCHAUER, FREE SPEECH: A PHILOSOPHICAL ENQUIRY 181-84 (1982). Sunstein recognizes that part of the feminist case for regulation of pornography rests upon the fact that pornography represents an ideology, one that feminists find abhorrent. To the suggestion that speech that amounts to an ideology should not be considered "low value" because such speech lies at the heart of politics, Sunstein replies that whether particular speech is low value does not turn on whether the materials contain an implicit ideology. If it did, almost all speech would be immunized. The question instead turns more generally on the speaker's purpose rather than how the speaker communicates the message. Sunstein, *supra* note 2, at 607-08. The pornographer's purpose to produce sexual arousal in disseminating pornographic materials can be determined by the nature of the material, and any implicit ideology is communicated indirectly and noncognitively. A distinction along these lines, says Sunstein, is an integral part of the Supreme Court's commercial speech doctrine. Paid speech addressed to social issues receives full first amendment protection; paid speech proposing specific commercial transactions receives less protection, despite any implicit political statement such speech may contain. A contention that the purpose of the speech is to transmit an ideological message is easily overborne by the nature of the speech itself. Furthermore, says Sunstein, the purpose of the speaker is central to the question. Someone who burns a draft card for the purpose of protesting a war is in a very different position from someone who burns a draft card as part of a general program of arson, even if the action of the latter is taken to have expressed an ideology to bystanders.

Again Sunstein is resting his case on thin reeds. In the first place, his example of draft card

do not believe the combination of these features succeeds in identifying such a category. Imagine, for example, that a certain rock formation conveyed a politically revolutionary "message" to a small number of its viewers, though it conveyed no message at all to most viewers. And suppose, out of fear of this revolutionary "message," the government banned visiting the rock formation. I would maintain that freedom of speech is indeed implicated by government's action, and that it is the "high value" category of freedom of speech at that.[20] The same would be true if the government sought to ban the public's viewing of the devastation caused by an accident at a nuclear power plant out of fear that the public would form the idea that nuclear power plants should not be built; if the government sought to ban the works of Hemingway because it believed them to contain subversive ideas, and it turns out that those works were the product of the proverbial thousand monkeys on typewriters; or if the government sought to ban communications from those, such as foreigners and corporations, whose own first amendment rights are in doubt.[21] In short, freedom of speech is at issue when, whatever action government is taking, its *reason* for taking the action is to prevent people from obtaining certain information or forming certain ideas.[22] For that reason, banning pornography for fear that some people will, upon viewing it, form the erroneous idea that women should be subjugated or abused, is a core freedom of speech concern.

I need finally to deal with the fourth element that Sunstein argues

---

burners is inapposite because the prosecution of the arsonist is not a prosecution based on the low value of his ideology, but on the medium of his expression. Moreover, he is not treated any differently from a person who burns a draft card to protest a war. Both are prosecutable. In the second place, trying to tell whether a piece of explicit sexual art is pornography based upon the intent of the speaker—that is, whether the artist intended to communicate a message or intended merely to create sexual arousal—is very difficult and problematic. One cannot, by definition, look at the art and make the distinction on that basis, since the same picture might be drawn with different intentions. Moreover, Sunstein advances no case for why the artist's intention should matter, especially when the government's concern in regulating the art is based on its fear of the message that the audience, or part of it, will receive, regardless of the artist's intent.

20 Note that this example has three of the four elements that Sunstein uses to distinguish government regulation of pornography from unconstitutional restrictions on speech—lack of intent to communicate ideas, no meaning conveyed to the majority of the audience, nonpropositional form of the medium that is meaningful for the minority of the audience. The fourth element—suspect government purpose—is dealt with in the next paragraph.

21 *See* First Nat'l Bank of Boston v. Bellotti, 435 U.S. 765 (1978) (corporate speaker); Kleindienst v. Mandel, 408 U.S. 753 (1972) (foreign speaker); Lamont v. Postmaster General, 381 U.S. 301 (1965) (same).

22 *See* F. SCHAUER, *supra* note 19, at 98-111, 159; Alexander & Horton, *supra* note 5, at 1330-34. I take no position here on whether freedom of speech is even implicated in situations where the governmental action at issue is not taken for the purpose of preventing receipt of a message. Orthodox doctrine does support some freedom of speech concern with content neutral regulation, but I am skeptical that any principled approach can be developed in this area. *See* Alexander & Horton, *supra* note 5, at 1348, 1349, 1352, 1354. The messiness of what doctrine there is supports my skepticism.

NORTHWESTERN UNIVERSITY LAW REVIEW

distinguishes "low value" speech from "high value" speech, namely, that government regulation of "low value" speech, in contrast with its regulation of "high value" speech, is most likely based on legitimate concerns. Frankly, I find this part of Sunstein's case the most baffling. It is true that protecting women from sex discrimination and sexual violence is a quite legitimate governmental concern, as are the concerns to protect against street violence (from fighting words), commercial deception (from commercial speech), and damage to reputation (from libel). But the governmental concerns behind unconstitutional regulation of "high value" speech have often been legitimate as well. In the paradigm case of unconstitutional suppression of "high value" speech, *Brandenburg v. Ohio*,[23] the government's concern, prevention of violence, was quite legitimate and weighty *qua* concern. The problem was the weak linkage between the speech and the feared harm, not judicial suspicion that the government's reasons were not in fact prevention of violence. Moreover, the very type of linkage that government relied on in *Brandenburg* is the type that Sunstein himself relies on to support anti-pornography laws. Indeed, the purely censorial motive of disapproval of the message rather than fear of imminent harm is *more* likely to lie behind anti-pornography statutes than behind statutes banning advocacy of violence.

My critique to this point has been entirely negative, a pure case of "trashing" an orthodox doctrinal distinction. I would like to conclude this comment on a somewhat more positive note. Whenever government seeks to prevent a harm by regulating the message that is being received—what others have called the communicative impact of speech—then we can respond in terms of freedom of speech in one of three ways. First, we can treat the realm of messages as an undifferentiated whole and distinguish protected from unprotected speech on the basis of the nature of the harm that is feared and the linkage between the message and the harm. Second, we can divide that realm of messages into "high value," "low value," or "no value" *ideas* irrespective of the media through which they are conveyed. Or third, we can divide *audiences*, perhaps into the trustworthy intelligentsia, the less trustworthy unwashed, and the completely untrustworthy. I am sympathetic to the first approach. It appears, however, that under the guise of the value distinctions among types of speech, the Court and commentators are really following either the second or the third of these approaches, or more likely some mixture of the second and third approaches. If so, then the full implications of these approaches must be faced, and the justifications for them tendered. The idea of "low value" speech is an unavailing dodge.

---

[23] 395 U.S. 444 (1969).

[14]

FREE SPEECH AND SPEAKER'S INTENT

Larry Alexander*

A few years ago, in an exchange with Cass Sunstein and Frederick Schauer, I criticized efforts to distinguish "high value" and "low value" speech, as the Supreme Court, Sunstein, and others have urged from time to time.[1] Any particular "unit" of speech, however such a unit is individuated, may convey an indefinite number of ideas to its audience. The ideas conveyed vary depending upon what the unit of speech is taken to be, the context into which it is placed, and the audience to which it is presented. Some ideas may seem more valuable than others—because we think some are true and important, while others are either false or banal—but we cannot locate the ideas that audiences derive from speech *in* the speech itself. We cannot ban "low value" ideas by banning, say, "low value" movies because audiences may derive low value ideas from high value movies and vice versa. A medical textbook may be neglected by physicians but eagerly sought by those who are sexually aroused by its pictures of sexual organs; a book of "pornographic" photographs may be profitably studied by psychologists and sociologists in whom it produces no sexual arousal whatsoever. The ideas that speech evokes are not locatable *in* the symbols employed.[2]

In the same exchange, I also argued against locating the "value" of speech in the intentions of its authors.[3] My reason was similar to my reason against locating value in the speech it-

---

* Warren Distinguished Professor of Law, University of San Diego.

1. Larry A. Alexander, *Low Value Speech*, 83 Nw. U. L. Rev. 547 (1989). See also Cass R. Sunstein, *Low Value Speech Revisited*, 83 Nw. U. L. Rev. 555 (1989); Frederick Schauer, *The Aim and the Target in Free Speech Methodology*, 83 Nw. U. L. Rev. 562 (1989).

2. This is not to say that we cannot predict with some confidence what ideas various audiences will receive from particular symbols. If we could not so predict, successful communication would be just a random event. It is to say, however, that the ideas symbols produce in audiences are as much a matter of the nature of the audience and the context as the symbols themselves.

This point also explains why there is no principled way to demarcate what is to count as a unit or item of speech for purposes of assessing whether the speech is high or low value. Consider (1) a photograph of two people fornicating (2) found within a medical textbook (3) being viewed by voyeurs (4) who are being studied by psychologists.

3. See Alexander, 83 Nw U. L. Rev. at 548-49 (cited in note 1).

21

self. Whatever the author intends to communicate by her speech, it is always possible and indeed highly likely that the ideas the audience receives will be different. *Das Kapital* may be a "high value" work for most of its audience even if Karl Marx meant it as a joke, or even if it was the product of the proverbial thousand monkeys on typewriters. Pornography intended by its author only for the audience's arousal and the author's profit may turn out to be highly useful in sociological and psychological studies, just as a medical textbook may end up being read mostly by voyeurs in search of "dirty pictures." (Popular culture in particular is a rich mine of works intended as "high brow" that end up as "low brow" entertainment and works intended as entertainment that end up being subjects of serious debate and discussion.)

I concluded that for purposes of first amendment jurisprudence, the principal focus should not be on the value inhering in some tangible item of speech or the communicative intentions of authors. Instead, the focus should be on the government's reasons for regulating.[4] If the government regulates because it wishes to prevent an audience from considering certain ideas, either as an end in itself or, much more likely, as a means to some further end, then the First Amendment is in play. If the government's reason for regulating is not to prevent an audience from considering certain ideas, the First Amendment is probably not in play (or at least the jurisprudence shifts to the less stringent time, place, and manner analysis). The government's aim to suppress ideas is both sufficient and necessary for invoking standard first amendment jurisprudence. Once the First Amendment is in play, however, the value of the targeted idea may be relevant (if the idea were a false factual proposition, for example, or revealed private, embarrassing facts).[5] Additionally, the way in which the possession of the idea leads to harm will be relevant and often determinative.[6]

In a recent article, Sunstein appears to agree with me that the locus of the value of speech is not any particular tangible item.[7] He rightly points out that all speech is "symbolic conduct," and that any conduct can be used to symbolize ideas.[8] Thus, it would be wrong to locate pornography's "low value" *in*

---

4. Id. at 553.
5. Id. at 554.
6. Id.
7. Cass R. Sunstein, *Words, Conduct, Caste*, 60 U. Chi. L. Rev. 795, 808 (1993).
8. Id. at 833-34.

the tangible work itself rather than in the message the author was intending to communicate and the audience was receiving.

Sunstein, however, ignores the remainder of my analysis and makes the author's intentions central to first amendment analysis. His position now is that "speech qualifies for protection if it is intended and received as a contribution to social deliberation about some issue."[9] More precisely, "conduct carrying a political message qualifies as speech within the meaning of the First Amendment . . . . When it is expressive and communicative but nonpolitical, such conduct belongs in a second tier of protection ["low value" speech] . . . ."[10]

In his latest article, as well as in the article to which I initially responded, Sunstein is searching for a way to justify suppression of pornography because pornography promotes a view of women that impedes women's achievement of equality.[11] In my view, if government attempts to suppress pornography for this reason, it is conceding the "political" nature of pornography. For first amendment purposes, bannning pornography for this reason is no different from banning political tracts that urge the subordination or sexual enslavement of women.[12]

Sunstein's present position is that unless the pornographer is intending to convey such a message, the pornography is not high value political speech and is more easily regulable. For him, the author's intent is central to first amendment analysis, whereas for me, the government's intent is central. Let me briefly list some of the problems with Sunstein's view.

First, Sunstein's view fails to bring within the First Amendment many governmental regulations that appear intuitively to raise first amendment concerns. I already mentioned the possibility that *Das Kapital* was intended, not as a serious political tract, but as a joke (low value entertainment), or that it was "written" by a thousand monkeys on typewriters (no authors' in-

---

9. Id. at 834.

10. Id. at 835. See also Cass R. Sunstein, *Democracy and the Problem of Free Speech* 130-31 (Free Press, 1993) (the highest level of protection goes to political speech, which is speech that is both intended and received as a contribution to public deliberation about some issue).

11. Sunstein, 60 U. Chi. L. Rev. at 804-13, 817-22 (cited in note 7); Cass R. Sunstein, *Pornography and the First Amendment*, 1986 Duke L.J. 589.

12. Alexander, 83 Nw. U. L. Rev. at 547-48 (cited in note 1). Catharine MacKinnon apparently accepts this conclusion, though for her it means that government should ban the political tracts as well as pornography, not that it should ban neither. See Catharine A. MacKinnon, *Only Words* 106-07 (Harvard U. Press, 1993). Sunstein, however, wants to stake out a middle ground in which pornography, but not political tracts, is bannable *because of its political message.*

tention). If government were to attempt to suppress it because of a fear that it would give readers subversive ideas, Sunstein's position would give government a first amendment green light. The fact that the audience is "receiving" the book as political does not help Sunstein's position. If an effect on the audience's political ideas were enough to bring the First Amendment into play in the absence of an author's political intent, then pornography could not be regulated on the feminist rationale.[13]

The same analysis applies if the government prohibits people from observing a rock formation because it fears they will be inspired by it to adopt socially harmful views, or if it bans military toys because it believes they inculcate militarism. There are no authors' intentions here, but there are surely free speech issues. The same applies to bans on political tracts written by those, such as foreigners, who have no first amendment rights.

Sunstein's approach also leads to a good deal of indeterminacy. Conduct, including but surely not limited to the production of books, movies, art, and so forth, will be regulable or not depending upon whether the actor intends to express some idea through the conduct and whether the idea is "political." The first amendment status of all conduct will depend in part on the actor's intention.[14]

Of course, merely because an actor intends a political message through his conduct does not mean that the conduct is constitutionally immunized from regulation. As Sunstein tells us, much politically expressive conduct is regulable notwithstanding its high value first amendment status because government has a compelling interest in regulating it.[15] That points to a third problem with Sunstein's approach, which is that the approach will trivialize the compelling interest test. Or, put differently, lots of governmental interests that we ordinarily would not think of as "compelling" will come out as such under Sunstein's approach. Sunstein himself gives an example of this when he says that political graffiti on public monuments can be prohibited (despite the author's political intention) because the government has a "powerful" interest in "protecting public monuments."[16] The point is that under Sunstein's approach, all of the multitude of everyday regulations which we do not believe people should be able to violate just because they have a political point to make will end

---

13. Sunstein is in fact explicit that speaker's political intent is necessary for deeming speech political. See note 10 supra.

14. See Sunstein, 60 U. Chi. L. Rev. at 834-36 (cited in note 7).

15. Id. at 834-35.

16. Id. at 834.

up being deemed to serve "powerful" government interests. The result will be that any government interest—including keeping people from sleeping in parks, preventing the destruction of draft cards, and so forth—will be a "compelling" interest, and the compelling interest test will be analytically useless.

Sunstein is not alone in the error of focusing on the speaker's intent in first amendment analysis. The Supreme Court itself in *Brandenburg v. Ohio*[17] appears to make the first amendment status of speech that incites imminent lawless action turn on whether the speaker intended the incitement. That position is counterintuitive, however. Although the speaker's state of mind should be material to criminal law analysis, it should be immaterial to the first amendment status of the speech, at least if there is no danger of chilling protected speech. If I know that my speech will "incite" someone to commit an illegal act immediately, before there is an opportunity for counterspeech, then it should be immaterial that I do not "intend" the illegal act. (When I do not know that my speech will incite others to illegal acts but am negligent in that regard, punishing me may be of first amendment concern because it may chill other, protected expression. In that sense, my mental state is material to the First Amendment in the same way that it is in defamation cases, derivatively and instrumentally, but not because it affects the first amendment status of the speech per se.)

It is not the speaker's intention in speaking but the government's intention in regulating that should bring the First Amendment into play. If the government closes a beach because conditions are unsafe, that should *not* be a first amendment case. If it closes the beach because people are getting subversive ideas from looking at the ocean, that *should* be a first amendment case. If government forbids destruction of draft cards because of the costs of reissuing them, that should *not* be a first amendment case, even if some who destroy draft cards do so to express political ideas. If government forbids destruction of draft cards to prevent those political ideas from being communicated, that *should* be a first amendment case, even if no one intends a political message in destroying a draft card.

Once the First Amendment is triggered by virtue of government's regulatory intention, the analysis should focus on the ultimate harm the government is seeking to avert by interdicting the receipt of a message and the causal mechanism through which receipt of the message leads to the harm. Traditional first

---

17. 395 U.S. 444 (1969).

amendment analysis largely does just this, and first amendment cases can be usefully grouped according to the types of harm messages cause and the causal mechanisms by which they cause those types of harm.[18]

Under my analysis, the First Amendment is not implicated by regulations that impact speech but that are based on speech-independent governmental reasons, those that Larry Tribe would call Track Two regulations.[19] (An example is government's closing the beach because of unsafe conditions when that closure prevents people from receiving political "messages" caused by viewing the ocean, or, more prosaically, prevents people from congregating and discussing politics.) My analysis implies a First Amendment with only one track. So whereas Sunstein's "speaker's intent" approach is underinclusive in the respects I have listed, my "government's intent" approach is underinclusive in others.

I have two responses to this point. First, Sunstein's approach handles Track Two cases badly by stretching the notion of a compelling governmental interest to the point of uselessness.[20] Second, I believe that Track Two jurisprudence has been an extremely unsuccessful jurisprudential exercise, with only a few very arbitrary victories for speakers in a period of over fifty years.[21] It should be dropped from first amendment analysis.

* * * * *

To paint with a very broad brush, there are two dominant views in the jurisprudence and the scholarly commentary regarding the nature of constitutional free speech. On one view—the

---

18.   For example, the harms government seeks to prevent through content regulation include: illegal actions; revelations of private facts, confidences, and secrets; invasions of copyrighted and related property interests; defamations; inflictions of emotional distress; offenses to sensibilities; disruptions of workplace relationships; coercion; and so on. The causal mechanisms can be usefully divided into those that require sanctionable listener choices in response to the content for the harms to occur (e.g., incitement to crime); those that require responsible but nonsanctionable listener choices in response to the content for the harms to occur (e.g., defamation; revelation of national security information to foreign powers); and those that do not require any listener choices for the harms to occur (e.g., revelation of embarrassing private facts).

19.   Laurence H. Tribe, *American Constitutional Law* § 12-2, at 791 (Foundation Press, 2d ed. 1988).

20.   See text accompanying notes 15-16 supra.

21.   See Larry A. Alexander, *Trouble on Track Two: Incidental Regulations of Speech and Free Speech Theory*, 44 Hastings L.J. 921 (1993). The two Track Two cases decided by the Supreme Court after publication of the cited article do nothing to call this observation into question. See *City of Ladue v. Gilleo*, 114 S. Ct. 2038 (1994); *Madsen v. Women's Health Center*, 114 S. Ct. 2516 (1994).

view I hold—free speech is about limitations on the government's authority *deliberately* to control what facts we know and what arguments and ideas we consider. On the other view, free speech is about the quality of public discourse. The primary shortcoming of the first view is that it has nothing to say about the myriad government rules and decisions that, though not aimed at our beliefs and attitudes, have profound effects on our beliefs and attitudes and ultimately the quality of our democratic self-rule and our personal autonomy.

The primary shortcoming of the second view is that it *requires* rather than forbids government deliberately to affect our information, arguments, and ideas; and thus it necessitates recourse to an Archimedean point from which information, arguments, and ideas can be evaluated.[22] Government policy, which depends for its legitimacy on being the product of the public discourse, is on this view to be directed toward structuring that very discourse.[23] Deliberate censorship, the core first amendment violation on the first view, becomes on this view a first amendment command.[24]

Sunstein's concerns seem to align him more with the second view than the first. Yet, the jurisprudential apparatus he employs—a hierarchy of types of speech, with "political" receiving the greatest protection; the reliance on speaker's intent to bring conduct within the First Amendment and to identify its place in

---

22. Reference to the lack of an Archimedean point may seem like a cheap shot. Is it really impossible to determine whether government is enriching or impoverishing public discourse?

Of course it is not impossible to do so from anyone's particular point of view. Each one of us knows what would be an improvement of the public discourse—which ideas should receive more play and which should receive less. Each one of us knows when the public discourse is "balanced" and "diverse" and when it is not.

The problem is that there is no noncontroversial overarching point of view from which these evaluations can be made. Would we be happy if the government decided that there was too much in the way of speech resources devoted to free market arguments, sitcoms, and baseball and too little devoted to monarchism, socialism, art history, and rugby? Some of us would, and some would not. From what or whose perspective should this government attempt deliberately to structure the public discourse be judged? The majority's? The Supreme Court's?

23. Again, I am not denying the obvious truth that under my view, government actions also structure the public discourse. All laws and governmental acts result in a particular distribution of resources and set of regulations that affect what gets said by whom and to what effect. On my view, however, these government actions may structure the public discourse not as a matter of deliberate aim but only as an unintended consequence of other goals. On my view, free speech is a deontological principle about the respect government must show for people's autonomy, not a consequentialist one about how to structure public discourse.

24. Whenever government determines that enough has been said on some topic, or that a given idea is really the same as one that has already been "adequately voiced," it is necessarily engaged in censorship.

the speech hierarchy; and the compelling governmental interest test for non-content-related restrictions on expressive conduct—does not fit neatly with either view. Perhaps he wishes to steer a middle course between the two camps and believes his jurisprudence produces the advantages of both views and the shortcomings of neither. From where I sit, however, Sunstein's jurisprudence, particularly his reliance on speaker's intent, has no such redeeming virtue. It is an approach in desperate need of a rationale.

Name Index